Nur Jahan

Nur Jahan

Empress of Mughal India

Ellison Banks Findly

OXFORD
UNIVERSITY PRESS

YMCA Library Building, Jai Singh Road, New Delhi 110 001

Oxford University Press is a department of the University of Oxford. It furthers the University's objective of excellence in research, scholarship, and education by publishing worldwide in

Oxford New York

Athens Auckland Bangkok Bogota Buenos Aires Calcutta Cape Town Chennai Dar es Salaam Delhi Florence Hong Kong Istanbul Karachi Kuala Lumpur Madrid Melbourne Mexico City Mumbai Nairobi Paris Sao Paulo Shanghai Singapore Taipei Tokyo Toronto Warsaw

with associated companies in Berlin Ibadan

Oxford is a registered trade mark of Oxford University Press in the UK and in certain other countries

Published in India
By Oxford University Press, New Delhi

First published 1993
Oxford India Paperbacks 2000

ISBN 019 565597 4

Reprinted by arrangement with Oxford University Press, New York for sale in India only

Printed in India by Pauls Press, New Delhi 110 020
Published by Manzar Khan, Oxford University Press
YMCA Library Building, Jai Singh Road, New Delhi 110 001

for
Caroline and Ross

Preface

After much consideration, I have decided to remove diacriticals from the text. Two issues weighed heavily on this decision: first, there is a substantial amount of quoted material with varying transliteration conventions that proved to be distracting to read (the variant English forms already add a certain fragmentation); and second, since most current histories do not use all diacriticals, especially in the case of Persian, Urdu, and Sanskritic words, the decision which to include and which not was somewhat arbitrary. Since this is not meant as a specialized textual study but rather a documentation of the early emergence of the Nur Jahan legend, omitting diacriticals seemed the best and most consistent course.

In stabilizing transliteration conventions, I have for the most part followed the *Cambridge History of India* (minus the diacriticals), leaving bibliographic references as they are published when they are not a part of the regular narrative. In passages quoted directly from a text, the spelling and grammar of the original have been preserved, and geographic and place names, where possible, follow currently preferred spellings. For the ease of the reader, finally, some names have been run together (without hyphens) and others left to stand as separate words (for example, Itimaduddaula and Nur Jahan).

Verb tenses, generally, are as follows: information from primary sources is in the past tense, that from secondary sources is in the present tense. Such differentiation highlights the many layers of an unfolding tradition.

Hartford, Conn.
April 1992

E. B. F.

Acknowledgments

To all those who have had some small hand in this work, I extend my thanks, and especially

to Trinity College for an exploratory grant from its 1980's Fund from the Andrew W. Mellon Foundation in the spring of 1985, and to the National Endowment for the Humanities for an NEH Fellowship for College Teachers in 1987–88;

to Robert Skelton, Betty Tyres, David James, Milo Beach, and Jim Wescoat for their helpful expertise in the Indian arts;

to M. C. Joshi, Ali Sardar Jafri, K. A. Abbas, Pran Chopra, Balwant Gargi, Kumkum Singh, and A. N. Khanna for their time, their efforts, and their great wisdom in things Mughal; and to Bilkiz Alladin, Galib and Noshina Bachooali, Ashok and Renu Bhandari, and Gian and Lalita Sachdev for their kind hospitality and continuing generosity in the details of finding things;

to Wheeler Thackston and Syed N. Haq for translating selected passages;

to Pat Bunker, Linda McKinney, and Peter Knapp of the Trinity College Library's reference department for tireless efforts on my behalf;

to Gay Weidlich, mid-wife to this project, whose expert eye, deft hand, and gracious industry have lightened the task immeasurably;

to Craig, whose patience, commitment, and sense of humor have never flagged;

and, finally, to Caroline and Ross, in whose laughter, energy, and affection this work has flourished.

Contents

Prologue: Standing in the Legend, **3**

1. The Immigrant Persians, **8**
2. Death of Sher Afgan and Marriage to Jahangir, **19**
3. Rise of the Junta (1611–1620), **43**
4. "The World Conqueror," **62**
5. Life in the Women's Palaces, **88**
6. The English Embassy, **128**
7. Breakup of the Junta (1620–1627), **161**
8. Nur Jahan and Religious Policy, **184**
9. Arts and Architecture of Nur Jahan, **218**
10. In the Gardens of Eternal Spring, **244**
11. The Rebellion of Mahabat Khan, **260**
12. Death of Jahangir and Retirement to Lahore, **275**

Appendix I: Selected Members of Jahangir's Family, **288**

Appendix II: Selected Members of Nur Jahan's Family, **289**

Appendix III: Brief Chronology of the Jahangir Era, **290**

Notes, **292**

Abbreviations and Selected Annotated Bibliography, **371**

Index, **391**

Nur Jahan

"Portrait of Nur Jahan." Indian painting; Mughal, Delhi School, ca. 1675.
By courtesy of the Board of Trustees of the Victoria & Albert Museum, London
(1.M.37-1912; Neg. no. HE. 1201).

Prologue

Standing in the Legend

This is the story of an immigrant girl from Kandahar, born on a caravan traveling from Tehran to India. Noble in lineage, her parents had fled misfortune in Persia but soon flourished again at the Mughal court of Akbar. Married early to a Turkish soldier, Mihrunnisa was widowed in 1607 and was taken in as a handmaiden by the imperial harem in Agra.

After four years of obscurity, the woman who came to be Nur Jahan met Jahangir at a palace bazaar in the spring of 1611 and the two were married a few months later. She was in her midthirties, had already had one child, and was to be Jahangir's last and most influential wife. Almost at once, Nur Jahan and her cohorts took control of the government as Jahangir bowed to the effects of alcohol and opium. She minted coins, traded with foreign merchants, managed promotions and finances at the court, orchestrated new developments in art and religion, and laid out many of the Mughal gardens we now know. Her power over the emperor and in government affairs was almost complete, but came at the cost of internal tensions. Midway through the reign, her stepson Shah Jahan went into open rebellion and her ruling coalition fell apart as the couple increasingly spent their months in Kashmir. By the time Jahangir died in 1627, splintering at the familial center was so substantial that she had no real chance for power in the next reign. Nur Jahan was exiled to Lahore where she lived in seclusion with her daughter until her death in 1645.

I

The story of Nur Jahan is, in part, a story of ambition, power, military skill, and courtly endurance. Like other prominent women of the medieval period—Raziyya Sultan, Rani Durgavati, and Chand Bibi, for example—Nur Jahan came to power through the auspices of a male relative who recognized in her great personal strength and the skills necessary for a sovereign. And like most other women who had political influence, she knew how to work the system to its greatest advantage and then how to stop when the limits of acceptable behavior had been reached. Nur Jahan was distinguished from other comparable women, however, by the exceptional good fortune of her circumstances, by the very peculiar relationship she had with her second husband, and by the great number of her skills. By luck, perhaps, she happened to be married to the most powerful man in India, and she happened to live at a time of great cosmopolitan and international diversity: Europeans, for example, made their first considered appearance on the subcontinent during her time, and trade in luxury items was at a record high. Moreover, her relationship with Jahangir appears to have been exceptionally intimate, its complex structures giving rise to many of the policies and achievements now known singularly to be Nur Jahan's. Finally, her personal abilities extended well beyond politics and economics into areas of art and architecture, literature and religion, travel and gardening and were such that the range of contributions she made to Indian culture remains almost unparalleled by any other person today. As so many contemporary writers have said of her, there was nothing she could and did not touch.

Exactly what all these contributions of hers were, however, is sometimes hard to verify. Almost everyone seems to have a Nur Jahan story—about her jewelry now in someone's private collection, about textile designs passed down in tact from her own original patterns, about verses she wrote with superb wit and imagery, about the boundlessness and munificence of her charity—but most of them belong to an undocumented oral legacy. This legacy has become so potent and authoritative, in fact, that although much of it remains unsubstantiated in text and artifact, it endures as a dynamic and indisputable undercurrent in the Mughal heritage of India. Situated at the vortex of two powerful and distinguished families (her father's and her husband's) and possessing an extraordinary personality, Nur Jahan continues to hold sway over India's mythmaking culture with decided though elusive persistance. In every generation, and from Indian and non-Indian pens alike, reworkings of the Nur Jahan story have appeared. And as the forms of cultural expression have changed, so have the means of presenting Nur Jahan with the result, for example, that Indian cinema now carries her material in many of its modern languages.

Why has there been such a fascination with Nur Jahan? Certainly being a key figure in the relatively short-lived Mughal dynasty (1526–1707) is central, for, if the "only glory accepted in India is the Mughal glory" and if things Mughal represent a superior aesthetic,[1] then the progenitress of so many Mughal forms would naturally acquire a stature of her own. More than this, however, Nur Jahan was exemplary not because she perfectly fit established ideals for women, but precisely because she stood outside of the traditional Indian prototypes of circumstance, role, and sentiment. Her image did not inherently conform to enduring cultural models but rather came to be seen in the form of a distinct personality, singular in its talents, consuming in its ambitions, and passionate in its tastes. As an individual, Nur Jahan had led a life known to us in many of its details, and it was these, perhaps aberrantly, fascinating details that allowed such endless speculation. Finally, it may be that as Nur Jahan worked her way through the social and cultural conventions of her day, she came to be seen as pushing these conventions to their greatest limits. She found ways in being a good wife and queen to exploit the various structures of power available to her without violating their integrity and in that has won considerable admiration. We will argue later, as well, that Jahangir worked at some level out of the prevailing images of Khadija, the Madonna, and Parvati in his relationship with his last wife, and there can be no doubt that she not only allowed this but fostered it as well.

Who, then, was Nur Jahan? Or better, what was she for that rich stew we call the Indian tradition? Conventional mythology in India ordinarily focused on young girls and their physical and emotional coming of age that led to marriage for in this move from public to private, young girls (and allegorically, souls) acquired a much-valued spiritual maturity. In contrast, there were no readily available models in Indian culture for the middle-aged woman, who happened in this case also to be Muslim, a widow, and at the same time a decidedly public figure. By the time she entered the historical arena, Nur Jahan's persona was fully formed and she was too old to be treated gently and reverently by tradition. At her age no matter who she was she could not be innocent, and so it was the manipulative quest for power that was the only thing left through which the tradition could envision her. And although that quest for power would most naturally fall to the known pattern of mother-in-law, it could not fit without a son. Age-model structures for Nur Jahan, then, had to be worked anew.

One pattern Nur Jahan did fit was that of consort, but even here the exact dimensions were slightly askew. While in traditional Christian models the primal tie of women was to their children, in Hinduism it was to their husbands. The preeminence of the consort in an Indian woman's vision of her self became complicated, however, in Nur Jahan's case. On the one hand, although she came to the marriage already with a child, this child remained without siblings and remained only a minor figure in the narrative. This left Nur Jahan to develop publicly the relationship most valued in the culture, that which she had with her husband. Part of the image of her, then, was the peculiarly seductive nature of that relationship: she was by reputation an exceptionally beautiful woman who made the emperor fall at her feet by sway of her charisma and intelligence. The relationship was complicated, however, by its not conforming exactly to the consort type, that is, by its concomitant acceptance of exactly what had been purged, the mothering ideal. With Jahangir, Nur Jahan was not only the marriage partner supreme, but also one who had to praise and scold, nurse and protect as well. The tradition would see in her, then, the consort ideal broken wide open, testing strengths and emotions hitherto devalued.

Through marriage, finally, Nur Jahan wielded personal and societal power associated in general only with unmarried women and goddesses. The power issue, so ubiquitous here, had an emasculating quality, which allied her with Hindu figures like Kali. Traditionally, unmarried women were dangerous because inherent powers of eroticism and violence could be unleashed at will. The institution of marriage tamed these powers and rendered their bearers socially useful and decent. With Nur Jahan, however, marriage was seen as not taming anything but rather as working to the opposite effect: as amplifying and augmenting her asocial tendencies beyond what might be seen as acceptable proportions. As in the cases of the age-model problem and the consort ideal, then, the function of marriage was also out of kilter for it did not leave Nur Jahan safe as it should have, but made her dangerous instead and a threat to those nearby.

II

This book began as an attempt to recover Nur Jahan's lost reputation. It had been my hope to discover a more authentic and, I had assumed, a more unblemished persona behind the traditional delineations and, in portraying it, to rectify the scars of history. I am sorry not to have done so. Early in the sifting of materials it became clear that each layer had its own bias, whether it be celebratory, critical, or intimately possessive, and that an original, unprejudiced, and entirely sympathetic account was a phantasm of no recourse. Nur Jahan left no memoir of her own, no paintings attributed to her hand, and poetry said to be hers only by later sources. Even if there had been some more personal document, however, it too would have carried the complementary veil of a performer in history and would have brought me no closer to whatever truth I imagined to uncover. To be sure, then, what she really thought and felt and why she did what she did are lost, and we are left with substantially less than an intimate portrait. In the end, we cannot see the world fully as she saw it or, more heinous, as it really was. But that in fact may not be the point. Since it is the images that consume us anyway, how others saw her may be the most important thing to know.

Images may be everything, but whom to trust, nevertheless, remains an issue. The most important text we have is the memoirs of her husband, the *Tuzuk-i Jahangiri*, an uneven chronicle of most of his reign, which moves alternately between descriptions of things and events and personal musings on items of interest. Jahangir emerges from this text as such an interesting and complex man that he himself often becomes the central character of the book. Cumulatively, he does not tell us very much about Nur Jahan, but when she does appear she is clearly pivotal in his life and a dominant force at court. We would also expect to find a good deal about life in the harem from that woman's rarity, the *Humayunnama*, compiled by Gulbadan, sister to Humayun and aunt to Akbar, who at Akbar's insistence wrote down what she knew. Although there are some intimate anecdotes and substantial amounts of information, the account is disappointing in its lack of the right details and in the overall fullness it avoids. As we know in doing women's history, however, everything must be interpreted including, and especially, the silences.

The best sources, aside from the wonderfully rich *Tuzuk*, are the contemporary Persian and European sources. Ordinarily, the semiofficial Persian chronicles sought to portray the emperor in power (who was, of course, the author's main patron) in as complementary a light as possible. Many of these sources have been used but many have not, and I defer here to two other secondary works that in different ways have more fully mined the Persian/Urdu archives: the Shujauddins' *The Life and Times of Noor Jahan*, which, though fairly objective, is biased hagiographically in favor of Nur Jahan, and Chandra Pant's *Nur*

Jahan and Her Family, which is wonderfully documented, though poorly proof-read, and openly argues against the political effectiveness of Nur Jahan as a single person and instead for the prior and ubiquitous preeminence of her family as a whole.

Much greater use has been made here instead of European sources. Modern Indian opinion runs high against the reliability of Portuguese, English, and Dutch travelers in recording accurately what they saw before them. Note, for example, Saksena's remark in the introduction to his 1931 doctoral dissertation on Shah Jahan:

> Unfortunately their [European travelers'] narratives are vitiated by an attempt on their part to cater to the imagination of their readers. Moreover a majority of them were obsessed with the idea of race superiority, and were thus unable to appreciate properly the institutions which they describe. Their common epithet of "barbarian" to Indians is a clear proof of their narrow outlook.[2]

While a measure of these charges may be true, on the whole they are excessive, and it is a more honest evaluation to say that the issue of bias and perspective is present in every text. To balance them, however, note what van den Broecke has said as he closed his 1627 account:

> Although I wished to give the correct year and date of events (I have not been able to do so) on account of the carelessness of the Indian historian from whom I had to translate what occurred before my time. I hope that this will not cause any disinclination to read, but may be liked as a change of food. Farewell.[3]

To be sure, contemporary European writers were sometimes shocked and amazed at things that they saw for the first time, but their accounts were full and detailed, and often as richly anecdotal as the imperial authors were spare. They complemented their Persian counterparts by reflecting stories heard on the street and in the bazaars, and in that were often the earliest documentation for scandalous portions of today's oral traditions. One wonders if they faithfully reflected current information and opinion that had been rejected by official chroniclers as too unreliable or too risky, or more serendipitously, if their material (whatever the veracity) was somehow fed back in at a later date enhancing and enriching an already densely woven local culture.

Whatever the case, I have used European sources more fully than they have been in the past, but certainly not so much as they could be. I have made extensive use of quotations from original texts in order to ground opinions, events, and people and to make as clear as possible what was known and thought, and when and by whom. I have drawn on as many characters as was necessary for the story, but have not included everyone; the narrative is already heavy laden. And I have used a few miniature paintings of the period to enhance the textual descriptions that we have and to fill in gaps where crucial texts, like the *Tuzuk*, were negligent or consciously exclusive.

In all, I hope I have been faithful.

1

The Immigrant Persians

. . . he took her out of the dust, from a very mean family.

Edward Terry,
A Voyage to East-India

Nur Jahan was born in 1577 in Kandahar, a trading town on the border of Persia by the upper reaches of the Mughal empire.[1] Her father, Mirza Ghiyas Beg, had fled the poverty and destitution of his native Persia and, with her mother, known to later tradition as Asmat Begam, and her two brothers and one sister, was on his way to the Mughal court at Fatehpur Sikri in India. It was well known that Akbar, the third Mughal emperor (r. 1556–1605), had created a court of great tolerance and learning, where people of all faiths, races, and nationalities could meet. Already other members of Ghiyas Beg's family had traveled to India in hopes of prospering in ways impossible in their homeland, and Ghiyas Beg had similar hopes for himself and for his children.

Mirza Ghiyasuddin Muhammad was originally from Tehran. His father, Khwaja Muhammad Sharif,[2] had been a poet writing under the name Hijri or Yazdi and had earned a reputation for being a man of great character and good background, "famous for his simplicity, cool thinking, gift of conversation and straight forwardness."[3] Muhammad Sharif had come to Khurasan after the death of his own father and had been appointed *wazir* to Tatar Sultan, son of Muhammad Khan Sharifuddin Ughlu Taklu, who then held the office of *beglarbegi*, "lord of lords," or governor of Khurasan. Ghiyas Beg's father had profoundly impressed the governor with his manner and skills and in time had been given complete power to carry out the affairs of the state. When Tatar Sultan died, Muhammad Sharif had been kept on by the governor's son, Qazaq Khan, and then, upon the son's death, was appointed by Shah Tahmasp Safawi to be *wazir* of Yazd. After seven years, and in recognition of his excellent service, Muhammad Sharif had then been made a courtier of the shah and was appointed *wazir* of Isfahan, one of the best posts in the territory. In carrying out his duties at Isfahan, Muhammad Sharif became known for his judicious treatment of citizens and for his excellent ability to mediate disputes. He had died there in 1576.[4]

Muhammad Sharif had had two sons. The elder son, Muhammad Tahir, was a scholarly man who wrote poetry under the name Wasli. The younger son, Ghiyas Beg, was also well-educated in the literary arts, but had decided to leave Persia immediately after his father died in 1576. For unknown reasons, his family had suffered a reversal in fortune that year and soon found circumstances in their homeland intolerable.[5] Drawn to the favorable climate of Akbar's court in India where Persian elite were highly regarded as bearers of an enviable culture and literary tradition, Ghiyas Beg took his wife, the daughter of Mirza Alauddaula, son of Aqa Mulla, and children and began the move southward. Descended as both of them were from illustrious families—Ghiyas Beg from Muhammad Sharif and Asmat Begam from the Aqa Mulla clan[6]—the future parents of Nur Jahan headed for an empire as large and as powerful as it was newly ambitious and hungry for substance. Although Persians were known "for favouring their own nation [when] in the Mogul Empire" and for exaggerating greatly about themselves and their origins,[7] they were welcome as immigrants nevertheless. The empire they came to was already more than just a loose collection of faiths and clans, but not quite yet the tolerant and pluralistic culture of which Akbar dreamed.

For their journey Ghiyas Beg and Asmat Begam joined a caravan traveling southward under the leadership of a merchant noble named Malik Masud. While still in Persian territory, less than half the way to their destination, Ghiyas Beg's party was attacked by robbers and the family lost almost everything it owned. Left with only two mules, Ghiyas Beg, his expectant wife, their sons, Muhammad Sharif and Abul Hasan, and one daughter took turns among themselves riding on the backs of the animals.[8] When the group got to Kandahar, Asmat Begam gave birth to her fourth child and second daughter, Mihrunnisa, "the Sun of Women."[9]

Chroniclers of the period emphasized the great impoverishment of Mihrunnisa's parents. According to their accounts, the unexpected plundering of the bandits was so thorough that soon after their daughter's birth, Ghiyas Beg and Asmat Begam had to give up Mihrunnisa by the side of the road. Khafi Khan, writing almost one hundred and fifty years after the event, gave the earliest narrative of what has come to be known as "the abandonment of Nur Jahan." According to his account, mother and father were utterly penniless and in a moment of desperation relinquished their child to the elements. The caravan leader Malik Masud, however, happened upon Mihrunnisa's small bundled form on the road and was so struck by her charm and beauty that he picked her up and brought her back to the caravan. Searching out a suitable nurse he, by chance, found the baby's own mother and, giving her the child to raise, promised the family that it would never be destitute again.[10]

According to the version of Alexander Dow, drawn from a variety of later Persian texts, Mihrunnisa's parents became afraid one night as darkness approached for they knew that wild beasts would be roaming about. Ghiyas Beg, moreover, had become too tired to move.

> A long contest began between Humanity and Necessity: the latter prevailed, and they agreed to expose the child on the high-way. The infant, covered with leaves, was placed under a tree; and the disconsolate parents proceeded in tears.
>
> When they had advanced about a mile from the place, and the eyes of the mother could no longer distinguish the solitary tree under which she had left her daughter, she gave way to grief; and throwing herself from the horse on the ground, exclaimed, "My child! my child!" She endeavoured to raise herself; but she had no strength to return. Aiass (Ghiyas Beg) was pierced to the heart. He prevailed upon his wife to sit down. He promised to bring her the infant. He arrived at the place. No sooner had his eyes reached the child, than he was almost struck dead with horror. A black snake, say our authors, was coiled around it; and Aiass believed he beheld him extending his fatal jaws to devour the infant. The father rushed forward. The serpent, alarmed at his vociferation, retired into the hollow tree. He took up his daughter unhurt, and returned to the mother.[11]

This story belongs to the rarefying tradition that arose as Nur Jahan became the dominant queen of Jahangir. As her personal influence and charisma were more widely felt, Nur Jahan's shadowy childhood and youth were used as sources for her later strength and stamina as well as to foretell the events of her time on the throne. In Dow's account, Mihrunnisa's personal resilience and power of endurance were so substantial that any danger, even parental abandonment and the approach of a black snake, could be overcome by simple sway of personality. And in the very confrontation with the snake's life-threatening behavior, the young girl was prepared for the often sinister and crisis-ridden future we know she had from contemporary chronicles.

Whatever the circumstances of their journey, however, Ghiyas Beg and his family continued on to the court of Akbar at Fatehpur Sikri. It was a custom at the time for a newcomer to be presented to the emperor by someone of influential standing. Because of the friendship that had arisen between Malik Masud and the immigrant Persian family, and because of Masud's notable background, the caravan leader was the natural person to make the introductions to Akbar. Contemporary sources do not mention any of these facts about Ghiyas Beg's introduction at the court of Akbar, but based on slightly later sources like Khafi Khan, Blochmann, for example, notes that Masud "is said to have been known to Akbar . . . [and we] are left to infer that it was he who directed Ghiyas Beg to India" and to the court at Fatehpur Sikri.[12] From the *Iqbalnama* we know simply that in "the city of Fathpur, he [Ghiyas Beg] had the good fortune to be presented to the Emperor Akbar," and that it was at this time that his considerable rise to power began.[13]

Akbar's India was at the moment centered in Agra, known to European travelers as "the Mogul's . . . chief city."[14] Agra had for a long time been a small and undistinguished village, but when "Akbar chose it for his residence in the year 1566,"[15] it suddenly grew into a teaming sprawl of municipal buildings, residences, and gardens. Monserrate noted that Agra had an advantage over many of the other cities of the region because of its fertile soil and its centralized location on the great river Yamuna, both of which were optimal for the laying of gardens and the control of trade.[16] Although quite irregular in its plan,[17] Agra became an exceedingly large city with street after street of noble palaces, a magnificent fort build right on the river, and a "luxuriance of . . . groves all round [which] makes it resemble a royal park rather than a city." The market-places in Agra could not, unfortunately, be compared to those in Lahore, Burhanpur, or Ahmedabad, but there was always a great deal of commercial activity, the population being very dense "by reason of the great Mogolls keeping of his Court heere"[18] and "Hindus mingled with Moslems, the rich with the poor."[19] In fact, "in the Bazare ordinarilye there is such a throng that men can hardly passe without much trouble."[20] Foreign travelers were not always complimentary of the disorder that was Agra—note Withington's remark in 1614 that "this cittye hath gone much to decaye and is nowe verye ruynous"[21]—but in its prime the city was a vibrant, bustling, and attractive place to be, and for Akbar's son, Jahangir, it would remain "one of the grand old cities of Hindustan."[22] Agra would continue to be so important to him, in fact, that during his reign he would plant a double row of trees on the sides of the road connecting it to Delhi.[23]

The emperor Akbar himself was the grandson of Zahiruddin Muhammad Babur, who founded the Mughal empire with the battle of Panipat and the overthrow of Ibrahim Lodi Afghan, emperor of Hindustan, in April of 1526.[24] Babur was descended through his father from Timur the Turk, by way of Timur's son, Miran Shah, and through his mother from Chingiz Khan the Mongol, by way of Chingiz's son, Chaghatai. Both families represented influential lines in Central Asian aristocracy,[25] each made noble by their conquests, imperial visions, and (in time) single-minded profession of Islam. Of the two, however, it was the Timurid ancestry that made Babur most proud because, in contrast to the barbarism of the Mongols, Turkish culture was considered more sophisticated and refined. Babur himself, in fact, wrote and spoke in Turki and so encouraged its use that it remained a domestic language of the Mughal family until the mideighteenth century.

Such a separation between lines, however, was not so easily made, for Timur himself was at least part Mongol, as he came from a tribe known as the Barlas Turks, who were a subgroup of the Chaghatai Turks—"a contradiction in terms since Chaghatai was a son of the Mongol Jenghiz Khan."[26] To make matters more complicated, Timur was especially attached to the Mongol connections he had made firm by a marriage into one of the noble Chingiz Khan lines: "This *Tamerlan*, so celebrated for his conquests, married a kinswoman, the only daughter of the prince who then reigned over the people of *Great Tartary* called *Mogols*; a name which they have communicated to the foreigners who now govern Indoustan, the country of the *Indous*, or *Indians*."[27]

Akbar, the current and most distinguished Mughal to date, was in appearance an agreeable man: "This Prince is of a stature and of a type of countenance well-fitted to his royal dignity, so that one could easily recognise, even at the first glance, that he is the King."[28] Marked by a well-built and robust body, a tilt of the head to the right, a limp in the left leg, and a mole on the upper left lip, Akbar impressed all foreigners with his serene dignity, his ease of anger, his openness to all subjects, and his tolerance of religion.[29] Du Jarric recounted that he and the other Portuguese Jesuits present at the court were privy to "a man of sound judgment, prudent in affairs, and, above all, kind, affable, and generous." Not only was Akbar interested in undertaking the large enterprises needed to expand and sustain his empire, but he was at the same time, "well disposed towards foreigners . . . and curious to learn about many things."[30]

It was to this court at Fatehpur Sikri, then, that Ghiyas Beg first came and received the greetings of the emperor. Family members from Persia had already been present in the chambers of Akbar and had already rendered substantial service prior to Ghiyas Beg's arrival. Mirza Ghiyasuddin Ali Asaf Khan (II), the uncle of his wife Asmat Begam, and Asaf Khan (III) Jafar Beg, Ghiyas Beg's own cousin and the grandson of Aqa Mulla Dawatdar Qazwini, for example, had each been employed in the provincial ranks of Akbar. Although not always model servants of the government, both relatives eventually distinguished themselves on behalf of the emperor and were amply rewarded.[31] Of all the Persian immigrants, however, it was Ghiyas Beg who would eventually leave the greatest mark for not only would he be a wise and trusted minister to two emperors, but he would also hold together a brilliant but cantankerous collection of relatives as they pursued power and place in their new country.

Ghiyas Beg began his own career in India in 1577 with an appointment by Akbar to a modest *mansab*, or government rank, of 300 and shortly thereafter to the post of *diwan* or treasurer of Kabul.[32] For someone so recently arrived in the country, the appointment to Kabul was an honor. Although no doubt a provincial post, Kabul was nevertheless a chief city of the empire, lying on the northern Mughal border in the foothills of the mountains.[33] Not only was Kabul important for trade and defense but, owing to its river, which ran southward into subcontinental India, farming and gardening there brought forth consistently abundant produce as well. We don't know how long Ghiyas Beg and his family were in Kabul nor the details of their accomplishments there, but it was certainly a successful stay for in 1596 the minister was promoted to a *mansab* of 700 and appointed *diwan-i buyutat*, in charge of buildings, at the imperial court.[34] Although these offices were clear marks of recognition and although the *Iqbalnama* mentioned at length the intelligence and courtly skill with which Ghiyas Beg performed his service to Akbar—he "was considered exceedingly clever and skilful, both in writing and in transacting business"[35]—he was not yet so important or so indispensable a minister as he later came to be. Despite Guerreiro's attribution that Ghiyas Beg was "the King's chief minister and a very powerful lord,"[36] it was not until after Akbar's son, Jahangir, acceded to the throne in 1605 that Ghiyas Beg acquired all the power and influence for which he was to become famous.

Some think it was the accident of his daughter's birth that eventually brought Ghiyas Beg to Akbar's court. It might be, they would argue, that the friendship and then patronage of Malik Masud on behalf of the Persian immigrants might never have occurred had the unfortunate parents not forsaken their child on the road from Kandahar.[37] Although the abandonment narrative may have intended to make Mihrunnisa the catalyst of her father's subsequent rise to power, the story is almost certainly legendary, being absent as it is from the earlier sources. We would argue instead that the initial successes of Ghiyas Beg cannot be laid upon the shoulders of his young daughter, at least insofar as the contemporary texts are concerned. Rather, whatever initial fortune Ghiyas Beg might have had in India, he would undoubtedly have caught the emperor's attention at some time anyway, for he was a man of impeccable character, astute and gracious diplomacy, and exquisite taste: "His leisure moments were devoted to the study of poetry and style, and his generosity and beneficence to the poor was such that no one ever turned from his door disappointed."[38] In a court so receptive to new talent and so accessible to people of all backgrounds, we can be almost certain that Ghiyas Beg would have found a place there no matter what his manner of entry.

In these early years, Mihrunnisa must have flourished among a nobility as accomplished as it was in the arts and letters. We know almost nothing of her life before her first marriage, but we can assume that while her father was in Kabul as *diwan* for Akbar, she enjoyed all the pastimes available to children of well-appointed families. Growing up in the women's quarters of her house, Mihrunnisa would have played mostly with children of her own family, though children of servants and retainers would have lived there as well. She would have learned the arts and literatures of her Persian past from the resident tutors and would have been part of the seasonal festivities and gatherings that marked her Shia heritage. Undoubtedly as well her family would have been curious about its new surroundings, so she might often have traveled the countryside and seen some of the garden sites so important to her later on and have come in contact with other Muslim and Hindu practices of her adopted land.

Later tradition says that it was during these early years that Mihrunnisa first met Salim, the future emperor Jahangir (r. 1605–27), and that their love for each other emerged out of the romantic intrigues of adolescence. This would have happened not in Kabul, most likely, but in Agra or Lahore where Akbar had established fairly permanent courts and where he would certainly have brought the family after Ghiyas Beg had served out his post at the northern station. The earliest source to project a youthful affair onto this period was the Dutch trader Pieter van den Broecke, whose *Hindustan Chronicle* was finished in 1627, just about the time of Jahangir's death.[39] Van den Broecke relied heavily on material collected by one of his subordinates, Francisco Pelsaert, but since Pelsaert's own document made no mention of the early love between Mihrunnisa and Prince Salim, we may assume that these late rumors were of van den Broecke's own finding, perhaps from gossip in the bazaar.[40]

Tradition tells us that there had been an "old affection" between Mihrunnisa and Salim.[41] Khafi Khan related that whenever Mihrunnisa visited the palace with her mother, she would be pursued by Salim, who at least once found her alone and pulled her aside into an embrace. The young girl was so surprised that she went to her mother, who then complained to the emperor. Not wanting such an affair to develop, Akbar immediately made plans for Mihrunnisa's marriage to another man.[42] Dow's sources, of course, being late and highly interpretive, inflate the narrative and redirect the legend by casting Mihrunnisa, not Salim, as the tender seducer.

> The ambition of Mher-ul-Nissa aspired to a conquest of the prince. She sung—he was in raptures: she danced—he could hardly be restrained, by the rules of decency, to his place . . . . When his eyes seemed to devour her, she as by accident, dropt her veil; and shone upon him, at once, with all her charms.[43]

Even restrained by princely decorum, implies Dow, the boy Salim could hardly resist such advances.

Young Mihrunnisa's hypnotic personality was idealized nowhere better perhaps than in the relatively modern story of the two pigeons. One day the adolescent prince Salim was walking through a garden after he had visited the Mina Bazaar. He wanted to pick some flowers but was carrying two pigeons and so handed them both to a young girl who was passing by. After picking the flowers, he returned to the girl to reclaim the birds but found that she now had only one. Seeing that the first pigeon had flown away, he asked her how it happened and she said, "Like this!" and released the other pigeon into the air. Salim's anger was immediately overcome by the young girl's wit and charm, and he inquired about her amongst his courtiers. Very soon thereafter, the story goes, Mihrunnisa began regularly visiting the palace.[44]

Narratives like these filled the vacuum of information that surrounded Mihrunnisa's childhood and youth. Although none of them were documented in the very early sources, they reflected a tradition's vision of Nur Jahan as a compelling and charismatic woman who was loved to a fault, even at a young age, by the man who would become her second husband. This unrestrained and obsessive love must have begun at some point, later sources assume, and the seeds of romance were soon woven into the silence of history about her early years.[45]

We do know that in 1594, at the age of seventeen, Mihrunnisa was given in marriage to Ali Quli Khan Istajlu, a Persian adventurer. Ali Quli had been a *safarchi*, or table attendant, to Shah Ismail II of Persia (1576–78), but on the Persian king's assassination had fled through Kandahar to India.[46] In Multan he joined the army of Abdur Rahim Khankhanan, who at that time was marching on Tatta in his conquest of the Sind.[47] Ali Quli distinguished himself so much during the Tatta campaign that on the Khankhanan's return to the imperial court in Lahore, he brought Ali Quli with him and secured a *mansab* for him under Akbar as a reward.[48] Jahangir noted in his memoirs that Ali Quli "having performed services in that campaign was promoted to a rank in accordance with his condition and was a long time in the service of my revered father."[49] The marriage of Ali Quli to Mihrunnisa was, at least in part then, a tribute to the young soldier's exceptional service, first under the Khankhanan and then under Akbar.

There is every reason to believe that the match between Mihrunnisa and Ali Quli was an ordinary and unremarkable one made between two members of the extended imperial family and approved, as all such marriages had to be, by the emperor Akbar himself. Mihrunnisa was after all of the right age and from a good family, and Ali Quli had just triumphed in the service of his military commanders. A tradition grew up, however, beginning as early as Jahangir's later years, that the marriage had been arranged in order to cut short the growing affection between Mihrunnisa and Salim. Writing in 1627, for instance, van den Broecke said: "While Akbar still lived, and this Jahangir was Prince he had been attracted by Mehr-un-Nasa, before she had been betrothed to the Turk Sher Afghan.[50]" According to Khafi Khan, when Akbar heard of the love between the young Mihrunnisa and Prince Salim, he urged Ghiyas Beg to move quickly to betroth his daughter, thereby avoiding a scandal, and himself provided Ali Quli as a suitable husband. Immediately thereupon, said Khafi Khan, Ali Quli was given a post in Bengal to which, we are to assume, he took his wife.[51] The problem with this story, however, is that Akbar would have had no reason to refuse a marriage between Mihrunnisa and Salim. She was from an excellent Persian family and would have borne him heirs of good lineage, character, and stamina. Moreover, more reliable sources have told us that immediately after the marriage, Ali Quli was sent not to Bengal but on an expedition against the Rana of Udaipur and was under the command of none other than Salim himself.[52] Had there been any early rivalry between Ali Quli and Salim for the same woman, Akbar would never have sent the two men into battle as fellow soldiers.

Other sources placed the beginning of Salim's love in the period after Mihrunnisa's betrothal to Ali Quli but before Ali Quli's death. Van den Broecke, for example, said that when Jahangir asked for Mihrunnisa's hand, "Akbar was not at all willing to permit this marriage. He said, 'She is already betrothed to Sher Afghan [Ali Quli]. Are there not women enough that you should marry a retainer, who is [already] promised to one of my Turkish soldiers?' "[53] Dow's sources, once again, add a slight twist. Salim, "distracted with passion" for Mihrunnisa, was in a quandary because she had already been pledged to Ali Quli. "He applied to his father Akbar, who sternly refused to commit a piece of injustice, [even] though [it would be] in favour of the heir of his throne."[54] We have in this version, then, not only Salim's early affection but also, more importantly, a motive for Akbar's refusal to the marriage: he was a just emperor and could not breach a contract he himself had made with one of his subjects.

Manucci, the romantic Venetian writer of 1656 onward, reported yet another story, that of Jahangir first seeing Mihrunnisa on a boat. While in Lahore once and watching from his palace on the Ravi River, Jahangir saw a boat pass with its curtains down.

> When it arrived near the royal seat, he saw that in the boat was a beautiful woman. He fell so violently in love with her that he had no sleep nor rest; but the woman replied firmly to all the solicitations made to her on behalf of the king, that she was the wife of a soldier of position named Xir Afgam (Sher Afgan) . . . nor would she hear a word from any other man so long as her husband remained alive.[55]

Unlike Dow's story, which places the beginning of the romance after the Ali Quli betrothal around 1594 and before Akbar's death in 1605, Manucci's story placed it after Jahangir's accession to the throne in 1605[56] and before Ali Quli's death in 1607 [see Figure 1–1]. Such inconsistency certainly undermines the veracity, but in no way compromises the sentimental power, of any of these tales.

It seems quite certain, however, that even at this point there was no love, and probably not even any acquaintance, between Mihrunnisa and Salim.[57] After his marriage to the daughter of Ghiyas Beg, Ali Quli was, according to early sources, placed on the staff of Salim, who had just been appointed to undertake a campaign in Mewar.[58] In routing the Rana of Udaipur, Ali Quli displayed immense courage and ability and quickly won the admiration of his commander, Prince Salim. For this Ali Quli received an appropriate *mansab* and in time was given the title of Sher Afgan, or "Tiger Slayer."[59]

Although Jahangir noted in his memoirs that it was he himself who bestowed the title of Sher Afgan on Ali Quli, the title by which the soldier was to become famous in Indian tradition, he made no mention of the circumstances that brought it about. Modern novels like that of Jyoti Jafa, for example, provide background about the bestowal of the title that, though surely inflated by a zealous tradition, is totally in keeping with Salim's character. The prince, she tells us, had long loved to tame and rear wild animals and, coming upon some unprotected tiger cubs one day, bent down to take them back to the palace with him. When the mother tigress ripped out of the tall jungle grasses at Salim, aiming to open his neck with her teeth, Ali Quli raced in on horseback and beheaded her with his scimitar.[60] However he actually received the title, Sher Afgan was clearly a favorite member of Salim's retinue for some time, and it was only when the forces of rebellion against Salim under the prince's eldest son, Khusrau, became too powerful for Sher Afgan to resist, that Mihrunnisa's first husband broke alliances with the future emperor.

The legend of Sher Afgan as a tiger slayer was to follow Nur Jahan for the rest of her life. She herself became famous as a markswoman in her later years (perhaps the best in Jahangir's entire retinue) and, during one particularly good shoot, brought down four tigers with a total of six bullets. According to Sayyid Ahmad, there was a poet in attendance at this particular hunt who composed an impromptu verse in her honor:

> Though Nur Jahan be in form a woman, /
> In the ranks of men she's a tiger-slayer.[61]

Her own habits and expert skills, then, were in part responsible for the lifelong ties that bound her to her first husband. He was a bold and daring young soldier of fortune whose own story was one of intrigue and romance. Nur Jahan's later reputation would become so powerful a force in Indian imagination, however, that any independent assessment of Sher Afgan as a military or political figure in his own right was certain to be eclipsed in its sway.

We can assume that the well-decorated Sher Afgan and his wife had very little home life together. As a member of Salim's retinue, and later as a defector

FIGURE 1–1. Gateway to the tomb of Sher Afgan, Barddhaman, Bengal. Courtesy of the Archaeological Survey of India, New Delhi. Note the erroneous date.

to the imperial side (ca. 1600–1605), that is, to Akbar, there were without doubt few moments he could spare from his involvement in various campaigns to be with Mihrunnisa. Although she was probably with him at the time of his death in Bengal and may certainly have followed him on his campaigns, his personal style seems, from what little we know, to have been more as adventurer and man-at-arms than as husband and courtier.

The couple did have one child, however, a daughter, named Ladli Begam,[62] born about the time of Jahangir's accession to the throne in 1605.[63] This was to be not only their only child but the only child we know of ever born to Nur Jahan. For whatever reasons, Nur Jahan and Jahangir never had any children together,[64] and although as empress she was to play a decisive nurturing role with regard to both Jahangir and his own children born of his other wives, Nur Jahan's contributions to history stem not from any role as biological mother, but from that as wife.

We know very little about the child Ladli Begam. We do not know if she was talented or charismatic in any particular way. We do know that she became a pawn in her mother's later intrigues at court, rejected by Prince Khusrau as a prospective wife, but in time successfully married to the prince's younger brother, Prince Shahryar. Sadly, Shahryar was to die in 1627 after Nur Jahan failed to set him up as a puppet on the throne at the time of Jahangir's death. With Shahryar and Jahangir passing on at the same time, mother and daughter were, ironically, to live out their long years of widowhood together in Lahore. They were buried side by side in a tomb of Nur Jahan's own design in a garden across the river from the main city.

2

Death of Sher Afgan and Marriage to Jahangir

Fate had decreed that she should be the Queen of the World and the Princess of the Time . . .

Ikbal-nama-i Jahangiri of Mutamad Khan,
translated and edited by H. M. Elliott and John Dowson

Jahangir came to the throne in 1605. The struggle that put him there, however, had brought the empire deep divisions, repressed hostilities, and large numbers of Hindu and Muslim partisans dead. As Akbar had grown more enfeebled and weak, and as all of his sons had shown signs of severe dissipation from wine and opium, concern had arisen as to who would inherit the Mughal throne. Two of Akbar's sons, Murad (d. 1599)[1] and Daniyal (d. 1604),[2] were dead or dying of alcohol abuse and his eldest son, Salim, was showing signs of a similar affliction. Afraid that a power vacuum would result, efforts had begun sometime in 1603 among certain factions of the nobility to consolidate support for the accession of Salim's own eldest son, Khusrau, in the event of the emperor's death. Although Salim himself would have been the likely heir, in his impatience to rule (he was thirty-six when he eventually became emperor) he had alienated most of the nobles at court and, through unpredictable displays of violent temper, religious intolerance, and general inebriated frenzy, had undermined any popular appeal he might have had.

Although Salim's estrangement from Akbar dates at least from 1591 when Badauni recorded the emperor's fear of being poisoned by his son,[3] open discord did not begin in earnest until the last five years of Akbar's reign. Feeling the advancement of age and wanting the empire for himself, the prince staged a revolt against his father, setting himself up in court at Allahabad.[4]

It was in the wake of the campaigns in Mewar that Salim had first been moved to revolt. His brother Murad had died in 1599, eliminating one contender for the throne, and Salim, far from the influence of his father and the imperial army, who were now occupied to the south in the Deccan, had come under the sway of ambitious and misguiding associates.[5] Salim had been persuaded that the north was vulnerable to insurrection and could easily be taken from Akbar. So with loyal friends like Khubu (Qutbuddin Khan Koka),[6] grandson of Shaikh Salim Chishti; Sayyid Abdullah; and Zamana Beg (later Mahabat Khan), he had pulled together an army and, after a failed attempt to take the imperial treasure in Agra,[7] had by 1601 marched on Allahabad, where he established an independent court so autonomous it even produced its own miniature paintings.[8] To reinforce the seriousness of this move, Salim gave himself a title—Sultan Salim Shah, or simply Shah Salim or Salim Shah—and passed out *jagirs* (revenue-producing land-holdings) to his followers.[9] All attempts to reconcile Salim with his father in Agra, however, were futile, and except for a brief easing of tension in 1603, the prince would remain in Allahabad until November of 1604 when he returned to his father's court to wait out the impending death.

Not knowing what to do in 1602 as the tension heightened between father and son, Akbar recalled Abul Fazl, his own faithful counselor, religious colleague, and biographer, back from the Deccan for advice.[10] Abul Fazl was a man of "superior wisdom and vast learning" who was considered by some to be "the most distinguished of all the Shaikhs of Hindustan." He had become, however, said Kamgar Khan, "intoxicated by the wine of fortune, and vain of the influence he had obtained over the Emperor's mind" and had begun to act, at least from Salim's point of view, "with rancour and animosity against his master's son."[11] Fearing now that Abul Fazl would counsel against him and perhaps even urge his own disinheritance, Salim decided to move against his father's close friend.[12]

To this end, then, he solicited the aid of a fearless Bundela chief named Bir Singh Deo who at that time, in August 1602, was already in revolt against the imperial government[13] and "whose territory lay on the road which the Shaikh must take."[14] Bir Singh Deo agreed to organize and carry out the assassination of Abul Fazl, who though forewarned of the attack and despite urging from his friends to change the route by which he was to travel, went ahead as planned anyway. Although the initial attack of the Bundelas was repulsed, subsequent ones succeeded, and in the end, on August 12, Abul Fazl's murder was complete and his head was sent to Salim in Allahabad.[15]

Akbar was overcome with grief when Shaikh Farid Bukhari, his *mir bakhshi* (paymaster general), conveyed the news of his friend's death to him.[16] "His face bore marks of sorrow . . . and he remained indoors for three days,"[17] and for the remaining years of his life, he pursued to the death (though unsuccessfully) the murderers of his friend.[18] In spite of Salim's delight at the fate of Abul Fazl,[19] however, Akbar wanted only peace and reconciliation with his son. Salim was the natural heir to the throne and Akbar wanted the succession to take place with as little bloodshed as possible. To ease the tension between father and son, Salim's stepmother, Salima Sultan Begam, Akbar's favorite wife and an extremely accomplished woman, went to Allahabad to recover the prodigal child.[20] Salim received her warmly and agreed to go back with her to Agra. Upon his return, he met first with his grandmother, Maryam Makani, and then finally, peacefully, with his own father in April of 1603.[21]

> The mother of the King, who was ninety years of age, was sorely distressed at this discord. She was devoted to the young Prince; and fearing that he would be vanquished in an encounter with a veteran warrior like the King, she tried her utmost to turn the latter from his purpose. But her efforts were of no avail.[22]

The reconciliation was short-lived and by late 1603, Salim was back in Allahabad again under the tutelage of his errant advisors presiding over an independent court.[23] The immediate effect on Maryam Makani was substantial and shortly thereafter she became irreversably ill and died.

It was amidst the strain of these last years that the plot to succeed Akbar with Khusrau had begun. In increasingly precarious health, Akbar dearly wanted a reliable heir, but his eldest son was proving weak, treacherous, and dissolute. Moreover, many nobles realized that if Salim did accede to the throne their own fate was tenuous. A good number, including Mihrunnisa's husband, Sher Afgan, had already openly sided with the imperial forces of Akbar after Salim went to Allahabad and would, under any rule of Salim, be doomed as traitors.[24] To provide an alternative, the mantel fell to Khusrau who, though only seventeen, had already distinguished himself on the battlefield and, with his moderate manners and pleasant demeanor, was extremely popular at court.[25] He had excellent family ties, being the nephew of Raja Man Singh and the son-in-law of Mirza Aziz Koka, and was more than willing to throw himself wholeheartedly into the quest for the throne. Khusrau's own mother, Man Bai, the sister of Man Singh, however, was beside herself with grief at her son's decision to move against his father and was eventually so overcome with the disgrace of it that she took a large dose of opium and, on May 6, 1605, she died.[26]

As the polarization between Salim and Khusrau developed, many at the court and in official positions in the countryside began to take sides. At one time apparently, Akbar did actually suggest that Khusrau was his heir, for the English travelers Hawkins and Finch, as well as the Reverend Edward Terry, each resoundly proclaimed the passing over of Salim for his son in the line of succession.[27] As the nobles filed in behind their candidate, a division between the "old" guard (pro-Khusrau) and a "new" group of nobles (pro-Salim) took place.[28] The group on behalf of Khusrau was led by his uncle, Raja Man Singh, appointed governor of Bengal by Akbar in 1599,[29] and his father-in-law, Aziz Khan Koka, and was supported by the efforts of, among others, Mihrunnisa's husband, Sher Afgan, who had early on served the noted Khusrau supporter Abdur Rahim Khankhanan in his conquest of the Sind. Much of the pro-Khusrau activity took place in Bengal where Man Singh was stationed and where dissident activity seemed to flourish naturally in a place far from the imperial center. The other group, formed on behalf of Salim, included the family of Shaikh Salim Chishti, a Sufi who had successfully prophesied the birth of Salim to his father. One of his descendants was an especially beloved foster brother, Qutbuddin Khan Koka, [see Figure 2–1] whose loyal service now and later would serve Salim well.[30]

To complicate matters, however, a second Sufi *silsila*, the Naqshbandis, had begun trying to garner power recently in the hopes of supplanting the liberal and religiously erratic Akbar with a more stable and orthodoxly Muslim emperor.

FIGURE 2–1. "Jahangir Receiving Qutbuddin Khan Koka at Lahore in 1605." Indian painting; Mughal, ca. 1605; fr. the *Wantage Album*; inscr. to Manohar. By courtesy of the Board of Trustees of the Victoria & Albert Museum, London (I.M.111–1921). Note the fur-lined coat of Jahangir and the shawl on the retainer.

Although one of their leading members, Shaikh Ahmad Sirhindi, had written letters regularly to a number of Akbarian courtiers (including the pro-Khusrau Mirza Aziz Koka) to request support, it seems that they finally decided to throw their lot behind Salim in exchange for what the Jesuits at court clearly described as a promise to promote traditional Islam. As Du Jarric reported:

> Accordingly, the leading noble, having been sent by the others as their representative, came to the Prince and promised, in all their names, to place the kingdom in his hands, provided that he would swear to defend the law of Mahomet, and to do no ill or offence either to his son, to whom the King wished to leave the kingdom, or to those who had sought to secure his son's succession.[31]

And as Guerreiro confirmed:

> For he had sworn an oath to the Moors to uphold the law of Mafamede [Muhammad], and being anxious at the commencement of his reign to secure their good will, he gave orders for the cleansing of the mosques, restored the fasts [*ramesas*] and prayers of the Moors, and took the name Nurdim mohamad Iahanuir, which signifies, "The Splendour of the Law of Mafamede, Conqueror of the World."[32]

The "leading noble" in Du Jarric's passage was Shaikh Farid Bukhari, a trusted minister in Akbar's court and an increasingly supportive partisan of Salim's. Shaikh Farid had been receiving letters from Sirhindi and was by now a prominent Naqshbandi agent, and it seems from these passages at least that Salim had been chosen as the most likely hopeful by the Sufis. It is not clear whether Salim in fact did promise the Naqshbandis favor for a future time or not, but Nizami argues that "one is constrained to conclude that Shaikh Ahmad Sirhindi and others of his school of thought did play some part in the accession of Jahangir."[33]

A final group of lobbyists were the Christians. Portuguese Jesuits had for some time been at the Mughal court, for a while hoping to convert Akbar to Christianity and to maneuver a place in what promised to be some lucrative trading agreements with the Mughals. The Jesuits did not want to cross Akbar, whom they saw as the key to their negotiations, and so they tried to stay as neutral as possible. Although they knew that Khusrau would be favorable to their Christian cause,[34] they also knew they could win Salim to their side with European pictures of Christ and the Madonna. Although Jahangir was often charged later with favoring the Jesuits only in the hopes of getting Portuguese help in acceding to the throne, Salim appears not to have placed much stock ultimately in their support. As Guerreiro put it rather bitterly: "Of the Fathers he took no more notice than if he had never seen them before."[35]

Khusrau's early move to outbid his father for the throne was eventually unsuccessful, due as much to the bungling of his own people as to the factional alliances drawn up against him.[36] As Akbar's life neared its end, the emperor's youngest son, Daniyal, died in April 1604 of alcohol consumption and general debauchery. Although his death was no surprise, it was nevertheless a sad event, followed as it was shortly thereafter by the death of Akbar's revered mother, Maryam Makani.[37] Realizing that an important intercessor was now gone and with the Man Singh/Aziz Koka conspiracy still brewing in Bengal, Salim decided once more to reconcile with his father.[38] When Salim arrived in Agra in November 1604, Akbar received him in public honorably and graciously. In private, however, Akbar raged with anger.[39] Seeing that his son was heavy with wine and opium, Akbar had him confined to a room for ten days so that he could dry out under the watchful eyes of a physician. Upon his release Salim was then fully and finally received by Akbar and showered with honors and accolade at his father's court.[40]

Although Salim and Akbar were in cordial relation with one another from this point on,[41] Salim and Khusrau were increasingly hostile. At an elephant-fight between Salim's elephant Giranbar and Khusrau's elephant Apurva on September 20, 1605, for example, fighting broke out between this next generation of father and son.[42] Giranbar was by far the superior elephant, and when an assisting elephant was sent in by Khusrau, Salim's followers stoned it and wounded the driver, resulting in an angry dispute between the two sides. Akbar was so enraged at the behavior of the two that it "increased his illness" beyond repair,[43] and he sent messages to Salim to restrain his men. Akbar's efforts were ultimately to no avail, however, and the elephants continued to struggle until Giranbar, prophetically, was victorious.

In the end it was too much for Akbar. Surrounded by intrigue, plots, and counterplots, he grew decidedly worse. In spite of conspiracies to the contrary and dangers to Salim, Akbar maintained now to the end that his eldest son was indeed his heir to the throne. On his last visit to his father, Salim bowed at Akbar's feet and was invested with the sword of Humayun and with the turban and robes that had been prepared for him by his father's assistants.[44] This done, Akbar died in October of 1605,[45] and soon after that Salim was proclaimed emperor of Mughal India, taking the name Nuruddin Muhammad Jahangir Padshah Ghazi.[46]

Upon his accession in 1605, Jahangir vowed to start anew and began by pardoning criminals, raising the allowances of the women in his harem, and bestowing numerous honors upon his faithful followers and supporters.[47] One of those honored was Mirza Ghiyas Beg, father of Mihrunnisa, who received the title Itimaduddaula, "Pillar of the Government," and a *mansab* of 1,500. Itimaduddaula's service to Akbar as *diwan-i buyutat*, master of works, had been long and distinguished, and it was for this that Jahangir was now so generous.[48] Shaikh Farid Bukhari, the *mir bakhshi* under Akbar and a key player in the presumed Naqshbandi accession maneuverings on Jahangir's behalf, was confirmed again in his post and given some honorary titles.[49] Zamana Beg, a friend and colleague from Jahangir's childhood, was also honored, given at this time the title of Mahabat Khan, raised to a *mansab* of 1,500, and made *bakhshi* of Jahangir's private establishment.[50] Bir Singh Deo, the murderer of Abul Fazl, was called out of hiding and given a *mansab* of 3,000 for his past services.[51] And finally, and perhaps most surprisingly, Sher Afgan was honored with a *jagir* in Barddhaman in Bengal. Of this appointment, Jahangir said in his memoirs:

> When I came from Allahabad to wait on my revered father, on account of the unfriendliness that was shown me, most of my attendants and people were scattered abroad, and he [Sher Afgan] also at that time chose to leave my service. After my accession, out of generosity I overlooked his offenses, and gave an order for a jagir for him in the Subah of Bengal.[52]

Bengal, at that time, was not a premier post. The province was plagued with an erratic and unhealthy climate and was as vulnerable to drought and famine as it was to floods and typhoons. It was also on the eastern fringes of the Mughal empire and, being far from the luxurious and elegant lap of the court, ministers posted there could not easily enjoy the fruits of their position. Moreover, the great distance from the center of the empire had turned Bengal into a breeding ground of dissident activity, where men who were sent when out of favor at the court could easily commingle with those who wanted to be out from under the watchful eyes of the emperor as they schemed and plotted against him. Although it was an honor, then, for Sher Afgan to be sent to Bengal—perhaps only a man of his caliber could control some of the seditious activity there[53]—it was a muted honor, as the post could well have been in retribution for his defection to Akbar's side during Salim's revolt.[54]

Not everyone was so fortunate on the occasion of Jahangir's accession. Mirza Aziz Koka, father-in-law to Khusrau and co-mover of the preaccession Khusrau conspiracy, was allowed to retain his titles but was stripped of his power and dignity.[55] Raja Man Singh, Aziz Koka's colleague on behalf of Khusrau who had been relieved of his eastern post in the wake of his anti-Salim activities, was at first forgiven and reinstated as the governor of Bengal with a new *mansab* of 2,000.[56] But in August of 1606, as a result of his role in Khusrau's 1606 revolt, Man Singh was relieved of his Bengal post again, and Qutbuddin Khan Koka, a favorite foster brother of Jahangir's, was appointed in his stead.[57]

Despite the partisan shuffling on behalf of Khusrau at the time of his father's accession,[58] the first few months of Jahangir's rule were relatively tranquil. This peace was not to last long, however, for Khusrau soon grew agitated and, on "account of certain grievances and suspicions"[59] and unable to bear his consignment to oblivion,[60] the elder son went into full revolt on April 6, 1606. Khusrau had been under house arrest in the fort at Agra since Jahangir's accession and, in spite of his father's desire to treat him leniently, he had remained there unmollified.[61] So, on the night of the sixth on the pretext of going to visit the tomb of his grandfather Akbar in nearby Sikandra, Khusrau left the fort and, taking with him 350 horsemen, made his way toward the Punjab.[62] He was met by Husain Beg, Mirza Hasan, the son of Mirza Shah Rukh, and Abdur Rahim, son of Bairam Khan and the *diwan* of Lahore. The ranks of the rebel followers quickly swelled to over 12,000, and the makeshift army took to living off the land, mostly by looting, as they wound their way to Lahore. Reaching the city, Khusrau and his rebels found that the residents had already been forewarned and had brought it up to a state of defense. The rebels attacked anyway, but after eight days were unsuccessful and soon withdrew.[63]

By now Jahangir had discovered that his son was gone and, making sure that

Khusrau was not with his maternal uncle Man Singh in Bengal, left Agra in the charge of Itimaduddaula[64] and Wazirulmulk and took a large army with him in pursuit of Khusrau.[65] Outside of Lahore, negotiations between the rebels and the imperial forces broke down, and the two sides joined in battle. Although the rebels outnumbered the imperialists, Khusrau's men were without order or discipline and soon fell in great numbers, due in large part to the valorous fighting of the Barha Sayyids, who had come on behalf of Jahangir,[66] and of Shaikh Farid, who was said to have "wonne the battle of Lahor by a stratagem."[67] Jahangir himself had given orders that Khusrau was not to be treated leniently just because he was the emperor's own son, saying that "kingship regards neither son nor son-in-law,"[68] and the resulting professionalism of his army was noteworthy. Says Payne:

> I do not think Jahangir has been given sufficient credit for the energy he displayed in this crisis . . . . From a military point of view his pursuit of Khusrau was a notable performance; and it speaks well for the organisation of his troops that they were ready, at a moment's notice.[69]

Nevertheless, Khusrau eventually escaped with Husain Beg and Abdur Rahim, and after some confusion as to what to do next, the rebels decided to retreat to Kabul. Unfortunately for Khusrau, however, the move to escape included crossing the Chenab River at night by boat with the help of a boatman who, distrusting Khusrau, abandoned ship midway.[70] When dawn came, the rebel party saw that it had been surrounded by Jahangir's forces and had no choice but to submit to being taken to the emperor's temporary court in Mirza Kamran's garden near Lahore.[71]

Khusrau was brought before Jahangir "weeping and trembling between" his two friends Husain Beg and Abdur Rahim, bound in chains "after the manner and custom of Chingiz Khan." Then sending Khusrau off into confinement, Jahangir "ordered these two villains to be put in skins of an ox and an ass, and that they should be mounted on asses with their faces to the tail and thus taken round the city."[72] Because the ox-hide dried more quickly than the ass-hide, Husain Beg died shortly afterward; his head was cut off and sent to be fixed to the gate in Agra. Abdur Rahim, however, who had been given refreshment during the ordeal, remained alive and after some time was freed and restored to his former dignity.[73] Jahangir then ordered wooden posts set up along the road from Mirza Kamran's garden into the city and on them had his men impale the bodies of Khusrau's rebels.[74] To make his humiliation complete, Khusrau was led on elephant-back down the road to receive the "homage" of his former supporters.[75] As van den Broecke reported:

> When all the nobles had been hanged or impaled, the King personally went to see the sight as a pastime, taking his son Sultan Khusrau, mounted on an elephant, with him. They rode through the dead nobles, who filled both sides of the road . . . . Mahabat Khan, was seated behind the Prince, in order to introduce . . . [each] head to Khusrau.[76]

Jahangir's next order of business was to take care of all those otherwise involved in the 1606 revolt. Among those punished was the Sikh Guru Arjun, well known to Akbar during his reign for extreme piety, who in his kindheartedness had blessed Khusrau and his rebels in Gobindwal on their way to Lahore.

> On account of his reputation for holiness, the Prince went to see him, hoping apparently that this would bring him good fortune. The Goru congratulated him on his new royalty, and placed his tiara on his head. Although the Prince was a Moor, the Goru deemed it lawful to bestow on him this mark of dignity . . . and the Prince accepted it, believing the Goru to be a saint.[77]

For this, however, Guru Arjun was summarily executed and all of his property was confiscated[78] in a martydom that eventually raised him to mythical stature within the Sikh tradition. Others such as Mahabat Khan were rewarded with large *mansabs*, and local supporters of the imperial position were given land or other suitable recompense.[79]

Jahangir's attention now turned, in mid-1606, to the conquest of Kandahar, a province of crucial importance as a commercial center and as a strategic outpost for military activity.[80] Although Jahangir's affair at Kandahar ended in a muted stalemate in March 1607, his return stop in Kabul proved most interesting. It happened that while he was resting in Kabul, Jahangir heard of the murder of Qutbuddin Khan Koka by Sher Afgan and of the subsequent retaliatory killing of his former friend and soldier.

Both men had, in earlier times, been recipients of Jahangir's largesse. Qutbuddin Khan Koka had succeeded Raja Man Singh as governor of Bengal in August of 1606,[81] and Sher Afgan had been granted the *jagir* of Barddhaman in Bengal as part of Jahangir's accession honors in 1605.[82] For reasons that are not altogether clear,[83] Jahangir suddenly became suspicious of Sher Afgan's activities in Bengal and in March 1607 ordered Qutbuddin to check up on the former recruit, who had been posted in his province. Said Jahangir:

> Thence came news that it was not right to leave such mischievous persons there, and an order went to Qutbu-d-din Khan to send him to Court, and if he showed any futile, seditious ideas, to punish him.[84] The aforesaid Khan had reason to know him (his character), and with the men he had present, immediately [when] the order arrived, went hastily to Bardwan, which was his jagir.[85]

The imperial instructions were, then, that if Qutbuddin were convinced of Sher Afgan's harmlessness, the soldier was to be allowed to remain in his post; if, however, the charges of sedition were proved true, the governor was to send him back to court immediately. And, if Sher Afgan resisted, Qutbuddin was to bring him "to punishment."[86]

According to Jahangir's account, Qutbuddin went to Sher Afgan at his *jagir* in Barddhaman and upon his arrival Sher Afgan and two of his attendants came out to meet him. Seeing that the governor had brought a large army with him and becoming convinced "that there was a design against him," Sher Afgan demanded to know the purpose of the visit. When Qutbuddin, "a corpulent man," moved forward alone to explain, Sher Afgan drew his sword as if in defense, but then—perhaps in fear or perhaps in anger—he struck the governor in the "belly, so that his bowels gushed out." One of the governor's men, Amba Khan of Kashmir, rushed toward Sher Afgan and hit him on the head, but Sher Afgan quickly turned and fatally wounded his assailant.[87] At this point other retainers of Qutbuddin came forward and attacked Sher Afgan, now finally killing him and cutting him to pieces with their swords.[88] The wounds to Qutbuddin that he had received were fatal, and the governor died within twelve hours of the encounter.[89]

A slightly different version was given by Haidar Malik, author of the *Tarikh-i Kashmir*, who himself was among Qutbuddin's men that day and who gave what we are to presume was an eyewitness account. According to Malik, it was he who barred the way of Sher Afgan as he was rushing toward Qutbuddin, and he who received substantial injuries to his face and upper body as he tried to prevent a confrontation. After Sher Afgan successfully struck down others and fatally wounded Qutbuddin, Malik continued, Mihrunnisa's husband tried to escape but wounded an elephant and lost his own horse in the attempt. At this point Amba Khan of Kashmir began to abuse Sher Afgan verbally, and angered, Sher Afgan delivered a fatal blow. In revenge, Yusuf Khan came forward and decisively struck down Sher Afgan,[90] whose head, some say, was removed and sent to Jahangir.[91]

The news of Qutbuddin's murder disturbed Jahangir immensely. Not only had he been Jahangir's foster brother, but over the years had become a loyal and supportive friend as well: "What can I write of this unpleasantness? How grieved and troubled I became! Qutbu-d-din Khan Koka was to me in the place of a dear son, a kind brother, and a congenial friend."[92] As Akbar had Abul Fazl, Jahangir so loved his friend that he felt nothing but bitterness and derision for Qutbuddin's murderer. Characterizing Sher Afgan as a man of "natural wickedness and [in the] habit of making mischief," Jahangir cursed "this black-faced scoundrel" to a permanent place in hell.[93] Following on the heels as it did of the natural death of Qutbuddin's mother, a dear foster mother to Jahangir, the emperor was doubly aggrieved: "After the departure of the late King and the death of that honoured one, no two misfortunes had happened to me like the death of the mother of Qutbu-d-din Khan Koka and his own martyrdom."[94] He was moved to reassert this theme later for Qutbuddin, saying in 1612 that he had "attained to martyrdom at the hand of one of those mischievous ones,"[95] someone who remained unnamed in the text, out of deference perhaps for his present queen, Nur Jahan.

In time the story of Sher Afgan's death was romanticized by tradition almost beyond recognition. Later sources saw in Jahangir's hostile words for Sher Afgan not the bitterness of his loss of Qutbuddin, but Jahangir's own malicious feelings toward the husband of the woman with whom he was secretly in love. According to the story, the visit by Qutbuddin's men to Barddhaman had been for the sole purpose of murdering Sher Afgan and freeing Mihrunnisa for marriage to Jahangir. The earliest Persian source to suspect Jahangir of planning

Sher Afgan's murder was Sujan Rai, author of the *Khulasat ut-Tawarikh* (ca. 1695–96), who reported: "Under these circumstances [that is, the narrative as we know it], it is not strange that Sher Afgan might have been killed at the Imperial insistance."[96] His only evidence seems to have been the remarkable sequence of historical events beginning with Sher Afgan's murder, Jahangir's marriage to his widow, and the extraordinary relationship that grew up between the emperor and his new wife. Khafi Khan also suggested a suspicious connection between Sher Afgan's death and Jahangir's later love for the soldier's wife but did not directly charge the emperor with a premeditated murder.[97] The first to actually make such a charge was the European writer, Niccolao Manucci (ca. 1656), who said:

> The king, who was deeply in love with her, sent an order to the governor of the city of Patana (Patnah) that as soon as Sher Afgan should arrive there with a letter he must be slain. This was done, but the valorous soldier, although taken unawares, killed five persons in defending himself. Sher Afgan being dead, Jahangir took the woman into his palace.[98]

This recasting of a simple coincidence of events into a causally dependent sequence is further amplified by the later sources found in Dow. According to Dow's rendition, not only had the prince known and loved Sher Afgan's wife from a very early age, but even after the Persian soldier's marriage to Mihrunnisa, he continued to feel the ill effects of Salim's old affections. Refusing to give her up, Sher Afgan endured the disgrace cast his way by imperial retainers, but in the end was overcome with the need to escape to Bengal. When Jahangir came to the throne in 1605, he recalled Sher Afgan to court. Sher Afgan still refused to give up his wife, however, and in his resistance to imperial pressure garnered popular support for his cause. Meanwhile, Jahangir had been devising ways to get rid of Sher Afgan. He organized a tiger hunt and, because Sher Afgan had already proven his bravery before such animals, invited him to come along. When the tiger approached, Sher Afgan was goaded into fighting it with his bare arms, but to Jahangir's chagrin, the soldier emerged victorious and only slightly wounded from the struggle. Thus rebuffed, Jahangir tried again to kill Sher Afgan, this time with a stampeding elephant, but once again was outwitted.

Finally, Dow continues, after sending Sher Afgan back to Bengal, he allowed Qutbuddin, "one of these convenient sycophants,"[99] to hire forty assassins to attack Sher Afgan at his home at night. As the story goes, Sher Afgan and his family had already gone to bed when the assassins arrived and, just as they were about to strike, one of their number, an old man overcome with remorse at what they were about to do, called out that it was unfair to attack as they were forty against one. Sher Afgan awoke and beat off the assassins and gratefully sent the old man out to spread the story abroad. Jahangir now expressly demanded that Qutbuddin get rid of Sher Afgan, and on a "state visit" to Barddhaman, the governor had one of his men pick a fight with him. A melee ensued during which both Sher Afgan and Qutbuddin were killed. Sher Afgan himself took six balls from a musket but died only after having turned, dramatically, toward Mecca in prayer.[100]

Other, earlier, sources were less suspicious of the events surrounding Sher Afgan's demise. Two Dutch traders whose information dated roughly from the time of Jahangir's death (1627), van den Broecke[101] and De Laet,[102] both mentioned the old love that had arisen between Jahangir and Mihrunnisa in the time of Akbar, but neither made the connection between that love and Sher Afgan's death. In other even earlier and more reliable sources not only was there no suggestion of Jahangir's brutal attitude toward Sher Afgan, but there was also no mention of young romance between Jahangir and Mihrunnisa. Relatively trustworthy European sources like William Hawkins,[103] Thomas Roe,[104] Edward Terry,[105] Pietro Della Valle,[106] and Peter Mundy,[107] for example, and equally reliable Persian sources like the *Iqbalnama* and the *Maasir-i Jahangiri* were all silent on any romantic intrigue involving the trio prior to Jahangir's meeting of Mihrunnisa in March of 1611. Silent as well was Jahangir's *Tuzuk*, which is not as obvious as it might seem, for any memoir that so blatantly exposed its author's base motivations in the 1602 murder of Abul Fazl might have exposed equally low behavior in the murder of a beloved's first husband—creating, in the process, at least the semblance of an official rationale.

These sources were all contemporary, and as others have pointed out, they would certainly have picked up and recorded scandalous gossip circulating in the streets.[108] The European sources would have everything to gain from discrediting the Mughal court, which was dragging its feet in concluding trading agreements, and the Persian sources would have been quick to offer official discussions of any weaknesses in the imperial memoirs, which could be used by future disparagers of the emperor. There was no sign of either concern anywhere in these texts.

From this, then, we can conclude three things. First, Jahangir did not order the murder of Sher Afgan so that he could marry his widow. While he may have been pleased that Sher Afgan's death now freed him of one more discontent in Bengal, it was not a death linked in any way to romantic intrigue. The murder narrative most probably evolved as a way to tie historical events together into a sequence that would plant Nur Jahan's future charismatic hold over her husband securely in circumstances of the past. Furthermore, as a story line, the murder narrative was especially appealing, as it supported all that India was coming to know of imperial Mughal behavior.

Second, the murder narrative most probably developed during the reign of Shah Jahan (r. 1627–58), sometime between the van den Broecke/De Laet report of a young love with no murder (ca. 1627) and the earliest report by Manucci of young love coupled with a premeditated attack (ca. 1656). Certainly by the time Manucci arrived in India the connection had already been made and was in the creative hands of mythmakers. That the elaboration happened under the reign of Shah Jahan is no surprise. His animosity toward Nur Jahan and what he saw as her power-mongering ways was legendary, and scholars have ascribed apocryphal narratives such as these to an established anti–Nur Jahan campaign[109] that was designed to prevent her return to power during her exile years before her death in 1645 and to tarnish her potentially well-worshipped image thereafter. No love was lost between Nur Jahan and her stepson in the last years of Jahangir's reign, and Shah Jahan's encouragement of stories such as these was a legacy of his continued effort to thwart her dominant personality. Ironically, they served only to enhance it.

Third, the first sources to report romanticized narratives about Jahangir and Mihrunnisa were European, indicating perhaps that Europeans were not only the most eager to announce any scandal emanating from the court, but were especially close to popular channels of gossip as well. As traders they were in a particularly good position to gather information brought by their agents from commercial centers and trading outposts, and they selected, we presume, only stories with a clear human interest and only those of benefit to their European sponsors. Although they would have had no reason to make up the stories themselves, they must certainly have been instrumental in the amplification and proliferation of them (in both Europe and India) once the seeds had been sown. And they most certainly would have published whatever information they had as soon as it came to them.

Returning to the narrative, the death of Sher Afgan brought immediate consequences for Mihrunnisa and her family. Early sources told us only that, after Sher Afgan died, Jahangir ordered his former comrade's widow back to court in Agra and "entrusted her to the keeping of his own royal mother," Ruqayya Sultan Begam. "There she remained [for] some time without notice,"[110] continuing on "for a long time without any employment."[111] This bare skeleton of narrative is probably all that can be gleaned of the historical sequence of events before Mihrunnisa's 1611 marriage to Jahangir. Because of its meagerness, however, it has been a convenient structure for later storytellers who have found in it ample room for spurious tales of their own.

Khafi Khan's story elaborated the moments before Sher Afgan's death with intrigue involving Mihrunnisa herself. Severely wounded and knowing that he was going to die, apparently, Sher Afgan rushed back to his house intending to kill Mihrunnisa, thus depriving Jahangir of his coveted prize. Realizing Sher Afgan's intent, Mihrunnisa's mother Asmat Begam began to cry out as if in mourning, telling her wounded son-in-law that Mihrunnisa had thrown herself in a well the moment she learned what had happened to her husband. Collapsing in despair on the ground, the Persian Romeo died on the spot.[112]

Peter Mundy's version, mindful of Nur Jahan's later prowess in battle, reported that Mihrunnisa had actually been on the field with Sher Afgan at his death, riding in on an elephant and encouraging him in his attack on Qutbuddin. When he was killed, she was imprisoned by the imperial army and brought before Jahangir, presumably for complicity in treason. Showing herself arrogant and haughty, Mihrunnisa was sentenced "to the common stews, there to be abused by the baser sort." This never came to pass, however, and in time Jahangir fell in love with her and made her his wife.[113]

Haidar Malik portrayed a more docile Mihrunnisa, whose plight stirred up surprising reserves of chivalry. After fatally striking Sher Afgan, Malik said, Yusuf Khan returned to the fort at Barddhaman and plundered the houses of

Sher Afgan's mother and widow. When Haidar Malik heard the news, he rushed to Barddhaman and took Mihrunnisa and her daughter back to his own house where he had them looked after by his Kashmiri kinsmen. After forty days, imperial orders came for Mihrunnisa to be sent to the court in Agra. For his kind protection and care during these moments of great stress, Haidar Malik was rewarded with a letter of recommendation on his behalf from Mihrunnisa to her father Itimaduddaula at court.[114]

The trip to Agra was not uneventful either. According to van den Broecke and De Laet, Mihrunnisa and her family were to go there to join her father, Itimaduddaula, who was then at court. Receiving the summons from Jahangir, the local official, Islam Khan, set out with Mihrunnisa, her daughter, and Sher Afgan's brother Qumar Sultan. At a point near Hajipur and Patna, Mihrunnisa stopped to consult the saint Shah Hamadan, whose prophesies "always came to pass." He told her of great happiness in the future, "saying that she would be given to the King Jahangir and (would receive) many other marks of unexpected good fortune which she herself could never believe." In time the party made its way safely to Agra, and Mihrunnisa was taken, as prophesied, before the king.[115]

Despite such apocryphal tales, it seems quite certain that Mihrunnisa was brought back to the court in Agra after her husband's death and placed in the care of one of Jahangir's stepmothers, Ruqayya Sultan Begam,[116] as a lady-in-waiting. It was the custom in Mughal times for the widow and immediate dependents of an imperial retainer to be provided for in some way at the time of their loss.[117] Given the precarious political connections of Sher Afgan before his death, his family would be in certain danger with him gone from those seeking to avenge Qutbuddin's murder. For her own protection, then, Mihrunnisa needed to be at the court in Agra. Moreover, her natural family was employed there, and it was normal for a daughter in her circumstances to be reunited with her paternal lineage. That she was brought back in honor (presumably because of her father's position at court) was clear from her new post with Ruqayya Begam. Ruqayya was the most senior woman in the harem and, by stature and ability, the most capable of providing the protection Mihrunnisa needed.[118] She had been Akbar's first and principal wife, a daughter of Mirza Hindal, but had had no children by him, though among her charges had been Prince Khurram, third child of Jahangir and his successor as Shah Jahan.[119] The relationship that grew up between Mihrunnisa and Ruqayya Begam appears to have been an exceedingly tender one. Said van den Broecke: "This Begam conceived a great affection for Mehr-un-Nasa; she loved her more than others and always kept her in her company."[120] It was under the senior Begam's care, then, that Mihrunnisa was able to spend time with her parents and occasionally to visit the apartments where the emperor's women lived.

Mihrunnisa's life in the women's palaces in service to Ruqayya Begam did not begin auspiciously, however. About the time of Sher Afgan's murder of Qutbuddin and his own death, Mihrunnisa's father Itimaduddaula, who was then the *diwan* to an *amir ul-umara*, was charged by one of his underlings ("a heathen in his service named Uttam Chand") of embezzling Rs. 50,000. When told of this, Jahangir placed Itimaduddaula in the custody of the informant,

Diyanat Khan.[121] This was followed, according to van den Broecke, by the murder of Qutbuddin by Sher Afgan, Itimaduddaula's son-in-law, and then in late August of 1607, by the uncovering of a plot to assassinate the emperor, masterminded by nearly five hundred pro-Khusrau activists,[122] who included among them Itimaduddaula's son and one of Mihrunnisa's elder brothers, Muhammad Sharif. According to the *Tuzuk*, the plan had been to attack Jahangir while he was hunting in Kabul, kill him, and raise Khusrau, whom the would-be assassins had been entrusted to guard, to the throne. The plan, however, had been unsuccessful.[123]

Needless to say, Jahangir was outraged by all of these offenses, especially as they involved members of the same family. He returned to Lahore from Kabul, where he had first heard the news of Qutbuddin, and demanded that Itimaduddaula, his son Muhammad Sharif, and three others—including Mirza Nuruddin (son of Ghiyasuddin Ali, Asaf Khan [II]) and Mirza Fathullah (son of Hakim Abul Fath)—appear before him. When Jahangir ordered the execution of the traitorous group, Diyanat Khan interceded on behalf of Itimaduddaula and argued for a reprieve, claiming that it would be more advantageous for the emperor to keep the *diwan* alive and to extract from him two *lakh* rupees in payment for his crime. Jahangir conceded and returned Itimaduddaula to Diyanat Khan's custody in exchange for the sizable purse.[124] Four of the ringleaders of the assassination plot, however, were executed.[125] They included among their number a distantly related kinsman to Mihrunnisa, Nuruddin, as well as her brother, Muhammad Sharif.

The final punishment, however, was to be handed out to Khusrau himself. Khusrau had up until this time been living a life of comparative ease in Lahore; he had been allowed to walk freely in his garden without chains and had apparently been given all the comforts due a man of his noble birth.[126] With this new assassination attempt, however—clearly perpetrated "at Khusrau's instigation"—something more serious had to be done with Jahangir's errant son. Since neither the emperor nor the women of his harem would consent to Khusrau's execution,[127] it was decided, at Mahabat Khan's urging, that Khusrau be blinded. Blinding was a common form of punishment in cases of sedition[128] and, although Jahangir himself did not mention the blinding of Khusrau in his memoirs,[129] other early sources did, and it is the consensus of modern scholars that the blinding in some form and by some agent did take place.[130]

Father Fernao Guerreiro, in an account published in 1609,[131] for example, stated that Jahangir took his son from Lahore to Agra "in a cage on the back of an elephant," and on the way stopped at the place where the battle between them had been fought and had him blinded with "the juice of certain herbs, which had the appearance of milk."[132] Finch, in 1611, recorded two stories: one, that Jahangir took Khusrau to Kabul "where the battell was fought" and had his eyes burned out with a glass, and the other, that Jahangir only blindfolded his son with a napkin.[133] In 1613, Hawkins likewise reported that Khusrau was in prison in the king's palace, having been blinded in some form at the command of his father.[134] Terry, sometime before 1622, placed the blinding immediately after the 1606 rebellion and said that Khusrau was cast "into prison, where his eyes were sealed up (by something put before them which might not be taken off) for the space of three years; after which time that seal was taken away, that he might with freedom enjoy the light, though not his liberty."[135] Della Valle's account of 1623 to 1624 described the sewing up of Khusrau's eyes, a condition that remained for two years until the eyes were commanded to be ripped open again,[136] and van den Broecke, in 1627, returned to the earlier version of a blinding by the juice of poisonous leaves.[137] Finally, Tavernier, sometime between 1640 and 1643, recorded the use of a hot iron, which was passed before the eyes "in the manner which . . . is followed in Persia,"[138] and the *Intikhab-i Jahangir-Shahi*, written by a contemporary companion of Jahangir who himself accompanied the emperor on several trips, described Khusrau as blinded by a wire inserted into his eyes, which caused a pain that was "beyond all expression."[139]

The blinding stories are clearly at variance on several points: first, whether the blinding took place in the wake of the 1606 rebellion or of the 1607 assassination attempt; second, whether the blinding was carried out with poisonous juice, glass, wire, needle and thread, or a simple blindfold; and third, whether, how, and after how long partial sight was restored. That there ever was a blinding is probably not at issue, for Jahangir's silence was to be expected if he, as all accounts indicate, ordered the blinding himself; and Roe's inattention to Khusrau's injured sight when he saw him in 1617[140] may be due to any number of things, mere courtesy at least. As to the issue of the restoration of Khusrau's sight, both Prasad and the Shujauddins prefer the *Intikhab-i Jahangir-Shahi* account,[141] which stated that Jahangir eventually called in outside physicians and that one of them, Hakim Sadra of Persia, was able to restore full vision in one eye.[142] It is probable, however, that aside from strong evidence that the blinding itself did take place, little can be conclusively known about the details of the event.

As for Mihrunnisa, the ultimate consequences of the disgraceful actions of her family from possible embezzling and during the assassination attempt were minimal. She had come as lady-in-waiting to Ruqayya Begam in 1607 and continued to live there with her daughter in relative obscurity for the next four years. Later tradition, of course, filled these years with budding attention from the emperor, but it seems quite clear that even at this point neither one had more than a passing awareness, if that, of the other. The stories preserved of this period, however, portrayed a Mihrunnisa full of schemes and hardened dealings. Della Valle recorded a story of her first meeting with Jahangir shortly after she arrived in Agra in the wake of Sher Afgan's death.[143] Luck was with Mihrunnisa, he told us, for "as it falls out many times to some handsome young Widows I know not how," Jahangir noticed her and fell in love with her. The emperor wanted to keep her in his harem with his other concubines but being a "very cunning and ambitious Woman," Mihrunnisa refused saying that to do so "was unsuitable to her noble condition." She continued by suggesting that the emperor might even make her his wife, thus ennobling his own position through an alliance with her family. Jahangir was at first infuriated by this suggestion and in his anger decided to marry her to a local scavenger. Mihrunnisa persisted, however, vowing to die if Jahangir did not give in to her demands, and in the end the emperor was won over by her determination—aided, said Della Valle, by the sorcery she practiced on him. Although she did not have any other charms as a woman, apparently, she was able to persuade Jahangir to take her as his lawful wife and was eventually made "Queen above all the rest."[144]

The Dutch chronicles also preserved stories about this period, one of which became stock in trade for Mughal raconteurs: an incident involving Nur Jahan's child and the subsequent nocturnal meetings of the lovers by boat. The story recorded an encounter between Mihrunnisa and Jahangir at what must have been the 1611 Nauroz, or New Year's festival. The emperor, who had already seen Mihrunnisa a few days before and was by now in love with her, saw her here again with her young daughter and jokingly said to her, "I am the father of that child." Mihrunnisa replied with unlegendary humility: ". . . Who am I that should please the King and be included among the King's women? Permit me, a poor, innocent widow, to live in the same condition under your shadow. But be kind to my poor daughter and remember her."[145] With this Jahangir fell even more in love with her and began to go every evening by boat to the house of her father, Itimaduddaula, where he would stay the whole night returning only by morning to do his business in the palace.[146]

In spite of such tales, reliable sources placed the first meeting of Mihrunnisa and Jahangir at the Nauroz of 1611. The Nauroz was one of the two annual holidays celebrated with special pomp at the Mughal court, the other being the emperor's birthday. It had been introduced by Akbar in 1582 in imitation of the Persian custom, was later abolished by Aurangzeb (presumably because it was pagan), but was eventually revived by the latter's Mughal successors. The Nauroz originally lasted for nine days, but in Mughal times it had become a festival of eighteen days.[147] Marking the commencement of the new year, it began on the day the sun moved into Aries and ended eighteen days later, on the nineteenth of the month, with two days being special days of gift giving and favors, the first day of the month of Farwardin and the nineteenth, the time of Sharaf.[148]

Nauroz was ordinarily a time of merrymaking and abandon.[149] It had as its centerpiece, however, a formal celebration of the majesty and generosity of the emperor. As Jahangir celebrated Nauroz, a throne was erected in the middle of the *darbar* courtyard four feet above the ground. A rectangular space, measuring 56 by 43 feet, was closed around by fine curtains and canopied over by awnings of gold cloth, silk, or velvet—"the like [of which] cannot bee found in the world."[150] At the upper end, on the inside, the enclosure was decorated with pictures Jahangir had received from Europe,[151] and on the ground underfoot were placed fine Persian carpets. The throne itself was made of wood inlaid with mother-of-pearl, and it was hung over with a costly canopy, supported by four columns covered with silver and sporting a fringe strung with pearls and hollow pomegranates, apples, and pears made of pure gold.

Around the throne, where the emperor sat on a cushion embroidered with pearls and gemstones, were tents for the chief ministers of the court where they could display with appropriate extravagance whatever treasures they might possess. In earlier times, the emperor would go into each of the ministers' tents, take what he pleased, and return to his throne, but now he waited for gifts to be brought to him.[152] According to Jahangir, who was perhaps our best source here, Akbar had had each of his great nobles prepare an entertainment on each of the seventeen or eighteen days of Nauroz, and on their day present him with gifts from which he would choose what he wanted. Jahangir seems to have forsaken this custom and to have opted for a more informal exchange of presents and good wishes.[153] In special places prepared for them, the women of the court could sit and watch the men's proceedings without themselves being seen. Near the end of the feast, the emperor distributed small gifts and favors to the courtiers who had pleased him, and frequently used the occasion to announce promotions at court and on the battlefield.[154]

The Nauroz was an especially festive time for women. As a part of the celebrations a fancy bazaar (the Mina Bazaar), like the monthly Khushruz or "pleasure day,"[155] was set up in the women's apartments, where wives of the nobles and other "better sort of . . . women"[156] could shop at stalls as in an ordinary market. "In manner of a faire,"[157] wives of tradesmen would bring in items of merchandise from all over the country and sell them. With no other men present, the emperor would go among the open stalls, acting as "broker for his women," haggling and flirting with all the ladies "and with his gaines that night make his supper."[158] He could also learn from the gossip of the tradeswomen who had come from every part of the region "what is said of the state of the empire and the character of the officers of government,"[159] and learn as well the specific grievances of the tradespeople. It was clearly a time, then, of great pleasure, as well as of economic and political gain for all those who participated including, and perhaps especially, the emperor.[160]

The Nauroz festival of 1611 was held, as many others were, in the emperor's palace at Agra. It was during his playful rounds through the women's bazaar on or shortly after March 21,[161] that Jahangir first came upon Mihrunnisa, who was there to shop with her patron, Ruqayya Begam. Gazing upon her unveiled face as she stood in the bazaar, Jahangir fell in love with her and decided then and there to make her his wife. According to the most reliable Persian source, the *Iqbalnama*, "it happened that on the celebration of New Year's Day in the sixth year of the Emperor's reign, her appearance caught the King's far-seeing eye, and so captivated him that he included her amongst the inmates of his select harem."[162]

Mihrunnisa was, by tradition, a remarkable beauty. Few contemporary sources actually comment on her physical appearance and most early miniaturists depict her, as they do all noblewomen secluded by the custom of *parda* whom they could not paint from life, according to the current standards of female beauty. Nevertheless, authors like the Shujauddins confidently describe her as "a tall, attractive woman of proportionate limbs . . . [who even] at the age of thirty-five . . . had such charm and grace that the Emperor Jahangir . . . [became] enamoured of her."[163] Dow's later sources suggest that "in beauty she excelled all the ladies of the East" and, with an extraordinary education in the arts, "had no equal among her sex."[164] Although to describe Mihrunnisa as tall and even statuesque may, to some, explain her dominance, two contemporary paintings [see Figures 3–1 and 5–2] suggest that she may instead have been rather small and diminutive in comparison to the other women at the court.

We know, in any case, that Jahangir was captivated by the radiance and charm of Mihrunnisa as he saw them then in the Mina Bazaar, so much so, in fact, that two months after their initial meeting, on May 25, 1611,[165] the two were married. Very few details are known of their first meeting, of their short courtship, or of the marriage ceremony itself. Van den Broecke, whose information on such issues is highly suspect, nevertheless said that Mihrunnisa and Jahangir were married by a *qazi*, judge,[166] and that great celebrations were held during which the couple received many presents and gold and silver from the nobles.[167] Most other sources were silent on these matters, however, but since Mihrunnisa was Jahangir's last legal wife, taken at a time when he was in full powers and had all the luxuries of the empire at his command, it is likely that the ceremony was extremely lavish. Both Terry and Pelsaert noted that ordinary Muslim marriages were carried out with great festivity and entertainment,[168] and it is quite probable that noble marriages like this were equally grand.

There was little that stood in the way of Jahangir's marriage to Mihrunnisa. She was from a good family whose members had established themselves, though not altogether consistently, as eminently useful to his empire.[169] In addition, her early marriage to the murderer of one of his best friends did not prove to be a major barrier, as he had already married other women closely related to men he had despised.[170] Neither her family background nor her previous marriage seem to have been half as important as her beauty, which as Terry has noted, was the preeminent requirement of any potential partner of Jahangir's.

The further issue of Mihrunnisa's widowhood was not an obstacle either. Unlike Hinduism, which enforced a strict ban on widow remarriage, Islam allowed and even encouraged widows to take up a new husband.[171] Remarriage was useful to Islam in making the new personal alliances so needed in a religion of conversion and especially useful to the Mughals, who frequently saw marriage as a way to serve political ends. Moreover, the remarriage of a widow eliminated one more person who would some day draw upon the financial resources of charity for the poor made available by the Islamic *umma* through the *zakat*.

For Mihrunnisa's own immediate family, marriage to Jahangir became a great boon since several members received sizable promotions and endowments in 1611 as a result of her new alliance. Her father, Itimaduddaula was promoted from the rank of 1,500, which he had received some time between 1608 and 1611,[172] to 1,800 *zat* and then to 2,500 *zat* and 500 *suwar* in 1611, the second promotion coming with an additional gift of Rs. 5,000.[173] Jahangir apparently no longer felt any bitterness over the previous indiscretions of Itimaduddaula in making these lavish presentations to his new wife's father. Shortly thereafter, Mihrunnisa's surviving elder brother, Abul Hasan, received the title Itiqad Khan and one of Jahangir's special swords called Sarandaz ("Thrower of Heads").[174] He was later, in 1614, given the title Asaf Khan (IV),[175] under which he became famous as a member of Nur Jahan's ruling junta and then as a leading minister in Shah Jahan's court.

What is most surprising about this year is that Jahangir made no mention at all of his marriage to Mihrunnisa in his memoirs. In fact, the very first mention of her in the *Tuzuk* was over three years later, in the summer of 1614, when having come down with a fever and headache, Jahangir said he told no one but Nur Jahan "than whom I did not think anyone was fonder of me."[176] The absence of any notice of his nuptials with Mihrunnisa, coupled with her abrupt entrance into the *Tuzuk* in 1614—where she appeared under the name Nur Jahan, a title Jahangir himself said he did not give her until two years later in 1616,[177] and with an intimacy with the emperor unparalleled for any other queen—is odd indeed. Why would Jahangir have omitted mention of this marriage, when many of his other marriages where recognized so appropriately in his memoirs?[178]

Unfortunately, there is no good explanation for the omission. One might argue, perhaps, that Mihrunnisa's presence and importance were immediately accepted as fact, and that Jahangir was silent in his memoirs about what he assumed was universally known—"an omission," A. S. Beveridge might say here, "of the contemporarily obvious."[179] Or, one might argue that the omission was an oversight; it simply slipped his mind to note in his memoirs that he had married yet again another wife. Or, perhaps he was trying to conceal this marriage; she was after all, at least by one story, the daughter of an embezzler or worse yet the former wife of his good friend's murderer. Although in these cases there was nothing so illegal or shameful about the circumstances that would make him want to hide his new alliance, there might be if, as another alternative, he really did order Sher Afgan's death in order to marry an old love. In such a case, his omission of both his retrieval of Mihrunnisa from Bengal after the murder of her husband and his marriage to her four years later, "after the dust had settled," could be understandable. Each of these attempts at interpreting his silence, however, has little evidence to support it. At the very least, the omission simply confirms that the peculiar process by which Jahangir selected what he would discuss in his memoirs and what he would leave out is not altogether consistent or clear.

That he did in fact marry Mihrunnisa in May of 1611 is not only reported in contemporary Persian texts,[180] but is confirmed by a Persian inscription inside a cistern (or bath) in the court opposite the *diwan-i am*, or public audience hall, in the fort at Agra. This *hauz-i jahangiri*, or cistern of Jahangir, is cut out of a single block of sandstone and records in it the name of Jahangir and the date of 1611, leading "one to suppose that the bowl has some association with the Emperor's marriage to Nur Jahan in 1019 A.H. (1611 A.D.) and might have served as a curious present from or to the Imperial bridegroom."[181] As confirmation we also have Hawkins' remark in mid-1611 that he had "sent my broker to seeke out for jewels fitting for the kings . . . new paramour,"[182] a note made apparently just about the time of the marriage.

Although there was no overt mention of Jahangir's marriage to Mihrunnisa in the *Tuzuk*, there are clues in the text nevertheless that something interesting was happening during the year 1611. Conflating Jahangir's own chronology in the *Tuzuk* with dates mentioned in other manuscripts,[183] we can conclude at least two things. First, we know that Itimaduddaula was promoted, with others, to the rank of 1,800 *zat*[184] after Jahangir met the Persian's daughter but before he married her. Second, we know that Itimaduddaula became *wazir*, and that his son Abul Hasan was given the title of Itiqad Khan, after the actual marriage ceremony took place. What we do not know is whether Itimaduddaula was raised to the rank of 2,000 *zat* and 500 *suwar* and given Rs. 5,000 before, after, or on the occasion of the wedding, perhaps as part of Jahangir's "bride price" to Mihrunnisa's father. It is clear no matter what that, even if Jahangir did not mention the marriage itself, his excessive generosity to Itimaduddaula and his family in 1611 for vague and unspecified reasons (especially given their recent "questionable" behavior in the service of the emperor) indicates some fresh new sentiment being extended in their direction.

The chronology of the *Tuzuk* also raises new questions about the greatest mystery of all in Jahangir's relationship with Mihrunnisa: the possibility that they knew each other beforehand. On April 30, 1612, Jahangir's son Prince Khurram married Arjumand Banu Begam, later called Mumtaz Mahal, the beloved woman for whom he began the Taj Mahal in 1631. Their betrothal had taken place five years and three months earlier when Khurram was fifteen and the future bride almost fourteen, that is, around January 30, 1607.[185] Arjumand Banu was the daughter of Abul Hasan, one of Mihrunnisa's elder brothers, and therefore, her own niece. The 1607 betrothal took place four months before Mihrunnisa's husband, Sher Afgan, was killed, around May 30, 1607.

Is it possible, first of all, that with his son pledging marriage to Arjumand Banu, Jahangir came to know his future daughter-in-law's aunt at the same time? He certainly would have presided over the negotiations, meeting with the father, Abul Hasan, and the grandfather, Itimaduddaula, and perhaps attending festivities where the veiled, or even unveiled, women in the family would be present. Would it not also be possible, then, that Jahangir fell so in love with the aunt that he plotted to murder her husband, who was at that time far off in treacherous Bengal? The timing is certainly supportive of the argument, for if Jahangir first met Mihrunnisa in late 1606 or early 1607, four or five months would have been time enough to plan and execute her husband's demise. The only immediate argument against this possible sequence of events is that Mihrunnisa would probably have been in Bengal with her husband at the time, far from the intrigues of the imperial court and definitely far from the wandering eyes of Jahangir. If the argument for an early acquaintance could be substantiated, however, it would help explain Jahangir's failure to mention his marriage to Mihrunnisa in 1611; that is, the omission could have been an attempt to conceal the marriage and cover, perhaps, his own guilt for the circumstances it involved.

There seems to be little clear evidence, however, to support a previous acquaintance between the two. Although we could argue that Jahangir knew of Mihrunnisa long before their marriage—a case based, first, on Khurram's betrothal to her niece in 1607 and, second, on Sher Afgan's early service on behalf of Jahangir beginning around 1599—there is no evidence at all that Jahangir ever actually saw Mihrunnisa. If at any time physically in his presence, she would have been covered with a veil, as was the custom for noble women then, unless the circumstances were extremely intimate family ones, which, except perhaps in the case of the Khurram betrothal, were not likely. Granted, the emperor had rights to women unknown to any other man in the empire, but there would have been no reason for him to want to know the appearance of the wife of one of his minor retainers. One would further have to explain why Jahangir waited four years to marry Mihrunnisa, a eventuality hardly accounted for by Della Valle's spurious story of her long refusal to make alliance with the emperor unless it be to her full advantage.[186] Far more likely was the story of the early sources, that Jahangir saw Mihrunnisa only in 1611 at the Nauroz festival, when she happened to have her face unveiled as part of the informal amusements.

On the occasion of their marriage in 1611, Jahangir bestowed upon Mihrunnisa the title Nur Mahal, "Light of the Palace."[187] She was known by this name (as testified by the Europeans at court) until 1616, when the emperor gave her a new title Nur Jahan, or "Light of the World."[188]

These new names were in keeping with an old fetish of Jahangir's, and an old fetish of Akbar's in fact, of reverence for the sun. At the center of Akbar's eclectic religious faith had been the symbol of light, the perfect form of divine manifestation, which eventually would shine through the vagaries of human experience and unite the divisions separating men.[189] As his new religion developed, called the *din-i ilahi*, Akbar increasingly took to worshipping the sun. Badauni, an orthodox Muslim opponent of the new religion, reported that for a short time in his career Akbar would turn to the sun in prayer four times a day and that, at the noon worship, he would recite Sanskrit names for the sun accompanied by gestures borrowed from Hinduism.[190] Worshipping the sun for Akbar was apparently "a way of exhibiting gratitude" to the heavenly body for regulating his affairs as a ruler,[191] for as a symbol it reflected the wisdom and constant presence of the divine.

Although worship of the sun was not a consistent part of Akbar's religious formalism, it was adopted, along with other symbolic trappings, by Jahangir upon his own accession to the throne in 1605. At that time Jahangir gave himself the title Nuruddin Jahangir Padshah, "Light of the Faith, World Conqueror, Lord on High," because, he said immodestly, "my sitting on the throne coincided with the rising and shining on the earth of the great light (the Sun)."[192] This sun imagery became even more apparent when Jahangir minted gold coins that year calling them, in decreasing values, *nurshahi* (100 *tola*), *nursultani* (50 *tola*), *nurdaulat* (20 *tola*), *nurkaram* (10 *tola*), *nurmihr* (5 *tola*), and *nurjahani* (1 *tola*). At the same time, Jahangir had couplets imprinted on the coins, which had been written by contemporary poet-nobles and which linked the emperor's reign to the brilliance of the sun.[193] He also minted silver coins in equivalent denominations, with the 1 *tola* silver coin being called, of all things, a *jahangiri*.[194] It is clear, then, that the name "Nur Jahan" was in use by Jahangir long before he knew of or was married to Mihrunnisa and that, by coincidence perhaps, the *nurjahani* (gold) and *jahangiri* (silver) coins were paired from the very beginning as coins of equal weight if not of value. Note, however, that in time, presumably after 1611, the *nurjahani* gold piece was upgraded from a 1 *tola* piece to a 100 *tola* piece.[195]

Light or sun imagery appeared sporadically in the memoirs later on as well. Jahangir named at least two elephants "*nur*," Nur Gaj in early 1606[196] and Nur-i Nauroz in 1619,[197] and several edifices connected with Nur Jahan carried similar "light" names: the Nur Manzil garden and buildings in Agra,[198] the Nur Mahal Sarai travelers' house and garden in Jalandhar,[199] and the Nur Afshan garden in Agra.[200] Moreover, Jahangir reported with obvious pleasure a Hindi poem written in his praise that likened him to the son of the sun,[201] and he had many later visionary paintings made of him in which he shone forth against a brilliant gold nimbus suggesting his identification with, or at least external repose within, the glory of the celestial light.

In bestowing the title Nur Jahan on his last legal wife, then, Jahangir was not only paying a great compliment to Mihrunnisa's exceeding beauty and obvious personal charisma, but allying her, the wife of his middle years, with the symbolic center of his sovereign world [see Figure 2–2]. She was not only the "light of his world," illuminating his private life with physical radiance and personal charm, but the "light of the imperial world" as well, united with him as one and together with him the source of all benevolent power and authority. That he first recorded her name as Nur Jahan in 1614, two years before he said he officially bestowed it on her, is either a case of textual interpolation, or an indication that it was a private name for some time before it was made public (perhaps as a contemporaneous alternate to Nur Mahal). In either case, the new title betokened what in fact Mihrunnisa was almost from the beginning, the legal and emotional wellspring from which the strength of this generation of rule was to emanate.

FIGURE 2–2. "Lovers Embracing." Indian painting; Mughal, attr. to Govardhan, ca. 1615; ink, color, gold on paper: 13 1/8 × 8 1/4." Courtesy of the Los Angeles County Museum of Art, from the Nasli and Alice Heeramaneck Collection, Museum Acquisition Fund (M.83.1.6). Said to be of Nur Jahan and Jahangir.

3

Rise of the Junta (1611–1620)

I saw now the faction, but was irresolute what to doe . . . [for I feared that] the Power of a wife, a sonne, and a fauorite, would produce reuenge.

The Embassy of Sir Thomas Roe to the Court of the Great Mogul,
edited by William Foster

Day by day her influence and dignity increased. . . . No grant of lands was conferred upon any woman except under her seal. . . . Sometimes she would sit in the balcony of her palace, while the nobles would present themselves, and listen to her dictates. Coin was struck in her name . . . [and] on all *farmans* also receiving the Imperial signature, the name of "Nur Jahan, the Queen Begam," was jointly attached. [Until] at last her authority reached such a pass that the King was such only in name.

Ikbal-nama-i Jahangiri,
translated and edited by H. M. Elliott and John Dowson

It has been said that there are no more poisonous ties than those of a family,[1] and Nur Jahan's immediate acquisition of power made the best and worst of such alliances. It is a usual remark among the "writers of the affairs of Hindostan . . . that no family ever rose so suddenly, or so deservedly, to rank and eminence, than the family of" Itimaduddaula.[2] Moreover, concerning the rise of that family, there is no question more controversial than the exact role played by Nur Jahan.

The proposition that the good fortune of Itimaduddaula's family was due solely to the influence of Nur Jahan has been put forth by such early chroniclers as Mutamid Khan, Shahnawaz Khan, and Muhammad Hadi and fixed in history by later writers.[3] Recent scholars, however, like Nurul Hasan[4] and Chandra Pant[5] have challenged this theory by arguing that the rise of the family was a "natural phenomenon," which had begun long before, during the reign of Akbar, and had been cemented in place by numerous matrimonial alliances and the good hard work of loyal government service. What has come to be called "the junta debate," however, is in fact no debate at all. While some could argue that

Nur Jahan single-handedly engineered the promotion of her family into high positions, others could argue that Nur Jahan's ascendancy was just a part of the normal emergence of an already distinguished family into positions of merit. Since the evidence can be weighted to serve either side, it is wiser to maintain simply that this talented and charismatic woman made the very most of an already good situation.

Long before her entrance into the life of Jahangir's court, Nur Jahan's relatives occupied high posts in various of the Mughal capitals. Imperial recognition of merit within the family had begun with Mirza Ghiyasuddin Ali, an uncle of Nur Jahan's through her mother, who received the title Asaf Khan (II) from Akbar in 1573 for distinguished fighting and who was, until his death in 1581, recognized for services within the provincial administrations.[6] Jafar Beg, a cousin of Nur Jahan's, was introduced to Akbar in 1577 by his uncle, Ghiyasuddin Ali, and, making his way up the ranks, received the title of Asaf Khan (III) in 1583 and a *mansab* of 3,000 *zat* in 1599.[7] Upon Jahangir's accession in 1605, Asaf Khan Jafar Beg (d. 1612) was named *wazir* of the whole dominion and given a *mansab* of 5,000 each[8] and in 1607 was appointed *vakil khilat-i khas*.[9] This was in part for his role in detaining the rebellious Khusrau and in gathering intelligence about the unsuccessful assassination attempt made on the emperor's life in 1607. Other family members were rewarded as well for their brave loyalty and meritorious service in the 1606 Khusrau affair. Given sizable promotions in the wake of that event, for example, were Aqa Mulla, Ahmad Beg Khan Kabuli, and Abdul Qasim Namakin.[10]

Nur Jahan's own father, too, had done exceptionally well as a new immigrant in the years under Akbar and in the early period just after Jahangir's succession. In a letter dated February 2, 1604, for example, Brother Benedict Goes reported that "he was sent for by Merisachias . . . the King's [Akbar's] chief minister and a very powerful lord,"[11] and the *Iqbalnama* noted that "owing to his devotion to the King's [Akbar's] service, and his intelligence," Mirza Ghiyas Beg was early on made *diwan*, or "superintendent of the household."[12] This honor was later reconfirmed upon Jahangir's accession to the throne when Ghiyas Beg was made *wazir* (*diwan-i kul*) of half the dominion and granted the title of Itimaduddaula.[13]

One could argue, however, that it could only have been the marriage of Nur Jahan to Jahangir in 1611 that accounted for the rather dramatic rise in fortunes of the Persian-born family of Itimaduddaula. Nur Jahan's father was given a substantial increase in *mansab* and made *wazir* of the whole dominion in 1611 and by the time he died in 1622 had been raised to a *mansab* of 7,000 each.[14] Her brother, Abul Hasan, of whom no meritorious accomplishment was recorded definitively prior to this year, received the title Itiqad Khan in 1611,[15] a good *mansab* the next year, and the title Asaf Khan (IV) in 1614. By the time Jahangir died in 1627, this Asaf Khan had been promoted to 7,000 each and had held high posts in Gujarat, Bengal, Orissa, and the Punjab.[16] Another brother, Shapur, who had also been given the title Itiqad Khan (by which he was best known), received his first *mansab* in 1615 and by the time Jahangir died had been promoted to at least 4,000 *zat* and 3,000 *suwar*.[17] Finally, an uncle, Ibrahim

Khan, brother of Nur Jahan's mother Asmat Begam, was promoted to 1,500 *zat* and 600 *suwar* in 1614 and, by the time he died in 1624, had been raised to 4,000 each and given the title Fathjang.[18]

Nur Jahan's sisters also fared well after her marriage to the emperor. A brother-in-law, Mir Qasim, for example, known as Qasim Khan Juvaini, husband of Nur Jahan's sister Manija, was given a *mansab* of 500 *zat* in 1611 and by Jahangir's death in 1627 had been raised to 4,000 *zat* and 2,000 *suwar*.[19] During that time, in 1623, he was made governor of Agra, a position that would be contested later during the rebellion of Mahabat Khan. The husband of another sister Khadija Begam, a man named Hakim Beg, was in time honored with the title Hakim Khan and with the usual presents due "one of the household of the Court."[20] A third brother-in-law, Sadiq Khan, was given a *mansab* of 1,000 *zat* and 500 *suwar* in 1614 and by 1618 was ranked at 2,000 each.[21]

Judging by the figures, then, Nur Jahan's role in the rise of her family's fortunes was significant, but it may not have been, as some have argued, absolutely essential. It is true that although before 1611 no family member held a provincial governorship under Jahangir, between 1611 and 1627 about twelve such members did. It is also true that although the Itimaduddaula family held almost 8 percent of the *mansab*s in 1621, they already had about 2 percent of them by 1605.[22] Based upon inconclusive evidence like this, one might hesitate to attribute the increase in position and status of the family solely to either natural accretion within the system or the 1611 marriage. But one matter alters the balance dramatically because it highlights, as nothing else can, the significance of the role of Nur Jahan: that is, the particular set of circumstances of the family just prior to the marriage.

In the years preceding the marriage, Nur Jahan's family had fallen into disgrace. Her first husband, though formerly in service to Salim, had during the preaccession skirmishes sided with Akbar (and probably with Khusrau) and had subsequently murdered a childhood friend and foster brother of the emperor's. That same year (1607), her father, who had been a trusted minister under both Akbar and Jahangir, had succumbed to his only weakness, money, and had been charged with embezzling by an energetic underling.[23] Finally, the pro-Khusrau assassination attempt on Jahangir in 1607, though ill-fated, had led to the execution of one of Nur Jahan's brothers and a cousin of her mother's. The resulting eclipse of her family over the next four years was to be expected, then, and their reemergence into the light a surprise if attributed only to their own accomplishments. Had the marriage not taken place, we can only guess at the undistinguished pattern the careers of her family might have followed. But had her family not been somewhat well-positioned already, despite the disgrace, the meeting at the Nauroz festival might not ever have happened. We argue, then, that her family's fortunes under Jahangir were due to not one but many things: to strategic positioning, to meritorious service, and also to the beauty and charisma of one of its members.

History has bequeathed us an impressive list of the accomplishments of the woman known as Nur Mahal and later Nur Jahan. The first phase of her ascendancy was marked not only by a prodigious acquisition of power and a disposal of uncountable political and social favors, but also by the awe and almost total disbelief of onlookers at the speed, efficiency, and advantage that characterized Jahangir's retreat and Nur Jahan's appearance. Hawkins reported specifically that he had "to seeke out for jewels fitting for the kings . . . new paramour" in order to gain favor with Jahangir.[24] This was in 1611, and this early date means that within the first six months of her marriage, Nur Jahan had already begun to hold petitioners and courtiers in account to her.

Despite the negative sentiment that often marked the contemporary analysis of this shift in rule,[25] Nur Jahan's growing powers were applied uniformly to benefit an empire that was to experience peace and exceptional prosperity during her reign. Dow, late though he is, has captured the remarkable nature of what she did:

> Her abilities were uncommon; for she rendered herself absolute, in a government in which women are thought incapable of bearing any part. Their power, it is true, is sometimes exerted in the haram; but, like the virtues of the magnet, it is silent and unperceived. Noor-Jehan stood forth in public; she broke through all restraint and custom, and acquired power by her own address, more than by the weakness of Jehangire.[26]

The channels of authority she had to hand were almost endless.[27] Nur Jahan approved all orders (*farmans*) and grants of appointment that went out under the king's name, ordering her own name, "Nur Jahan, the Queen Begam," to be jointly attached to the imperial signature.[28] She controlled all promotions and demotions that issued from the royal government.

> Her former and present supporters have been well rewarded, so that now most of the men who are near the King owe their promotion to her, and are consequently under . . . obligations to her. . . . Many misunderstandings result, for the King's orders or grants of appointments, etc., are not certainties, being of no value until they have been approved by the Queen.[29]

She put her seal on all grants of land "conferred upon any woman," and took special interest in orphan girls, promoting many of them through generous dowries in marriage.[30] She habitually sat at the balcony of her palace (*jharoka*) receiving petitions from nobles[31] and was a lenient and sympathetic judge to those who sought protection under her. She had coins struck in her name, which bore the twelve signs of the zodiac.[32] She collected duties on goods from merchants who passed through her lands near Sikandra from the eastern provinces[33] and traded with Europeans who brought luxury goods from the continent.[34] She assessed and approved the credentials of all visitors who came to court.[35] She engaged in international diplomacy with high-placed women of other countries.[36] And she routinely erected expensive buildings—rest houses for travelers (*sarais*), gardens, palaces, and tombs—"intending thereby [said Pelsaert] to establish an enduring reputation for herself."[37]

Nur Jahan was careful to encourage the paraphernalia of power around her as well. Dow notes that she was distinguished from the other wives by the title of Shahi or "empress,"[38] deriving undoubtedly from the title Shah Begam, given to her either, according to Prasad, in 1613 after the death of the reigning Shah Begam, Salima Sultan Begam, or, according to C. Pant, in 1622.[39] She enjoyed the display of public fanfare and affection for her and did nothing to discourage the easily manipulated popular mythologies; "Nur Jahan Begam used to ride out, with people playing and singing before her, [and] she was received by every one with marks of excessive honour and reverence, even like a goddess."[40] Finally, she gathered wealth to her as a natural perquisite of her position, spending it lavishly on herself and her family, but using it as well to lubricate the gears of the empire.[41]

In the end, her powers grew so vast that she acquired all the rights of sovereignty and government normally due the emperor. She managed "the whole affairs of the realm, and honours of every description were at her disposal,"[42] such that she was absolute monarch in all but one thing—that of having the *khutba* read in her name.[43] The *khutba* was an announcement of sovereignty made before the Friday noon prayers in the mosque and after those of the *id*, and its reading would have made her absolute ruler in name as well; it would also have required absolute obedience to her from all subjects.[44] Here, however, its absence was only a religious and political formality as she already wielded all the power there was. Jahangir, still the hereditary holder of the throne, prided himself on having successfully passed over to her not only all the responsibilities of maintaining the empire, but most of its privileges as well, for he was known to brag that having bestowed sovereignty on Nur Jahan, he required nothing else but a *sir* of wine and half a *sir* of meat.[45] Sir Thomas Roe, in fact, was to write to a fellow Englishman in January of 1617 as follows:

> But I fear he [Jahangir] will not long stay anywhere, whose course is directed by a woman, and is now as it were shut up by her so, that all justice or care of anything or public affairs either sleeps, or depends on her, who is more unaccessible than any goddess, or mystery of heathen impiety.[46]

In Shah Jahan's reign, according to Bernier, Nur Jahan was known as the queen "who . . . wielded the sceptre, while her husband abandoned himself to drunkenness and dissipation," as her "transcendent abilities rendered her competent to govern the Empire without the interference of her husband."[47] She was in short, said Manucci, eminently "worthy to be a queen."[48]

Her rise to power, however, did not have the unanimous support of all the nobles and at least one of them, Mahabat Khan, reportedly went to Jahangir later and made known his opposition to the rule of the queen. The *Intikhab-i Jahangir-Shahi*, for example, said that when Mahabat Khan finally realized that "the entire management of the Empire . . . [had been] entrusted to her hands," he spoke to the emperor as would a loyal friend. "The whole world is surprised," he said, "that such a wise and sensible Emperor as Jahangir should permit a woman to have so great an influence over him." What would future kings say?

After considering Mahabat Khan's concerns in private, "the Emperor for some days became more reserved in his demeanor towards the Begam."[49] Nur Jahan, however, did not take Mahabat Khan's opposition to her power lightly, and even though he was opposed, it seems, only on principle—"it was indecorous to let a woman govern the empire"[50]—she held this noble personally in contempt for much of her time on the throne.

Nur Jahan could not have exercised the authority she did without a structure that funneled power naturally and immediately to her. The "junta," or the "faction" as Roe called it, was a skillful outgrowth of the needs and circumstances of the time, comprising at its height Nur Jahan; her father, Itimaduddaula; her brother, Asaf Khan; and her stepson and the eventual heir to the throne as Shah Jahan, Khurram. The power of the junta was substantial and could be carried, as it often was, to extreme excess. "They still strive for an impossible advancement," said Pelsaert, "for the world cannot sustain their eminence."[51] Nevertheless, the group managed, by an intricate network of communication and vested interest, to promote their own concerns while at the same time protecting the king from unnecessary responsibility. The junta worked as follows:

> If anyone with a request to make at Court obtains an audience or is allowed to speak, the King hears him indeed, but will give no definite answer of Yes or No, referring him promptly to Asaf Khan, who in the same way will dispose of no important matter without communicating with his sister, the Queen, and who regulates his attitude in such a way that the authority of neither of them may be diminished. Anyone then who obtains a favour must thank them for it, and not the King.[52]

The specific configuration of the junta was, then, extremely important. The group could not have worked without a strategically placed son around whom courtiers could vie for attention, and in whom the hopes for a brilliant succession could be invested. Thus, while the function of the junta was to provide benefits to its members in the present, its rationale was to give caretaker governance to the current emperor in preparation for a glorious succession in years hence. The choice of sons, therefore, was especially significant. Although no real power struggle ever actually took place among them, as Khurram, who had been much loved by Akbar and was his choice to succeed Jahangir,[53] had been the heir apparent in all but name for years, the appearance of a struggle and the constant jealousies were intense.

The eldest son, Khusrau (1587–1621), was "a Prince of much expectation, [and] well-belov'd."[54] He was apparently a very handsome man and the beauty of his face was matched only by "a very lovely presence."[55] He had been hailed by some nobles at the court as the successor to his grandfather Akbar before his father's accession,[56] but the bitter struggle of those years had brought out a bleaker side of his personality.

> [Khusrau] was a prince of haughty disposition. He was governed by furious passions. His mind was in a perpetual agitation. . . . He was now volatile and

> cheerful; now dark and sullen. He often laughed at misfortune; he was often enraged at trifles; and his whole conduct betrayed every mark of an insanity of mind.[57]

Jahangir often expressed the strong affection that he had for this firstborn son who, he knew, had obvious charisma and personal magnetism,[58] but he recognized that Khusrau was easy prey to both ill-minded courtiers[59] and the hereditary melancholy of his ancestors.[60] To him Khusrau became "that graceless one,"[61] "that unfortunate one,"[62] yet a son whose life he couldn't end no matter how despicable the behavior.[63] The struggle for power between father and elder son continued to be so strong and so eratic that Jahangir could find no way to bequeath him the throne,[64] and ultimately Khusrau was left with the support of only a few nobles and of the women of the harem.

Jahangir's second son, Parviz (1589–1626), was reportedly dull and incompetent, "a man of poor spirit, aspiring to no state or display,"[65] who though full of pride and ambition found his greatest pleasure in drink. Roe visited him at his court in Burhanpur once in 1615, and in spite of Parviz's willingness to contract business, the ambassador found him running the Deccan campaign in name only, the real work being carried out by his guardian the current Khankhanan (Abdur Rahim). Roe had given the prince a number of presents at the time but found that Parviz had interest only in the case of liquor, and by the time Roe stood to leave, Parviz had become completely incapacitated by drink.[66]

Jahangir's fourth and youngest surviving son, Shahryar (1605–28), was born of a concubine at the time of Jahangir's accession. Although famous for his youthful patience and restraint in the face of his father's cruel and violent treatment of him,[67] Shahryar was known to be easily manipulated. Reportedly "the most beautiful of all the princes,"[68] he would eventually become the puppet of Nur Jahan, married to her daughter Ladli Begam in an attempt to secure imperial longevity for another branch of the Itimaduddaula family. Shahryar's "tender age, docile nature, feeble mind, and imbecile character,"[69] however, precluded any real chance he might have had in the final struggle for succession.

It was Jahangir's third son, Khurram (1592–1666), who proved to have the character, stamina, and cunning necessary for the political intrigues that would carry him to a successful place on the throne. Born of a favorite early wife, Jagat Gosaini (a harem rival of Nur Jahan's), Khurram was educated in the broad, liberal tradition of the court. He had a restrained streak that manifested itself most notably in a youthful abstinence from drink, which would be seriously compromised on his twenty-fourth birthday when his father introduced him to wine.[70] Although it was with much hesitation that he drank his first cup that day,[71] he eventually took to the wine, beginning in this way a lifelong, though not always tempered habit.[72]

As is evident from the exquisite beauty of such buildings as the Taj Mahal, built for his favorite wife upon her death in 1631, Khurram loved fine things. An extraordinarily handsome man himself, Khurram had a strong proclivity for jewels, and Manrique reported that even when, after a banquet, twelve dancing girls appeared with "lascivious and suggestive dress, [and] immodest behavior and posturing," he continued to inspect the jewels Asaf Khan had brought for him.[73] It was primarily through a taste for fine gemstones, then, that he relished without regret the fabulous lifestyle of the court.[74] He was a well-trained and experienced general as well, whose reputed skill and tactical expertise earned him rewards for his campaigns in Mewar, the Deccan, and Gujarat.[75] But though he spent much time in military campaigns, fighting did not become him quite as much as it did his son and eventual successor, Aurangzeb, and Khurram seems to have accepted the stints in the field only as a way to return to the luxuries of the court.

For his promise as a well-rounded and competent sovereign, then, Khurram had been much loved by Akbar, who "always recommended him to me [Jahangir] and frequently told me there was no comparison between him and my other children. He recognised him as his real child." Khurram himself had returned the favor, for by Jahangir's own admission, Khurram was "more attentive to my father than all (my) other children."[76] Though third in birth, Khurram was considered by Jahangir to be in all respects "the first of my sons,"[77] and his father watched as "gradually, as his years increased, so did his excellencies."[78] In his early years, this son was called Baba Khurram, "Darling Khurram," "inasmuch as the signs of rectitude and knowledge of affairs were evident in him."[79] In 1616, Jahangir bestowed on him the title of Shah Sultan Khurram just before he departed for the Deccan,[80] in recognition not only of his military prowess but also of his eventual fitness for the throne.

Khurram, then, was the natural son around whom the junta could build its structures of power. The dynamics of the junta's pivotal relationships, rooted as they were in the kinship ties of father, daughter, and son, rested more precariously, however, upon the nature of the bond between Nur Jahan and her stepson. We do not know when the collaboration between them actually began (perhaps in the early years under Ruqayya Sultan Begam), but it must surely have been as much at the instigation of Khurram as it was of his stepmother. Nur Jahan had early on secured the lasting favor of Jahangir and, if Khurram were to have any chance of prevailing over his brothers for the throne, he must find favor with his father in the most profitable way possible. It was to his advantage, then, to acquiesce to or even to promote the maternal bondings so desired by his father and so central to the harem's involvement in governing; and if Nur Jahan was his father's chosen among the women of the palace, then, clearly her favor was crucial. As Roe said: "Sultan Carroone is as absolute by Normahall's power, as she, who is all."[81]

It comes as no surprise, then, that one of the first times we see Khurram and Nur Jahan together was when, in the wake of Khurram's victories in Mewar in early 1615, Jahangir ordered his son "to go and wait on his mothers."[82] As a part of the festivities, Nur Jahan presented Prince Karan, son of Amar Singh and heir apparent to Mewar, now a negotiated part of the Mughal empire, "a rich dress of honour, a jewelled sword, a horse and saddle, and an elephant"[83] [see Figure 4–2]. The presentation was not only a personal compliment to Khurram from Nur Jahan for his tactical finesse in the negotiations with the leadership of Mewar, but an act of imperial recognition on the part of the junta for one of its own.

The tightness (and tension) within the junta rested in part upon a series of marriage negotiations undertaken between the families of Itimaduddaula and Jahangir. The most important marriage, without doubt, was that between Khurram and Arjumand Banu Begam, Nur Jahan's niece and daughter of her brother Asaf Khan. The ceremony took place on April 30, 1612, and was accompanied by the usual bestowal of lavish presents, made particularly grand by those to the women of the palaces. Das claims that the arrangement of this marriage was one of the first acts of Nur Jahan as empress,[84] but according to the *Padshahnama*[85] the betrothal took place five years and three months before, that is, sometime in 1607.[86] Nur Jahan's role in contracting this marriage, then, was minimal, and for the ceremony she had to settle for the lesser role of aunt of the bride.

As it happens, the marriage may have been the cause of some ill-feeling between Khurram and Nur Jahan. Some have hinted at Nur Jahan's early attempts to get Khurram to marry her own daughter by Sher Afgan, Ladli Begam. Such a marriage was never a possibility, however, as Khurram was unquestionably devoted to Arjumand Banu Begam.[87] He loved Asaf Khan's daughter so much, in fact, that on her death in 1631 he went into seclusion for two years, reappearing, according to legend, with eyeglasses and hair now completely gray.[88]

Nur Jahan had also been unsuccessful in marrying Ladli Begam off to the eldest son, Khusrau. According to Della Valle:

> *Nurmahal*, who had apprehended that *Sultan Chosrou* would succeed his Father in the kingdom, and desir'd to establish herself well, had frequently offer'd her Daughter to *Sultan Chosrou*, before she married her to *Sultan Scehriar*, but he, either for that he had another Wife he lov'd sufficiently and would not wrong her, or because he scorn'd Nurmahal's Daughter, would never consent.[89]

While in prison, it seems, Khusrau was told that if he would consent to marry Nur Jahan's daughter he would be set free but, despite the pleadings of his own much-beloved wife, who had negotiated to live with him as his servant in confinement, Khusrau continued to refuse the offer.[90] This was apparently the reason why "*Sultan Chosrou* remained always much in the hatred of *Nurmahal*" and why she was later so malicious in her dealings with him.[91]

Despite the tensions over marriage arrangements, however, the alliance between Nur Jahan and Khurram remained exceedingly strong for a number of years. Its official high point came with the feast Nur Jahan prepared for him in 1617 in Mandu marking his victorious return from campaigns in the Deccan [see Figure 3–1]. It was during this campaign that Khurram earned the title Shah Jahan, "King of the World," and the right to sit on a chair near his father's throne during Jahangir's assemblies.[92] At her feast, Nur Jahan presented Shah Jahan with robes, a turban, a turban ornament, a waistbelt, a sword, a dagger, and a saddle—all richly decorated with rare and costly gems—along with two horses and three elephants. She also presented his women and children with substantial presents, thereby bringing the total cost of the entertainment to

FIGURE 3–1. "Jahangir and Prince Khurram Feasted by Nur Jahan." Indian painting; Mughal, 1617; school of Jahangir; from an album of Shah Jahan; color and gold on paper: 25.2 × 14.2 cm. (9 15/16 × 5 5/8"). Courtesy of the Freer Gallery of Art, Smithsonian Institution, Washington, D.C. (07.258). Note the Chinese porcelain imports, the Madonna picture, and the nimbus around Jahangir's head. Copies of this painting can be found in the Victoria and Albert Museum, London (I.M. 115–1921), and in the Maharaja Sawai Man Singh II Museum, City Palace, Jaipur (A G 823).

about Rs. 300,000.[93] In return, Shah Jahan gave Nur Jahan presents worth Rs. 200,000 and Rs. 60,000 to "his other mothers and the Begams."[94]

The early relationship between Nur Jahan and Shah Jahan seems to have been one marked by respect, collaboration, and enduring counsel. The only contemporary chronicler to even hint at anything more was Thomas Roe (followed by Peter Mundy) who, observing that Shah Jahan seemed distracted during one meeting, noted the following:

> If I can Iudg any thing, hee hath left his hart among his fathers women, with whom hee hath liberty of conuersation. Normahall in the English Coach the day before visited him and tooke leaue. She gaue him a Cloake all embrodered with Pearle, diamondes and rubyes; and carried away, if I err not, his attention to all other busines.[95]

There is no evidence whatsoever to suspect Nur Jahan and Shah Jahan of anything other than the most filial of bonds, and the distraction Roe observed here was easily the result of the presents or, more likely, a political matter currently occupying their joint attention. From all the evidence, stepmother and son were at best platonically friendly and at worst warily on guard.[96]

The elder statesman of the junta was Nur Jahan's father, Itimaduddaula (d. 1622). Itimaduddaula was known as the "open ear" of the court, who by reputation was fair, just, and compassionate. He was exceptionally well educated and "considered exceedingly clever and skilful, both in writing and in transacting business." Having studied the classical Persian poets, he "had a nice appreciation of the meaning of words; and he wrote *shikasta* in a bold and elegant style."[97] He had the complete trust of Jahangir, and the emperor, being "very closely connected with his family," held Itimaduddaula's goodwill toward him "very dear,"[98] bestowing upon him the title Madarulmulk, "Pivot of the Country"[99] [see Figure 3–2]. At the counsellor's death, Jahangir eulogized him with an unusual perceptiveness and acuity:

> He was a wise and perfect Vizier, and a learned and affectionate companion . . . . Though the weight of such a kingdom was on his shoulders, . . . no one ever went to Itimadu-d-daula with a petition or on business who turned from him in an injured frame of mind. He showed loyalty to the sovereign, and yet left pleased and hopeful him who was in need. In fact, this was a speciality of his.[100]

Nur Jahan's father was not only a loyal courtier fond of the normal round of gift giving and promotions,[101] but a minister whose services, as Jahangir noted above, were singularly wise and reliable. His advice to Jahangir was priceless, especially on matters of promotions for loyal subordinates, pardons for criminal offenders, and general issues of patronage in which Itimaduddaula was known to be a particularly compassionate touch.[102] He regularly urged conciliation during moments of family tension,[103] acted as messenger and courier at Jahangir's behest[104] (as he had for Akbar),[105] and maintained a house forever open to the

FIGURE 3–2. "Emperor Jahangir and his Vizier, Itimaduddaula." Indian painting; Mughal, ca. 1615; fr. the *Kevorkian Album*; inscr. to Manohar. Courtesy of The Metropolitan Museum of Art, New York, Purchase, Rogers Fund and The Kevorkian Foundation Gift, 1955 (MMA 55.121.10.23).

frequent and often unannounced visits of the emperor.[106] Itimaduddaula's compound had a reputation as "a delightful place and enchanting residence"[107] and was often lavishly decorated as a part of his contribution to the empire's entertainment.[108]

Itimaduddaula was rewarded substantially for his part in Jahangir's rule, with honors bestowed upon him the likes of which no other minister on record had ever seen. In 1615, he was given a standard and drums to be beaten after the emperor's entrance to the court.[109] In 1616 he was called upon to help write the memoirs when Jahangir himself was so overcome with the death of one of Shah Jahan's daughters that he couldn't lift his pen. At the beginning of 1617, Jahangir ordered the women of the harem to go unveiled before Itimaduddaula as he was now "an intimate friend" of the imperial family.[110] Later that year, Jahangir removed the imperial turban from his own head and placed it on Itimaduddaula's as a sign of special favor[111] and gave him one of his own private elephants, named Jagjot, in honor of his work in governing the Punjab.[112] Finally in 1618, Itimaduddaula was one of only three people to receive a personal copy of the *Jahangirnama*, a record of the first twelve years of Jahangir's reign. The other two recipients were Shah Jahan and Asaf Khan.[113]

Famous as he was for his sense of fairness and accessibility, Itimaduddaula was also famous for the weakness that made this accessibility possible: greed. According to the *Tatimma-i Wakiat-i Jahangiri*, the charitability toward which the minister was so well disposed and which allowed "no one [to] ever . . . [leave] his door dissatisfied" was also the liberality which drew him toward offbeat financial arrangements, for "in the taking of bribes he certainly was most uncompromising and fearless."[114] Itimaduddaula's propensity for monetary persuasion was not so well known as to be found in all the early sources, but there must have been some truth to the rumors about it for the Dutch seemed quite confident cf the minister's weaknesses here. Van den Broecke routinely recounted the early story of Itimaduddaula's "misappropriation" of Rs. 50,000 and the trouble it caused for the family when coupled with the seditious activities of the elder son Muhammad Sharif.[115] De Laet's derivative account confirmed the embezzling charge, as well as the reprieve granted Itimaduddaula in exchange for a substantial purse[116] and a temporary loss of rank. Certainly later tradition knew of the weakness, but tempered it to suit an overall laudatory assessment. Says Dow, for example, "an economist in every thing, but in charity, he was only covetous of wealth to relieve the needy and the poor."[117]

The final player among the principals in the junta was Nur Jahan's brother, Asaf Khan (d. 1641). He was the last of the junta members to come into power under Jahangir and the only one to move relatively unscathed through the bitter years of succession, emerging in the years after 1627 as the most powerful man in Shah Jahan's government. Asaf Khan became prominent in the junta as the point man for Europeans in the efforts to establish trading contracts and exhibited over the years a habitual duplicity in matters of loyalty that was motivated entirely by opportunism. Born Abul Hasan, he received the titles of Itiqad Khan in 1611[118] and Asaf Khan (IV) in 1614.[119] Because of his family ties and because of his expertise as a courtier, Asaf Khan was taken in by Jahangir as his "adopted son" (*farzandi*)[120] and, like his own father, was known as "that pillar of the kingdom"[121] who "fulfilled the duties of homage, and of offerings, and thereby acquired eternal bliss."[122] Says Dow:

> In his private character, he was mild, affable, humane, generous; in his public, severe, reserved, inflexible, exact. He never excused negligence; he punished disobedience. His orders, therefore, were no sooner issued than they were executed; his very nod was respected, understood and obeyed. . . . He was uniform in his conduct, impartial and dignified in his actions, consistent with himself. He courted not popularity by his measures: justice, propriety, and the ultimate good of the state, and not the applause of the vulgar, were his objects in all his decisions.[123]

Perhaps even more than in the case of his father, Asaf Khan's house and gardens were Jahangir's second home. Known as "a very fine and pleasant place," Asaf Khan's house had a reputation for beauty and luxury and was often the site of Jahangir's own rest and entertainment.[124]

Of all the members of the junta, Asaf Khan was perhaps the only one intimately known to European traders.[125] Farthest of the four from the throne and therefore closest to the world outside the palace, Asaf Khan developed good relations with several of the Englishmen who courted trade, a tie that became a decided advantage for him at court. He and Hawkins, for example, "were great friends, he [Asaf Khan] having beene often at my house,"[126] and the Mughal minister frequently entertained Roe at his own home during the ambassador's official stay in India.[127] The English saw Asaf Khan as a man whose high station was the result primarily of family alliances, and one who sought to aggrandize his material worth by using these alliances to his own best advantage,[128] as seen in his purchase of a fine, large pearl.[129] There could be no better person, then, through whom to negotiate what promised to be exceptionally lucrative trading agreements.

The general state of affairs under the rule of the junta, it seems, was one of peace and prosperity for the empire and mental relief for the emperor. The junta formed a strong party that was loyal to Jahangir, but that freed him from the major responsibilities of governing. Although Jahangir was fearful of losing too much power to the provinces—hence his policy of frequently moving governors and their ministers around so that these "his substitutes may not in any place grow popular"[130]—he himself did not relish administration. The junta, then, was the ideal structure, for it allowed Jahangir all the trappings of state but extricated him from the powers and obligations attendant upon his office. The popularity of the junta fluctuated, however, and, in spite of a real dislike for Nur Jahan by the other women of the harem,[131] the business of the group was such that no matter what the personal style of the players, the faction in power was sure to be seen as cunning and avaricious and as having duped an innocent, if lame, emperor into its hands. Sympathy, then, ran high for Jahangir and notoriously low for the group actually in power.

The interworkings of the junta members were perhaps nowhere more clear than in their collaboration on the domestic issue known as the "Khusrau problem."[132] The Khusrau issue was not of the junta's own making for Jahangir's eldest son had made himself troublesome to his father from an early age in the succession struggles of 1603 to 1605, in his rebellion of 1606,[133] and in the assassination attempt of 1607. Since that time Khusrau had been imprisoned in the palace near Jahangir, under vigilant guard, blind or partially blind, and attended by a loving and faithful wife. In the years following the junta's ascendancy, however, Khusrau became a passive pawn in the jostling for power that took place. Although Jahangir had made efforts not to have Khusrau treated exactly like a prisoner, providing "everything necessary for his comfort and convenience in the way of eating and clothing,"[134] he was nevertheless watchfully concerned that old Khusrau loyalties did not foment once more into rebellion. For this reason, and because of Nur Jahan's growing frustration with Khusrau's imperviousness to her pleas for marriage to her daughter, Khusrau was forbidden in 1614 to come to court to pay his respects to the emperor.

Khusrau's life in prison was, with the exception of his wife, a miserable lot. Coryat observed that once during this period, when Jahangir was to go away for four months on a hunting expedition, he had Khusrau walled up in a tower to keep him safe during his absence. The tower was "without gate, doore, or window, except some small holes to let in ayre, higher than he could come into," and while there he was allowed only a small number of servants.[135] His wife had pleaded with the king to be shut up with her husband and, refusing the liberty offered by Jahangir, she would have nothing but to be a companion to her husband in his misery.

It was in 1616 that Khusrau was handed over to Asaf Khan for safekeeping.[136] Roe described in detail the story of the junta's efforts in bringing about this change. With "impudent bouldnes . . . that dare attempt anything," the faction now worked to use its extraordinary liberty with the emperor to remove Khusrau from any possibility of imperial favor. Resolved that "it was not possible for them to stand if the Prince Sultan Corsoronne liued, whom the nobilitye loued, . . . [they] Practised how to bring him into their Power, that poyson might end him."[137] Nur Jahan, said Roe, went to work on Jahangir, using "the false teares of womans bewitching flattery" to convince her husband that Khusrau still entertained seditious thoughts.[138] When this failed, Shah Jahan, Itimaduddaula, and Asaf Khan went to the King when he was drunk and persuaded him that for Khusrau's safety and honor "it were fitter he were in the keeping of his brother," whose company would be pleasing one to the other.[139] Jahangir agreed and then fell asleep. Roe's story did not conclude with the successful handing over of Khusrau to Asaf Khan, however, and later, on October 21, 1616, we find Roe reporting that six of Shah Jahan's servants came secretly to murder Khusrau, "but were refused the key by the Porter."[140] Eventually the forces of the junta must have won out, for it was on October 25, 1616, that Jahangir announced the transfer of Khusrau to Asaf Khan on account of "certain considerations."[141] A month later, in November, Roe noted that when Jahangir and Nur Jahan called upon the now reassigned Khusrau, he appeared before them with a beard "grown to his middle, a signe of disfauour."[142]

In 1617, with Khusrau still in "protective custody," efforts were made to heal the breach between him and the junta. Roe reported that on August 21, 1617, Itimaduddaula advised Nur Jahan and Asaf Khan "to make a peace with Corsoroone," as a part of his enjoying his first day of hoped-for liberty in Roe's company.[143] Later on August 25, Asaf Khan had a feast prepared for Nur Jahan and Khusrau in order to make a "firme alliance" in the expectation, said Roe, of Khusrau's future full freedom.[144]

Freedom came at last in 1619 when Jahangir, having decided that Khusrau's imprisonment had been long enough, took him out of confinement and allowed him to pay his full respects at court.[145] Until his death in 1621, Khusrau himself never made any other move that might have been interpreted as seditious. Nevertheless, with the power structures as fragile and precariously balanced as they were, members of the junta could not take a chance. Despite earlier rumors of an alliance between Khusrau and Asaf Khan,[146] Nur Jahan, Shah Jahan, Itimaduddaula, and Asaf Khan worked keenly and, as they saw it, in their own best interests, against any permanent restoration of Khusrau. Whatever Jahangir himself may have wished—and we cannot discount the possibility that the 1619 grant of freedom was a publicity play on the part of the junta—Khusrau's chances for renewed stature at court, or even for rights to succession, were extremely small.

Information gathering and policymaking were the two mainstays of the junta's operation and Nur Jahan's central role in them could be found in all parts of the government. It was she, for example, by Jahangir's own account, who first informed the emperor of Shah Jahan's 1617 victories in the Deccan, for which he rewarded her the *pargana* of Toda with revenues calculated to be about Rs. 200,000.[147] It was she who dissuaded Parviz in 1616 from paying his respects to the emperor, presumably because the prospect had caused Shah Jahan extreme anxiety, despite the fact that "the king had fallen downe and taken his Mistris by the feete to obteyne her leave to see his sonne."[148] And it was she who held meetings, like the one in 1617, where differences and breaches that had grown up among government workers could be worked out in an amiable atmosphere.[149] The junta operated so effectively and so single-mindedly during these years precisely, as these examples show, because of her smooth regulation of its internal affairs.

The operation of the junta was seen to particular advantage by Roe, who was present at the court during the height of its power (1616–18) and who learned quickly the best, though not always the most successful, way to manipulate its parts. Roe originally became aware of the junta within the first month of his stay in the Mughal king's presence and knew immediately that, whatever his fortune, it depended solely upon the good auspices of these four people. At the end of January 1616, after having been first received at court on only January 10, Roe reported:

> I saw now the faction, but was irresolute what to doe. Asaph Chan was a broken reede; the Prince gouerned by him;[150] the King was my only refuge, from whom I was sure of Iustice if I Complayned, but I feard I should drawe vpon me the hate of Normall the beloued queen.[151]

Roe discerned at once the nature and relations of all the characters arrayed before him and believed full well that in the peculiarities of their familial alliances lay his fate: "The Prince Sultan Coronne, Normahall the deare queene, Aunt to his wife, Asaph chan his father-in-law, brother to the Queene, and Etiman Dowlett, father to them both, beeing they that now gouerne all and dare attempt anything."[152]

Powerless before what he called the "treacherous faction,"[153] Roe found that there was another equally as powerless as he: the emperor. While Jahangir was his only refuge and source of justice, he was, nevertheless, also at the mercy of the faction's whims. Jahangir, for whatever reason, had given them "liberty beyond eyther the law of their owne Condition or the limitts of Policye and reason,"[154] and now had to suffer the consequences of having withdrawn in the face of their increasing ascendancy: "[Jahangir] is soe good of disposition that he suffers ill men to gouerne. . . . [He] had yeeilded himself into the handes of a woman, [and] could not defend his sonne [Khusrau] from their Practises. Hee either sees not the ambition or trustes it too farr in Confidence of his owne Power."[155] Roe seemed to be of two minds as to Jahangir's complicity in the junta's power, not being able to decide whether the king willingly gave up authority or had had it tricked or stolen from him. Whatever his final assessment of Jahangir on this issue, Roe seemed to be well-disposed toward the emperor, casting him as a gracious, curious, and compassionate man who, though weak, was still the majesterial head of the empire.[156]

The real center of the government, however, as Roe saw, was Nur Jahan. On January 12, 1616, when he first arrived at court, Roe was asked to give up his letter of commission to one of Jahangir's couriers so that the queen could see his official seal,[157] and from that moment forward the ambassador knew that this woman, who in time came to be the "protectresse" of the English, "wholly gouerneth" the king and all his affairs.[158] He tried, therefore, not to make any mistakes in seeking to conciliate her or her allies. Very soon, however, the particular power of Nur Jahan, and the way it was manifest in the workings of the junta, reflected a larger pattern for Roe:

> Normahall fullfill[ed] the observation that in all actions of Consequence in a court, especially in faction, a woman is not only alwayes an ingredient, but commonly a Principall drugg and of most vertue; and shee showes that they are not incapable of Conducting busines, nor herselfe voyd of witt and subtiltye.[159]

What made the centrality of Nur Jahan even more difficult for Roe was that he was denied the intimacy with her he clearly enjoyed with all the other members of the junta, save Itimaduddaula, whom he described as distant and "always indifferent."[160] As a Muslim woman, Nur Jahan was screened from him behind the walls of *parda*, and this inaccessibility only enhanced the loss of control Roe experienced with regard to his own affairs at court.

Roe was able to work closely with other members of the junta, however, and soon developed productive, if not always mutually respectful, relations with Shah Jahan and with the prominent courtier, Mahabat Khan. His main point of contact with the junta, though, was always Asaf Khan, with whom he was in touch almost daily and who served as the conduit for information and opinion on trading agreements between Roe and the government. Roe knew that Asaf Khan was, at least at this time, the puppet of his sister[161] but since his connections were excellent, through both his sister and his daughter (the wife of Shah Jahan), and since he was by nature a man of greed and connivance, Asaf Khan was as effective an agent of negotiation as the ambassador could have. Roe worked hard to separate Asaf Khan from the rest of the junta so that the trading contracts could more easily be settled—entertaining him, praising him, and being conciliatory—but the fickleness of the Mughal court continued to work to his disadvantage. As he noted on September 5, 1616: "Mochrebchan sent to speake with mee, who reauealed to mee in great friendship that Asaph Chan was our enemy, or at beste a false frend: that hee had faltered with mee in my business with the king."[162] Although Roe had no choice but to go on with Asaf Khan, the process of negotiation with a man of his character was frustrating and, in the end, a failure.

Negotiation could only take place in an atmosphere of openness and receptivity, and Roe found that entrance into the court and into the good will of its members was possible only if he bought it, and with presents of extremely high value and quality. As Best said: "The Portuguese will do their utmost, both by gifts and by force, to expel us from this place. It is therefore necessary for us to gain the goodwill of the King and of certain principal persons; the which may be obtained with some trifles from our country."[163] Bribing eventually became a way of life for Roe and his people,[164] and he routinely had to bring presents for all members of the junta whenever he came to court.[165] Often the presents were not good enough and not frequent enough,[166] and Roe occasionally found himself wanting to break all rules by having no presents at all. He never did, however.

> If the Queene must be presented (which I will not aduise too, and doe purpose, as well out of necessytye as Iudgment, to breake this Custome of daylye bribing) fine needle woorke toyes, fayre bone lace, cuttworke, and some handsome wrought wastcote, sweetbagges or Cabinetts, wilbe most Convenient. . . . I would add any faire China Bedsteeds, or cabinetes or truncks of Japan are here rich presentes.[167]

The generosity of the Mughal court to Roe in return was apparently substantial, though given at whim and with great condescension. In addition to being entertained in the palaces and at the homes of leading junta participants, Roe used to receive spontaneous gifts like that of muskmelons from Itimaduddaula—"with this Complement that they came from the handes of the Queene his daughter"[168]—or that of a female slave, a former servant of Nur Jahan's "who for some offence was putt away."[169] "Loathe to receiue" a former offender, Roe tried to refuse the woman but was forced to keep her the night in his dining room before negotiating her departure to friends the next day.[170] He was also granted courtesies at court, presumably because of his official high standing at the court of the English king, and Jahangir, characteristically, treated him intimately on any number of occasions. Nevertheless, Roe's pains were for nothing, and in spite of all the efforts at personal and material cultivation of those in power, his own advice would have been well worth taking: "I did aduise our little Common wealth to keepe close and neare togither, to attend the issue, to know no syde, to make few debtes, and to keepe as few residencyes as the necessitye of their affaires will suffer."[171]

Even if Roe was eventually outmaneuvered in his bid for trading contracts, he was eminently successful in approaching the junta and in observing it close to hand. Because his tenure at the court (1616–19) coincided roughly with the height of the junta's power (1614–19), and necessarily with the height of favor for Shah Jahan (1617–19), Roe was able to confirm by his own participation what others knew only at a distance. He knew, for example, that Pelsaert's claim was true: that the king was "King in name only, while she and her brother Asaf Khan hold the kingdom firmly in their hands . . . [and that many] misunderstandings result, for the King's orders or grants of appointments, etc., are not certainties, being of no value until they have been approved by the Queen."[172] He could also draw his own firsthand opinion of the players and, in as discreet a manner as his public journals would allow, cast support for his own personal candidates. Roe was sure that fratricidal fighting would break out over the issue of succession, but he was not sure that Shah Jahan would win; his own choice, we know, was the pro-Christian elder son, Khusrau. Since even at its height, the cracks in the junta were perceptible to Roe,[173] we are not surprised that, given his bad treatment at the hands of the "faction," he dreamt of a different lay of land in the years to come. We are surprised, however, that he miscalculated the staying power of Nur Jahan so completely. Given all that he knew of her pivotal dominance at court, he must surely have foreseen that she would stand by the controlling reins until the very end.

4

"The World Conqueror"

. . . for sometimes he was barbarously cruel, and at other times he would seem to be exceedingly fair and gentle.

Edward Terry, *A Voyage to East-India*

The ease with which Nur Jahan took control was as much a function of the personality of Jahangir as it was of her own clear sight and charisma. The man she married as her second husband, and with whom she spent more than a third of her adult life as consort, was an odd mix of traits often much at war. It has become commonplace to say that Jahangir had contradictory elements within his personality, that he was as Terry noted above both barbarously cruel and exceedingly fair and gentle,[1] weak and yet amiable,[2] and as given to scrupulous, severe, and exact behavior as he was to caprice and whim.[3] Modern scholars, too, generally characterize Jahangir as a man of contrasts saying, for example, that he was a "strange mix of savagry and kindness," a not altogether harmonious blend of whimsical temperamentalness and sympathy, or of intolerance and understanding.[4] While the view that Jahangir was a man plagued by inconsistency is fair—great cruelty and random punishment did alternate with a love of justice and odd affections—these inconsistencies masked another, greater vision. The world peculiar to Jahangir grew, apparently, from a perspective that was clear and satisfying and that seemed, internally at least, to be as reasonable and coherent as any of those held otherwise.

Above all else, Jahangir's ties to the world were aesthetic. His orientation toward his environment, his perception of his experience, and the guiding structures of his relationships with people derived directly from his senses and, of these, primarily from the visual. What most satisfied Jahangir was what gave him pleasure, and what gave him most pleasure were things he could see. He was guided not by principles of right or wrong or standards of good behavior, but by an affective and material order, which could be known, admired, and manipulated by him as viewer. And pleasure arose when this aesthetic vision fell into place around him confirming that he was, if not its creator, at least its caretaker.

Jahangir "the aesthete," as Das calls him, was most susceptible to items of form. From his decision to pierce his ears in 1614[5] to his fascination with Karnatic jugglers throwing up balls the size of oranges,[6] Jahangir loved the visual frenzy of life at court. He was a connoisseur of almost every aspect of Mughal life. He loved the mangoes grown around Agra;[7] he knew all the flowers in north India and Kashmir;[8] he helped create the delicacies of the Mughal kitchen and could distinguish between fish that were almost identical in appearance and taste;[9] he had a collection of jade wine cups in various designs and sizes to match his extravagant drinking habits;[10] he wore magnificent clothes of embroidered silks and brocades and invented a special coat called a *nadiri* to be used only by those he gave it to;[11] he fancied himself a poet like the other Persian-speaking rulers of his time;[12] and he orchestrated elegant parades and mannered royal camps that became a part of Mughal court in motion.[13] All this, Roe noted, was part of the theater-like quality of Jahangir's court:

> Three times a day hee sitteth out in three places: once to see his Elephants and beasts fight, about noone; after, from foure to fiue or sixe, to entertaine all that visit him; at night, from nine till mid-night, with all his great men, but none else, where he is below with them, in all familiaritie. I visited him in the second of these, where I found him in a Court, set aboue like a King in a Play, and all his Nobles and my selfe below on a state couered with carpets—a iust Theater; . . . Canopies ouer his head, and two standing on the heads of two wooden Elephants, to beat away flies.[14]

His love of life at court was not pure hedonism,[15] however, for Jahangir's proclivity for pleasure was often refined by his intellectualism into a keen sense for beauty. Says Das: "He was an aristocrat with the eye of a naturalist, the vision of a poet, the taste of a connoisseur and the philosophy of an epicurean."[16] This made Jahangir a patron of all forms of art. His strong interest in what was new and unusual and his exquisitely discriminating taste found room in the current schools of Mughal art to take the creative impulse in all its variety out of the constraints of a growing empire and allow it to flourish as the luxury it came to be. Of all the arts, however, Jahangir loved miniature painting the best and it was under him that European influences in perspective and shading, his own interest in nature and naturalism, and Akbar's encouragement of character delineation began to flower. Unlike his father, who had depicted the momentous sequences of a civilization in adolescence, and his son, who was perhaps no more than a glorified jeweler, Jahangir encouraged his artists to make paintings of people in events rather than of events with people, to portray objectively yet sympathetically the ordinary foibles of the great and the unusual, and to preserve for posterity his own ideals and visions as well as reality as he, perhaps alone, found it.

Jahangir's aesthetic vision came at a cost, however. It was fortunate for him that he had been given a large and well-run empire by his father, for he had neither the desire nor the temperament to tinker with regional boundaries or with the machinery of government. Many contemporary travelers saw him as the great

King of the East. Roe, for example, noted that "this king is one of the mightyest Princes in Asia, as well in extent of territory as in revenew";[17] Terry called him "the greatest and richest master of precious stones that inhabits the whole earth";[18] Hawkins said he was "the greatest emperour of the East for wealth, land, and force of men, as also for horses, elephants, camels, and dromedaries";[19] and Withington conceded that "the greatnesse of this Kinge, the Greate Mogul, . . . is soe greate in comparison of most Christian Kinges that the report would bee almost incredible."[20] That he was an emperor of great wealth is undisputed; that his wealth was of his own making, however, is a grave misconception.

It is true that Jahangir ruled over a large and prosperous empire, but it had been a gift to him not a reward. He did not love hard work, as his father did, and he was not willing to dirty his hands in the building and maintenance of a political state. He was, however, the perfect emperor for his time: a ruler who, precisely because he had inherited a stable domain from Akbar,[21] did not have to work hard at governing and who could more appropriately spend his hours in pursuing artistic dreams. A second Akbar, with that emperor's determined perseverance, might well have brought more war and overextended the Mughal enterprise, while an aesthete like Jahangir might have been better suited to the leisure time afforded by the unparalleled peace of the first years in power. The later Das, in fact, says: "This slow and languorous lifestyle helped Jahangir to be a great patron of all kinds of creative arts."[22]

Politically, then, Jahangir's reign was of little note. His tendency toward the arts and to pleasure meant that there were no spectacular successes on the battlefield and no great innovations in the workings of Mughal government. Although some contend that there was in fact a loss of territory—Kandahar to the Persians, for example[23]—what change there was in the configurations of the empire or in the basic structure of Akbar's system was immaterial. Indeed, as H. Beveridge notes, Jahangir's "peaceful temper, or his laziness, was an advantage, for it saved much bloodshed."[24]

Jahangir's aesthetic vision gave him a place at the center of a pleasure-giving world, which encouraged and infused a second tendency more fundamental perhaps than the first: self-absorption. From the beginning, Jahangir lived in a world that had, quite literally, been waiting for him, that had adored him when he arrived, and that had existed for nothing else from then on than to please him. When he opened his memoirs with the story of his birth—of how a father had been deprived of a son and heir for some time, but on visiting a saint had been granted not one but three sons, the first of whom was Salim[25]—it was not an ordinary statement of historical facts, but an opening testament to the extraordinary event of his existence. That he had come into the world as a result of remarkable circumstances meant that from that time on he was to be the object of special attention and regard.

Envisioning the uniqueness of his own appearance in the world, Jahangir became self-centered and self-indulgent. He developed grand and inflated views of himself and in time was less and less able to make connections with reality. His exaggerated view of himself was perhaps nowhere more evident than in the political allegory paintings he commissioned later in life, which depicted the emperor not only as the grand prince of Asia, benevolently patronizing the lesser rulers of lesser nations, but also as a sovereign whose rule was divinely inspired.[26] At court, he easily dismissed visitors who didn't please him,[27] and he routinely sent back gifts from travelers and supplicants that were inferior in any way—damaged, wrong in color or size, or simply inextravagant.[28] He was able without qualms to rewrite history, to consign to oblivion by his silence whole peoples, incidences, nuances of events if they did not fit the way he wanted to see the sequence of his life. There is little mention in his memoirs, for example, of the European merchants, especially the English, who were for years (1615–19) well placed at court, conversing with Jahangir, receiving presents from him when they were sick,[29] and traveling with him when and wherever his camp moved.[30] Nor is there mention of his marriage to Nur Jahan, surprising in view of his later dependence upon her and explainable only perhaps with A. S. Beveridge's wonderful phrase "an omission of the contemporarily obvious."[31] His description of the murder of Abul Fazl related the appropriate facts but in no way indicated grief or remorse on his part,[32] and his eloquent vision of his father did not betray the strain and tension that marked their last few years.[33] Finally, there was no overt notice of the blinding of Khusrau, an odd omission given the great attention paid to the issue of his eldest son's transgressions over the years.

It may be that history has judged Jahangir as a lazy and indulgent wastrel of a man who was jealous of his brothers and sons, who shirked the sovereign responsibilities bestowed on him by his father, and who gave in too easily to the positive gratification of his senses.[34] But he was also an utterly appealing character. His aesthetic vision beautified the court with its symbolic trappings and ritual posturings and created in the Mughal arts, especially in painting, a lasting expression of the refinement, sophistication, and luxurious repose the Mughals have come to exemplify. His grandscale egoism, though damaging to the political empire, gave rise to a diplomacy as pleasing and gracious as it could be random and retributive and to a memoir that is as immediate and naively self-reflective as it is selective and self-celebrative. Roe's verdict, though forged of his own humiliating and eventually unsuccessful bid for trading contracts, was clearly and surprisingly eulogistic:

> He is very affable, and of a cheerefull countenance . . . and not proud in nature, . . . for at nights he is . . . full of gentle conversation. . . . The wisdome and goodness of the King appeares aboue the malice of others . . . [and] all [are] reconciled by a Patient King, whose hart was not vunderstood by any of all these [members of the junta].[35]

That Jahangir was an essentially good man misjudged and manipulated by his retainers may not be an altogether accurate estimate of him, but foreigners who knew the court felt that as a sovereign he was open, hospitable, and a lover of fine things. Said van den Broecke:

> Jahangir was a handsome man in his youth, but not tall of stature. He was very ambitious, always striving after more and greater (things). . . . He was a great

> friend of all foreginers, and artists, whom he loved and treated generously. . . He was a great lover of all novelties which he had never seen before, and was excessively fond of jewels.[36]

His aesthetic vision and interior repose, for all their dangers, had shaped a man who was at once extremely materialistic and self-indulgent, but who could exhibit the taste of a true connoisseur and the open frankness of only the most naively self-aware. He must surely be, as Gascoigne has noted, "the most sympathetic of [all] the Great Moghuls."[37]

Of Jahangir's behavior, perhaps the most conspicuously repulsive was his cruelty. He appears to have inflicted pain at random, condemned to punishment on whim, and watched acts of brutal savagery just for the morbid fascination of it. What is most disturbing, perhaps, is that Jahangir did not punish or inflict pain out of principles of right or wrong or according to the mandates of civil law, but only if the crime offended his aesthetic sensibility or somehow violated his ennobled view of himself. For example, he ordered the thumbs of a servant to be cut off for taking down some *champa* trees; these trees were "above the bench alongside the river" and their removal apparently offended some personal appreciation Jahangir held for the area.[38] He had a maidservant of Nur Jahan's executed by placing her in a pit with her feet tied to a stake and "the Earth hard ramed" around her up to the armpits, to stay without food and water with her head and shoulders continually exposed to the sun. If she survived after three days and two nights she was to be pardoned, though she lived in fact only a day and a half "crying out most lamentably," "Ah my head, my head!"[39] She had been a former concubine of Jahangir's but had passed the age of thirty when most men's women were set aside in favor of others. Her crime in this "old age" had been to kiss a eunuch.[40]

Jahangir had men beaten and killed for breaking a china dish.[41] He made two Armenian children who had been raised as Christians become Muslims, forcing them to be circumcised and to eat pork.[42] He had Hindu icons smashed because he considered them ugly.[43] He had rackish youths locked up with women of low caste who were "dirty, malodorous, and covered all over with filth."[44] He killed servants who interfered with a good hunt. He condemned a man convicted of killing his own father to be dragged for miles by the hind leg of an elephant.[45] He desecrated the grave of another man, Nasiruddin, who had also murdered his father, by ordering the remains thrown into the fire.[46] And he condemned a man to die for killing his mother, judging "him to be stung to death by snakes."[47]

Jahangir's special ire at a criminal's parricide[48] did not prevent him, however, from inflicting pain upon his own kin. In about 1612, Hawkins recounted the famous example of Jahangir baiting his seven-year-old son, Shahryar,[49] to see if he would cry. When Shahryar, under instructions from his nursemaid to restrain himself, refused to give in Jahangir got even angrier, beat the boy, and had a bodkin thrust through his cheek.[50] This was odd behavior for a man who condemned most vehemently those others of his acquaintance who violated the sacred bonds of parent and child. Note again his irrational hatred for a man like

Nasiruddin, who poisoned his father, as well as his curious incomprehension of his colleague, Shah Abbas of Iran, who had had his own son killed in January of 1615. When Jahangir's spies could bring no satisfactory reason for Shah Abbas's action, he reluctantly put the matter aside by saying, "The killing of a son must have some powerful motive in order to do away with the disgrace of it."[51] Jahangir himself had resolutely refused to kill his own son Khusrau at the time of his rebellion and ordered him blinded instead, saying in 1607, "my fatherly affection did not permit me to take his life."[52]

Nevertheless, Jahangir did live by the bloody rules of the Mughal dynasty, and if there were concessions to things like "fatherly affection," these were counterbalanced by a swift recourse to punishment, a refusal to allow transgression of imperial whim, and a belief that gory retribution would not only be "a warning to others,"[53] but a visually powerful spectacle as well. Only rarely do we see Jahangir recant a punishment he had ordered: once, for example, when he allowed Khusrau's blinded eyes to be treated by a physician for sight again,[54] and on another occasion when he interceded, too late apparently, in the infliction of a death penalty. On this occasion, a huntsman, Subhan Quli, had just been condemned to die for seditious activities when the executioner hurried him away and carried out the emperor's orders. Jahangir meanwhile had decided that cutting off the offender's feet would be punishment enough, but when he realized he was too late, "[he] regretted the circumstance, and directed that whenever an order was given for anyone's execution, . . . they should wait till sunset before putting him to death. If up to that time no order for release arrived, he should without fail be capitally punished."[55] Such regret is reflected in a later incident when Jahangir, in a moment of jest, encouraged a love-stricken blacksmith named Kalyan to fling himself off the roof of a house in confirmation of his love for a reluctantly beloved widow. When the blacksmith's injuries from the fall proved fatal, Jahangir was greatly repentant and "grieved in my mind."[56]

Jahangir's reputation for cruelty was widespread in both its magnitude and its randomness. Said Terry, "when he did wickedly, none could do worse," and he punished "to his will and passion, not justice."[57] Although the streak of sadism in Jahangir[58] hardly affected the foreigners at court or in the surrounds,[59] it severely compromised whatever appeal with his people Jahangir might have had. According to Hawkins, "hee hath raigned in quiet, but ill beloved of the greater part of his subjects, who stand greatly in feare of him."[60]

In assessing Jahangir's capacity for cruelty it seems clear that, however susceptible his violent responses were to his own variable temperament and unstable emotions, his cruel acts were occasioned either by violations of his own aesthetic sensibilities or by transgressions of a very personal sense of self. They were not, we would argue, brought on by the offender's breach of a moral code, written or unwritten, or by his derision of a principle sacred to the Mughal system. The crimes, for example, of cutting down *champa* trees, or of breaking china, or of being an ugly icon were each distasteful to Jahangir because of his own quest for visual order. Equally integral to his aesthetic vision were the punishments he commanded: being crushed or dragged for miles by elephants or being buried in the ground up to the neck and roasted alive, each carried with it an aesthetic appeal that pleased the eye and, in its extreme brutality, confirmed the majesty of Jahangir's reign. Likewise, other crimes disturbed his exaggerated view of himself. Khusrau's seditious acts were an affront to Jahangir's sovereignty; a maidservant's kissing a eunuch violated his own possession of women as well as the protective structures of his personal harem; parricide offended the parent-child bonds so ambivalently symbolized in his own strained relationship with Akbar and Khusrau; Christian children who resisted conversion profaned the sanctity of the religion he called his own; and a child like Shahryar who refused to rise to the bait belittled the direct power of Jahangir's own personality. His cruelty, then, was not simply an example of contradictory forces at work, but an expression of a self so inwardly focused that the beauty and order of the world depended for their perfection upon nothing other than his own sensual satisfaction.

On the other side of cruelty was Jahangir's love of justice. Among contemporaries at the court, he was acknowledged as a supreme example of a king who in "his greate justice"[61] "did relieve continually many poor people."[62] When he acceded to the throne, said van den Broecke, "Jahangir was at first very severe. He meted out strict justice to all evil doers, for which he was called Adil Padshah, or the 'Just' king."[63] In that year, 1605, Jahangir decided to turn against his reckless past and vowed "my justice . . . [will] not put up with oppression from anyone, and . . . in the scales of equity neither smallness nor greatness . . . [will be] regarded."[64] With this in mind he instituted new practices in the structure of Mughal administration that would, he avowed, ensure fair treatment of all his subjects. In keeping with his character, however, these new practices became mere symbols, for he could in the end be a lover of justice only in appearance. Jahangir came to be known as "just" not because he was in fact a moral king or because he genuinely had his peoples' interest at heart, but because he was able to surround himself with the trappings of the fair and the right. His reputation for justice came to be carried by things outside of ongoing acts of clear and responsible judgment; instead it was built and maintained by visual symbols, which endured as reminders to him and to others of the vision he had originally created of himself [see Figure 4–1]. Moreover, these symbols were perfectly attuned to the man they represented, for not only were they simple, clean, and aesthetically appealing forms, but they also placed him, Jahangir, at the very center of the system, in this way circumventing the existing structures of grievance and redress.[65]

To this end, then, Jahangir opened his administration by pardoning all long-term criminals and by issuing twelve edicts known as the *dastar ul-amal*.[66] These edicts were to guide and encourage the good conduct of his subjects by, for instance, setting up way stations (*sarais*) on roads normally frequented by robbers, forbidding the search of merchants' goods without their permission, ensuring the passing of a dead man's property on to his heirs, prohibiting the manufacture or sale of intoxicating spirits and drugs, and establishing certain days of the week and year as days free of animal slaughter for food.[67] Although these edicts would appear to have infused the system with a sense of fairness, they were in fact only cosmetic—paying homage to a sensitivity to justice, but hardly offering

FIGURE 4–1. "The Emperor Jahangir with Bow and Arrow." Indian painting; Mughal, ca. 1605; opaque watercolor, ink and gold on paper mounted on board: 14.8 x 7.5 cm. Courtesy of the Arthur M. Sackler Gallery, Smithsonian Institution, Washington, D.C. (S86.0408). Probably painted at Jahangir's accession, this traditional standing portrait shows a youthful, though robust, emperor with the symbols of his new sovereignty. The red turban and dark green ground make this an exceptionally pleasing image.

radical change in the way things worked. In fact, as the reign proceeded, they themselves were frequently violated.

More importantly, as his very first order of business, he had a Chain of Justice fastened up, "so that if those engaged in the administration of justice should delay or practise hypocrisy in the matter of those seeking justice, the oppressed might come to this chain and shake it so that its noise might attract attention."[68] This chain was made of pure gold and hung with sixty bells, and was fastened at one end to the battlements of the Shah Burj of the fort at Agra and at the other to a stone post on the riverbank of the Yamuna.[69] It was to stand as a symbol of his readiness to hear every complaint of every subject no matter how petty the issue or how mean the supplicant. Hawkins saw this chain and described it as follows:

> A long rope is fastened unto two pillars, neere unto the place where the King sitteth in justice. This rope is hanged full of bels, plated with gold, so that the rope beeing shaken the bels are heard by the King; who sendeth to know the cause and doth his justice accordingly.[70]

The second tangible and visible sign of Jahangir's justice was his custom of sitting at the *jharoka,* or inspecting window of his palace, and hearing the affairs of the poor and miserable.[71] It was a custom that developed early in his reign and that he honored three times a day (after morning prayers, between noon and three in the afternoon, and just before sunset)[72] no matter how sick his body had become or how unfortunate the weather. According to Coryat:

> The King presenteth himselfe thrice every daie without faile to his nobles; at the rising of the sunne, which he adoreth by the elevation of his hands; at noone; and at five of the clocke in the evening. But he standeth in a roome aloft, alone by him selfe, and looketh uppon them from a window that hath an embroidered sumptuous coverture, supported with two silver pillasters to yeeld shaddowe unto him.[73]

In theory, Jahangir envisioned himself as a second Solomon, who occupied "the throne of the wind, and hastened out, and released the people of God from this pain and trouble."[74] Said Roe: "On Tuesday at the *Jarruco* he sitts in Judgment, neuer refusing the poorest mans Complaynt, where hee heares with Patience both parts."[75] The immediacy of Jahangir's judgment was remarkable, apparently, and Terry was often impressed by the swiftness of the hearing and the directness of the sentence: "The Great Mogul will sit himself as judge, in any matters of consequence that happen near unto him: and there are no malefactors that lie more than one night in prison and many times not at all."[76] *Jharoka* sitting was an ideal custom for Jahangir, for it allowed him the appearance of being a just and concerned king without requiring him to exert any effort in the back corridors on behalf of the often tedious maintenance of a fair and equable system. It also placed him squarely at the center of his subjects' vision of Mughal rule, creating the perception of a unique intimacy with each and every one of them and of a visible presence at the very source of power from which the peace and order of the empire emanated. At the window, then, Jahangir was indeed the sun upon whose radiance his subjects depended for their sustenance.[77]

Jahangir's reputation for justice was enriched by the particular cases he saw fit to adjudicate. There was, for example, the case of the widow's daughter who had been forcibly taken in the port on the Gulf of Cambay by one of Muqarrab Khan's servants. When inquiries were made, the widow discovered her daughter had died what was called "an unavoidable death." On learning of the affair, Jahangir ordered the servant put to death, Muqarrab Khan's *mansab* reduced by half, and the widow recompensed for her loss.[78] In another instance, probably apocryphal, the son of one of Nur Jahan's sisters whom she had adopted as her own accidentally trampled a child to death while riding through the streets on an elephant. Concerned, as any good Muslim might be, that the punishment fit the crime, Jahangir eventually had the offending boy himself trampled to death by another elephant.[79] Again, Jahangir once noticed a Rajput being taken away to be hung. Asking his offense, the emperor was told that he had violated a Muslim woman. Jahangir called the woman in and asked her "if the Rajput's body was hairless, like he was in the face." Supposing that he shaved the hair on his body as he did his beard, the woman answered yes, whereupon Jahangir ordered an examination. Finding the woman to have raised a false complaint, the emperor released the Rajput and ordered the woman to die.[80]

By tradition, the most famous example of Jahangir's justice, however, was his response to a crime committed by Nur Jahan herself. In a story that is almost certainly not historical, Nur Jahan was standing unveiled in an inner courtyard one day when a low-caste man happened by accident to wander in. Incensed by this intrusion, the queen quickly drew an arrow and killed him. Notwithstanding who she was, Jahangir sentenced Nur Jahan to prison, bound and chained, to be executed.

> Ah! Is it the same Nur Jahan who /
> behind the curtain of Jahangir /
> was but the true Ruler of the Time? /
> Is it the same Lady /
> that if her delicate forehead creased /
> the leaves of governance creased too? /
> [No], this Nur Jahan, now, /
> is not the same. /
> No more her conceit, cruel charms, /
> devastating coquetry! /
> A criminal, /
> she has no supporter, no advocate: /
> forlorn, homeless, belonging nowhere!

The emperor would have carried the requirements of justice out to their very end, according to the story, and executed Nur Jahan had not she paid a hundred thousand *dirhams* blood money to the poor man's heirs.[81]

Even though this story is probably the product of a tradition obsessed with the excesses of its king, Jahangir was himself responsible for his reputation of impartially implementing justice. He said, for example, after ordering the death of a nobleman's son who had committed "an unjust murder," "God forbid that in such affairs I should consider princes, and far less that I should consider Amirs. I hope that the grace of God may support me in this."[82] Not only did Jahangir agonize over inflicting punishment on the high-placed and noble, deserving though they might be, but he also visibly recoiled in horror when he heard of the cruelty and injustice of others. When he heard, for example, that Abdullah Khan had ordered the head of a man cut off who at a wine party was drunk and in his "state of drunkenness . . . had uttered some improper expressions by way of a joke," he was outraged and ordered that Khan's holdings be drastically reduced.[83]

If Jahangir's reputed love of justice put him at the visual center of a domestic system of redress and grievance, then it was a kindred diplomatic policy that dreamt of placing his empire, with him as its symbol, at the center of all the other nations of the earth [see Figure 4–2]. Here, Jahangir's self-indulgence demanded that popular sentiment be focused directly upon him and be as firm in appearance as he hoped it might be in reality. Terry, for example, told the touching story of Jahangir's encounter with the Mercator map book. Among the travelers and merchants at the court, Jahangir had fed himself "with this conceit, that he . . . [was] Conqueror of the world." Roe once gave Jahangir a copy of Mercator's atlas when the emperor arrived unannounced and the Englishman had nothing more suitable to give.[84] At first Jahangir appeared to be much taken with the map book looking for his own territory and asking questions about those that surrounded it. He soon gave the book back, however, saying "that he would not rob him [Roe] of such a Jewel." But, said Terry, "the truth, is that the Great Mogul might very well bring his action against Mercator and others who describe the world, but streighten him very much in their maps, not allowing him to be lord and commander of those provinces which properly belong unto him."[85] Jahangir was no fool here and well understood the message the maps had to tell. His response, however, was completely in character. He did not want to know anything that might undermine the carefully crafted vision he had of himself; even less was he willing to change, by conquest or treaty, the boundaries reflected in Mercator's maps so that they might more accurately match the world as Jahangir had envisioned it. Better to keep intact his inflated sense of himself than to tamper with the reality it was supposed to mirror.

Jahangir's self-centered geography was perhaps best reflected in the series of miniature paintings he had commissioned later in life to portray, among other things, his benevolent patronage of area rulers and emissaries. Unlike his early paintings, which reflected a vigor and restlessness characteristic of youthful impatience, and unlike the paintings of his mature rule, which showed him politically responsible, managing in due course a daily life surrounded by sons, friends, and nobles, the political allegory paintings of Jahangir's old age eulogized him outrageously, flattering him beyond proportion as a mighty yet benevolent sovereign, just short of divine stature.[86] These paintings of his old age functioned for Jahangir in a number of ways. In cases such as "Jahangir as the

FIGURE 4–2. "Durbar Scene of Jahangir." Indian painting; Mughal, ca. 1615; school of Jahangir; by Abul Hasan; color and gold on paper: 16.9 × 12.3 cm. (6 11/16 × 4 7/8″). Courtesy of the Freer Gallery of Art, Smithsonian Institution, Washington, D.C. (46.28). Note the footed globe under Jahangir's feet with a keyhole and the key hanging from his sash. Arranged around him *mandala*-style are courtiers, including Karan Singh, Hindu prince of Mewar, a Europeanized "emperor of Rum," Shah Jahan, Mahabat Khan, Asaf Khan, and Itimaduddaula.

Queller of Rebellion"[87] and "Jahangir Shooting the Head of Malik Ambar,"[88] they transformed acknowledged fears and failures into decided victories. In a case such as "Jahangir Embracing Shah Abbas,"[89] they established Jahangir as the preeminent ruler of Asia, generously patronizing and receiving homage from neighboring rulers. And in cases such as "Jahangir Preferring a Sufi Shaykh to Kings"[90] they showed Jahangir making a clear choice away from secular authority and toward the life of the spirit.[91]

Notwithstanding the wonderful intimacy and self-revelation of his memoirs, it was these later paintings, perhaps, that best showed the dynamics of his "mature" character. Even as they shored up icons to protect him from a failed reality, they worked as well to a counter purpose: to betray (certainly not unbeknownst to him) his impotence and vulnerability to the court and to the people of his realm. Not only do we see an aging and increasingly corpulent physical body but also personal dreams too grandiose and impossible ever to be true. Are these paintings, then, more than just the excessive visions of an old man helplessly out of touch with reality? Could they also be a kind of mockery of the great abyss between what was and what was hoped to be, hopes so futile and preposterous that now the visions could be played out in the open without any threat to the integrity of the holder? It would have taken a substantial personality to allow such a mockery to unfold over so many years, but perhaps by his later life he was just such a man: hopelessly entangled in fantasies about his political rule, yet clear enough about himself to let a public in on the wild and errant dreams that had replaced any real efforts of his own to govern.[92]

Whether or not these paintings reenvisioned reality or self-consciously poked fun at the patron who held such views, one of the central icons of most of them was the nimbus around Jahangir's head, recalling the sun imagery so prevalent in his use of the name *nur*[93] and in the symbolic structures of his love for justice (for example, the gold chain and the radiantly central *jharoka* window). Use of sun imagery for religious and political purposes had begun in earnest with Akbar and with Jahangir had become so much a part of his public persona that the emperor had come to truly believe he was, as a Hindi poet had told him, the son of the sun.[94] His royal standard, preserved in an engraving by Terry, showed "a couchant lion shadowing part of the body of the sun,"[95] and his daily rituals were increasingly attuned to the movements of the sun, thus affirming the association, if not the identity, of the two.[96] These paintings of his later years, then, not only brought to completion the presumptions of his earlier reign, but tied him as well to the symbols of Akbar and, in the case of at least one painting ("Jahangir Embracing Shah Abbas"), allowed him to become so overwhelmed by the solar icon as to be personally absorbed within it.

That Jahangir loved justice for the aesthetic qualities and self-indulgence of that love is clear. That this lore meant separation from the world for the preservation of justice was tolerable to him so long as his idealized perception of himself as just remained intact. This love's distance from reality became counterpoised, however, by an oddly objective scrutiny of nature that was, if not intimate, at least highly curious and wonderfully attentive to particulars. Says Varadarajan: "Jahangir may have lacked the charisma of Akbar but he had a finer eye for observation than his illustrous father."[97] We have seen that Jahangir's aesthetic vision produced in him a desire for the appearance of order and that his self-absorption required a world that seemed to revolve around him. These two tendencies found expression again in a naturalist's sympathy for the unique and curious in nature. He took pity, for example, on elephants in winter, who had to bathe in cold water, and provided for them water heated up to the temperature of lukewarm milk.[98] He had suits and shawls made for some jackals who had called out craving "some protection against the cold." [99] And he erected a *manar* or tower on the grave of a favorite antelope, who had excelled in fighting other antelopes.[100]

He loved new and unusual animals,[101] noting, for example, that the zebra looked as if "the painter of fate" had colored it "with a strange brush,"[102] and he recorded seeing the albino of any number of species;[103] he watched cranes mate[104] and a mad dog inflict fatal wounds on two elephants;[105] and he recorded in detail all the animals he had killed while hunting—not out of morbidity but as a naturalist might list populations.[106] He had Inayat Khan, a courtier dying from opium and wine, brought into his presence so that he might watch the ravages of nature work their course;[107] he marveled at a gardener's daughter who had a moustache, a thick beard, hair on her chest and no breasts but who was in every other way an ordinary woman(!);[108] he noted being given an outrageously over-sized peach[109] that proved to be as sweet as any he had ever tasted; and he was astounded at the appearance of snow in the lower Himalayas on the way to Kashmir after so many years of its absence.[110] His naturalist's instinct and his sympathies for the quirks in the world were thus revealed with amazing accuracy and attention to detail. Jahangir prided himself so much on his capacity for detail, in fact, that he boasted that he could tell in a moment which of his artists had painted a certain picture.[111] This attention to little things and to the realia of nature was best reflected in the honesty Jahangir asked for himself in all his miniature paintings. In image after image, we can see him grow increasingly wide in girth, and we can see the slackening skin of his jowls, the sometimes unshaven skin of his cheeks, the shortish stature, and the eyes heavy with drink.[112] Jahangir never shied from having himself shown as he was, and if these imperfections were part of his place in a larger scheme, his art would make them known.

Two of the things that gave Jahangir great pleasure were wine and opium. Although intoxication had been a habit of the early Mughal emperors[113] and was the habit of all of Akbar's sons (both Murad and Daniyal had died of its excesses),[114] Jahangir might have drunk anyway because wine augmented his aesthetic vision and reaffirmed his self-indulgence, while unfortunately magnifying his other faults and frailties [see Figure 4–3].[115] By his own admission, Jahangir began drinking in his eighteenth year.[116] Except occasionally when sick as a child,[117] Jahangir did not drink until about January of 1586, when he became involved in a campaign to put down a disturbance of Afghans at the fort of Attock. Leaving the camp that had been set up on the bank of the river, young Salim went out on a hunt. As he grew tired, one of his uncle's (Mirza Muhammad Hakim) gunners suggested that a little liquor might relieve his exhaustion

FIGURE 4–3. "Portrait of Jahangir." Indian painting; Mughal, ca. 1620; opaque watercolors on paper: 10.8 × 5.4 cm. (4 1/4 × 2 1/8″). Courtesy of the Los Angeles County Museum of Art, from the Nasli and Alice Heeramaneck Collection, Museum Acquisition Fund (M.83.1.5). Note the wine cup.

and, feeling well-disposed to it, Salim took a cup and a half of sweet yellow wine. Finding "its quality agreeable," he began drinking regularly, increasing the quantity day by day until wine no longer intoxicated him and he had to change over to spirits (*araq*).[118]

During the next nine years, until he was twenty-six, Jahangir's "potions rose to twenty cups of doubly distilled spirits, fourteen during the daytime and the remainder at night," while his food consumption diminished drastically.

> In that state of matters no one had the power to forbid me, and matters went to such a length that in the crapulous state from the excessive trembling of my hand I could not drink from my own cup, but others had to give it to me to drink.[119]

In the wake of this period of heavy adolescent drinking, and at the insistence of one of his father's physicians, who told him he had six months left in which to turn his life around,[120] Jahangir began to cut down his consumption. Over the next seven years, he reduced his intake of liquor to six cups a day, each portion containing two parts wine and one part *araq*.[121] This reduction was facilitated by the use of *filuniya*, a drug of unclear identity,[122] whose quantity increased as the liquor decreased. With certain exceptions for given days of the week,[123] Jahangir continued at the rate of six cups of liquor a day for the next fifteen years, or until he was forty-seven. It was at the same time, at some point during this twenty-two-year period, that Jahangir substituted opium for the *filuniya*, and by 1615, when he gave this detailed account of his history of drinking, he was taking opium twice a day, eight *surkhs* (a red berry being used as a measure) after five *gharis* of day and six *surkhs* after one watch of night,[124] in addition to his liquor.

As might be expected, Jahangir's consumption of wine and opium severely affected his health. Although he admitted that after the first nine years of heavy drinking his body was ready to give out, he continued drinking despite its ill effects. In mid-1614, for example, he came down with a fever and headache, but drank his usual wine at night just the same, even though "it brought on greater weakness."[125] Later, in 1618, when doctors again assessed his state of health, Jahangir was told that: "As soon as you moderate your habit of taking wine and opium, all these troubles of yours will disappear."[126] Jahangir did, in fact, reduce his intake of both intoxicants this time and noticed "a great gain on that first day." A week and a half later when his headache returned, he reduced his liquor again, but with the consent of his doctors, had to resume his normal pattern of drinking after three days. It appeared that the withdrawal symptoms from reducing his liquor had only exacerbated his illness, which was already quite advanced.[127] Although later again in that year he was advised by his physicians to reduce his usual number of cups of wine because of the harshness of the climate of Gujarat where he was then staying,[128] it appears in general that until the end of his life he continued his habit of daily wine and opium.[129]

It seems odd that a man who could be at once so obsessed with his own health,[130] could also be so stubborn in holding onto those very things that devastated his body. We know that he had a powerful capacity for delusion about drink, as he rationalized in 1605 that now "I drink only to digest my food."[131] But he also must have known what wine and opium were doing to him. While there is no doubt that his life was foreshortened by these intoxicants, there can be no doubt as well that their consumption helped to stave off the feelings of inferiority he held in the face of the powerful memory of his father and helped also to sustain the high standards of his own aesthetic vision.

We are not privy to Jahangir's inner feelings about his addiction, but he did leave us with one story that suggested a deep sense of the knowledge of the power of drink. In his 1618 memoirs, he related an event previously narrated to him by Akbar. Once in his early youth, apparently, Salim had had two or three cups of wine and, mounting an elephant, urged the beast to charge and fight another elephant. The fight took both elephants to the head of a bridge over the Yamuna and Salim, who was pretending to onlookers to be even more drunk than he actually was, wondered to himself whether to hold his own elephant back.

> I thought that if I held him back from the bridge the people would regard those drunken ways (of mine) as a sham, and would believe that neither was I beside myself, nor was the elephant violent and headstrong. Such pretences on the part of Kings are disapproved of, and so after imploring the aid of God—Glory be to Him—I did not restrain the elephant.[132]

Even though the story was told by Akbar, and betrayed Akbar's clear moralistic sense as well as his knowledge of his own son's temperament, it was completely characteristic of Jahangir to have kept the facade he had created for his audience intact. This early story about Jahangir's drinking indicated, moreover, that alcohol may have been one sure way for Jahangir to encourage in himself a personal recklessness large enough to compete with the courage and fearlessness of Akbar. Wine and opium, then, besides being an expected custom of the family, were both a source of shame before his father and the very agent by which he fended off Akbar's powerfully competent image. They provided perhaps the only medium by which Jahangir could feel comfortable as Akbar's son, for they afforded him not only a mental screen to cloud out his filial memories, but also an avenue for contributing to the empire—the aesthetic—that was impossible for his father's generation as the evolution of the empire had not yet fully provided for the luxuries of leisure. Jahangir's addiction, then, was a complex structure—part family habit, part indulgence in the sensual, part manipulation of those who cared for him, part blind against his father, part false courage for his father, and part stimulant for the arts. It seems quite certain in any case, that it was not to be given up.

If Jahangir did, in fact, exercise little control over his own drinking habits, he was quite vocal about those of others. At the beginning of his reign, as one of his twelve orders, he forbade the manufacture or sale of any intoxicating spirit or drug;[133] he openly criticized one of his commanders, recently dead, who "had been maddened with wine and drank immoderately," assuming, probably rightly, that it had been this habit that had brought about his destruction;[134] and he appeared belatedly pleased when another noble had been able to give up "this man-destroying intoxication" in one stroke without leaving "it off gradually" as Jahangir had advised.[135] Others were aware of Jahangir's apparently high standards as well, and Roe noted that drunkenness was strictly forbidden at the court where one's breath was tested upon entering and a positive result meant a whipping.[136]

The puritanical streak in Jahangir that moved him to ban tobacco[137] as well as drink at court, but did not seriously limit his own indulgence,[138] was not strong enough to include his own children. It was in 1615 that Jahangir turned to his son, Khurram, then twenty-four and with wife and children, and observed, certainly not proudly, that he had "never defiled himself with drinking wine." On his twenty-fourth birthday, then, and on the occasion of his yearly weighing, Khurram was introduced by his father to the pleasures of wine.[139] Why this son had not yet ever drunk is somewhat of a mystery, but his long restraint may have stemmed from poor health,[140] from a general prohibitionist personality, from his increasingly orthodox Muslim ways, or from the negative modeling of his father. Whatever the reasons for his earlier abstinance, however, Khurram, though reluctant, eventually took the wine.[141] Although we have no further record of his reaction to the liquor that day or to the windy speech on moderation delivered by his father, Khurram was now indulgent for life. Why Jahangir felt it necessary to initiate Khurram into the mysteries of wine is unknown, but he might have felt, as he certainly did for himself, that Khurram was no man without it.

Some may suggest that Jahangir's addiction clears up one of the puzzles of his relationship with Nur Jahan. Although she had one daughter by Sher Afgan, Nur Jahan had no children by her second husband and Jahangir himself recorded no more children born after the births of Jahandar and Shahryar in 1605 to concubines.[142] It is certainly possible that Jahangir's heavy consumption of alcohol and opium rendered him either impotent or uninterested. Equally possible, however, is an early menopause for Nur Jahan, concern by her doctors for her advancing age and therefore of an increased risk in childbirth, or the custom, noted by Terry, of putting women aside sexually after their thirtieth year, presumably when they had lost their youthful bloom.[143] This last possibility is not likely: although Jahangir married Nur Jahan when she was thirty-five, he was, from all accounts, truly smitten by her beauty. The effects of Jahangir's addictions, then, may well have included their childlessness.

Jahangir's basic proclivity for the orderly structure and self-reflective quality of his world was voiced, finally, in his durable interest in signs and portents. Jahangir saw the natural world as at every point invested with a unique meaning tied directly to the experience of men. Each sphere—the human and the natural—was a map whose points had significance, and each map in its turn mirrored the constantly changing movements of the other. As emperor, Jahangir played a special role in the correspondence between these two spheres, for not only could his future well-being or demise be read in the manifestation of natural omens, but his own human actions were thought to be especially powerful in altering the flow of events in nature. Beginning with the prophetic origin of his own birth,[144] Jahangir's life was in many ways ruled by the proclamations of soothsayers and fortune-tellers. Pelsaert, for example, said: "Some of the brahmans are very ingenious, good astronomers . . . indeed the present King generally kept one at Court, whose prophecies, or most of them, proved quite accurate."[145] Jahangir, we know, minted zodiacal coins;[146] he weighed himself in gold and silver, vegetables and animals, and gave "his weight" to the poor in order to stave off the ill effects of an eclipse of the sun;[147] his premonition to hold back from a trip to Agra was confirmed by an outbreak of the plague in that city;[148] and he used astrologers to fix auspicious hours for his marches.[149]

He noted with unabashed satisfaction that Shaikh Salim Chishti accurately foretold the occasion of his own death—that it would be when he, the child Salim, learned and recited something from memory;[150] that an astrologer, Jotik Rai, foretold the fall and safe recovery of Jahangir's grandson, Shah Shuja;[151] that this same astrologer foretold the death of one of the emperor's wives, Padshah Banu Begam, which had been perceived in Jahangir's horoscope two months earlier;[152] that this same astrologer again accurately foretold that Shah Shuja would not die from a sickness but that it would take some other child instead;[153] that a female soothsayer predicted the recovery of a valuable pearl lost in the harem;[154] and that a gold tray used to carry refreshment to a hunter, which had fallen from a servant's hand as he was crossing the river, was recovered the next day, still in the river, right side up, "and not a drop of water had got into the cups"![155] Jahangir, moreover, operated in a system where some days were lucky and others unlucky. Nur Jahan, for example, had lost a valuable necklace of pearls and rubies on a hunt in 1618. Huntsmen who looked for them on a Wednesday, an unlucky day for the emperor, could not find them but then successfully recovered them on Thursday, one of his lucky days.[156] Van den Broecke reported that soothsayers were consulted for the most auspicious day on which to bring a treasure of gold and silver out of Agra and away from the reach of Shah Jahan,[157] and Pelsaert noted that Jahangir slept in different palaces each night according to the "day name of the" building.[158]

Jahangir was drawn to signs and portents, then, because this system of referents had an intrinsic order and beauty and provided him a central position in the allocation of meaning. Like the *jharoka* window, the sciences of auspicious prophecy catapulted Jahangir to the head of an ordering system that made him an essential component in linking together the human and natural spheres. And again like the *jharoka* window, it was Jahangir's position not his person that was important, for he did not actually have to do anything to make the system work; he simply had to be in place and let the system set him forth. The science of signs and portents, moreover, perfectly suited Jahangir's temperament, for it was based on an aesthetic sense of a vague and distant divine order not fully knowable to man. Man's only access to it was through secondary markers and, because these markers always had a specific referent, it was easy for Jahangir to center the system on himself. Believing in signs and portents, then, gave him an established order that was visible, tangible, and material and that could be comfortably explained and sometimes manipulated by persons from within.

It was this personality, self-absorbed and sensual, superstitious and prone to excess, that found its ideal match in Nur Jahan. Theirs was a real love, no doubt, born of a physical attraction and personal allure powerful on both sides, but also an alliance of perfectly suited talents and needs. Nur Jahan was by the time of her second marriage an experienced woman, no longer prey to adolescent desires and already successful in bearing a child. Hers could be a mature love, sometimes nurturing, sometimes scolding, sometimes relinquishing, but always a partner to her husband's idiosyncrasies. Jahangir, as well, was past his prime. Already hopelessly under the influence of wine and opium, he had spent too many youthful years enjoying the fruits of a noble birth and scheming his way onto his father's throne. He had married many women already, sported a surplus of heirs, and was surrounded by courtiers who fawned, physicians who nagged, and poets and seers who too readily offered their words. Why, then, did he marry Nur Jahan? He did not need an heir; he did not need to firm an alliance with Persian nobility; and he did not lack for beautiful faces in his *zanana*. This already aging woman, herself the victim of a tragically ended first marriage, was somehow able to clear out the debris and stave off the emptiness of Jahangir's life. She came to him in his middle age and, thus deprived of any memories of a firmer, more handsome, and more hospitable consort, she had to accept her new husband for what he had become. Knowing him from no other time than 1611, she could offer him unconditional approval and out of that affirmation could create a marriage in which she accepted yet refined, celebrated yet transfigured, attended yet ruled.

It is because it was a mature marriage for both, shaped by the peculiarities of men and women in their later years, that the alliance of Jahangir and Nur Jahan has received such devastating press and that the reputation of Nur Jahan in particular has suffered the most damage. The needs of a Jahangir in his middle years and the experienced abilities of a Nur Jahan easily lent themselves to the regressive dependency that surfaced so readily in the accounts of contemporary writers. Mutamid Khan and Kamgar Khan, for example, both stated that Jahangir passed the affairs of state on entirely to Nur Jahan and that he was able to remain emperor of India only in name.[159] Terry, who called Nur Jahan Jahangir's "most beloved wife," also said "she made such a thorough conquest on his affections, that she engrossed almost all his love, [and] did what she pleased in the government of that empire."[160] Van den Broecke, whose opinion of Jahangir was almost always critical, said that soon after his accession Jahangir "gave himself up to pleasures, allowed himself to be misguided by women, and became addicted to drink, caring very little about his kingdom."[161] More specifically, however, "he got into the clutches of this woman, who has ruined his fair name" and who kept "very much . . . in check" his natural inclinations and generosity.[162] And Della Valle, sometime in 1623 to 1624, noted that Jahangir "hath one Wife, or Queen, whom he esteems and favours above all other Women; and his whole Empire is govern'd at this day by her counsel."[163]

Although the view that Jahangir simply abandoned his government to the power-mongering hands of his middle-aged wife is frequently recapitulated in secondary sources,[164] there is another, equally persuasive view to the contrary. Many argue that "it is a mistake to think Jahangir was reduced to a cipher"[165] and that, while Nur Jahan did exercise considerable authority, Jahangir retained much of his control over the government. The balance was tenuous, no doubt, and given the weakness of the central authority system and the strengths of the internecine struggles, some rightly believe that "Jahangir's credit lies [instead] in the [very] fact that he survived."[166] If we examine Jahangir's memoirs it shows in fact that, in his relationship to Nur Jahan, there lurked a personality that had always depended upon advisers for support and that had always elicited doting affection from its intimates. It is only with Nur Jahan, however, that all these tendencies took up rest in a single person. The vacuum of government left by Jahangir's aesthetic interests and physical debilities was filled, in this marriage, by a capable, strong, and aggressive woman, who provided a shield behind which Jahangir felt safe but who could also hold him up squarely in his office.

There is no doubt, however, that the power he gave up to her was founded upon a real affection. He noted in his memoirs, for example, a time when Nur Jahan had fallen sick. She had been attended by both Muslim and Hindu doctors but had shown no signs of recovery when Jahangir ordered in Hakim Ruhullah. Under this man's expert ministrations, by "the aid of God (Glory be to His name!), in a short time she quite recovered," and Jahangir rewarded the successful physician most amply.[167] Such concern was shown for no other wife and only rarely for a stricken son. On other occasions, what took Nur Jahan's fancy also took his and when she built "a lofty house, and . . . royal garden," calling it Nur Mahal Sarai and celebrated its completion in early 1621 with a feast, Jahangir showed great pleasure.[168]

Later in January of 1622, when Nur Jahan's father Itimaduddaula died, Jahangir's concern was not that he was losing his most trusted and loyal minister, but that his favorite wife was losing her father: "The next day news came that his state had undergone a change, and that the signs of hopelessness were apparent. I could not bear the agitation of Nur Jahan Begam, and considering the affection which I bore towards him, I returned to the camp."[169] Just before Itimaduddaula finally passed on, Nur Jahan beckoned Jahangir to come close to her father's pillow, and when she asked the dying man if he recognized her husband, he responded with a couplet that praised his son-in-law's splendor as evident even to a man blind from birth. Had Itimaduddaula not been Nur Jahan's father, Jahangir would probably not have sat so attentively by his pillow for the last two hours of his life, and although the posthumous praise might have come in any case, he certainly would not have responded so touchingly to other members of the mourning family.[170]

Following the Mughal custom of escheat, of bestowing a dead man's fortune upon whomever the emperor so designed, Jahangir then gave Itimaduddaula's entire estate, including all his political holdings, to Nur Jahan "and ordered that her drums and orchestra . . . be sounded after those of the King."[171] In so bypassing the expected heir, Itimaduddaula's eldest living son, Asaf Khan, Jahangir was exercising a prerogative that was his indeed, but one which in this instance made no friends for Nur Jahan. Not only was this substantial gift an expression of Jahangir's love for his wife but it resulted in a consolidation of power evermore firm, evermore influential, and evermore feared as it went into hands that were increasingly closed. With this gift, though, the declaration Jahangir had made of his wife just earlier in 1621 seemed to have been confirmed: "From the date on which Nur Jahan Begam entered into the bond of marriage with this suppliant . . . she had made such arrangements as were becoming to the State, and knew what were the requirements of good fortune and prosperity."[172]

Nur Jahan's response to the personal affection and largesse bestowed on her by Jahangir was to give back in kind. In all she did for Jahangir, at least by his own account, she was as generous, as hospitable, and as nurturing as any mother might have been for a child. It seems most appropriate that Jahangir's very first mention of Nur Jahan in his memoirs was some three years after their marriage when, in 1614, he came down with a fever and headache. Fearing that knowledge of his illness might throw the country into an unstable state, he did not tell his family nor any of his doctors. He did not tell anyone, in fact, except Nur Jahan, "than whom I did not think anyone was fonder of me."[173] Jahangir continued to turn to Nur Jahan in his other sicknesses and, in 1621, when his health succumbed, as it often did, to the evils of hot weather, he found his most satisfying repose with her, for her "skill and experience are greater than those of the physicians."[174]

It was in Jahangir's drinking that Nur Jahan was probably most helpful, for his own natural restraint was quite low and her powers of discipline notoriously high. On this same occasion in 1621, in fact, Nur Jahan's remedy for the ill effects of heat was a reduction in Jahangir's cups of wine. She had not approved the prescriptions of the attending physicians and, by measures Jahangir did not record in his memoirs, "she, by degrees, lessened my wine, and kept me from things that did not suit me, and food that disagreed with me."[175] Pelsaert went even further and recorded an evening scene that must have taken place almost every night at the close of Jahangir's business hours. After the last of the wine had been drunk, he said, the king went to bed and there the queen with her female slaves undressed him, "chafing and fondling him as if he were a little child." Having so completely disposed him into her powers, Nur Jahan now took advantage of his intoxicated state—"his wife, who knows so well how to manage him that she obtains whatever she asks for or desires, gets always 'yes,' and hardly ever 'no,' in reply."[176] The debilitating control Nur Jahan acquired over Jahangir's drinking habits became legendary and, said Manucci: "It was enough for the queen to deny him a drink of wine to drive him to tears, and to dry them . . . [she] had only to present him a glass well filled with liquor."[177]

In another story recorded by Manucci, a physician called on Jahangir's court when the emperor was drunk. Deciding to kill the man, Jahangir called for a bow and arrow, but Nur Jahan, "who was behind a screen," had arrows made of cane sent so that "the king might not kill him." When the arrows failed to do their job, Nur Jahan had the courtiers motion to the physician to fall down as if dead to bring, thereby, the emperor's drunken displeasure to an end.[178] On yet a different occasion, Jahangir was listening to the singing of his musicians when he came to the end of his allotted nine cups of wine. He turned to Nur Jahan to ask her for more, and when she said no, "he fell into a passion, laid hold of the queen and scratched her, she doing the same on her side, grappling with the king, biting and scratching him, and no one dared to separate them." The musicians devised a ploy to end the scuffle and themselves, in the outer room, began to weep and cry out and tear their garments. The couple heard and, coming out to see "that it was a feigned plot, . . . they fell a-laughing, and the fight ended." The musicians were rewarded, but Nur Jahan could be placated only by having Jahangir fall at her feet, which he did by having his shadow cross her path one day in the garden.[179]

Much of what the later Europeans recorded may be exaggerated local tradition, but van den Broecke, writing in 1627 or so, must have preserved some of what was authentic, even in his radically critical account of their relationship:

> He suffered in his mind because he found himself too much in the power of his wife and her associates, and the thing had gone so far that there were no means of escaping from that position. She did with him as she liked, his daily reward being pretended love and sweet words, for which he had to pay dearly.[180]

Somewhere between the fond, almost idealized, accounts of Jahangir and the debasements of contemporary merchants like van den Broecke, then, lies the truth of Jahangir's rapport with Nur Jahan. It is fair to say that the relationship was intimate, that of all Jahangir's wives, Nur Jahan was his most trusted and most solicitous; and that for all the power that seems to have passed between them, there was real affection there indeed. The mercenary vision projected onto Nur Jahan by her detractors stemmed from the control she really did exercise within the government and over her husband, but it was a control drawn, by all the evidence, from marital bonds of decided strength.

If we believe what contemporary accounts have told us, we find that Nur Jahan fits smoothly into the overall pattern of Jahangir's character developed earlier. That she was an exquisite beauty is attested by many,[181] and given Jahangir's aesthetic vision, he could only have been animated and emboldened by her entrance into his life. Her beauty would have exemplified the very best the natural world could offer and, now in his service, would confirm that he did indeed preside over a visually perfect order. Moreover, the particular constructs of their marriage were testimony to Jahangir's power of self-preoccupation, for Jahangir and Nur Jahan fit together as a unit each half of an inseparable whole.[182] Absorbed together in one personality, when Jahangir ruled so did Nur Jahan and when she did, so did he. Proclamations of *farmans* in her name were testimony of Jahangir's rule, while decisions about the fate of Khusrau issued through him were testimony of Nur Jahan's power. While we can only guess at the appeal such a vision of marital unity would have had for Nur Jahan, it may have been the only way Jahangir was able to integrate his wife's increasing sway (and his own enfeeblement) into the overall structure of his world.

The pattern of their relationship fit most easily, however, into that of mother and child. While it was rare that the Indian tradition cast Nur Jahan into a decidedly maternal role, noting even so that she was the mother of Ladli Begam and the tender of such charges as Shah Shuja,[183] her tie to Jahangir seems more than anything else to have been nurturing. Since the primary role of Mughal women was that of child care, a mothering role was natural for a woman normally past her sexual prime and newly married to an innately needy, somewhat absentminded, and certainly self-indulgent king. In the end Nur Jahan's essential appeal may have been her parental charisma, which so perfectly fit the increasingly child-like dependencies exhibited by her husband. In this regard, then, it is fair to say that Nur Jahan responded to the filial needs extended to her, but in fulfilling her role, she in no way violated or unduly transgressed the personal requirements made of her as a Mughal queen.

In his attachment to Nur Jahan, Jahangir expressed a strength of affection familiar in his relations with other, especially older, women who were close to him. We note, for example, the important role Maryam Makani, Jahangir's paternal grandmother, and Salima Sultan Begam, one of Akbar's favorite wives, played in Jahangir's reconciliation with Akbar during the last years of the elder Mughal's reign. In addition, Jahangir's affection for his own mother, Maryamuzzamani, was exceptional and his memoirs are filled with tales of the stature and largesse he bestowed upon her,[184] of the birthday weighings (both lunar and solar) he held at her house,[185] of the marriage ceremonies he hosted there,[186] and of the powerful sentiment which he had for her.[187] Said Terry: "Not seldom would [he] shew many expressions of duty and strong affections to his mother, . . . so that he who esteemed the whole world as his vassals, would help to carry her in a palankee upon his shoulders."[188]

The mother-son relationship was typically strong in Muslim families because it was seen as the bond that outlasted all others. Given the structure of Mughal households, where religious custom obligated providing shelter for any older unattached women and where "multiple mothers" (wet-nurses, barren aunts and foster mothers of all types) were the norm, Jahangir found it easy to feel strongly for the older women around him. When Qutbuddin's mother, Salim's wet-nurse as an infant, died in 1607, Jahangir noted that she was "as a mother to me or even kinder than my own kind mother,"[189] and he went so far as to place the feet of her corpse on his shoulders and carry her part of the way to her grave. When Nur Jahan's mother Asmat Begam died in 1621, Jahangir said, "I did not value her [any] less than my own mother,"[190] and spent considerable time in consoling her natural son, his own minister Asaf Khan. A Mughal son's reverence of his mother was total and without bounds and in all reigns was colorfully shored up by the customary trappings of Indian life. Akbar, for instance, gave great honor to his mother, Maryam Makani, when he chose to carry her litter while on a journey.[191] Coryat suggested of this account that it was exceptional for Akbar to burden himself with the actual portage of his mother and that the gesture here, as in most other instances like this, was a genuine and spontaneous burst of affection for the woman who had given him birth as an infant and who continued to nurture him throughout his adult years.

Jahangir's own expression of the filial bond was manifest especially in his preoccupation with the Christian image of Madonna and Child. It comes as no surprise that Jahangir, when afforded the chance to order prints and paintings from Europe, included in his lists (as Akbar had) numerous copies of the Virgin Mary and Christ Child. Even before his accession to the throne he pursued this quest, and as Du Jarric said: "The Prince showed the Fathers, with whom he was on intimate terms, many proofs of his devotion to our Savior and His holy Mother, whose images he held in the highest veneration. Indeed, the Fathers could make no more acceptable present than a well-executed representation of either."[192] The use of Christian imagery in his palaces became even more pronounced after Jahangir acceded to the throne, and there is good evidence that he closed his official documents with seals bearing images of Christ and of Mary,[193] that he prayed on a black slate throne with pictures of both Christian figures graven into its stone,[194] and that paintings of both hung continuously on the walls of his galleries.[195] It would not be unexpected that most of the pictures brought by the Jesuits to the court were religious in nature, and given the strongly biblical origins of Islam, it is clear that pictures of the Madonna and Child would find great appeal among the Muslims of India.[196] Moreover, it is often charged that Jahangir curried favor among the Jesuits—to the point, they hoped, of conversion to Christianity—in the last years of the sixteenth century because he feared he might need Portuguese assistance in his attempt for the throne.[197]

Nevertheless, above and beyond any general cultural interest in the Marian pictures, the Madonna imagery fit quite naturally into the Mughal reverence for the mother-son relationship and even more naturally into the peculiar strength of this relationship for Jahangir. Aside from the testimony of European donors of pictures at the court, however, and the numerous examples of Madonnas prominently displayed in Mughal galleries [see Figure 3–1], we do not have evidence enough to substantiate the claim of a personal cult of the Virgin Mary at Jahangir's court. But we do contend that the Madonna and Child imagery we know was available to Jahangir must certainly have fed his natural inclination toward reverence of the mother, and that his attachment to and sympathy for older women must have found easy expression in the maternal symbolism of Mary, Mother of God.

The mother-child patterning of Jahangir's relationships with the senior women of his household and of his interest in Madonna paintings culminated, of course, in his powerful attachment to Nur Jahan. There can be no doubt that when later Indian tradition tried to remold Jahangir's love for Nur Jahan into an adolescent obsession born of the romantic frenzy of youth, it had completely misunderstood both Jahangir's character and the quality of the woman he married in 1611. We do not in fact know anything of Nur Jahan's adolescent fantasies, but that she had married and born a child long before meeting Jahangir at the Nauroz festival of 1611 means that she came to Jahangir at a time when the passions of youth were long rechanneled and, at age thirty-five, were now transformed into more mature emotions. Given what we know of their daily relationship, of the tending in sickness, of the curbing of wine, and of the exercise of ripened skills like patronizing the arts and marksmanship, it seems clear that Nur Jahan was completely miscast as the seductive vamp of later novels and cinema. Instead, all evidence of the period points to a middle-aged wife, still no doubt very beautiful and personally charismatic, but whose claim on Jahangir was not by way of adolescent romance, but of a mature partnership heavily colored by Jahangir's vision of ideal maternal care.

What can we say, finally, of Nur Jahan herself? We do not, quite remarkably, have any firsthand personal account of her thoughts and feelings. We have no memoirs, no authentic poetry, no miniature paintings verified to her hand. All we can do is project onto her what might be reasonable responses to the course of life she experienced. Nur Jahan, we assume, must have been flattered to have been brought with her daughter into Ruqayya Sultan's service after the death of Sher Afgan. She had relatives at the court, to be sure, but her husband had gone down in ignominy and she could have rightly expected only the worst. She must have been flattered even more to have been married to the emperor and in no time elevated to be his chief queen. She certainly loved, or had great affection for, her second husband and, despite vague, unfounded rumors about Shah Jahan, was faithful to Jahangir and to his memory throughout her life. She loved the acquisition of power and was, without any doubt, exceptionally good at wielding it. She was radical enough to stretch the limits of a Mughal queen's life—through trading, issuing *farmans*, overseeing promotions at court, designing tombs and gardens, and influencing religious policy—but she was not radical enough to actually overstep the boundaries accepted by custom for women related to high office. She accepted, apparently authentically, the psychological, emotional, and philosophical rapport that was supposed to exist between husband and wife and, recalling perhaps the unit concept of Hindu marriage, she moved smoothly, if creatively, through the duties assigned a king's consort. Most importantly, however, she knew how to match the needs and quirks of the difficult personality of her husband with talents and abilities that were now assuredly her own.

If Jahangir was a king whose grand conceit of a just rule and often ignominious behavior in and out of office were governed by an aesthetic vision that was at best amoral, then Nur Jahan was a queen who knew quite clearly the moral limits of her role. We have argued earlier that Jahangir's character, in its need for a visual and pleasure-giving order with him at the center, was beyond any sensitivity to ethical or even legal standards of right and wrong and that his reality was more often than not a cerebral world not readily shared by others but surprisingly responsive to the details of natural life. This amoral stance was matched by his consort's decided susceptibility to moral laws and to the pleasures of virtuous judgment. When Nur Jahan did what was right, she did so knowing it was good (dowries to five hundred orphan brides, for example),[198] and when she did what was wrong, she knew full well she had overstepped the boundaries of corruption. Manipulating the fate of her eventual enemy, Shah Jahan,[199] or actively encouraging a young Jain monk to break his monastic vows[200] were conscious intrusions into an otherwise orderly and acceptable world, and Nur Jahan certainly knew that in cases like these she was playing counter to a moral code acknowledged by others. Nevertheless, such knowing breeches of righteous behavior must have been tempting against a background that was so completely immune to concepts of virtue. Living under the shadow of a king as oblivious to morality as Jahangir was must have frustrated, if not actively terrified, all those in any way affected by the movements in his sphere. Nur Jahan, it seems, was neither frustrated nor terrified, for she had acquired early on exceptional powers of orchestration and survival.

5

Life in the Women's Palaces

Oh yes, I shall marry someone; but he shall be a man whose collar my hand can touch, and not one whose skirt it does not reach.

(Hamida Banu Begam, hesitating on her marriage to Humayun)
The History of Humayun, by Gulbadan Begam, translated by A. S. Beveridge

We have heard that prosperity and bad luck depend on four things: first, upon your wife; second, upon your slave; third, upon your house; fourth, upon your horse.

The reflection of the lamps fell on the water and had a wonderful appearance. I passed the most of that night with the ladies of the mahall on the bank of that tank.

The Tuzuk-i-Jahangiri, translated by A. Rogers
and edited by Henry Beveridge

I

Three things sustained the power of a Mughal emperor: his army, his treasury, and his women. Of these, the army was perhaps the least fixed and the most distant from the king, large parts of it being entrusted to underlings to whom rank was assigned for purposes of honor and income. The treasury, which rose and fell with the vagaries of politics, was also an impersonal, if fairly stable, symbol of the majesty of state. But the women of the *zanana*, the women of the inner apartments, were as constant, as unfailing, and yet as demanding a touchstone as any head of state could claim. Not only were they the closest to him in proximity and affection, but they could offer the emperor more personal pleasure, more unchallenged support, and more wise counsel than any other person or group.[1] The *zanana* women went with the emperor everywhere, and if A. S. Beveridge can marvel at "how fully the fate of the ladies was involved in that of the Emperor,"[2] then we must note with Roe that the emperor was in turn just as dependent upon the whims and the schedules of his women, for no court business could take place until after their needs had been fully satisfied.[3]

An uncritical vision of the harem might suppose that its women were, like the treasury, simple possessions of the king. Jahangir certainly spoke at times as if that were the case—"I sent back Dust Muhammad . . . to take charge of the fort of Agra and of the zanana and the treasuries"[4]—and Mughal lifestyle often depended upon being able to send large groups from the *zanana* quickly to various parts of the country or to dispatch small groups to a court as tokens of allegiance and support.[5] The basis for this, argues Dow, was that a noble's or emperor's "affection for the woman" was not bound up in his private pledges of fidelity to her but in the sovereign honor that he placed "in her person," and that he then made over to his own custody.[6] Women and the honor of their lord were thus inextricably bound, and the medieval codes of etiquette linking these two set the future of the empire unfailingly upon their bonds.[7]

Although the women of the palaces were ultimately under the jurisdiction of their male principal, they were a diverse, internally mobile, and highly vociferous group who exercised enormous freedom in reworking the configurations of their restraint. The palaces in which the *zanana* women lived were self-sufficient cities with a full range of castes, occupations, and administrators, and were as cosmopolitan a mix of religions, nationalities, and artistic talents as to be found in any metropolis of the time.[8] But, while an emperor like Jahangir may have found his central support in the strength of the harem—he did, after all, like other young boys of class, grow up in the *zanana*—for an individual woman the central issue was not how much power she could exert at court but how she could fit into the complex lives of the others immediately around her. Finding a productive and satisfying place in a society where pleasure (in all its forms) was the main competitive commodity was a substantial task, but this process was surely a more vibrant and honest affair given that it took place in the company of women.

The public lives of women of nobility were governed by the laws of seclusion. The practice of *parda*, or the sequestering of women behind a veil or wall, had already been known to ancient and medieval India and had been used throughout history by many of the upper classes.[9] By the time of the Mughals, seclusion was an accepted way of life for aristocratic families, and the institution as practiced by Jahangir had come to be a sign to foreign travelers of a strict adherence to Islam. Said Roe at the beginning of his tenure:

> All the People are strickt Mahometans, . . . They are veary Jelous to let their weomen . . . be seene; of which we had experience by an alarum of one of their Priests, who espied one of ours comming toward a village, who shutt vp all the woemen, and cried out if we came neare them or their church they would kill us.[10]

Terry reported that he never "had . . . sight of those [women] of the greatest quality,"[11] and it appears that no one at court was allowed to see the women housed there except the principal man and a few select male relatives:[12] "There are none admitted, strangers or others, to have a sight of those houses, while the King's wives and women are there, which must not be seen by any but by himself, and his servants the eunuchs."[13] Such women, said Terry, "as have the reputation of honesty, [are not] to be seen at any time by any man, besides their own husbands, or by those before named, and by them but very seldom."[14] Those men given special, if brief, privileges included the brothers and fathers of the women inside, but even these men were not allowed to come to the harem or to speak to the women except in the presence of the husband.[15] It must have been a very great honor, then, when Jahangir decreed that Nur Jahan's father Itimaduddaula had become such "an intimate friend" that "the ladies of the harem [were] not to veil their faces from him."[16]

As practiced by the Mughals, then, seclusion was a religious, social, and class arrangement. Dow speculates as to the causes of *parda* and concludes that it had a sexual origin: women were kept in seclusion, he argues, in order to protect their modesty and thereby the honor of the family. And India, especially, was prone to the practice of seclusion because of her climate, "where continence is a more arduous virtue than in the bleak regions of the north."[17] No doubt *parda* was supported by the quasi-religious rationale of the time that a woman's honor needed protecting by a socially enforced institution rather than by the force of her own character, but *parda* had much more important ramifications in the area of work. The practice of seclusion in a family was a sign of high economic standing: a family able to afford so many servants that its women were not needed to work could cloister them off in a harem. Moreover, the lord of a family who was himself free from the everyday demands of labor could spend his leisure time in pursuit of pleasure with his women. The harem, then, became the ultimate mark of social standing, and for the king, who had the largest supporting staff and the most leisure at hand, women were the real symbol of his imperial sovereignty.

We do not really know what it was like to be an inmate of a *zanana*. Gulbadan, whose *Humayunnama* is one of the few chronicles of Mughal history written by a woman and who spent some time detailing the activities of women of her time, did not, unfortunately, reveal much of the feelings and sentiments of those behind the walls. There is no doubt, however, that as far as the times permitted women were regarded highly and treated with great respect by their men.[18] Women's advice was sought, their material needs attended to, and their community supported by whatever staff was required to meet the individual eccentricities of its members. But we don't know if women inside saw their lot as better or worse than those who exercised more freedom outside, nor do we really know what effect seclusion had on the psychological and spiritual development of those it embraced. We suspect, however, given the diversity of personnel and the wide range of activities open to them behind the walls, that the women of the *zanana* were, as a group, sophisticated, self-assured, and by most accounts happy.

The physical residences in which royal women lived were lavish. During the Mughal period, the apartments reserved for the use of the emperor's women were called *mahals*, and because there were so many women involved, these *mahals* took up large portions of the main palace area. In Agra, for example, which Jahangir called "the centre of the State, the abode of the ladies of the holy harem, and the depository of the world's treasures"[19] and where earlier Babur himself had had special buildings erected for the use of the harem,[20] there were separate palaces for each of the important female relatives of Jahangir. Along the bank of the Yamuna could be found, for example, the individual residences of Shahzada Khanam, sister of Jahangir and the wife of Mirza Muzaffar Husain, at one time governor of Gujarat, Gulazar Begam, and Ruqayya Sultan Begam, one of the widows of Akbar and a senior woman in the harem—as well as the Shaikh Pura, "a large enclosure inhabited by the [other] widows of the late King Akbar."[21] Inside the Shah Burj itself, the royal bastion of Agra fort, was the palace of Nur Jahan and near it other palaces for women of the *zanana*. Three of these *mahals* were called respectively the *Itwar* (Sunday), the *Mangal* (Tuesday), and the *Sanichar* (Saturday) indicating the day on which the emperor slept there, and a fifth palace inside the enclosure, called by Akbar the Bengali Mahal, was "occupied by ladies of various nations."[22] "Internally then the Fort is built over like a city with streets and shops, and has very little resemblance to a fortress, but from the outside anyone would regard it as impregnable."[23]

Behind the high walls of the *mahals* were tanks and gardens, as well as separate apartments for each wife and for "her slaves, of whom there may be 10, or 20, or 100, according to her fortune."[24] Running water through the rooms was standard, and it flowed into the various courtyards via troughs or pipes where it was released through elaborate fountains and waterfalls [see Figure 5-1] Water often came from spring-fed wells beautifully "wrought up with firm stones, [and] laid in fine plaster," and was drawn fresh each day by oxen turning large wheels with many small buckets.[25] The tanks of the *mahals* were usually large and quite deep and were designed so that those used for bathing offered some degree of privacy.[26]

Plants also were an important "refreshment and recreation" within the *mahals* and, when carefully placed throughout the gardens, provided a welcome antidote to the often uncomfortable vagaries of the climate.[27] Fruit trees gave "daily yields" of produce,[28] squares of flowers provided continual beauty, and shade trees placed conspicuously apart kept off the hot sun. "They have no furniture of the kind we delight in, such as tables, stools, benches, cupboards, bedsteads, etc.," but instead the women (and men) sat on cushions, rugs, or low cots, which "are lavishly ornamented with gold or silver."[29] The spaces, then as now, were open and clean and laid out so as to encourage cool winds and diffuse light, and to minimize the effects of the persistent heat and dust.

The wealthier and more noble the lord, the more ornate the decoration inside the *mahal*. Surface ornament has always been valued in Indian aesthetics, and the extended courtyard style of residence with its pillared verandas, open halls, and turreted gazebos was optimal for the application of paint, inlay, mirror-work, and carved molding that came to be the single most desirable way of relieving the visual sameness of the *mahal* interior. Roe had a chance to look inside a *mahal* room once and, although it was very rich, it overwhelmed him with its patchworked appearance: the room decoration, he said, was "so diuers . . . [and its pieces] so vnsuteable that it was rather patched then glorious, as if it seemed to

FIGURE 5–1. Interior water-chute, Red Fort, Delhi. Courtesy of the Archaeological Survey of India, New Delhi.

striue to show all, like a ladie that with her plate sett on a Cupboard her imbrodered slippers."[30] Again, according to the ungenerous Pelsaert: "Their *mahals* are adorned internally with lascivious sensuality, wanton and reckless festivity, superfluous pomp, inflated pride, and ornamental daintiness."[31]

The hanging of paintings on palace walls was also fashionable, among

Mughal emperors, and the art gallery style of decoration eminently suited the need for variety inside the harem as well as the burgeoning trade with Europe and the Far East in paintings and objets d'art. Finch reported that in the *mahals* of the palace at Lahore, for example, Jahangir had hung pictures in his interior galleries "of Banian dews, or rather divels, intermixt in most ugly shape with long hornes, staring eyes, shagge haire, great fangs, ugly pawes, [and] long tailes." The creatures in the paintings were so deformed, he said, "that I wonder the poore women are not frighted therewith."[32] There was plenty of room to escape unwanted sights, however, and in spite of Terry's claim that "these Mahometans . . . [have] so many wives, . . . [that] they keep [them] pent up in little cottages or tents,"[33] the *mahals* were spacious and comfortable.

In the fort at Lahore described by Finch, there were three *mahals* constructed during the reign of Jahangir. The first of these was a small two-storied palace, each story containing "eight faire lodgings for severall women, with galleries and windowes looking to the river and to the court."[34] The second palace was a large square building called the "New Moholl" which could accommodate two hundred women "in state," presumably with all their baggage and personal paraphernalia.[35] The third palace was "the stateliest of the three" and contained sixteen "great lodgings, each having faire lodgings, a devoncan (or hall), a small paved court, each her tanke, and enjoying a little world of pleasure and state to herselfe."[36] The walls in these *mahals* were decorated with mirrors and pictures and, as Finch noted, "[all] the doores of these chambers are to bee fastened on the out-side, and none within."[37] Anything the women could ever want, presumably, was already inside the enclosure.

The women within the *zanana* were numerous. Estimates of the total number in Jahangir's harem ranged from that of Hawkins of "three hundred wives, whereof foure be chiefe as queenes,"[38] to that of Terry of "four wives, and . . . concubines and women beside, . . . enough to make up their number a full thousand."[39] Where the exact figure lay is not altogether clear, but it was certainly in the hundreds and may have fluctuated at the outer reaches as Jahangir continually gave away and brought in women of lesser place. We know, however, that he probably did not have women in the greater thousands, for he was aghast to learn of Nasiruddin "that he had collected 15,000 women in his harem."[40]

Those in the inner palaces came from a variety of religious, ethnic, and class backgrounds.[41] In addition to the wives to whom Jahangir was legally married and to his various female relatives—for example, daughters, sisters, mothers, and aunts—Jahangir's harem housed ladies-in-waiting of all sorts who were in attendance upon the queens and female relatives there. These noblewomen were joined by concubines, servants, slaves, female guards, spies,[42] entertainers, soothsayers, and stray women of all classes brought in under a variety of circumstances for stays of indeterminate length. In addition, the *zanana* housed eunuchs and all the children of the women inside, including young boys until they were old enough to move into quarters of their own. Women came into the harem either through marriage, birth, purchase, appointment, gift, or other accretive process, and the resulting mix was astonishingly international. Hamida Banu Begam (Maryam Makani), wife of Humayun, for example, "had amongst her household slaves a Russian of Moscow and his Polish wife, with their two children,"[43] and Hindu women of Rajput families were a consistent and conspicuous presence in the predominantly Muslim harem from the days of the Sultanate period onward.[44] Moreover, Jesuits at court firmly believed that Jahangir's motive in encouraging the sons of Daniyal to be baptized Christians was "to introduce Portuguese women of good position into Jahangir's own zanana."[45]

Noblewomen who came into the *zanana* were often given new titles as a special mark of honor or privilege.[46] Mihrunnisa, of course, was the most famous, receiving the name Nur Mahal, "Light of the Palace," upon her marriage in 1611 and Nur Jahan, "Light of the World," in 1616.[47] Said Terry: "His most beloved wife (when I lived at his court) he called Noor-Mahal, which signified the light of the court; and to the other of his wives, and women which he most loved, he gave new names unto them, and such names as he most fancied."[48] Akbar gave his mother the title Maryam Makani, "Mary of Both Worlds,"[49] and Jahangir's mother was known as Maryamuzzamani, "Mary of the Universe."[50] Shah Jahan's mother was called Bilqis Makani, "the Lady of Pure Abode,"[51] after her death and his wife, Arjumand Banu Begam, was popularly known as Mumtaz Mahal, "Exalted One of the Palace,"[52] and Malika-i Jahan, "Lady of the World." After Arjumand Banu's death in 1631, Shah Jahan's favorite daughter Jahanara was given the place of honor in the harem as well as the title Sahibatuzzamani, "Mistress of the Universe."[53] The most important title in the *zanana*, however, was that of Padshah Begam, the "Imperial" or "First Lady" of the realm. Begam was a general title of respect given to ladies of rank, "which signifies that they are void of care,"[54] and seems to have been conferred upon women of the royal family as a mark of special favor or at some momentous occasion like the birth of a son.[55]

The normally friendly relationship between women in the harem, ostensibly shaped by the courtesy of the seniority system, was often undercut by routine jealousies, which "dusted the poison of gossip on the intricate web of internal relations."[56] A. S. Beveridge notes that women frequently entered the *zanana* bound by old political allegiances, which would occasionally flare up and cause great friction among the other women there.[57] This friction would then be exacerbated into a constant level of "animosity and quarrel," Dow contends, by the simple fact that there were a great number of wives and concubines present at one time.[58] Each consort desired the exclusive attention of the emperor but had to subject these feelings to the exacting structure of harem life, thus making any relationship within the *zanana* a routinely mannered affair. "Jealousy itself, that most violent of the feelings of the soul, is curbed within the walls of the haram. The women may pine in secret, but they must clothe their features with cheerfulness when their lord appears."[59] Pelsaert noted that, in Agra at least, all food for the *zanana* came from one kitchen but "each wife takes it in her own apartments; for they hate each other secretly, though they seldom or never allow it to be seen, because of their desire to retain the favour of their husband."[60] The emperor tried to be fair to all by visiting a different wife or apartment each night, but if it happened that he took a fancy to a pretty slave girl at any time and enjoyed her, the wife did not dare "to show any signs of displeasure, but dissembling, . . . [took] it out on the slave-girl later on."[61] Women were thought to lose their sexual appeal at a fairly young age (thirty) and, because of this, Muslim families felt "the law for a multiplicity of wives . . . [was] necessary for the support of the human race." But, as Dow further notes, the children of these many women often inherited the petty squabbles of the *zanana* and "the jealousy between mothers in the haram grows into hatred among their sons."[62] On the other hand, however, we must note the many examples of adult male friendships in the Mughal period—like that of Akbar and Mirza Aziz Koka (Khan-i Azam),[63] and Jahangir and Qutbuddin Khan Koka[64]—that originated in obviously supportive relationships between *zanana* women. Here the prince in each set was nursed by the mother of his friend, a tradition that in almost all cases made lifetime alliances between the two men.

By Jahangir's time the structure of the Mughal harem had become an elaborate affair, far surpassing in complexity the earlier Turkish or Sultanate harems or anything found in contemporary Indian households. From Akbar, Jahangir had inherited a system based on seniority that was designed to keep a large number of women in the best possible order. Akbar's harem, for example, had five thousand women in it, each of whom was given a separate apartment. The women were divided into sections headed by "chaste women" superintendents known as *daroghas*, whose duty it was, apparently, not only to keep order but to make sure all the women were "attentive to their duties."[65] One woman was selected as writer and it was her responsibility to keep an accurate record of *zanana* life.[66] The most important office for a woman in the harem, however, was that of *mahaldar*, who was "like a female major domo . . . [acting] as a spy in the interest of the Emperor."[67] The *mahaldar*, it seems, coordinated most of the relationships between the harem and the nobles at court. This was a delicate task and she had to try to avoid any friction such as that which often arose when she was overly zealous in reporting to the emperor on the activities of the young princes in the *zanana*.[68] Just which of these roles the woman Aqa Aqayan had in Jahangir's harem is not clear, but the emperor noted with pride that this female relative of his, who had been taken from his sister Shahzada Khanam at the time of his first marriage and placed "in charge of my zanana" by Akbar, had been in his service for thirty-three years and, he said, "I esteem her greatly, for she has served me with sincerity."[69]

The harem was guarded on the inside by "sober and active women." Armed with bows and arrows and short daggers, women guards, such as the *urdubegis*[70] from Kashmir and Central Asia,[71] were placed throughout the *zanana*, "the most trustworthy . . . [being stationed in] the apartments of his Majesty."[72] Over these guards presided a chief armed woman, in the manner of Bibi Fatima, who held the post during the time of Humayun.[73] Jourdain noted that the guards around Jahangir, both men and women, were changed every twenty-four hours,[74] presumably to keep them alert and to prevent internal conspiracies. Beyond them eunuchs guarded the *zanana* from outside the enclosure of the apartments,[75] and "at a proper distance" from them stood a guard of loyal Rajput soldiers. Porters patrolled the palace gates and beyond even them were guards of nobles, including the famous quiver-bearing Ahadis, who were arranged according to rank.[76] At sunset the doors of the *zanana* were closed and torches were left burning to restrict any secret intrigue involving members of the harem. Each woman guard then sent a report to the *nazir* or supervisor detailing the activities of the women during the day or, alternately, as Manucci noted, a report was read by women of the *mahal* themselves once a week in the presence of the emperor around nine o'clock at night.[77] The twenty-four hour security around the *zanana* was kept so strong that if ever a noblewoman from the outside wished to come into the harem to visit someone who lived there, she first had to tell the servants of the *zanana* in the hopes that they would bring her a quick reply. She then sent on her request to the officers of the palace, who would let only those "who are eligible" into the harem. Permission to visit was generous, however, and some women visitors of rank were granted stays in the harem for as long as a month.[78]

Order within the harem was maintained by a strict system of salaries and allowances. Akbar's salaries to the women in the *zanana* were "sufficiently liberal," and we can assume that Jahangir's were as well. In Akbar's time, women of the highest rank received between Rs. 1028 and 1610 a month, while servants received salaries in ranges given alternately as Rs. 20 to 51 and Rs. 2 to 40.[79] A special accountant, or writer of the harem, was attached to the *zanana* to oversee the flow of cash and to keep check at all times on the reserves. Under him were the *tahwildars* or cash keepers, who granted almost all the requests they received from women, provided the desired amounts were within the limit of the women's salaries. The *tahwildar* would then send on the request to the writer, who checked with the general treasurer before making the payment in cash. The writer was also in charge of drawing up an annual budget, writing out a receipt for it, and having it countersigned by the ministers of state. This receipt was then stamped with a seal used exclusively for grants for the harem. Money designated by the receipt could only be paid out by the cash keeper of the general treasury, who gave it to the general *tahwildar*, who under instruction from the writer of the harem, divided it among the harem *tahwildars* to be distributed as designated among the women.[80] In all, the expenses of the harem were apparently extraordinary, with the "best and most costly" of all items reserved "for the king's person, the queens, and the princesses."[81]

Women of rank seemed to have acquired more control over their wealth as the Mughal period progressed. Not only did they probably have more wealth to begin with—Jahangir, for example, "increased the allowances of all the veiled ladies of my father's harem from 20 percent to 100 percent, according to their condition and relationship"[82] upon his accession in 1605—but they had more of their own officers to administer it. Manucci noted that during Shah Jahan's reign each lady of rank had a *nazir*, who was responsible for looking after her property, land, and income.[83] Nur Jahan had her own *vakils*, who supervised her *jagirs* and the construction of buildings on various of her properties,[84] and the emperor's mother, Maryamuzzamani, had numerous agents in and out of the harem appointed to help her oversee her trading activities and to advise her on investments. Moreover, many of the women of the Shah Jahan and Aurangzeb eras had men of note supervising their holdings and accounting for the cash and goods that flowed in and out of the harem under their egis.

While guards at all levels insured the physical protection of the harem, and a routine of salaries and allowances secured at least a minimum of order and adherence to duty, it was the seniority system that was the harem's most powerful guarantor of personal civility, internal cohesion, and generational compatibility. Ordinarily there was a senior wife who among the wives and female relations of the emperor commanded the most respect,[85] had the final word in harem matters, and had the special attention of the emperor at court: such senior women, says Lall, "enjoyed an authority on tradition and etiquette that was virtually supreme."[86] Under the most senior, all the other wives and female relatives, ladies-in-waiting, and concubines were arrayed according to their length of time in the *zanana* and to that often precarious element, the special favor of the male principal. Rank in the harem was indicated by any number of things, allowance, quality of presents, and title being three of the most obvious. But it was in the living arrangements of camps and in the hierarchy of parties, however, where rank was seen to be a most jealously guarded arrangement. Gulbadan's high standing with Humayun, for example, was shown clearly "by the record of the place assigned to her tent in the encampments. It was pitched next to Hamida's well within the great enclosure, and not far from the Emperor's own."[87] Gulbaden also preserved a detailed account of the Mystic Feast, which commemorated Humayun's accession, and of the feast accompanying Mirza Hindal's wedding, in which the seating arrangement reflected the harem hierarchy at large. During both parties Humayun and his "dearest lady" sat on a gold-embroidered divan in front of a gold throne in the forecourt of the house. To their right, on cushions, sat their elder female relatives and other senior women, and to their left sat women of lesser status including nurses and wives of the *amirs*.[88] Although there was certainly some flexibility and mobility within the ranks, harem seniority was a fairly stable system and may have accounted, at least in part, for the long period Nur Jahan remained unnoticed by Jahangir in the *mahal*.

One of the special privileges of women of rank was to care for ranking children not their own. All young children of the palaces were brought up in the harem, and this included young princes who lived with the elder women of the *zanana* until they were old enough to have palaces of their own.[89] Often childless women of rank would adopt the children of other women—even over the objections of the natural mother—in order to satisfy their own maternal instincts, to have something to do, and to acquire legitimacy in the generational struggle for power. Gulbadan, for example, was taken from her natural mother, Dildar, a younger wife of Babur, when she was about two and, with her brother, Hindal, was given to Maham Begam, the senior wife of Babur (and mother of Humayun) who had lost four children in infancy.[90] Maham Begam died, however, when Gulbadan was ten and the young girl was then given back to her natural mother for care.[91] Jahangir's sisters were given the care of Daniyal's children, two boys and four girls, at the same time as the third and eldest boy, Tahmuras, was taken in to wait on the emperor himself.[92] Ruqayya Sultan Begam, of course, the childless first wife of Akbar and daughter of Mirza Hindal, took Mihrunnisa in after the young woman's first husband was murdered and cared for her during her next four years.[93] She was also given charge of Shah Jahan in his early years[94] and then of Parhez Banu, one of his daughters by his first wife.[95] Nur Jahan herself was, except for her daughter by Sher Afgan, a "childless wife" of Jahangir's and was given Prince Shuja, a son of Shah Jahan, to raise in the harem. The new responsibility was the result as much of her own political ambition as it was of the emperor's affection for her, but it was an honor nevertheless as the young boy was a special favorite of Jahangir's.[96]

Within the structure of the harem, there was perhaps no one more important to its smooth running than that all-purpose servant, the eunuch. Neither fully man nor fully woman, the eunuch could travel freely throughout the *mahal* and to the world beyond, thus serving as an accessible conduit of favors and information. He has been described as a "sort of brute," prey to his own base emotions of greed, pride, and hypocrisy,[97] but in fact the eunuch was most often a loyal retainer caught in the irreconcilable tensions of *mahal* life. Each woman of rank had two or more eunuchs, head eunuchs being called *nazir* ("guardian" or "superintendent"), who were "usually faithful to their master, . . . [but were] appointed for each wife, to ensure that she is seen by no man except her husband."[98] Said Terry: "The women there of the greater quality have eunuchs, instead of men, to wait upon them, who in their minority are deprived of all that might provoke jealousy."[99] Eunuchs were often purchased as slaves from Bengal[100] and, in spite of the fact that at the beginning of his reign Jahangir "had repeatedly given orders that no one should make eunuchs or buy or sell them," saying "whoever did so would be answerable as a criminal,"[101] they were a staple in the harem and given significant roles in and out of the *zanana*. Not only were they part of the protective system used by the emperor to safeguard his women[102]—keeping as able a control over the locked doors as possible[103]—but of all the servants of the women, they had the most freedom to arrange contacts outside the *zanana* on matters of trade, military maneuvers, courtly intrigues, and secret communications. Eunuchs also accompanied *mahal* women when they traveled and on their various adventures and expeditions, serving both to protect them from being seen by men while out in public and to transmit messages to them from outsiders come to call.[104] Pelsaert noted that "the whole management of the *mahal* is in their [the eunuchs'] hands, and they can give or refuse whatever is wanted." They were so important, in fact, that "they can get whatever they desire—fine horses to ride, servants to attend them outside, and female slaves inside the house, [and] clothes as fine and smart as those of their master himself."[105]

The most important duty of the eunuch, however, was to manage the delicate relationship between the emperor and his women. On the emperor's side, the eunuch's responsibility was to make sure that the women saw no men in the harem except the principle male, and if he failed in this he, in addition to "everyone else to blame for the stranger's presence," was "in danger of losing his life."[106] The eunuch was equally responsible to the women, however, for he was uniquely able to keep whatever happened in the *zanana* concealed from the husband and was amply rewarded when the protective cover he gave allowed women freedom of movement and meeting. The chief eunuch or *nazir* of

Jahanara, for example, was famous for his complicity in her affairs and, rather than restrain her would-be lovers from entering the apartments (as Bernier has suggested), "the man obeyed her, and sought every mode of gratifying her, seeing the great interest he had not to work against her."[107] Eunuchs themselves were often involved in their women's love lives, and Pelsaert was quite explicit in his description of what happened in the *mahal* when the principal male went on a trip. Those women left at home, he said, "allow the eunuch to enjoy them according to his ability, and thus gratify their burning passions when they have no opportunity of going out."[108] Eunuchs, then, had an advantageous position that could be both remunerative and satisfying if the delicate balance between husband and wife were kept intact. But, if the husband's need to safeguard and the wife's desire for freedom were not properly synchronized, the eunuch's position could be most dangerous, his life itself at considerable risk.

The sexual life of the eunuch was supposed to be nonexistent. Deprived at a very young age "of all that might provoke jealousy," they were "a soft tender people . . . that never come to have any hair on their faces."[109] Eunuchs were, despite Pelsaert's observation above, officially forbidden from having liaisons with the women of the harem, but many of them did, and Bernier, for example, preserved the story of a eunuch in Aurangzeb's time who carried out a long affair with a beautiful Hindu neighbor. Her brother, it seems, was "a scrivener by profession," who, discovering the affair, attacked and killed the couple with a knife—it being a brother's duty to do so in cases of family honor. The harem was filled with "horror and indignation" at the deed, and women "and eunuchs entered into a solemn league to kill the scrivener" in turn. The orthodox Aurangzeb, however, was content, to have the perpetrator convert to Islam.[110] Roe and Terry recorded an equally fateful end to another eunuch liaison during Jahangir's time. A "gentell woeman of Normalls"[111] was found kissing a eunuch and was buried alive in the ground up to her armpits to die by the scorching of the hot sun. The eunuch she had met was then killed as she watched from her burial spot.[112] Liaisons like these of some sexual nature certainly must have developed between eunuchs and the women they guarded, but there was pressure equal to the opportunity from within the *zanana* to keep any such relationship seriously circumspect.

The sexual life of *mahal* women was governed by general rules of religion. Undergirding all intimate activity was a code of modesty that held that the physical protection of a woman was of utmost importance to the maintenance of her moral virtue. Says Dow:

> Women are so sacred in India, that even the common soldiery leave them unmolested in the midst of slaughter and devastation. . . . The haram is a sanctuary against all the licentiousness of victory; and ruffians, covered with the blood of a husband, shrink back with confusion from the secret apartments of his wives.[113]

The modesty of a woman was so important, in fact, that during times of war if a man were in danger of imprisonment or of death he often killed his women beforehand lest they suffer the shame of abuse by the enemy.[114] Because a woman was thought to carry not only the honor of her husband but the safekeeping of her entire family in the quality of her conduct, a life that was blameless and above reproach became the very measure of womanhood.

Within the *zanana*, women who were not married far outnumbered those who were. While the status of wife applied only to those legally espoused to the emperor, many hundreds of others around him, including female relatives, concubines, ladies-in-waiting, and servants of all types, were required to live the same lives of virtue and in the same restricted circumstances as their more legitimate colleagues. Perhaps the most unfortunate victims of this system were the princesses, the sisters and daughters of a reigning king, who by reason of their relationship to the throne were prohibited from marrying. Said Manucci: "Akbar bequeathed to his descendants the rule not to give their daughters in marriage. This rule remained in force up to the time of Aurangzeb, who gave his daughters in marriage upon their insisting."[115] The reasons why princesses were not allowed to marry had as much to do with the stability of the crown as it did with the virtue of the royal family: "the marriage of a Princess . . . [is] of rare occurrence in *Hindoustan*, no man being considered worthy of royal alliance; an apprehension being entertained that the husband might thereby be rendered powerful, and induced perhaps to aspire to the crown."[116] Any husband of a princess, who was herself (had she been male) in line for the throne, was considered a threat not only to the real sons at the time of succession but to the father as well, who was in constant fear of filial insurrection. In fact, a son-in-law, precisely because of his lack of consanguinity, would be more fickle, it was thought, than real sons when given a chance at early power. Princesses, then, had to be content with the material luxuries of the harem and the platonic affections of fathers and brothers, which, as all knew, were as constant as anything available at the court. There were exceptions to this prohibition, however, such as the marriage of a daughter of Prince Murad to Parviz,[117] of a daughter of Daniyal to Mirza Wali,[118] and of several daughters of Aurangzeb (e.g., Zinatunnisa Begam and Badrunnisa Begam) to nobles.[119] Tavernier noted that when princesses married nobles "they became the rulers of their husbands" and, if these men displeased their wives in any way, the princesses would go to the emperor and "persuade him to do what they please, to the disadvantage of their husbands; most frequently asking that they be deprived of their offices."[120] In general, however, marriage remained a luxury prohibited to women of immediate royal blood.

The institution of marriage for Mughal emperors was primarily a political affair. Akbar had made a practice of marrying women, especially Rajput daughters of renowned families, in order to enhance his political alliances and to stabilize his empire.[121] Jahangir himself was born of a Rajput mother who had come into the *mahal* as a result of just such an alliance, and he certainly continued his father's practice of using the daughters of political colleagues to further his negotiations with them. But Jahangir moved beyond the purely political context of marriage and introduced into it an element of love. As Terry noted, Jahangir was less interested in the genealogical background of his wives than in the beauty they brought with them to court.

> For that great monarch, the Mogŭl, in the choice of his wives and women, he was guided more by his eye and fancy, than by any respect had to his honour, for he took not the daughters of neighbouring princes, but of his own subjects, and there preferred that which he looked upon as beauty, before any thing else.[122]

And it was precisely because Jahangir chose his wives for their beauty and not necessarily their parentage that Nur Jahan came into his harem, for Itimadud-daula was already, without further persuasion, a close associate in counsel.

Whatever romantic views of marriage Jahangir might have had, the actual experience of his wives and women was far from ideal. Sexual life in the harem was a barren mix of occasional visits from the emperor, secret trysts with visitors or eunuchs, and a shadow cult of fantasy and creative practice. Foreigners of the period who imagined what it must be like for women in the harem drew devastating pictures of life inside. For Pelsaert: "These wretched women wear, indeed, the most expensive clothes, eat the daintiest food, and enjoy all worldly pleasures except one, and for that one they grieve, saying they would willingly give everything in exchange for a beggar's poverty."[123] The general lack of sexual satisfaction among women of the harem, ascribed to their frequent and long separations from men, led many to speculate, as Tavernier did, "[that] it is not difficult to imagine that strange things take place in the enclosure where these women and girls are shut up."[124] The most important focus of a woman's attention, of course, was her husband or consort, for whom she dressed and anointed herself, learned the courtly arts of music and poetry, and competed against her equally fervent sisters. To give a noble, or especially the emperor, his firstborn son was a great honor and was sure to catapult a woman to a position of high standing and affection. Competition for this honor was great and often resulted, unfortunately, in a woman's trying to miscarry the pregnancies of the other women around her.[125]

The sexual graces of a woman were considered expendable, however, and she was soon beyond the age considered physically attractive. Neither the emperor nor his nobles, Terry noted, "came near their wives or women, after they exceed the age of thirty years,"[126] the women "never [being] much regarded by those great ones, after the very first and prime of their youth is past."[127] Although many childbearing years and much satisfaction were thus wasted, older *mahal* women still provided companionship and wise counsel for their male principal. Nevertheless, together with their less desirable comrades, they were consigned to looking elsewhere for sexual intimacy and physical pleasure.[128] Perhaps the most risky of options available was adultery, and it appears, at least from the writings of the Europeans, that its risk attracted rather than restrained women from its practice. As Pelsaert said, *mahal* women "spare no craft or trouble to enable them to enjoy themselves outside,"[129] and women of high as well as low rank were drawn into the lure of relationships with men beyond the harem walls.

> Some of the nobles, again, have chaste wives, but they are too few to be worth mentioning; most of the ladies are tarred with the same brush, and when the

husband is away, though he may think they are guarded quite safely by his eunuchs, they are too clever for Argus himself with his hundred eyes, and get all the pleasure they can, though not so much as they desire.[130]

Although popular culture of the time assumed that women in *parda* engaged in frequent liaisons with eunuchs, male servants, visitors to the court, and local nobles—indeed Indian literature and miniature painting of the seventeenth and eighteenth centuries portrayed an adulterous population as prominent, if not more so, than its faithful counterpart—the dangers of extramarital relations were great. Terry noted that a woman's dishonor of her husband in adultery, like an unmarried woman's wanton behavior, deserved "the severest punishment" and that it was her own brother's hand that would be the first to take away her life.[131] Adultery was dangerous not only for the *mahal* woman involved but also for the adulterer himself. Tavernier, for example, preserved a story of an affair between Raushanara Begam, Aurangzeb's sister, and a handsome young man whom she had allowed into the *zanana* for almost twenty days. When "she was tired of him," she found she could not let him out without the emperor discovering the tryst and so told her brother that the man had entered the harem to rob and kill her. Since the eunuchs were clearly at fault for not sufficiently protecting her, she argued, they should be punished as well. When Aurangzeb came to the spot, however, the young man jumped out of the window into the river. A crowd had gathered to catch him, and the emperor, aware of the ruse and of his sister's fault, asked that the erstwhile lover not be killed but taken instead to the chief judge.[132]

In another story, preserved by Bernier who got it from "an old woman, a half-caste *Portuguese*, who has been many years a slave in the seraglio," Raushanara again had to let two men out of the *zanana* with whom she had been secretly carrying on. One was found wandering in the gardens and treated lightly by Aurangzeb but thrown from the top of a wall by the eunuchs who "exceeded their master's instructions," while the other (also found in the gardens) was allowed to leave by the way he said he had come in. The eunuchs, however, were severely punished for allowing the harem to go unguarded and for bringing dishonor thereby upon the Mughal house.[133] As in all things, however, an emperor was himself exempted from the normal punishments given to an adulterer (or to an unwary eunuch), for Shah Jahan was well known for his later dalliances among the wives of his nobles, particularly with the wife of Jafar Khan.[134]

Other practices, besides adultery, were known. Although we have no explicit reference to lesbian relationships, we cannot discount them in a society where women spent so much time with one another. Physical affection and contact within genders has always been a part of both Hindu and Muslim India, and this may have served to lessen the potential for explicitly lesbian relationships within the *mahal*. Terry, however, has twice made reference to the possibility of Jahangir's bisexuality. In the first, he mentioned some boys who had been called to court to help with the tricks of a divining ape: these boys "he was conceived to keep for such use as I dare not name."[135] In the second reference Terry was more explicit, saying that in order "that he [Jahangir] might raise up his beastly and unnatural lusts even to the very height, he kept boys."[136] Although we have no other specific charge of sodomy against Jahangir, the *Sribhanucandraganicarita* implied at one point that the emperor was physically attracted to handsome male youths. At court once was a young Jain monk named Siddhicandra, who was so pleasing and perfect in form that Jahangir spent some time in trying to woo him (unsuccessfully) from his vow of austerity. Although it may have been that Jahangir's great anger at not being able to persuade Siddhicandra from his vow[137] had nothing to do with being denied special physical favor in this one case, we must honor in general Terry's clear suggestion of Jahangir's bisexual tendencies.[138] Terry seems convinced of some activity divergent from ordinary English standards, but what that activity was and who it involved remains unknown. That regular life in the palaces may have been conducive to homosexual relations between men and between women must remain a possibility and would be especially so for the women there whose lives were perforce oriented one towards another.

Nor can we discount the possibility of incest involving members of the *zanana*. Although there is only one case in which incest has actually been charged, that between Shah Jahan and his favorite daughter, Jahanara, others may simply not have made it into the texts. Of this case, Tavernier was quite outspoken in his condemnation of the princess, whom he fully suspected of "improper relations with Shahjahan,"[139] and who "had full power over him in consequence of the intimate relations which existed between them."[140] Certainly other foreigners, like Mundy[141] and Bernier, suspected the same as did the gossip brokers in the countryside, and Bernier even offered a rationale for the liaison: the *mullas* argued that it would be "unjust to deny the King the privilege of gathering fruit from the tree he had himself planted."[142] Manucci, however, argued persuasively against the charge.

> It was from this cause [Shah Jahan's affection for Jahanara] that the common people hinted that she had intercourse with her father, and this has given occasion to Monsieur Bernier to write many things about this princess, founded entirely on the talk of low people. Therefore it is incumbent on me, begging his pardon, to say that what he writes is untrue.[143]

Although we have no reason to believe that incest occurred between other relatives of the imperial household, it may be that the notoriety of the suspected Shah Jahan/Jahanara relationship masked other, less prominent, liaisons.

Women of the *mahal* were also thought to have made creative use of objects brought into their apartments. Certainly, romance of the mind was part of the appeal of the fantasy-oriented poetry, dance, and music of the surrounding culture. That it may have existed alongside some unusual practices has been suggested from the very early days of European contact with Indian courts. In a famous passage about the Nauroz festival, Coryat noted that care had to be taken with items brought into the fair: "whatsoever is brought in of virill shape, as instance in reddishes, so great is the jealousie, and so frequent the wickednesse of this people, that they are cut and jagged for feare of converting the same to some unnaturall abuse."[144] Certainly, European imaginations embellished (perhaps overly) the sexual possibilities of what they knew was taken behind *zanana* walls, and when Manucci noted that the eunuchs refused to allow "radishes, cucumbers, or similar vegetables that I cannot name"[145] into the harem, Gascoigne consigns the information to unfounded rumor and bazaar gossip.[146] Paintings of the period by Indians, however, depict a life of such scintillating luxury and ease that it is not hard to imagine some truth to these early European suggestions.

The laws of *parda* restricted those who were allowed to visit the women's apartments. Women visitors were carefully screened by a formal process of written request and supervision,[147] but men visitors, except in a few special cases, were prohibited any entry at all.[148] Except for the ubiquitous eunuch[149] and the intimately regarded male relative, like Itimaduddaula,[150] "safe" men were relatively few. Into this category fell monks like the Jain Siddhicandra who came into the harem for educational reasons, to read works on grammar, poetry, logic, rhetoric, prosody, and dramaturgy,[151] as well as teachers and poets who were patronized by high-placed women like Zebunnisa and brought in to instruct interested *mahal* members in certain subjects.[152] Service men, like "masons or carpenters, or other workmen [who] are wanted to carry out any job" were also allowed in, but the eunuchs guarding the doors would take down "the descriptive marks on their faces, and so forth" so that they could be sure each male worker who entered also left as soon as the job was done.[153] An occasional European was allowed in, but as in the case of a Master Steele who (as reported by Purchas) was needed to interpret for a painter at court, when passing through the women's quarters he wore "a cloth ouer his head [so] that he should not see the Women (which hee might heare as hee passed)."[154] Special friends of the male principal were also invited in in the hopes that they would be so flattered by a reception in the *zanana* that they would grant anything the principal desired. Shah Jahan, for example, brought the Khankhanan into his female apartments in "order to please him and strengthen his promises and oath," thus making an intimate of him,[155] and Dara Shikoh allowed his wife to invite Raja Sarup Singh into the harem where she could, by sweet words and gifts, try to persuade the Raja to support her husband against his brother Aurangzeb.[156] Such cases were rare, however, and were often not as politically successful as they were intended to be.

Although not routinely allowed into the harem, Europeans were nevertheless curious and Bernier recounted using two stratagems in order to see "these hidden treasures . . . the finest burnettes in all *Indies* . . . justly renowned for their fine and slender shapes," housed in the homes of the noble. In the first (learned from townsmen), he would follow the steps of "richly harnessed" elephants through the streets, "because the ladies no sooner hear the tinkling of the silver bells suspended from both sides of the elephant than they all put their heads to the windows." In the second (used in Kashmir), Bernier needed the help of an old man with whom he had read Persian poetry. The Frenchman would buy large quantities of sweetmeats and accompany the scholar to houses "to which he had freedom of access," pretending that he himself was a "kinsman lately arrived from *Persia*, rich and eager to marry." As soon as the two entered a house the scholar would pass out the sweets among the children, "and then everybody was sure to flock around us, the married women and the single girls" hoping to get a share for themselves. Although Bernier spent many rupees doing this, the practice "left no doubt on my mind that there are as handsome faces in *Kachemire* as in any part of *Europe*."[157]

The most important of the regular nonfamily visitors to the harem was the doctor, often the court physician or some specialist, who came when one of the women fell ill. Illness usually put a woman out of commission, and if she were of high rank it often affected harem business, politics, or travel tremendously, so the care of a reputable physician was essential.[158] Nur Jahan, for example, was seen by both Muslim and Hindu doctors when she became sick in 1618,[159] and Maryamuzzamani, too sick that same year to come out from Agra to meet Jahangir, had to stay behind (presumably under the care of physicians) until she had recovered.[160] The conduct of doctors in the harem was, by design, extremely circumspect. Whether the doctor was foreign or Indian, he was not allowed actually to see his patient. Ordinarily, he had his head covered and was led into the harem by a eunuch;[161] there an elaborate curtain was set up around the sick woman and she was diagnosed either by extending the afflicted part out from under the cover, or by allowing the doctor to put his hand inside and touch her where necessary. Tavernier noted the case of a particular young Dutch surgeon named Pitre de Lan, who was called in by Shah Jahan in 1652 to bleed the king under his tongue in four places in order to relieve a chronic headache. De Lan's operation was so successful that the "young Queen and the Queen-dowager"[162] became extremely curious about the doctor—"for he was a young and well-made man, and probably in their lives they had not seen a stranger at close quarters"[163]—and they decided each themselves to be bled for the same thing. So, "they drew a curtain, and the young Queen putting out an arm through a hole, the surgeon bled her, and he afterwards did the same for the Queen mother."[164] More explicitly, Manucci reported that when a doctor came to visit the women in the harem he

> stretches out his hand inside the curtain; they lay hold of it, kiss it, and softly bite it. Some, out of curiosity, apply it to their breast, which has happened to me several times; but I pretended not to notice, in order to conceal what was passing from the matrons and eunuchs then present, and not arouse their suspicions.[165]

Such elaborate subterfuge may not always have been the case when a doctor came to call, however, and it is quite likely that often enough conditions did not warrant a curtain and a doctor was allowed to see his patient in the open. Bernier, for example, was called in to examine one of Shah Jahan's wives who had a bad wound in one of her legs. As Tavernier recounted: "Monsieur Bernier went to his tent, where he saw this lady and examined her ailment, for which he gave a remedy and quick relief."[166] In general, however, most male visitors were turned away from *zanana* quarters. Should there be a petitioner who wanted to pay his respects to a woman in the harem or to solicit her help or intercession on his behalf, his best recourse, if he were an important enough noble, was to enlist the appropriate eunuch at the harem gate and send his compliments inside along with a generous present. If the woman was pleased and became well-disposed toward him, she would send back a jewel or an ornament as a sign of her good-will accompanied, perhaps, by the promise of assistance. All other men with whom she had relationships, however—be they traders, soldiers, and even to a point, lovers—were subject to the layers of grillwork that enclosed the business of women.

Travel for Mughal women of rank was a way of life. Because so much of the emperor's time, or for that matter the time of most nobles, was spent in military maneuvers, guarding widely scattered family holdings, hunting wild animals, or simply escaping seasonal temperatures, whole families spent much of their time on the move. Often women were subjected to dangerous routes, lack of adequate provisions, and difficult weather conditions, but in the end they had no choice but to make do with whatever the male principal could provide. While on the move women could, under proper supervision, go off for brief excursions to see natural wonders like waterfalls or fruit stands, to visit nearby buildings and gardens, or to make pilgrimages to local religious shrines. Always, however, except when on pilgrimage to Mecca, women had to confine themselves to the traveling party of their lord, for modesty and family honor were uppermost at all times.

Wherever the emperor or a noble went, his women went. Whether Jahangir was going sight-seeing[167] or to visit a melon bed[168] or to hunt,[169] or Khusrau was on one of his flights,[170] or Shah Jahan was fleeing a flood,[171] the whole camp moved, women and all. On the road, the women always traveled behind the men,[172] and their presence severely reduced the pace the group might otherwise have gone.[173] Although women slowed down travel time considerably, they nevertheless made the whole party more conscious of safety and in this way averted many accidents. Men, for example, often went down the Kabul River on rafts, doing in twelve hours "what ten marches [ordinarily] covered," but because women were not expected to make this dangerous journey, it was always passed over for the longer, more tedious, but perhaps safer, road route.[174]

When the group made camp during a maneuver, placement of the women was second only to the establishment of the central offices and apartments of the emperor. Just inside the grand enclosure (*gulalbar*) (where Akbar, for example, had a two-storied pavilion of painted wood and canvas for worship and for audiences with nobles) were elaborate tents for the women and their servants, the important women making camp "with her own establishment and within her own enclosure."[175]

> Adjoining the royal tents are those of the *Begums*, or Princesses, and of the great ladies and principal female attendants of the *Seraglio*. These tents are also enclosed on every side by rich *kanates*; and in the midst of them are the tents of the inferior female domestics and other women connected with the *Seraglio*, placed generally in much the same order, according to the offices of the respective occupants.[176]

None of the women were allowed to enter the emperor's pavilion—no "one connected with the seraglio enters this building without special leave"[177]—and around the women were placed sturdy guards of both genders. When traveling with the army, overcrowding became a major problem[178] and Akbar devised a plan whereby tents for the harem, the audience hall, and the *naqarkhana* were pitched in the middle of a flat plain and surrounded on three sides by an open space patrolled only by guards. On the fourth side were the offices and workshops of the emperor, and at the four corners of the encampment were bazaars. Around the whole, nobles and their soldiers arrayed themselves according to rank.[179] The result was often an arrangement as big and as regularly organized as a full-size town, and duplicate tents for the king and nobles were made so that one series could always be set up at the next stage ready for the entourage to move in.[180]

Because of the needs of *parda*, however, the manner of travel for a woman of rank was substantially different from that of a man.[181] While most ordinary women traveled about on foot[182] noblewomen, and certainly women of the imperial harem, traveled by a variety of conveyances, the most prominent perhaps being the *palki* or palanquin. The palanquin was "a kind of bed, 6 or 7 feet long and 3 feet wide, with a small rail" around it and was usually made of bamboo and roofed over with satin or brocade. It was carried on poles by men at each corner—who could "travel in this way faster than our chairmen in Paris"—or between two camels or two small elephants, and was accompanied by servants with fancy umbrellas who could shield the occupant from the sun.[183] The palanquins of princesses were covered over with "a rich cloth or net of gold, sometimes ornamented with precious stones or pieces of looking glass,"[184] or with a net made of the finest silk. When a princess like Jahanara went out for a ride, eunuchs with peacock feathers drove away flies and men in front threw down water to lay the dust. Said Bernier: "I have sometimes seen *Rauchenara-Begum* pursuing her journey, and have observed more than once in front of the litter, which was open, a young, well-dressed female slave, with a peacock's tail in her hand, brushing away the dust, and keeping off the flies from the princess."[185] Guards in front and behind carrying sticks of gold or silver pushed away the crowds, and servants near the palanquin carried various perfumes for the use of whomever was inside.[186] If on the road a princess met a nobleman, any of whom would have been most "anxious to acquire such protectors at court," she accepted his compliments and gifts. If she was pleased, she gave him betel in an ornamental bag and, if she was not, she ordered that he "receive a shower of blows which makes him run."[187] In general, however, it was only with great difficulty that women in procession could be approached.

> Woe to any unlucky cavalier, however exalted in rank, who, meeting the procession, is found too near. Nothing can exceed the insolence of the tribes of eunuchs and footmen which he has to encounter, and they eagerly avail themselves of any such opportunity to beat a man in the most unmerciful manner.[188]

Women also traveled in *haudas* strapped like little towers on the backs of elephants. As throughout Indian history, elephants were important in Mughal times for conveying tents and baggage over long distances, and each animal was strong and wide enough to carry a good number of women (often eight) as well.[189] The *hauda* was a square construction "all most richly furnished" with gold, with screens of gold on every side so that the women could look out and a canopy over the top for protection which was made "of Cloth of siluer."[190] Jahangir estimated that the gold-covered *haudas* in use by the imperial family were each worth Rs. 30,000.[191] An excellent description of the *haudas* for women in use by Akbar was given by Monserrate.

> The queens ride on female elephants, hidden from view in gaily decorated howdahs. They are guarded and escorted by five hundred old men of very dignified and venerable appearance. Great care is taken to drive away to a great distance all who are found in the line of the queens' march. The higher the rank and dignity of these old men, the more careful they are in fulfilling their functions.[192]

A third type of conveyance for women was the carriage. These carriages were usually drawn by oxen not by horse, according to Terry and Tavernier,[193] and were closed on all sides to maintain *parda*.[194] Women could and did go out in open carriages under their own veils, but such public travel was a mark of considerably lower status. A famous and much more elaborate carriage was the English coach given to Jahangir by Roe in 1616. Jahangir had given this coach to Nur Jahan, who had had it "newly couered and trimed rich,"[195] whereupon the emperor had made an exact copy of the vehicle for himself. Both coaches, to the delight of the English ambassador, were given regular use as part of the imperial entourage. Faster travel for women could be found on horseback[196] either by riding directly on a saddle or by using a horselitter.[197] The advantage of the horse over the elephant, or over the man-powered *palki*, was that it was not only faster but more efficient on the rough terrain of the northern hills and mountains, and it was often a normal mode of travel, for example, when the Mughal family went on trips up to Kabul. Camels and camel litters (*kajawas*) were also used,[198] although Terry consigned these to passengers "of the meaner sort [who] ride in cradles, hanging on the sides of dromedaries, all covered close, and attended by eunuchs."[199] Tavernier noted, however, that these side-slung *kajawas* were used not only by women but also by soldiers who could hide in the closed compartments and, as at the siege of Troy, jump out off the camels in a surprise attack.[200]

Although women ordinarily traveled with the party of the male principal, it often happened that a woman or a group of women traveled alone with their ladies-in-waiting, separate from the larger *zanana* group. Women could be sent on ahead, for example, to keep the emperor's journey a secret,[201] to forego a long and tedious wait while he hunted,[202] or to get a head start by horseback on a rough journey.[203] Or, certain women could be allowed to delay their start until after the emperor left if they, like the elderly Maryamuzzamani, were sick or wanted to travel at a more leisurely pace.[204]

Women's lives inside the harem were a rich mix of art, religion, and leisure. Although Gascoigne has cautioned us against thinking of the harem "as nothing more than a gilded cage full of pretty but idle women,"[205] it is difficult to imagine what normal hardships lay in store for a woman who belonged to the *zanana*. It is true that the emperor could not attend to each and every women on a regular basis and that the time actually spent in his company was relatively small.[206] It is also true that the women as a group were at his beck and call and that they had to subject their own lives to his rigorous yearly calendar of hunting, visits to Kashmir, and continuous military and political maneuvers. At the same time, however, inmates of the *zanana* had most of their material needs met, did not have to work for a living—except insofar as the business of pleasure was work—and in their splendid isolation from the general public[207] were free to pursue whatever pastimes took their fancy.

Food, for example, was always available in the *zanana* and the pantry, at least in Akbar's time, was open from morning till night.[208] As Pelsaert noted, all meals for the *mahal* came from one kitchen, but because there were often squabbles between the women, they tended to take their food each into their own apartments.[209] Most of the cooking was done by servants hired for that purpose, but as today, women of rank occasionally enjoyed cooking themselves, and Jahanara, in fact, wrote of preparing many kinds of dishes for the saint Hazrat Mian Mir.[210] Eatables for the harem were of the "daintiest" sort,[211] and most food was served with gold and silver serving pieces used only in the *mahal*. Such serving utensils were "seen by scarcely anybody except women,"[212] probably to forestall theft as well as to be kept counted as part of the imperial treasury. "Before eating they first wash their hands; then the tablecloth is brought and spread on the floor."[213] Dishes consisted of great varieties of spiced roast meat and fish, dressed rices, vegetables and fruits from all over the subcontinent, and sweet puddings and pastries.[214] No eating utensils were used and Pelsaert noted that "they besmear [their five fingers] up to the knuckles soldier-fashion, for napkins are not used, and it is very bad manners to lick the fingers." As in Hindu custom, no food was touched with the left hand and little or nothing was drunk with the meal—wine and water being saved until after the washing of hands and prayers.[215]

Although much time was spent in the preparation and taking of meals, *zanana* women had a wide range of activities available to them outside of the kitchen, many of which depended upon the acquisition and expenditure of wealth. In addition to their regular allowances, which were based upon duties performed in the *mahal* and relationship to the king (by either kin or affection), women could acquire wealth in a number of ways.[216] There were often special gifts from the emperor, who periodically gave land and money to women he deemed worthy[217] and who often used the proceeds from his lunar and solar birthday weighings as presents for the inmates of the harem.[218] Special-occasion gifts of money, jewels, dresses, and ornaments were also given to individual women by their male relatives, such as Shah Jahan's gifts to Nur Jahan at the time of his 1617 victories in the Deccan[219] and Itimaduddaula's gifts "to the Begams and other ladies of the Palace" at the time of the 1619 Nauroz.[220] Women also received presents from visiting traders, nobles, and other petitioners who hoped that a fortuitously placed offering would gain precious time at court. Wealth could come to women through inheritance as well, and although women were not guaranteed equal shares by Islamic law, they sometimes faired well through the favor of the emperor. The most famous example here, of course, was Jahangir's transfer of the late Itimaduddaula's holdings to Nur Jahan when the emperor received the estate through the process of escheat.[221] Finally, women often received substantial return on investments they made in the currently burgeoning business of inland and overseas trade. Profits on the sale of textile, mineral, and agricultural goods, as well as duties taken from merchants crossing lands belonging to *mahal* women, were collected by specially appointed officials and brought to the *mahal* for proper distribution.[222]

Women spent their wealth, and spent it lavishly, almost as soon as it reached their hands. Although most women paid out money freely in the normal course of life at court—none so extravagantly as the profligate wife of Jafar Khan, a longtime lover of Shah Jahan[223]—some, surprisingly, tried to keep their costs to a minimum. Khafi Khan, for example, preserved an exchange between Nur Jahan and Jahangir, which idealized the queen as a paragon of thrift.

> Once the royal elephants were being displayed before the Emperor. All the animals were decked with coverings of a very fine brocade. The Emperor was so much impressed by them that he inquired from Khan-i-Saman (the controller of establishments) about the cost of the coverings.
>
> "Your Majesty, I know nothing about it. They were prepared in the harem and Her Majesty the Empress has sent them to me."
>
> The Emperor now turned to Noor Jahan. The Empress smiled and said, "Your Majesty, I did not purchase any cloth for them. These coverings have been made by palace tailors from the bags in which letters and petitions of the mansabdars and nobles are received, spending practically nothing on them."
>
> The Emperor was immensely pleased on the information.[224]

Nur Jahan did, however, like to spend money, and like most of her colleagues in the *zanana*, she used her money first and foremost on luxury items for her own personal use. Perfumes, hair ointments, jewelry, silks, brocades, mirrors, glassware, and small porcelain vessels were necessities in any woman's toilet and were the most common purchases in the harem. Money also went to pay for parties, marriages, feastings, and religious festivals for which food, decorations, presents, and new clothes were needed each time.[225] Especially important was the extravagant cycle of gift giving women had with each other and with those outside. Presents were given not only to fellow members of the *mahal* and to male relatives—such as the two large pearls Nur Jahan gave to Jahangir[226] and the new dress, horse, and elephant she gave to Parviz[227]—but to those who came to birthdays,[228] marriages, weighing ceremonies, accessions, and special political occasions.[229]

Women also used their money to lay out gardens and waterways and to build buildings like *sarais* for travelers,[230] or mosques for worshippers,[231] or tombs for relatives.[232] The *sarai* built by Jahanara, for example, was said by Manucci to be "the most beautiful *sarae* in Hindustan," and there were "put up none but great

Mogul and Persian merchants.[233] Women's money was also given in charity, generally to the needy and impoverished at large,[234] but occasionally to individual persons or establishments that seemed worthy of *mahal* indulgence. And finally, women spent their money in trade, buying ships and carts, hiring captains and middlemen, and procuring all manner of goods that might be wanted in other parts of Asia or Europe. Nur Jahan, Maryamuzzamani, and Jahanara were three women especially involved with overseas trade, and the ships they ran often took pilgrims to Mecca along with their cargo.[235] Women invested in inland trade as well; Nur Jahan, for example, had officers stationed in Sikandra, across the Yamuna from Agra, to collect duty on goods that came from Bengal and Bhutan before they crossed over the river.[236] This duty was in addition, it should be noted, to monies she collected as revenue from tenants on these lands, as well as to profits she made on the sale of her goods.

A special part of a woman's wealth was allotted to her in outright gifts of land. Manucci reported that usually a woman's allowance was paid half in cash and half in the grant of a land assignment (*jagir*) from which she could collect an often sizable amount of money.[237] These *parganas* granted to women could be fairly large[238] and were often scattered throughout much of Mughal-held India. The practice of granting *parganas* to women appears to have begun with Babur,[239] was continued under Humayun, abated somewhat during the time of Akbar, and became a considerable practice under Jahangir.[240] Jahangir gave many of his women grants of land as part of their regular allowances and also at times of their special service to the empire. Nur Jahan, for example, received the *pargana* of Toda with a revenue of Rs. 200,000 as a result of having passed on the news of Shah Jahan's 1617 victories in the Deccan to her husband,[241] but later had another *pargana*, that of Dholpur, seized as a political ploy by Shah Jahan at the time of his 1622 rebellion.[242] More often than not, however, the land-holdings of his women provided personal pleasures for the emperor and were often sites of entertainment whenever Jahangir and his party happened to be passing through.[243]

How women spent their time after their financial affairs had been settled was a matter of choice. All women, it seems, had to have an interest in clothes since the elegance of their finery reflected and legitimized the authority of the empire. These clothes, Pelsaert noted, were "the most expensive" of anything available,[244] with women often having so many outfits that once-worn garments were reportedly buried in the ground "there to rot."[245] Each member of the *mahal* was provided with apparel and jewels "according to the extent of . . . [the man's] affection"[246] for her, and clothes and jewelry became an easy indication of class and religion. In public (that is, out on the street, in a coach, or on horseback), Mughal women generally wore white veils covering their faces, while the unveiled Hindu women "commonly use no other colour but red [for their dress], or certain linnen stamp'd with works of sundry colours . . . but all upon red."[247] Terry noted that Muslim women "abroad" wore clothes very much like their men—"coats and breeches one very like the other"—and had long hair down their backs that had been bound with fillets.[248] Pictures of Jahangir's harem [see Figures 3–1 and 5–2], however, indicate that most women inside his *zanana*, Muslim and Hindu alike, wore short tight bodice tops with the midriff showing, ankle-length loose pants under a thin, long skirt, and a large veil covering their heads but not faces—all made of silk or cotton in striped, brocaded, or stamped designs rendered in a great variety of colors.[249]

Jewelry was an essential part of women's adornment, and much time was spent putting it on and admiring it in tiny mirrors set in pearls that were worn by ladies on their right thumbs.[250] All women wore pierced earrings, the wealthier having large pendants of gold or silver, the less wealthy ones of brass or iron. The left nostril of each nose was pierced and a stud or nose ring of pearls or precious stones was passed through it at all times.[251] Elaborate pendants, bracelets, and anklets of metalwork and gems were worn around the neck, arms, and legs of each woman, providing not only ornament but concealment for parts of her body left uncovered by her clothes.[252] Head ornaments were worn as well, and Manucci reported that when they wore turbans, they often had in them "a valuable aigrette, surrounded by pearls and precious stones."[253] Terry did not, he claimed, observe the dress of women inside the *zanana*, but he imagined based on what he saw outside that "doubtless, the women of the greatest quality (though I saw it not) are bedeck'd with many rich jewels."[254] Jewelry and jeweled decorations on clothing were certainly a sign of wealth and leisure, and women of the harem, who did not need to labor in the fields for their keep, would have indulged in them as much for their own as for the emperor's pleasure.

Women's toilet in the Mughal harem was a complicated affair. Manucci reported that unguents and sweet-smelling pastes used before and after the bath and hair oils used to enhance the many twists and rolls of hair were commonplace.[255] In addition, colored pastes decorated many parts of the body: black (collyrium), for instance, on the eyes and eyebrows,[256] red (vermilion) on the hair parts of married Hindu women,[257] red (betal leaf) on the lips and (henna) on the hands and feet,[258] and all colors (for example, red, yellow, white, and black) as *bindu* on the forehead.[259] Flowers were often used as body ornaments as well and popular varieties such as marigolds and jasmine were freely woven into the hair, while ribbons, bells, tassels, and mirror-work decorated clothes and jewelry all over the body. A woman's toilet could be a daylong task and a proper routine of bathing, anointing, dressing, and adorning might normally have filled most of the hours any woman had at hand.

Many women did, however, take advantage of the education available in the *zanana*. Women competed among themselves in various fields of learning, spurred on by each of the emperors, who valued high standards of intellectual life in all parts of the court. Of the subjects studied, certainly one of the most popular and important was language. In the harem, the language of everyday use was Turki for the Mughal women, and Hindi or some other regional language for the Hindu women. Persian was the language of literature and poetry, as was Sanskrit, and to master either one of these in some degree was indeed an accomplishment.[260] Gulbadan and Salima Sultan were both known to have been well-versed in Persian, and Nur Jahan knew Persian and Arabic and herself had a library rich in their classics.[261]

Other subjects were available in the *mahal* as well, and a good sampling was given by the Jain monk Siddhicandra. He had apprenticed himself in Jahangir's harem and while there had studied Sanskritic texts on grammar, poetry, logic, rhetoric, prosody, and drama. At the instigation of Jahangir, he also studied Persian and Persian literature[262] and knew that mathematics, astronomy, and calligraphy could be had should he want them. All of these subjects were available to *mahal* women also, and if they were interested they could have studied with female tutors or with knowledgeable male relatives.

In the *mahal*, women were encouraged not only to learn from texts but also to make substantial contributions in the arts. Poetry was a popular pastime and a number of women are known to have written some verse. Gulbadan and Salima Sultan Begam both composed poetry, and Nur Jahan not only wrote poetry herself but also held contests for other women poets of the *mahal* and patronized outside poetesses who were especially renowned. A particularly able Persian poetess, who had been sponsored and brought up by Nur Jahan, wrote under the name of Mehri and of her works at least the Persian *mathnawi Sarapa-i Mehri* survives.[263] Other women used pen names (*takhallus*), too—Salima Sultan Begam wrote under the often-used name *makhfi* ("concealed," as in *parda*),[264] as apparently did Zebunnisa[265]—and what survives under these names indicates that *zanana* women often achieved a remarkable proficiency in composition.[266]

Women were also acquainted with music and were often entertained by male and female singers who would be a part of larger entertainments brought in for their amusement.[267] Gulbadan reported that dancing girls had been sent in once by a friend of the emperor's and passed out among the women as gifts to be enjoyed as each woman saw most fit[268] and that the ongoing presence of players and singers was a common feature of all festive gatherings.[269] Finch noted that professional singers and dancers were always at the beck and call of Jahangir and his women, waiting just outside one of the palace gates,[270] and Manucci reported that Jahanara especially "treated herself to many entertainments, such as music, dancing, and other pastimes."[271] Just how many or how often women of the harem themselves took up singing or a musical instrument is not known, but paintings of the period do show princesses, their companions, and their ladies-in-waiting playing instruments like the *vina* or singing to an accompaniment,[272] and Manucci reported that there were female superintendents of music and their women players in the harem who presumably would be available for instruction.[273] Dancing may have been a different matter, however, for it was not as respectable an art as music and was usually left to various groups of professionals.

Women of the *mahal* engaged in other arts as well. Miniature painting appears to have been popularly appreciated, judging from the number of paintings that show women holding or looking at such images up close, but we have relatively little evidence that *mahal* women themselves became prominent as artists. Nur Jahan, however, took an active interest in working with Jahangir's atelier, and we know that she herself ordered considerable drawings, paintings, and engravings from foreign traders, especially the English, to be brought back to the royal couple from Europe.[274] Women certainly had many paintings hung around them on *zanana* walls,[275] or in their makeshift galleries at camp, and it would be no surprise if some of them received instruction from the painters in residence at the palace.

With much of their wealth women also created buildings and gardens, elaborating and extending quite considerably the architectural heritage of their empire. Women built tombs for themselves or their male relatives—such as Salima Sultan Begam for herself;[276] Nur Jahan for her father, Itimaduddaula, and for herself;[277] and Zinatunnisa, a daughter of Aurangzeb, for herself[278]—as well as *sarais* for travelers, garden houses, mosques, wells, bazaars, monasteries, poorhouses, reservoirs, and gardens.[279] The *sarai* that Jahanara built, as noted before, was called by Manucci "the most beautiful *sarae* in Hindustan,"[280] and Jahangir often walked through what he called "the famous gardens of Kabul," three of which had been made by his women relatives: Bika Begam, grandmother of his father, Maryam Makani, mother of his father, and Shahr Banu, an aunt of Babur's.[281] In addition, Jahangir's mother, Maryamuzzamani, built a garden and well in Jusat in 1613, and when the emperor himself inspected them a few years later, he pronounced the *baoli*, or step-well, "a grand building . . . [which] had been built exceedingly well" and found that his mother had spent a mere Rs. 20,000 in constructing it.[282]

Nur Jahan likewise was an extravagant builder and two of the most famous and historically important sites were the Nur Manzil garden outside of Agra, reworked around 1618 to 1619 and called by Jahangir "that garden of delight,"[283] and the Nur Sarai near Jalandhar, a travelers' house and royal garden completed in late 1620.[284] Jahangir also noted the constructions of Aqa Aqayan, a female relative who, at the time of his first marriage, was put in charge of his *zanana* by Akbar where she remained for thirty-three years. In her old age, she had been sent to Delhi for a rest and there had built a garden, a *sarai*, and a tomb, all of which she had been constructing "for some time past" when Jahangir visited her in late 1619.[285] Later Mughal women like Jahanara, Raushanara, Zebunnisa, and Bibi Akbarabadi (a wife of Aurangzeb's) built gardens as well and, as earlier, these became extravagant places for dalliance and pleasure.

Women's pursuit of pleasure was epitomized in their experiments with the making of perfume, a mix of science and sensuality relying as much upon the olfactory tastes of the emperor as upon the technological skills of his staff. Of Jahangir's time, Pelsaert noted that women studied "night and day how to make exciting perfumes," some of which were derived from the red *falanja* seed,[286] and we know from Abul Fazl that the imperial kitchen areas were elaborately equipped for all kinds of techniques that might be needed in the process—drying, extracting, fermenting, distilling, and straining.[287] Akbar had taken a keen interest in the making of perfume and encouraged it, said Abul Fazl, "from religious motives," and the court hall of his palace was "continually scented with ambergris, aloewood, and compositions according to ancient recipes, or mixtures invented by his Majesty."[288] The chronicler listed thirty-four different types of perfumes together with their current prices and included detailed recipes for the preparation of some of the most popular fragrances at court, including among them those made from *ambar*, camphor, *zabad* (civet), *chuwa* (aloe), and sandalwood.[289]

The most famous perfume story was that in the *Tuzuk*, which attributed the discovery of attar of roses to Nur Jahan's mother, Asmat Begam. "When she was making rose-water" once,[290] Jahangir noted, "a scum formed on the surface of the dishes into which the hot rose-water was poured from the jugs." Little by little Asmat collected this scum and discovered that it was so strong "that if one drop be rubbed on the palm of the hand it scents a whole assembly, and it appears as if many red rosebuds had bloomed at once." It was such a good perfume that Jahangir "presented a string of pearls to the inventress," and Salima Sultan Begam gave the oil the name "*Jahangiri itr.*"[291] This story circulated widely, but in time the discovery was falsely attributed to Nur Jahan rather than to her mother. Manucci, the main beneficiary of this misattribution, said in his version that in the aftermath of a scrap between husband and wife (over drinking) Nur Jahan decided to please Jahangir by giving him a large banquet. She filled all the reservoirs in the palace and garden with roses in water and prohibited anyone from washing his hands in them. She happened, however, to fall asleep by one of the tanks and when she awoke she noticed that a film of oil lay on top of the water. Furious at the thought that "someone had thrown fat into this tank," she had the oil tested on the fingertips of a companion. Finding that it smelled very sweet and that it must have come directly from the rose petals, Nur Jahan rubbed some all over her clothes and ran to awaken the king who became "lost in admiration at such a fine perfume." "It was thus," concluded Manucci, "that the secret of essence of roses was discovered in Hindustan."[292]

The enjoyment of palace life was enhanced as well by the frequent use of drugs and alcohol. Intemperance was the Mughal family's main affliction, and despite continued public abjurations and the clear ban on the use of liquor by Islam, it remained not only a private curse but a public habit.[293] Women were not immune from the effects of intoxicants, either from the customs that allowed or encouraged them or from the negative consequences of their addiction. With inebriants a regular part of their daily lives and of the lives of the Hindu population around them,[294] it should be no surprise that when Man Bai, first wife of Jahangir, came to feel so dishonored by her son Khusrau's revolt against his father in 1605, she "swallowed a quantity of opium, and quickly passed away."[295] Pelsaert related that *mahal* women experimented with "efficacious preserves . . . containing amber, pearls, gold, opium, and other stimulants" and ate them during the day because they produced "a pleasant elevation of the spirit." At night, he said, women drank wine—"the women learn the habit quickly from their husbands"—and did it increasingly in Jahangir's time as "drinking has become very fashionable in the last few years."[296] Manucci, always the voyeur of the habits of women, reported that Jahanara liked to drink wine, which she imported from Persia, Kabul, and Kashmir. "But the best liquor she drank was distilled in her own house," being "a most delicious spirit" made from wine and rosewater and spiced with flavors and aromatic drugs. "Many a time," said Manucci, "she did me the favour of ordering some bottles of it to be sent to my house, in sign of her gratitude for my curing people in her harem."[297] Opium and hashish were also commonly used, and miniature paintings of the period attest to the frequent practice among women of smoking from a water pipe or *huqqa* as part of their social or private meditations.[298]

For the most daring of the women, hunting and military activities provided an adventurous diversion from what might have seemed like the humdrum roll of harem life. By necessity, to be sure, those armed guards in the *mahal* who were women came to know the intricacies of armaments and protective weapons,[299] but knowledge of weapons was also an accomplishment of their friends of leisure. Gulbadan reported, for example, that some of the younger women present at the Mystic Feast "used to wear men's clothing and were adorned by varied accomplishments, such as the making of thumb-rings and arrows, playing polo, and shooting with the bow and arrow."[300] If women did learn to shoot, however, either with a bow and arrow or more probably with a gun, it was most likely so that they could participate with the emperor and other nobles in the hunt for wild animals. Gulbadan noted that hunting by women was popular in Humayun's time,[301] and it was most certainly a regular pastime of several women in Jahangir's harem.

The most famous markswoman, of course, was Nur Jahan, who from at least 1616 onward came to be known as an excellent and consistent shot. In that year, Jahangir reported, she shot a huge *qarisha* "the like of which for size and beauty of colour had never been seen,"[302] and the next year in 1617 she shot four tigers with a total of only six shots. Said Jahangir of this feat, until

> now such shooting was never seen, that from the top of an elephant and inside of a howdah (*amari*) six shots should be made and not one miss. . . . As a reward for this good shooting I gave her a pair of bracelets (*pahunchi*) of diamonds worth 100,000 rupees and scattered 1,000 ashrafis (over her).[303]

Nur Jahan also made a record shoot in 1619 when a tiger reappeared after having troubled a village neighborhood and its byways for some time. Jahangir had recently taken a vow of nonviolence,[304] and as "I had vowed that I would not injure any living thing with my own hand, I told Nur-Jahan to shoot at him." Nur Jahan was, as usual, in a *hauda* on top of an elephant, a perch that was ordinarily very awkward as an "elephant is not at ease when it smells a tiger, and is continually in movement, and to hit with a gun from a litter (*imari*) is a very difficult matter."[305] Mirza Rustam, in fact, who next to Jahangir was unequalled in the empire for shooting,[306] "has several times missed three or four shots from an elephant. Yet Nur-Jahan B. so hit the tiger with one shot [this time] that it was immediately killed."[307]

Nur Jahan's legendary shooting ability was deflated, however, by later writers, and Khafi Khan, for one, preserved an apocryphal story implying that she only learned to shoot in order not to be outdone by a rival wife, Jagat Gosaini. According to him, both women were shooting once and when the party was confronted by a lion "Noor Jahan was left perplexed and spell-bound" while Jagat Gosaini quickly picked up a gun and struck the lion's chest with a bullet. The emperor, who had been asleep through all this, woke up and applauded his one brave wife and chastised the other, the cowardly Nur Jahan. He only forgot his displeasure when Nur Jahan's mother intervened and reminded Jahangir that women were supposed to be delicate coquettes and that bravery in arms was reserved for soldiers on the battlefield.[308] The story is certainly a product of the anti-Nur Jahan tendency of Shah Jahan chroniclers, and of this emperor's promotion of his own mother, but it does show that women did hunt regularly under Jahangir and that Nur Jahan was apparently so good that some explanation of her expertise had to be sought.

Other sports helped pass the time as well. It is clear that horseback riding was known by women and, as Gulbadan has noted, polo was a popular recreation for some of the younger and more active members of the *mahal*,[309] although the laws of seclusion would have checked involvement by any except the most courageous. Less physically strenuous games also filled the leisure hours, and from the substantial information given to us by miniature painting, we know that a variety of board games were common in the inner chambers.[310] Women also kept pigeons and falcon hawks and flew kites of various shapes when the weather was right. Fireworks were known, too, and appeared as large torches of wax and oil lit at night, or actual displays from powdered pieces set against the evening sky.[311]

The religious practices of women in the *mahal* were diverse and depended to much extent upon the sectarian background of each member. The general tone of religious life was pious and tolerant, with an overall flexibility to religious observance that had been set from the time of Akbar. Badauni, for example, described Akbar's official policy as: "No man should be interfered with on account of his religion, and everyone should be allowed to change his religion, if he liked."[312] This policy was applied judiciously to the women in the harem, and it was a tradition of emperors through most of the Mughal dynasty not only to marry women of different faiths, but to allow them freedom of practice as well. By the Shujauddins' count Jahangir had eleven Muslim wives and seven Hindu,[313] and from all we know, they and all the other women of his harem lived together in what must have approximated ecumenical harmony. That there was bound to be some discord, however, was evidenced from the time of Gulbadan: "Hamida-banu is named by the Father as protesting, with other ladies of the *haram*, against the royal countenance of Christianity, and assuredly Gul-badan would swell the chorus of complaint, in which, too, Hindu wives would join the Moslim lamentation."[314] Moreover, it is quite possible that the language barrier between Muslim and Hindu wives precluded any serious communication about their mutually exclusive religious lives. Nevertheless, each woman was bound into the one community by her particular relationship to the emperor, and tolerance, if not affirmation and understanding, made that community work supportively for each of its members.

Perhaps the most difficult of issues for a Muslim woman to understand was the *sati*, the devoted Hindu wife who immolated herself on her husband's funeral pyre. Although the practice of immolation would not have directly affected women of a Muslim emperor, it might have affected some of their servants and would certainly have been a custom the *mahal* women knew from the countryside.[315]

> When the Rasbooche dies, his wife, when his bodye goes to bee burned, accompanieth him, attyred with her beste arrayments and accompanyed with her frends and kyndred, makinge much joye, havinge musicke with them. And

> cominge to the place of burninge, the fyer beeinge made, sitteth downe, havinge twice or thrice incompassed the place. Firste, shee bewayleth her husband's death, and rejoycinge that shee is nowe reddye to goe and live with him agayne; and then imbraceth her frends and sitteth downe on the toppe of the pile of wood and dry stickes, rockinge her husband's head in her lappe, and soe willeth them to sett fyer on the wood; which beeinge done, her frends throwe oyle and divers other things, with sweete perfumes, uppon her; and shee indures the fyer with such patience that it is to bee admired.[316]

The *sati* was a common figure in Akbar's time,[317] and many of the European travelers who came during Jahangir's reign knew of the custom's frequent observance and of the emperor's disdain for it: Hawkins,[318] Withington,[319] Terry,[320] Della Valle,[321] and later Mundy,[322] Bernier,[323] and Tavernier[324] all knew the details of this elaborate Hindu ritual and of the role played by the wife's relatives and priests in the making of her decision to burn with her husband.

Jahangir frequently admired the piety and devotion of the Hindu wife who died with her husband, saying in late 1608 that few "women among the Musulmans have ever shown such fidelity,"[325] and was thoroughly acquainted with the Hindu view of marriage by which "no good deed can be thoroughly performed by men in the social state without the partnership of the presence of a wife, whom they have styled the half of a man."[326] Nevertheless, he abhorred the violent consequences of this philosophy of marital unity and in late 1620, concerning the practices of both widow immolation and female infanticide, he "gave an order that hereafter they should not do such things, and whoever was guilty of them, should be capitally punished."[327] While Jahangir's views may seem fairly enlightened to the modern reader, they certainly indicated some willingness to interfere with indigenous religious life. Although A. S. Beveridge's interpretation of earlier Mughal harems—that these "Hindus can never have been welcome inmates of the palace to any of the Moslims"[328]—was certainly not true by Akbar's or Jahangir's times, there was probably some small residue of condescension in the attitudes of the Muslim wives to their Hindu colleagues. Nevertheless, we do have a painting of Jahangir playing Holi with the women of his harem [see Figure 5–2],[329] and the universally festive ambiance of the piece confirms the general view that religious tolerance and widespread participation in all major religious holidays by the women of the *zanana* were the norms.

The religious lives of *mahal* women moved against a background of magical practices overseen by sorceresses and women astrologers permanently attached to the court. At the beginning of 1619, for example, Jahangir described an event that happened to him when he was a child of two years and seven months. He was visited then by a sorceress who "used to burn rue constantly in order to avert the evil eye, and on this pretext had access to me." Shaikh Salim Chishti, who had foretold to Akbar the birth of his three sons, had also prophesied that he himself would die when the eldest, Jahangir (then Salim), memorized and recited a verse. Because of his attachment to the *shaikh,* Akbar had given strict orders that no one should teach the prince anything either in prose or in verse. The sorceress, however, was able to enter the boy's quarters on the pretext of

FIGURE 5–2. "Jahangir Playing Holi with his Women." Indian painting; Mughal, fr. the *Minto Album*, fol. 4. Courtesy of the A. Chester Beatty Library, Dublin (ms. no. 7, no. 56; CB86–200601). Note the nimbus around Jahangir's head, the traditional box-like hat of one of his supporting women (probably Nur Jahan), the four metal squirts for shooting red liquid, the wall niches with imported porcelain, and the large cat in the upper left doorway. An obviously inebriated Jahangir is being led, perhaps, to his bed.

forestalling some black magic and there taught him a couplet. The young Salim did not, apparently, know of the prophecy and went to the *shaikh* to tell him what he had just learned. Within a day of the recital, the *shaikh* came down with a fever and, after taking "his turban from his head" and placing it on the boy's, he died.[330] On another occasion, in 1622, a pearl valued at Rs. 14,000 or 15,000 was lost in the harem, and one astrologer (Jotik Rai) and two soothsayers, one of whom was a woman, each gave prophesies as to the manner of its recovery. The female soothsayer "represented that it would soon be found, and that a woman with white skin would bring it in a state of ecstacy" and give it to the king. "It happened that on the third day one of the Turkish girls found it . . . and all in smiles and in a happy frame of mind gave it to me."[331] Misra speculates that this office of female soothsayer came into being because male soothsayers were not allowed into the women's apartments.[332] Moreover, as we saw in the case of Jahangir, the first experience of young princes with soothsayers would also be with women, as their early personal encounters were primarily those of the *mahal*.

Little is known about the private side of women's religious lives, but we assume that it followed the normal daily and seasonal routines of their male counterparts. For a Muslim woman, this would mean a regular schedule of prayers five times a day, study of the Quran, and faithful observance of such things as Ramadan and, for Shias, of the dramas of Muharram.[333] For a Hindu woman it would mean the daily practice of *havan*[334] and/or of *puja* to whatever gods or goddesses (*ishtadevata*) she ordinarily worshipped and yearly participation in such festivals as Holi, Navaratra, and Divali.[335] Both traditions encouraged charity and, given the goodly amount of *mahal* women's income and given among other things the important political consequences of such acts, we can assume that most women gave generously and at frequent intervals. A. S. Beveridge, for example, notes that Gulbadan's charities, especially as she got older, "were large, and it is said of her that she added day unto day in the endeavor to please God, and this by succouring the poor and needy."[336] Nur Jahan was also noted for her generosity, and of her openhandedness the *Iqbalnama* said:

> Whoever threw himself upon her protection was preserved from tyranny and oppression; and if ever she learnt that any orphan girl was destitute and friendless, she would bring about her marriage, and give her a wedding portion. It is probable that during her reign no less than 500 orphan girls were thus married and portioned.[337]

Hindu women, as well, would be under religious obligation to give to the poor and, as Abul Fazl has noted, there were many ways according to contemporary practice by which to fulfill the Hindu duty of *dana* or almsgiving.[338]

Perhaps the most public of a woman's religious observances was the pilgrimage, a practice shared by both major faiths of the *mahal*. For Muslim women the preeminent pilgrimage (*hajj*) was to Mecca, and it became the special pleasure of the emperor, particularly in the early days of the dynasty,[339] to encourage and support such journeys with substantial largesse. Unmarried women were forbidden by tradition from going, however, so "the younger women, who go in as large numbers as the older, all get married beforehand, so as not to break the law."[340] One of the most famous women's pilgrimage parties of the era left for Mecca in 1575 under the fortunate auspices of Akbar and included a large number of high-ranking members of the harem: Gulbadan Begam, Salima Sultan Begam, Sultanam (widow of Akbar's uncle Askari), Haji and Gulazar Begams (two stepnieces of Gulbadan), Umm Kulsum (a granddaughter of Gulbadan's), and Salima Khanam. The party left Fatehpur Sikri on October 15, 1575, and after taking a year to get to the sea, set sail for Mecca on October 17, 1576. They were said to have spent three and a half years in Arabia and made the *hajj* four times, returning home to Agra in March of 1582.[341] Women continued to make the *hajj* under Jahangir, and Roe reported that in September of 1617 the emperor sent his sister, presumably Shahzada Khanam, to Mecca;[342] Tavernier reported later in the century that the Queen of Bijapur had stopped at Isfahan on her way back from Mecca.[343]

Women also made pilgrimages to their father's tomb, as Ruqayya Sultan Begam did in 1607 to the tomb of Mirza Hindal,[344] and to the tomb of other ancestors, as Jahangir and his ladies did in late 1619 to the mausoleum of Humayun.[345] But the practice was not confined to Muslim pilgrims as Hindu women in the *mahal* would have journeyed equally far to visit their sacred spots throughout India as well.[346] Although we have little evidence that these women did so, the imperial policy was such that, under Jahangir at least, pilgrimage to Hindu sites would have been a normal part of harem life. Finally, however, we must note that pilgrimage was not always religious in intent. It was Pelsaert who reported that religious journeys were often the cover for romantic liaisons: "Under pretext of a pilgrimage, they used to come without reproach to see, and perhaps even speak to their lovers. Assignations were made in the gardens, . . . [and on] such occasions new passions were aroused by the sight of a handsome youth."[347] Whether for love or for religion, then, pilgrimage was a regular part of women's lives, and it was perhaps primarily because of its hardship and duration that through it some women were able to achieve a measure of autonomy and independence.

Direct political influence at the court was ordinarily a power outside the realm of the harem, but physical proximity behind a screen at court while the emperor did business meant that women could give their own opinions on the matters at hand. We know, as well, that important imperial issues were often brought before the emperor while he was in his women's chambers,[348] and that foreign travelers were routinely astounded to find themselves the object of intense inspection by women they could not see. Roe's description of this is perhaps the most famous.

> At one syde in a window were his [Jahangir's] two Principall wifes, whose Curiosity made them breake litle holes in a grate of reede that hung before yt to gaze on mee. I saw first their fingers, and after laying their faces close nowe one eye, Now another; sometyme I could discerne the full proportion. . . . When I lookd vp they retyred, and were so merry that I supposed they laughd at mee.[349]

The scrutiny of women from behind the screen was rarely silent, however, and a wonderful story was preserved of Salima Sultan Begam who interceded most vociferously on behalf of Mirza Aziz Koka. Aziz Koka had been a foster brother of Akbar's and consequently a great favorite in the harem for decades. One of his daughters had married Khusrau and when Khusrau revolted against his father Jahangir, Aziz Koka was discovered to have been involved in the plot from the very beginning. Aziz Koka would surely have received capital punishment had not Salima Sultan Begam yelled out from behind the screens:

> "Your Majesty, all the Begams are assembled in the *Zenana* for the purpose of interceding for Mirza Aziz Koka. It will be better if you come there, otherwise they will come to you." Jahangir was thus constrained to go to the female apartment, and on account of the pressure exercised by the Begams, he finally pardoned him.[350]

The pressure exerted by the women in the *zanana* was apparently so strong in this case that Jahangir could do nothing but treat Aziz Koka with some leniency.

Women intervened on any number of issues and it is safe to say that their advice and counsel, or even their earnest persuasion, changed the course of many events. Khanzada Begam, for example, was sought "to mollify Humayun and smooth the way for Askari when the latter should submit,"[351] just as later Maryam Makani and Salima Sultan Begam interceded in 1603 when Jahangir, then Salim, revolted against his father Akbar.[352] Women like Haram were put in charge of calling up extra forces for the army while the emperor Humayun recuperated from a wound,[353] and women like Nur Jahan corresponded with other women in foreign government as she did with the mother of Imam Quli Khan, the ruler of Turan.[354] Moreover, Nur Jahan was a powerful force in the Khusrau affair of 1616, working hard to make sure he would not be a contender for the throne when the time came, just as the other women of the harem were working equally hard on Khusrau's behalf. Said Roe: "[Jahangir's] sister and diuers weomen in the *Seraglia* mourne, refuse their meate, crye out of the kinges dotage and Crueltye, and professe that if hee dye ther will 100 of his kindred burne for him in memorye of the kinges bloudines to his woorthyest sonne."[355] Maryamuzzamani, in fact, was so worried about the danger to Khusrau's life at this time that she "is gone to the king with an ouerture of all the Practice."[356] Women were also, as we noted before, heavily involved in the political and economic decisions of inland and overseas trade, and because their ships were not only cargo ships but pilgrimage ships and international messengers as well, knowing the political protocol of every detail must have been extremely important to their success.[357]

Finally, some women of high rank were often allowed to issue edicts and royal orders (*farmans*), which carried all the weight and obligation of other imperial commands. Nur Jahan was the only other person under Jahangir, besides his mother, who was allowed to issue an imperial *farman* and, although she did so only in moderation, several of them still exist: concerning the financial affairs and legal debts of a certain Raja Surat Singh (1617); concerning the disposition of the woman Ganga Bai's relatives in confinement (1619); and again concerning the proper disposal of the affairs of Raja Surat Singh.[358] According to the *Iqbalnama*, on "all *farmans* also receiving the Imperial signature, the name of 'Nur Jahan, the Queen Begam,' was jointly attached."[359] Several women were allowed to issue other kinds of edicts as well, such as *hukms* (issued by prime ministers), *nishans* (issued by royal princes), and *sanads* and *parwanas* (issued by other court officials), and these women included in their number Hamida Banu Begam (Maryam Makani),[360] Maryamuzzamani,[361] Nur Jahan,[362] and Jahanara.[363] As Misra notes, however, although the various edicts were not always confined to the women's own *jagirs*, their scope was fairly limited as they dealt primarily with personal favors to individual petitioners.[364] Every *farman* that went out was stamped with the royal seal, which was usually kept under the protection of the queens and therefore stored in the harem. Nur Jahan, however, had her own seal and, as the *Iqbalnama* noted, no "grant of lands was conferred upon any woman except under her [the queen's] seal," and gold coins were struck in her name as a symbolic (if also real) affirmation of her political power.[365]

II

The Mughal family had many talented women, and in each generation the character of the harem emerged as a distinct interweaving of the personalities it contained. Central to Jahangir's *zanana*, of course, were his wives, and any list of the real loves of Jahangir must begin with the legendary Anarkali. Anarkali was a title presumably given to a woman named Nadira Begam or Sharifunnisa, whose tomb in Lahore dates to 1615, being completed sixteen years after her death in 1599. According to the story popular among the European travelers of Jahangir's time, Anarkali ("Pomegranate Kernel") had been a wife of Akbar and, as suggested by Finch, the mother of Daniyal.[366] Jahangir, then Salim, had taken notice of her and had incurred the wrath of his father "for climbing up into the bed of Anarkelee, his father's most beloved wife."[367] As Finch noted much more subtly, she was the wife of his father "with whom it is said Sha Selim had to do."[368] Latif's version, based perhaps on popular legend, says simply that Anarkali, a favorite of the harem, had returned a smile given to her by Salim and that Akbar, noticing it in the mirrors of his inner hall, had suspected the worst.[369] In any event, Akbar had become very angry at the liaison or suspected liaison between his wife and his son and had caused Anarkali "to be inclosed quicke within a wall in his moholl, where shee dyed,"[370] subsequently changing the succession over to bypass Salim in favor of Khusrau. Salim was overcome with grief at her death and "in token of his love" had built for her "a sumptuous tombe . . . of stone in the midst of a foure-square garden richly walled, with a gate and divers roomes over it."[371] The popular version says that Anarkali was placed alive in an upright position and that the wall was built up around her brick by brick. When Jahangir ascended the throne he then had an immense structure raised over her sepulcher.[372]

If the dating of Anarkali's death is correct, then Jahangir had already married several wives and fathered three of his sons by the time of his suspected affair. What he had imagined the outcome of the relationship would be, given its clear incestuous nature (at least by some traditions), is not altogether certain and, in light of Jahangir's known maternal respect and affection for Akbar's wives, the relationship seems somewhat out of character. On the other hand, however, Jahangir was capable of falling madly in love and the Anarkali legend is most significant, perhaps, precisely because it pays tribute to this capacity. Whether the legend of Anarkali is historically true or not, it does not seem to have curtailed his marital alliances in any way. The following is an account of Jahangir's wives, ordered for convenience by the Shujauddins' list, but not necessarily depicting the correct chronology of the women's marriages to Jahangir:[373]

1. *Man Bai, daughter of Raja Bhagwan Das of Amber and sister of Raja Man Singh* (Hindu). Salim's "first marriage and that at the commencement of my adolescence" was with his cousin, the Hindu girl Man Bai, made officially his wife on February 13, 1585, after the two families had settled upon a very rich dowry.[374] Man Bai's first child was a daughter, Sultanunnisa, born April 26, 1586, amidst great rejoicing[375] and her second, Jahangir's first son, Khusrau, was born August 6, 1587, in Lahore;[376] on his birth, Man Bai received the title of Shah Begam.[377] Man Bai was a charming and intelligent woman who seems, however, to have been prone to frequent depression. When Khusrau continued to exhibit an unrelenting tendency to rebel against his father and suspicion of involvement fell on her brothers, Raja Man Singh and Madho Singh,[378] she grew so despondent that on May 6, 1605, just before Jahangir's accession to the throne, she "killed herself by swallowing opium (*tiryaq*)." Said Jahangir of her character:

> What shall I write of her excellences and goodness? She had perfect intelligence, and her devotion to me was such that she would have sacrificed a thousand sons and brothers for one hair of mine. She constantly . . . urged . . . ([Khusrau] to be sincere and affectionate to mee . . . [but] When she saw that it was of no use . . . she from the indignation and high spirit which are inherent in the Rajput character determined upon death. Her mind was several times disturbed, for such feelings were hereditary, and her ancestors and her brothers had occasionally showed signs of madness, but after a time had recovered.[379]

Jahangir was so attached to her that, when she died, "I passed some days without any kind of pleasure in life or existence, and for four days . . . I took nothing in the shape of food or drink."[380] Man Bai was buried in "a sumptuous tombe"[381] in Allahabad where later, in 1622, her son Khusrau, was buried after his mysterious death in the Deccan.[382]

2. *Jagat Gosaini, daughter of Udai Singh, Mota Raja* (H).[383] Jagat Gosaini was also a Hindu princess, and though it may well have been a political marriage, she was known not only for her beauty and charm but for her wit, courage, and spontaneity of response—all of which greatly endeared her to her husband and to the Indian tradition. Known most popularly as Jodh Bai, the Jodhpur prin-

cess,[384] Jagat Gosaini was married to the emperor on June 26, 1586, and on January 5, 1592, gave birth in Lahore to what would be Jahangir's third son, whose "advent made the world [so] joyous (*khurram*)" that they named him Khurram. The prince who was to become Shah Jahan "was more attentive to my father [Akbar] than all (my) other children. . . . He recognised him as his real child."[385] Aside from being mother of Khurram, Jagat Gosaini was known chiefly for her quick tongue and dexterous repartee. The Shujauddins preserve two stories of her verbal defeat of her archrival Nur Jahan. In the first story, both women were in royal company once—Nur Jahan dressed in white and Jagat Gosaini in colors—when Nur Jahan pointed out to the emperor that the other wife, that rustic Hindu woman, was, as usual, clothed in gaudy rather than the more sophisticated subtle tones. Jagat Gosaini replied that while a married woman could wear clothes of all colors, a widow could wear only white, a reference not only to Nur Jahan's previous marriage but also to the rigidly upheld Hindu ban on widow remarriage. In the second story, Nur Jahan once flattered Jahangir by telling him that his breath was sweet and, when he mentioned this to Jagat Gosaini, she told him that only a woman who had been around many other men could judge the sweetness or sourness of any one man's breath.[386] Jagat Gosaini died in 1619 in Agra[387] and was buried in Dahra Bagh as was her wish. After her death, Jahangir ordered that she be called Bilqis Makani in all of the official documents.

3. *Sahib Jamal, daughter of Khwaja Hasan and cousin of Zain Khan Koka (Muslim)*.[388] Sahib Jamal was one of the four chief queens of Jahangir mentioned by Hawkins, having married the future emperor in 1586. She gave birth to Parviz, Jahangir's second son, in November of 1589 in Kabul and on her death she was buried in Lahore. The Shujauddins argue that her tomb was the same one that has been otherwise attributed to Anarkali.[389]

4. *Malika Jahan, daughter of Raja Kalyan of Jaisalmer* (H).[390] Kalyan was a Rajput chieftain whose family had maintained a strong alliance of patronage with the Mughal government. Jahangir himself noted that he married Kalyan's daughter while still a prince and that he gave her the title Malika Jahan ("Lady of the World"). The marriage was primarily a political one made, as Jahangir noted, because "the ancestors of this [her] tribe had come of ancient loyal people."[391]

5. *Nurunnisa Begam, sister of Mirza Muzaffar Husain* (M).[392] Mirza Muzaffar Husain was married to Jahangir's sister, Shahzada Khanam.

6. *Saliha Banu, daughter of Qaim Khan* (M).[393] This wife was from a well-placed family in the government as her brother, a man named Abdur Rahim (titled Tarbiyat Khan), was said by Jahangir to be "of the hereditary houseborn ones of this Court."[394] For much of Jahangir's reign, she was the Padshah Banu Begam, also called the Padshah Mahal, and when she died in 1620,[395] the title was passed on to Nur Jahan.[396] Jahangir noted that Saliha Banu's death had been foretold by the astrologer Jotik Rai; grief stricken at her loss, he nevertheless marveled at the accuracy of the prophecy, which had been taken from his own horoscope.[397] She was one of the four chief wives attributed by Hawkins to Jahangir.[398]

7. *Karamsi, daughter of Raja Kesu Das* (H).[399] This Rajput wife came from the

Rathor clan and gave birth in September 1590 to one of the two known surviving daughters of Jahangir, a girl named Bihar Banu Begam. Bihar Banu was later married to the ill-fated Tahmuras, eldest son of Prince Daniyal, when the young man was in his twentieth year.[400]

8. *The daughter of Ali Rai, ruler of little Tibet* (M).[401] Her marriage to Jahangir took place in 1592.[402]

9. *The daughter of Mubarak Chak of Kashmir* (M).[403]

10. *The daughter of Husain Chak of Kashmir* (M).[404]

11. *The daughter of Raja Ali Khan, king of Khandesh* (M).[405]

12. *The daughter of Khwaja-i Jahan of Kabul* (M).[406]

13. *The daughter of Mirza Sanjar and granddaughter of Khizr Khan Hazara* (M).[407] In that Khizr Khan was married to Gulbadan, Jahangir's great aunt, this wife would be Jahangir's second cousin.

14. *The daughter of Rai Singh of Bikaner* (H). Rai Singh was one of the great *amirs* and according to Nizamuddin his daughter married Salim on June 28, 1586.[408]

15. *The daughter of Said Khan Ghakkar* (M).[409] A possible daughter of this union, Iffat Banu, is mentioned.

16. *The daughter of Jagat Singh, eldest son of Raja Man Singh* (H). In the spring of 1608 Jahangir sent Rs. 80,000 as a marriage present (*sachaq*) to Jagat Singh so that he, the emperor, might marry his daughter. The wedding ceremony took place in the early summer in the house of Maryamuzzamani, and on that occasion Raja Man Singh sent sixty elephants as part of the wedding present accompanying his granddaughter.[410]

17. *The daughter of Ram Chand Bundela* (H). In 1609 Jahangir married the daughter of Ram Chand of Bundela at the request of her father.[411] The bride's father had recently submitted to the sovereignty of the Mughal government after a revolt, and we can assume from this that the marriage was primarily a political one.

18. *Mihrunnisa, daughter of Mirza Ghiyas Beg (M).*

Jahangir's harem was, from all accounts, a rowdy and exuberant place to live and Nur Jahan's fulsome charisma played out profitably against its many walls. There is no doubt that she was not universally liked for her obvious political affiliations and her strident acts for power. The Khusrau affair, for example, only accentuated her style, and in her overt efforts to dispense of this first obstacle to fully shared authority, she made many enemies among her colleagues in the *mahal*.[412] There is no doubt either that she tangled with the other wives for Jahangir's affection. The stories preserved of her rivalry with Jagat Gosaini, for example, suggest not only the animosity felt toward her and her ascendancy by others equally legally espoused, but also the need of later tradition to put her in her place in the face of her clear talent, wit, and enduring presence.[413] Nevertheless from the time of her marriage to Jahangir in 1611, she was indisputably the chief wife, whose gifts of management, courtly etiquette, and perseverance had combined with her beauty to compel her husband to hand over to her not only the major responsibilities in the *zanana*, but in the larger court as well. Della Valle's assessment of her role in the harem was, thus, singularly critical:

> And as such she commands and governs at this day in the King's Haram with supream authority; having cunningly remov'd out of the Haram, either by marriage, or other handsome wages, all the other Women who might give her any jealousie; and having also in the Court made many alterations by deposing, and displacing almost all the old Captains and Officers, and by advancing to dignities other new ones of her own creatures, and particularly those of her blood and alliance.[414]

Unfavorable as these comments are, however, they show the ease with which Nur Jahan could take the structures of power offered by the harem and reshape them without violation to their integrity, thus giving them life for purposes entirely her own.

6

The English Embassy

The disposition of the King is to bee very familiar with strangers if they bee in Cash.

The Embassy of Sir Thomas Roe to the Court of the Great Mogul,
edited by William Foster

Of the channels to the outside world, the most enticing for women were the possibilities opened up by foreign trade. The local marketplace and the palace fairs of the Nauroz had always provided women of means the chance to buy and sell, but the coming of European merchants in substantial numbers to the Mughal court made available a life beyond the harem walls that could also, fortunately, be totally in keeping with domestic practices. Although India had traditionally been a self-supporting country,[1] trade had been a consistent part of her history and had served not only to disperse raw materials and luxury items among various parts of the subcontinent, but to bring goods from more distant parts of Asia, Africa, and the Middle East, as well.

In Jahangir's time, as in others', overseas trade was inextricably bound to the pilgrimage needs of the Muslim population. Ordinarily, Muslim pilgrims from India could travel to Mecca by one of two routes: either by caravan on the overland road through Iran, or by sailing ship from Gujarat across the Arabian Sea. Either way was filled with danger, for the overland route had bandits and undesirable contact with unbelievers and the sea route had the menace of the Portuguese pass system and the vagaries of the monsoon.[2] Nevertheless, pilgrimage and its suffering were obligatory to the Muslim community and no amount of abuse could curtail its practice among the religious. Moreover, Mecca itself was a central market[3] and ships trafficking in pilgrims also brought goods to be exchanged for things from all over Europe, Africa, Arabia, and Asia. Almost all trade for Mecca from India came through the Red Sea port of Mocha,[4] which acted as the main distribution point "for all Indian commodities"[5] that had passed across the sea. Because of the monsoon[6] and of the difficulties of sea voyage, however, the trip to Mocha was usually made only once a year and, for Mughal trade at least, these voyages emanated primarily from the port of Surat.

Surat was located on the Tapti River about fourteen miles up from its mouth and up from the more coastal town of Swally. It was, in Jahangir's time, "one of the chief ports of India, and the centre of trade with the Red Sea,"[7] made even more important because the harbor of its more northerly rival on the Gulf of Cambay, Cambay itself, was fast silting up with sand and dredge. Surat had its own problems, however, the chief being that its deep water anchorage off the bar at the mouth of the river was especially exposed during the monsoon,[8] but it was a well-built city[9] with good access to the major marketplaces of the interior[10] and afforded both native and foreign traders an excellent center for business. In fact, in March of 1616, Surat was officially designated the chief factory of the English East India Company in India.[11]

The story of the first official English embassy to the Mughal court and of its difficult relations with Nur Jahan and her junta is irrevocably bound to the history of the other main European presence, the Portuguese. The Portuguese and their Roman Catholic agents, the Jesuit missionaries, had first come to India some time before the Mughals in order to ply their religion in the countryside. In time they had gotten involved in the lucrative business of exporting textiles and indigo from the local markets, using their holdings in and around Goa as a primary base, and had gained control over the shipping lanes in the Arabian Sea. Relations with the Mughals had been fairly friendly, as the Jesuits could provide the much-loved Christian images to the nobility, engage in theological discussions with other religious at court, and give some protection at sea. But because they had cultivated a monopoly in trade, they could be equally offensive to their hosts and in time acquired a reputation for considerable brutality. Portuguese banditry at sea, diversion of Arab and other trade away from the subcontinent, curbs on export goods and the consequent stunting of local industry, exuberant proselytizing at every level, and stinginess in gifts to the court all eventually wore away at Indian good will[12] and caused the government to begin to look elsewhere for trading partners.

Most offensive, however, especially to orthodox Muslims, was the Portuguese development of a pass system. In order to travel in Portuguese waters, each Asian ship had to obtain a *cartaz* or pass by paying customs at a Portuguese port or by keeping an agent in residence there. Listed on the pass were all the ports the ship was allowed to visit and the specific articles of trade the ship was allowed to carry on board. If a ship did not carry the pass or if it was in violation of the conditions there listed, it could be seized by any Portuguese agent on patrol.[13] Particularly distasteful was that each pass carried stamped on it pictures of the Virgin Mary and Jesus, and for orthodox Muslims to travel under such conditions, especially if on pilgrimage, "would mean to countenance idolatry."[14] Often, for strict interpreters of Islamic law, this meant the periodic suspension of the obligation of pilgrimage; although given the freer religious milieu of the Akbar and Jahangir eras, pilgrimage to Mecca did, in fact, continue at a healthy rate despite the religious problems of the journey.

All of these issues, however, did not curtail the relatively friendly relations with the Portuguese, which continued until well into Jahangir's reign. Although Moreland cites the decay of Portuguese commerce in India as beginning about

1610 (coinciding with the rise of Dutch and English interests), there was one incident in particular a few years after this that permanently turned the Mughals away from their early European friends. In September of 1613, an exceptionally large and well-known pilgrimage ship called the *Rahimi* belonging to Jahangir's mother, Maryamuzzamani, was captured by the Portuguese at Surat and taken with all her goods and all seven hundred people on board down to Goa:

> The shippe, which arrived at the barre of Suratt the 13th of September, 1613 . . . was taken by the Portungales armado of friggotts, notwithstandinge theire passe which they had of the Portungales. This shoppe was verye richlye laden, beeinge worth a hundred thowsand pounde; yet not contented with the shippe and goods, but tooke allsoe 700 persons of all sorts with them to Goa.[15]

As Withington noted, the ship was carrying the necessary pass and was apparently not in violation of any of the terms posted on it, yet out of pure greed, or anger at the new Mughal friendship with the English,[16] the Portuguese acted "contrarye to theire passe." Jahangir's reaction was one of outrage: "takinge yt soe haynosly that they should doe such a thinge"[17] in blatant disregard of their own rules and, perhaps worse, against the ship of his own mother. His response was to move quickly to curtail the activities of the Portuguese in India and to undermine the privileges they had enjoyed up to now. When it became clear that the Portuguese had no immediate intention of returning the Queen Mother's ship or its cargo, however, Jahangir sent Muqarrab Khan, his governor at Surat, down to stop all shipping traffic and to lay seige to the Portuguese town of Daman. The Jesuit church in Agra was closed and the Jesuit Fathers were taken off the allowance they had been receiving up to that point.[18] According to Thomas Aldworthe and William Biddulph in a letter to the East India Company dated August 19, 1614, Jahangir's reprisals against the Portuguese were complete:

> The king caused a city of the Portingals called Damaen (Damaun) to be besieged, and hath likewise taken order for the seizing of all Portingals and their goods within his kingdoms. He hath likewise sealed up their church doors and hath given order that they shall no more use the exercise of their religion in these parts, and beyond all this he hath caused Xavier the great Jesuit, whom before he loved, to be sent down hither unto Mocrob Chan, who now layeth siege unto Damaen, to do with him as he shall see good.[19]

The Portuguese capture of Maryamuzzamani's ship thus served to bring about a major change in the relationship between the two governments and was by fortunate accident a substantial windfall for the English. After this, English letters home referred to "the wars that is between the Mogul and the Portingals, which proceeded of the Portingals taking of one of the Mogore's ships richly laden."[20] In this same letter Edwards noted that the Portuguese offered to return the *Rahimi* if the Mughal king would "deliver the English that were here into their hands," but Jahangir refused.[21] Thereafter "the wars betwixt the Portingals and the Indians" continued for several years stopping virtually all Portuguese trade in the area[22]: "the Great Mogul's mother was a great adventurer, which caused the Great Mogul to drive the Portingals out of this place."[23]

The fortunes of the *Rahimi* herself, however, went down with those of the Portuguese, for in a letter dated December 16, 1614, from Surat Thomas Elkington reported that Portuguese frigates had been in Goa and "there burned 120 ships." Of that large number, ten ships were classed as "great" and one of them, perhaps not by chance, had been Maryamuzzamani's *Rahimi*.[24] The Portuguese later agreed to compensate the Mughal government for the loss of the Queen Mother's vessel and "to grant certain additional passes to native vessels proceeding to the Red Sea," but since the agreement was contingent upon the expulsion of the English, Jahangir balked. Eventually an agreement was made by the emperor by which the Portuguese had to pay "three lecks of rupees for the ship taken," but the issue of English expulsion was left hanging as Jahangir was increasingly aware of English power at sea.[25]

After the *Rahimi* incident in 1613 through 1614, the Portuguese became a relatively insignificant factor in trade. They continued to maintain a presence at the Mughal court, but their harrassments of the English, which had earlier been so prominent and so successful,[26] were no longer seemly with the English quickly gaining the upper hand at court. Tension remained between the English and the Portuguese, especially at the lower levels, and Jahangir himself reported on the sea fight between the two in the Swally channel in January of 1615 during which the English burned most of the Portuguese ships.[27]

The only other major European contenders for trade at the court were the Dutch, and of the three they were clearly the least significant in Jahangir's time. Unlike the Portuguese and English, the Dutch were not in the business of offering protection of the seas or any other such privilege to the Mughal government.[28] Rather, having found that a good and steady supply of cotton goods from Gujarat was indispensable to their commercial operations[29]—which revolved primarily around spice trading in pepper, cloves, nutmeg, and mace[30]—the Dutch wanted to set up a base at Surat to manage their business. After some only mildly successful attempts at sea trade early on, little was done in India until Pieter van den Broecke established a factory at Surat in 1616.[31] Another Dutch envoy under Pieter Gillesz van Ravesteyn arrived at court in January of 1618 and obtained from the Mughal government terms of trade very similar to those of the English. Although troubles for the Dutch had brewed in the Far East during these years, with the conclusion of a peace there, attention could be turned once again to India and at the end of 1620 van den Broecke reappeared at Surat as the Director of the "Western Quarters" comprising north and west India, Persia, and Arabia. He remained around Agra presiding over a growing Dutch indigo and cotton goods trade for the next seven years.[32]

The Europeans who were most important in the time of Nur Jahan, however, were the English. Unlike the Portuguese, the English had not come to India to proselytize[33] but to establish trading contracts at the highest levels with the Mughals. Although English interest in a sustained and exclusive friendship was in the profits derived from a commercial relationship, Mughal interests were not in the direct benefits of commerce. Rather, the Mughals wanted protection of the seas for those of their subjects who went on pilgrimage. Indian ships, despite courtly shows of friendship, had long been under the threat of Portuguese attack and although Roe could say somewhat wryly of Jahangir's court, they "feare the Portugall, they feare vs, and between both patch vp a friendship,"[34] the Mughals saw clearly that the Portuguese were their most dangerous enemy. The English recognized this immediately and used the difference between their own good intentions and those of the Portuguese who "robd and abused the subiectes of this kingdom" as a decided diplomatic tool. Although Jahangir denied there was a problem and continued in his fashion to play the various interests off against each other, he did recognize that his country's trade and pilgrimage needs were at the mercy of whomever controlled the seas.[35] The Portuguese folly in the capture of the *Rahimi*, then, tipped the scales in favor of the English, and whenever the English could win a sea engagement against the Portuguese[36] or whenever the English could play the peaceable European in the face of "the wars betwixt the Portingals and the Indians,"[37] Roe's prospects for binding the Mughal government to a long term commercial agreement soared.

An examination of the first official English embassy (1615–19) to the Mughal court does more than simply provide another example of how Nur Jahan's junta operated in the years it sustained its greatest power. Women of the harem had wealth and time, and the newly burgeoning European trade provided a means by which to both enhance that wealth as well as develop relations beyond the *zanana* walls. Nur Jahan was preeminent among the women traders of nobility, and the details of her relationship with Thomas Roe's embassy help reveal, first, to what degree she or any other women in the harem obstructed or facilitated the opening up of trade with the Europeans and, second, to what degree the women themselves traded. It is not initially clear, for example, why the foreign trade of the Europeans would have appealed to Nur Jahan and her colleagues, or why conversely the women might have seen it in their best interests to work against it. Of all the Europeans present, Roe and company were the most familiar by proximity and privilege to Nur Jahan and, although he never actually saw the chief queen face on,[38] he did do business with her and did feel the presence of her and her junta in every dealing he had at court. Roe's chronicle, then, by timing and familiarity, comes the closest to any available of a European eyewitness account of Nur Jahan in power. And in examining the relations he developed at court, many reasons emerge as to why Roe had to leave India without obtaining the formal trading agreements he had so desired.

I

English interest in India began to take shape at the time of the defeat of the Spanish Armada in 1588. Confident of their abilities at sea, a group of English merchants got permission from Queen Elizabeth to send trading ships to India, and in 1591 three vessels, under her aegis, left the English shore. Although only one ship completed the voyage, that under James Lancaster, its success opened the way for other expeditions to follow. In December of 1600, a charter was granted to the East India Company allowing member English merchants to trade in the name of the crown and in the next year, 1601, the first official East India Company voyage set out to the East Indies for spices under Captain Lancaster's command.[39] The English move to set up factories or posts in India, specifically at Cambay and Surat, in order to trade in calicoes followed soon thereafter, and on August 24, 1608, the first ship to fly the English flag off the coast of India dropped anchor in the Tapti River near Surat. Its captain, William Hawkins, left his ship the *Hector* at Surat with instructions to proceed without him and himself went on to Agra with letters for Jahangir[40] in order to solicit from him specific trading privileges. Hawkins knew Turki, the language of the court, and received immediate and familiar attention from the emperor.[41]

Despite his encouraging reception, however, Hawkins's mission would not succeed. The Portuguese were adamant about not sharing their trade in India and, still strong at court during this period, used their influence to intrigue against the Hawkins mission. Muqarrab Khan, an old friend of the emperor's soon to convert to Roman Catholicism, was the primary opponent of the Englishman, but Hawkins knew that, despite Muqarrab Khan's giving orders, it was "the Jesuites and Portugalls [who] slept not, but by all meanes sought my overthrow."[42] Eventually Hawkins' petitions for trade were rejected, and in spite of the fact that Jahangir offered to keep him in comfort should he decide to stay on, Hawkins left Agra on November 2, 1611: "to stay I would not amongst these faithlesse infidels."[43]

On September 26, 1611, ships under the command of Sir Henry Middleton anchored off the bar at Surat. Although repulsed by the Portuguese, Middleton found a way to land some of his men and merchandise. Muqarrab Khan, knowing full well that Jahangir still wanted the goods promised to him by Hawkins, obtained as many of the items as he thought worthwhile and then, entirely under the sway of the Portuguese, ordered the English to leave without any hope of future trade. Middleton was angry and after he left Surat in February of 1612, with the erstwhile envoy Hawkins now on board, he forced the Indian vessels he met in the Red Sea to trade with him at his own rates and, in the case of some, to pay a heavy ransom for passage.[44] This retaliation against the Surat traders of the Red Sea was likely, many thought, "to make the breach irreparable" between the two governments[45] and to undermine any future attempts at establishing trade.

Nevertheless, unaware of the Middleton problems, Thomas Best and his fleet arrived at the mouth of the Tapti in September of 1612. Middleton had left a letter behind with Jadu his Indian broker indicating the difficulties awaiting anybody in search of trade there, but he had apparently so terrified the local merchants that his successor received an exceptionally cordial welcome. Best was able initially to enter into a written agreement for English commerce in Gujarat, an agreement that so angered the Portuguese that they then attacked Best's ships. This first attack was repulsed, and when Best moved his ships out to get more sea room, the Portuguese attacked twice more but were twice again defeated. The Mughal government, now swayed by the demonstrations of English power at sea, sent Best an imperial *farman* on January 6, 1613, confirming English trade in Gujarat.[46] The terms of the agreement were apparently vague but did give general approval to the arrangements with the English that were already set and did, most importantly, stipulate that an English representative of some high standing should be sent to reside at the Mughal court to represent his country's interests.[47] With the agreement in place, Best departed Surat on January 17, 1613, leaving behind Thomas Aldworth as chief of the factors in Surat and Paul Canning, his second in command, to be a provisional English representative at court. Canning died on May 27, 1613, however, just following his arrival in Agra, but not until after he had presented his two musicians to Jahangir. His cousin, Lancelot Canning, played the virginals and Robert Trully the cornet, and although the virginals made no favorable impression, the cornet did.[48] Paul Canning's death (just weeks after his cousin's) left temporarily vacant the formal representation of the English at court; the post envisioned by the Best agreement would not then be officially filled until the arrival of Sir Thomas Roe in January of 1616.

The mechanics of English trade at this time were set by the factory system. Young men who had departed England with the various East India Company voyages were left behind in India as agents or factors to collect articles of trade and to prepare them for the next fleet out. The men lived in houses or factories, each one separate from the other and each one functioning as an autonomous unit.[49] Factors were given general guidelines about the goods to collect, but since at least in the early stages there was no central control, English posts were often characterized by personal rivalries and the individual hoarding of goods. To make matters worse, the factors had no standing with Jahangir for as merchants, who in their own country were middle class at best, they stood on par only with the low-caste Indian traders the emperor most despised.[50] What was needed was a central office to give cohesion to the commerce undertaken at the various scattered settlements and to give prestige not only to the English presence in this part of India but to the general business of foreign trade as well. During this period factories came to be set up in the four cities of Surat, Ajmer, Burhanpur, and Ahmedabad. In time other factories were established, such as those in Agra, Baroda, Broach, and Cambay, but all remained subordinate to the powers in Surat.

Best's agreement with the officials in Gujarat had been that the King of England would be allowed to keep "his embassador at the courte of the Greate Magoll" during times of peace, "there to compound and end all such greate and waightie questions" as may come up.[51] Aldworthe had further written to the Company in November of 1613 requesting that "a sufficient man" be sent to the king in Agra "whose person may breed regard, for they here look much after great men."[52] The Company scouted around and found that "none were esteemed soe fittinge for that seruice as Sir Thomas Roe, yf hee may bee had."[53] Thomas Roe (1580/81–1644) was by personality, education, and connection a perfect choice [see Figure 6–1]. Called by Terry "that most noble gentleman,"[54] Roe came from a substantial city family and was, when called upon by the Company, a member of Parliament for Tamworth. He was a man "of a pregnant vnderstandinge, well spoken, learned, industrious, and of a comelie personage," his fleshy appearance of later years only just beginning to show. Handsome,

FIGURE 6–1. Sir Thomas Roe (ca. 1581–1644). Line and stipple engraving by M. Mirevelt (artist) and G. Vertue (engraver). Engraving published London, 1740. By permission of the British Library (P 634), London.

dignified, well-spoken, and tactful, Roe was also shrewd and his broad knowledge and experienced common sense made him an excellent choice to represent his country's interests at a foreign court.[55]

For his part, Roe was happy to go to India. Though a member of Parliament, his liberal views were not in keeping with those of his king and may, in fact, have prevented further advancement at home. Moreover, his moderate fortune of earlier years had been wasted away and he was now fallen on hard times. From India he would later write: "I had fully ended and wasted my patrimony and saw no way but scorne . . . [but here] beeing as it were newborne, hee [God] restored mee to a new Inheritance and sett me right."[56]

In his midthirties when he set out on the mission, Roe had recently married a woman of good position. The marriage had been a secret one, however, with no one at home knowing of it except her uncle "to whose discretion I haue referrd her and the revealing of the marriage."[57] For unknown reasons, Roe kept the information from Jahangir and the other courtiers as well, and this position of his gave rise to a humorous interchange with the emperor once over the subject of a picture in Roe's possession. Jahangir had heard that Roe had a picture he had not shown him and demanded it be presented. It was of a very lovely lady and the emperor, confessing, "hee neuer sawe so much arte, so much bewty," wanted to know who she was. Roe replied that the picture was of a friend of his now dead, and Jahangir, seeing that the ambassador was very much attached to it, agreed only to borrow the picture for his painters to copy.[58] Although the reasons for Roe's secrecy are unclear, he was, nevertheless, a faithful if long-distance husband, returning all female servants given to him and proclaiming in 1618: "You see I desier noe weomens company, but labour to leaue such incumberances behynd."[59] Upon his return to England, however, Roe resumed what was to be an enduring, fruitful, and exceedingly tender relationship with the subject of the painting Jahangir had had his artists copy.[60]

Roe's official position in India was as an ambassador.[61] William Hawkins had used this title before, as had William Edwards, a merchant in Nicholas Downton's expedition of 1614 who was the English agent at court when Roe arrived (though, as Roe said in a marginal note in *The Embassy*, "I heare Master Edwards disavowes it").[62] Because of Hawkins's unfortunate experience, however, the Company had prohibited any of its later employees in India from assuming it as a personal form of address.[63] Roe, then, was the first Englishman sent expressly as "an Embassador . . . by the king of England," and he made it quite clear upon his arrival at Surat that he came in a very different capacity than had his predecessors: "they must not esteeme me in the qualetye of my forerunners,"[64] he noted, for he was not an ordinary merchant but an official representative of the English king. Furthermore, Roe clearly believed that he had come with the full understanding and consent of Jahangir's government to carry out negotiations at the highest level.[65]

That Roe had come as "a man of qualetye,"[66] however, did not insure him of deferential treatment. Using the title, in fact, put him in an awkward position for his predecessors had "almost made yt ridiculous to Come vnder that qualetye," and with the title he was initially treated as "an Imposture."[67] Although he was eventually received at court and was eventually accorded many of the privileges he thought due his office, he came to the conclusion early on not only that his job could have been done as easily by someone of lesser stature, but that the Indian context itself was an inappropriate one for the ambassadorial office as conceived of by the English: "This place is either made, or [is] of itselfe vnfitt for an ambassador."[68] This lament would be heard in his letters home throughout his tenure in India, and he often complained that, though authorized by the Mughal *farman* issued to Best to be present as an official at the highest level, the same or better results could have been obtained through a lower level official: "A meaner Agent would among these proud Moores better effect your busines. My qualety often for Ceremonyes eyther begettes you enemyes or suffers vnwoorthely."[69]

Roe's most well-known colleague in India was the Rev. Edward Terry (1591–1660), who acted as Roe's chaplain during much of the embassy [see Figure 6-2]. Roe's original chaplain was John Hall, who had died suddenly on August 19, 1616, to Roe's "great greife and discomfort."[70] At that time Roe had written immediately to Surat for another clergyman, not wanting to live in India as an atheist without "the Comfort of Godes woord and heauenly Sacraments." When the factors' original choice turned down the position, the matter was postponed until a new fleet arrived with two young ministers on board. A letter to Roe of September 26, 1616, recommended the "graver" of the two, Edward Terry, who was then about twenty-five years old and very eager to stay on in India and do service to the English embassy.[71]

The mission of Roe and Terry was colored by the differing desires and expectations of three governments. Through Roe, the English, who had become dazzled by the prospects of expanded international trade, hoped to bind the Mughal empire to a long-term commercial agreement. Roe had early on stated his country's position to the Portuguese Viceroy of Goa: "It is not the Purpose of the English to roote out or hinder your trade; but to Continew theyr owne in frendship, and wilbe ready as Christians to doe you any curtesye or assist your Excellence or nation in any want."[72] To this end, then, Roe presented Jahangir, through the emperor's agent, Asaf Khan, a list of demands that might constitute "a solemn treaty" between England and the Mughals.[73] Included in the demands were free access to Mughal ports for English merchants, free passage for English goods with only the usual payment of customs dues, free access to buy and sell goods, rent factories, and hire boats and carts, and freedom from confiscation of dead factors' possessions and from unlawful search and seizure.[74] All that Roe asked of Jahangir, said Terry, was "that his countrymen, the English, might have a free, safe, and peaceable trade in his dominions."[75] In desiring "absolute trade in any partes within the Dominions of the greate Mogore,"[76] Roe made clear that his vision of the region was not exclusive trade for the English but "open trade for all nations,"[77] including the Portuguese, contracted mutually as Roe was trying to do now for his own country. In return the English would help preserve the peace and offer protection of the seas to representatives of the Mughal government should they need it.

On Jahangir's part, English overtures were welcome on two accounts. First,

FIGURE 6–2. Portrait engraving of Edward Terry, then Chaplain to the Right Hon. Sir Thomas Row. Frontispiece to 1655 Terry, *Voyage*. By permission of the British Library, London.

he was excited by the prospect of English and European goods—not so much, however, as articles of trade in India but as presents for himself and his courtiers. The promise of goods, then, or more realistically of personal presents, were responsible perhaps more than anything else for opening the way for the English at court. Jahangir was receptive as well to the English promise of protection against Portuguese attack. More belligerent now than ever before at sea and on land, the Portuguese posed a real danger for Indian trade, and English pledges of security were considered timely and exceedingly welcome. Although Jahangir was genuinely open to the English, Roe's embassy had to overcome a long history of negative Portuguese influence against them, and it was to Roe's credit that by the time he left India in 1619 most of the danger from the Portuguese had passed.[78] During his stay, however, Portuguese harassment was a persistent presence: even as Roe arrived, the Portuguese were tendering treaties with the Mughals conditional upon English banishment;[79] Portuguese friends in Cambay continued to badger Mughal officials against trading with the English;[80] and Portuguese rhetoric against the English crown increased proportionate to their own decreased influence.

Roe arrived in Surat in September of 1615, but because of quarrels with local authorities over ambassadorial etiquette, he did not leave for Ajmer, where Jahangir had set up court, until October 30, 1615.[81] On the way he paid a visit to Parviz in Burhanpur, and as one of the presents Roe had brought was a case of liquor, the meeting ended amicably with the ambassador receiving the promise of a major factory in that town and the prince retiring to bed quite "drunck." That night, November 18, Roe came down with a fever,[82] and severe sickness plagued his journey and subsequent early stay in Ajmer so continuously that he was prevented from officially calling on Jahangir until January 10, 1616.[83] When he did finally present his credentials [see Figure 6–3], Roe made a good impression on the emperor, and Jahangir offered him his own physicians should he need them and blanket permission to ask him for anything he desired. Ever wary of new points of power, however, the queen Nur Jahan asked to see the ambassador's seal, keeping it overnight,[84] and Shah Jahan, who was in charge of the province where Surat was, gave Roe an audience on January 22.[85]

From these and other early instances, Roe soon saw that to have any of the grievances of the English in Surat redressed or to effect any negotiations on trade whatsoever he was going to have to deal with "the faction" under the leadership of "the beloued queene."[86] Knowing that, he went about his task graciously and firmly, presenting the specific demands to be met by a treaty to Jahangir on March 26, 1616. Although Roe did not speak the language of the court and needed an interpreter throughout his stay,[87] he "prepared my demandes perfect and in the Persian Toong"[88] in the hopes of a good reception. As it happened, Jahangir was less than anxious to conclude the treaty and months passed with haggling over only minor issues as the emperor waited for new presents from the English. Caught between Shah Jahan's desire for specific powers over trade in Surat, and Asaf Khan's general duplicity, Roe's efforts were increasingly frustrated as Jahangir's interest was taken up by other things.

In November of 1616 Jahangir left Ajmer heading for Agra but turned south

FIGURE 6–3. "Jahangir Investing Courtier with a Robe," ca. 1616. By permission of the British Museum, London (OA 1933–6-10–01). The European figure in the audience may well be Sir Thomas Roe.

instead to Mandu, important to the Mughals as a home of Persian culture, reaching "this desolate spot" in March of 1617 and staying on until October to watch the campaign of his son. Roe had no choice but to go with Jahangir, and there in Mandu found residence in a deserted mosque—"My Roome and House was good"—and water from a spring on the hillside.[89] Little of consequence happened for Roe's negotiations during the stay, and when Jahangir left Mandu, Roe proceeded on ahead of him to Ahmedabad,[90] the principal city of Gujarat, where Roe spent the remainder of his tenure at the Mughal court. When Roe made his yearly report to the Company in February of 1618, all hopes of a formal treaty were gone, despite assurances by Jahangir to the contrary.[91] "You can neuer expect to trade here vpon Capitulations that shalbe permanent," he said, because "the Gouerment dependes vpon the present will."[92] So sure was Roe that he had no chance of getting any concessions that he "was fully resolued to returne by this fleete,"[93] but was prevailed upon at the last minute to stay. During his last year in India he visited Burhanpur and, returning to Ahmedabad, miraculously escaped infection from an outbreak of plague there. When Jahangir prepared to move on to Agra in August of 1618, Roe took formal leave of him and departed for Surat in September. On February 17, 1619, the English fleet put to sea, with Roe on board the *Anne*.[94]

Trade with Indians at that time was governed by both the special interests of a consuming ruling class and the social boundaries of the lower castes. Those in power had enormous personal wealth, but were dependent (as in the law of escheat)[95] upon the ruler's good will for the stability and increase of what they possessed. Moreland had observed that, as elsewhere in Asia, "the ruler was the principal merchant of the country,"[96] investing in trade the wealth he acquired through revenues, through presents, and through the estates of his nobles.[97] According to the calculations of merchants like van den Broecke,[98] Akbar left behind enormous wealth, which was then reflected in the contemporary accounts of Jahangir. Hawkins, for example, gave Jahangir's annual income from his lands as fifty crore rupees (or five hundred million rupees) and detailed by type the gold and silver coins, the jewel stones, and the wrought jewelry he had in his treasury.[99] Coryat noted that "in his revenue he exceedeth the Turk and the Persian his neighbour by just halfe,"[100] and Roe continually marveled "that this King is one of the mightyest Princes in Asia, as well in extent of territory as in revenew,"[101] and that Jahangir "was so rich in Iewelles that I must confesse I neuer saw togither so vnvaluable wealth."[102]

Involvement in trade took place on a number of different levels. Patronage came most often from the ruling family and from the noble classes, whose investment delineated the extent of trade and whose peculiar interests shaped the quality of imports from overseas. Shah Jahan, for example, ran his own ships to Mocha in the Red Sea and had a substantial interest not only in developing commercial structures friendly to him but also in amassing sizable profits for his own bid for the throne.[103] Below them were middlemen who acted as agents for the patrons and who, though having had neither the money nor the goods themselves, were indispensable in connecting the courts with the commercial outposts. A famous middleman was the *baniya* Jadu, who acted as principal broker for Roe and his embassy and who was for many years the chief Indian agent employed by the English. Finally, there were the merchants themselves who, as either administrators of provinces and factories or their shifting underlings, were directly responsible for the procuring and dispersal of goods. The English would have had most contact with the Muslim merchants, for example, who were spread out along the shores,[104] but might also have had some direct dealings with the craftsmen themselves, the dyers and weavers, for example, who belonged to both Hindu and Muslim craft guilds.[105] Jahangir had traditionally held a low opinion of the merchants he had dealt with, but their contacts and perspicacious endurance were essential to his style of life.

Of the officials in the Mughal government, Roe and his embassy had most contact with three men, each of whom used his relationship with the English to bolster his own personal position, and among whom Roe had to maintain a most fickle and chameleon-like balance:[106] Shah Jahan, Asaf Khan, and Muqarrab Khan. Shah Jahan was in charge of the province containing Surat and therefore had control over the governorship of the port.[107] Officially it was he who was the imperial sponsor of the English mission, but he was suspicious of all foreigners and held the English in particular in great contempt.[108] Although Roe cast Shah Jahan as an "enemy to all Christians,"[109] "a . . . hater of all Christians,"[110] and "one that by an inveterate hatred wisheth ill to all Christians,"[111] Shah Jahan was in fact regularly partial to the Portuguese cause. Perhaps because the alliance with the Portuguese was an older one, or because the current English representative was a more successful match for the prince,[112] Shah Jahan was consistently hostile to English concerns and more open instead to those of their European rivals.

It was no surprise then that Roe quickly developed a preference for the fickly disfavored Khusrau, who was seen not only as an advocate of all Christians, but a genteel and well mannered diplomat as well. Observing the faction's endless dealings, Roe noted that "if Sultan Corsoronne preuayle in his right, this kingdome wilbe a sanctuary for Christians,"[113] a situation that would also have appealed to Roe's English inclination toward primogeniture. Nevertheless, Shah Jahan was the man to deal with, "for his favour is as necessary for you as the King's,"[114] and despite later times of celebration when this prince fell out of favor with Jahangir,[115] Roe had to make the effort to win Shah Jahan to his side. He rejoiced then whenever the prince appeared to be on "new termes of frendship," knowing himself privately, however, that his own hospitable conduct was often a matter of pretense.[116]

The man Roe had most to do with, however, was Asaf Khan, whom Jahangir had made the chief negotiator with the English and through whom all English business had to pass. In a letter to King James of August 8, 1618, Jahangir said: "The care of this matter [i.e., trade] has been committed to Asaf Khan, who has been instructed to grant the English all their desires."[117] Asaf Khan had been a principal agent at court for Hawkins, being entertained by the Englishman "often at my house,"[118] and was also the point man for the English during Edwards' stay.[119] Both envoys seem to have been on good terms with Asaf Khan, who quickly proved to be an exceptionally adept courtier and an unctuous servant to the king. There is no doubt, however, that it was in part through the Persian minister's malice that Hawkins' mission was a failure.[120] It appears that Asaf Khan was often under the sway of the Portuguese,[121] who brought more "curious toyes for the king" than did the English,[122] and that he loved to treat whomever he could, in this case the English, as a pawn in his daily joust for power and wealth at the court.

On the whole, however, Asaf Khan proved to be a less than diplomatic mediator whose least sin seems to have been "barberisme" and "vnmannerlye" behavior[123] and whose greatest sin was outright duplicity. Although Asaf Khan often protested his allegiance to the English with cries "that he was neuer [a] lyar nor of a double hart,"[124] and although Roe often had to pledge his absolute trust in the minister,[125] the truth was that Asaf Khan only moved to the English side when he needed this foreign allegiance against Shah Jahan. As the junta began to strain at the seams, Asaf Khan sought to use the English as a means of outmaneuvering the king's third son, his own son-in-law. In hopes of obtaining some extra English goods in 1617, for example, Asaf Khan was willing "to betray" Shah Jahan with sweet talk about the benefits of an English alliance[126] and later to defend the English against being "vsed very rudely by the Princes seruants."[127] Roe was wise to the ploys, but was as always powerless to reshape the channels of patronage.

Subordinate to Shah Jahan was the governorship of Surat, an office filled from 1611 to 1618 by Muqarrab Khan. Muqarrab Khan had been "a great favourite" with Jahangir since the emperor's youth, "having won his regard by his skill in surgery and by his usefulness in the field sports to which that monarch was so much addicted."[128] Muqarrab Khan was in charge of the customs for the Gujarat ports—in particular, of those monies going directly into the royal treasury[129]—and for this reason had much to do with early English trade. Like those of his colleagues, then, Muqarrab Khan's dealings with the English were particularly fickle and inconstant, and foreigners often experienced outright abuse at his hands:

> By Mocrob Chan, chief governor of Surat, we had many wrongs done us, ourselves stayed so that we could have no recourse to our ships, our goods taken and used at his pleasure, our arms that we brought for our defence taken from us, and [he] forced us to show the king's presents.[130]

Many Englishmen complained of bad treatment from Muqarrab Khan who, though he had religious ties to the Portuguese (having converted to Christianity about 1610 under their influence) and often schemed with the Portuguese against the English,[131] seemed to act most often out of self-interest.

Finally, Roe's work with the three officials of the Mughal government was facilitated by a man whose whole career was spent furthering the business interests of the English in India. Jadu "the broker" had been the principal agent of the English for years, having served Hawkins and Middleton as well as others during the first voyages of the Company.[132] He became Roe's chief agent upon the ambassador's arrival, and Roe's dependence upon him is evident from the many references to Jadu in *The Embassy*. Not only did this *baniya* undertake the tedious and routine errands involved in negotiation, but he often acted as Roe's interpretater at the court as well.[133] Jadu was not known, however, for his mental or physical swiftness, and Keridge had complained earlier that a Portuguese servant "one An.de Guerra . . . can dispatch more business in an hour than this banyan in a day."[134] Roe later noted that Jadu was "lazy and offers voluntary to quit our business," but the Englishman needed him too much in the end and would not accept a resignation. Said Roe: "Necessity enforceth me to bear,"[135] a lament as fitting for Roe's whole experience in India as it was for the one man Jadu.

II

At the heart of the relationship between the Mughals and the English were the goods offered up in trade. Because it was the English who most wanted a trading agreement, it was the goods they desired that formed the nucleus of the discussion. India of the early seventeenth century could offer the European and Asian market a substantial variety in natural resources. Among them in good quantity were gum-lac,[136] iron,[137] copper,[138] brass,[139] and silver,[140] though, as Terry noted, the Indians "need not open" their silver mines "being so enriched from other nations of Europe, and other parts, who yearly bring thither great quantities of silver to purchase their commodities."[141] Diamonds were also available, coming primarily from mines in the Deccan. These stones were "accounted [the] most precious" and formed much of the yearly tribute paid to Jahangir by minions in his empire;[142] skill in procuring and buying diamonds was highly prized and there were many "natives [who] know very well how to value" the stones.[143]

The shipment of "drugs" from India was also brisk and several items were a regular part of European trade. Borax came from "the Eastern mountains" (in Tibet) and was mined there from the Manasarowar Lakes. The supply, said Pelsaert, "is very large, sufficient to satisfy the whole world."[144] Another resource was the plant spikenard, used to treat stiffened limbs, and since it only grew wild in the mountains it, like borax, had to be harvested and taken some distance to Agra to sell.[145] A third item, however, saltpetre (a saline earth used in gunpowder and to cool water), was found close by in Agra—as it was in other places—and could be refined there directly from abandoned villages. Although originally cheap, saltpetre's price rose, Pelsaert noted, when Indian peasants realized how desired it was by both the Dutch and the English.[146] Opium, from markets in Malwa and Benares, for example, was brought for trade through the west coast ports,[147] and spices of astounding assortment came from all over India: pepper,[148] ginger,[149] tumeric, and Kasmiri saffron,[150] for example, were sold in quantity in Agra, the biggest spice-market then on the subcontinent.[151] Sugar in great stores was ranked among the chief Indian commodities desired by the English,[152] and musk from the muskcat was widely available "in good quantity . . . [from] the Mogul's provinces."[153]

Articles manufactured in India's local industrial sectors were marketable abroad as well, and boxes,[154] trunks,[155] chess sets,[156] and pottery all became part of the growing overseas trade. Roe was disappointed, however, that more curios were not available, for soon after his arrival he lamented: "I thought all India a China shop, and that I should furnish all my Frendes with rarietyes; but this is not that part,"[157] what he saw being not as good as articles already available in England. There were carpets, though, and of good quality and in great abundance[158] from markets in cities like Lahore and Srinagar. They could be made to order, "fine or course as required,"[159] and the variety of color, material, and design meant that European and Asian consumers had a good and serviceable range from which to choose.

By far the two most important commodities for export, however, were indigo and cotton goods.[160] Indigo was a dark blue vat dye used to color cottons, wools, and silks in gradient tones widely pleasing to the English and Asian markets. The dye came from a plant that grew well in places like Bayana, a town just southwest of Agra, because of the brackish water that was found in the wells nearby.[161] Indigo was made by soaking the leaves of the plant in large containers of water for about a day and a half until the blue dye had seeped out. The water was then drained off and "the indigo which has sunk down is taken out, and laid on cotton clothes until it becomes as firm as soap, when it is made into balls." The round blue "gobbets" were then stored in earthen jars for shipment.[162]

Standing indigo plants, still in the ground, were subject to a precarious fate, being "liable to many more accidents or misfortunes than other crops or products." Too much or too little rain, insubstantial sunshine, extreme cold, and plagues of locusts each threatened the vulnerable stalk, and Pelsaert noted that many men who had planted large fields for years and had reaped great rewards from their crops had been reduced to poverty by a single act of nature.[163] Moreover, the quality of indigo produced depended upon the cycle of the plant—the second crop being a superior cut with "a violet infusion" in its dye that was missing in the coarser brown results of the first crop[164]—and cultivators had to be extremely careful in the planning and working of their harvest.

Because of the water issue, most of the best indigo available to European merchants came from the vicinity of Agra.[165] Indigo prices in that city fluctuated depending upon the vagaries of the season and the demands of the market, and Roe was kept consistently apprised of the current price in that key factory so as to insure a good profit to the Company: "I am of opinion if the Indico will make mony it is no ill bargayne."[166] In the days before the coming of the English, however, a chief market for indigo was Lahore, as merchandise was carried by caravan to points north and west out of the commercial lanes of this city. Indigo reaching Europe from the Levant, for example, was known as Lauri or Lahori even though it might have been produced in a place like the Bayana region.[167] Lahori indigo did, however, also travel by ship, for the English factor Richard Cocks noted in 1613 that two bales of the indigo were taken from the Queen Mother's vessel, the *Rahimi*, and put aboard the English ship the *Hector*.[168]

Trading from India, however, was to be primarily in cotton cloth. Said Roe: "The trade here will doubtlesse in tyme bee very profitable for your Maiesties Kingdomes, and may vent much cloth."[169] The general term used by the English for cloth was calico, deriving from the port city of Calicut from which many loads of stuffs were shipped to the west and east.[170] Calicos or cotton wools came in many "divers sorts;" as white cloths they could be broad or narrow and coarse, fine, or very fine—some of them being so delicate that Terry said, "I believe [they are] as fine as our purest lawn." The coarser cloths were dyed or printed with "well-shaped and well-coloured flowers or figures, which are so fixed in the cloth, that no water can wash them out." This art of staining or printing cloth belonged so peculiarly to India, he concluded, that countries far and wide brought "their money to fetch them hence."[171] *Pintadoes*, the Portuguese term for "painted" cloths, were so popular, in fact, that they became a staple in the decoration of European and early American homes.

Finally, the shipping lanes to Europe and Asia carried Indian silk—the best coming from Bengal, where it was sold either in skeins or cloth bolts[172] and could be procured at reasonable rates.[173] Silks were woven as fine or coarse materials and were also made locally into velvets, satins, and taffetas "either plain or mingled, or striped in party-colours." Although India could offer a wide variety of silk cloth by weight, dye, and design, European traders, however, often found that the highest quality came from weaving centers elsewhere. Said Terry: "the best of them [Indian silks], for richness and goodness, come not near those which are made in the parts of Italy."[174] Persia, likewise, was a good source, for "the greatest quantity of that rich commodity, that any place in the whole world affords, comes out of Georgia, a province belonging to the King of Persia,"[175] and Persian silk in time even came to be procurable "at a more reasonable price."[176]

Cotton weaving, then, remained the most extensive industry in India and that which produced the most exportable product. It is important to remember, however, as Moreland has pointed out, that even though the average quality of the cloth made then was probably higher than it is now, the proportion of cloth traded overseas was very low compared to the total produced. Moreover, the upper classes in India consumed a relatively insignificant quantity of cotton, most of that woven being "similar to the coarse but durable fabrics which are still produced"[177] and consumed by the Indian populace at large. Nevertheless, a great deal of Indian cotton goods soon began making their way overseas by ship, and as Roe said, Jahangir made no complaint "that wee [English] buy not their Comoditie, but Contrarie, that wee buy so much that their owne Merchants want for the Red Sea."[178]

In return for Indian indigo and cotton cloth, the English sought to trade articles of their own, or alternately articles produced in other countries they had access to through established commercial channels. On the whole those things that aroused the most interest at court, however, were not what could be traded and sold broadly in local Indian markets, but the presents the English brought, or could bring, for the emperor and his nobles at court. For the most part, these constituted luxury items and, in addition to some one-of-a kind presents like a ruby-studded gold whistle that made its way into the *zanana*[179] and a fully appointed English coach Jahangir had dismantled to copy for a second coach and then reassembled and reupholstered with new velvets and gold work,[180] English presents to the court formed an unusual and somewhat motley list: mirrors,[181] swords and knives,[182] liquor or "hot waters,"[183] precious stones,[184] dogs (especially large powerful ones),[185] and horses and saddles.[186] Certain cloths found favor with the Mughals, such as "french Muff or veluett,"[187] woven gold cloth,[188] and English broadcloth that was red "for that is the colour they most love."[189] On the whole, however, there was a limited market for each of these items, and even that depended upon imperial whim.

The only presents Roe brought that truly impressed Jahangir were pictures—prints at first, then paintings, done of human faces and figures in either secular or religious settings. European art had been known and admired for some time at the court, and it had been because of their capacity for giving pictures, especially of Christ and the Virgin Mary, that the Portuguese had been able to preserve so firm a place in the Mughal entourage. Jahangir was fond of hanging these images on the walls of his inner chambers, and pictures played an important role in decorations for the Nauroz[190] and in maintaining the domestic spaces of his encampments when on tour. Galleries, in fact, were often set up in his many gardens, and bowers hung with pictures were intended to complement and to enhance the beauties of nature.

Roe sensed immediately that pictures may provide him an entree like nothing else he could give, and only two weeks after he met Jahangir he wrote to the Company asking for pictures, "lardge, on cloth, the frame in peeces." But "they must be good," he added, "and for varyetye some story, [and] with many faces."[191]

The subjects of the pictures Jahangir eventually requested from the English were different from those he asked from the Portuguese. Terry noted that instead of pious renderings of Christ and the Virgin Mary, what "pleased the Mogul very much" were portrayals of fair and beautiful women. He liked portraits, especially of noblemen and noblewomen when the workmanship was very fine, and scenes representing biblical or mythological stories; landscapes do not appear in the lists of requests per se, but battle scenes, banquet scenes, maps of the world, comic incidents, and pictures of Parliament do.[192] Roe found out, however, after a particularly prickly session, that care had to be taken in choosing each image in order to avoid giving a damaging message. In one of his shipments of gifts, for example, were three pictures, the first two of which proved to be innocuous portraits of two English noblewomen. The third, however, was a picture of Venus and a satyr, showing "the Satyres hornes, his skinne, which was swart, and pointed to many particulars." Wanting an interpretation of the painting, Jahangir at first asked the English to remain silent, and turned instead to his own men, each of whom "replyed according to his fancie." The emperor thought they were all deceived and turned back to Roe and Terry, neither of whom in the end could speak to the meaning of the image. Jahangir then gave his own explanation, implying that it showed "a scorne of Asiatiques, whom the naked Satyre represented, and was of the same complexion, and not vnlike; who, being held by Venus, a white woman, by the Nose, it seemed that shee led him Captiue." Although the emperor graciously accepted the picture as a gift, Roe concluded that from then on the Company had "to be very wary what they send [that it] may be subject to ill Interpretation."[193]

Pictures proved to be excellent presents, however, both for their workmanship and for their ease of imitation by Jahangir's painters. At the conclusion of his stay, Roe noted that they "imitate euery thing wee bring,"[194] and Terry said that they "are excellent at limning, and will copy out any picture they see to the life." "The truth is", he continued, "that the natives of the monarchy are the best apes for imitation in the world, so full of ingenuity, that they will make any new thing by pattern."[195] Edwards had noticed the same thing but with one picture, apparently of Sir Thomas Smith, Governor of the Company, Jahangir's painters "confessed that none of them could anything near imitate the same which makes him prize it above all the rest."[196] Keridge noted that pictures of women, presumably high-born ladies of good English stock, were not esteemed by the Mughals "according to their value," but were only prized "for the rarity of the workmanship."[197]

Aside from presents to the Mughal court, the English brought articles they hoped to sell in trade at the local markets. Chief among these was their own English broadcloth, which Best had said "sells here fairly well, much of it for cash down."[198] But Best's later experience with Jahangir's governor (who told Best "the Kinge would not esteeme" the cloth)[199] was far more prophetic. After extensive efforts, Roe found that "our Cloth will neuer vent" here,[200] and even though for "one yeare gould or siluered veluettes, Grogrames, Chamletts and silk stuffes may serue vs, but constantly noething."[201] Terry attributed the Indian indifference to English cloth to "that country's immoderate heat," saying that the broadcloth was "not fit to make habits for that people." What was sold, he noted, was red in color and was used to make trappings for local elephants and horses and to cover over coaches.[202] Representatives of the Company in the past had warned against sending English cloth, which "would in no sort vent" in India,[203] and Edwards had even hoped that a letter, asking that 1,000 broadcloths be sent over, would be lost at sea "for more experience hath since showed [him] . . . the error."[204] Although when English cloth did come, some colors sold more popularly than others—in addition to Venice reds, popinjay and grass greens and yellows in deep tones[205]—in the end it was good advice to counsel against sending over broadcloths for "our cloth is but a dead commodity" here.[206]

There were four staples, however, that did sell well in India: quicksilver, lead, elephants' teeth (ivory), and vermilion.[207] The demand for these items was variable and depended upon their availability from local sources, but during the early English tenure in India, at least, there was a healthy market for these materials.

On the whole, however, the English had to pay for the merchandise they took out with them not in goods in kind, but in silver bullion, which was then melted down and made into coins with Jahangir's stamp and Persian inscriptions minted on them. Said Terry: "yet the greatest part by far of commodities brought thence, are caught by the silver hook. . . . And this is the way to make any nation of the world rich, to bring, and leave silver in it, and to take away commodities."[208] That the balance of trade in India's favor was paid in silver did not set particularly well with the English, who feared a widespread sapping of their monetary strength into South Asia as a result of their need for textiles. No one was more aware of this than Roe, who concluded in April of 1616: "Seeing our state cannot beare the exportation of mony, except some new trade can be discouered from the East to serue this Kingdome, it must fall to ground by the weaknes of itts owne leggs."[209]

It became clear early on, then, that the market for English goods in India was very limited, and that England simply did not produce anything that India really wanted and could buy in large quantities. "I see no Comoditye that will proue staple and certaynly vendable, able to returne a ship yearly," said a depressed Roe.[210] On the other hand, there were large supplies of indigo and cotton goods England wanted to ship out of India, and short of dumping huge supplies of silver bullion into the subcontinent, English merchants had to rely on the large trading networks in other parts of the world. In this way, the English could use the goods they received in trade from Africa, Sumatra, and China, for example, to pay for their wares from Indian merchants. Thus, India could get porcelain from Macao, camphor from Borneo, and spices from Achin and Bantim.[211] From Thailand could come raw silk, benzoin (benjamin), and lignum aloes,[212] from Africa ivory and amber, and from Japan silver[213] for, unlike China, this last source had no embargo on the export of the precious metal. Moreover, English ships could bring examples of each of the goods sold at the huge markets in Mecca—cloths, drugs, spices, metals, precious stones, and so forth[214]—all the time making a profit in goods, while theoretically, expending as little as possible of their own short supply of bullion. Being a relatively self-sufficient country, however, India had the upper hand in any trading agreement, and European merchants coming over found that trinkets pleased as much as anything else: "Things best for presents generally with all the people of these countries are novelties and things of little worth, and are esteemed for their rarity and not for their value."[215]

Noblewomen were among the major consumers of goods brought into India, and although it was rarely specified which articles were expressly for them, many of the luxury items brought into court ended up in the *zanana*. Roe once, in decrying the need to bribe Nur Jahan daily in order to gain favor at the court, went on to offer a list of possible presents that would be suitable for women if indeed they did need to be given things: "fine needle woorke toyes, fayre bone lace, cuttworke, and some handsome wrought wastcote, sweetbagges or Cabinetts, wilbe most Convenient. . . . I would add any faire China Bedsteeds, or cabinets or truncks of Japan are here rich presentes."[216]

The one item expressly imported for women, however, was hats. In a letter to the East India Company dated September 10, 1614, Keridge asked for "half a dozen of coloured beaver hats, such as our gentlewomen use, . . . for the king demanded for such things of me for his women to wear a-hunting."[217] He requested them again of the Company in a letter dated March 20, 1615: "two or three beaver hats also for his chief women, and half a dozen of felts would be liked of, for they wear them on hunting."[218] And Roe as well received a request for hats from Jahangir "for that his women liked them'[219] and was forced to give up the few that he had when the emperor discovered them among his things. That it would be hats that would be expressly brought for noblewomen is significant, for the Indian body image designates the head as the most sacred part of the figure. Head coverings as ornamentation and protection were then, as now, an important part of any dress, and women especially found modesty and purity essential attributes in treating that sovereign part of the body.

It is not clear whether non-noble women were direct recipients of imported goods as well, though it is likely that they were not. Women of all classes, however, were major consumers of products internal to the country and in that had a certain decided influence on the market. The millions of yards of cotton and silk materials produced in India every year were bought primarily by women for their own use, and the "copper pots, dishes, basins, and other articles for use in Hindu houses" were ultimately scrutinized by women of all classes for their quality and value.[220] Likewise the craft industries that produced gold and silver jewelry and set stones for earrings, bangles, necklaces, and nose ornaments all had women's tastes in mind, and drug and cosmetic vendors knew that it was women who would be the primary purchasers of their commodities. In this way, then, specific articles successful in both domestic and foreign trade were dependent upon the tastes and demands of women in the Indian marketplace who, at least as consumers, could exert substantial influence on the nature of commerce.

III

While we can fairly assume that the goods available in bazaars and through private traders were subject in large part to the needs and judgments of the women who bought them, we must also allow for the contributions of women in other areas of trade as well. Beyond their role as consumers, women were known to take a more active interest in commerce as traders themselves, and during the Jahangiri period, wealth and opportunity increasingly allowed women access to the channels that directly selected and moved merchandise. One of the most distinguished of the early women traders was Jahangir's mother, Maryamuzzamani, whose ship, the *Rahimi*, was captured by the Portuguese in 1613 and burned in 1614. Known as "a great adventurer"[221] and as a woman of high-spirit with a taste for the unusual, Maryamuzzamani was the most famous of all women shipowners running vessels in Jahangir's time. From descriptions left us by a subordinate to Sir Henry Middleton in the summer of 1613, we know that Maryamuzzamani's greatest ship, the *Rahimi*, had a sail area so vast that it was identifiable to sailors from miles away, its main mast reaching up a full forty-three or forty-four yards. This ship could displace up to fifteen hundred tons and ordinarily carried fifteen hundred passengers, many going as pilgrims to and from Mecca.

The *Rahimi* was home-ported in Surat but often traveled to Jiddah, the port near Mecca on the Red Sea, where she carried merchandise for the vendors of the holy city and trafficked in pilgrims on various parts of their journey.[222] One of the most controversial aspects of the *Rahimi*'s passage was the amount her officers had to pay the Portuguese for a *cartaz*. Finch preserved one account in which the *Rahimi* was held up on a trip to Mocha because the Portuguese demanded a huge sum; the principals eventually settled on a smaller sum, but the Mughals "were faine to give" the presents that were demanded of them in accompaniment.[223] The *Rahimi*'s "sum" became, in English reckoning, a standard by which other vessels were taxed, and Middleton's subordinate, who was apparently in charge of setting rates, noted the following:

> The ground that I had to work by was the sum formerly agreed on by general consent and that in the forenoon agreed on for the Remee . . . and according to that rate by my nearest esteem to myself set down rates on other ships . . . [not] out of proportion to the Remee sum.[224]

Exactly what the *Rahimi* carried is not now known—except that she did take on indigo[225]—but we can presume that her cargo, undoubtedly arranged for by Maryamuzzamani herself, covered the whole of what was offered up in trade at the time. When the *Rahimi* was seized by the Portuguese[226] and burned along with 119 other ships,[227] an era in overseas trading came to an end. Not only did these acts effectively ruin the future commercial prospects of the Portuguese in India, but after the *Rahimi*'s time, trade, while becoming more complex, was also governed more increasingly by the English sense of fair play.

Like her mother-in-law, Nur Jahan engaged in substantial commercial activity. We do not know the names of the ships she owned and ran out of the western ports, but the evidence available suggests that her trading network was an extensive one entailing domestic markets as well as foreign ones. Pelsaert was the only foreign merchant who specifically detailed Nur Jahan's domestic trade and then only that which he could have himself observed around the city of Agra. He told us that in Sikandra, across the Yamuna from Agra, Nur Jahan's officers collected duty on goods before they were crossed over the river to be sold, presumably in the profitable markets of the main city. The goods that arrived there came mainly from the east and northeast, from Bengal and the Bhutan mountains, and included in their number: "cotton goods from Bengal, raw silk from Patna, spikenard, borax, verdigris, ginger, fennel, and thousands of sorts of drugs, too numerous to detail in this place." Many of these goods were intended for foreign markets, but grain, butter, and "other provisions" also came in great quantity for consumption locally. "Without these supplies," said Pelsaert, "this country could not be provided with food, and would almost die of hunger, so that this is a place of great traffic."[228] Agra was "at the junction of all the roads from distant countries," and since all goods from all directions had to pass through the city to markets either there or elsewhere, Nur Jahan's officers were in a position to take in substantial monies. Being at such a crossroads of commerce, then, the Agra stations not only provided Nur Jahan with a sizable income, but also allowed her some control over the types of goods that passed through the gates and were then dispensed to local and foreign merchants. Moreover, although there is little mention of customs collection elsewhere, we can assume that Nur Jahan had similar control over commerce in other areas, especially in the *jagirs* that were her own like Ramsar and Toda and even perhaps in the lands managed personally by the king.

Nur Jahan was also involved in negotiations for overseas trade, and during the time of the embassy, developed a firm, if prickly, relationship with the English ambassador. In the fall of 1617, Roe received a servant of Nur Jahan's who announced that with Shah Jahan's consent the queen had obtained a *farman* "that all our goods might bee in her protection, . . . and [that she] was readie to send down her seruant with that, to see and take order for our good establishment: that shee would see that wee should not bee wronged." The servant had actually been sent by Asaf Khan who, at least officially, wanted to circumvent the prince Shah Jahan's reluctant behavior toward the English. The order, however, came from Nur Jahan herself, Roe was told, and she had "charged her seruant to assist our Factors, so that we should haue neuer more cause to complaine of Surat." As he could do nothing else, Roe accepted the change in patronage—coming as it did with special requests from the queen for "some toyes"—but saw clearly that it rested on a consistent avarice at court now newly awakened by the stores of additional goods Roe could provide. Nevertheless, Nur Jahan was from this moment on a regular buyer through the English trading networks, for which purpose Roe declared, "I haue ordered your Factory [at Surat] to sell to the seruants of Normahall and her brother whatsoeuer may bee spared."[229] Roe reiterated the terms of the new relationship with Nur Jahan some days later—"His Sister I haue promised to visit, whom hee hath made our protectresse"[230]—seeming to acknowledge outright that Nur Jahan was an independent figure in commercial dealings now with whom he must cement firm trading ties.

Roe never saw Nur Jahan, protected as she was from foreign view by *parda*, but he clearly found her as central a trading partner as any in the government. Her reasons for wanting the official sponsorship of English trade were more than apparent: first, with the very earliest rifts in the junta now just beginning to show, Nur Jahan, in taking English commerce out from Shah Jahan's jurisdiction, gained a symbolic and perhaps real advantage in power over her stepson; second, the financial benefits due her from her patronage were to be substantial, and if they happened to turn out otherwise, she had nothing to lose; and, third, sponsorship of the English would win her protection at sea from the Portuguese, who still threatened vessels sailing under Mughal dominion. It is hardly likely that Asaf Khan masterminded the shift against Shah Jahan without his sister's consent or encouragement. Not only must she have approved the move, but more likely, urged her brother to make it. The effects on the English chances for successful negotiations were probably minimal: without Shah Jahan there would be less blockage, but with Nur Jahan there would still be a self-serving interest on the part of a government and a country that, ultimately, could manage very well without European contracts.

Other evidence that Nur Jahan traded for overseas goods came from incidental letters written to the East India Company. John Browne, writing to the Company on February 10, 1617, noted that toward the end of the year 1616, now that peace with the Portuguese had been concluded, "there are many buyers, and never so many great ones as now, viz. the Queen, Prince, Muckrob Chan, Meir Joffer, etc."[231] Danvers, in his note, assumes that the Queen Mother,

Maryamuzzamani, was meant here because Roe often referred to her trading activity, but three elements indicate instead that this reference was probably to Nur Jahan: first, this occurred about the same time, between 1616 and 1617, that Nur Jahan began making serious overtures to Roe about involvement in the English trading networks; second, by this time Maryamuzzamani had more or less retired from trade, her primary ship burned[232] and her own health not as good as it used to be;[233] and, third, to list the Queen and Prince together as Browne did was to indicate nothing else but the junta, very powerful at this time and with Nur Jahan as the woman at the helm. Likewise, James Bickford's reference in his March 4, 1617, letter to Sir Thomas Smythe, which mentioned "the Queen" among the "divers others beginning to buy,"[234] must for the same reasons have referred to the current chief queen on the throne rather than to her mother-in-law, the Queen Mother. A later reference, in a document dated November 23, 1621, which made note of "goods . . . sould the Kinge and Quene," indicated beyond question that Jahangir and Nur Jahan were buying things through the English factors in Agra and Surat[235] and that they had been for sometime. From these we can conclude that the overtures to Roe made by the queen were neither the beginning nor the end of Nur Jahan's business dealings with the English.

Indeed, it is clear that, even after Roe left, Nur Jahan continued to engage in overseas trade despite the fact that it meant submitting to the still-present yoke of the Portuguese. In a letter dated March 12 and 13, 1619, to the Company, Kerridge and his colleagues reported that Nur Jahan was once again running ships and once again paying huge sums for the privilege:

> The Portingalls, that incroacheth as much on them [the Mughals], permitt none of their shipps to sayle without lysence, and even now since the *Anns* departure have forced the Goga junck, appertaineing to the beloved queene, to pay them 65,000 mamoodes for custome to the porte of Dieu (an antient dutie), which striveing to infringe loste her voyage the laste yeare, and made greate shew off warrs; yett after much contention have submitted againe to the yoake.[236]

Some time later, consultations among the factors of Surat indicated that the English there were still grievous over injuries suffered earlier and had planned, as a result, to seize some of the trading vessels sailing for the Mughal government. In a letter received March 7, 1623, for example, a ship destined for Mocha was mentioned, "and thatt the shipp and goods onely belonged to the Kinge, the Normall [Nurmahal], Assafcon, Suffichan, and other greatte men." It was given out that the English were going to seize this ship belonging in part to Nur Jahan, but subsequent provisions seem to have been made for her secure passage.[237] Nevertheless, there is no doubt that Jahangir's chief wife continued to trade in channels of overseas commerce and did so despite the obvious danger to her charges even if from her erstwhile allies of the embassy.

More time-consuming, more frustrating, and ultimately more debilitating than the trade negotiations with any member of the Mughal government, however, was the gift-giving cycle Roe found himself caught up in almost from the start, a cycle that as time went on increasingly involved Nur Jahan. Others before Roe had noted that Jahangir did not like to see his visitors come without gifts. Hawkins, for example, had said "there is no man that commeth to make petition who commeth emptie handed."[238]

> His custome is that when you petition him for any thing, you must not come empty handed, but give him some toy or other, whether you write or no. By the gift you give him he knoweth that you demand some thing of him; so after enquiry is made, if he seeth it convenient, he granteth it.[239]

Terry described Jahangir as having "a covetous heart . . . [that was] so unsatiable, as that it never knows when it hath enough; being like a bottomless purse, that can never be fill'd."[240] Although Roe expected to have to come bearing presents,[241] he always felt that the gifts he brought were inadequate, and once at the beginning gave Jahangir a present "but not in the name of his Majestie, it beeing too meane."[242] Again, at the beginning of Roe's stay after Jahangir had accepted some things, the emperor took aside the resident Jesuit and asked him "whether the King of England were a great Kyng that sent presents of so small valewe."[243] Somewhat later Roe's tone reflected the weary humiliation of being constantly deficient in his gifts: "The Presentes sent this yeare were too good; but (to deale playnly with my frendes) soe farr short of their greedy expectation that they rather disgrace then helpe mee."[244] Several times Roe tried to lay down the law on gifts, telling Asaf Khan that if he didn't like what he brought to write down a list of what would please,[245] but ultimately became so discouraged that he began to counsel against any presents at all: "[because] our trouble is all aboute the presents . . . I am inforced by experience to change the Course."[246]

To make matters worse, Jahangir was not simply a passive recipient of the gifts Roe brought but often interfered with the process and changed its course. As in the case of other petitioners,[247] Jahangir often gave back to Roe the things he didn't like, complaining as always about the poor quality of gifts coming from presumably so great a man as King James I of England. Nobles at the court often said that better presents came from the Portuguese,[248] and Roe lamented halfway through his tenure that the English were now "the scorn of nations" because of their gifts that were "so unworthy of merchants that our enemies have moved upon that advantage to turn us out."[249] Asaf Khan had warned Roe that the English had brought all the trouble on themselves for, had they come merely as merchants, nothing would have been expected of them "but to buy."[250] Moreover, Roe himself always seemed to be having money problems both professionally, when at the outset he didn't have enough silver to cover even a third of the cloth and other goods[251] the English needed, and personally—as he said in November of 1616: "I was vnfitted with Carriadge, and ashamed of my Prouision."[252] And having come to India out of wasted financial circumstances, such poverty was humiliating. It is a surprise, then, that Roe did not try to line his own pockets on the sly, remaining instead ever a gentleman and good sport:

"I neuer gaue a knife for myne owne endes, nor vsed the least basenes of begging; my riches are accordingly."[253]

Almost from the start, Roe knew that a substantial draw on his presents came from Nur Jahan. In 1611, Hawkins had noted that Jahangir's new bride was already powerful enough to be asking for gifts for herself. Knowing the obvious, that he would get nowhere at court without the necessary bribes, Hawkins said: "I sent my broker to seeke out for jewels fitting for the Kings sister [Shahzada Khanam] and new paramour, and likewise for this new Vizir and his sonne."[254] To be so powerful so soon after her marriage was a sure sign that, in the future, Roe could not forget the pleasures of the chief queen. Nur Jahan's needs were immediately apparent to the English ambassador who in January of 1616, shortly after his arrival at court, noted that "the Queene must be presented" with something whenever he came even though he did not approve of this "daylye bribing."[255] During Jahangir's famous seizure of Roe's goods, Roe protested at the beginning that some among his things had been "entended for the Prince and Normahall." Jahangir's response, that since "the Prince, Normahall and he were all one" all presents should go to him, brought no reply from Roe who knew full well that Nur Jahan must be remembered for presents personally—as with one of the two glass chests he noted later during that same exchange.[256] Afterward he would be advised by Asaf Khan "to giue his sister Normahall some toy,"[257] which he would do posthaste.[258] Roe complained early on that the queen's expectations of him were extravagant: "they did expect ten times as much from me as from Mr. Edwards, and spake it openly: that now an ambassador was come, a great man, they should receive proportionable gifts."[259] And when Nur Jahan's expectations were not met, Roe was fully apprised for, as he said of her late in 1616, the "neglect of her last year I have felt heavily."[260] Without her favor, however, Roe could make no headway at court and he left each time knowing that "toys for presents . . . above all things prevail with the King and stop the mouths of all the aforesaid," that is, of Nur Jahan and her faction.[261]

Roe's gifts of wine, pictures, knives, precious stones, mirrors, and fancy cloths[262] were not left unrequited, however, for Jahangir and his family returned gifts that were, they judged, in kind. Roe, for example, received several servants from the emperor and his queen, some of whom came to the ambassador as slaves, whom he refused to buy for himself but instead offered to ransom as free citizens.[263] Jahangir also sent Roe various kinds of food, deeming fresh fruits like muskmelons,[264] wines,[265] and freshly slaughtered animals like elk,[266] wild pig,[267] and venison,[268] some of which he had killed himself in hunting, as especially prized rewards for his efforts. Roe did not often refuse a present of food, as his own board had been at best a flexible item on the Company's provision for him, but he did refuse other grander gifts from the emperor, believing them not to be a part of his office's protocol. Said Terry, asked why "he did not desire some good and great gifts at his hands . . . the Ambassador would reply, that he came not thither to beg any thing of" the emperor,[269] his only reward being, quite sincerely, good service to the Company.

Roe's overall views of his embassy to India were generally negative. He was, first, highly frustrated by the gift-giving needs of the court and overwhelmed with feelings of inadequacy because the expectations of him were so much more than he could produce. His final advice to the Company was to downgrade the post in the future to that of a merchant so that imperial desires, and indeed involvement, would be comparably low.[270]

Second, from the start Roe saw the Indians he dealt with, and indeed the Mughals themselves, as woefully indifferent to what he felt was proper protocol and etiquette. From their initial attempt to search his men even after an agreement to the contrary was made,[271] to a list of abuses in Surat to himself, his goods, and his men,[272] to the general rudeness and bad manners he felt affronted him everywhere, Roe responded with what he hoped was a tempered demeanor. If at first he vowed to change the behavior of those around him—"I was resolued to bring these People to a better vnderstanding or to perish in yt"[273]—he later sank back into a passive resignation that felt abuse almost to its limits but did not try to change it. As he said in early 1618: "My toyle with barbarous vniust people is beyond patience,"[274] a major revision of his earlier view that English treatment in India was "so bad . . . that [it] will require much patience to suffer, much Industry to sett vpright."[275] Roe did not often take personally what he saw as insults, attributing mismatches of cultural behavior instead to peculiarities in the Indian perception of the English ambassadorial office.[276] Some time later, however, Della Valle would charge the English with mismanaging their business in India, assuming somewhat mistakenly as they did that the Mughals "hath great need of the Sea" when in fact most of Jahangir's revenues came from his lands. What was seen as insulting behavior, the Portuguese trader continued, arose rather from the English sense of self-importance, "for it is not possible for a few strangers and immigrants to contest with and get the better of a great King in his own Country."[277]

Roe's experience in India was colored, third, by an increasing anger at the power of the junta. Certain at the beginning that to win the king he must win the junta and convinced at the end that it was the junta that had done him in—"the faction I knew was too strong"[278]—Roe increasingly identified Nur Jahan as the chief obstructionist. To focus thus on specific people, indeed on a specific person, as the cause of his frustration allowed Roe the luxury of an easy rationale for his somewhat more complicated grievances. Fourth, Roe was beset with a strong dislike of the country to which he had been sent. Terry entitled an early section in his *A Voyage to East-India*, "Of the Discommodities, Inconveniences, and Annoyances, that are to be found or met withal in this Empire," and proceeded to describe at length the myriads of "venomous and pernicious creatures" to be encountered, the fickle and destructive monsoon rains, and the excessive temperatures that are "so hot to us English, that we should be every day stewed in our own moisture."[279] Roe's early sickness[280] and the "house of Mudd" that he lived in "which I was enforced to build halfe"[281] did nothing but encourage his view that "this is the dullest, basest place that euer I saw"[282] and that while there he was forced to "liue a miserable life."[283] The "base . . . Conditions"[284] in which he found himself coupled with the perceived lack of civility to him and to his entourage often resulted in earnest pleas to be recalled to England. Said Roe to the Company toward the end of his first year at court: "I assure you I can doe you better seruice at home" and so hope that you will send for me soon.[285] And Terry ended his *Voyage* with an apology "for the leanness and lowness of my stile" but hoped that his readers would understand for it was the Indians among whom he lived "which made me rude."[286]

The harshness with which Roe and his embassy viewed their whole Indian experience was balanced, however, by three important elements. First was the ever-present hope for trading contracts for England that, though it dimmed over time, did provide a continuous source of stability and inspiration, especially with the knowledge of the Company's great resources at home and the potential bonanza in profit should they succeed. Second was Roe's increasing facility at maneuvering elements in the Mughal court. As he saw the junta weakening, for example, he learned how to use each opportunity to his best advantage: when a fine pearl was acquired by the English factors, Roe sold it at substantially less than cost to Asaf Khan in the hopes of buying favor,[287] and whenever the issue of injustices suffered by the English came up before the emperor, Roe knew how to play successfully to Jahangir's sympathy for him against various junta members.[288] Finally was Roe's genuine affection for Jahangir, which was apparent from the very beginning and which lasted throughout the duration of his stay. "He is very affable, and of a cheerefull countenance, without pride,"[289] said Roe of the emperor, and he "respectes vs very well and is ready to grant all reasonable demandes."[290] Roe's good feeling toward Jahangir was based on the king's receptive demeanor toward him, "I stand . . . in extraordinarie Grace with the King, who is gentle, soft, and good of disposition."[291]

In assessing the reasons for Roe's inconclusive results at the Mughal court, we must raise the issue, central to our larger concerns, of whether Nur Jahan actively obstructed the efforts of the English ambassador. Roe openly described the work of her stepson Shah Jahan in blocking the trade of the English ships in early 1616: "He [Shah Jahan] had a ship to set out for the Red Sea and was willing to wink, yea, to encourage his ministers to molest and hinder the despatch of our fleet until his ship were clear."[292] Roe did not, however, record any acts of the queen herself that were as blatantly hostile to the English enterprise as this, but he did continually refer to her definitive influence over the others in positions of power. Nur Jahan, recorded Roe of Jahangir, "conducts all his actions" and each one of his decisions or directives "depends on her."[293] While some, like Roe's modern chronicler Michael Brown, see in the *Embassy* references a substantial case against Nur Jahan, a clear argument in fact that, because "she had grown accustomed to reaping handsome profits," she felt "threatened by the European powers whose purpose was to lure the trade of India into their own ships" and therefore "used her influence against the foreign representatives in her husband's court,"[294] another reading of the text gives less conclusive results.

We will argue below that there were a number of reasons why Roe left India without the treaties he wanted and that Nur Jahan's influence may or may not have had anything to do with his lack of success. As for what she actually did with regard to the English, we have no way of knowing precisely except that she was a presence behind the *parda* screen whenever Roe paid court to Jahangir and that she did have considerable, and perhaps even final, power over the junta's directives at this time. But based on these generalities, we cannot charge her with specific acts of hostility or obstruction as we can in the case of her brother and stepson. The evidence just isn't there. As for the motivations she may have had, the possibilities are likewise inconclusive. On the one hand, she may admittedly have wanted exclusive or at least a proportionately larger share of the rights to the profits from overseas trade, but on the other, she may, being the shrewd businesswoman that she was, have seen that there was far more to be gained by expanding her trading networks to include the English than not. We do know that she wanted to use the English channels available to her to procure goods and that, in fact, because of this, the English were to her a commercial opportunity not a commercial foil. In the end, it is probable that Nur Jahan was more indifferent to the English than anything else. Her time and energies were taken up with so much other junta business that Roe's perception of obstruction may simply have been benign unconcern.

Roe's inability to formalize trading relations between England and the Mughal government before he left in 1619 may have had as much to do with historical circumstance and the personality of Jahangir as it did with the quality of Roe's efforts or any malicious dealings on the part of Nur Jahan. Historically, the English were not the first Europeans of recent times to try to set up trading arrangements with the Mughals. The Portuguese had gotten there first, and when the English came, the earlier arrivals did everything they could to belittle their new European competitors. Moreover, when Roe's embassy did succeed in getting a foothold in Jahangir's court, ambassadors from rival governments continued to show up with larger and better presents for the emperor. Although in general Roe seemed to have captured Jahangir's ear during his stay in India, representatives not only from Portugal[295] but from Holland[296] and Persia[297] as well only heightened the Englishman's anxiety each time they approached Jahangir with the gifts. Finally, since the English came in the interest of trade, their concerns fell in naturally with those of a lower strata of Indian society. In spite of the fact that Roe was an official ambassador and a direct representative of his country's ruler, Jahangir may not ever have been able to see him as more than a glorified merchant. Try as the emperor might to change his expectations of Roe,[298] the Englishman's ultimate desire for a trading agreement permanently cast him amongst those bound strictly to commercial concerns and therefore beyond Jahangir's imperial purview.

Jahangir himself and the habits of Indian culture may have contributed just as much, if not more, to Roe's undoing. First, and perhaps most important, there was no real market for English goods in India. English cloth was too heavy and too hot for the Indian climate[299]—even though it came in the beautiful scarlet red so admired by Hindus—and knives, leatherwork, mirrors, and fancy textile work could not be sold in great quantities as there were abundant industries in these crafts already on the subcontinent. Second, rumors of unruly English behavior on the streets of Surat—"drincking and quarreling . . . and draweing swoordes in the Custome house"[300]—had reached the imperial family and, despite Roe's defense of his countrymen, the image of brawling foreigners on his shores may have set Jahangir against any trade that might be disruptive. Third, in spite of the fact that Roe had wanted a civilized etiquette to prevail over a fair and just agreement that would obligate each party to items of mutual interest, the need for a binding "legal" contract was neither understandable nor desirable to Jahangir. As Brown has observed, the kind of agreement put forward by Roe "was repugnant to the Mogul's idea of sovereignty because, by binding him to the performance of certain provisions, it sought to limit his future freedom of action." To make matters worse, such an agreement would be "with the representative of an obscure and distant state"[301] and would subject Jahangir to certain obligations on his own sovereign soil. For an emperor who increasingly thought of himself as ruler of the whole immediate world, the possibility of such a treaty, just as he was, was not only unthinkable but outright insulting as well.

All of these resulted, finally, in a general indifference to the English mission. Although there was mild interest in overseas trade, in particular for the luxury items procurable for the court, and although Muslims did need the protection of English ships for the pilgrimage to Mecca, Mughal benefit from a sustained relationship with the English did not hold considered promise. Jahangir did not once mention the English mission in his *Tuzuk*,[302] in spite of the fact that at least one miniature painting of the period showed an Englishman at court [see Figure 6–3]. In this painting, Jahangir invested a courtier with a robe of honor before an audience, which included a European who, though not identified, was almost certainly Sir Thomas Roe. Another painting, "Jahangir Preferring a Sufi Shaykh to Kings," now in the Freer, had along its edge a likeness of King James I of England. Although Roe preserved letters from Jahangir to James in his *Embassy*,[303] Jahangir made no mention of any such correspondence and, in the Freer painting, clearly meant to downgrade the English king's significance in the ultimate scheme of things.

Roe's mission, then, was incomplete. He was not in the end able to get Jahangir to sign a formal treaty covering the wide-ranging issues in English–Mughal trade he had outlined earlier. But he was able to get Shah Jahan to issue a *farman* covering the more specific province of the English factory at Surat, over which the prince still had jurisdiction. Roe successfully got Shah Jahan to agree to free trade for the English factors there, general respect and courtesy for their business dealings, freedom of worship and of arms, and the grant of considerably substantial living conditions.[304] By Roe's own account, he had also "gotten many bribes restored, many debtes, many extortions, and Commandes to take noe more,"[305] but when it was all finally assessed, Roe knew that though "I shall trauell much in myne owne eies . . . [I shall] performe little in yours."[306] Of the aftereffects of Roe, Pelsaert said: "Formerly the English maintained an ambassador at the Camp, an arrangement which was very expensive to their Company; but it has now been abandoned, because a factor who sells their goods at Court can also look after all their incidental business, and obtain farmans, or rescripts, from the King."[307] More important than the specifics of his accomplishments, however, were the seeds of future ties that were sown. The Company was now more realistically apprised of the conditions necessary for any future attempts at commercial agreement, and the Mughal government was now privy, more than ever before, to the particulars involved in international trade with Europe. After this encounter, Nur Jahan's personal dealings with the English were somewhat diminished, but her role in the activities of this early envoy, however two-faced it might have been, contributed substantially to the slow and perhaps evenhanded fashion by which the Indian entrance into larger international markets took place. On the one hand, her hedging of an early contract with Roe's embassy may well have helped protect the current flourishing of Mughal culture and, in the process, have forestalled a ravaging of Indian resources. But on the other, the considerable trading that she did do, with and without the facilities of the English, may well have helped infuse new elements into Mughal culture that, in part, gave it its health.

7

Breakup of the Junta (1620–1627)

When ["the wretch," Shah Jahan] . . . acts in this manner, I appeal to the justice of Allah that He may never again regard him with favour.

The Tuzuk-i-Jahangiri translated by A. Rogers
and edited by Henry Beveridge

The effectiveness of the alliances made within Nur Jahan's junta began to wane around the turn of the decade in 1620. Coming off the victories of Shah Jahan in the Deccan in 1617, the group was heady now with a sense of limitlessness to its power and rightness to its course. These victories, it seemed, signified the ascendancy of rule by counsel and wisdom through consensus, but revealed little of the turmoil possible when counsel would become command and consensus cartel. Bubonic plague had broken out in 1616, introduced into northern India most probably from Central Asia,[1] and it continued to devastate the country during cold weather for the next eight years.[2] Moreover in November of 1618, two heavenly phenomena appeared that lasted for about a month: one, in the southern sky, was shaped "like a pot boiling out fire"[3] or "a sickle"[4] and the other, in the northern sky, was a comet.[5] The monsoon failed that year and the famine, pestilence, and mortality that came in the years following were blamed on the appearance of these astrological signs.[6] In the wake of these occurrences, the power of the junta declined, and the *Iqbalnama* went so far as to say that "through the effects of this [heavenly] phenomenon . . . a misunderstanding arose between His Majesty and the fortunate Prince Shah Jahan. The disturbances which thus originated lasted seven or eight years. What blood was shed in the country! and what families were ruined!"[7]

Whatever the connection between the junta's decline and heavenly disturbances, it was clear that the alliance was weakening as early as 1617. On October 21, Roe noted the dangerous rift he saw between Shah Jahan and Nur Jahan over patronage for English trade when Asaf Khan came to promise that, with his sister now as "Protectresse" of the English, "the Prince would not meddle."[8]

This rift would widen in the next few years, and with the second phase of Nur Jahan's ascendancy, Shah Jahan would pull decidedly away from his early benefactress and become steadily and more clearly a contending power in his own right.

At the height of the junta's influence, the four protagonists—Nur Jahan, Shah Jahan, Itimaduddaula, and Asaf Khan—ruled over as prosperous and extensive an India as ever was to be under the Mughals. The capital city of Agra, for example, had become a large, open, and sprawling trade center of great traffic, where Hindus mixed with Muslims, rich with poor, and foreigners with natives. Trade, both domestic and foreign, passed through the great markets of the city and her surrounds and tied this particular seat of Mughal power to provinces in all parts of India and, therefore, to much of the prosperity of the realm.

The decline of the junta was linked perhaps to no sequence of events more than to the successive loss of parents by junta members. The first to die in this illustrious series was the mother of Shah Jahan, known as Jagat Gosaini in the *Tuzuk* and earlier as the daughter of the Mota, or "Fat," Raja.[9] She died in the spring of 1619, and Jahangir noted the death succinctly, saying simply that she had "attained the mercy of God."[10] Whatever his own grief for his wife was, it went unnoted in the memoirs, but the grief of his son for the mother was apparently substantial. Shah Jahan's need for solace was so strong, in fact, that he had to be brought back to the main palace to mourn his loss.[11]

The events of this period took place against the background of Jahangir's increasingly poor health. Jahangir had never taken good care of himself, but he had a robust constitution and seemed to be able to avoid, sometimes treacherously closely, the calamitous ends that befell both his brothers. The years of wine, opium, and general excess, however, began to catch up with him, and in 1620 while on one of his trips to Kashmir, he noted in his memoirs a shortness of breath and difficulty in breathing.[12] Later, in 1621, the difficulty in breathing returned, now severely intensified, and he drew about him the best physicians known in the country. One of his own physicians who had accompanied him to Kashmir, Hakim Ruhullah, gave him some medicine that worked for a time but could not prevent the return of Jahangir's painful symptoms when he came down from the hills. Another personal physician, Hakim Rukna, who had been excused to stay in Agra, now joined Jahangir and gave him "warm and dry" medicines, but these too did not help as Jahangir's pain increased and he became considerably weakened.[13] To make matters worse, Hakim Sadra, one of the chief physicians of Persia whom Jahangir had honored extensively at court and to whom he had given the title Masihuzzaman, "Messiah of the Age," refused at this point to treat the emperor saying, "I have no such reliance on my knowledge that I can undertake the cure."[14] Hakim Sadra's reluctance, whether for professional or personal reasons, was compounded by that of a fourth physician, Hakim Abul Qasim, who said that he was "suspicious and afraid . . . terrified and vexed" and could not, therefore, help Jahangir out of his affliction. Jahangir then gave up all professional advice and yielded his care to the Supreme Physician,[15] deciding to drown himself in wine in what appeared in his memoirs to be suicidal excess.

As the weather became hotter, Jahangir's condition grew worse, and Nur Jahan—"whose skill and experience are greater than those of the physicians"[16]—took over complete control of the nursing. Although she had previously approved of the remedies ordered by the court physicians, Nur Jahan now tried a new course: regular decreases in Jahangir's cups of wine coupled with attention so obsessive it could only have suited a child. Nur Jahan's watchful control over her husband's consumption of wine and other unsuitable foods was successful. In return for a year of "severe illness" that ended "well and in safety," Jahangir allowed his wife great extravagance in preparing the festivities for his solar weighing, at which all supporters who had been loyal to him during his infirmity were to be rewarded.[17] Jahangir's illness, in the long run, however, did not abate, and he continued to ask for divine mercy and to search for healthy climates (like Kashmir) for the rest of his life.[18] His physical condition later deteriorated to such a point, in fact, that at the beginning of 1623 he had to give over the writing of his memoirs completely to Mutamid Khan, "who knows my temperament ana understands my words."[19]

The increasing severity of Jahangir's illness—his weakness, his shortness of breath, and at times his mental debilitation—posed a dilemma for Nur Jahan. On the one hand, as his health faded she could have taken efforts to consolidate power in her own hands and to shape the government and array of alliances to her best advantage. On the other, however, her marriage to Jahangir was the very reason she had power and if he died of his excesses Nur Jahan would no longer have a sovereign base of her own from which to work. As Jahangir became sicker, then, Nur Jahan, had to shore up those alliances she did have and to establish new ones fruitful to her and her lineage should the worst happen, all the while trying to preserve and extend the life that had already, for so many years, given her the throne. Central to this drama was Shah Jahan, who was becoming increasingly powerful and independent and who, she realized, would probably not allow her comparable supremacy at the court if he were to succeed his father. As Shah Jahan began to drift away, Nur Jahan was obliged to turn to others she might use as tools, others whose claims were equal to those of Shah Jahan and who she thought, in their pliancy to her, would be willing to fight the current contender for the throne.

If the condition of Jahangir's health provided the backdrop for the decay of the junta, three more or less contemporaneous events acted on the junta's alliances to bring them to an almost complete state of collapse: (1) the marriage of Nur Jahan's daughter to another son of Jahangir, Shahryar; (2) the deaths of Nur Jahan's parents, which deprived the junta of its elder advisers; and (3) the revival of problems in the Deccan and the ensuing death of Khusrau. The deciding event, perhaps, was the marriage of Nur Jahan's daughter, Ladli Begam, by the empress's first husband, Sher Afgan, to Jahangir's youngest surviving son in April of 1621.

The marriage between Ladli Begam and Shahryar was by no means a love match. Years of negotiated matchmaking had consumed the time of Nur Jahan, who had wanted her daughter to marry into her second husband's lineage so as to ensure the presence of her own descendants at the imperial court as well as the continued prominence of her own advice and counsel on sovereign matters. There is little evidence that Nur Jahan seriously approached Shah Jahan as a future son-in-law. He had married her niece, Arjumand Banu Begam, in a love match that was consummated in April of 1612, and although there were other wives and although there is a tradition that maintains that Ladli Begam was Arjumand's rival for Khurram's hand,[20] Arjumand was clearly his chief wife in all respects. Instead, the most talked about "negotiations" were those that took place in 1616 and 1617 between Nur Jahan and Jahangir's eldest son, Khusrau.

Della Valle's famous account of these negotiations stated that Nur Jahan had frequently offered her daughter to Khusrau, who had refused each time either because he loved his first wife too much or because he "scorn'd" Nur Jahan's daughter. At this time Khusrau was in prison, and Della Valle said that Nur Jahan promised him immediate freedom if he would consent to marry her daughter. Khusrau continued to refuse, despite the protests of his wife, and continued to enjoy an imprisonment voluntarily shared by this wife, who never ceased "to persuade him to marry *Nurmahal's* Daughter."[21] The love between Khusrau and his wife, in fact, was well known to all chroniclers of the tradition, and the English adventurer, Thomas Coryat, told the story of Jahangir's building an escape-proof prison for Khusrau so that the imperial entourage could hunt in peace and of Khusrau's wife begging on bended knee to be put there too. As Coryat effused, "she utterly refused any other comfort then to be the companion of her husbands miseries."[22] Despite these obstacles, Nur Jahan's marital negotiations on behalf of her daughter continued, becoming well known to the English as well, with Roe noting on August 25, 1617: "This day Asaph Chan feasted Normahall [and?] the Prince Sultan Corsoroone; as is reported, to make a firme alliance, and that he will bring away a Wife, by his Fathers importunitie. This will beget his full libertie, and our proud Masters ruine."[23]

The brokering was eventually a failure, however, and in despair over not successfully persuading Khusrau to marry her daughter, Nur Jahan turned to Shahryar. She had hopes of finding in him a well-placed husband for Ladli Begam and of bringing him forward, in the face of Shah Jahan's willful independence of her, as an alternate successor to the throne. Shahryar was the youngest surviving son of Jahangir, having been born to a concubine in 1605. By reputation he had shown little promise of greatness and had, as Prasad notes, a "docile nature, feeble mind, and imbecile character."[24] According to van den Broecke, Shahryar was "without sense or understanding, and not fit to govern a kingdom"[25] and again, to the *Padshahnama*, was in "want of capacity and intelligence, . . . [and had therefore] got the nickname of *Nashudani*, 'Good-for-nothing.' "[26] One anecdote, however, preserved by Hawkins suggested instead that Shahryar was a young man capable of showing great restraint and courage. When Shahryar was seven, apparently, his father asked him if he wanted to accompany him on a short trip, and the child replied he would go or stay depending upon his father's desire. Jahangir was not pleased by this diplomacy and struck Shahryar, who refused to cry. When Jahangir pressed him on this restraint, Shahryar replied that his nurses told him it was shameful for a prince to cry when pained, at which point Jahangir, so infuriated by this speech, had a bodkin pushed through his son's cheek. Although Shahryar bled profusely, he did not cry, and Hawkins pronounced, ironically, that there "is great hope of this child to exceed all the rest."[27]

Certainly Nur Jahan had her own hopes for Shahryar, and perhaps because of the qualities earning him the nickname of "Good-for-nothing," Ladli's mother thought he would serve as an excellent puppet in her efforts to keep the throne in the family. Accordingly, Shahryar and Ladli Begam were betrothed in December of 1620 and a great exchange of gifts in honor of the tie took place, with feasts and entertainment provided by the bride-to-be's grandfather Itimaduddaula.[28] The two were married in April of 1621 in Agra at the usual places for such family gatherings—the putting on of henna took place in the home of Jahangir's mother, Maryamuzzamani, and the marriage feast itself took place in the home of Itimaduddaula. In honor of the occasion, a happy Jahangir gave his son a jewelled coat, turban, and cummerbund, and two horses with fancy saddles,[29] and raised his son's *mansab* to 8,000 *zat* and 4,000 *suwar*.[30] At the time, both bride and groom were about seventeen.

As a result of the marriage between Ladli Begam and Shahryar, the prestige of the Nur Jahan family was greatly enhanced. Nevertheless, an irreparable cleavage in the solidarity of the lineage was now visible as Asaf Khan, whose daughter was married to Shah Jahan, became increasingly anxious and mistrustful of his sister's activities. Itimaduddaula was able to prevent the cleavage from becoming too cancerous, but he was old and, with his death in early 1622, the now fragile bonds of the junta fell apart. More important than the simple realignment the marriage involved, however, was the surge in activity that from this time on propelled the Asaf Khan/Shah Jahan faction forward as its members adjusted and compensated for the shift in power the new marriage lines had brought about.

The second set of occurrences that overwhelmed the junta was the deaths of Nur Jahan's parents. Asmat Begam, Nur Jahan's mother, who had traveled impoverished out of Persia with her husband and their young children and had watched over her family as its members had secured increasingly influential positions at the court, died in October of 1621. Jahangir's eulogy of her "amiable qualities" was touching, and he wrote: "Without exaggeration, in purity of disposition and in wisdom and the excellencies that are the ornament of women no Mother of the Age was ever born equal to her, and I did not value her less than my own mother."[31]

Itimaduddaula's grief at this wife's death was considerable, and it became even greater when he saw the sorrow of their son Asaf Khan, who in his distress had abandoned all conventions of society. Nur Jahan's grief is mentioned only briefly, but we can be sure that the loss of so important a mainstay in her personal and social affairs was devastating. Jahangir himself, by his own account, rose to the occasion and administered "the balm of kindness" to all aggrieved survivors for many days thereafter.[32]

Itimaduddaula's grief, born with the great resignation expected of an old but courtly man, eventually took its toll. He had outwardly controlled his emotions over the loss of his wife,[33] but the inward cost was substantial and at the end of January of 1622 he himself succumbed. The death of Itimaduddaula occurred as Jahangir's entourage was camped at the village of Bahlwan near Kangra during the imperial couple's second tour to Kashmir. Jahangir had gone out to inspect the fort at Kangra, leaving his sickened father-in-law behind in the tent. When, on the next day, he heard that Itimaduddaula had gotten worse and that his condition was now thought hopeless, Jahangir returned to camp immediately, noting that he did so not only because he bore great affection for the old man, but also because he "could not bear the agitation of Nur Jahan Begam."[34] Jahangir and Nur Jahan stayed by her father's pillow for two more hours and finally, that evening, Itimaduddaula died.[35] He was eventually buried in an exquisite tomb of marble and *pietra dura* inlay in Agra [see Figure 7–1], which was designed and built by his daughter in her father's memory.[36]

The family's grief at the chief minister's death rivaled only the great sense of loss felt by the kingdom. Itimaduddaula had been, except for occasional suggestions of financial misdealing, a man of impeccable character. He was exceptionally learned, excellent at letter writing and conversation, and especially skilled at running the affairs of the empire. His advice to Jahangir was greatly valued, and

FIGURE 7–1. General view, tomb of Itimaduddaula, Agra. Courtesy of the Archaeological Survey of India, New Delhi.

he had been particularly helpful to the emperor in deciding matters of individual reparation: to release Diyanat Khan from the Gwalior fort and return his confiscated property in 1615,[37] to appoint Raja Man as the leader of the attack on the fort of Kangra in 1616,[38] to request that the negligent Itiqad Khan be allowed to pay his respects to the emperor in 1617,[39] to allow Allahabad Khan to return to the court after fleeing the country without permission, and to appoint Abdullah Khan, son of Hakim Nuruddin of Tehran, among the personal servants of the emperor.[40] In this way Itimaduddaula had become known for his generous and compassionate response to all petitioners. Jahangir noted, for example, that "no one ever went to Itimad-ud-daula with a petition or on business who turned from him in an injured frame of mind,"[41] for he was always pleasing and hopeful to him who was in need. The high esteem in which Itimaduddaula was held by the emperor was marked by his frequent raises in *mansabs*, his free roaming before unveiled women in their palaces, and his receipt of the emperor's turban from Jahangir's own hands.

Immediately after the death, Jahangir moved to transfer the minister's holdings to an appropriate heir. Following the rule of escheat, all that Itimaduddaula owned reverted back to the crown, which could then do with the estate as it pleased.[42] Jahangir had regularly conferred such estates accrued by death upon the offspring of the noble, but in cases past these offspring had usually been male.[43] Jahangir now bestowed "the establishment and everything belonging to the government and Amirship of Itimad-ud-daula . . . [upon] Nur Jahan Begam" and ordered her drums and orchestra to be played immediately after those of the King.[44] What was unusual about this was not so much that he passed on an inheritance to a woman, but that he passed on all of it to her. Ordinarily, the women and children belonging to the family of a deceased noble were "given enough to live on, but no more," and since every part of the property in question had been carefully and publicly inventoried, no chance for concealing part of the fortune or of tampering with the "designated needs" of the survivors was possible.[45] In passing everything on to Nur Jahan, then, Jahangir completely bypassed a logical recipient to a major portion of the estate, her brother Asaf Khan. The emperor immediately compounded the insult by appointing Khwaja Abul Hasan, a noble not related to Itimaduddaula who had distinguished himself in the Deccan, to the position of *diwan-i kul*, or supreme *diwan*.[46]

We can only guess at Nur Jahan's role in the making of these decisions. Jahangir was, to be sure, grief-stricken over the loss of his chief minister and still, as always, suffering from indulgence in wine and opium. Nevertheless, he must have at least approved if not encouraged the outright neglect of Asaf Khan and his daughter, the wife of Shah Jahan. The inheritance decision, suggested if not actually enacted by Nur Jahan, not only reflected the existing rift within the inner circle of Itimaduddaula's family, but also served, by design to be sure, to cut off those members of the junta whom Jahangir and his wife already suspected of seditious loyalties or whose growing power and independence they were coming to fear: Asaf Khan and, indirectly, Shah Jahan.[47] With Itimaduddaula dead, and with this insult so blatantly and publicly handed down, moreover, Asaf Khan and Shah Jahan would now become increasingly opposed to the interests of Nur Jahan, who would begin to act more frequently on her own. For the remaining years of Jahangir's reign, then, five years of slow but consuming debilitation in the emperor's physical and mental state, Nur Jahan would rule much more closely from within the walls of the women's palaces.

The third and final affair to weaken the bonds of the junta was the revival of problems in the Deccan and the subsequent death of Khusrau. By 1620 the situation in the Deccan had again become critical. Jahangir's enemy, Malik Amber of Ahmadnagar, had fashioned coalitions with leaders in Bijapur and Golconda and had recruited about sixty thousand troops, including rebellious Maratha bands, to defend the Deccan. He had violated the treaty he made with the Mughals only two months earlier, and as a result of the outbreak of hostilities, a good deal of the territory conquered by the Mughals had been liberated by Malik Amber's army.[48] The Mughal commander Abdur Rahim, the Khan-khanan, had repeatedly asked Jahangir for reinforcements, and because of his past military successes in Mewar, the Deccan, and Gujarat, Shah Jahan seemed the natural choice to head such an expedition to the south.

Jahangir had become suspicious of Shah Jahan of late, however, for his seditious alliances had now grown strong and he had built up an experienced army of his own.[49] Under Nur Jahan's urgings, though, Jahangir finally decided to send Shah Jahan anyway in the hopes that this second time his son could match his successes of 1617. Shah Jahan, however, refused to go unless Jahangir send along with him his eldest brother, Khusrau, arguing from the tender affection he held for him.[50] Jahangir "justly doubted his sincerity"[51] here, and the general consensus of the time and later seems to be that Shah Jahan was, in fact, worried that if he were to be so far away from the center of power, his brother, who was now being treated a bit more leniently at court, would be a clear contender for the throne should Jahangir die. Shah Jahan was worried, and rightly so, that in his absence, at the very least, various factions would consolidate their power behind his back and, at the most, he would lose what he thought to be the just dessert of his labors. And so he pressed for Khusrau to accompany him to the Deccan, in the hopes of depriving Nur Jahan of his popular brother as a candidate for the throne. As Terry had reported in 1618: "Sultan Caroom . . . raised and kept together very great forces, and stood upon his guard, and would not disband 'till his father had delivered his eldest son, Sultan Coobseroo, into his hands."[52]

Nur Jahan, however, already had a history of trying to get rid of Khusrau. During the period when Khurram was still her favorite stepson, she had tried several times to get Jahangir to put Khusrau in Khurram's care and, if we believe Roe's 1616 account, to engineer with the help of the rest of the junta Khusrau's death.[53] Khusrau's refusal to marry Ladli Begam, it seems, permanently embittered Nur Jahan toward him and this rancor continued for some time after the period 1616 through 1617.[54] Moreover, Nur Jahan did not need Khusrau's partisanship for she now foresaw a puppet all her own in the person of her future son-in-law, Shahryar, whom she could manipulate freely and mount quickly to the throne should her own husband pass on. And so it was that for the last time in their joint careers Nur Jahan, Shah Jahan, and Asaf Khan acted unanimously in their bid to see Khusrau accompany Shah Jahan to the Deccan. "Nur Jahan and her brother, Asaf Khan, begged the King to put Khusrau in the charge of his brother Sultan Khurram, and to send Khurram on an expedition to the Deccan."[55] It was apparently against his better judgment and under much pressure from this oddly reunited junta that Jahangir capitulated and gave his permission to Shah Jahan to take Khusrau along with him. The gravity of the situation in the Deccan necessitated, he felt, some kind of precipitous action.

> *Sultan Chorrom*, after the alliance that he made with *Asaf Chan*, so wrought by the means of his Father in law, and *Nurmahal*, his Aunt, that the King granted him the prisoner Sultan Chosrou into his own power, taking him out of the hands of him that kept him, and committing him to keep, yet with order to use him very well and have great care of him.[56]

Thus, toward the end of December in 1620, Shah Jahan was dispatched by his father with many gifts of honor, including an elephant from Nur Jahan, and with many troops to the Deccan.[57]

It is in all likelihood that Nur Jahan knew what might happen to Khusrau while in the charge of Shah Jahan and far away from the watchful eye of the emperor. The Shujauddins are quite convinced that Nur Jahan knew, and perhaps even hoped, that Khusrau would meet some unnatural end, thus doing away with his candidacy for the throne altogether. They also argue that Nur Jahan actually planned that Shah Jahan would be so clearly perceived as the instigator of the foul deed that his candidacy would thereby be permanently discredited.[58] C. Pant does not agree with this "two birds" theory, however, saying that "Nur Jahan definitely played in the hands of the faction without probably knowing its consequences,"[59] but given what we know of the empress such naivety is highly unlikely. That Nur Jahan should not know the consequences of sending Shah Jahan and Khusrau far away from the court together does not fit well with the general picture of her as an astute and careful manipulator of power. Although her strong hatred of Khusrau is hinted at by several sources,[60] it was probably her growing apprehension of Shah Jahan that above all made her urge Jahangir's final decision. "She saw the great lines of ambition," says Dow, "and an unrelenting perseverance in pursuit of power, in all his conduct."[61] With Shah Jahan and Khusrau out of the way where nature might take its barbarous course, then, the empress would have a freer hand with which to arrange the remaining lines of power around her.

Shah Jahan was sent off with great fanfare. He left from his father's court in Lahore and this meeting, in December 1620, in which Jahangir gave him many supplies and presents preparatory to the trip into the Deccan, was to be the final one, the last time Shah Jahan and his father ever saw each other. For most of the next seven years after the Deccan affair, Shah Jahan was a rebel, a fugitive, and a nonentity with regard to his father's rule, not surfacing again until his own accession to the throne from 1627 to 1628.

Leaving Lahore, Shah Jahan proceeded southward, routing the rebels and pushing them farther away from their strongholds of power and, in so doing, scoring major victories near Burhanpar, in Khirki, and in Ahmadnagar.[62] His expedition was without a doubt a success, taking him only six months to recapture power in the Deccan and receive Malik Amber's surrender, and his father, grateful for his son's triumph, rewarded him and his men with fine presents of jewels and clothes.[63] Shah Jahan, in his turn, sent on to Jahangir all those presents of tribute given to him by the now-subject kings of the Deccan.[64] Celebrating their victory, Shah Jahan and his men then returned to Burhanpur to rest and to consolidate their newly reestablished base of power.

Jahangir's reaction to his son's second set of victories in the Deccan was curious. Although he noted the victories in his memoirs and gave presents in due course, the *Tuzuk* prose was neutral and the gifts paltry. Jahangir's somewhat cold response here can be attributed either to his increasingly poor health (but notice how inspired the prose was in the same pages when he saw a zebra for the first time[65]) or to the dampening influence of Nur Jahan. Although by 1621 there was not yet an open struggle between Shah Jahan and the throne, there was certainly a struggle of wills. Jahangir may have increasingly feared his powerful son, whose ambitions he knew were on the throne, and therefore did not, for seeming a fool, celebrate the Deccan successes too much.

What happened next was given only three lines in the *Tuzuk*, but made much of by other contemporary sources. Shah Jahan and his entourage had been staying in Burhanpur in the Deccan, and from there in the north, on January 29, 1622, Jahangir received word from his third son that Khusrau had died of colic pains (*qulanj*).[66] At first everyone accepted the official story that Khusrau had died a natural death.[67] Jahangir made only short and neutral notice of the death in the *Tuzuk* before passing on to report other news of the time. European sources, however, and a few Persian sources were suspicious, and in their final drafts were quick to level charges of murder at the victim's younger brother. Terry, for example, said simply that Shah Jahan "strangled that most gallant Prince his eldest brother,"[68] but the Dutch sources of a slightly later period went into much greater detail.

The most popular version of the story was that while he consulted his ministers and then himself left on a hunting trip, Shah Jahan had ordered a slave named Raza Bahadur[69] to go into Khusrau's room in the middle of the night. Knocking on the door, Raza pretended that he and his companions had brought letters from the king and imperial robes for Khusrau to try on. When Khusrau refused to open up, not believing the story, Raza and his men unhinged the door, rushed in, and attacked the sleeper. Although the still partially blinded Khusrau defended himself bravely and screamed loudly to awaken his party, it was to no avail. His attackers were able to wrap a cord or a cloth around his neck and strangle him. After Khusrau was dead, Raza's men lifted his body up onto the bed and arranged the bedclothes to look as if his death had been natural.[70]

This same story appeared in slightly altered versions in other sources. Della Valle included the murder by strangling, noting that it was done instead with a bowstring, but preceded the actual murder with Shah Jahan's attempt to poison Khusrau by sending him tainted meat. Each time the poisoned meats arrived,

Khusrau refused them knowing they were meant to kill him. The nighttime strangling was then plotted by Shah Jahan's party only as a last resort and only because "there was no other remedy"[71] to the Khusrau problem. Peter Mundy mentioned the strangling as well, but focused his attention, in the short narration, upon others killed in the action surrounding Khusrau: a porter outside Khusrau's door "for denyeing entrance" and one of Raza's own men before the main murder took place.[72] The later account by Dow goes so far as to relieve Shah Jahan of most of the criminal responsibility. Raza, he claims, was "a notorious villain" in his own right, and because he was worried about Shah Jahan's chances for the throne and in the hopes of receiving a substantial reward, took it upon himself to rid his hero of a rival for power by stabbing the sleeping Khusrau in the heart.[73] Persian sources as well, except for those which were entirely silent on the matter, held Shah Jahan responsible for Khusrau's murder,[74] and Aurangzeb himself, Shah Jahan's own son and heir, assumed his father's murder of his uncle to be a stated fact of family history.[75]

Few, if any, contemporary sources actually refuted the charges levelled against Shah Jahan. Although many Persian texts were silent, presumably to preserve the facade of the line's good breeding within the official chronicles, the indictment of the middle son was clear. H. Beveridge, apparently, doubts the story of the murder,[76] but Foster believes the evidence is too strong to be ignored.[77] But because so many contemporary sources include the story, and because the circumstances and motive seem perfectly appropriate, the probability of Khusrau's death being of unnatural causes—and at the indirect hand of his brother, Shah Jahan—is very high.

In the morning after the murder, Khusrau's wife, a much-beloved[78] daughter of Aziz Khan Koka, foster brother to Akbar,[79] came from her room to Khusrau's and finding the door open went in. At first she thought her husband was just sleeping but touching his face with her hand and finding it cold and still, she "ran out and began to scream and cry whereupon all maid servants and others came running to her."[80] The shrieks and cries were so loud that soon everyone in the area knew that Khusrau was dead, and news was sent on ahead to Shah Jahan. The prince at that time was out hunting, but upon hearing the report ("that [his plan] had succeeded"[81]), he returned to Burhanpur, and as van den Broecke said, had all his ministers bear witness to the letter he wrote Jahangir about the sudden demise of his brother, Khusrau. As Dow notes, Shah Jahan, "shewed such apparent symptoms of grief, that he was believed, for some time, innocent of the murder."[82] Out of the confusion that followed, Khusrau's son by Aziz Khan Koka's daughter, Prince Bulaqi, was placed in the care of his maternal grandfather and given a considerable *mansab* by Jahangir.[83] The whole of the immediate family, including the widow and son, was then brought to Lahore.

Khusrau's body was at first buried in a local garden near Burhanpur, but Jahangir, becoming suspicious later of the circumstances of his son's death, had it exhumed and sent to Agra and then on to Allahabad to be buried beside his mother[84] in what is now known as Khusrau Bagh. Jahangir's early reaction to the news of his son's death seems to have been fairly neutral. In spite of the fact that Terry reported Khusrau's death "did so trouble his father, that the grief thereof, as it was strongly believed, shortened his days,"[85] Jahangir showed neither pleasure nor grief in his memoirs at the news from Burhanpur.[86] What seems to have made him most angry was the process by which he was informed of the death and the possibility that his other son, Shah Jahan, was trying to deceive him about the true sequence of events. Jahangir was told of it on January 29, 1622; how much earlier than this it actually took place is uncertain.[87] It seems clear that Shah Jahan at some point wrote Jahangir a letter informing him of what had happened and affixing to it the signatures of all his chief nobles in witness to the truth of the contents[88]—"in order the better to conceal his own crime."[89]

It happened that one Matab Nuruddin Quli, who was present at that time in Burhanpur, also wrote to Jahangir with a full account of events, evidently suggesting that Khusrau's death may have been planned. Upon receiving this second letter, Jahangir became furious and wrote back to the nobles in Burhanpur "a very angry letter . . . enquiring why they had failed to write to him the truth, whether his son had died a natural death or been murdered by some one."[90] It was then that Jahangir ordered Khusrau's body exhumed and brought to Allahabad and committed Khusrau's surviving family to the care of his still living father-in-law. Jahangir's final course of action was to order Shah Jahan himself to come back to court and to give in person his account of Khusrau's death. Shah Jahan refused to obey his father's summons and instead gathered together his forces "to withstand his Father" and with the help of local alliances moved toward Agra.[91]

Although this Deccan affair began auspiciously for Shah Jahan, it ended with his complete and willful disenfranchisement from Jahangir. Reacting perhaps too hastily to the news of his father's illness in 1621, Shah Jahan had put into effect, quite clearly and premeditatively, plans for his brother's death, thereby clearing his own way to the throne. When his plan backfired on him—that is, when his father didn't die and began to suspect instead, quite accidently, that his middle son had in fact murdered his eldest—Shah Jahan had to flee, no longer ever welcome at the court and by his own actions now a seditious rebel. With these events in the Deccan, then, Shah Jahan went into open and permanent struggle against the court.

The complicity of other members of the junta in the final Khusrau affair, however, is not altogether clear. Certainly Nur Jahan and Asaf Khan agreed to and encouraged entrusting the care of Khusrau to Shah Jahan. That they had a hand in his actual murder is doubtful, though their courtly manipulations behind the scenes certainly made them accessories to the crime in some degree. That they were pleased with the results is beyond doubt for Khusrau's permanent absence now allowed each to mount seriously the cause of a protége: Nur Jahan that of Shahryar and Asaf Khan that of Shah Jahan. From this point forward, however, brother and sister would be on opposite sides. With Shah Jahan in rebellion, Asaf Khan could not openly champion his cause, but could and did work secretly on his behalf. Moreover, the Khusrau murder cast the whole ruling family, except perhaps for Jahangir, into a bad light and whatever popularity Nur Jahan had garnered up to now began to wane as her partisan activities became more prominent.

Imperial attention now turned to Kandahar. Proceeding from Khurasan, Shah Abbas of Persia, perhaps sensing a momentary weakness in the Mughal administration, moved to capture the important border post of Kandahar.[92] Jahangir received the news in mid-June 1622 while at the royal camp at Rawalpindi and, because of past friendly relations with the shah, refused at first to believe the report. Finding it to be true, however, that the shah was moving to lay siege to Kandahar with troops from Iraq and Khurasan, Jahangir ordered his high-ranking commanders with armies from the Deccan, Gujarat, Bengal, and Bihar to proceed toward the area.[93] Aziz Khan was currently governor of Kandahar on behalf of the king and was ordered by Jahangir to "fortify the place and furnish it with provisions, and that he [Jahangir] would send reinforcements."[94] As he was increasingly under attack, Aziz Khan made sorties out daily to fend off the Persian forces as best he could. It was not good enough, however, for he "wrote to the King many times that he should quickly send relief or Kandahar would fall, since they were hard pressed."[95] Jahangir had written to Khan Jahan, governor of nearby Multan, "to procure large supplies of rice, butter and salt to go with all his forces to assist Asaf [sic] Khan,"[96] but it is not clear what the emperor instructed Khan Jahan to do about the timing of his move on Kandahar. The *Tuzuk* said that Jahangir ordered Khan Jahan to stay in Multan until the reinforcement armies from the south arrived,[97] but van den Broecke said that, although Jahangir repeatedly ordered Khan Jahan to proceed and give aid to Aziz Khan "with all his forces," the governor of Multan, "always raised difficulties."[98]

When he had first heard the news of the seige of Kandahar, Jahangir had ordered Shah Jahan and the Khankhanan Abdur Rahim, then still in the Deccan, to proceed toward the northern post to check the progress of the shah. About the time the situation was getting critical, however, Jahangir received a messenger with a letter from Shah Jahan that stated in no uncertain terms that the prince was going to "pass the rainy season in the fort of Mandu [in Malwa], and then come to Court."[99] Moreover, Shah Jahan made as the conditions of his return to court that he be given full command of the imperial army, full command of the Punjab, and the fort of Ranthambhor for the safety of his family.[100] Jahangir was offended by the letter and said: "I did not like the style of its purport nor the request he made, and, on the contrary, the traces of disloyalty (*bi-daulati*) were apparent."[101] The emperor had no choice, however, but to let his son wait before coming to court until after the rains had stopped. Jahangir then ordered Shah Jahan to send instead the great commanders and armies who were assisting him in the south—especially the Sayyids of Barha and Bukhara, the Shaikhzadas, the Afghans, and the Rajputs—on to support the defense of Kandahar.[102]

One could argue, with little evidence to the contrary, that Shah Jahan fell into rebellion gradually and that his revolt came as a result of Nur Jahan's conscious policy of forcing him out of the lines of power. It is quite possible that Nur Jahan, now securely in power herself and with the decisions for the administration of the empire almost totally in her hands, saw Kandahar as a way to get Shah Jahan into trouble. There can be no doubt that Jahangir's orders to his son to proceed to Kandahar and to aid in its defense were instigated by his wife. Furthermore, we assume that Nur Jahan intended these orders to place Shah Jahan in a difficult situation: if he refused to go, he would be denounced as a rebel and crushed, most likely, by the imperial armies; but, if he left the Deccan for Kandahar he would lose the base of power he had spent so long in cultivating. Moreover, if he was far off in Kandahar fighting and Jahangir died, Shah Jahan might miss his chance for the throne. His response, then, from his point of view was a balanced one. He would delay and make time for himself by spending the monsoon in Mandu, yet fend off the rage of his father with the promise to Jahangir of proceeding later to the north. Shah Jahan must also have seen through the ruse of the orders; they could have no other intent than to be a subtle declaration of war upon him by his stepmother, who was clearly provoking a seditious response on his part in order to secure her own place after Jahangir's death. Shah Jahan must have come to see that this woman, with whom he had so ably negotiated a favorable relationship early on in order to impress and eventually eclipse Jahangir, was now negotiating to outclass him for ends that were openly self-interested. Such a vision of Nur Jahan was the only one possible given the evidence available to Shah Jahan.

Believing he knew who his enemy really was now, Shah Jahan tested his power. Shortly after the confrontation with Jahangir over Kandahar, in the summer of 1622, Shah Jahan forced the issue of ownership over some property that belonged by right to Nur Jahan and Shahryar. Among the contested properties was the *pargana* of Dholpur, some miles to the southeast of Agra, which was in a *jagir* assigned to Shahryar.[103] Shah Jahan had petitioned for Dholpur for himself and, anticipating that his request would be granted, had sent one of his men, an Afghan named Darya Khan, with some assistants to take charge. In the meantime, Nur Jahan had procured Dholpur for Shahryar, who had sent his own men there. Upon arriving, then, Shah Jahan's men met Shahryar's and, when the two sides clashed, many men from both camps were killed. Jahangir was furious when he heard the news of the confrontation and sent a servant to Shah Jahan to hear "the cause of this boldness."[104] Because Shah Jahan was deemed "unworthy of all the favours and cherishing I had bestowed on him," Jahangir ordered his son to behave more appropriately, to be content with the property he already had, and to refrain from coming to wait on the emperor.[105]

As punishment for his insolence, and because it was clear that Shah Jahan had no intention of ever proceeding to Kandahar, Jahangir now gave the appointment to the Kandahar expedition to his "fortunate son," Shahryar.[106] This appointment must have been made at the instigation of Nur Jahan and was accompanied, as expected, by a raise in *mansab* for Shahryar to 12,000 *zat* and 8,000 *suwar*. Nur Jahan, however, though certainly happy at the turn of events, could not have been their sole author. Shah Jahan was himself responsible for his part in undermining the Mughal frontier policy at Kandahar and in deliberately provoking the Dholpur clash. Nevertheless, his misguided judgment played right into the hands of his stepmother, and she was able to make the very best of the events as they were presented to her.

Jahangir now proceeded in managing the Kandahar affair as if the possibility of Shah Jahan's taking up command in any manner were no longer at issue. He continued to appoint new people to join the armies in the north, and in order to alleviate some of the wartime expenses, he ordered his finance ministers to pay the salaries of the men involved out of the northern *jagirs* of Shah Jahan, which he had transferred to Shahryar. The reason for this action is not altogether clear, especially when Jahangir immediately followed it with a blanket proposition to Shah Jahan that he might take possession, as recompense, of almost any district in the south that he desired: "An order was passed that the Subahs of Gujarat, Malwa, the Deccan and Khandesh should be handed over to him (Khurram), and he might take up a permanent residence wherever he might wish, and employ himself in the administration of those regions."[107] This order was followed, however, by a repeat command that Shah Jahan send the requisitioned troops from the south to help out where they were needed.[108] If the reprimand behind the confiscation of Shah Jahan's *jagirs* was redeemed by the granting of new ones, then the halfhearted repetition of his request for reinforcements from his third son was an equally futile and perhaps consciously hollow demand. Jahangir, though he desperately wanted his son's good will and obedience, was helpless now either to buy or to command them.

The Kandahar affair proceeded from here on of its own accord with the result, however, that the city "fell again into the hands of Shah Abbas."[109] Unaware of this, however, Jahangir, had been planning to send Abdullah Khan, secretly sworn in allegiance to Shah Jahan, with some other men on to assist the cause there. To help out he had decided to have the imperial treasury brought from Agra to Lahore[110] and had appointed Nur Jahan's brother, Asaf Khan, to be in charge of the move.[111] The decision to remove the treasury from Agra was based either, as van den Broecke has argued, on the need for the wealth in resolving the Kandahar affair,[112] or as Della Valle has argued, on Jahangir's desire to keep it away from Shah Jahan,[113] who was at that time moving toward the city, having vowed to take decisive action against his father.

Whatever the motive, the issue of the Agra treasury served to crystallize Jahangir's relationship with his son. He had until this time still harbored a secret hope that Shah Jahan's rebellion was a temporary whim, that his third-born really was still Baba Khurram and "my worthy son Shah Jahan."[114] When he realized, however, that Shah Jahan's intentions were now seriously seditious, Jahangir christened him Bidaulat, "the wretch," and referred to him by this name from then on.[115] Although at this time Jahangir was so sick that he could no longer write his own memoirs, entrusting them to his faithful minister, Mutamid Khan,[116] he nevertheless continued his last, futile propitiations of his son as well as his fairly clearheaded oversight of what was now the Agra affair. Civil war loomed on the horizon, and Jahangir saw with ominous foreboding that he must work to consolidate the empire that he had and prevent the internal forces focused around his rebellious son from destroying the bonds of the immediate union.

With the situation in Agra becoming critical, then, Jahangir turned his attention from what he must have known was an impossible cause in Kandahar to the more pressing familial concerns at home. Judging that the "momentous affair of Qandahar must now be postponed"[117] and assuming, if he did not already know, that Kandahar was to be lost to the Persians, Jahangir became caught up in the incoming and increasingly depressing reports about Shah Jahan. Itibar Khan sent news from Agra that Shah Jahan had left Mandu and was on his way to the city. The prince had apparently heard that the treasury was going to be removed and, "having let fall from his hand the reins of self-control," decided to proceed and seize the wealth himself before it left Agra. Van den Broecke and others have argued that Shah Jahan learned of the impending removal of the treasury from none other than Asaf Khan, his father-in-law and most ably connected supporter. Asaf Khan, the Dutchman continued, had sent word to the prince that as soon as the store had left Agra, he "should rapidly follow him [Asaf Khan] in the region between Agra and Delhi, and (there) he would hand over the treasure to him."[118] If van den Broecke was right, and if the removal of the treasury from Agra was to keep it away from Shah Jahan, then to have appointed Asaf Khan to oversee the operation was either a very stupid move or a very brilliant one, designed deliberately to provoke the prince into action.

Nevertheless, seeing that his son was on the move, Jahangir was himself forced to act. At the beginning of February 1623, having urged another son, Parviz, to assist, Jahangir marched out with his troops from Lahore toward Agra. Reports from Itibar Khan continued to come in and, because Shah Jahan's march on the city was becoming increasingly decisive, the ministers in Agra decided that it was not advisable now to move the treasury, but instead to work on "strengthening the towers and gates, and providing things necessary for the defence of the fort."[119] Asaf Khan, consistently intent on good appearances despite what were clearly devious designs, also wrote a report to Jahangir, saying that Shah Jahan had "torn off the veil of respect" and, as it was not safe to move the treasury, was himself on his way to attend Jahangir.[120]

Receiving reports that servants once faithful to him had gone over to Shah Jahan's side, Jahangir moved to punish and disenfranchise them and called once more for the help of his other son, Parviz. In the middle of February 1623, the imperial army arrived at Nur Sarai, one of the way stations built by Nur Jahan, and Jahangir received there the report that Shah Jahan had arrived at Fatehpur Sikri near Agra in the hopes of catching the imperial army unawares. Shah Jahan discovered, however, that intelligence moved quickly and that the gates of the fort had already been closed to him: Itibar Khan had "fortified the castle (of Agra) and put it into a state of defence, mounting all the guns in the arsenal on the ramparts, and walling up all the gates."[121] Being unable to confiscate the treasury as hoped, he had his men loot and plunder valuables from the surrounding local houses.[122]

Rebuffed now after their unsuccessful attack and having failed to capture the royal treasury, Shah Jahan and his men, after almost a month, turned away and moved northward toward Delhi. He was resolved, said van den Broecke, "to offer battle to his father."[123] Hearing of this, and in a move that would have wide-ranging repercussions, Jahangir placed Mahabat Khan, a trusted friend and adviser, in charge of managing his affairs and of the army,[124] and himself began the advance down from the capital toward his son. Jahangir knew not only that Shah Jahan had paid his men well, thereby ensuring their loyalty, but that many who had formerly been the emperor's allies had gone over to the other side.[125] Nevertheless, he proceeded southward from Delhi receiving reports all the time as to the whereabouts of his son's advancing army:[126] an army that was, though nominally under Shah Jahan's command, in reality led by Raja Bikramajit, or Sundar, a fearsome *brahman* leader from Gujarat.

The decisive battle between Jahangir and Shah Jahan took place in the neighborhood of Baluchpur on March 29, 1623. The day before, the tail end of the imperial march under Baqir Khan had been attacked by the rebels, but Baqir Khan had successfully turned the skirmish to the king's advantage. The next day, under forces led partly (and ironically) by Asaf Khan,[127] or alternately Shahryar and Mahabat Khan,[128] the imperial troops routed the rebels. In the process they killed many of Shah Jahan's important commanders, including his chief commander, Sundar. Those not killed turned in disgrace and ran from the field until they came to Shah Jahan, himself stationed some distance from the battle.[129] Jahangir, of course, was overjoyed at the victory, and the next day received Sundar's head as a sign of rebel submission. "In consequence of his [Sundar's] destruction," said Jahangir, "Bi-daulat did not gird his loins again."[130] The emperor rewarded all those who had helped in the routing of the rebels and, although Baqir Khan, Itibar Khan, Shahryar, and Mahabat Khan were among those immediately honored, Asaf Khan, oddly, was not.[131]

On April 10, 1623, the imperial party rested on the bank of the lake at Fatehpur, postponing their pursuit of Shah Jahan until the arrival of Parviz. Parviz came and as new news was received about the whereabouts of Shah Jahan, in May Jahangir sent Parviz out "in pursuit to overthrow Bi-daulat." To keep Parviz in line and to ensure military success, Jahangir appointed Asaf Khan's staunch enemy, Mahabat Khan, to have the "reins of authority over the powerful Prince, and (to be) the centre of the ordering of the victorious army." The campaign's orders were to capture Shah Jahan alive, but if that did not prove possible, they had the full permission of the court to kill him.[132] With Parviz and Mahabat Khan in pursuit of Shah Jahan, Jahangir was now free to attend to other matters. He appointed Dawar Bakhsh, Khusrau's son, to the government of Gujarat, with a *mansab* of 8,000 *zat* and 3,000 *suwar*, and placed him under the tutelage of his now much aged maternal grandfather, Aziz Khan Koka, as *ataliq*. Aziz Khan Koka then led the Dawar Bakhsh campaign directly to Ahmedabad to recover successfully the *suba* of Gujarat; the Khankhanan was to die there in Ahmedabad during the next year.[133] Jahangir himself now proceeded to Ajmer to wait out the various campaigns, reaching it on May 9, 1623.[134] As Prasad says, "There he had once resided to support Shah Jahan's Mewar operations. There he now resided to support a campaign against him."[135]

About this time, Jahangir's own immediate family experienced some changes. His mother, the charismatic and adventurous Hindu widow of Akbar, Maryamuzzamani, died early in the summer of 1623 in Agra and was buried in a tomb in Sikandra near her husband, Akbar. Maryamuzzamani had played an important social role in Jahangir's life by hosting most of his family celebrations at her own home, and she had, in the larger arena, helped chart the role of Mughal women in the newly expanding business of foreign trade.[136] Though Jahangir must have grieved immensely at her death, his notice of it in his memoirs was very short, saying only that "I trust that Almighty God will envelop her in the ocean of His mercy."[137] She was the last in the illustrious series of parents to die in this period, and her death came, strangely, only four years before Jahangir's own.

Also at this time, on September 4, 1623, a daughter was born to Ladli Begam and Shahryar. The child's name has been given alternately as Arzani Begam, Lardili Begam, and Wali Begam in the manuscripts, and Jahangir heralded her birth by saying, "I hope that her advent will be propitious and blessed to this State."[138] Because Shahryar would die violently in the climactic and crisis-ridden period around Jahangir's death, this girl would be the only known offspring of the marriage, and because Ladli was not known to have married again, the baby would be the only known grandchild of Nur Jahan. Since Nur Jahan and her daughter spent the last years of their lives in Lahore and were buried together there when they died, any true descendants of Nur Jahan are likely to have old Lahori ties.

After his defeat at Baluchpur, Shah Jahan had retreated to Mandu in Malwa.[139] Hearing now of the advance of Parviz and Mahabat Khan, he marched out toward them, but because his forces were light, he was easily subdued and, in time, many of his key men deserted to Mahabat Khan. "Mahabat K. was continually capturing, by messages and letters, the afflicted hearts of a number of men who out of timidity and confusion had accompanied Bi-daulat." The forces of Parviz, under the able guidance of the older general, continued in their push to undermine the campaign of Shah Jahan,[140] and as more and more of the rebellious troops turned treacherously on their leader and came over to the imperial side, Shah Jahan had to consolidate his base of power. He therefore, in September of 1623, crossed the Narmada River and made for the fort of Asir, a fort now under the rule of Mir Husamuddin, the husband of a cousin of his wife's. It happened that the ruler was also the husband of a niece of Nur Jahan's, and the queen wrote a letter to him strictly urging the following:

> Beware, a thousand times beware, not to allow Bi-daulat and his men to come near the fort, but strengthen the towers and gates, and do your duty, and do not act in such a manner that the stain of a curse and ingratitude for favours should fall on the honour or the forehead of a Sayyid.[141]

Mir Husamuddin did indeed strengthen the fort well, but when Shah Jahan arrived he sent one of his attendants, a man named Sharifa, to seduce the ruler into submission "by means of promises and threats." This Sharifa did and, by the end of the assault, Mir Husamuddin had surrendered the fort of Asir without resistance to Shah Jahan in return for a title and a sizable *mansab*.[142] Shah Jahan planned to use the fort as a retreat for himself and his family, but the post did not, in fact, serve as a strategic center for very long.

Leaving Gopal Das, a Rajput, in charge of the fort, Shah Jahan took his family and went to Burhanpur. Realizing that his retreat toward the Deccan had seriously jeopardized and weakened his efforts in Gujarat, Shah Jahan now tendered proposals of peace to Mahabat Khan. Through letters and messengers, it became clear that Mahabat Khan would not grant peace until Shah Jahan turned over the old Khankhanan, Abdur Rahim, "that head of deceivers who was the ring-leader of trouble and sedition."[143] Shah Jahan, who had imprisoned the ever duplicitous Khankhanan himself, took him out of prison and made him swear an oath of loyalty to the prince on the Quran. Then, taking him into the women's palaces, Shah Jahan beseeched him to act sincerely on his behalf: "My times are hard, and my position difficult; I make myself over to you, and make you the guardian of my honour."[144] The Khankhanan then left Shah Jahan's camp, but before he got to the southern bank of the Narmada River where he was to correspond in writing with Mahabat Khan, some imperial troops crossed over the river at a point where the rebel commander Bairam Beg's men had been careless. Bairam Beg's rebels could not repulse Parviz's men, and they scattered in all directions, some deserting to Mahabat Khan. The Khankhanan, himself finding confusion, then went over to Mahabat Khan's side and made his cause, despite the pledge to Shah Jahan, with the imperial forces of Parviz.

With the virtual desertion of the Khankhanan, the flight of Bairam Beg and his men, and the crossing of the Narmada River by the imperial side, Shah Jahan lost all courage.[145] In spite of heavy monsoon rains and flooded waterways everywhere, Shah Jahan "in a state of wretchedness" left Burhanpur and, in the middle of September 1623, crossed the Tapti River to the south, going off from there toward the Deccan. In the confusion, he was separated from some of his men but pushed on with his family anyway despite the rains, leaving aside excess baggage as each piece became too much to carry through the mud. Under orders from Jahangir and Nur Jahan to persist, Parviz and Mahabat Khan then took up pursuit of Shah Jahan and, reaching Burhanpur, they too crossed the Tapti.[146] Shah Jahan moved as quickly as he could, and in October of 1623 he escaped into Golconda, foreign territory happily outside the purview of Mughal rule. Once there he could rest easily, as Mahabat Khan could not pursue him, and the imperial forces, certainly weary now from their marches, returned to Burhanpur to wait out the rains. Finally "at ease with regard to the affair of Bi-daulat," Jahangir proceeded in November of 1623 to Kashmir, where he could escape "the heat of Hindustan" and pamper his badly broken constitution.[147] Before going, however, Jahangir appointed Asaf Khan as governor of Bengal stating as he did so that he "had taken a great liking to his society . . . (and) regretted separation from him."[148]

Now in the Deccan with his family and close associates, Shah Jahan began making alliances with the Golconda government and the new English factories of the south. While some of his former followers like Jagat Singh in the north were seeking protection and patronage from Nur Jahan, Shah Jahan had procured the firm alliances he wanted and had decided to move on. In mid-November, with the help of Golconda officers, he marched northeast and entered Orissa.[149] Although he lost some of his men in the process of reentering Mughal territory,[150] Shah Jahan found the conquest of Orissa relatively easy. The governor of the province, Ahmad Beg Khan, a cousin of Nur Jahan's, had been uninformed of Shah Jahan's march and, when he finally heard of the prince's safe passage into Orissa, "was struck with terror and leaving everything took to flight."[151] Orissa's treasures and many ministers falling thus to Shah Jahan, the prince went on toward Barddhaman and wrote to Ibrahim Khan, Nur Jahan's uncle and at that time still governor of Bengal, who was then in Dacca, that he wanted to hold Bengal and would grant Ibrahim Khan any *jagir* in the country in return. Nur Jahan's uncle rejected the offer, maintaining loyalty to the imperial throne, and Shah Jahan proceeded to beseige and take Barddhaman and then move on to Akbarnagar (Rajmahal) where Raja Man Singh had formerly built his stronghold.[152]

There, in the spring of 1624, Shah Jahan faced off against Ibrahim Khan, who had fortified the area and substantially strengthened his troops. During the battle of Rajmahal, both sides lost considerable men in the fighting that took place there on the banks of the lower Ganges. Eventually, however, the tide turned in the favor of Shah Jahan and his men, and Ibrahim Khan's forces, who "disliked him, as their pay was in arrears,"[153] began to desert him. Left with relatively few men, Ibrahim Khan, brother of Asmat Begam, was attacked and killed by the prince's forces on April 10, 1624, and all of his property and holdings fell to Shah Jahan.[154] With the prince's victory at Rajmahal, the leading nobles surrendered, and Shah Jahan now held Bengal and Orissa firmly in his possession. He then successfully advanced to take Bihar and to swear the allegiance of its nobles to his cause. When he moved further on to take Oudh and Allahabad, however, he was at last checked by the counteradvance of the imperial forces. Parviz and Mahabat Khan had, it seems, at the news of Shah Jahan's successes, set off for Allahabad in March of 1624 and there again on the banks of the Ganges engaged in heavy skirmishes with the prince, during which the son and grandson of the old Khankhanan were killed. In time, Shah Jahan was beaten back from Allahabad and fled with his men to Orissa.[155]

Parviz and Mahabat Khan had, meanwhile, secured alliances with the king of Bijapur in the Deccan. This had left Malik Amber, of rivaling Ahmadnagar, with no one to support, ironically, but Shah Jahan. Malik Amber, however, was greedy on his own behalf after receiving back tribute from Qutbulmulk, and set out in seige upon Bijapur. In spite of imperial reinforcements on the other side there, he was able to make substantial headway against the Mughal alliances. When Shah Jahan, who had passed quickly back through Orissa and Telingana, arrived in Golconda, he was welcomed by Amber and, on "the basis of common enmity to the Imperial government," the two former enemies then laid seige together to Burhanpur.[156] The joint assaults might have succeeded had not Parviz and Mahabat Khan arrived with substantial forces and had not Shah Jahan fallen seriously ill.

Assessing his strengths and realizing that his cause was futile, Shah Jahan now saw the "error of his conduct . . . and . . felt that he must beg forgiveness of his father for his offenses."[157] So he wrote a letter to Jahangir, who had returned to Lahore from Kashmir, "expressing his sorrow and repentance, and begging pardon for all faults past and present."[158] At the instance of Nur Jahan,

Jahangir replied in March of 1626 that if Shah Jahan surrendered Rohtas and the fort of Asir and sent his sons Dara Shikoh and Aurangzeb to court, he would give him full forgiveness and the province of Balaghat. Shah Jahan felt he had no other choice but to comply, so he made arrangements for the surrender of Rohtas and Asir, sent his two sons to court, and proceeded with his wife and youngest son, Murad, to Nasik near the coast.[159] Thus with this pardon, Shah Jahan's civil war against his father ended. It had lasted over three years, cost millions of rupees and thousands of lives, and left in its wake an empire deeply broken along its borders in Afghanistan and in the Deccan. Shah Jahan was now to remain in exile in the Deccan for most of the time until his father's death in October of 1627.

Nur Jahan's role in the events of Shah Jahan's rebellion are probably much greater than contemporary texts reveal. She was certainly instrumental, first, in sending Shah Jahan to the Deccan in 1621 and, thus, in setting up the context for Khusrau's murder.[160] Although she had nothing to do with Shah Abbas's seige of Kandahar, it afforded her, second, an excellent opportunity for putting Shah Jahan in a position that would push him into seditious activity—a position Shah Jahan saw as one of her own design.[161]

Third, the clash over the *jagir* of Dholpur was undoubtedly a setup by Nur Jahan who, in her efforts on behalf of Shahryar, had been more persuasive with Jahangir than Shah Jahan over whom should finally be given the rights to the *jagir*.[162] Nur Jahan had also had, no doubt, a decided hand in the appointment of Shahryar to the ill-fated Kandahar expedition, and in the confiscation of Shah Jahan's northern *jagirs* for her new son-in-law. Fourth, in removing the treasury from Agra and in deciding whom to put in charge of the operation, Jahangir was clearly swayed by Nur Jahan. To entrust Asaf Khan with the task meant either that the queen was on good terms with her brother again and hoped to cement family loyalties in the act or, more probably, that being in certain collusion with Shah Jahan, Asaf Khan's obvious presence in Agra would draw the rebellious stepson out into the open.[163]

Fifth, although the appointment of Parviz to head the pursuit party of Shah Jahan in the wake of the battle of Baluchpur did not further the Shahryar cause, it did continue to deepen the divisions between the rebel prince and Jahangir's other sons, thus undermining the power behind Shah Jahan's eventual bid for the throne. Consistent with the divide and conquer strategy, the appointment of Mahabat Khan, made certainly with Nur Jahan's approval, set his staunch enemy, Asaf Khan, at odds with the imperial cause. Asaf Khan's deep loyalties to Shah Jahan were openly known to Nur Jahan and the designation of his enemy as the official general overseeing the pursuit of his protégé undoubtedly tested his public show of allegiance to the crown. Finally, Shah Jahan's defeat and surrender at Burhanpur must have been joyful news to Nur Jahan, and his subsequent pardon at her hands a bitter turn for him.[164] To be in a position to pardon her erstwhile colleague while thus compounding the pain of his submission was all Nur Jahan could have hoped for from the lengthy struggle, which was, more than anything else, a contest of nerves. For Shah Jahan the pardon made the humiliation complete, and he refused to return to court not so much because "he was ashamed to see a father whom he had so much injured," but because "he was actually afraid of the machinations of the favourite Sultana."[165]

While Nur Jahan could be openly supportive of Shahryar, the other courtly partisan, Asaf Khan, had to be more covert in his loyalties. Although he could remain quietly consistent in his allegiance to Shah Jahan, in order to ensure his family's stable goodwill in the eyes of the throne, he had to give lavish and public support to Jahangir. On the one hand, then, Asaf Khan was often in a position of advantage for Shah Jahan: in urging Jahangir to send Khusrau to the Deccan with him,[166] or in passing on intelligence to him while in Agra concerning the removal of the treasury,[167] or in commandeering a sensitive position in Bengal.[168] But Asaf Khan had to play a game of balance, for as Della Valle suggested of the Agra affair, "the King still entrusts him [Asaf Khan], and consequently either he is not in fault, or . . . his fault is not yet known."[169] Clearly Asaf Khan had to make sure that the latter condition prevailed and, to this end, worked extremely hard at a "suave game of diplomacy"[170] to keep Jahangir convinced of his good faith and free of all suspicion.

Asaf Khan's efforts at court, then, were critical and, as evidence of his great success in duping the emperor, were his continued raises in *mansab*,[171] his official reports to Jahangir about the doings of his rebel son "the wretch [who] had torn off the veil of respect,"[172] and his general acts of courtly obeisance.[173] His excellence in deception probably went only so far as the emperor, however, for van den Broecke reported that Itibar Khan, during the maneuvers in Agra, "did not wish to entrust the royal treasure to Asaf Khan" and consequently went about his work of compiling the treasury very slowly and deliberately so as to prevent, in this delaying technique, any hasty action on the part of the queen's brother.[174] In the end, the rebellion of Shah Jahan not only tested Asaf Khan's emotional and diplomatic reserves of duplicity, but severely weakened his own position of power. Not only was he rightly suspected by many to be double-dealing, but he had risked his standing, and perhaps his life, on behalf of the expected, though not necessarily secure, heir to the throne. If Shah Jahan had been killed in one of the many skirmishes or if he proceeded to mishandle the accession bid when it came, Asaf Khan's traitorous intentions would have been immediately acknowledged, and he would have been fortunate to get away with only his life. His public massaging of Jahangir, then, was crucial and so was his increasing inclination to disengage himself from open scrutiny and to stand aloof from the court. In the end, we know, the queen's brother was very lucky.

As it happens, the surrender and ruin of Shah Jahan crystallized the realignment of loyalties that had resulted from the slow but certain breakup of the junta. By the spring of 1626, each of the remaining sons of Jahangir sat in the camp of a crucially placed and actively patronizing benefactor. Parviz (b. 1589), the eldest surviving son, was championed by the able general Mahabat Khan, and old and trusted wartime colleague of Jahangir's from before the time of the emperor's own accession to the throne. Shah Jahan (b. 1592), the favorite grandson of Akbar and by ability the expected heir to the throne, was championed by his father-in-law, Asaf Khan, who was, at the end, well placed at the court as *vakil*. This appointment, made in mid-1626 in the wake of the rebellion of

Mahabat Khan, was due primarily to the administrative gifts of his father and to the charismatic charms of his sister, but as well, of course, to his own considerable courtly ways. Shahryar (b. 1605), the youngest surviving son and the one of most meager ability, was championed by Nur Jahan. Although least likely to succeed militarily if given the chance, Shahryar's patron was the most advantageously placed at court and the most well-suited to manipulating the lines of power. At this point, however, none of the three sons was the obvious heir to the crown.

The breakup of the junta, so visibly played out in Shah Jahan's rebellion (1622–26), brought a decided shift in the working habits of Nur Jahan. Until the death of her father Itimaduddaula, Nur Jahan, though certainly the craftiest of the operators in the main palace, had submitted nevertheless to the accepted code of courtly decorum which encouraged good manners, high entertainment, and above all cooperation. With the deaths of both her parents, the failure of her preferred marriage negotiations, and the increasing autonomy of her erstwhile protege, however, the oil in the machinery dried up and the delicately crafted bonds of the junta fell apart. Despite the seeming indivisibility of the junta as a family clique,[175] the hidden grievances and budding ambitions of the early years had finally become full-blown as Nur Jahan entered the second half of her rule.

With the dislocation of old loyalties, then, Nur Jahan had to rework the sources of her considerable power. Jahangir's growing incapacity had left her with greater total authority and the death of her father had left her with greater total wealth. This authority and wealth, coupled with her virtually complete isolation—now without her father, her husband, and her stepson—could have set Nur Jahan seriously and dangerously adrift. Instead of succumbing to paralysis, however, Nur Jahan used increasingly overt tactics to consolidate her resources at court and, in the vacuum that was left behind by the loss of the junta, to create at least the semblance of a strong sovereignty. In doing this, Nur Jahan strained at the boundaries of the roles usually allotted to women of place and, because she had to, did things ordinarily done by men. Said Dow:

> Her abilities were uncommon; for she rendered herself absolute, in a government in which women are thought incapable of bearing any part. Their power, it is true, is sometimes exerted in the harem; but, like the virtues of the magnet, it is silent and unperceived. Noor-Jehan stood forth in public; she broke through all restraints and custom, and acquired power by her own address, more than by the weakness of Jehangire.[176]

The shift in power, then, served on the one hand to intensify old traits like her desire to survive at all costs, her greed, and her manipulative charm. It also, however, allowed new skills in policy-making to emerge, without which the substantial developments in trade, religion, and art so central to the period might not ever have taken place.

8

Nur Jahan and Religious Policy

> I cannot forget that memorable pietie, when at Asmere hee went afoot to the tombe of the prophet Hod. Mundin there buried, and kindling a fire with his owne hands and his Normahal under that immense . . . brasse-pot, and made kitcherie for five thousand poore, taking out the first platter with his owne hands and serving one; Normahal the second.
>
> Coryat in Foster, *Early Travels in India,* edited by William Foster

By reputation, Nur Jahan was not an especially religious woman, but like Jahangir she was fond of charitable acts. Whether her charity was the result of her own generous benevolence or of her intuitions about policy best befitting the government may not ever be clear, but it is apparent that she took a decided interest in religious matters at the court, both by way of the administration and of the functionaries who appeared before her from time to time. What is crucial to discern here is the nature of the influence she exerted over Jahangir: was she responsible, for example, for an increasing religious conservatism in the regime, for a movement away from her father-in-law Akbar's universalist sentiment to a more narrow, exclusivistic view consonant with her Shia background? Or did she exercise a somewhat liberal influence, judging that as a minority she and her fellow coreligionists would benefit more from a tolerant, open-ended policy?

Surprisingly, her influence may have generated more flexibility at court than confinement, and yet whatever specific configuration it took, we can be sure it accommodated, or at least expertly complemented, Jahangir's own view and treatment of religion. Moreover, not only may Nur Jahan have weighed precipitously on Jahangir's judgment of a number of religious matters, but his affinity for her may have been patterned by certain religious structures of his own that had had a strong hold on him since youth and that provided a neat and fitting mold for her own personality in the later years of his life. In a sense, then, Nur Jahan's influence on the development of religious policy was a function of the way in which Jahangir himself was religious, and his vision proved to be a variegated and often contradictory meld, which derived as much from his relation to his father as from the cultural assortment of his surroundings.

I

Jahangir's religious vision was characterized by three pervasive patterns of temperament. First, he had a predilection for holding onto forms that were already established, in this way structuring both his seasonal life and his sense of place within the family tradition: for example, the yearly festival of Nauroz, introduced in 1582 by Akbar in imitation of the Persian custom;[1] the reverence of Shaikh Muinuddin Chishti by regular visits to his tomb in Ajmer; the weighing ceremonies on Jahangir's solar and lunar birthdays at which he would pass out the proceeds to the local poor; the policy of open admission for almost any religious to his court in preservation of Akbar's provisions for religious tolerance; and his veneration of the sun, as clear symbol of power and visibility, which though it became preeminent in his own reign was, in fact, a holdover from his father's. All these practices helped to legitimize Jahangir's administration by pinning it up with religious forms from the past and by providing Jahangir himself with some sense, at least early on, of the religious direction he ought to take.

Second, Jahangir's own interest in religion was less theologically and philosophically informed, and much more aesthetically inclined. What pleased him and kept his attention in religious matters was form and form, more than anything else, that he could see. When he visited the Jami mosque in Mandu in the winter of 1617, for example, what appealed to him most was not what he felt or thought but what he observed: "A very lofty building came to view, all of cut stone, and although 180 years have passed since the time of its building, it is as if the builder had just withdrawn his hand from it."[2] In the winter of 1619 he visited the tomb of Shaikh Salim Chishti at Fatehpur Sikri, and after recounting the circumstances of the *shaikh*'s death, Jahangir gave at length the dimensions of the gateways, the domes, the verandas, and the cells, and said of the lamps on holy days that "they are enveloped in coloured cloths, so that they look like lampshades."[3] And again, we have an account of Jahangir as he listened to the Jesuit fathers debate Muslim scholars on the significance of religious matters raised by paintings that had been brought to court. Said Guerreiro: "The occasion arose out of the pleasure which the King took in looking at the coloured pictures of sacred subjects which the Fathers, knowing his interest in these things, had presented to him."[4]

Finally, the religious quest of Jahangir—not apparent to any, not even to himself, until just about the middle of his reign—revolved in many ways around his unspent feelings of both admiration and inadequacy before his father. Whatever the pattern that emerged as Jahangir's own religious vision, it came, in part, out of an internal battle with his father's image. Jahangir's history with his father, at least in Akbar's later years, had been one of insurrection and murder: the death of Abul Fazl at the hands of Salim's henchmen had occurred during the years of his independent court at Allahabad, and with it Jahangir had violated, almost irreparably, the trust invested in him by his father for future sovereignty. The guilt and remorse Jahangir felt over his behavior during the years from 1600 to 1604 had become even more intolerable, however, in the face of his father's unquestionable greatness.

There is no doubt that Jahangir admired Akbar to an extraordinary degree. As a part of the opening remarks of the *Tuzuk*, he lionized his father's appearance saying, "the glory of God manifested itself in him."[5] Of his father's character, however, he made only one point: that he was illiterate. By way of an offhand compliment, he proclaimed that his father had conversed so often with learned men "that no one knew him to be illiterate,"[6] but to Jahangir this lack of book learning was crucial. Whatever his own feelings of inferiority before the greatness of his father, they paled in the knowledge that his father was flawed. And to announce it now, at the beginning of his own reign, was to prepare the way, by some form of negative magic, for the rule of what he hoped would be his own unsurpassed administration. It was partly out of this contradictory tie to Akbar, then—out of the need to vanquish and to please him, to win over him and to win him over—that Jahangir's religious views developed, and no one knew that change was coming until the turmoil began to erupt around the middle of his reign [see chart, Figure 8–3].

Against these patterns of temperament, Jahangir's view of Islam appeared to range from fervent veneration of the saints to open contempt for the interference of Muslim scholars in his government. Some claim that Jahangir had come into power in large measure because of the support he received from the newly emergent Naqshbandi *silsila* and especially from the Sufi activist Shaikh Ahmad Sirhindi (1564–1624) and those nobles in Akbar's court he had won to his side through letters. Men such as the Murtaza Khan Shaikh Farid Bukhari (d. 1616), Abdur Rahim Khankhanan, and Mirza Aziz Koka Khan-i Azam were all beneficiaries of Sirhindi's correspondence, and some, like Nizami, claim "that in the later years of Akbar's reign, under the influence of Shaikh Ahmad Sirhindi, a definite ideological cleavage had developed between Akbar and his nobles."[7] This cleavage[8] pitted the supporters of Khusrau against those of Jahangir and, given the substantial honors and presents bestowed on Naqshbandi adherents just after Jahangir's accession—on Shaikh Farid Bukhari,[9] Abdur Rahim,[10] Qulij Khan,[11] and Khwaja Abdullah,[12] for example, it is argued that Jahangir was beholden in some way to this religious faction for the throne. In support of this, Nizami mentions the account of Shaikh Husain Jami, a disciple of "the dervish of Shiraz," who had written to Jahangir from Lahore to tell him of a dream in which he had seen that "saints and pious men had delivered over the affairs of the kingdom to that chosen one of the Court of Allah (Jahangir)."[13] Appended to this account came a petition to pardon the faults of one Khwaja Zakariya, a Naqshbandi who was in disgrace—a petition that Jahangir, in fact, did grant.[14]

And then there is the claim by the Jesuits Du Jarric[15] and Guerreiro[16] that Jahangir made a commitment upon his accession to orthodox Muslim leaders to uphold and encourage the practice of Islam. The first passage of Du Jarric's, especially, suggested that a bargain was reached with those who might have supported Khusrau[17]—said to have been pro-Christian anyway[18]—to withdraw their support and throw it to Jahangir in return for a pledge of loyalty on his part to uphold orthodox Islam. We know in fact that two of the early correspondees of Sirhindi, Mirza Aziz Koka, father-in-law to Khusrau, and Abdur Rahim, were involved in pro-Khusrau activity, the former before Jahangir's accession[19] and the latter in Khusrau's revolt of 1606, for which he was severely punished by Jahangir when the revolt failed.[20] (Ironically, and perhaps by some shrewd design of Jahangir's, it was Shaikh Farid Bukhari who was placed in charge of the imperial forces of 1606 that were sent in successful pursuit of Khusrau.[21]) Some sort of pact with the Naqshbandi's upon his accession, then, may well have taken place,[22] primarily to ease his worries (unsuccessfully as it turned out) about the threat of any renewed Khusrau activity. And his honoring of these Naqshbandi associates in 1605 could then have been as much a genuine gesture of appreciation for past services as an expected guarantee of future political harmony.

Jahangir, however, was not one to tie himself inflexibly to any one religious institution or group, and his post-accession honors showed that he saw himself as equally beholden to the non-Khusrau supporting family of Shaikh Salim, the most recent luminary of the much older Chishti *silsila*. The Sufi lineage of the Chishtis had had long ties to the Mughal family and Chishti saints had been venerated in the imperial household from the time of Babur.[23] Shaikh Salim Chishti held an especially important place in Chishti hagiography for the Mughals because once, when in the pursuit of the blessing of sons, Akbar had made a foot pilgrimage to Ajmer to visit the tomb of Shaikh Muinuddin Chishti and had happened to visit Shaikh Salim in "his abode on a hill near Sikri."[24] Shaikh Salim had correctly prophesied that Akbar would have three sons and in gratitude Akbar had named the first of these sons (in 1569) after the illustrious Sufi and had moved his capital to the *shaikh's* village of Sikri. Named Fatehpur Sikri, this city did not last long as a central pivot of Akbar's reign, primarily because of water problems,[25] but Shaikh Salim Chishti's (d. 1572) tomb had been built there by Akbar and remained a pilgrimage place for members of the Mughal family.[26] Jahangir had been tied thus from birth to Shaikh Salim had grown up thereafter in the company of many of the *shaikh's* descendants.[27]

Akbar himself had promoted Shaikh Ahmad, the son of Shaikh Salim, and had patronized as well a nephew of the *shaikh*, Shaikh Ibrahim.[28] In the years just before he died, the emperor had also promoted Shaikh Bayazid Muazzam Khan, a grandson of the *shaikh*, to a *mansab* of 2,000.[29] Bayazid's mother had been the "first person who gave me [Jahangir] milk, but for not more than a day" and, tied thus to Bayazid as a foster brother, Jahangir continued to promote him during his own reign.[30] Jahangir also promoted as part of his accession gifts Shaikh Kabir, another member "of the family of the venerable Shaikh Salim," whom he had honored with the title of Shajaat Khan while still a prince "on account of his manliness and bravery." Now he gave him the rank of 1,000.[31] And he gave another grandson of the *shaikh*, Shaikh Alauddin, "who had strong connections with me," the title of Islam Khan and the rank of 2,000.[32]

Most dear to Jahangir, however, was a son of Shaikh Salim's daughter,[33] a man named Qutbuddin Khan Koka, who was destined to play a crucial, if ambiguous, role in the legends of the early Nur Jahan. Qutbuddin's mother had nursed Jahangir as an infant, making the two boys foster brothers, and on her death in 1606 Jahangir celebrated her by saying: "I have not so much affection for my own mother as for her. She is to me my gracious mother, and I do not hold him

[Qutbuddin] less dear than my own brothers and children." Jahangir was much attached to her son, who was "the foster-brother . . . most fit for fosterage,"[34] and promoted him grandly at the beginning of his reign.[35] One of his promotions was to the *subadar*-ship of Bengal, and it was there at Barddhaman that Qutbuddin had died in the fray with Sher Afgan.[36] Qutbuddin's role in Sher Afgan's death would come back to haunt the family of Shaikh Salim Chishti, for scholars like Husain are of the opinion that Nur Jahan did not easily forget Qutbuddin's hand in the slaying of her first husband and because of this systematically shut out others of the Shaikh Salim family from promotion in the years that were to come.[37]

The bonds cemented at Jahangir's accession did not pull him toward one Muslim group or another, and it seems quite clear that he was determined to remain a mainstream Muslim, eclectic and antinomian to be sure, and that he intended his reign and its symbols to be bearers of the truth of Islam here on earth. While he was not fond of Islamic leaders or institutions transgressing the boundaries of his political rule,[38] he did manage to maintain the general Muslim organization of his father's administration.[39] He encouraged converts to Islam[40] but prohibited conversions into the faith from being forced.[41] He consorted with any number of religious teachers from different Muslim sects,[42] but he moved against those (like the Afghan Shaikh Ibrahim Baba[43] or Shaikh Ahmad Sirhindi[44]) who he felt were speaking out of turn or accumulating too much power. He celebrated Muslim festivals like Ramadan[45] and the Ramadan *id*,[46] the Muharram,[47] and the Shab-i Barat,[48] and observed dietary restrictions consonant with Islam.[49] He visited mosques,[50] tombs of Muslim saints,[51] and tombs of his own ancestors as acts of religious and aesthetic veneration,[52] and he had the Quran translated "into plain language without ornament," saying that the new version should be in a "simple language (*lughat-i-rikhta*) [done] word by word into Persian."[53] He took pains in his memoirs to note the types of Islam in Kashmir,[54] and he held assemblies for mystical dancing and singing[55] as the ultimate in Muslim religiosity.

Jahangir was most involved, however, in the friendship and patronage of Muslim dervishes. He was fond of the company of these men and often gave them money,[56] watched them dance in ecstatic religious ceremonies,[57] and conversed with them on theological matters.[58] His spiritual ties to them were summed up in the following hope for transferred religious merit: "I walked round . . . in this neighbourhood, with the idea that I might see some faqirs from association with whom I might obtain grace."[59] He sent verses he himself composed along with some money to a dervish in Transoxiana, one Khwaja Hashim, who had written to him reaffirming his alliance to the Mughal family,[60] and he took interest in the condition of a certain "Miyan Shaikh Muhammad Mir by name," whose spirit he finally judged to be "too high" for the gift of money, so he left him, after an interview, with "the skin of a white antelope to pray upon."[61] Finally, Jahangir, urged on by his "truth-seeking mind," summoned holy man Qazi Nasir of Burhanpur to court but finding, apparently, that although the dervish was well-read, he preferred to be alone, "I respected his feelings, and did not give him the trouble of serving me."[62]

Jahangir's personal religious feelings, however, were tied to no figure more than to Khwaja Muinuddin Chishti, the founder of the Chishti *silsila* in India and an object of veneration in the Mughal family for generations. Jahangir opened his memoirs with a tribute to the Sufi, calling him "the fountainhead of most of the saints of India,"[63] and in late 1608 he recalled his father's pilgrimage with Maryamuzzamani to Muinuddin's shrine in hopes of sons by making his own pilgrimage to Akbar's tomb in Sikandra.[64] Further, he supported Khwaja Husain, a descendant of Muinuddin's, who had been persecuted by Akbar at the instigation of his rival Abul Fazl,[65] and in 1610 Jahangir gave Khwaja Husain Rs. 1,000 "as was usual for the half-year."[66] Finally, in early 1611, he dedicated a blue bull (*nilgau*) caught on a hunt to the soul of Khwaja Muinuddin, its flesh to be given "to eat to poor people."[67]

In the fall of 1613 Jahangir moved his court from Agra to Ajmer in order better to oversee Khurram's Mewar campaign against some local Rajput chieftains.[68] He eventually stayed in the town for three years, from November 1613 to November 1616,[69] and there took advantage of being close to Muinuddin's shrine, "from the blessing of whose illustrious soul great advantage had been derived by this dignified family."[70] By his own count he visited Muinuddin's mausoleum nine times during his three-year stay in Ajmer,[71] and during that time he had a large caldron made in Agra to be used in ritual ceremonies held at the *khwaja's* shrine [see Figure 8–1]. On the first occasion of its use, Jahangir said:

> On this day it was brought, and I ordered them to cook food for the poor in that pot, and collect together the poor of Ajmir to feed them whilst I was there. Five thousand people assembled, and all ate of this food to their fill. After the food I gave money to each of the dervishes with my own hand.[72]

One such festival during these same years, and perhaps the very one noted above, was observed by Coryat and in his description he marveled that the emperor performed so much of the ritual himself:

> [Jahangir] went afoot to the tombe of the prophet Hod. Mundin there buried [in Ajmer], and kindling a fire with his owne hands and his Normahal under that immense and Heidelbergian—aequipollent brasse-pot, and made kitcherie for five thousand poore, taking out the first platter with his owne hands and serving one; Normahal the second; and so his ladies all the rest.[73]

During the three years in Ajmer, Jahangir buried a Naqib Khan and his wife and a Mirza Ali Beg in Muinuddin's mausoleum as these servants of his had developed a great affection for the saint.[74] In the summer of 1614, he went himself to the shrine to pray for personal restitution from an illness that was marked by an excessive fever and headache.[75] When he recovered, he bored holes in his ears for pearl earrings in thanksgiving to Muinuddin for his new health; this action placed him among the saint's "ear-marked slaves" and started a custom that would be imitated by his retainers far and wide.[76] In the summer of 1615, he went to the Ajmer shrine at night on the anniversary of Muinuddin and stayed there until midnight with the attendants and Sufis who were in "ecstatic

FIGURE 8–1. "Jahangir Dispensing Food at Ajmer." Indian painting; Mughal, ca. 1614. Painting on paper: 31.8 × 20.8 cm. Courtesy of the Trustees of the Prince of Wales Museum of Western India, Bombay (29.6257). Not to be reproduced without prior permission of the Trustees.

states,"[77] and in the summer of 1616 he placed a gold railing with latticework at Muinuddin's tomb for the cost of Rs. 110,000.[78] When Jahangir left Ajmer in November of 1616 for Mandu (to be even closer to the still-advancing Mewar campaign),[79] he paid tribute to Ajmer as being of a favorable climate and "the place of the blessed tomb of the revered Khwaja Muinu-d-din."[80] After this he did not record ever going back to Muinuddin's tomb, although he did visit the tomb of the Chishti saint, Shaikh Nizamuddin Auliya, in Delhi in 1619.[81] The year 1616, then, seems to mark the end of his direct attention to the esteemed saint of Ajmer.

While it is possible that Jahangir did occasionally stop at Muinuddin's tomb in later years to honor the man who for so long had been his patron saint, he left no record of such in his own hand. Moreover, the years just after the Ajmer stay, especially 1618 to 1619 [see Figure 8–3] appear to mark a profound change in the religious sensibilities of Jahangir, and the veneration of Muinuddin, as an inherited, although obviously sincere and heartfelt, practice may have fallen away as Jahangir moved from the religious forms of his family's past generations to ones more authentically his own.

One of the policies inherited by Jahangir from his father was that of religious tolerance. According to Jahangir, Akbar "associated with the good of every race and creed and persuasion, and was gracious to all in accordance with their condition and understanding."[82] Though some have said that Jahangir came to the throne substantially more orthodox than his father and liberalized only later on,[83] Jahangir's long opening section to the *Tuzuk* seems clearly to lay the ground for the continuation of his father's tolerant policies from the very beginning. Roe noted that Jahangir wanted it said of him: "Christians, Moores, Iewes, hee meddled not with their faith: they Came all in loue and he would protect them from wrong: they liued vnder his safety and none should oppresse them."[84] And, Terry as well found that under Jahangir "all religions are tolerated . . . [and] that a man might be happy and safe in the profession of any religion."[85] That Jahangir was both openly tolerant in his policy toward his subjects' practice of religion and equally open-minded in his own views on religion is clear. While some, like Das, have questioned how deeply Jahangir reflected on universal religious issues and how well formulated his own thinking on spiritual matters was, there is agreement at least that while the specifics of his personal preference in religion may have been vague, there was no "systematic hostility" toward any tradition during his reign.[86]

Against the background of such a general policy of religious tolerance, Jahangir's response to Hinduism, the religion of his mother, seven of his wives, his subjects, and many of his courtiers, was a mix of curiosity, admiration, and occasional vehemence. Much of the early part of his reign was taken up in observing the Hindu tradition and patronizing its holy men. Just after his accession in 1605, for example, he argued with Hindu *pandits* about the relation between a high god and the phenomenal forms through which it must be known,[87] and in 1607 he noted having walked around a worshipping place of the *yogis* in the hopes of receiving grace from them.[88] In 1613 he was able to give a detailed account of the Hindu caste system,[89] and in early 1617 of some of the

Hindu *samskaras*, in particular that of initiation for young boys (*upanayana*).[90] And he always seemed to have been charitable to the *brahman* priests and *sadhus* he met on the road,[91] and to have remembered Hindu festivals like Holi, Divali,[92] Shivaratri, and the reverence of the ancestors.[93] Bernier noted, finally, that it "was on account of the scarcity of cattle that *Jehan-Guyre*, at the request of the *Brahmens*; issued an edict to forbid the killing of beasts of pasture for a certain number of years."[94]

Jahangir was not always kind to Hindu practice, however, and erupted once unexpectedly at a temple dedicated to Vishnu. In 1614, while walking around the temple grounds, he came upon "a form cut out of black stone, which from the neck above was in the shape of a pig's head, and the rest of the body was like that of a man." Disgusted by this image of Varaha, the boar incarnation of Vishnu, Jahangir began to rile against the "worthless religion of the Hindus,"[95] and like a good Muslim and consistent with his earlier discussion with the *pandits*,[96] he went on to denounce the religion in which "the Supreme Ruler thought it necessary to show himself in this shape." Ever wary thus of idolatry, Jahangir then had "that hideous form" broken up and thrown into the tank. Seeing further that there was a white domed structure on a hill nearby where devotees flocked to visit a resident *yogi*, Jahangir, unable to control his anger when he heard that part of the worship was to put flour in the mouth and to "imitate the cry of an animal," had the building broken down, the *yogi* turned out, and the image inside destroyed.[97]

Oddly consistent with the aesthetic dimensions of his character, however, Jahangir then inspected the building to confirm or deny the rumor that it had no bottom. The building did have a bottom, however, and being Jahangir, he measured it.[98] This incident, sadly prophetic of Shah Jahan's later destruction of Hindu idols and temples,[99] was indicative less of Jahangir's disdain for Hindu practice—of which, in fact, there seems to have been very little—and more of his easily offended aesthetic nature. His main criticism of Hinduism was its idolatry,[100] and his main criticism of idolatry was not a theological abhorrence of giving the unknowable form, but a visual repulsion at the specific form this particular phenomenalization took. Unable to bear what didn't please his eyes, Jahangir destroyed, but in the act of this destruction, he unwittingly upheld the iconoclasm of the faith of his forefathers.

In 1617, however, Jahangir's seemingly incompatible relationship with the Hindu tradition changed radically, for at the beginning of that year he began a series of interviews with a Hindu *sannyasi* named Gosain Jadrup that lasted over two years and which profoundly altered his view of the religion. In these interviews—in the winter of 1617,[101] the fall of 1618,[102] and the fall of 1619[103]—Jahangir established an unusual rapport with the saint of whom he said, "he spoke well, so much so as to make a great impression on me. My society also suited him."[104] Akbar himself had known of Jadrup, and it was from his father, apparently, that Jahangir's appreciation of the *sannyasi* had first begun. Jahangir didn't actually meet Jadrup, however, until 1617 and found him then having "retired from the city of Ujjain to a corner of the desert . . . [to employ] himself in the worship of the true God." Jahangir reported that Jadrup at that time lived in a hole in the side of a hill whose entrance was so small that it was difficult even for a very thin person to use. Jadrup, apparently, bathed twice a day and went once a day into Ujjain for alms where, Jahangir said, he accepted five mouthfuls of food which he swallowed without chewing.[105]

The two conversed for long periods at a time during these two years, usually "in the retirement of his cell"[106] [see Figure 8–2], and from Jadrup Jahangir learned much of what he reported on Hindu caste, family custom, and ritual. By Jahangir's own accounting, Jadrup had "thoroughly mastered the science of the Vedanta" but how much of "the science of Sufism"—which Jahangir claimed was the same as Vedanta—Jadrup knew is not clear.[107] Jahangir's attraction to Jadrup was probably not due strictly to doctrine anyway, however, but rather to some lived spiritual ideal he perceived in the saint. Jadrup had, in 1618, been an ascetic living "in the garment of nakedness" for thirty-eight years, after taking this vow against external attachments when he was twenty-two.[108] Jahangir clearly admired the *sannyasi*'s tenacity and the consistency with which he maintained his austerities, as well as the modesty with which he taught, and it is fair to say that Jadrup's appeal for the emperor lay primarily in his saintly posture more than anything else. Jahangir's last account of the *sannyasi*, in fact, before he said good-bye in 1619, was of Jadrup's temperament: "[a man whose] heart [was] free from the attachments of the world."[109] The hedonistic and sensuous emperor, then, had found a spiritual comrade in someone who had put aside all that he himself had claimed. Again, it seems that Jahangir's choice was an aesthetic one: of a companion and mentor whose lifestyle was so authentically stark and uncompromised that its cleanness far outstripped the beauty Jahangir thought he had in his own colorful yet cluttered existence.

After the interviews with Jadrup, Jahangir's approach to Hinduism was substantially more open and forgiving. In 1620, for example, on the way to Kashmir, he came across merchants from the apple-growing village of Baramula, but even when he learned that their district was named for the boar incarnation of Vishnu,[110] he showed none of the vehement disgust he had earlier during the incident of the black Varaha image in Ajmer. Moreover, he continued to take an interest in Hindu theories of men and women as well as in that culminating act of marital unity, the creation of the *sati*,[111] although in late 1620 he became so overcome by the practice of the *sati* and of female infanticide among the Rajaur women, who "ally themselves with Hindus," that he prohibited any such acts of violence against women.[112] He continued to extend kindnesses to holy men[113] and to converse with learned *brahmans* on issues of theology and Hindu custom,[114] and at the beginning of 1622, he became so fascinated with a *sannyasi*'s powers of renunciation and persistence that he had the man brought to court and tested, successfully, with a drink of double-strength spirits.[115]

The most significant event of this period, however, and the one that most aptly showed the change in Jahangir's response to Hindu practice, took place again in early 1622. Jahangir had gone to visit a temple of Durga and, although he spent some time in the *Tuzuk* riling against "the desert of error"—noting as he did that crowds were made up of as many Muslims as Hindus, two things marked a more lenient attitude toward the idol-worshipping that he saw. First,

FIGURE 8–2. "Jahangir Converses with Gosain Jadrup." ca. 1616–20. Courtesy of the Musee Guimet (MG 7171; 71En 1900).

he himself was not moved to take any retaliatory action, such as the breaking up of images or the casting out of infidels (although he did relate that others had done it); and second, although he noted that the "Hindus, while knowing the truth, deceive the common people," he treated this deceit as a human trait common to all and not one reserved exclusively for Hindus. His new nonintrusive stance was perhaps best shown in his own conclusion to the narrative: "But God only knows!"[116]

A similar change in attitude took place in Jahangir with regard to the Jains, perhaps the most ambiguously treated of all religious groups under his rule. Known best by the behavior of the *baniyas*, a merchant caste primarily in Gujarat adhering to the principles of Jainism, this tradition was characterized by foreign travelers primarily as one of nonviolence. The *baniyas*, said Terry, "are the most tender hearted . . . of all that people," who believe that because "they cannot give life to the meanest of the sensible creatures . . . they may not take the lives of any of them."[117] Roe noted that the *baniyas* "will not kyll the Vermyne that bytes them,"[118] and Manucci said that not only do the *baniyas* "hold it as a great sin to kill any animal," but they are also "very timid, and object to carry arms."[119]

Jahangir's attitude toward the Jains was one of great ambiguity and seems to have been directed to their policy of nonviolence.[120] Like his father, Jahangir maintained, on the one hand, a more or less tolerant posture toward the Jains, to the point of making early pronouncements favorable to them prohibiting the slaughter of animals. His eleventh regulation issued at the beginning of his reign in 1605, for example, banned the slaughter of animals for food beginning in each year from the day of his birth and continuing for the "number of days corresponding to the years of my life," as well as on Thursdays (the day of his accession) and Sundays (the day of his father's birth).[121] Moreover, he had many Jain monks at his court, both as teachers and as students,[122] and he often granted special favors to them by way of private audiences or privileges in the countryside. Jahangir had himself been taught by the Jain monk Bhanucandra as a child[123] and later asked this same monk to give religious instruction to his own youngest son, Shahryar, in return for his settling some factional disputes internal to the Jain community.[124] During his reign many Jain images were consecrated, and "in the inscriptions of some of them the name of Patasaha Jahangira was also engraved."[125] Most important, however, were the edicts and *farmans* issued by Jahangir that promoted and encouraged the practice of Jainism in the countryside.[126] For example:

1. August 14, 1601, a *nishan* of Prince Salim's attached to a *farman* of Akbar's confirming an earlier *farman* which prohibited the slaughter of animals during nearly six months of the year, and ordering that respect be shown to Jain teachers and that their old temples and religious buildings be repaired and rebuilt.
2. 1605, a *farman* of Prince Salim again confirming a *farman* of Akbar which prohibited the slaughter of animals during nearly six months of the year and making a religious spot in Una tax-free.
3. 1608, a *farman* of Jahangir allowing repairs and rebuilding of Jain temples

and rest houses, allowing Jains to visit their Shatrumjaya *tirtha* tax-free, and prohibiting animal slaughter on specified days.[127]

4. 1610, a *farman* of Jahangir prohibiting animal slaughter throughout the empire during the twelve days of the Jain Paryushana festival.
5. 1615, a *farman* of Jahangir permanently granting ten *bighas* of land in Akbarpur near Cambay to Chandu Sanghavi,[128] a Shvetambara Jain monk, in order to make a temple and garden dedicated to his late teacher Vijayasena Suri.
6. July 1616, a *farman* of Jahangir allowing complete freedom of worship to monks of the Jain community throughout the empire.
7. August 1, 1618, a *farman* of Jahangir written as a sealed letter to Vijayadeva Suri "in a friendly way" requesting that he pray for the permanence of the empire.

Although Jahangir may well have issued these edicts for personal religious reasons, he was not above tying his own religious needs to economic benefit, for several European travelers noted that the financially endowed and notably vegetarian *baniyas* paid large sums in order to have animals saved from the slaughter. Roe, for example, noted that the *baniyas* "often buy many dayes respite in charety from kylling any flesh at all"[129] and Terry that the *baniyas* "gave yearly large sums of money unto the Mogul to redeem them [all living creatures] from slaughter."[130] Pelsaert reported:

> They also occasionally obtain by bribery a general order from the King, or from the Governor of a particular city, that no one shall catch any fish for several days, or for as long a period as they can secure; and, occasionally, that for some days no meat of any description, whether goat, sheep, or buffalo, shall be sold in the market.

Pelsaert went on to say, however, that such edicts, while extremely inconvenient for ordinary law-abiding people, were ignored by the wealthy who "slaughter daily in their own houses."[131] Jahangir was also effective in settling disputes within the Jain community, such as the one he agreed to mediate in return for the Jain monk Bhanucandra's instruction to his son, Shahryar, and the one that broke out between monks at Burhanpur over issues of authority.[132]

Jahangir, however, was not a wholehearted supporter of the Jains, and in spite of his official advocacy and personal proclivity toward the Jain tradition, he caused them to suffer even more than he did the Hindus. While still a prince, for instance, the administrators he had appointed in Gujarat revived animal slaughter, the *jizyat* tax placed on followers of religions other than Islam, and other taxes prohibitive to the Jains, in actions that were presumably sanctioned by Salim. When Akbar found out about these practices from a Jain monk, he stepped in and issued the 1601 *farman* with an attached corroborating *nishan* from Salim, renewing his pronouncements in favor of the Jains.[133] Some time during the years 1611 to 1616,[134] after Jahangir had acceded to the throne, another incident occurred that showed Jahangir's clear disdain for the ascetic vocation of the Jains. At the court was a handsome and exceedingly well-formed

Jain monk named Siddhicandra whose beauty and good manners so struck Jahangir (and Nur Jahan) that he requested the monk's regular company. Siddhicandra, by his own account, was so young and appealing that Jahangir embarked on a lengthy campaign to break him of his vows. "Your age is meant for the soft pleasure of contact with the body of red-blooded damsels," reasoned Jahangir, "Why, then, do you waste it upon the desert of severe austerities?" Siddhicandra argued that the strength of religious commitment knew no age—the young, in fact, have more energy with which to control themselves than do the old—and as far as his handsome body was concerned, an unattached mind was ordinarily unaffected by any worldly pleasure whether that pleasure be his own form or someone else's. Unable to sway Siddhicandra, Jahangir became so angry with the monk for not accepting his proffered life of a householder and the cumbent pleasures of women that he banished Siddhicandra to the forest and issued a *farman* stating that all other advanced sages should retire to the forest as well, as it was only there that their disinterest was appropriate.[135] Siddhicandra's teacher, the Upadhyaya Bhanucandra, was kept at court by Jahangir, however, and in time became so overcome with depression at Siddhicandra's absence that Jahangir, out of affection for the older monk, issued a *farman* recalling Siddhicandra to the court.[136] Later the other banished monks were allowed, by imperial *farman*, to return to their cities and villages and to practice there as they had before.[137]

The incident Jahangir himself gave most attention to, however, was the recall and death of the Shvetambara Jain monk Man Singh. Man Singh had been head of the Kanthal (Kartal) sect of the Shvetambaras, and when Akbar died and the newly crowned Jahangir had pursued his rebellious son, Khusrau, Man Singh had been asked by Rai Singh Bhurtiya, *zamindar* of Bikaner, "what would be the duration of my [Jahangir's] reign and the chances of my success." Man Singh, that "black-tongued fellow, who pretended to be skilled in astrology and the extraction of judgments," had told the *zamindar* that Jahangir's reign would last only two years, withdrawing confidence thereby in the new emperor's rule. Man Singh had in time been proved wrong, however, and developed leprosy so bad "that death was by many degrees preferable to life." Living thus in Bikaner, he was "remembered" by Jahangir, who was then in Gujarat, and called to court. Man Singh became so overcome with fear at that point that he took poison on the way "and surrendered his soul to the lords of hell."[138]

This event was recorded as given above in the *Tuzuk* in early 1618, but Jain accounts of the incident suggested that there may be problems with Jahangir's version. Desai notes first, for example, that Jain monks were actually prohibited from predicting anyone's future—thus raising a question about Man Singh's original transgression—and, second, that the story of his later leprosy may have been only a myth. According to Jain documents, Man Singh died what we presume was an ordinary death on December 15, 1617, leaving Desai to account for Jahangir's outburst in his memoirs by saying it was merely "the result of a fit of ill humour," his ears having been poisoned by courtiers "constantly telling him evil things about Mana Simha."[139]

While it is not altogether clear what caused Jahangir's abrupt digression in the *Tuzuk* on the death of Man Singh, the written context of the outburst indicates that it may have been a part of a larger and more general denunciation of the Jains. Having already called the Shvetambaras "a tribe of infidel Hindus" in his narrative of Man Singh,[140] Jahangir proceeded to slander the Jains and the *baniyas* by charging that they maintained "houses [which] are the headquarters of sedition." The *baniyas*, said Jahangir, sent their wives and daughters to the Shvetambara monks who, with "no shame or modesty," perpetrated all "kinds of strife and audacity" upon the women. As a result of this, Jahangir ordered all Shvetambara monks expelled from his realm: "I circulated farmans to the effect that wherever there were Sewras in my empire they should be turned out."[141]

Jahangir's conflation of the Man Singh death with his charges, surely false,[142] of adultery and sedition on the part of Jain monks make sense only as a part of a large-scale attack on the tradition. The death of the monk in 1617 seems to have acted as a touchstone around which Jahangir could then weave other issues concerning the Jains. But why he originally called Man Singh to court (assuming, of course, that his account here was correct) and why his *Tuzuk* discussion became so negative an attack on the Jains in general are not immediately apparent. Presuming that the "remembrance" of Man Singh belonged to an older wound of Jahangir's and that the Jains' policy of nonviolence was an inferred critique of the emperor's own cruel and aberrant behavior in the field, Jahangir's outburst against the Jains may well have been the result of a larger issue: the internal preparations for a vow of nonviolence he would make later in 1618.

In the middle of 1618, Jahangir took a vow of nonviolence whereby he renounced shooting with guns and injuring any living creature with his own hand: "Sixteen or seventeen years ago I had vowed with my God at Allahabad that when I reached fifty I would give up shooting with gun and bullet, and would injure no living thing with my own hand."[143] This vow brought to a conclusion Jahangir's long-standing feelings of guilt and remorse over having ordered the murder of his father's close friend and chronicler Abul Fazl in August of 1602, and in general over his own rebellious and destructive conduct toward his father during the last years of Akbar's reign when the then prince had set up an independent court in Allahabad [see Figure 8–3]. The dynamics of the vow, we have argued elsewhere, allowed Jahangir to identify with the nonviolent religious persuasions of Akbar, which Jahangir had held up to now only as a matter of policy. In fact at the time of taking the vow, Jahangir himself made the connection to Akbar by noting his need to visit his father's tomb and "by God's help, seek the confirmation of my resolve from my father's holy elements, and renounce the practice (of shooting)."[144]

The double effect of this act—identification with the father he had earlier so grievously wounded and espousal of a clear policy of nonviolence in the face of his own long-term aggression—served to countermine and assuage the disruptive behavior of his earlier years. And the public quality of the vow (all those at court and beyond would be the clear beneficiaries of the official pronouncement) would make certain that the resolving of private guilt could not be derailed by new ambiguities or old lethargies but would rather become the overt responsibility of his entire entourage. It is a powerful confirmation of the father–son structure of this vow of nonviolence, moreover, that Jahangir granted greater freedom to his first son, Khusrau, in 1619, the year the vow went into effect, but then revoked the vow in 1622 when his third son, Shah Jahan, rebelled against him.[145]

The timing of the vow, however, paralleled too closely for coincidence the tortuous patterns of Jahangir's treatment of the Jains. The Jains, who were subjected to an ambiguous mixture of compassionate advocacy and disdainful rejection from Jahangir's later years as a prince up until early in the imperial year of 1618, were then forgotten by the emperor after what was apparently his last *farman* concerning them in August of 1618.[146] Surely there was a connection between Jahangir's own internal conflicts between aggression and compassion and his mixed treatment of the Jains, the very symbol of nonviolent restraint, during those first two decades and his resolution of these conflicts through the vow and his newly inattentive attitude toward the Jains, both of which began in 1618. We can argue, then, that the Jains, through no fault of their own, save the very nature of their religious doctrine, got caught up in Jahangir's private struggles with the memory of his father that swept through the whole range of relations he had with religious groups in his realm and that, given Jahangir's personality, could not help but be projected into the public arena.

Jahangir's relations with the Christians, however, was the telling example of the way in which religious policy during his reign became a blend of personal whim and political expediency. The mix of Christians Jahangir found around him reflected the variety of much of Europe, the older, more long-standing Roman tradition of the Portuguese Jesuits vying with the more recently arrived Protestantism of the Dutch Reform merchants and the Anglican English Embassy. The burden of the religious quest for converts in India was carried primarily by the Portuguese Jesuits, the Dutch and the English being essentially concerned with the establishment of trading contracts for their home countries. Nevertheless, within the secular missions of the English there was certainly some proselytizing activity, and the presence of one so conscientious as the Reverend Edward Terry, chaplain to Sir Thomas Roe, was testimony not only to the religious needs of his English compatriots but also to his hopes for an increased flock.

Jesuit expectations for Jahangir had been genuinely hopeful when the emperor first came to the throne. His father, Akbar, had openly welcomed the priests to the court and had toyed, at least publicly, with the possibility of conversion for himself for many years. While still a prince, Jahangir had often professed an attachment to the Christian faith,[147] and Payne argues persuasively that because Salim knew "his succession to the throne was by no means a foregone conclusion," his association with the Jesuits was based on more than just religious affinity. Rather, the prince hoped that the Portuguese could offer him "very valuable assistance" in the event he should need it in his struggle for accession.[148] As it turned out Jahangir managed the throne without Portuguese help, but he continued to entertain the Jesuits courteously and encouragingly at his court throughout his life.

Father Francisco Corsi, for example, had been in Mughal country for the last five years of Akbar's reign and continued on at Jahangir's court until he was succeeded by Father Joseph de Castro in 1624.[149] Corsi and Roe, apparently, were on friendly terms, but the English ambassador saw right through the emperor's attempts to conciliate the Jesuits without binding himself irrevocably to them. Jahangir granted the Catholic Church many privileges, said Roe, and spent "euerynight for one yeare . . . in hearing disputation" amongst Christians and other theologians. He often cast "out doubtfull woordes of his conversion, but to wicked Purpose," for in the end he had no serious interest in the European doctrine. "And, the rather to giue some hope, he deliuered many Youthes into the hands of Francisco Corsy" for their education and religious instruction.[150] Terry noted, moreover, that in pursuit of such hopes Corsi lived at court "as an agent for the Portuguese" and not only had free access to Jahangir but was the recipient of gifts and great encouragement.[151] The surge of Jesuit optimism that accompanied such acts of benevolence, however, masked the real naivety with which the Roman Church often seemed to work.

Jahangir's most active interest in Christian doctrine was in the debates held at his court between the Jesuit fathers and Muslim *mullas*. In a letter sent from Agra to the Jesuit Provincial of Goa dated September 24, 1608, Father Jerome Xavier detailed a series of discussions that arose there out of Jahangir's viewing of some Christian pictures. The fathers "had long been anxious for an opportunity of disputing with the Moors before the King, that they might demonstrate the truth of our faith, and the falseness of the law of Mafamede."[152] The debate that ensued covered a variety of theological issues,[153] and the discussions often became loud and abusive, with the Muslims (according to Guerreiro) at times crying out: "It is a lie! It is a lie!"[154] For his part, Jahangir got along by asking questions of the fathers, questions that "were evidently meant to put our faith in a favourable light" and "to bring ridicule on Mafamede, and on his Moorish courtiers, who, during this conversation, stood grinding their teeth with rage against the Fathers." By Guerreiro's account, Jahangir's tactics were successful for "the Moors began to regard the Fathers with intense hatred, following them with evil looks wheresoever they went."[155] Although the Jesuits claimed great victory from these debates, which lasted over a month during the summer, no one (by the Jesuits' own admission) was converted, not even and especially the king.[156]

Roe and Terry both mentioned at a later date some debates lasting over a year that took place every night for two hours before Jahangir in his court.[157] Jerome Xavier was a major participant in them, and Terry noted that these particulars about Xavier's debates before Jahangir were given to him, the English chaplain, by Corsi in Latin and were so confirmed "by other people professing Christianity in that empire" that Terry believed they actually did occur.[158] Quite possibly Terry and Roe's accounts referred to the same 1608 Agra debates as described by Guerreiro.

By policy and personal assent, Jahangir allowed anyone to convert to Christianity who wanted to. Said Terry:

> The Jesuits in East-India . . . have liberty to convert any they can work upon, unto Christianity, etc. the Mogul hath thus far declared, that it shall be lawful for any one, persuaded so in conscience to become a Christian, and that he should not by so doing lose his favour.[159]

The Jesuits took to heart this blanket permission to ply their trade and filled their chronicles with case studies of individuals who had come over from Islam and Hinduism. Conversion to Christianity had taken place on a fairly small scale among the nobles and relatives of the Mughal court under Akbar[160] and continued, again at a slow pace, under Jahangir.[161] The most famous case of conversion among Jahangir's nobles, perhaps, was that of Muqarrab Khan. Formerly Shaikh Hasan, son of Shaikh Baha, Muqarrab Khan received his title while Jahangir was still a prince for service he had given the emperor since the days of his childhood. A frequent companion of Jahangir's when he hunted, Muqarrab Khan was skilled in the use of the bow and arrow and gun and was especially able in the practice of surgery,[162] a talent he used often in his position as personal physician to the emperor.[163] Muqarrab Khan had spent a good deal of the early part of Jahangir's reign in Cambay overseeing Mughal trading interests there and had often brought or sent extravagant presents to Jahangir that he had procured while on duty there.[164] He got into trouble, however, in 1610 when one of his attendants abducted a girl in the port of Cambay and was deemed responsible when she died "an unavoidable death." The attendant was executed and Muqarrab Khan's *mansab* was reduced by half.[165] It was perhaps from an ensuing imprisonment that he was saved by Father Emmanuel Pinheiro and reinstated as envoy to the Portuguese Viceroy in Goa. When he returned to Goa from Agra in 1611, Muqarrab Khan was reported by the Jesuits to have converted to Christianity and to have been baptised with the name John. His relationship with Christians after this remained, as expected, quite friendly and supportive,[166] but Jahangir, though he always honored and promoted his servant[167]—especially to the *suba* of Gujarat in 1616[168]—did not once mention Muqarrab Khan's Christianity.

Conversion to Christianity came closest to the Mughal throne, however, with the baptism of several of Jahangir's nephews, three sons of his late brother, Daniyal, on September 5, 1610, in a large public ceremony held at the Jesuit church in Agra and later at the imperial court.[169] Finch noted that for the baptism "Christian apparell" was made for the boys and, in a display put on with "the whole city admiring," the boys were conducted to the church by all the Christians in Agra. The boys each received a Christian name—Tahmuras became Don Philippe, Bayasanghar, Don Carlo, and Hoshang, Don Henrico—and were followed in their baptism by that of the grandson of Akbar's brother, Mirza Muhammad Hakim, who became Don Duarte.[170] Jahangir himself did not mention the baptism—only the earlier conveyance of Daniyal's children to him from Burhanpur by Muqarrab Khan[171]— but Finch noted that the emperor had given "daily charge to the Fathers for their [the boys'] instruction that they might become good Christians."[172] Hawkins, who was an eyewitness participant to most of these baptismal events, argued persuasively that Jahangir urged the conversions not "for any zeale he had to Christianitie," but because he had taken heed of a prophecy that his own sons would be disinherited and that he would be succeeded by the children of his brother. Therefore, in order "to make these children hatefull to all Moores," he had them baptized as Christians, in a faith so "odious . . . [that] they should find no subjects."[173] Their father, Daniyal, had been so loved, argued van den Broecke later, that the sons would be natural inheritors to the throne, and yet some years after the conversions, he continued, Jahangir brought them back into the Muslim fold,[174] presumably after the threat of succession scuffles had passed.

What, however, was Jahangir's own involvement with Christianity? Although Manucci later asserted the willingness of Jahangir himself to become a Christian,[175] earlier travelers were less certain as to the emperor's final disposition. To be sure, Jahangir loved to watch the Jesuits debate the *mullas*,[176] and he had a fascination for Christian images of Jesus and of Mary[177] that extended to other biblical figures as well.[178] Moreover, he had allowed and even patronized the building of Christian churches and cloisters[179] and had exhibited eccentrically supportive behavior of the tradition from the very beginning. To a servant of an Italian visitor while still a prince, for example, Salim was reported to have responded to the servant's avowal of Christianity as follows:

> "You have done well to embrace so good a law." Then, still addressing the Italian, he added these words: "I have a very great affection for the Lord Jesus"; and to show that these were not mere words, but that he spoke from his heart, he drew aside his robe, and showed him a cross of gold, which it was his habit to wear suspended from his neck.[180]

In spite of his attraction to the visual elements in Christianity, however, Jahangir still had irreconcilable problems with the tradition on at least two counts: aspects of the life of Christ and Christian monogamy. Jahangir had watched entranced once while an ape, later called the "divininge ape" had twice drawn the name of Christ out of a pool of twelve prophets but had come up empty-handed after the name of Christ had been removed;[181] nevertheless, he remained unconvinced of this "Son of God" 's absolute authority. Although Jahangir spoke respectfully of Christ, he was continually troubled by "his parentage, his poverty, and his cross,"[182] so much so that Christology was a central issue in the theological debates at the court. Jahangir was also put off, perhaps more decidedly, "by the severe discipline which our [Christian] law imposes" that forbade a man from taking more than one wife. It was because of "this prohibition," said Guerreiro, "that they find our faith so hard to accept."[183] Being part of "a carnal-minded race,"[184] Guerreiro continued, Jahangir ultimately found the domestic teachings of Christian monogamy the hardest to accept.

Jahangir's response to Christianity, then, was one of curiosity, of testing, of admiration of its arts, but eventually of rejection of its doctrine. Perhaps the most symbolically authentic image of Jahangir here was given by Hawkins, who described the emperor while at prayer once in Agra: in a private room, with a lambskin under him, fingering eight chains of luxuriously studded jewel prayer beads. Graven in stone on the upper end of his black slate throne, Hawkins reported, were "pictures of Our Lady and Christ," but the emperor's lambskin and his face were turned westward[185]—toward Mecca. Jahangir may not have been a Christian at heart, then, but he was certainly open to the tradition, at least as much as his own father Akbar had been and no doubt much more than his son Shah Jahan was ever to be.[186]

Like all those of his age, Jahangir had to respond to the many religions that appeared at the crossroads of his court. As religious questions were in the air, Jahangir was called upon to make personal and political choices that would, particularly in his case, be marked by the eccentricities of his own personality. He was not, by his own memoirs, an especially profound man nor was he moved to probe for the sake of knowledge the subtleties of foreign doctrine. But he was touched by religion and knew that it had to play some fairly central role in his life.

Based on evidence in the *Tuzuk* given so far, we can now divide Jahangir's spiritual chronology into three distinct periods [see Figure 8–3]: a pre-1618 period of adherence to religious policy brought forward as a whole from Akbar's reign but often expressed in wildly contradictory behavior toward the religious groups in question; a transitional two-year period marked internally by serious introspection about the past, but externally by a vehement calling to account of figures like the Jain monk Man Singh and the Sufi *shaikh* Ahmad Sirhindi (see the following), who had both questioned Jahangir's sovereign competence in years previous; and a post-1619 period of moderation, leniency, and above all detachment from the religious fray, marked by a sense of ease with himself and an affirmation of the policy of pluralistic tolerance as authentically his own.

When he first came to the throne, for example, and for some years thereafter, Jahangir's religious patterns followed by habit those of his predecessors: veneration of Muinuddin Chishti at his tomb in Ajmer; uneven but usually tolerant open-mindedness of the Hindus, Jains, and Christians he found around him; and studied detachment from the claims of the orthodox Muslim religious on the policies of his government. These particular postures, however, had been adopted more or less intact from the practices of his father, who had himself come to them after careful thought and reflection. Moreover, Jahangir's enactment of these policies was often riddled by thoughtless inconsistencies and wild swings of behavior that had every mark either of a desire to tease, flaunt, and mock or of a simple carelessness as sovereign.

Beginning with the years of 1618 and 1619, however, Jahangir began to settle into a more stable and moderate pose, characterized by a detached tolerance, leniency, and general affirmation of religious pluralism that more authentically mirrored the practices of Akbar. Sparked perhaps by his interviews with Jadrup or by the resolution of father feelings in his own vow of nonviolence, Jahangir moved neatly into a period of benign noninterference with the traditions around him. Although the move had been marked as well by the abruptly painful Man Singh and Sirhindi affairs of 1617 to 1618 and 1619, respectively, in which each of the two was called upon to answer for unkind remarks bearing on Jahangir's sovereignty made very much earlier, this period of transition brought with it a

	Chishtis	Sirhindi	Hindus
Pre-1618	*Open support* and promotions for the descendants of Shaikh Salim Chishti. *Veneration* of Shaikh Muinuddin Chishti by regular visits to and ritual practice at his tomb in Ajmer.	*Accession of 1605:* possible influence of Shaikh Ahmad Sirhindi and Shaikh Farid Bukhari. *1605–19:* Jahangir recorded no contact with Sirhindi.	*Curious but offended by Hinduism:* Jahangir learned about and even engaged in "infidel" practice, but in late 1613 lashed out at a statue of Varaha, ordering it as well as a nearby *yogi's* abode and the statue inside to be completely destroyed.
Transition (1618–19)	*November 1616:* last recorded visit to Muinuddin's tomb. *Early 1619:* visited tomb of Shaikh Salim and recounted story of his death. *Fall 1619:* recounted story of death of Islam Khan, grandson of Shaikh Salim, on his own (Jahangir's) behalf. *Fall 1619:* visited tomb of Shaikh Nizamuddin Auliya.	*Early summer 1619:* Sirhindi called to Jahangir's court to account for teachings and activities, including a possibly seditious letter written much earlier; imprisoned in Gwalior fort. *Early summer 1620:* released from the fort and given gifts of honor.	*Interviews with Jadrup:* during long, private conversations held in winter of 1617, fall of 1618, fall of 1619, Jahangir learned much of what he knew of Hinduism (and, he said, of Sufism) from a *sannyasi* living in a cave outside of Ujjain.
Post-1619	*After 1619:* very little reference to Chishti saints or Chishti family members.	*1620–24:* Sirhindi enjoyed pleasant, if ultimately unproductive, relationship with Jahangir instructing him in the teachings of Islam.	*Tolerant restraint:* after his interviews with Jadrup, Jahangir continued to record Hindu practice and to patronize local *yogis,* but showed remarkable restraint, forbearance, and even objectivity in attitudes toward Varaha, and worship at a temple of Durga.

FIGURE 8–3. Chart: "Summary of Selected Changes in Jahangir's Religious History."

decided closure to the anxieties of the past about Jahangir's fitness to rule. Aided no doubt by the foregathering rupture in the junta, his own declining health, and the turning of his attention toward Kashmir, Jahangir nevertheless seems to have come to some genuine ease with the traditions at work in his realm. Although we have no clear idea of his personal vision of religion after the transitional years, it was probably the same in form as it had been earlier yet was now sincerely his own.

II

Against the vast documentation of Jahangir's habits of religion, the particular persuasions of Nur Jahan remain almost unknown. We can be sure, with her family's Persian origins, that her general tendency in politics and religion was pro-Shia and anti-Sunni. What the particular manifestations of these loyalties were, however, can only be guessed at for the elitist, secretive, and cliquish style of Shia operatives, coupled with Nur Jahan's appearance only in others' memoirs, preclude a firsthand account of almost all her religious dealings.

Jains	*Akbar*	*Miscellaneous*
Policy swings: prohibited animal slaughter, ordered work on temples, allowed complete freedom of worship, but also encouraged animal sacrifice, tried to persuade a monk to break his vow of asceticism, and riled against Jain doctrine and practice.	*Ambivalent attitude before the accession:* while waiting for the throne, Jahangir rebelled against his father, set up independent court in Allahabad, and had Abul Fazl murdered; after the accession (and after Akbar's death), he celebrated and eulogized his father.	*Sons:* Khusrau rebellious, ostracized, and blinded; Shah Jahan ascendant. *Jahangir:* contradictory swings between acts of cruelty and displays of benevolence.
Late 1617/early 1618: Jahangir recalled the Shvetambara Jain Man Singh to court for a seditious prophecy he made much earlier at the accession, but the monk took poison and died on the way. *Vow of nonviolence:* citing the Allahabad years (and presumably the murder of Abul Fazl) of 1600–1604 as the origin of the vow, Jahangir renounced shooting with a gun and injuring creatures with his own hands in 1618; reiterated and activated the vow in 1619.		*1619–21:* Khusrau given greater freedom; Shah Jahan more distant from the throne. *Jahangir:* increasingly declining health; ever more power handed over to Nur Jahan as junta began to rupture; new attention to Kashmir.
After 1618: no significant proclamations concerning the Jains.	*Until 1622:* no hunting with a gun or injuring of living creatures.	*1622:* vow of nonviolence rescinded when Shah Jahan went into open revolt; Khusrau now recently dead. *Jahangir:* focus on greater personal pleasure (e.g., Kashmir) and greater distance from political realities; general tolerance and restraint.

There are two things, however, that we may attribute unhesitatingly to the at least formal aspect of Nur Jahan's spiritual life. First, she was, by Persian accounts, a generous woman who gave in charity to "all sufferers" and especially to "helpless girls" at the time of their marriage. It is said that "thousands were grateful for her generosity"[187] and "if ever she learnt that any orphan girl was destitute and friendless, she would bring about her marriage, and give her a wedding portion."[188] Nur Jahan's generosity stemmed, most certainly, from her position as chief wife of the reigning emperor and from her consequent vision of herself as the female dispenser of noblesse oblige. But it is quite likely that she also gave out of the Muslim conviction that each member of the community was responsible for the financial well-being of all others. Islamic obligations of charity would most certainly have molded her behavior as queen, but it may also have been an authentic religious persuasion that, happily, found extravagant outlet in her imperial position.

Nur Jahan was also known to have participated in the celebration of the *urs* festival at the tomb of Shaikh Muinuddin Chishti in Ajmer [see Figure 8–1]. Coryat recorded having seen Nur Jahan with Jahangir at Muinuddin's shrine, sometime between July 1615 and September 1616, passing out *khichri* from a huge brass pot to thousands of the poor.[189] Normally at the *urs*, held in honor of the death anniversary of a Sufi, a rich devotee of the saint paid for the preparation of a huge mixture of grain and spices that was cooked in the caldron there and passed out to pilgrims coming to the shrine.[190] At the festival Coryat observed, however, the emperor himself became that patron, and himself kindled the fire and served the first platter with his own hands. Nur Jahan was a major functionary at this meal, helping with the cooking fire and with the distribution of food, and Coryat was so overcome by the immense generosity of the event she participated in that he irreverently compared European forms to what he saw before him: "Cracke mee this nut, all the Papall charitie vaunters."[191]

Aside from charity and from ceremonies in Ajmer at the tomb of Muinuddin, Nur Jahan most surely must have taken part in the religious observances of the harem. Like her women colleagues of the *zanana*, Nur Jahan would have participated regularly in the five times daily prayers and in the seasonal celebrations of Islam that were carried out around her. Moreover, she may even have been a welcome participant in the Hindu festivals of the Rajput wives [see Figure 5–2] and certainly was an appreciative observer of those things of moment Jahangir may have been involved in religiously. Whatever else she may have thought, supported, or done, however, is absent from historical documents, and there is, therefore, very little that can be argued conclusively about her religious persuasions at the court. Nevertheless, there were four identifiable areas of religious policy in which Nur Jahan's influence may have been felt, although the evidence in most cases remains circumstantial: the abusive treatment given the Jains, the summons and imprisonment of Shaikh Ahmad Sirhindi, the decline in favor of Shaikh Salim Chishti's family, and the weakening of Jahangir's interest in Christianity.

Nur Jahan's contact with Jain monks at the court was surprisingly substantial. Siddhicandra, chronicler of his teacher Bhanucandra's activities and himself a Jain monk, used to visit the harem "sometimes by invitation of the Emperor and sometimes of his own accord" to read and study great works of grammar, poetry, logic, rhetoric, prosody, and dramaturgy.[192] He had caught the eye of Jahangir who, because of the monk's exceedingly handsome form, had asked him to come visit every day for some short while. Jahangir used to listen to Siddhicandra's sermons and in time vowed that he would do anything the monk asked him to do. Once while the court was in Agra,[193] Jahangir was struck by the fact that the exceptionally comely Siddhicandra had remained unmarried because of his ascetic vows and now, as a young man of twenty-five who should be enjoying the physical pleasures of a wife, was by choice a celibate. This observation was followed by lengthy conversations with Siddhicandra that were at times detached and abstract and at times personal and argumentative, but that ended with the monk's temporary banishment to the forest when he refused to take whatever wife Jahangir might find for him.[194]

At one point in the argument, Nur Jahan, "the beautiful and beloved Empress," stepped in to join Jahangir's attempt to persuade the monk. Her argument refined one Jahangir had suggested earlier in a more passionate and rambling fashion, by focusing on the incompatibility of controlled firmness with youth.

"Asceticism is meant for those who have had their fill of sensual pleasures," she argued, not for those who have not yet experienced them. The position she presented to Siddhicandra then developed two points: first, that normally a person will continue to hanker after pleasures until he has experienced them sufficiently to renounce them; and, second, that Siddhicandra was rebuffing, by his youthful vow of sustained asceticism, the Indian *ashrama* system, which laid out the most psychologically appropriate chronology of a life: initial renunciation, indulgence, and final renunciation. Siddhicandra responded to her implied introduction of doctrine by introducing some of his own—the spiritual decline that had taken place in humankind over the course of the *yugas* and had resulted in the young becoming more disciplined than the old. At this point Nur Jahan ceased raising objections, for reasons not preserved in the Jain text, and Jahangir took the discussion to its eventually stalemated conclusion.[195]

Nur Jahan's contribution to the Siddhicandra debate, on the face of it, had been to make the discussion more abstract and to legitimize it by referring to issues of doctrine. While she was not able to dissuade Siddhicandra from his resolve, the account of her role as depicted by the Jain document shows three things. First, the text portrays Nur Jahan as an accomplice, and even promoter, to Jahangir's harassment of the Jains on the grounds, we infer, that vows of lifetime asceticism set up authority systems separate to and rivaling those of the crown. Her influence on the development of religious policy here, then, was to bring reason to a discussion based primarily on emotion, thereby providing justifiable affirmation for a course Jahangir had already embarked upon. Second, the episode, if rightly reflective of the empress's views on the subject, reveal that her own religious persuasions were consonant with the Muslim ideals she grew up with. Siddhicandra represented Nur Jahan as inclined against religious vocations involving celibacy, and in favor of the affirmed householder life as the preeminent context for spiritual development. True to Islam, which unlike most other religious traditions, eschews the virginal life for its religious, Nur Jahan could not understand why Siddhicandra was unable to come to spiritual maturity as an ordinary citizen. Third, the account is unabashedly admiring of Nur Jahan as a personality, depicting her as a woman who could play a commendably intelligent role in the religious debates at court. Because Siddhicandra was not only an intimate of Jahangir's inner rooms but also of the harem as well, we can presume that this portrayal of Nur Jahan was one drawn from actual sustained and discerning conversation with her and not simply from the reified conceptions of bazaar gossip.

Nur Jahan's influence on religious policy came next to light in the 1619 episode involving Shaikh Ahmad Sirhindi. The Naqshbandi *silsila* had only recently become a force in sectarian Muslim politics, achieving prominence in the last few years of Akbar's reign. Politically and emotionally weakened by the rebellion of his son Salim and Salim's establishment of an independent court in Allahabad, and by Salim's murder of his friend, Abul Fazl, Akbar seemed powerless to prevent Naqshbandi activists from gaining an ideological hold among some of his high-ranking nobles.[196] Akbar's freethinking tolerance of many religious traditions at his court and his establishment of an emperor-based discipleship among some of his colleagues had angered many of his more orthodox Muslim ministers. The Naqshbandi agenda, then, at least in terms of what were ultimately to be minimal relations with the Mughal government of this period, had been to try to stem the influence of the Akbarian heresy and to give orthodox Islam more voice at the policy-making level of the administration.[197]

Shaikh Ahmad Sirhindi, like his teacher Khwaja Baqi Billah, was in the forefront of Naqshbandi criticism and by some accounts played a considerable role in bringing Jahangir to power in 1605 and in trying to extract a pledge from him to adhere more closely to Islamic law during his reign.[198] The exact role played by the Naqshbandis in Jahangir's accession has been open to much debate, but it is fair to say that after some token honors given to Naqshbandi associates at the beginning of his reign[199] and after placing Shaikh Farid Bukhari (a close correspondee of Sirhindi's who died in 1616) at the head of the army pursuing Khusrau in 1606,[200] Jahangir paid little heed to members of the *silsila* for well over a decade. His accession pledges to the Naqshbandis, then, had either been minimal or encumbered with such little power on the religious side that they were unenforceable. Sirhindi did, however, have an important intercessor at court in the figure of Shaikh Farid, who was the recipient of several letters from Sirhindi and who, apparently, tried to promote Sirhindi's cause with Jahangir.[201] One such incident took place when the emperor asked Shaikh Farid to recommend four *ulama* to be *sharia* advisors in his court. Sirhindi wrote to Shaikh Farid saying that if Jahangir went ahead with these appointments the outcome would be to employ four men who would end up quarreling with each other, as conciliatory peace-loving *ulama* were not now available; one man, he argued, would be far superior. The inference was, some presume, that Sirhindi himself wanted to be that one man appointed to that position,[202] but in the end Jahangir's plan to appoint the *ulama* to the court was never carried out.

Instead, we hear that in 1619 Jahangir abruptly called Sirhindi to court to account for his preaching activities in the countryside. Calling him "a loud talker . . . [and] a cheat" who was responsible for spreading "the net of hypocrisy and deceit," Jahangir wanted to hear from Sirhindi himself what was behind the *shaikh's* promotion of a worship "without spirituality" and of his false "selling of religious knowledge." Sirhindi had, by Jahangir's account, established *khalifas* in "every city and country" to further his cause and had written a book of letters (the *Maktubat*) full of "absurdities . . . [designed to] drag (people) into infidelity and impiety." When asked to respond to the issues, Sirhindi "could give no reasonable answer, and appeared to me to be extremely proud and self-satisfied, with all his ignorance." Judging that the *shaikh* needed some time to quiet "the heat of his temperament and confusion of his brain," Jahangir gave Sirhindi over to one Ani Rai Singh Dalan to be imprisoned in the fort at Gwalior.[203] Jahangir released Sirhindi a year later and gave him a dress of honor and Rs. 1,000 for expenses after the *shaikh* had made clear that he saw his punishment as "a valuable lesson to him" and had expressed his desire "to wait on me."[204] Thereafter, Sirhindi spent considerable time at the court exegeting Quranic verses for Jahangir and explicating the basic teachings of Islam. Although Jahangir seemed to have been open-minded about these theology lessons and was generous in his gifts to the *shaikh*,[205] Sirhindi apparently made little real headway in capturing the spiritual attention of the emperor.[206]

At least four issues may have been involved in the sudden call to Sirhindi to appear at Jahangir's court. Most scholars focus, first, not only upon the inflammatory style and widespread appeal of Sirhindi's public preaching, which seemed to have been a main problem for Jahangir,[207] but upon the content of his past and present discourse. Sirhindi had, some time before his teacher's death in 1603, written to Khwaja Baqi Billah describing a mystical experience in which he saw himself raised to a position above the four orthodox *khalifas*. The old letter had become public and had so infuriated the *ulama* that they had pressed Jahangir to take the action he did in 1619.[208] Why this action, based on the contents of so old a letter, did not occur until 1619 is usually accounted for by the vagaries of the process it took for things to become public knowledge.[209]

A second element in Jahangir's unexpected summons of Sirhindi to court was the religious transition the emperor himself was going through during the years 1618 to 1619[210] [see chart, Figure 8–3]. The Sirhindi incident, we have argued, falls into the middle transitional period when Jahangir was most fraught with doubt about the legitimacy of his accession to the throne and his own abilities as a ruler to carry out the obligations of the crown. The vow of nonviolence taken in 1618[211] had resolved long-standing ambivalent feelings about Akbar, but had come at the expense of frightening (to death!) in late 1617/early 1618 the Shvetambara Jain Man Singh, who at the beginning of Jahangir's reign had committed the unfortunate mistake of prophesying a short and unaccomplished rule for the emperor. The fact, however, that the vow had to be reaffirmed in 1619[212] indicates that finalizing the resolution had taken a while, and in view of this, it was in the last phases of the middle period that Jahangir abruptly turned to Sirhindi.

Like Man Singh, Sirhindi had a long time earlier questioned the authority of Jahangir; his letter to Khwaja Baqi Billah, benign and otherworldly as it was, nevertheless flaunted a second authority in the face of what Jahangir assumed was his own absolute rule. At any other time, this may not have been so troublesome to the emperor but, with his own anxieties at their height, any person in any way who doubted his competence at his job (Man Singh) or who set up alternate authority structures (Sirhindi)—even if those actions had taken place many years before—had to come to account for their positions before the king. Sirhindi's appearance in court occurred about two months after Jahangir's 1619 final and activating reaffirmation of his vow and must have signaled, thus, the emperor's last attack of worry before he settled into the relatively easy religious stance of his later years.

Sirhindi's implied threat to Jahangir in his elevation of himself to substantial spiritual authority was compounded, third, by his refusal to prostrate before the emperor. From Shia followers, apparently, Jahangir had learned that Sirhindi had done so on the grounds that it was "against the spirit of Islam." Although Shah Jahan, a supporter of Sirhindi's, had sent books on *fiqh* to the *shaikh* telling him that prostration before the king had been sanctioned by legal scholars, Sirhindi remained adamant about bowing down only before Allah.[213]

The Sirhindi incident could also be seen, finally (and to the point here), as a result of the political maneuvers of the Shia faction at court managed, for all intents and purposes, by Nur Jahan. Although we have no substantive evidence that Nur Jahan was directly involved, many have suggested that both the timing and vehemence of the Sirhindi incident indicate the presence of the empress's heavy hand on Jahangir to respond to the anti-Shia remarks of the *shaikh*.[214] Sirhindi had earlier, "in the pre-Sufi period of his life," written a document highly critical of Shia doctrine and texts. He had called the Shias heretics and infidels because of their, to him, baseless claim that Ali was the only true successor to the prophet and their refusal to acknowledge the consensus of the community (which had included Ali) as the authentic heritage of Islam. In their excessive adoration of Ali, Sirhindi argued, the Shias exhibited traits similar to the Christians in their idolatrous attitude toward Jesus. Moreover, their religious documents were unreliable and had been corrupted with spurious passages designed to promote the peculiarities of their doctrine.[215] In time, however, Sirhindi modified his rhetoric against the Shias, and the opinions expressed in his later *Maktubat* were less hostile and condemnatory and more diplomatic with regard to the role of Ali in Islamic religious history. Nevertheless, he continued to maintain his position that orthodox Mughal officials should not enter into relationships with any of the Shias whom they might meet at court.[216] Sirhindi's position, then, certainly well known and publicized during Nur Jahan's time, was less hostile in the middle of Jahangir's reign than it had been during the Akbar years, but it continued without doubt to be anti-Shia enough to infuriate the Persian faction at court.

Not only was the provocation sufficiently strong to elicit a response from Nur Jahan, but the timing as well suited the pattern of her career. In 1619, Nur Jahan was at the height of her power, having just some time before hosted the 1617 festivities honoring Shah Jahan for his victories in the Deccan.[217] The junta was as strong now as it would ever be, with the splintering effects of the marriage of her daughter, Ladli, to Shahryar[218] and the deaths of her parents,[219] so pivotal to whatever harmony there was in "the faction," still some time away. Now in 1619, Nur Jahan enjoyed both the full attention and permission of Jahangir as well as the undivided support of the Shias at court for whom she almost assuredly acted as chief counsel and spokeswoman during the height of the junta's power. Added to this, Shaikh Farid Bukhari, who had been such a cultured and diplomatic bearer of Naqshbandi influence at court, had died in 1616, leaving a vacuum that drew new and differently persuasive elements to the emperor's side. Although Nur Jahan most certainly would have seen that a doctrine of open tolerance for all traditions was the most beneficial in the long run to the Shia community in positions of power, she would nevertheless have had every reason to react with anger against anyone like Sirhindi whose anti-Shia remarks were directly insulting to her own tradition and whose proclamation of higher authority undermined what was at least a veneer of tolerant pluralism present in her and Jahangir's religious policy.

One could argue alternately, however, that although Nur Jahan was seemingly at the height of her power in 1619, there were cracks beginning to show in the solidarity of the junta. Most particularly, Shah Jahan, with substantial military victories to his credit and with an increasing irritation at his stepmother's upper hand, could have been hinting now at his clear needs for independence. Since Shah Jahan was an acknowledged follower of Sirhindi, Nur Jahan's provocation of the summons and imprisonment of the *shaikh* may have arisen either from her burgeoning efforts to consolidate power in her own right, outside of the junta, or from her anger at her recently divisive stepson. A substantial reprimand to Sirhindi, we might argue, would have been a strike at Shah Jahan as well and an attempt, before it was too late, to put the prince back in his place.

The evidence for Nur Jahan's involvement in the Sirhindi incident remains, however, circumstantial. We know that Sirhindi had been making anti-Shia remarks, and we know that Nur Jahan had both the power and the force of personality to get Jahangir to take the actions that he did in 1619. Whether there was a direct connection here or not may not ever be known, for not only is the wide-ranging extent of her opinions and political directives masked by the imperial persona of the *Tuzuk*, but so are the details of most of the factional disputes at court. Aslam has convincingly shown that the Shia response to Sirhindi was harsh and that the *shaikh* himself thought that the "charge was only a plot of the Shias to entangle him."[220] But since we cannot establish satisfactorily[221] whether Nur Jahan was an active participant in the Shia response or not, that she could have moved successfully against Sirhindi remains the only certainty.

A third issue suggestive of Nur Jahan's influence in religious matters was the decline in fortunes of Shaikh Salim Chishti's family. Because of his important prophetic role in Jahangir's birth, Shaikh Salim and his family had enjoyed the blessings and patronage of the Mughal court for several generations. Honors and promotions for his descendants had been a matter of course for years in the Mughal household, and the two families had shared nurseries and battlefields over most of Jahangir's lifetime. Beginning about 1621, however, there was a sharp and dramatic falling off in the appointments and recognition of Shaikh Salim's family members, and Husain argues (with some merit) that this was due in part to the increasing influence of Nur Jahan.[222]

One of Shaikh Salim's grandsons, a son of a daughter, was Qutbuddin Khan Koka, whose mother had been a wet-nurse to Jahangir and who had been held in special affection by the emperor. It had been Qutbuddin's party that had confronted Nur Jahan's first husband, Sher Afgan, in Barddhaman, Bengal in 1607 and that had been in the fray in which Sher Afgan had died. Although Qutbuddin himself had also been killed, Husain suggests that Nur Jahan had continued to harbor bad feelings for his family and was eventually successful in preventing them from getting substantial promotions at court.[223] Again, while such influence with Jahangir is highly probable—given the timing and Nur Jahan's motivation—there is no direct evidence of her role in the decline of Shaikh Salim's family at court. Nevertheless, if she did in fact so despise the family of her first husband's murderer, which is most likely given what we know of her personality, then her marriage to Jahangir must have carried with it a certain divisive tension: her desire to avenge Sher Afgan's murder set against Jahangir's undeniable love for the man who was responsible.

Nur Jahan, finally, was said to have played a role in Jahangir's reluctance to embrace fully the tradition of the Christian Jesuits. In a letter of 1623, the Superior of the Jesuit Mission remarked on the kindnesses shown to the Fathers by Jahangir. The emperor's consideration paid to the wearing of the cross and to the making of proper references to Christ elevated Christian hopes at the time that Jahangir might convert to the faith. But the Fathers suspected as well that for some time there had been a powerful influence working against them. From their intimate dealings at court, they believed that as long as the emperor's wives, and especially Nur Jahan, were prominent in influence over Jahangir, the Fathers would have no hope of converting him to Christianity. Their concern was expressed in the phrase *averterunt mulieres cor ejus*, "his wives turned away his heart,"[224] and caused them to shift their proselytizing attentions to one of Jahangir's sons, Prince Parviz. Several years later, however, in the summer of 1627, Father Joseph de Castro, who had accompanied the emperor on his last trip to Kashmir, remarked in some letters that Jahangir and Nur Jahan had visited the church in Lahore and had even expressed their desire to eat and drink in it.[225] We may assume, however, given Jahangir's lifelong teasings of the Jesuit community, that at this late date if he hadn't already converted to Christianity he wasn't going to. The need for political support was long gone and what remained, as the Lahore incident above shows, was the emperor's more authentic admiration of the Christian arts. We may assume also that Nur Jahan's role was probably minimal. She would have known that there was no chance of a conversion for Jahangir and had no need to campaign actively against the Church. Jesuit attributions of negative influence to Nur Jahan, then, must be seen as final and labored rationalizations of why Jahangir continued not to come over to Christianity.

The influence of Nur Jahan on religious policy, then, is only hinted at in the documentation of the texts. The imperial facade of court chronicles and the inaccessibility of life behind harem walls to other, mostly foreign, diarists mask any real knowledge of whatever involvement she did have. There is, however, strong circumstantial evidence in these several cases to suggest that her opinions were probably a considerable element behind much of what Jahangir did on the religious front. And the particular tendency of her influence turned, in all likelihood, away from seeing any religious claims as exclusive. A pluralistic court and a tolerant government policy would have ensured the greatest opportunities and the least hindrances for Nur Jahan's Shia family and colleagues. It was in her interest, then, to promote ecumenism at the highest levels in order to guarantee good fortune for Shia nobles throughout the empire. Although Nur Jahan wouldn't have wanted Jahangir to convert out of Islam, neither would she have wanted him to embrace Muslim orthodoxy. Instead, consonant with his increasingly authentic religious leanings, her own inclinations would have been to foster an open and tolerant interest in all traditions.[226]

III

While Nur Jahan almost certainly exercised some influence on the development of Jahangir's religious policy, her own positions at court as the beloved of her husband and the wife of this particular king may themselves have been the result of religious ideals intimately persuasive to Jahangir and to the people he ruled. Three structures seem especially compelling: the Islamic vision of Khadija, first wife of Muhammad, which offered the model of an older, more mature mate as an ideal; a possible cult of the Madonna peculiar to Jahangir himself and prescriptive of his love for Nur Jahan; and the goddess imagery prevailing at large in Hindu culture, which might have set the tone for popular adoration of the favorite queen. In the first case, the wife of the founder of Islam, who was both his senior in age and his patron in profession, may well have acted as a traditional, though perhaps unconscious, prototype in Jahangir's attraction to older women who sustained and guided as well as played and seduced. In the second, the mutual devotion of the Christian mother and son, so beautifully rendered in the European art Jahangir saw around him and so reflective of similar themes in Islamic culture, may have prefigured the adoring and nurturing relationship of the emperor with his eighteenth wife. In the third, the consort image of divine pairs in Hinduism—based on the human marriage as a necessary union of complements each incomplete on its own—may have shaped the appeal of the imperial couple in the eyes of their subjects and, indirectly then, the vision Nur Jahan may have come to have of herself.

In the first case, Jahangir's marriage to a woman older than the normal bride who quickly became his nurturing companion as well as his lover may well have been prefigured in the marriage of Muhammad and his first wife, Khadija. Although we have no remaining record of Jahangir's use of the Prophet's choice as a rationale for his own marriage to Nur Jahan, it is quite likely that the pattern of the religious founder's marrying his main patron, confidant, and religious backer gave a kind of traditional, if unspoken, authority to the emperor's espousal of 1611. Not only was Khadija some years older than Muhammad, but by the time they met, she was already an independent woman of property and the survivor of two previous marriages. Khadija had originally employed her future husband as an agent on her Syrian caravan, and it was when he successfully concluded the trip that she proposed marriage to him. While there is a limit to the comparisons that can be made, the suggestion that the Khadija pattern of close intimacy with a wise, influential, and mature woman remains quite strong.[227]

The Khadija argument is supported by three patterns. First, although aberrant in many ways, Jahangir was still nominally a Muslim. It seems clear that it was important for him to carry on the religious and cultural traditions of his forefathers and that, in relation to his religious heritage, he was essentially conservative—the veneration of Shaikh Muinuddin Chishti of Ajmer being perhaps the best example. The Khadija image, then, may have been influential simply because it was an Islamic one, and one that drew from the very earliest sources of that varied all-encompassing tradition.

Second, Khadija belongs with the general Islamic focus on the mature woman who guides and sustains a younger man, a structure normally expressed in the relationship of mother and son. The Mughal harem had made much of this emphasis and, as argued earlier, the older nurturing woman had many guises for Jahangir: for example, Maryam Makani (Hamida Banu Begam), Salima Sultan Begam, Ruqayya Begam, Maryamuzzamani, Qutbuddin Khan

Koka's mother, and Asmat Begam. That Jahangir did not marry again after Nur Jahan seems to indicate that he had finally found someone who, in her midthirties, could manage and even surpass the expectations and needs of this demanding older woman relationship.

Third, Khadija herself was no ordinary woman. Not only did she come with property and position, but in many ways she was much more willing, apparently, than even Nur Jahan to toy with the boundaries established for regularly accepted behavior in women. Her relationship with Muhammad, then, charted new areas for the marriage partnership: it allowed wife and husband greater working space in both their private and public arenas, and it recast the issue of dominance and control as given in customary female/male roles of the time. As inheritors of the tradition, then, Nur Jahan and Jahangir recapitulated the tone of this early relationship.

The Christian case continues that from Islam. From an early age as a prince Jahangir had been in contact with the paraphernalia of the Portuguese Jesuits at his father's court. Not only had he come to know a good deal about the central figures of Christianity, Jesus Christ and the Virgin Mary, but he had also developed a very positive appreciation of them as spiritual personae. Guerreiro, for example, noted that "the King is well versed in most of the mysteries of Christ our Lord and our Lady the Virgin, and openly prides himself on his knowledge." And again, "one cannot but recognise the sincere devotion of this King to Christ and our Lady, for whom he himself confesses his great love."[228] These affirmations of Jahangir's attachment to the central Christian figures are not just the unrealistic dreams of Jesuit missionaries, for the Protestant chaplain Terry, who as far as we know did not actively seek the conversion of Jahangir, said that the emperor "would speak most respectfully of our blessed Saviour Christ"[229] in the presence of a mixed and often discordant group of courtiers.

The basis of Christianity's appeal for Jahangir were the artistic objects of both Christ and the Virgin Mary that he had either been given by the Jesuits or ordered from Europe through the traders at court. Jahangir had learned of such wonders from his father and, like his father, he held these pictures in high esteem: "The Prince showed the Fathers . . . many proofs of his devotion to our Saviour and His holy Mother, whose images he held in the highest veneration. Indeed, the Fathers could make him no more acceptable present than a well-executed representation of either."[230] Finch reported that, in his palaces at both Agra and Lahore, Jahangir kept galleries in which were hung pictures of Christ to the king's right and of the Virgin Mary to his left.[231] These pictures, said Guerreiro, "which fill the Moors with astonishment every time they look upon them, are thus publicly displayed in this infidel King's chamber, which resembles the balcony . . . of a devout Catholic King rather than of a Moor."[232]

Jahangir had other Christian objects around him as well. According to Hawkins, Jahangir often prayed on a black slate throne that had on its upper end graven images of Christ and the Virgin Mary,[233] and Du Jarric noted that while still a prince, Jahangir had an "image of our Saviour crucified" engraved upon an emerald the size of a man's thumb, which he carried around with him on a gold chain.[234] Guerreiro reported that all letters and orders Jahangir sent out, whether they be to Muslims, Hindus, or Christians, bore on the inside the royal stamp but on the outside were sealed with the

> "effigies . . . [of] Christ and our Lady. . . . For he has an instrument like a small forceps made of gold, on the points of which are set two emeralds, square in shape and as large as the nail of the thumb, on which are engraved the figures of our Lord and the Virgin, and these are impressed on the wax with which the letters are fastened.[235]

Although Jahangir was attached to likenesses of both Christ and the Virgin Mary—indeed, one of Guerreiro's chapters focused entirely upon the king's reverence for Jesus Christ[236]—he was said to have reserved a special place of honor for the Madonna. Veneration of the Mother of Christ was common among Jahangir's subjects, for the power of Virgin Mary images was exceptionally strong among a Hindu populace conditioned to veneration of the creative and destructive gifts of goddesses like Devi and Kali, and among Muslim believers knowledgeable of their own Mariological heritage. Du Jarric noted, for example, that when a picture of the Virgin Mary was placed in the church in Agra in 1601 to 1602, thousands and thousands flocked to the church to "see this marvel." Guards had to be placed at the doors and, after talks had been given in the local language explaining who the Madonna was, all "went away full of veneration for the Virgin, and deeply impressed by her sanctity."[237] Hindu petitioners "frequently, and of their own accord," would come to the church in Agra to pray to the Madonna "that, through her intercession, their prayers may be heard,"[238] and the English chaplain, Terry, reported that when he went out, many begged alms of him in the name of the Virgin Mary.[239]

Against such widespread effusion, it was Jahangir of all the Mughals at court who showed the greatest attachment to the Madonna. He got very angry as a prince once when the Fathers did not bring him "any picture of our Lady from Goa" and charged another who was about to set off for the coast to make sure he brought back, as a personal gift, the Madonna he desired. Jahangir then had a Portuguese painter make "a copy of the picture of our Lady" that had been brought back[240] and took it with him into his private quarters. On tour with Akbar once, Du Jarric noted that Salim, with his eyes closed as if in meditation, burned candles in honor first of Christ and then of the Virgin Mary.[241] When he became sovereign, Jahangir always kept pictures of the Madonna around him and a number of miniature paintings show a Jahangir in *darbar* with paintings of the Virgin Mary placed in niches close by him.[242] The presence of a Madonna image around Jahangir had become so customary, in fact, that Della Valle reported with surprise the absence of an image of the Virgin Mary that "in one of the Balconies [had] stood expos'd to publick view," it having been placed there by the emperor "who, they say, was devoted to her." Presumably, the image had been taken away by Shah Jahan who was "reported [to be] an Enemy of the Christians and their affairs."[243]

The appeal of the Madonna image, which had so powerfully struck Jahangir when young and which had continued to play a role in the visual symbols of his later court, was probably not grounded in his simple desire to imitate his father, however, who was also an admirer of the Madonna. Although the young prince surely wanted the approval of his father, the veneration of the Virgin Mary seems to have been an internally authentic choice for Jahangir and in the end a spiritual, rather than a political or psychological, force in his life. And spiritually the great appeal of the image lay not in the isolated figures but in the relationship between the Virgin and Christ itself, and the particular familial role this relationship gave to the woman the emperor saw in the paintings.

Jahangir surely could have found solace, as millions already had, in the veneration of any of the prevalent Hindu goddesses—for example, Devi, Kali, Durga, Parvati, Sita, Shri, Lakshmi, but the quality of the relationship between devotee and divine here would have been substantially different. For Hindu goddesses, the primary relational mode was as consort, with connubial mating as the first order of activity and the subsequent act of giving birth and/or of mothering relegated only to secondary status. In the Hindu pantheon, for example, there were few if any divinely idealized mother–child relationships that did not bespeak violence, deformity, or abandonment. The Christian ideal, however, focused on the actual act of giving birth and the subsequent bonding of mother and child therefrom; the actual act of conception being repressed, ignored, and even denied. The effect of the virginity of the Madonna was to place preeminence not upon whatever relationship she had had with her consort, the father, but upon the mutually devoted and nurturing relationship that she had with the child and, importantly for Jahangir, that she had with the son.

That the Madonna image did in fact suggest to the Mughals the idealized relationship between mother and son is clear from a passage of Gulbadan's. Describing Maham Begam's great concern over the illness of her son Humayun, Gulbadan said: "To her experienced eye he seemed ten times weaker and more alarmingly ill than she had heard he was. From Mathura the two, mother and son, like Jesus and Mary, set out for Agra."[244] By Jahangir's time, then, the Madonna image conventionally expressed the nurturing self-sacrifice of a mother's commitment to her child. Jahangir's reverence of this ideal, however, in no way disclosed a weakness in his own relationship with his birth mother; in fact, Maryamuzzamani seems to have found just the opposite with her son. Rather, his veneration of the Madonna was quite likely the religious expression of the very strength of his relationship with his mother, which was for him not only an early and formative bond but certainly the continuing prototype for future personal ties.

It was this pattern, then, that may have been the most compelling to Jahangir as he made his final marriage. The middle-aged Nur Jahan, beautiful and charismatic as she was, fit more easily into the nurturant and mothering structures that Jahangir had long idealized and that were by now accessibly comfortable modes in the culture. With her competent and experienced strength, she would surely, he foresaw, safeguard and sustain as much as she would possess and enjoy. Jahangir's so-called Madonna cult, then, was in fact nothing but a vision that expressed in art what was already valued in the Muslim tradition. And Nur Jahan, by right of her history, personality, and experience, became, perhaps unknowingly, the primary legatee and beneficiary of the consequences of this vision in Jahangir.

Nur Jahan may also have benefited from the final case, the prevailing images in Hindu culture that depicted in myth the nature and relationship of divine pairs. Just as the Hindu man was thought of as incomplete—either socially or religiously—without a woman joined to him in marriage, so also was the male god only partially whole without a female consort. Functioning on the divine plane as a complete unit, then, the pair distributed between each of them all possible combinations of opposites, sometimes as in Radha/Krishna mythology giving the active role to the man, and sometimes as in Parvati/Shiva mythology giving it to the woman. Although we have little information about how Nur Jahan was received by her Hindu subjects, it is quite possible that her public persona was empowered by, at least to outside perceptions, the currently operative models of female divinity. Roe, for example, in his despair over lack of direct dealings with her, said that Nur Jahan was "more unaccessible than any goddess, or mystery of heathen impiety."[245] And van den Broecke noted that at the height of her popularity she was given "marks of excessive honour and reverence, even like a goddess."[246] Playing to the Parvati/Shiva ideal, then, Jahangir could have assumed the passive, cerebral persona of the male figure while Nur Jahan could have become the energetic female facilitator of her consort's vision, each incomplete without the other.

If this consort vision of Parvati/Shiva were to have been personally absorbed by the king and queen at all, it is possible to imagine the following. Drawn to the asceticism of the *yogi*, Jahangir would also have seen the erotic and rampant madness implicit in the dance of creation and destruction as the obligatory complement of the *yogi's* abstinence and mortification. His own contradictory tendencies of violence and nonviolence, sensualism and restraint, might have found ample repose in the contradictory nature of Shiva, in whom those tensions rested with equal ease and for whom resolution in favor of one or the other was unnecessary. To Jahangir's Shiva, then, Nur Jahan may have played Parvati, stabilizing and defusing his excesses and bringing his dysfunctional personal characteristics under the control of social institutions. The structure of marriage—suspend for the moment that Jahangir had been married much before—and of the rule of the junta provided acceptable channels, and escapes, for his sometimes chaotic tendencies and, as in the myth, his taming could only come at the expense of some of his powers.

There is no way of knowing the extent to which consort imagery shaped either the public perceptions of Nur Jahan and Jahangir or their own style of personal interaction. Should Nur Jahan have found a place among the Hindu divines, then the Parvati pattern of energetic partner within socially given institutions would have fit much better than the pattern, say, of Kali whose unrestrained use of sex and violence left her free, ultimately, from any point of acceptable social reference. Nur Jahan, certainly, like any newcomer to Indian soil, must have been reshaped in some substantial way by the many configurations of the foreign culture around her. Intriguing it would be, then, if this Muslim woman came to be queen of this Muslim king by virtue of the Christian and Hindu ideals among which she, almost by accident, found herself.

9

Arts and Architecture of Nur Jahan

Up to now, our perception of Nur Jahan has been filtered through the eyes of others. With her artistic achievements, however, we are able in a manner unlike any other to touch her personality unrefined by secondary receivers. In the architecture she designed and patronized and in the gardens she laid out, for example, we are as near as we will ever be to her own voice and vision. Many noblewomen of Nur Jahan's era had both the time and money to invest in the arts, as well as the technical advice and personal authority with which to plan and carry out their own projects. Of these women, those of the Jahangiri generation were certainly among the most prolific, and of these, it was Nur Jahan who made the contributions best known to history.

The fine arts and architecture of the Mughal tradition had already reached a well-cultivated stage by the time of Jahangir and Nur Jahan. The prosperity and splendor of Jahangir's court, however, had attracted even more talented craftsmen from the distant centers of Persia, Central Asia, and the subcontinent, who were then given the freedom to develop objects of the very finest quality under the watchful eyes of an inspired patron. The artistic productions of the time came, in this way, to be infused with an elegance and sophistication that reflected Jahangir's own luxurious tastes and discriminating instincts. Under him connoisseurship flourished and new elements unfolded yearly as additions to the Mughal repertoire grew: the use of the flowering plant as a design motif on buildings, vessels, and manuscript pages; the use of European styles of perspective, shading, and character delineation in miniature painting; the surfacing of buildings in translucent white marble; the development of jade carving as an art native to the court; and the appearance of costumes in ever finer cloth and ever more elaborate design within the imperial wardrobe.[1]

Although artistic innovations in these and other areas had been made under the aegis of the emperor, many feel that it was his favorite wife whose imprint they really carried.[2] A freshly Persian perspective and a genuine gift for aesthetic discernment together with a foreigner's newly appreciative eye for indigenous Indian decoration combined to produce in Nur Jahan an artistic force inventive and strong enough to influence much of the art of her husband's court. While we dare not speculate about the character of these arts without Nur Jahan, we do find her considerable presence in the widespread Persianizing of ornament, in the incorporation of more representational (Hinduized) figures, and in the general emphasis on opulence in material and on the embellishment of surfaces so prominent during Jahangir's reign.

While Nur Jahan may have encouraged Jahangir's penchant for the rich and luxurious, there was an emphatically populist streak in her patronage. Both in the designs she created and in the materials she used, Nur Jahan was careful to bring out items that would not only have broad appeal but, in some cases, be inexpensive enough for many to afford. Certainly most of her creations, by reason of cost and availability, would have benefited only the wealthy classes, but in her empathy for the common people, she did make designs for consumption outside the palaces. On her Nur Mahal Sarai, for example, we find an abundance of the realistic figures so avoided by the abstract tastes of stricter Muslims and so popular in the iconography of local Hindus: dueling elephants, pairs of peacocks, and three-dimensional lotus flowers. Moreover, Khafi Khan attributed an inexpensive dress for marriage ceremonies to the empress's hand, and it became known from that time on as the *nurmahali*.[3] Nur Jahan's populism, seen earlier in things like her many marriage dowries to Hindu orphan girls and confirmed in these two examples, reached as far then as her artistic developments, confirming once again the ubiquity of her touch and the realism of her sensibilities.

I

By legend, Nur Jahan made contributions to almost every type of fine and practical art. In many cases the attributions can be traced back no further than Khafi Khan, who seems to have been in the business of re-creating Nur Jahan's talents and accomplishments beyond all realistic possibility. While some of her work can be documented in extant material objects and in contemporary texts like the *Tuzuk* and early European memoirs, others were first recorded in popular oral tradition and, though perhaps not less authentic, are at least less verifiable. It is clear, however, that both popular tradition and contemporary texts and objects preserved an image of Nur Jahan as creating anew everywhere she turned, and she remained, in fiction if not in fact, a persona to whom new inventions were freely attributed with each succeeding generation. This tendency to ascribe cultural and artistic innovations to Nur Jahan was a reflection of the general Indian preference for tracing a tradition back to a single charismatic individual. We will not ever know for some items whether Nur Jahan was actually their author or not and, while there may be forms and techniques now lost to her canon, an overall appreciation of her work is still possible from the uneven remains of tradition.

Indicative as much of her political power as of her appreciative eye were the coins minted in her name. Jahangir had reworked the system of currency at the beginning of his reign[4] and, although the gold coin (*muhr*) of only one *tola* was called a *nurjahani*, this bore no actual relationship to the later empress.[5] (This particular coin, however, the *nurjahani muhr*, was upgraded later, presumably some time after Nur Jahan's marriage to Jahangir, to the highest value of one hundred *tolas*).[6] Pelsaert has told us that, like Jahangir, Nur Jahan minted coins in both gold and silver (a rupee) and that her coins were distinctive both in the inscription they bore and, in the case of some, in the signs of the zodiac printed on the sides of each coin: "The inscriptions [on Jahangir's gold coins] are similar to those of the rupees, except those which have been coined by the Queen; her coins, both rupees and mohurs, bear the twelve signs of the Zodiac, one sign on each coin."[7] Jahangir's coins, much finer and more bold[8] than those issued both before and after him, had a variety of inscriptions stamped on them taken from contemporary verse, sometimes written especially for the occasion. Nur Jahan's coins, however, all contained the following:[9] "By order of the King Jahangir, gold has a hundred splendours added to it by receiving the impression of the name of Nur Jahan, the Queen Begam."[10] Her zodiac coins were not substantially different from those of her husband, and, like his, the sign on each piece corresponded to the month of issue. Jahangir claimed, however that this use of the zodiac on tender had been an invention all his own:

> Previously to this, the rule of coinage was that on one face of the metal they stamped my name, and on the reverse the name of the place, and the month and year of the reign. At this time it entered my mind that in place of the month they should substitute the figure of the constellation which belonged to that month; for instance, in the month of Farwardin the figure of a ram, and in Urdibihisht the figure of a bull. Similarly, in each month that a coin was struck, the figure of the constellation was to be on one face, as if the sun were emerging from it. This usage is my own, and has never been practised until now.[11]

While we do not doubt that the appearance of the zodiac on Mughal coinage was indeed new under Jahangir, two factors suggest that the instigation for this design was as much his wife's as it was his. First, the introduction of zodiac coins, at least according to the *Tuzuk*, came in the spring of 1618, well after Nur Jahan's marriage to Jahangir and well into the period of her established power. Second, that Nur Jahan also had zodiac coins similar in value to Jahangir's suggests that she was at least an equal advocate if not the initial sponsor of the new currency. Because the use of zodiacal coinage is consistent both with Jahangir's dependence upon astrology for ordering his days and with Nur Jahan's affinity for representational symbols, however, it may be argued that its introduction was in full measure a joint venture.

Like Jahangir's, Nur Jahan's coins were minted at all the major points of issue and distributed throughout the realm from cities like Agra, Ahmedabad, and Lahore.[12] Pelsaert noted, however, that very "little trade . . . is done with these gold coins [of the Queen's], seeing that most of them must come from the King's treasures," and a large number of pieces came to be collected and hoarded by nobles as an embellishment of their own personal treasuries.[13] What is significant about Nur Jahan's mintings, however, is not so much the uniqueness of their design or form (even if she was instrumental in introducing the zodiacal coin) or the collector's status they acquired almost immediately upon issue, but the very fact that she actually sponsored pieces and that they were of an equal quality with the very best of her husband's exceptionally fine currency.[14] The minting of coins was, along with the use of the *khutba* and the issuing of *farmans*, the supreme symbol of sovereignty for a Mughal ruler. To have been granted the right of two of these (the use of the *khutba* remained the only power kept from Nur Jahan)[15] was a mark in itself of almost total sovereign responsibility.

If fine coins were one of Nur Jahan's most public creations, then her advancements in the domestic arts were some of her most private. As part of the assembling of feasts and festivities, Nur Jahan is reputed to have developed new ways to prepare and serve food. Jahangir, we know, was a gourmet, loving mangoes best of all fruits,[16] having a special predilection for the variety of fish that could be brought him,[17] and savoring especially the hearty meats taken on his many hunts.[18] These foods were shared with the women of the *zanana*, who often received not only a goodly portion of whatever was brought to court but, on regular basis, for example, the most succulent pieces of meat and the very sweetest of the muskmelons. We know from the 1617 festival in Mandu that, from such hoards as these, Nur Jahan made excellent preparations of meat and fruit, and Khafi Khan has noted that she contributed liberally to the development of new recipes of rare and distinguished taste. Culinary tradition in India today, in fact, attributes a number of specialty dishes to Nur Jahan and her contributions to Mughal cuisine appear on menus in the finest restaurants as well as in standard cookbooks. There is a tradition, moreover, that the finely carved jade and gem-studded fruit knife now in the Salar Jung Museum in Hyderabad belonged to Nur Jahan and was used by her, if not for the preparation of fruit, at least for its presentation.[19]

Central to the domestic arts was the appreciation of dress and fabric. Jahangir was, by all accounts, a lover of fashion and his costumes, turbans, and jewelry tended on the whole to be more luxurious and elaborate than those worn during his father's time.[20] He claimed to have "adopted for myself certain special cloths and cloth-stuffs" and apparently gave an order that "no one should wear the same but he on whom I might bestow them." One of these was the *nadiri* coat made to be worn over the *qaba*, a kind of outer vest.[21] It was considered so exceptional by the emperor, in fact, that it was given out to courtiers only on exceedingly honorable occasions. Jahangir made particular use as well of variations on the *qaba*: with a folded collar and embroidery on the ends of the sleeves, with fancy borders, and of special Gujarati satin.[22] Nur Jahan's hand in the design and execution of these outfits of her husband's, while not specifically mentioned in the *Tuzuk*, may have been substantial as their relationship encouraged the creation of a wondrous imperial image.

Women's clothing evolved as well during the Jahangiri period and the basic Mughal contribution to women's wear in India—stitched instead of wrapped clothing, longer skirt lengths, a type of tight trouser (*paijama*), and an overdress developed from the *jaguli* (a long, full empire-style gown with tight sleeves and an opening at the breasts)—were themselves influenced by the new extremes of climate and the aesthetic qualities of available goods.[23] Nur Jahan is said to have contributed substantially to these changes by introducing a variety of new textiles, among them silver-threaded brocade (*badla*), silver-threaded lace (*kinari*), flowered muslin (weighing just two *dams*, hence *dudami*) to be used for gowns, and *panchtoliya* (a cotton cloth weighing only five *tolas*) to be used for veils. She is also said to have introduced the *nurmahali* marriage dress, an inexpensive costume presumably to be used for wider consumption, and new patterns for gold ornaments. Moreover, the *farsh-i chandani* or sandalwood-colored carpet belonged as well to the Nur Jahan repertoire, being among those floor coverings famous throughout the country in her own time.[24]

Some of the best evidence of Nur Jahan's interest and innovations in textiles comes from the patterns she left to us on stone walls in her buildings. Embroidery is thought to have been a main passion of the empress's, who like many other Mughal women spent some of her free time stitching.[25] Styles of embroidery that were among Nur Jahan's favorites, or were even of her own invention, can be found, for example, on the interior surfaces of her father Itimaduddaula's tomb in Agra [see Figure 9–5].[26] Evident in them is a fineness of stitch and perfection of design that must have characterized much of her own handiwork.

Also present in the Agra tomb of Itimaduddaula is inlay work on the floor around the cenotaphs of the minister and his wife [see Figure 9–4]. This layout suggests the carpet designs prevalent in the early seventeenth century[27] and, again, may have come directly from Nur Jahan's own store of patterns. The floor's colors, moreover—hues of tans, golds, and browns—recall the sandalwood-colored *farsh-i chandani* attributed above to her hand. Note here the overlaid tendrils of different tones and the varied flower styles linking the stems one to the other.

Finally, we have evidence of costume design in the relief of a woman on the wall of the empress's Nur Mahal Sarai in Jalandhar [see Figure 9–1]. The woman is shown standing on a stool by the side of a large vase filled with flowers opposite a companion whose headdress and dagger suggest he was a palace servant. The couple are both dressed in the trousers and the sharp-pointed frocks that were popular among their class in Akbar's time,[28] and the woman has the commonly worn thin, diaphanous veil over her head and tasseled jewelry on both arms. Nur Jahan's decision to depict a servant couple on the walls of her *sarai* may have stemmed from the hospitality and comfort she hoped to offer travelers in this house for the worn and weary and confirms again her openness to popular sentiment. Whether she herself designed the clothes on these two is not clear, but that she did not personally dress this way is evident from Figures 3–1 and 5–2 where her fancy armlets are jeweled, not tasseled, and where she is wearing heavy ornament and a long elaborate outer sash.

More important, however, were the strictly visual arts and of these painting had a special place at the court of Jahangir. Under his enlightened patronage, miniature painting achieved unequaled stylistic levels of empathy, realism, and design, and his studios produced an impressive array of portraiture, animal and plant studies, and historical tableaus. Nur Jahan's marriage to such a connois-

FIGURE 9-1. Ornamental relief, western gateway, Nur Mahal Sarai, Jalandhar. Courtesy of the Archaeological Survey of India, New Delhi.

seur must have given rise to substantial mutual benefit. We can be almost certain that while she encouraged and helped inform the work of his ateliers, he allowed her and the other women of the *zanana* freedom to experiment here as they saw fit. Although scholars like K. S. Lal state convincingly that Nur Jahan "herself painted with some amount of excellence,"[29] there are no extant paintings which can be attributed unmistakably to her hand. Das notes that there were women under Jahangir who did paint and that in several cases their instructor was Aqa Riza,[30] a painter trained in Iran who came to work under Jahangir while the latter was still a prince sometime around 1588 to 1589. Aqa Riza had been prominent in the rebel court at Allahabad, where these women painters may have worked, and he died, it seems, around the time of Jahangir's accession in 1605.[31] Whether Nur Jahan was ever a student of a master like Aqa Riza[32] or more likely of his son Abul Hasan and his colleagues is not clear, but if there were any paintings of hers, they are not known.

Nur Jahan did, however, have other kinds of influence upon the development of painting under Jahangir. She was no doubt the appreciative beneficiary of many of the single images and illustrated manuscripts made in the imperial studios. A copy of Hafiz's *diwan*, for example, written by Khwaja Abdus Samad Shirinqalam during Akbar's reign and illustrated with miniatures under Jahangir, bears the seal of Nur Jahan, indicating that it was presented to her on some occasion by her husband.[33] Moreover, Nur Jahan may well have been behind the presentation of two copies of the *Jahangirnama* (having illustrations intended to accompany written entries in the emperor's memoirs[34]) to her father and brother. Itimaduddaula and Asaf Khan were each said to have received a copy of the album in 1619,[35] a year at the height of the junta's power, and there can be no doubt that Nur Jahan had masterminded this appropriate deposition of valuable imperial treasures.

Beyond her role as collector and curator of some of Jahangir's pictorial hoard, Nur Jahan may well have helped select the specific subjects of paintings requisitioned from European merchants. In Jahangir's earlier days, the European paintings he preferred were religious images of the Madonna and Christ, which he could procure most easily from the Portuguese Jesuits who traded and proselytized on India's western shores. After 1611, however (and perhaps in accord with the more worldly sources of the recently arrived English and Dutch), his taste or at least his collection became more secular. Moreover, the paintings he received had a greater variety of women subjects, many of whom were portrayed in various states of dishabille.

While in 1610, for example, Covert could still bring Jahangir a "picture of St. Johns head cut in amber and gold,"[36] by January of 1613 Best would be asking the East India Company to send a "good store of pictures, espetially . . . [of] Venus and Cupids actes."[37] Edwards had early on brought portraits of the English royal family, which were much appreciated at the Mughal court for political reasons,[38] but he was still asked for more pictures and especially for those which showed "some two faces or persons, and some three."[39] While in general those pictures "which pleased the Mogul very much" were those that had "fair and beautiful women pourtrayed in them,"[40] the most desired women subjects, it seems, were those in mythological settings. Stories close to the imaginative lore of home evidently were preferred, for as Keridge noted of the requested paintings: "Black hair or brown is most esteemed here, agreeing [best] with their [own] complexions."[41] In the wake of the decline in requisitions for Madonna and Christ images, then, mythological (and especially Venus) pictures were highly regarded, despite the almost disastrous consequences of Jahangir's audience with Terry and Roe before the Venus and Satyre picture in 1617, as described in Chapter 6.[42]

This shift in painting subject was due not only to the replacement of Roman procurers by Protestant ones, but to the addition of a very powerful influence in patronage. Nur Jahan's Persian origins and her preference for representational imagery helped stimulate and encourage the move away from traditional Muslim interest in pietistic Biblical subjects toward themes consonant with the more figurative tendencies of local Hindu culture. Moreover, the English were more likely to bring secular images that celebrated sovereignty—such as pictures of the English Court and of Parliament[43]—which fit neatly with Jahangir's later tendency to aggrandize his own political condition, however divinely inspired he thought it to be. Such secular encouragements to rework his own presentation of office must surely have appealed to Nur Jahan, whose place at court impelled her to preserve her husband's often fragile mental equilibrium. Finally, the increase in interest in the variety of female images available, whether they be of urban matrons, Roman goddesses, or feasting courtesans, must certainly have been at Nur Jahan's instance. Jahangir had always loved fine form in women, but these new requisitions were surely less to satisfy his own prurient interests than to meet the curiosity of his ever worldly queen. The woman who would send a letter and gifts to the mother of a neighboring ruler[44] must also have wondered about women's lives in the home countries of her commercial partners, and once again circumstance, here the mercantile resources of the English, obliged to offer Nur Jahan exactly what she wanted.

At the same time as more secular, more mythological, and more gender-specific pictures were coming into the court from Europe, women were being more frequently depicted in the miniatures produced at home and in ways different from the images of the Akbari period. Because it is likely that Nur Jahan could ask the painters in Jahangir's studios to paint any image that appealed to her, Pal has attributed the increase of women in Mughal paintings to her hand: "It was due perhaps to the influence of Nur Jahan, the favorite queen of Jahangir . . . that women became more popular as the subject matter of painting."[45] While this is certain to be true, it is also the case that local Indian paintings, specifically Rajput images, were exerting more influence on the work of contemporary Mughal artists. Mughal painters could hardly ignore the many *raginis* and *nayikas* who were beginning to appear so abundantly in paintings from Malwa and Mewar, much less the women depicted so elegantly in the centuries of Hindu sculpture that had preceded their ascendance. Nur Jahan's interests, then, would have been in complete accord with the growing presence of the Hindu celebration of women and the human body currently taking hold at the court.

Moreover, not only were women increasingly portrayed in miniature painting, but the manner of their portrayal was changing as well. Women under Akbar had traditionally been shown veiled or secluded behind the walls of the *zanana*. As bearers of a strict moral code of behavior, women had to uphold the honor of the family by restraining from any show of physical or emotional pleasure. Women deviating from this code, as adultresses, for example, were often depicted in paintings being devoured by wild animals or caught in the ravages of the sea. Under Jahangir and the joint influence of Nur Jahan and the increasing Hinduization of the subjects of painting, women came to be shown with open necklines and midriffs, comfortable postures, and pursuing pleasure in all its forms. This elegant cult of leisure that became a dominant image in the paintings of Jahangir's years, however, did not necessarily create an image of women's availability for the pleasure of men, but with the guiding hand of Nur Jahan, of women newly initiated into activities of pleasure undertaken directly for themselves.

Nur Jahan's hand in the arts extended to literature as well and, consonant with her own family background, she is said to have composed poetry of fairly competent quality. Nur Jahan belonged to a lineage known for its literary and scholarly achievements, and the composition of verse had long been a favored pastime for many of her relatives as it was for those at the royal court. Men like her grandfather, Muhammad Sharif "Hijri"[46]; her great-uncles Khwajagi Razi and Mirza Ahmad, a son of Khwajagi Razi's named Shapur;[47] her father's brother Muhammad Tahir "Wasli"[48]; as well as her father himself were all poets of varying quality, much of whose work has survived. Among her poetic male relatives as well was her brother-in-law, Qasim Khan. Married to the empress's sister, Manija Begam, Qasim Khan was not only a poet of very high order but a master of extempore verse. Poetry contests were popular at the Mughal court, and it was here that recognized poets could recite verses composed on the spot before an assembly of their peers. During these contests, Qasim Khan emerged as Nur Jahan's favorite sparring partner, in part because he was such a good poet and in part because, as a family member, and an exceptionally witty one at that, he made each occasion a lively and unrestrained affair.[49]

Women at the court were also encouraged to compose poetry, but none have been recognized as extensively as Nur Jahan. Like most other women of the court, she wrote under the name of *makhfi*, "the concealed one," referring to her life behind *mahal* walls, and the verses she composed were often part of a gentle tease she made with Jahangir, the tone of which is reflected in the following set of exchanges:[50]

1. Nur Jahan to Jahangir wearing a long silken coat buttoned with a ruby:

   You have a ruby button on your silken robe it is the drop of my blood that has seized you by the collar.

2. Jahangir sighting the *id* moon, marking the end of fasting:

   The crescent of the feast is apparent at the apex of the celestial sphere.

Nur Jahan responded:

The key to the tavern was lost but is now found.

3. Jahangir seeing tears of reunion in Nur Jahan's eyes:

A pearly tear from your eye is rolling [down your cheek].

Nur Jahan:

The water I drank (the tears I choked back) without you comes forth from my eyes.

4. Nur Jahan seeing a meteor on the horizon:

No star has ever raised its head so far; it is the celestial sphere, loins girded in service to the king.

5. Talib Amli, a poet out of favor with Jahangir to Nur Jahan:

I was so embarrassed I turned into water, and water cannot be broken; so I am perplexed why my honor ("face-water") has been broken.

Nur Jahan:

It [your honor] turned into ice and was shattered.

Also attributed to Nur Jahan are these lines:

6. I do not give my heart to form until the course of action is known;

I am a slave to love, and the seventy-two sects are known.
Ascetic, do not cast fear of doomsday into our hearts; we have suffered the terrors of separation, so doomsday is already known.

7. If the rosebud can be opened by the breeze in the meadow, the key to our heart's lock is the beloved's smile.

The heart of one held prisoner by beauty and affection knows not roses, color, aroma, face or tress.

8. When I lift the veil from my face, a cry rises from the rose; if I put the comb to my tress, a moan comes forth from the hyacinth.

When I pass through the garden in such beauty and perfection, a cry of "blessed" arises from the nightingale's souls.

9. We have purchased Lahore with our soul; we have given our life and bought another paradise.

Called "poetry of a high order," Nur Jahan's compositions gave reign to her broad knowledge of Arabic and Persian at all levels. Her expertise, moreover, seems to have been in extempore verse[51] where her quickness, sense of humor, and charm could be shown to their best advantage. Given the texts in which her pieces have been preserved and the extensive involvement of so many members of her family, past and present, in the literary arts, it can almost be certain that if these verses were not genuine, something like them must have been. Combined with her patronage of other poets, in particular women poets like Mehri, whose

Sarapa-i Mehri still survives, Nur Jahan's own literary accomplishments suggest a decided force in the cultural circles of her time.

II

The most permanent of all of Nur Jahan's artistic achievements, however, were the buildings she designed and patronized, for in them she made enduring contributions to the history of Mughal architecture. It is clear that she shared with her immediate family a love of the arts of a settled culture, and like the immigrant Itimaduddaula and his Persian-born son, Asaf Khan, she must have reveled in the chance to make monuments of stability and endurance in a country so recently her own. Her father and brother had created homes of substance and taste that had quickly become centers of imperial social life[52] and, like their's, her buildings and gardens came to reflect the epitome of Mughal style.

Although there is no direct evidence, the Shujauddins estimate that "the talents of Noor Jahan actively worked in the planning and execution of all the Royal buildings constructed between 1611 and 1627."[53] This may well be true given the broad extent of the powers she had and the long tradition of Mughal women's involvement in architectural projects.[54] That her constructions were extensive we know from Pelsaert for "she erects very expensive buildings in all directions—*sarais*, or halting-places for travellers and merchants, and pleasure-gardens and palaces such as no one has ever made before." Her intention in all this was "to establish an enduring reputation" and solidify the advancements she had already gained within the government.[55] Especially prominent among her constructions were those in Agra where "very handsome gardens" were mixed with buildings and "delightful . . . groves," many of which, noted Pelsaert, could be attributed directly to Nur Jahan.[56] Although even in the Dutchman's time her buildings, or any buildings for that matter, were not kept in especially good repair,[57] Nur Jahan's works were substantial enough to endure climate, accidental abuse, and for a while, marauders. Several have survived intact; others, however, have not withstood history.

Nur Mahal Sarai, Jalandhar[58]

As it developed, Mughal India became laced with a network of roads that connected one with another most of its important commercial and political centers. Along these roads government officials and private patrons built quarters for travelers (*sarais*) at convenient distances, and established wells and measured markers for the comfort and convenience of whomever might pass that way: merchant, soldier, or pilgrim. Said Jahangir in 1619:

> I now ordered that from Agra to Lahore they should put up a pillar (*mil*) at every koss, to be the sign of a koss, and at every three koss make a well, so that wayfarers might travel in ease and contentment, and not endure hardships from thirst or the heat of the sun.[59]

In late 1620, the *vakils* of Nur Jahan completed a large *sarai* in Jalandhar district, twenty-five miles east southeast of Sultanpur, sixteen miles south of Jalandhar proper, and thirteen miles west of Phalor. It was financed, no doubt, from Nur Jahan's own private purses, and was such an important *sarai* that, according to the Shujauddins, " 'Serai Noor Mahal' in local idiom meant some spacious and important edifice."[60]

> At this spot the Vakils of Nur Jahan Begam had built a lofty house, and made a royal garden. It was now completed. On this account the Begam, having begged for an entertainment, prepared a grand feast, and by way of offering, with great pains produced all kinds of delicate and rare things.[61]

The *sarai* was built on an old site of some previous use,[62] 551 feet square, with octagonal towers placed at the corners. The western gateway, alternately called the main or the Lahore gateway, was built double-storied and clad on the outside with red sandstone from the Fatehpur Sikri quarries. The whole of its front was divided into panels, with many of the surfaces ornamented in sculptured relief [see Figure 9–1]. Although Cunningham has called the workmanship on these reliefs "coarse," the "sides of the gateway . . . [being] in much better taste,"[63] the work is in fact quite delicate and remarkably well-preserved. His aversion is due not to the quality of work, it seems, but to its content; Nur Jahan had decorated this now most prominent facade with panels of figurative angels, nymphs, peacocks, lions, elephants, men on horseback, birds, and a wonderful array of stylized lotuses—all of which had appeal for the local Hindu populace. These representational scenes were set off, moreover, by the more traditional Mughal latticework and outlining abstract frets, treated here in a variety of patterns and used to divide the whole into what must have seemed like a multitude of borders. Cunningham's comment on the overall achievement—that "the design is much better than the execution"[64] is contentious, as Nur Jahan's attempt to combine Hindu figuratives with Muslim geometrics is, in fact, quite pleasing. Over the entrance to the gateway is an inscription, flanked by scenes of fighting animals (drawn, no doubt, from Jahangir's own such entertainments) and sculpted lotus-mounds similar to those on Humayun's tomb in Delhi. The inscription was written in four rhyming verses and reads as follows:

1. During the just rule of Jahangir Shah, son of Akbar Shah, whose like neither heaven nor earth remembers.
2. The Nur Saray was founded in the district of Phalor by command of that angel, Nur Jahan Begam.
3. The poet happily discovered the date of its foundation: this Saray was founded by Nur Jahan Begam 1028.
4. Knowledge of the date of its completion was found in the words: "This Saray was erected by Nur Jahan Begam" 1030.[65]

The courtyard inside the *sarai* had thirty-two rooms to a side, each measuring ten feet ten inches square, "with a verandah in front. In each corner there were three rooms, one large two small. The Emperor's apartments formed the centre block of the south side, three storeys in height."[66] Jahangir's quarters, once beautifully finished inside, were eventually covered in whitewash; his main parlor, a long room with half-octagon recesses on two sides, was big enough to hold about one hundred people, with room for overflow in a walled exterior court of about 2,000 square feet.[67] On the north side of the *sarai* Nur Jahan built a mosque for the use of her travelers, and in the middle of the courtyard she established a well. She also put in a bathhouse large enough to accommodate what must have been a substantial flow of visitors.

Jahangir was, from the text, quite pleased with the construction of the *sarai* and agreed most cheerfully to an entertainment there in late 1620, after the couple's first visit together to Kashmir, in honor of its completion.[68] He was to return to its rooms often in the future, as its location in the Punjab proved central and its accommodations were luxurious enough to hold court.[69]

There was apparently another Nur Mahal Sarai, perhaps one of many others, associated with a garden outside of Agra that Nur Jahan had been given to rework and build up. It was in a district known as the Nurmahal[70] and the building may well have resembled, in style and layout, Nur Jahan's more famous *sarai* in Jalandhar. Mundy stopped at this *sarai* on August 6, 1632, and finding it still in use, stayed over on the seventh in its gardens with several of his friends. This *sarai*, he said, "is a very faire one, built by the old Queene Noore mohol . . . for the accommodation of Travellers." It could take five hundred horses and two to three thousand people, he estimated, and was made all "of Stone, not one peece of Timber in it, the roomes all arched, each with severall Copula. It stands betwene Two gardens, built also by her."[71] According to Temple, Mundy's editor, the two gardens mentioned here are the Moti Bagh built by Nur Jahan herself and, he guesses, the Nawal (or Nawab) Ganj built during the reign of Shah Jahan.[72] Nur Jahan, of course, was still alive when Mundy made his visit to the Agra *sarai*, but would have been fully retired and in exile at her home in Lahore.

Tomb of Itimaduddaula, Agra

When Itimaduddaula died in January of 1622, a tomb fit to celebrate the magnitude of the late minister's service to the empire was begun. Although Jahangir does not mention it specially, the privilege of undertaking such an elaborate project may have been the greatest gift of all to his wife, for the tomb has been universally attributed to the hands of Nur Jahan.[73] Itimaduddaula's tomb took six years to finish (1622–28) and was completed at an enormous cost, much of the expense no doubt born by the empress's own treasuries.[74] Pelsaert, at the beginning of his stay in Agra, for example, estimated that the minister's "tomb has already cost fully 350,000 rupees, and will cost 1,000,000 more before it is finished."[75] According to one of the legends surrounding the tomb, Nur Jahan wanted to build a mausoleum of pure silver, but advisers convinced her to use white marble instead, as it would be a more stable and durable finish in India's notoriously damaging climate.

Itimaduddaula's tomb was built in his own garden on the eastern bank of the

Yamuna River across from Agra. The garden itself is of the *charbagh* type, divided into four squares and surrounded by a wall, and its gatehouse "approached by a straight drive, with orchards [planted] on either side." The regular establishment of orchard trees here reflected the traditional practice of using marketable produce to provide "funds for the upkeep of the garden after the death of the owner.[76] The mausoleum itself [see Figure 7–1] stands on a simple decorated platform with edges set forth in inlay and raised walkways leading squarely outward from the middle of each of the four sides: water was supplied for the pools, chutes, and channels of the garden by underground pipes. The relationship between building and grounds was designed to please, for "the harmony between the pale colours of the tomb and the reflected light from the broad pearly river" was achieved with a charm rare for its time.[77] Moreover, the dark trees around the tomb even now "act as a foil"[78] to the structure, leading at least two scholars to conclude that as "far as colour is concerned, this is probably the most sophisticated of all the Mughul gardens."[79]

The tomb itself is neither big nor massive, and given the intricate quality of the inlay on the surface of the white marble, one's eyes are drawn more immediately to its decoration than to its form. The building is a square measuring sixty-nine feet on each side, with four octagonal towers rising up one at each corner. Partway above the line of the continuous eaves (*chajja*) and latticed railing, each tower becomes cylindrical and is capped by a domed kiosk whose round edges mimic the circle of the balcony. The domed balconies themselves are reached by stairs leading directly up from the flat roof of the building and could as easily be function-specific as purely formal. In the center of the roof Nur Jahan placed a square pavilion (*baradari*) on a platform [see Figure 9–2] bearing a deep *chajja*, a low square dome, and four finials matching those on the corner turrets.[80] Three arches open out each side of the main portion of the building [see Figure 9–3], and they are separated one from the other by latticed lancets. Inside this lower story is a vaulted central chamber containing the cenotaphs of Itimaduddaula and Asmat Begam and walls decorated with paintings set in deep niches. The upper pavilion contains a second pair of cenotaphs [see Figure 9–4] arranged in a much more intimate space and surrounded on each side by large latticed windows. Says Andrews of the view from inside: "the quality of light from . . . [this pavilion's] lattices is enchanting."[81]

Perhaps the most appealing aspect of the tomb, however, is its surface decoration, which is so exquisite that it appears "bejewelled . . . like a brilliant casket."[82] On almost every area except the domes, the white marble surface of the tomb has been worked with polished inlays of semiprecious stones in a technique similar to that developed in Florence in the sixteenth century. Called *pietra dura*, it has been argued that both the concept and the technique of this inlay was brought from Italy to India where it was subsequently copied by Mughal builders.[83] Other scholars have argued, however, that the Florentine work is more figurative than the Indian, the former often being a direct copy of pictures made in other media while the Indian is more decorative and a direct development instead of earlier local patterned mosaics.[84]

The *pietra dura* of Itimaduddaula's tomb was one of the very earliest true

FIGURE 9-2. Central square roof pavilion, Itimaduddaula's tomb, Agra. Courtesy of the Archaeological Survey of India, New Delhi.

examples of the technique in India.[85] Workmen began by cutting geometric and figurative cavities into the smooth surface of the white marble. Into these cavities were laid precision-fit pieces of semiprecious stone like jasper, cornelian, topaz, and onyx, each ground to show the grain and markings of the mineral to the greatest advantage. The inlay was so intricate and the materials so hard, however, that the task of construction was much closer to that of a jeweler than that of a mason.[86] Geometrical designs and scrollwork predominate on the lower exterior of the tomb, while more representational images of ewers, covered cups, vases, cypress trees, creepers, grapes, and flowers are featured on the upper exterior and interior surfaces of the building. The color tones of blacks, browns, reds, golds, and tans against the white ground proved more varied and elaborate than the earlier styles of carved relief or of marble-inlaid sandstone, and the extensive use of stone-inlaid marble as a building clad was to become one of "the distinguishing features of [this] the greatest period of Moghul architecture."[87] For the most part, the *pietra dura* work of the Itimaduddaula was designed in

FIGURE 9-3. Latticed archway, exterior lower story, Itimaduddaula's tomb, Agra. Courtesy of the Archaeological Survey of India, New Delhi.

panels with an elaborate dado around the whole of the outside, and with inlaid brackets beneath the *chajjas* spaced to accent the vertical framing on both stories. "An extraordinary delicacy unites it all,"[88] and this along with "the chaste quality of its decoration places it in a class by itself." Itimaduddaula's tomb, says Marshall, truly "expresses . . . the high aesthetic ideals that prevailed among the Moghals at that time."[89]

Nur Jahan's great monument to her father is important as well because it reflected architectural transitions occurring in a number of areas that were to achieve full flower in the tomb of Arjumand Banu. We can identify at least five areas of the building that reflect this transition, some relating to design and some to ornament. First, the very use of white marble as an extensive building material was just coming into fashion, and although occasional other buildings of the period had already been reclad in marble, the Itimaduddaula was the first to use marble as an original outer surface. The tomb of Shaikh Salim Chishti, for example, which had been built of sandstone in 1580 to 1581, was recovered in marble in 1605 to 1606 as a part of Jahangir's accession activities, and Hoshang Shah's tomb (d. 1435) eventually appeared clad in marble although there is some doubt as to when and under what circumstances this work was originally done.[90]

FIGURE 9-4. Floor and lattice patterns around cenotaphs of Itimaduddaula and Asmat Begam in upper pavilion of Itimaduddaula's tomb, Agra. Courtesy of the Archaeological Survey of India, New Delhi.

Nur Jahan's decision to use white marble, regardless of the circumstances under which it was made, was in complete keeping with the general opulence and luxury of her tastes, with the goodly purse she had to hand, and with the current refinement of the Mughal court. Moreover, against the extraordinary visual success of Itimaduddaula's tomb, the subsequent need to use white marble was perhaps already a foregone conclusion by the time Shah Jahan began to plan for the Taj Mahal.

Second, in the *pietra dura* of this tomb marble inlay achieved its most intricate and elaborate expression yet, surpassing, say some, even the later work of the Taj. While geometric and representational designs had been worked earlier in fired mosaics and marble set in sandstone, and while semiprecious stones had already been set on a small scale into marble surfaces, the treatment of inlay in the Itimaduddaula was the first time these stones had been used for ornament over the entire surface of a building. Together with the innovative use of the white marble ground, these new surfaces created a color scheme more brilliant and varied than any seen before and, in its complex repeating earth tones, perhaps more subtle and sophisticated than those to appear later in the Taj. Moreover, the quality of the inlay was much more refined, for earlier mosaic had simply placed one piece of stone by the side of another on a flat ground, and earlier inlay had been used to outline areas rather than to lay forth entire panels, tower sides, and wall lengths. The builders of Itimaduddaula's tomb took on, says Gascoigne, "a considerably harder task, that of laying unsymmetrical and curved pieces of stone into a marble surface to make free figures of scrolls and flowers,"[91] and did so over decidedly larger expanses of ground.

New as well to the surface treatment of the tomb, third, were some of the figurative ornaments preferred by the queen. Daughter of an immigrant from Persia, intent on commemorating the cultural heritage of her father, Nur Jahan drew upon her Safavid roots both in her basic preoccupation with surface as well as in the Persian motifs she placed throughout. M. C. Joshi has noted that in the Bada Batashewala Mahal, an early Mughal tomb just north of the tomb of Humayun in Delhi, Persian ornament similar to that found in the Itimaduddaula tomb is present on a long panel above the entrance to the mortuary chamber. Built to commemorate the remains of Mirza Muzaffar Husain, son of Ibrahim Husain and husband of Jahangir's sister, Shahzada Khanam, who died in 1603, the Bada Batashewala Mahal has considerable significance in the history of Mughal architecture because, in eschewing the superimposed dome, it "is amongst those few early Mughal . . . sepulchres . . . [which are] flat-roofed."[92] Prefiguring thus the Itimaduddaula's flat roof, this *mahal* is also just antecedent to the Agra tomb in its Persian-style designs: the pieces of note in the its front panel being the cypress, the sprinkler, and the cup and saucer.[93] On the surface of the Itimaduddaula, however, Nur Jahan has given much more. Here the cypress is now encircled by twining creepers, a Rajput element thought to symbolize the love of Nur Jahan and Jahangir, and in addition to the perfume sprinkler and uncovered cup and saucer, the walls carry covered scent boxes, Chinese vases, wine cups, double-bodied planters [see Figure 9–5] and stylized renderings of grapes and pomegranates.

FIGURE 9-5. Carved and inlaid archway, Itimaduddaula's tomb, Agra. Courtesy of the Archaeological Survey of India, New Delhi.

The Itimaduddaula also advances beyond Bada Batashewala in its carved reliefs, which so admirably suggest the textile patterns loved by contemporary designers. As noted earlier, the elaborately worked surfaces above arches such as in Figure 9–5, indicate the kind of chicken-work embroidery that Nur Jahan and her colleagues must have crafted by course as a part of *zanana* life, their three-dimensional plans mimicking and relieving the framed surfaces of inlay below. Moreover, the stylized flowers carved inside friezes suggest the traditional sculpted surfaces of Indian carpets such as Nur Jahan herself may have designed and give additional expression to the empress's passion for gardening so evident in the pleasances of the hills and the plains. Joshi argues that, apart from the geometric designs, all the decorative motifs of the Itimaduddaula tomb must have been inspired directly by Nur Jahan,[94] and despite the precedent-setting patterns on the Bada Batashewala Mahal, such a conclusion is happily inevitable. Andrews, in fact, has described the overall surface of the Itimaduddaula as having "a recognisably Iranian quality, here attributed to the influential taste of his daughter, the Queen Nur Jahan."[95] While the cypress is indeed an old Persian symbol, the twining creeper is decidedly Indian, and in the collective achievement of ornament on the tomb we see not only an interweaving of these two design styles but, perhaps more importantly, a reflection of the genuine refinement and sophistication particular to life at the Jahangiri court.

The Itimaduddaula tomb is transitional, fourth, not only in its approval of the flat roof design of the Bada Batashewala Mahal, but also in its freezing of the portable upper awning of the earlier tomb into marble on the Agra piece. As Andrews has pointed out, the stone constructions now remaining of the Mughal architectural heritage "are mere skeletons, deprived of the soft furnishings which gave them useful life."[96] As a part of Mughal living chambers, awnings and canopies would ordinarily have been stretched from rings and poles and used thereby to define space by giving shade, protection, and privacy. Their flexibility allowed occupants to manipulate light and air at will and their portability gave them a usefulness unknown to more permanent structures. The flat roof of the Bada Batashewala Mahal has the remains of twelve such masonry rings mounted along the inner edge of the outer parapet, one at each of the four corners and two spaced evenly on each of the four sides. Joshi argues that these rings were used to support a central awning mounted on four poles whose top and sides covered the platform of the upper cenotaph. This type of awning, "a canopied structure on the roof-terrace of a tomb," was borrowed from the pleasure pavilions used in early Mughal gardens for entertainments. Moreover, like the Itimaduddaula, the Bada Batashewala was situated in a garden of the usual *charbagh* type surrounded by a walled enclosure,[97] thus enhancing the garden origins of its rooftop awning.

In this way, the tomb of Itimaduddaula developed the second-story garden-house structure by freezing the portable canopy known to the Bada Batashewala. Four sided and with a deeply protruding awning-like *chajja* [see Figure 9–2], the square marble pavilion on the roof of the Agra tomb is reminiscent of the Delhi building's cloth awning even more because of the four finials that protrude like tent poles from the top of the Itimaduddaula dome. There was thus, says Joshi of the later tomb, "a transformation of the canopied structure of cloth on Bada Batashewala-Mahal into a permanent surmounting pavilion of more durable material."[98]

Finally, we find structural transition in the development of the four attached corner towers in the Itimaduddaula, which become in the Taj fully detached minarets. The earlier Bada Batashewala has vaulted diagonal alleyways inside each corner of the main level that are set against the quoins of the central mortuary chamber. Perhaps because this arrangement lacked strength and because it "produced a complicated interior of little utilitarian value and, aesthetically, an unimpressive exterior," the quoins were changed in the Itimaduddaula to attached octagonal towers,[99] which housed in each a "regular corner-apartment"[100] and whose open upper balconies could assume the proper religious function of a public Muslim tomb. The towers, whose upper portions have been unflatteringly called "squat,"[101] are in fact in perfect keeping by height and volume with the rest of the building, continuing as they do the interplay between planed and curved surfaces whose harmony contributes substantially to the tomb's visual success. The position of the turrets here recalls the design of Akbar's tomb in Sikandra,[102] but in their form they are derived from the turret atop the Hiran Minar near Lahore, built by Jahangir in memory of his pet antelope.[103]

There is, as P. Brown has noted, no other building in India quite like the tomb of Itimaduddaula.[104] As a pioneer work in surface ornament, it established white marble cladding firmly in the repertoire of Mughal architecture and achieved levels of inlay technique and color tone not ever equalled in subtlety or sophistication again.[105] As a transitional piece, it experimented with the flat roof, with the fixed garden pavilion on the upper story, and with the placement and use of attached corner towers—all of which resulted in a form as pleasing to the eye as an exquisite "gem [set] within its casket [of a garden]."[106] The overall effect of the tomb, however, results from an interplay of all its elements: of flat with curved, bare with decorated, airy with thick, short with tall, dark with light, public with private. Nur Jahan created here, in her pocket-sized memorial to her father, a piece so personal as to be free of time and place, and yet so bound to history that, if it did not exist, it would have to be supposed.

Pattar Masjid, Srinagar

Nur Jahan's later forays into Kashmir, taken as much for pleasure as for health, became known primarily because of the gardens they produced. They also yielded some buildings, however, lesser known than the gardens, but nevertheless of some importance. Among the varied products of the Mughals' prolific building spree in Kashmir was a mosque constructed by Nur Jahan and known alternately as the Shahi Masjid (Royal Mosque), Nau Masjid (New Mosque), and Pattar Masjid (Stone Mosque). Most buildings in the mountain valley were, as had been true for some time, made of wood, but consonant with their imperial designs and perhaps with a view toward immortality, the Mughals decided to revive the ancient practice of building in stone, and Nur Jahan's new mosque became as noteworthy for its building material as it was because it was hers.

Made of the gray limestone that was available in Kashmir, the Pattar Masjid has a front facade of nine arches including a central arched portico [see Figure 9–6]. Each of the side arched openings is enclosed in a "shallow decorative cusped arch," which is in turn enclosed in a shallow rectangular frame while the deep front central entrance hall has carved vaultings framing a scalloped doorway.[107]

Associated with the mosque is a curious story, which though surely apocryphal, was undoubtedly circulated to account for the later degradation of the site. When the mosque was completed, Nur Jahan was asked how much it cost. She is said to have pointed to her slipper and replied, "as much as that." Upon hearing of her reply the *ulama* were incensed and, believing the mosque to be sullied at the mere mention of footwear, prohibited its use for religious purposes. While the Shujauddins have rejected the truth of this story,[108] it is certainly in keeping with at least the traditional view of Nur Jahan's wit and extended sense of proportion, and does give some rationale, if late, for the mosque's subsequent use as a rice granary.

Tomb of Nur Jahan, Lahore

After Jahangir's death and her own exile to Lahore in 1627, Nur Jahan's public role and sovereign duties diminished. She is said to have spent her remaining years in retirement attending to whatever domestic, charitable, and religious affairs she could and to the construction of her final edifice, that to house her

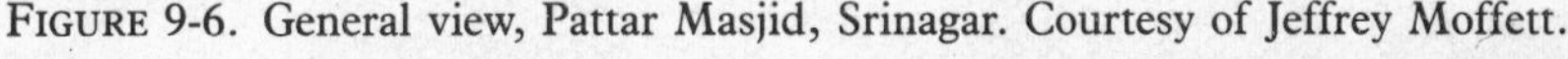

FIGURE 9-6. General view, Pattar Masjid, Srinagar. Courtesy of Jeffrey Moffett.

own remains. Although several have argued that Nur Jahan took some of these last eighteen years to supervise the design and building of Jahangir's tomb,[109] it is not likely that her involvement was extensive given her close guard by the officers of Shah Jahan as well as the new emperor's resolve, now that Jahangir was really dead, to build as fitting a memorial to his father and as grand a testament to his own sovereignty as possible. However, Nur Jahan may well have frequented the site of her husband's tomb, as the Shujauddins have suggested.[110] And as she watched the building go up there, and as she noted the severely reduced quality of her own life in seclusion, she must have known that Shah Jahan would not provide comparable sanctuary for her. Her monument, then, she would have decided, would have to come entirely from her own hands. Funds for the project were undoubtedly drawn from her yearly allowance (two *lakh* rupees[111]) and from what she could requisition of her own treasuries in Agra. She began construction of her tomb after her brother, Asaf Khan, died in 1641 and had presumably finished a good part of it by the time she herself died in late 1645.

Nur Jahan placed her tomb in a garden of the Shahdara near Jahangir's mausoleum [see Figure 9–7]. The Shujauddins note that the garden, formerly in the possession of Nur Jahan, became a public garden when Jahangir was buried there and suggest that "Noor Jahan either founded a new garden for her[self] in the vicinity of the mausoleum of her husband, or . . . already possessed another garden at Shahdara" among the many Mughal sites along the banks of the river

FIGURE 9-7. General view, Nur Jahan's tomb, Shahdara, Lahore. Courtesy of James L. Wescoat, Jr.

Ravi.[112] Like the tomb of Itimaduddaula, Nur Jahan's tomb was set on a square plinth in a walled area of the *charbagh* type, with water channels dividing the *charbagh* from pools that had been set in each side of the platform. The original garden, none of which now survives, was said to have been four hundred yards square, containing within its boundaries the house where Nur Jahan was left to live.[113] The Shujauddins note that cypress, tulips, roses, and jasmine were originally planted alongside the brick pathways, canals, waterfalls, tanks, and fountains that laid out the garden, and that fruit trees, especially date palms, provided marketable produce.

Judging from the tomb as it stands today in restored form, Nur Jahan's mausoleum was a square construction, probably of one permanent story, with seven arches like those of the Itimaduddaula, opening out the corridors on each of the four sides. Covering the central arch of each side was a protruding exterior archway, and at each of the four corners were octagonal towers, reminiscent of those attached to the Itimaduddaula—their height now, however, rising no further than the level of the roof of the building. The Shujauddins hypothesize that "there must have been either towers or minarets on the four corners"[114] topped by balconies and domed and finialed kiosks following the pattern of the tombs of Itimaduddaula and Jahangir, and perhaps a pavilion (*baradari*) on the roof like her father's. This is likely in at least the first case, though not certain, given the low profile that Nur Jahan had to maintain while her tomb was being constructed.

There is no doubt, however, that the design of the three tombs is of one mind.[115] Each is one main story with a flat roof, each has four attached octagonal corner towers, and the sides of each are perforated by arches: Itimaduddaula's by three, Jahangir's by eleven, and Nur Jahan's by seven. Moreover, the roofs of the first two tombs are surrounded by a short and latticed railing, a feature that may well have been found on Nur Jahan's also. There are two features, however, which Nur Jahan's tomb may have held in common with her husband's but not with her father's: an absence of latticing in the outside arches and an absence of the upper pavilion mounted permanently on the roof. Unlike on the Agra tomb, the side arches are closely spaced on Jahangir's tomb and open directly into the interior corridor; moreover, there is no permanently enclosed structure on the roof. Despite the hypothesis of the Shujauddins on this latter,[116] Nur Jahan's tomb was more likely to have copied the bare-roofed plan of Jahangir's as they were husband and wife and their tombs were to share space in Shahdara. Structurally, then, her tomb may have been a smaller version of his. Such a conclusion would suggest that even if not directly involved in the design of her husband's tomb, Nur Jahan was at least in close contact with its construction.

The interior of Nur Jahan's tomb is arranged in a series of three arched and columned galleries. In the center is a square room with a central platform on which are mounted cenotaphs for Nur Jahan and her daughter Ladli [see Figure 9–8]. The arched walls of this inner room together with arches of the three outer galleries allow a substantial amount of light to enter the central chamber, but if there ever were any latticework in the arches, the effect early on would have been much more subdued. This series of galleries around the central chamber

FIGURE 9-8. Cenotaphs of Nur Jahan and Ladli Begam, Nur Jahan's tomb, Shahdara, Lahore. Courtesy of James L. Wescoat, Jr..

served both to filter light coming in and to remove its inhabitants from the outside world, thus giving the effect of secluding its women within a reduced form of the *zanana*.

The surface decoration on the outside of the tomb has been recently restored with red sandstone inlaid with marble. The sarcophagi, the Shujauddins believe, were once covered with *pietra dura* work executed in either multicolored stone on white or black on white, and it "is certain that her sarcophagus was adorned with the attributes of God and appropriate verses from the Holy Book."[117] Their conclusions are drawn from the existing work found in the tombs of Itimaduddaula, Jahangir, and Asaf Khan, but do not take into account that Nur Jahan had a limited purse, and was laboring as well under a hostile regime. Old remnants of interior surface decoration are still to be found in Nur Jahan's tomb, however, but they are of a painted design rather than of inlaid stone. On several of the interior walls and ceilings are "very nicely executed panels of fine floral work and geometrical designs," one of these latter pieces being a *gulkari* on part of the ceiling of the second gallery.[118] But since so much of the ornament is now gone[119] and since it may be that the tomb was not ever completely finished,[120] we cannot tell the full scope of this last of Nur Jahan's personal quarters.

Nur Jahan's tomb remains a mystery. We do not know if it had corner towers above the first story roofline or how high, if present, they might have been. We do not know if she had a central upper pavilion to cover the rooftop cenotaphs, or what kind of cladding covered the brick and mortar on the outside of the whole. We do not know if she used much inlay and if so what type or color it was. We do not know how much of the interior was painted, and how much and what kind of latticework was used on the windows. We do know, however, that the tomb fell decidedly within the tradition of her father's and husband's, but that unlike theirs, hers was not protected by imperial immunity from the onslaught of marauding bands.

10

In the Gardens of Eternal Spring

For places of pleasure they have curious gardens, planted with fruitfull trees and delightfull flowers, to which Nature daily lends such a supply as that they seeme never to fade. In these places they have pleasant fountaynes to bathe in and other delights by sundrie conveyances of water, whose silent murmure helps to lay their senses with the bonds of sleepe in the hot seasons of the day.

Edward Terry, *Early Travels in India*, edited by William Foster

Kashmir is a garden of eternal spring, or an iron fort to a palace of kings—a delightful flower-bed, and a heart-expanding heritage for dervishes.

The Tuzuk-i-Jahangiri, translated by A. Rogers and edited by Henry Beveridge

The most alluring and influential of all the arts of Nur Jahan, however, was the most ephemeral, that of gardening. Villiers Stuart has ranked Nur Jahan along with Babur as the best and most prolific of all those who inspired and designed Mughal gardens[1] and even goes so far as to call Nur Jahan herself "the greatest garden lover of them all."

Nur Jahan's entrance into the landscape arts as Jahangir's chief agent in the field did not necessarily break new ground for women, for Mughal women had been laying out gardens for years. In 1607, for example, Jahangir recorded having walked through several of the better-known gardens of Kabul, among them gardens constructed previously by Bika Begam, his great-grandmother; Maryam Makani, his grandmother; and Shahr Banu Begam, an ancestral aunt.[2] Again, in early 1613, Jahangir recorded the death of Salima Sultan Begam, widow first of Bairam Khan and then of Akbar, and his order to Itimaduddaula to bury her in the Mandakar garden, "which she herself had made"[3] sometime earlier. Later, at the beginning of 1619, Jahangir stopped at a garden near Bayana southwest of Agra set out previously (in 1613) by his mother, Maryamuzzamani, and remarked at this time that the building she constructed within the grounds was impressive and exceedingly well made.[4]

It was Nur Jahan, however, who made possible the elevation of what had been merely a minor personal pastime to a major imperial pursuit. Drawing initially upon the natural conjunction between the private focus of Persian gardens and the secluded life of the harem, Nur Jahan broadened the concept of the garden, giving it an official sovereign function and then opening it up, at least in part, for popular use. In this way, gardens proliferated throughout the empire under her patronage and were designed and executed with increasing refinement and elegance. Moreover, the imperial couple used their gardens not only for the private pleasures of parties, family celebrations, art displays, and meditations, but increasingly for diplomatic and political functions as well: Jahangir brought rebellious sons to task there, he met with groups of religious there, and he held open court with foreigners there. This bursting forth of gardens and the expanded repertoire of their use could only have happened, however, in conjunction with another change Nur Jahan was encouraging at the time: the reorientation of travel by women primarily for the sake of leisure.

Before Jahangir, special travel time for leisure was allocated only to men in order that they might pursue such amusements as the hunt or polo. Women traveled as well but only, for example, to make a pilgrimage, accompany military and diplomatic campaigns, visit family, or escape the dangers of an approaching enemy. Women went with men when they went out for fun, to be sure, but only as part of the household accoutrements, to add to the pleasure and well-being of the male principal or to be protected from a greedy neighbor made bold by an absent lord. Women could and did make short excursions by themselves for picnics and tours of local sights, but these were rare and seem to have been reserved for exceptional occasions.[5] With Nur Jahan, however, such confining circumstances for women began to fall away. As the prevailing Hindu ethic of *kama* for the householder became not only tolerated but affirmed as an official Mughal norm, women who had previously symbolized tightly controlled family honor and the closure of dynastic morality now became the vehicles for an open ethic of courtly pleasure. We have seen that a comparison of paintings from the Akbar era with those commissioned under Jahangir shows women in the earlier period depicted either as veiled and secluded matrons or, individually, as adulterous or profligate deviants to this model. In the later period, however, women became confident sensualists whose open attire and epicurean habits were fully accepted in the growing cult of material luxury at court. It was this code of pleasure, presided over and inspirited by Nur Jahan, that opened the way for greater travel by women for the sake of leisure.

As women now went out more often for their own amusement—whether it was to see a local waterfall, taste the melons of the region, or simply get some fresher air—rest stations and gardens began to proliferate to the far reaches of the Mughal countryside in order to accommodate the expanding needs of the harem. Organized and orderly travel had been a mainstay of Akbar's journeys, to be sure, but now under Jahangir it became a matter of course. On the road between Delhi and Agra, for example, Jahangir had a double row of trees planted[6] for the pleasure of travelers in a symbolic linking of two main Mughal capitals. He ordered special buildings set up on the hillside for the journey out of

Kashmir in order that he and his women would not have to stay in tents during the cold weather.[7] And one of Nur Jahan's most memorable buildings was her Nur Mahal Sarai in Jalandhar built for the accommodation of travelers moving through the region. Travel, then, which had formerly been a leisure pursuit only for men, now became an accepted and even preferred mode of pleasure for women, and gardens, whether as way stations or as journey's end, now became the symbol of women's more sensual lifestyle as encouraged under Jahangir.

I

The gardens of Mughal India took their pattern from centuries-old Persian antecedents. The standard form of the paradise garden used idealized treatments of irrigated water as the symbols for the spiritual and physical source of life and exceptional species of living things to mark out space along perfected lines. In its most basic form, the Persian garden had four water channels, each crossing into the center of the garden and creating four orderly quadrants (hence the name *charbagh*). These channels were ordinarily placed above the level of the surrounding grounds so that their waters might feed the lines of trees planted along their banks as well as the fruits and flowers growing out within the quadrants and beyond. A wall was built around the entire garden to keep the dust at bay and to ensure privacy and protection for those within, and in the center, at the meeting of the four channels, a *baradari* was often constructed to provide shade and rest amidst the cooling waters.[8]

The Mughals adopted this basic plan of the Persian garden, changing it as needed to fit the vagaries of the Indian plains and of the mountainside sites of Kashmir, and in doing so, they played increasingly with the intricate geometric possibilities of the given prototype. By combining the shape of the square (representing material life) with that of the circle (representing eternal spiritual life), the Mughals developed the octagon as a symbolic pattern reconciling the two spheres; and by dividing the garden into eight parts, they could represent the eight divisions of the Quran. Moreover, the ten-by-ten cubit water tank so often referred to by Mughal builders was carried over from the ablution tank used in Persian gardens for ritual washing by the pious before their worship.[9] Finally, the outside wall around the garden became, in Mughal hands, a highly embellished rampart, often with serrated battlements and parapets and imposing entrances opening up each of the four sides with large and ornate gateways.[10] Added to the widened water channels, the enlargened tanks, and the water-set pavilions, these exaggerated enclosures became a standard mark of the Mughal style in India.

Essential to the garden always was water, and despite the proliferation of gorgeous plants and exquisite buildings, water flowing or at rest was the heart of what was seen, heard, and felt. The two main functions of water, to irrigate the plants and to cool the air, were addressed primarily by stone and brick canals, which ran through the garden and around its edges. Large receptacle tanks (*hauz*) were placed strategically at different levels to retain sizeable loads and often to change or stem the water's movement. These large tanks often housed elaborate display fountains, water plants, and fish and, with the canals, were connected by concealed irrigation pipes to all the areas needing infusion. Moving water often fell down water chutes (*chadar*) whose surface was carved in intricate patterns designed to play with the streams moving over it. Pavilions were usually placed on or by the water and were coolest when set at the confluence of canals or just opposite a large *chadar*. The water chilled the stone floors, walls, and roofs, and if the building were open enough, the wind could move calming, scent-laden breezes through all the rooms.

The variety of plants found in Mughal gardens was great and, by some accounts, there were so many different types that the gardens could be kept in continuous bloom all year. The "fruitfull trees and delightfull flowers," said Terry, "seeme never to fade."[11] This variety became even greater after Nur Jahan began going to Kashmir, for upon her return she quickly introduced types known only to the hills into the plains. Many of these new varieties, such as the blue Kashmir iris, have been immortalized in the inlaid panels of the Taj Mahal, where Shah Jahan followed Akbar's portraits of men and Jahangir's portraits of animals with his own portraits of flowers. Popular trees in the full-blown Mughal garden included the chenar or plane tree, the willow, and the cypress, as well as a great variety of fruit trees the sale of whose produce helped to pay expenses incurred in maintaining the gardens. By Peter Mundy's account of 1632, the fruit trees included "Apple trees (those scarse), Orenge Trees, Mulberrie trees, etts. Mango trees, Caco [cocoanut] trees, Figg trees, (and) Plantan trees,"[12] as well as cherry, apricot, pomegranate, and guava. In Kashmir, the usual orange and citron trees were replaced by the hardier apple and plum. Flowers, however, were the ultimate ornament and Mundy began the list with the following: "Roses . . . French Mariegolds aboundance; Poppeas redd, carnation and white; and divers other sortes of faire flowers which wee knowe not in our parts, many groweinge on prettie trees, all watered by hand in tyme of drought, which is 9 monethes in the Yeare."[13] Other flowers used in turn included the narcissus, lily, crocus, iris, tulip, dahlia, jasmine, and lilac—many found in such abundance in Kashmir that Jahangir had a series of paintings of Kashmiri wildflowers commissioned by the artist Mansur. The flowers of Kashmir so struck Nur Jahan and Jahangir that, upon their return from their first joint trip there in 1620, not only were new varieties introduced into the gardens of the plains, but the flower—rendered individually and in loving detail—became an important design motif in art as well. Said Jahangir prophetically in 1605: "From the excellencies of its sweet-scented flowers one may prefer the fragrances of India to those of the flowers of the whole world."[14]

II

Some claim that all gardens established by Jahangir after 1611 were in fact laid out jointly by the imperial couple.[15] This may well be true given the speed with which Nur Jahan took power and the affinity she so clearly had for growing things. We do know that the gardens of the plains were among the first designed by or belonging to Nur Jahan and that it was in Agra where many of the best of these were located. Pelsaert, for example, noted late in Jahangir's reign that in Agra there were "many very handsome gardens, with buildings as delightful as the groves, among them those of . . . Nurjahan Begam."[16] The principal Mughal gardens of Agra, that "grand old" city "of Hindustan,"[17] were set along the banks of the Yamuna within the habitable part of the city, with most of the sites extending along the river's eastern curve.

Nur Afshan Garden (Ram Bagh), Agra

Some time after their marriage, Jahangir gave Nur Jahan an old garden of Babur's for her own. Babur had not liked the site originally—thinking it ugly and unpleasant because it was flat, irregular, and at times quite swampy—but he needed a resting post outside of Agra and there was no better place than this spot on the eastern bank of the Yamuna now known as Ram Bagh (Aram Bagh or "Garden of Repose"), a name given to it some say by the Marathas in the eighteenth century.[18] After fortifying the bank with stone and earth there, Babur built a large well to supply water for his hot bath, various tanks for public and private use, and houses for himself and his entourage. Although Babur did not ultimately take to India, the garden he created there with its local resources proved a delightful and much-used place. Even though it was on what Jahangir called "improved land," few places were its "equal in beauty"[19] and Gul Afshan ("Flower Scattering"), the name by which it was known to Babur's immediate descendants, endured as a tribute to the master's lasting hand at the land. In Jahangir's 1605 description of it, Gul Afshan sported a small building cut of red stone and a mosque on one of its sides but lacked the lofty building on its other side that Babur had always planned to erect but never did. At this time, just after Jahangir's accession, Gul Afshan was especially known for its excellent fruit trees and vines, among them melons, grapes, tamarinds, mangoes, and pineapples, and Jahangir's early court often enjoyed its produce.[20]

Just when Nur Jahan was given the garden—or when she appropriated it as her own—we do not know, but we do know that by early 1621, it had already become an established spot for the couple and had acquired the name of Nur Afshan ("Light Scattering"). Since Jahangir was still calling the garden Gul Afshan when he visited it in 1619 and rewarded its keeper Khwaja Jahan (an honorary title for Dust Muhammad, the engineer responsible for laying out Jahangir's gardens in Agra and the fort in Lahore) for his fine care of the fruit and flowers there,[21] Nur Jahan must not have taken over patronage and direction of the garden until some time shortly after that. The first mention made of the garden as Nur Afshan in the *Tuzuk* is following Nur Jahan's 1620 trip to Kashmir when she and the emperor halted there for three days before marching on into Agra at an auspiciously appointed hour.[22] Two weeks later Nur Jahan and Jahangir held an entertainment in the Nur Afshan during which they passed out gifts of honor to attendants,[23] and in March of 1621, as part of the New Year's festivities, Jahangir retired to the Nur Afshan by boat with his ladies for a rest.[24]

The stay was not long for Jahangir seems to have returned almost immediately to his palace in Agra proper, but the women of the harem went back to the garden later that year.[25]

The Nur Afshan, or Ram Bagh, has the distinction of being one of the oldest recognizable Mughal gardens in India.[26] Many alterations have been made to it over the years, and it is not clear which of these can be attributed to Nur Jahan. The original orderly and geometric patterns of the site remain, as do many of the water channels, the well, the platforms, and the pavilions.[27] It is possible that Nur Jahan ordered some new building at the site, but it is much more probable that most of her innovations lay in the types of flowers and trees that grew inside the grounds, influenced as she was by seeing so much in Kashmir.

Nur Manzil Garden (Zahara Bagh), Agra

About the time Jahangir began to mention the Nur Afshan in the *Tuzuk,* he also began to make reference to the garden of Nur Manzil (Abode of Light), likewise in the vicinity of Agra and likewise, we presume, under the purview of Nur Jahan. H. Beveridge notes that the Nur Manzil was the same garden as Dahra Bagh,[28] the garden Jahangir often stayed in when he left Agra to go on hunting expeditions or diplomatic missions as he did in 1613 and 1614.[29] This Dahra Bagh is almost certainly the same garden with pavilion built by Babar for a daughter of his named Zahra, which is known today as the Zahara Bagh and is located just south of the Ram Bagh.[30] If this attribution is correct, then the Nur Manzil of the *Tuzuk* lay just below the Nur Afshan, on an adjacent plot along the eastern bank of the Yamuna. Although Jahangir never actually said that the Nur Manzil belonged to or was patronized by Nur Jahan, we can assume from its new name and from the time of its ascendance that it was, in good measure, one of the main projects of the queen.

The garden of Nur Manzil, and its newly erected buildings, first appear in the *Tuzuk* in the spring of 1619. Having heard much praise of the recently begun work there, Jahangir decided to visit and found a substantial wall of brick and cement surrounding a large building and a "highly decorated" residence. Reservoir tanks had already been made and thirty-two pairs of bullocks continually drew water from a large well just outside the gate. Other wells and numerous canals passed water into the garden plots and "all kinds of fountains and cascades" allowed water collected from rain in the middle tank, or from wellwaters, to cool the air for visitors. Although Rs. 150,000 had already been spent by the time of Jahangir's first visit, the garden was not yet finished, and he noted at that time that canals and walls needed to be strengthened, avenues laid out, and plants set in—a task that would raise the total cost of the project to about Rs. 200,000.[31]

The great pleasure Jahangir took in this garden must have increased substantially the next few times he visited when more of the site was finished. Returning to the Nur Manzil later in 1619, Jahangir said, "I passed the time in enjoyment in that rose-garden of delight,"[32] and in early 1621 he noted an entertainment put on there about the same time as he first mentioned the Nur Afshan. The narrative of the *Tuzuk*, then, places the Nur Manzil and the Nur Afshan in close physical, as well as temporal, proximity, and it would make sense to assume that Nur Jahan appropriated both these old and adjacent gardens and reworked them as her own.

Moti Bagh, or Moti Mahal, Agra

Two European travelers have attributed another garden around Agra to Nur Jahan based on information they were privy to in their journeys. In the latter half of Jahangir's reign, the Dutch merchant Pelsaert noted that among the many fort-like gardens on the eastern bank of the Yamuna "with handsome walls and great gateways" were two that belonged to the king (that is, Jahangir): "one named Charbagh, the other Moti Mahal."[33] Although Pelsaert said nothing more about it, this Moti Mahal must certainly be the Moti Bagh ("Pearl Garden") mentioned by the English traveler Mundy, who in late 1632 noted the many gardens he saw in and around Agra. Of these, he found, there were three that were great: "Darree ca baug (Dehra Bagh) and King Ecbars (Akbar's) on this side the river and Mootee ca baag on the other side, the latter built by Noore mohol."[34]

Earlier, in August of 1632, Mundy had also noted two gardens on the eastern bank of the Yamuna and had said they had between them a *sarai* built by Nur Jahan: "I departed from . . . Agra . . . and crossing over the river, I came to Noore mohol ca Sara . . . built by the old Queene Noore mohol [Nur Mahal] for the accomodation of Travellers. . . . It stands betwene Two gardens, built also by her."[35] In his note to this passage Temple identifies these two gardens as the Moti Bagh and, perhaps, the "Nawal (or Nawab) Ganj, erected in Shah Jahan's reign."[36] This information corroborates what Pelsaert had told us about the Moti Mahal/Bagh being among the gardens on the eastern bank of the Yamuna,[37] and part of what the later Mundy passage noted about the location of gardens: that, from Agra, "Mootee ca baag [was] on the other side" of the river. The rest of this passage, however, is problematic for it places on the western bank both "Darree ca baug (Dehra Bagh) and King Ecbars (Akbar's)." Temple notes that by "Akbar's Garden Mundy apparently means the garden attached to the Emperor's tomb at Sikandra,"[38] a fair identification as it leaves the Moti Bagh on the eastern bank, but does not solve the question of the Zahara (Dahra) Bagh, which we know is also on the eastern bank. The only possible explanation is that Mundy made a mistake at some point in his geography.

Another recasting of the Moti Bagh is possible as well. In Agra Fort there is a Moti Masjid built, according to the inscription, by Shah Jahan in 1654. An alternate view of Mundy's late 1632 passage might locate Zahara Bagh where we know it to be on the eastern bank, Akbar's garden as any of the other gardens located nearby, and Moti Bagh as a garden associated with an earlier layout on or near the grounds of the Moti Masjid across the river. These identifications, however, seem unlikely, and we leave Nur Jahan's Moti Bagh where modern scholars place it: among her other gardens on the eastern bank.

Mundy's description of the Moti Bagh added some other unusual elements.

After detailing an architecture typical to this period and some parterre layouts of sumptuous fruits and flowers, he then noted several specific things unique to the Moti Bagh: that marigolds were scarce there, and that in "Mootee ca baag were many roomes painted, which wee might perceive to bee drawne from Europe prints (of which they make accompt heere). Alsoe there was the picture of Sir Thomas Roe, late Ambassadour heere, as it was told us."[39] Temple presumes that this picture of Thomas Roe is "a fresco on the wall of the garden palace."[40] Whether painted by English agents in residence (Roe was never actually in Agra himself, skirting the city instead as he followed the court between Ajmer, Mandu, and Ahmedabad), or more likely by Indian painters privy to the company of Roe's embassy, the painting serves, fairly acceptably, to date the palace to the middle of Jahangir's reign.

Itimaduddaula Garden, Agra

The garden of the Itimaduddaula, which along with the tomb was almost certainly the primary responsibility of Nur Jahan from 1622 on, is a classic small-scaled example of the old Persian plan. Set right up next to the edge of the Yamuna, the Itimaduddaula garden has false gateways in the middle of three sides of the surrounding wall with a waterfront pavilion to the outside of the structure on the river side. The main gatehouse is opposite the river wall and is at the end of a straight drive with orchards once planted regularly on either side. The garden itself is in the traditional *charbagh* form, with water channels dividing the square into four equal quadrants and the mausoleum placed in the center at the confluence of the streams. There are four small tanks on each side of the central platform, each of which contains a single fountain, and there are angular channels that carry water to all four corners of the small enclosure. Originally Nur Jahan would have made great use of the pale colors of the tomb and the reflections of light off the river in designing the overall scheme of plantings in the garden, using dark cypresses, for example, to provide contrast and rose bushes to soften the harshness of the geometric forms.

Garden of Jahangir's Tomb, Shahdara, Lahore

In addition to lining the road between Agra and Delhi with trees, Jahangir also planted trees along the roadways that led up from Agra to Lahore. This he did, said Mundy, "for the ease of Travellers and for shade in hott weather," and chose for this purpose trees that "continue all waies greene."[41] The city that lay at the end of the road was a favorite spot of Nur Jahan's, being closer than any other imperial capital to the lands of her origin, and it was here where she laid out numerous gardens along the river Ravi and here where she and Jahangir were eventually buried.

The garden of Jahangir's tomb at Shahdara lies on the right bank of the Ravi, five miles north of Lahore. It was once an old pleasure garden of Nur Jahan's and was used frequently by her and Jahangir during the emperor's lifetime. When he died near the hill station of Rajauri on the way down from Kashmir in

1627, Jahangir was not taken back to the garden at Vernag to be buried in the mountains, as was by legend his wish, but instead to the Shahdara garden where the new emperor, Shah Jahan, could more easily oversee the building of the tomb and the activities of the now-dethroned, but still powerful, queen. How much of the new workings of the garden and of the mausoleum itself actually came under the direct purview of Nur Jahan is not clear—her immediate incarceration and her limited purse and movement suggest minimal firsthand involvement—but the fact that the design of Jahangir's tomb itself was taken from that of the Itimaduddaula in Agra indicates strong, if indirect, Nur Jahani influence.

The outer courtyard of Jahangir's tomb garden at Shahdara is a *sarai*, having a series of arched alcoves around the walls where travelers, pilgrims, guards, and servants would have been able to rest overnight. Inside, in the center of a second enclosure and reached by a tall gateway, is the tomb itself built on an enlarged scale after the tomb of Jahangir's Persian father-in-law. The large garden that surrounds the tomb recalls the plan of the garden at Sikandra and has regular fountain tanks around the mausoleum. The canals are wider here than at the Sikandra site and the causeways are done in the large brickwork patterns traditional to Lahore.[42] Villiers Stuart notes that often in extended *charbaghs* there is the danger of monotony and that frequently, as would have been the case at Shahdara, each of the four divisions was laid in different designs or was planted with its own broad mass of single flowers: tulips, roses, or violets, for example.[43] Such may have been true originally of the tomb garden, either during Jahangir's lifetime or after, where gardens dedicated to only one flower probably rivaled each other for the patron's attention.

III

Despite the beauty of the plains, it was Kashmir that drew the royal couple as no other place ever had. Although Jahangir had been going to the Himalayan valleys since his boyhood with Akbar, it was only under the influence of Nur Jahan that their immense appeal became realized.

Kashmir was an ideal spot for gardens. The abundance of water there could take on many forms and lent itself easily to the show and refinement of a man-made garden. In addition, the natural diversity of the terrain allowed for the combination and recombination of features in an unending variety. Gardens here, the Mughals discovered, no longer had to be flat, but could be terraced and layered in any number of ways to suit a hillside site; and the abundance and versatility of the many natural bodies of water were infinitely superior to the artificial tanks and canals of the plains. Jahangir and Nur Jahan thus found in Kashmir a natural paradise, a landscape needing nothing more than what it offered to be an ideal refuge. But they also found a countryside that could be shaped and changed and made even more beautiful as suited their own particular needs and forms of patronage. Moreover, in making what came to be a yearly pilgrimage to Kashmir from the time of the middle reign on, Nur Jahan and

Jahangir established a precedent that would render the valley a holiday refuge for their countrymen for centuries to come.

Jahangir did much to establish Kashmir as a center of Mughal culture. By his own account, he went there twice with Akbar and even then was fascinated with the natural life he found around the spring at Vernag.[44] Although all of his later accounts of Kashmir in the *Tuzuk* are highly romanticized, it is the very first narratives which indicate just how idealized he found life in the Himalayas. In 1607, for example, Jahangir noted the great purity of the water at Vernag, the extraordinary abundance of saffron at the nearby village of Pampur, and the immunity of Kashmiri workmen to headaches derived from the scent of the saffron flower.[45] Although he was to mention Kashmir subsequently in the early *Tuzuk*,[46] it would be his memories of his youthful visits that would provide the vision for his later preoccupation. In all, Jahangir would go to Kashmir six more times—for the springs and summers of 1620, 1622, 1624, 1625, 1626, and 1627—and each time the adventurous spirit of Nur Jahan would lead the royal entourage deeper and deeper into the secluded and enchanting recesses of the valley.

By the time the trips had become regularized, Jahangir was leaving Lahore in March or April and reaching Kashmir in May.[47] Jahangir's early trips with his father had always been in the fall—"I witnessed the Autumn season [there], and it appeared to me to be better than what I had heard of it"—but he had never seen Kashmir in the spring. "I have never seen Spring in that province," he said in 1607, "but hope to do so some day."[48] Thus, when he began to go with Nur Jahan, he was determined to go in the spring, and so loved that season there that his schedule remained the same to the end. The journey was tedious, risky, and very expensive, however, and the preparations so prolonged that in these later years the court was either in Kashmir, in transit to or from Kashmir, or packing or unpacking from the trip. Although horses and elephants would certainly have been used to cross the melting snows, sometimes, as Pelsaert noted, "pack-animals cannot cross the mountains, and practically everything must be carried on men's heads." The Kashmir trips, then, were for many a hardship, "but apparently," continued Pelsaert, "the King prefers his own comfort or pleasure to the welfare of his people."[49]

Aside from the beauty and sensual delights that drew the court to Kashmir, Jahangir made the trip for two reasons: to escape the heat of lower India and to improve his health. The scorching summer heat of the plains was usually moderated by changes in clothing, diet, and activity level and was further alleviated by the cooling courtyards and alleyways built into traditional homes. For the Mughal court, however, with the luxury of a large treasury and a willing and supportive staff, a retreat to the snow-cooled mountains was the ultimate antidote to plains life during an Indian summer.[50] Jahangir, however, also had problems with his health that were increasingly compounded by the effects of alcohol and opium. Fever, asthma, and general lethargy were increasingly reason enough for him and his doctors to see a move northward for a change of air as beneficial. With trips to Kashmir, the hot and stagnant air of the plains (Gujarat and Agra were especially noteworthy here)[51] could be replaced by the cleaner and cooler air of the hills, and the bland sameness of the flatlands by a variety of splendiferous surroundings.

The specific attractions of Kashmir were many. The most immediate, and ultimately the most enduring, were the flowers: "The flowers of Kashmir are beyond counting and calculation," Jahangir said, "Which shall I write of? And how many can I describe?"[52] Many of the flowers he knew of already, such as the varieties of lilies, tulips, narcissus, violets, roses, irises, and jasmines, and many others he had to learn or invent names for. Fields of single blossoms stretched out before him and Nur Jahan as they made their way over passes and by meadows, and side excursions revealed heady sweet smells unknown to the plains. The "place most worth seeing in Kashmir," according to Jahangir, was Kurimarg[53] where as "far as the eye could reach flowers of various hue were blooming, and in the midst of the flowers and verdure beautiful streams of water were flowing: one might say it was a page that the painter of destiny had drawn with the pencil of creation."[54] The violet-colored saffron flower was among the most amazing to the couple, for it grew in field after field around the village of Pampur. "I do not know if there is so much saffron in any other place in the world,"[55] noted Jahangir, and in "the whole country of Kashmir there is saffron only in this place." The smell of the saffron flower was especially fragrant—"The breeze in that place scented one's brain"—and both Jahangir and his attendant's got headaches from the sharp scent after picking the stems.[56]

Nur Jahan and Jahangir delighted in other things as well. The dramatic landscapes of lakes,[57] waterfalls,[58] and deep valleys[59] soothed and inspired them and fed the emperor's love of excess and natural detail. Fruit grew abundantly in Kashmir and, although many of the varieties were "inferior to those of Persia or Kabul,"[60] their freshness and diversity were nevertheless a great luxury to the court: apples, pears, melons, peaches, apricots, cherries, guavas, grapes, pomegranates, mulberries, walnuts, and almonds,[61] as well as some with unfamiliar names. It was perhaps because of the fruit that the ever-disparaging Pelsaert noted that "foreigners usually suffer from the flux, and many die of it."[62]

The fish of the region were also of interest, particularly those kept in garden tanks. In 1607, for example, Jahangir noted that he had seen many fish through the clear water in the tank of the spring at Vernag.[63] These fish became a preoccupation of Nur Jahan's some fifteen years later, and Bernier, during the reign of Aurangzeb, remarked on them when he visited Vernag: "One of its ponds contains fish so tame that they approach upon being called, or when pieces of bread are thrown into the water. The largest have gold rings, with inscriptions, through the gills, placed there, it is said, by the celebrated Nour-Mehalle."[64] Again, at the spring at Andha Nag (or Anantnag, "Place of Countless Springs"), there were fish known by the Mughals to be blind. Jahangir and his entourage stopped there one day and threw in a net and drew out twelve. After examining them, he determined that of the dozen fish only three were blind and that the blindness was, perhaps, the result of something in the water.[65]

Nur Jahan and Jahangir were not just passive receivers of Kashmiri bounty, however, but gave in return many times over. Their contributions to the valley included palaces, mosques, bridges, and aqueducts,[66] and with these they helped turn local construction temporarily away from wood to stone.[67] Their greatest contribution, however, was the network of gardens laid out near main thoroughfares and around Dal Lake, which forever changed the way plains India would look at this northern province.

Darogha Bagh (Lalla Rookh's Garden), Manasbal Lake

Among the many mountain gardens of the Mughals is one by Manasbal Lake called Darogha Bagh ("Lalla Rookh's Garden") containing a palace that, some say, was originally built for Nur Jahan. Set on terraced walls and planted with poplar trees, Darogha Bagh juts out into the clear calm water "like some great high-decked galleon"[68] as a hedge against the ravaging floods that often course through the region.[69]

Bagh-i Bahar Ara, Dal Lake

On the western arm of the Dal Lake at Sadurkhun was a now-vanished garden said to have been laid out by Nur Jahan in 1623. The Bagh-i Bahar Ara had two terraces, one approaching the lake and the other on a higher level, both with excellent views of the water. Each of these terraces was prepared in the famous *chahar chanar* pattern[70] with four chenar trees distributed evenly over a square plot in order to provide shade the whole day long.[71] A stone pavilion was built in the center, and water to irrigate the plants on all levels came from the Sind Canal.[72]

The Nur Afza Garden, Hari Parbat Fort, Dal Lake

Inside the palace-fort built by Akbar on the small Hari Parbat hill to the west of Dal Lake is a little garden "with a small building in it in which my revered father used constantly to sit." When Nur Jahan and Jahangir went to Kashmir for the first time together in 1620, they noticed that it was in ruins. Much disturbed by this "neglected state," Jahangir had Mutamid Khan "make every effort to put the little garden in order and repair the buildings," and in a short time the garden had acquired a "new beauty." Mutamid Khan added a terrace thirty-two yards square, in three divisions, and restored the building so that it could be hung "with pictures by masterhands, and so [be] . . . the envy of the picture gallery of China." Jahangir declared as well that the garden was now to be called the Nur Afza ("Light Increasing"),[73] probably because Nur Jahan had had a good hand in its restoration and was from this time on to be its main patron.

During their stay that first year, Jahangir observed that there were four cherry trees growing in the Nur Afza, planted presumably by Nur Jahan. These trees proved to be so productive, that Jahangir "ordered the officials of Kashmir to plant *shah-alu* (cherry) trees in all the gardens."[74] Later, at the end of the 1622 trip, Jahangir (or Nur Jahan) had a canal built into the Nur Afza to bring in extra water to irrigate the plants there. Haidar Malik was sent to Srinagar to cut a canal from the valley of Lar into the garden and was given Rs. 30,000 for the materials and labor to do it.[75] Malik, who had written a history of Kashmir and was ostensibly the one who protected Nur Jahan immediately after the death of Sher Afgan in 1607, was originally from the village of Chardara, and it was his request in 1620 that his native village be renamed Nurpur, the City of Light.[76] The relationship between Malik and the queen must have been one of deep affection, and we can only presume that her initial interest in Kashmir was encouraged by the strengths of this early and enduring friendship.

Shalamar Bagh, Dal Lake

The most famous and secluded of all the Jahangiri gardens on Dal Lake is the original Shalamar, built on the old Hindu grounds of Pravarsena II. We presume the Jahangiri garden was first struck in 1620, just after the refurbishing of the Nur Afza, for it was then that the emperor recorded the following:

> In these two or three days I frequently embarked in a boat, and was delighted to go round and look at the flowers of Phak and Shalamar. Phak is the name of a pargana situated on the other side of the lake. Shalamar is near the lake. It has a pleasant stream, which comes down from the hills, and flows into the Dal Lake. I bade my son Khurram dam it up and make a waterfall, which it would be a pleasure to behold. This place is one of the sights of Kashmir.[77]

Just how much was done on the site each year that the couple visited is not clear, for Jahangir does not make any more mention of Shalamar in the *Tuzuk* after 1620. The best contemporary description of the garden is given by Bernier, who went to Kashmir with the court of Aurangzeb and who found it to be the "most beautiful of all these gardens" he saw. The site is approached by an entrance canal off the northeast corner of Dal Lake, which was, in Bernier's time, bordered by grass and rows of poplar trees and led to a large *baradari*, which had been placed in the middle of the garden. A second canal connected this building to another pavilion at the end of the site and was set with fountains, as were the large reservoirs off to the sides. The two pavilions in the midst of the canals were built in the form of domes with galleries open on all four sides, large central rooms, and smaller apartments in each corner. The interiors were painted and gilded, with Persian calligraphy on the walls, and surrounded by magnificent stone pillars and doors, some of which had been taken by Shah Jahan from the Hindu temples he had had destroyed.[78]

When Jahangir first laid out the Shalamar garden, he almost certainly had the help of Nur Jahan,[79] and although Shah Jahan was responsible for the famous black marble work done in the pavilions, the overall design reflects the tastes and innovations of his father's queen. Shalamar is divided into three main areas: an outer or public garden, which contains the grand canal leading from the lake and ending with the first large pavilion, the *diwan-i am* (for public audience), which contains a small black marble throne; the emperor's garden, stretching from the first pavilion past the *diwan-i khas* (for private audience) and the royal bathhouses (*hammam*) to an upper wall with small guardrooms at each end; and, finally, the *zanana* garden for the women of the harem, containing the large black marble pavilion and the elaborate waterworks set in a cross around it. A traditional *charbagh*, the *zanana* garden was the climax of Shalamar and, when its many fountains and watery arcades were lit up at night with lanterns, the spectacle would surely have been overwhelming.[80]

Nur Jahan's hand in this design is seen most clearly in the functional divisions of the individual terraces. No longer just a place of private pleasure, the Mughal garden had newly imperial duties as well and, in providing the public and other higher petitioners official access to the emperor, Nur Jahan was extending the symbols of state Jahangir laid down at the beginning of his rule into areas formerly reserved for intimacy. The just, divinely connected king was now, even in leisure, available to mediate issues of local concern and to stand as visual center of an effective empire. Moreover, exemplary of her opening up of travel to women for leisure's sake, Nur Jahan's *zanana* garden at Shalamar stood as perhaps the greatest symbol of all of women's transformation: here women were no longer veiled bearers of morality but visible paradigms of the affirmation of the body and its sensual attributes. To be sure, Shah Jahan, who had had some hand in the garden as a prince,[81] would have agreed to both the development of imperial Mughal symbols and the introduction of sensuality and romantic love in the context of women. Nevertheless, the original inspiration for these, at Shalamar and in the empire at large, was Nur Jahan, whose vision and energy had already redirected the aesthetic efforts of imperial taste.

Achabal, southeast of Srinagar

Close to the old direct road from Jammu to Srinagar on the southerly side of the city is one of the two most favorite gardens of Jahangir and Nur Jahan. At the point where the valley of Kashmir abruptly ends and the great hills begin to descend, lies the garden of Achabal. Says Villiers Stuart: "It is an ideal site. If I were asked where the most perfect modern garden on a medium scale could be devised, I should answer without hesitation, Achibal."[82] Built around a powerful mountain spring that rises out of the Sosanwar hill, Achabal had earlier marked an ancient Hindu site of worship named Akshavala. Known to Akbar as both a delightful place to visit and a source of religious refuge, Achabal drew the early Mughals because of the stupendous fountain of water springing up from the limestone earth and the beautiful yellow spotted fish that appeared in the fountain's natural reservoir.[83] Jahangir and Nur Jahan visited Achabal often — captivated by the "fine waterfall," the "lofty plane-trees and graceful white poplars," and the beautiful *jafari* flowers in bloom—and were at one with Jahangir's sentiment that "it was a piece of Paradise."[84]

As usual, the best contemporary description of the garden was given by Bernier, who singled out the fountain, "whose waters disperse themselves into a hundred canals round the house . . . and throughout the gardens," as the obvious attraction of the site. "The spring gushes out of the earth with violence, as if it issued from the bottom of some well, and the water is so abundant that it ought rather to be called a river than a fountain."[85] The water from the spring, he reported, was "excellent . . . and cold as ice," and was harnessed by various man-made jets, tanks, and cascades into a wonderful sight. The main fall took "the form and colour of a large sheet, thirty or forty paces in length, producing the finest effect imaginable," especially at night when clay lamps with oil and a wick were placed in parts of the wall close by. Bernier also found the regular walkways of the garden very handsome, and in his day the garden plots were laid out, in part, with a variety of fruit trees: apple, pear, plum, apricot, and cherry.[86]

Today, Achabal is smaller than it was originally when Jahangir and Nur Jahan designed it, as the road northward has destroyed the lowest of the terraces. What remains are the two upper levels corresponding to the emperor's garden and the *zanana* garden, this latter having the spring and waterfall at one end and a bathing tank for women in the center. Many of the Mughal structures are now nothing but stone foundations with Kashmiri pavilions of wood and plaster built on top, but the play of light and dark in the pavilions, through the trees, and on the water remains much the same.[87] Ancient chenar trees still provide shade at Achabal, and it is said that Jahangir brought the chenar from Iran to Kashmir in order to please Nur Jahan.[88] Although the legend has no historical foundation (Jahangir himself reported the existence of plane trees in Kashmir in 1607[89]), it does seem to underscore Nur Jahan's legendary influence on horticulture. At one time actually called Begamabad after Nur Jahan, Achabal now stands as a reminder not only of her initial insight into the many possibilities of place, but of what she could do with a site once found.

Vernag, further southeast of Srinagar (Shahabad)

The garden most beloved of Nur Jahan and Jahangir, however, was the simple and immensely appealing site at Vernag farther down the Jammu road from Srinagar. Perhaps the most dramatic example of a natural feature tamed for use in a Mughal garden, the deep blue spring at Vernag was thought to be the fountainhead of the Bihat or Jhelum River.[90] For centuries prior to Jahangir, it was a religious retreat for Hindus, and in 1607 the emperor noted there "the remains of a place of worship for recluses; cells cut out of rock and numerous caves." The name *virnag* means snake, indicating that perhaps a large snake had once inhabited the site of the spring[91] and had been worshipped there[92] or that the Jhelum River was itself in origin a "snake recoiled." In any case, Vernag had always been the centerpiece of Jahangir's Kashmir vision and remained, at least by legend, the place he wanted to be buried.[93]

Jahangir had gone to Vernag twice during Akbar's lifetime and soon after his accession in 1607 had ordered stones to be built up on the sides of the spring and a garden made around it with a canal. At this early time as well, Jahangir had halls and houses built and a place made "such that travellers over the world can point out few like it."[94] The octagonal reservoir he had had constructed to contain the pool from the spring[95] formed the center of the palace buildings, and the twenty-four arched recesses built around it had stairways that led up to rooms on the second floor. Rushing out from the chief palace facade, the stream from the spring entered a long canal, which ran the length of the garden. Twelve feet wide, this grand canal was cut across just below the building by another waterway that ran from side to side.[96]

The pool held water that was exceedingly clear and, by Jahangir's account, "a grain of poppy-seed is visible until it touches the bottom,"[97] or alternately, "if a pea had fallen into it, it could have been seen."[98] Fish had lived there for some long time before Jahangir, and he remarked several times on their great number. Bernier, of course, preserved a famous account of the tameness of these fish and that the largest of them had gold rings through their noses with inscriptions on them, put there "by the celebrated Nour-Mehalle."[99]

In Jahangir's day, trees grew in abundance in the garden, and he remarked that on the hill rising behind Vernag, none of the fertile soil could be seen because there was so much greenery. The greenery on the hill, in fact, was so strong that its reflection in the water gave the surface "a hue of verdure,"[100] which was amplified by the herbs and flowers growing in profusion along the canal and by the side of the reservoir. Among these plants must have been the plane trees Jahangir had ordered to be set bordering the canal in 1620.[101]

Here in Vernag, the "most delightful pleasure-resort . . . in the whole of India,"[102] Jahangir and Nur Jahan could have it all. Half enclosed by mountains, half open to the sky, Vernag was both private and secluded and stately and imperial, and no divisions broke the garden into discrete functions as was the case in many of the other gardens. Arriving at Vernag before reaching Srinagar gave the garden an uncanny connection to the plains below, and yet clearly the spot was in Kashmir and, in "short, in the whole of Kashmir there is no sight of such beauty and enchanting character" as Vernag.[103] The power of the experience must have been overwhelming to Jahangir and Nur Jahan: the extraordinary greenness, the dramatically simple great canal, and the betwixt-and-betweenness of the valley and the mountain behind. No wonder, then, that Jahangir would have wanted to rest here in eternity.

Jahangir had been taken in by Vernag long before he knew Nur Jahan. And long before Nur Jahan as well, he had had the garden site built up and cultivated. No doubt, however, she shared in the depth of his attraction to the place and in the experience of expansive freedom and quite calm it afforded. Surely she was involved in the decisions about the plantings there, and surely she knew that it was her friend Haidar Malik who had brought the masonry work to completion there some time around 1616.[104] Vernag, then, was as much Nur Jahan's as Jahangir's—if not through history then certainly through affection. And it was this affection that made it the last garden of the mountains either one of them was ever to see.

11

The Rebellion of Mahabat Khan

> Apprehension and fear for his life so distracted the traitor, that his deeds and words were not at all sensible. He neither knew what he said nor what he did, nor what was to be done. Every minute some design or some anxiety entered his mind, and caused regret. His Majesty made no opposition to any of his proposals.
>
> *Ikbal-nama-i Jahangiri* of Mutamad Khan, translated and edited by H. M. Elliot and John Dowson

As Jahangir's reign came to a close, one last upheaval broke out in the calm before the confusion of the succession days. Mahabat Khan, an old and trusted friend of Jahangir's, pushed beyond restraint by the courtly infighting around him, rebelled against the emperor and held out in a "reign of a hundred days."[1] The rebellion of Mahabat Khan is significant not only because the story is a contained and vibrant one about an old allegiance gone awry, but because one of the principal actors was Nur Jahan. For most of her public life, Nur Jahan had maneuvered events from behind the walls of seclusion, giving directives and shaping opinion from the palaces reserved only for women. In this rebellion, however, the last of the principal events of her husband's reign, Nur Jahan was herself a real and active participant, providing not only the motive and impetus behind major narrative turns but the visual performance so central to the story as well.

The action took place in the months roughly from March to September 1626, on the banks of the Jhelum River, on the way to Kabul, in Kabul itself, and then on the way from Kabul to Lahore. The main sources of the story are an eyewitness account by Mutamid Khan in the *Iqbalnama* and a contemporary (1627) but secondhand account in van den Broecke (with its later transposition in De Laet). These two descriptions, plus the derivative and extended one of Dow's, provide somewhat conflicting sequences of narrative and motive, but are clearly in agreement that with this event, Mahabat Khan, who had been waiting in the background for some long time, now moved quickly into prominence.

Mahabat Khan, or Zamana Beg, came from a family in Kabul and had served Jahangir onward from the prince's childhood [see Figure 11–1]. At an early point, he had joined the ranks of the Ahadis[2] from which he had risen to a high place on the personal staff of Salim. He had endeared himself to the prince as a devoted, honest, and forthright friend who spoke freely, fought bravely, and displayed excellent talents in organization and service to the empire. He was, said the decidedly partisan van den Broecke, a "praiseworthy" man "whose brave deeds surpass those of all heroes of our time . . . [and were done] because of his love for the King and his Empire."[3] When Jahangir took the throne in 1605, he gave Zamana Beg the title of Mahabat Khan, raised his rank to 1,500, and made him *bakhshi* of his private establishment.[4] From then on the minister regularly received promotions[5] and was often sent by Jahangir to do various kinds of dirty work,[6] the most despicable perhaps being the reputed blinding of the emperor's eldest son, Khusrau.[7] Mahabat Khan became most famous, however, for his role in Shah Jahan's rebellion when in early 1623[8] he was assigned chief command of Parviz's eventually successful campaign to root out and "overthrow Bi-daulat."[9] Throughout all of this, the emperor noted, Mahabat Khan was "the pillar of the State,"[10] the conciliatory leader who controlled and organized his men with integrity and forbearance.

Mahabat Khan's alliance with Parviz, however, may have ultimately been his undoing. Though by 1623 he had been recognized repeatedly for his substantial contributions to the empire, the trusted minister had never achieved the spotlight his long-suffering allegiance seemed to have warranted. After the battle of Baluchpur in late March of 1623, when Shah Jahan retreated to Mandu and eventually to the Deccan, a tired and weary Jahangir decided to pass the reins of pursuit over to his eldest surviving son, Parviz. Parviz, though himself an insignificant prince and in no way a real contender for the throne, was nevertheless decidedly superior to Shahryar for the job and had by birth a better claim to the throne.[11] But because Parviz was an ineffective commander, Jahangir chose the only possible candidate to be his chief advisor: proven after years of service, Mahabat Khan was militarily skillful and historically loyal to the crown.[12] The alliance, then, had meant to combine the weight of the crown with known success and, in the process, with the choice of these two particular principals, to ease the emperor's mind about any further rebellion. For his part, Mahabat Khan must have been delighted to be entrusted with so important a task and, if we believe the accounts, to have again a significant chance to serve the empire.[13] How he felt about going against Shah Jahan, however, is not altogether clear.[14]

If the choice of Mahabat Khan to run Parviz's campaign against Shah Jahan was an astute one tactically for Jahangir, then the results of the campaign were disastrous for Mahabat Khan. Though he was eminently successful in pursuing and disabling the rebellious third son, his good show only provoked envy and disdain at the court. Especially concerned was Nur Jahan. She had first brought Mahabat Khan in to crush Shah Jahan's rebellion,[15] but now grew wary and suspicious of the minister's ensuing power and prestige.[16] In spite of the fact that his recent conduct had "raised sentiments of gratitude in the breast of Jehangire," these sentiments could not overpower the envy of his "great many enemies,"[17] and

FIGURE 11-1. "Portrait of Zamana Beg, Mahabat Khan." Indian painting; Mughal, ca. 1605–28; attr. to Manohar. Courtesy of The Metropolitan Museum of Art, Purchase, Rogers Fund and The Kevorkian Foundation Gift, 1955 (55.121.10.3).

in particular of Nur Jahan. She and her brother, Asaf Khan, says Dow, "had been long the enemies of Mohabet"[18] and she now resolved to undermine his new and enhanced power. Nur Jahan was especially fearful, apparently, of the minister's alliance with Parviz, who, with the notoriety of his recent military success, now became a more serious contender for the throne. Hearing "that Mohabet was forming designs to raise Purvez to the throne,"[19] then, Nur Jahan had to move quickly to protect the goal that, with Shah Jahan's recent disenfranchisement, she was so close to reaching.

Mahabat Khan, of course, had not himself been neutral toward Nur Jahan. According to the *Intikhab-i Jahangir-Shahi*, Mahabat Khan had for some years chided Jahangir about entrusting so much power to a woman. Always beginning his remarks by reminding the emperor that he (Mahabat Khan) cared for no one else but the emperor, "he now begs truly and faithfully to represent what he thinks proper, instigated by his loyalty, and for the sake of His Majesty's good name." Never, he would continue, has there been a "king so subject to the will of his wife. The whole world is surprised that such a wise and sensible Emperor as Jahangir should permit a woman to have so great an influence over him." Such remarks, apparently, would be repeated regularly,[20] and whatever Nur Jahan's feelings for Mahabat Khan, his for her only became more entrenched in their hostility as her power grew.

There was also animosity between Mahabat Khan and the queen's brother, Asaf Khan. As early as September 5, 1616, Roe noted that Mahabat Khan had revealed to him "in great frendship that Asaph chan was our enemy, or at beste a false frend: that hee had faltered with mee in my busines with the king."[21] Although on Roe's part he continued to deal with Nur Jahan's brother, not knowing how trustworthy Mahabat Khan was, there was no further indication in the English document what the source of the hostility between the two men might have been. From their recent past, however, Asaf Khan had excellent cause for wanting to ruin Mahabat Khan: Jahangir's longtime comrade had led the forces that had overpowered Asaf Khan's own protégé and had virtually exiled this prince to the Deccan. If it were only this, many argue, Mahabat Khan's role in suppressing Shah Jahan's rebellion was reason enough for Asaf Khan to harbor perhaps not so secret desires to move against the emperor's faithful retainer.[22]

For these various reasons, then, both Nur Jahan and Asaf Khan with the help of others sought to poison Jahangir against the minister. Unbeknownst to Mahabat Khan, "as soon as the King was rocked to sleep, the . . . dissemblers began to work, and . . . they were determined to poison the King's mind by bringing false charges against him.[23] At the instigation of his close advisers, Jahangir became "much vexed and thought that Mahabat Khan was plotting some evil in spite of his great and faithful service."[24] As Jahangir became more and more convinced of Mahabat Khan's ill intentions, Nur Jahan and her brother formed a plan by which to separate the minister from his charge, Parviz, thereby undermining the chances of this son for the throne.

It happened that Mahabat Khan, having left Burhanpur, had been staying in his castle of Ranthambhor near Agra with his Rajput forces and with Prince

Parviz.[25] According to the story, a royal *farman* now arrived from the emperor via his imperial messenger, Fidai Khan,[26] ordering Mahabat Khan "to proceed to Bengal [as governor] and to hand over the fort to Baqir Khan."[27] This order, according to De Laet, came directly from Nur Jahan.[28] Khan Jahan Lodi who was at that time in Ahmedabad was instructed to proceed to Parviz and join the prince as his *vakil* in the place of Mahabat Khan.[29] Parviz and his minister were not fooled by the request, however, and became convinced that Mahabat Khan's transfer "was owing to the instigation of Asaf Khan, whose object was to bring him to disgrace, and to deprive him of honour, property, and life."[30] Parviz refused to give Mahabat Khan up and, when Fidai Khan communicated this rejection of the *farman* to the imperial court, Nur Jahan and Asaf Khan issued a new *farman* strongly discouraging Parviz from uncooperative conduct and demanding that Mahabat Khan, if he refused to go to Bengal, must come immediately to Jahangir's court. Parviz, seeing that Khan Jahan Lodi was already on his way to take up his new post with him and being hesitant to share the fate of his rebellious brother Shah Jahan, gave in.[31]

For his part, Mahabat Khan was anxious to answer the charges of his accusers and was therefore happy to proceed and appear before Jahangir.[32] They were reminiscent of those once brought against Itimaduddaula and came in the benign form of a request to send back the elephants and to account for the money he had obtained during the period of Shah Jahan's rebellion.[33] These requests, however, amounted to accusations of embezzlement and had been made by Nur Jahan and Asaf Khan in order to undermine Mahabat Khan's great fame for honesty. By questioning his integrity in this way, these two had hoped to provide moral grounds to shift imperial and popular support away from the minister and, by implication, away from Parviz.

Mahabat Khan's response was to write Jahangir a letter announcing his desire to appear before him and redeem his honor. All he had ever wanted, he argued, was Jahangir's favor,[34] and it appears at this point in the narrative that Mahabat Khan had no conscious intention of going into revolt. He proceeded from Ranthambhor, then, with an army of 4,000 or 5,000 Rajputs and marched on to Lahore with the purpose of seeing Jahangir.[35] Jahangir, meanwhile, had left Lahore in March of 1626 and was on his way to Kabul when he reached the Jhelum River and made camp on the near shore. Hearing the news of Mahabat Khan's impending arrival, "Nur Jahan Begam and Asaf Khan urged the King to order that since Mahabat Khan was bringing with him his army and about 200 elephants" in defiance of Jahangir's orders, he should leave his army behind and wait until summoned to appear before the king, sending on ahead only his elephants and a few attendants.[36]

Mahabat Khan complied and, on March 17, 1626, sent his son-in-law on ahead with the elephants and a letter to Jahangir asking why he was now in such disfavor, much regretting "that the king distrusted his old servant." He was ready, apparently, "to hand over his wives and children as a pledge: but . . . could not permit himself to be dragged into the royal presence like a guilty criminal."[37] It happened that this particular son-in-law, Khwaja Barkhurdar, the eldest son of Khwaja Umar Naqshbandi, had married Mahabat Khan's daughter but that the "marriage had been contracted without the royal consent."[38] Jahangir had been much offended by this breach of the rules of royal permission,[39] and when the young man arrived at court with his father-in-law's elephants, the emperor had the young Khwaja's hands tied to his neck and taken directly to prison. Jahangir then ordered Fidai Khan to seize all that had come from Mahabat Khan as dowry to Barkhurdar and to put it in the imperial treasury.[40]

It was this brutal handling of his son-in-law and the wanton confiscation of the youth's personal property that finally provoked Mahabat Khan into action. He now saw that his honor and his life were in danger and, having no well-placed spokesman for his cause near the emperor, he decided to make his case in the only way possible. Jahangir was camped on the near shore of the Jhelum by the bridge passing over to the high road to Kabul and had with him Nur Jahan and a few attendants, one of whom was Mutamid Khan, the author of the *Iqbalnama*. Asaf Khan, in what turned out to be the great blunder of the coup—"notwithstanding the presence of such a brave and daring enemy . . . [and] so heedless of his master's safety"[41] —had already crossed over the bridge to the other side of the river and taken with him the women and children, the attendants and officers, as well as all the baggage, all the weapons, and the imperial treasury. Finding this situation to be most advantageous, Mahabat Khan went to the head of the bridge and left 2,000 men there to guard it with instructions to burn the bridge should anyone try to cross back over.[42] He then proceeded to Jahangir's quarters.

As Mahabat Khan approached, a cry went out and Mutamad Khan went to meet him as he came to the door of the private quarters. After inquiring for the emperor, Mahabat Khan rode through to Jahangir's rooms and, refusing to honor the normal courtesies offered by Mutamad Khan and tearing off some of the boards protecting the emperor's chambers, Mahabat Khan finally forced himself into Jahangir's presence[43] and placed his case before the king:

> I have assured myself that escape from the malice and implacable hatred of Asaf Khan is impossible, and that I shall be put to death in shame and ignominy. I have therefore boldly and presumptuously thrown myself upon Your Majesty's protection. If I deserve death or punishment, give the order that I may suffer it in your presence.[44]

As he spoke, Mahabat Khan's Rajput soldiers surrounded and filled the royal apartments quickly outnumbering all of Jahangir's attendants. Eventually he suggested that the imperial group make ready to go out hunting with Jahangir's "slave" (for example, Mahabat Khan) in attendance so that "it may appear that this bold step has been taken by Your Majesty's order."[45] After a brief scuffle over which horse to ride, Jahangir was given an elephant to mount, and went out guarded in the *hauda* by Rajputs in front and behind. Arrayed thus, Mahabat Khan took his imperial group back to his own camp.[46] According to Manucci, however, the way out was posted with "armed horsemen sent to slay Mahabat Khan; but no one attempted to use force for fear the Rajput might decapitate the king."[47]

It occurred to Mahabat Khan at this time that in all the confusion of getting Jahangir securely within his grasp, he had forgotten Nur Jahan. In order to "make himself safe on that side also," he had the emperor remount and turned the party around to go back to the imperial camp. Arriving there, Mahabat Khan and his men searched everywhere for Nur Jahan but discovered that she had already gone. Now very nervous about the security of his plan, Mahabat Khan "bitterly repented of the blunder he had made in not securing her."[48] He next remembered Shahryar and went to his house, but found that he, too, was missing, presumably now in flight.

Nur Jahan, in the meantime, had been busy. After Jahangir had left in the custody of Mahabat Khan, she had crossed over the bridge to Asaf Khan's camp on the other side. She went either to make a simple visit to her brother, thinking Jahangir to be out on a hunt and her now with some free time,[49] or more likely, knowing what had happened, to consult with her brother about strategy.[50] It is probable that she went to the camp in disguise, but how she got over the bridge with the Rajput army under orders to let no one across is not altogether clear. Whatever the case, Nur Jahan reached Asaf Khan's house late that afternoon and convened a meeting of all the nobles. She reproached them severely, especially her brother, for being so lazy and inattentive and to the whole assembly said:

> This . . . has all happened through your neglect and stupid arrangements. What never entered into the imagination of any one has come to pass, and now you stand stricken with shame for your conduct before God and man. You must do your best to repair this evil, and advise what course to pursue.[51]

Scolded for their fault in the emperor's abduction and fearful that his life might be in danger,[52] the nobles together agreed with Nur Jahan that they would cross back over the river the next day and lay seige to Mahabat Khan's camp and rescue Jahangir. When the emperor heard news during the night of this "unwise resolution," he sent successive messengers over to Asaf Khan and the nobles to warn them against any action that would be "productive of nothing but evil and repentence."[53] To insure the sincerity of these warnings Jahangir also sent over his own signet ring with Mir Mansur, but because Asaf Khan suspected that all the messages were a ruse instigated by Mahabat Khan, he ignored them.[54] The honor of the imperial forces was at stake and there was no other way to redeem their fault than to do battle with the abductors.

It was also during that night that Fidai Khan, who had already crossed over to the far shore, took a horse and went down to the river hoping to cross back over to the emperor. By this time, however, the Rajputs had burned the bridge and Fidai Khan found he had no alternative but to swim. Six of his men drowned in the river on the way over, and others who were too cold to go on turned back, but Fidai Khan himself made it to the near shore. There four more of his few remaining men were killed by Mahabat Khan's soldiers and Fidai Khan's party, now very severely reduced, could not reach Jahangir, ensconced for the night in the home of Shahryar. Tired and disappointed, the loyal servant swam back across the Jhelum to Asaf Khan's camp, there to wait until morning.[55]

The next day, March 18, 1626, Nur Jahan, Asaf Khan and the other nobles, "being resolved upon giving battle,"[56] began their march "with day."[57] Searching for an appropriate ford in the river by which to cross, Ghazi the boat commander found one he thought suitable. It happened, however, that this ford was one of the worst in the river with several large pits filled deep with water. As the imperial party began to cross over "all order was lost,"[58] and as chaos descended on the army many men fell to the river or were scattered. Mahabat Khan's Rajputs were still on the other side of the Jhelum, but had gathered seven or eight hundred strong "with a number of war-elephants in their front" and stood "in firm array" on the bank.[59] As the enemy held the bank in many places, Asaf Khan's forces began to look for other places by which to make their crossing and, in the middle of all the turmoil, several new fords downstream were found allowing, "each party . . . [to get] over as best it could."[60] When some of the enemy began to advance, Asaf Khan's men recoiled[61] and whatever organization and discipline they had left quickly disappeared: "everyone who was in front fell back, and those who went on together fell. The officers, in a panic, rushed off in disorder, not knowing whither they went, or where they led their men."[62]

From the very start of the assault, Nur Jahan had been in the middle of battle alongside her brother and all of the nobles. Not "a tame spectator on the occasion, . . . [she had] mounted on an elephant . . . [and] plunged into the stream with her daughter by her side."[63] It was she, it seems, who was the real commander of the forces,[64] and when she noticed that Mutamid Khan and Khwaja Abul Hasan had crossed over one branch of the river and now stood on the brink of crossing the second, she sent her eunuch Nadim to urge the two on into the fray. "The Begam wants to know if this is the time for delay and irresolution," he said, "strike boldly forward, so that by your advance the enemy may be repulsed, and take to flight."[65] They jumped in immediately and were among those men who successfully met the enemy's swords at the near shore. Nur Jahan's party, however, was not so fortunate. She had gone into battle "on account of her great bitterness [and] she [had] wanted to show her woman's courage to Mahabat Khan."[66] Riding with her in her *hauda* were her daughter Ladli, her granddaughter (the child of Ladli and Shahryar), and the child's nurse,[67] who happened to be the wife of Abu Talib Shayista Khan, son of Asaf Khan, and the granddaughter of the old Khankhanan, Mirza Abdur Rahim, through his son, Shahnawaz Khan. During the struggle, the nurse received an arrow in the arm, but Nur Jahan "herself pulled it out, staining her garments with blood."[68] The empress in return then "emptied four quivers of arrows on the enemy," but when the Rajputs "pressed into the stream to seize her," she turned her party away.[69] The elephant on which they were all riding received substantial wounds from Mahabat Khan's soldiers, and when its drivers took it into deep water, the accompanying horsemen turned back for fear of being drowned. The elephant, however, was able to swim to shore on its own, and Nur Jahan, on reaching dry land, proceeded to her own royal quarters.[70]

The battle, continued for several hours and eventually left Mahabat Khan victorious. Although the imperial army had outnumbered the Rajputs by 50,000 to 5,000, the Rajput army was a seasoned force emboldened in battle by the regular use of opium; moreover, Mahabat Khan's name had apparently sent fear into the hearts of everyone. Van den Broecke estimated that about 2,000 of the imperial forces were killed by the Rajputs and another 2,000 drowned in the river, now covered with elephants and horses.[71] Nur Jahan's men had met strong opposition and in their great panic had separated into small, isolated groups and become by consequence paralyzed. Now, in the wake of the battle, the army was demoralized and many men fled.

During the battle there had been an attempt to rescue Jahangir. Fidai Khan, by all accounts one of the most impressive personalities in Nur Jahan's camp, had taken some of the emperor's attendants and had successfully crossed the river. Once on the other side, he had proceeded to attack the Rajput forces who opposed him. Having bravely driven back the enemy, he reached Jahangir at Shahryar's house and, stopping outside, sent arrows into the courtyard. When in the skirmishes that followed, however, a number of his men were killed, Fidai Khan realized he could not rescue Jahangir and the next day went up the river to his sons at Rohtas.[72]

Van den Broecke's account of the battle sequences differed somewhat from that of the *Iqbalnama*. According to the Dutch version, when Mahabat Khan arrived at Jahangir's camp, he offered to send his women and children ahead to Nur Jahan as a pledge of good faith. Because of the hatred that Nur Jahan and her brother had developed for Mahabat Khan,[73] however, they refused to see him and decided instead to attack his army in the hopes of killing him or bringing him back to Jahangir as a criminal. The battle ensued and Mahabat Khan won. The victorious minister then crossed the river, and when he made his way to Jahangir's tents, found the emperor sleeping. Taking him by surprise, Mahabat Khan had Jahangir get dressed as if for hunting and brought him out in haste to his own camp. His Rajput men then searched for Nur Jahan and, finding her, surrounded her tents and kept her there in confinement.[74]

Meanwhile, according to both accounts, Asaf Khan had vanished during the course of the battle. The *Iqbalnama* stated that Nur Jahan's brother, "who was the cause of this disaster, and whose folly and rashness had brought matters to this pass," had panicked when he realized he could not offer substantial resistance to Mahabat Khan. Afraid for his own life, and thoughtless about his responsibility for what he was leaving behind, Asaf Khan fled the battle scene with his son, Abu Talib Shayista Khan, taking with him two or three hundred soldiers. He went to the fort of Attock, which was in one of his own *jagirs*, and in his great cowardice closed up the fort around him, leaving Nur Jahan and the other imperial nobles to deal with the Rajput army on their own.[75] His flight from battle came just at the end of the encounter, for Mutamid Khan reported seeing him just before Khwaja Abul Hasan left for Nur Jahan's quarters: "Asaf Khan now came in sight; his companions were scattered, and his plan had failed, so he departed."[76]

For her part, Nur Jahan had successfully reached her camp on the near shore. When she saw that so many of her men had been killed, however, and that Asaf Khan had taken flight, she decided to surrender to Mahabat Khan. Mutamid Khan, author of the *Iqbalnama*, had himself already gone over and Nur Jahan's capitulation, given the situation, was now nothing more than a cosmetic gesture. It did complete, however, Mahabat Khan's ascendancy and, having the government under his sole command, he proceeded to make firm his position. After the "shouting and shrieking . . . [which] filled the heaven and earth" had died down, Mahabat Khan had his Rajputs plunder all the gold, silver, and jewels in the camp, taking anything that was of any value. He placed into heavily guarded custody all the members of the royal family, including Jahangir, Nur Jahan, Shahryar, Prince Bulaqi (son of Khusrau), and a son of Daniyal.[77] Of Nur Jahan's confinement, van den Broecke now said:

> When formerly Nur Jahan Begam used to ride out, with people playing and singing before her, she was received by every one with marks of excessive honour and reverence, even like a goddess. This was forbidden by Mahabat Khan, saying that honour was due not to her but to the King.[78]

Thus restrained, Nur Jahan was subject to all the bitter feelings Mahabat Khan had harbored for years and especially those injuries he had received most recently. Dow preserves a story of this confinement that, though believable, is certainly not authentic. Mahabat Khan's bitterness was so great, Dow relates, that he decided to publicly accuse Nur Jahan of treason. She had, he said, estranged the emperor from "the hearts of his subjects;" she had authorized by "her capricious orders . . . the most cruel and unwarrantable actions . . . in every corner of the empire;" she had made many "public calamities" by "her haughtiness" and ruined many individuals by "her malignity;" and, finally, she had sought to undermine the whole empire "by favouring the succession of Shariar to the throne."[79] Because of her wickedness, then, Nur Jahan must be made a public example of and, knowing Jahangir's legendary passion for justice, Mahabat Khan had the emperor sign a warrant for her death. "Being excluded from his presence, her charms had lost their irresistible influence over him; and when his passions did not thwart the natural bias of his mind, he was always just."[80] In her quarters, Nur Jahan herself heard the sentence without emotion, but asked for permission to see the emperor one last time so "to bathe with my tears the hand that has fixed the seal to the warrant of death." She was allowed to come to Jahangir, but only in the presence of Mahabat Khan, and when the emperor saw her beauty, which "shone with additional lustre through her sorrow," he begged his captor for his wife's release. Mahabat Khan, his dishonor now assuaged and looking perhaps for a way out, replied that any emperor of the Mughals "should never ask [a thing] in vain" and released Nur Jahan with the wave of a hand.[81]

Having consolidated his power on all but one front, Mahabat Khan now proceeded to Attock to root out Asaf Khan. He sent on ahead of him some of his Ahadi guards, some of his own followers, and some landlords (*zamindars*) under the command of his son Bihroz and a Rajput, to capture Asaf Khan and to bring him out alive. Attock Fort was "reduced," and seeing that he could not escape,

"Asaf Khan bowed to Fate"[82] and gave himself up—but only "on receiving the promise that his life would be spared."[83] When the imperial party under Mahabat Khan arrived, Asaf Khan and his son, Abu Talib, were brought before Jahangir and given "into the charge of . . . [their] own adherents."[84] Under his amnesty agreement with Mahabat Khan, however, Asaf Khan could not be executed for his cowardice, but Jahangir could and did have him "thrown into chains" and placed in Mahabat Khan's prison.[85] Several of Asaf Khan's followers were then put to death.

With this the imperial retinue, under the sovereignty of Mahabat Khan, resumed their erstwhile march to Kabul. Under the control now of the old minister, the whole household of Jahangir arrived in the northern post without further incident in May of 1626. Once there, Mahabat Khan allowed his detainees some freedom, and Jahangir, upon arriving, was able to visit the tomb of his ancestors[86] and, with Nur Jahan, to make a visit to Shah Ismail of Persia.[87] During what came to be a fairly peaceful interlude, an issue arose that concerned one of Nur Jahan's sisters, Manija Begam, wife of Qasim Khan.[88] Jahangir had appointed Muzaffar Khan to be governor of Agra in the place of Qasim Khan. The reason for this change in personnel is not altogether clear, and De Laet himself could not decide whether Qasim Khan resigned or whether he had been deprived of his post.[89] Manija, in any case, "was not willing to leave Agra" and so went to her sister in the north in order to persuade her to allow the family to remain there in the city as before. Seeing that Nur Jahan "now possessed very little authority," however, Manija had to go on to Mahabat Khan with her request; he granted her desire and issued a *farman* confirming Qasim Khan as governor of Agra.[90] "Poor Muzaffar Khan," said van den Broecke, he "was in office for only three days"![91]

The imperial camp in Kabul now received news of three events. The first was the death of Malik Ambar in his eightieth year, news received by Jahangir in the middle of May 1626. Ambar had been an Abyssinian slave and had made himself Jahangir's most feared enemy as a military spokesman for the powerful forces in the Deccan. He had no equal, said Mutamid Khan, in "warfare, in command, in sound judgment, and in administration," and history "records no other instance of an Abyssinian slave arriving at such eminence."[92] The second news to come was of Shah Jahan's movements. Having "supposed [that] he was as good as dead and buried,"[93] the imperial court had not paid attention to the prince's whereabouts, but it now became clear that he had left the Deccan and had proceeded to Ajmer. From there he had gone by way of Jaisalmer to Tatta and was looting and laying seige to what he could find.[94] The court, though not now in the most opportune position to head Shah Jahan off, did, however, start from Kabul toward Hindustan in August of 1626,[95] presumably in response to the Shah Jahan issue. The third news to arrive was of Parviz's illness. Languishing in Burhanpur, he had been attacked by colic and, after becoming insensible, had fallen into "a heavy sleep." He had been cauterized by the doctors in five places on the head, but apparently to no avail. "His illness was attributed to excessive drinking; the same malady of which his uncles . . . had died."[96]

Although Jahangir "in his good nature and gentleness" had now become, at least on the surface, reconciled to the situation with Mahabat Khan,[97] he and his wife laid plans for escape. "At the instigation of Nur Jahan Begum and with the permission of the King,"[98] the Ahadis while still in Kabul picked a fight with the Rajputs of Mahabat Khan. The minister lost "some of his best men" in the violent fray that ensued,[99] some having been "slaughtered . . . like sheep" and others sold "like dogs" to traders in Kabul,[100] and he was justifiably mad. He complained to Jahangir, who handed over two of the perpetrators for imprisonment, but it was clear that the minister was not going to get any more satisfaction from the affair than that.[101] Because of his arrogance and general unpopularity among members of the imperial party, Mahabat Khan had been having trouble effecting peace with those in his camps. Jahangir and Nur Jahan became more courageous now with the Ahadi victory, and as the peace efforts faulted, they pushed actively to set up a mechanism for freedom.

The first part of the plan was for Jahangir to get Mahabat Khan into his complete confidence. Pretending to be fully open with his captor "so that Mahabat felt quite secure on that side,"[102] Jahangir said he would to hand over all the information he received to the general. "Whatever Nur Jahan Begam said to the Emperor in private, he unreservedly repeated to Mahabat Khan, and he bade him beware, for the Begam had a design against him."[103] He also let on to Mahabat Khan that Asaf Khan's daughter-in-law, the daughter of Shahnawaz Khan married to Abu Talib Shayista Khan and a nurse to Nur Jahan's granddaughter, planned to assassinate him whenever she got a chance. "By these means he set Mahabat's heart at rest, and removed that doubt and suspicion with which Mahabat had at first regarded him."[104] As a result, Mahabat Khan relaxed his defenses, becoming less careful about security measures around the palace and loosening the control he had exercised over the activities at court.

As Jahangir lulled the suspicions of Mahabat Khan and convinced him that he was actually pleased with the arrangements,[105] Nur Jahan set about her plan "to revenge herself."[106] The number of bodyguards around the palace had been greatly reduced, and with Mahabat Khan now off his guard, Nur Jahan was able to bring together an army of substantial proportion. She began every day by "conferring with [the] secret enemies of Mahabat Khan"[107] and by buying their loyalty with money and promises.[108] She wrote to her eunuch, Hoshiyar Khan, the *faujdar* of the Bajwaral and Dasuha districts, "to secretly recruit on her account 5,000 Pathan, Sayyid or Shaikh-Zadas horse and to hold them with her other old soldiers in readiness to join her when she should have passed Attock."[109] This he did, paid them in advance, and proceeded on to meet her.[110] Nur Jahan also secured soldiers from Lahore, paid for from her own money, as well as the "secret enemies of Mahabat Khan [who] had now begun to throw off the veil and openly join her."[111]

Confident now that their own forces were strong enough to make a play for the liberation of the imperial court, Nur Jahan and Jahangir took action. The court had already left Kabul for Lahore and was one day's march from Rohtas. Jahangir, no longer needing to act tactfully, sent a message to Mahabat Khan asking him to postpone his usual parade as he, the emperor, was going to make a review of Nur Jahan's cavalry. Khwaja Abul Hasan went personally to the minister to reinforce the request and, directing Mahabat Khan to go ahead so that the two parties would not clash, went on to join Jahangir. Although Mahabat Khan was "aware of what was passing, his mind had been so shaken by the fight with the *ahadis*, that he did as he was ordered, and marched forwards."[112] Unrestrained by the now outwitted and demoralized Mahabat Khan, Jahangir and his party proceeded on to Rohtas "where he found a Court ready to receive him."[113] Thus, having crossed over the Jhelum, "the emperor regained his liberty on the bank of the river where he had lost it a few months before."[114] From Rohtas, Jahangir sent orders to Mahabat Khan to follow Shah Jahan to Tatta and assist in matters there, and to send Asaf Khan, his son, Abu Talib, and the sons of the late Prince Daniyal, Tahmuras and Hoshang, to court.[115]

If Mahabat Khan were to delay at all in sending Asaf Khan, said Jahangir, an army would be sent after him. The general complied in returning the sons of Daniyal but decided to keep Asaf Khan because, without him as hostage, "he was not safe as regarded Nur Jahan."[116] His plan, Mahabat Khan said, was to hold the queen's brother until he had safely passed Lahore, at which point he would set him free. Nur Jahan was furious, her honor now more than ever at stake, and she sent a report back to Mahabat Khan demanding without delay, and with full threat of retaliation, the return of Asaf Khan. Mahabat Khan finally agreed, but did not release Asaf Khan until the prisoner had sworn an oath of loyalty to him.

> [Mahabat Khan asked Asaf Khan] to swear on the Book (the Quran) that he would always be as a brother to him, since he was setting him at liberty, and had spared his life. "For" he said, "it was in my power to kill you," and in support of this, he showed to him several letters of the King, making it clear that he was commanded ten times to kill Asaf Khan and not to spare his life. . . . Asaf Khan promised on oath that henceforth Mahabat Khan would be much more to him than his own natural brother.[117]

Having released Asaf Khan on oath of extreme obligation to him, Mahabat Khan kept the minister's son, Abu Talib, for some days. Then, releasing the son after his men crossed the Chenab, Mahabat Khan marched off as if his intention were to proceed to Tatta on the business of Shah Jahan as ordered by Jahangir.

Now free, the court went on to Lahore where, in late October of 1626, its members began to reassemble the machinery of the government. There, ever forgiving, Jahangir received Asaf Khan, and as the emperor "sympathised with him in his misfortunes and the great hardships that he had endured,"[118] he honored his wife's brother with the *subadari* of the Punjab and the office of *vakil*. He also ordered him "to preside permanently over the administration of all affairs, revenue and political."[119] Her brother's safe return did not assuage Nur Jahan, however, for she was still angry that she had not been able to avenge herself completely against Mahabat Khan. She scolded Asaf Khan for not having had more patience for, if he had only waited, she said, "she would have fought and rescued him by force, made Mahabat Khan like dust of the earth and punished him in a manner so as to make him an object-lesson for the whole world."[120] Asaf Khan appeased her by saying that he was lucky to be alive, but when Jahangir asked him if he realized how obligated he now was to Mahabat Khan, Asaf Khan duplicitously replied that he would forget what he owed or repay it benignly.[121]

Nur Jahan was still not satisfied, however—raging as she was "with a fruitless passion for revenge[122]—and when she got word that a convoy with twenty-two *lakh* rupees was coming to Mahabat Khan from Bengal and was now near Delhi, she sent out a confiscation party. When the men in charge of the convoy discovered the impending attack,[123] they barricaded themselves in a *sarai* near Shahabad and held out for some time against the imperial forces. Nur Jahan's army prevailed, however, and, setting fire to the *sarai*, retrieved the treasure when the men fled.[124] The queen then bribed the old Khankhanan, Abdur Rahim, with a large reward to go in pursuit of Mahabat Khan. The minister had, she argued, put to death the Khankhanan's son and nephew "without any order from the King."[125] When the Khankhanan protested that he was now too old and enfeebled for the trials of war, Nur Jahan insisted and, in the end, the Khankhanan had no choice but to take up Mahabat Khan's pursuit.[126] Abdur Rahim died in Delhi, however, in the winter of 1627 before he could seriously attend to the issue.

Although Mahabat Khan had been given a nominal "severance pay" of a dress of honor, some elephants, and some horses by Jahangir,[127] he was now for all intents and purposes a fugitive. Knowing that he was still the object of revenge by Nur Jahan and that his only "friend" at court Asaf Khan could do nothing to help him as his "power depended upon his sister,"[128] Mahabat Khan at first took the route toward Tatta, but before he got there went off into Hindustan. There he "concealed himself for some time in the hills of the Rana's country,"[129] waiting apparently for the final events of Jahangir's reign to unfold.

Mahabat Khan remains even now an appealing character. Although he did, without doubt, act seditiously toward Jahangir and his court, it seems clear that he was badgered and harassed into treason. One could argue, as van den Broecke did, that all of Mahabat Khan's actions were instigated by his enemies, who for the sake of their own interest, were "trying to bring about the fall of his power and his death."[130] His only mistake was that, believing too much in the imperial office, he was overly merciful and "did not act with that severity which was necessary in view of their offence." Nur Jahan was made his most implacable enemy, who saw in him not only a major threat to her imperial designs for her daughter, but a living symbol of rebuff to her own honor: the queen "wished to conquer him, who had conquered her, and who smarted because she had not been able to do with him as she liked, to cool her lust with him."[131] Nevertheless, Mahabat Khan did act inopportunely, even if it were for reasons of his injured reputation. And although Jahangir was known to value old friendships, he had to let this one fall given the pressing circumstances of his marriage and the empire.

For Nur Jahan's part, however, we find that she exhibited here as always a finely honed instinct for survival that allowed her to meet the occasion with whatever resources she found at hand. The rebellion did serve an interesting function, however, for in one strike it crystallized the loyalties of Asaf Khan, Mahabat Khan, and Shah Jahan away from the camp of the queen and ultimately toward one another. Ironically, had not Mahabat Khan been forced at the beginning to account for himself before Jahangir by the queen, Nur Jahan may have been in a better position one year hence to oversee the wars of succession in which her people, as it turned out, fared so very poorly.

12

Death of Jahangir and Retirement to Lahore

Nothing can be stated with certainty as the issue still belongs to the future. We may, however, discuss the question as to whose chances (of succession) are the greatest. In regard to the choice of a new king the nobles may be divided into three groups accordingly as they are inclined in favour of Sultan Bulaqi, Sultan Shahr Yar or the eldest Sultan Khurram.

A Contemporary Dutch Chronicle of Mughal India by Pieter van den Broecke, translated and edited by Brij Narain and Sri Ram Sharma

On the grave of this poor stranger, let there be neither lamp nor rose. Let neither butterfly's wing burn nor nightingale sing.

epitaph on Nur Jahan's tomb, translated by Wheeler Thackston

Nur Jahan's heroic role in the rebellion of Mahabat Khan was short-lived. Having come out of seclusion for the climactic episode of her political life and having maneuvered her husband out from the hands of his abductor, she had proven herself capable of an exquisitely executed victory. She had not become victorious, however, by fighting in battle but by the means she had always used best: strategy measured out from behind the palace walls. Her skills at duplicity, her easy use of charm at all levels of government, and most of all her tenacious powers of endurance had proved their mettle. But with the close of the rebellion of Mahabat Khan, Nur Jahan's role as manager of political events came to an end. She would now be forced, most reluctantly, to pass the brokering of power over to her brother, Asaf Khan, and, more particularly, to his protégé the future king, Shah Jahan.

Shah Jahan had not been well-off in the last two years of Jahangir's reign. Back in the Deccan after his unsuccessful revolt against his father, he had fallen ill[1] and had found few followers for support or security. Hearing the news of Mahabat Khan's coup, however, Shah Jahan left Ahmadnagar on June 7, 1626, and marched north through the pass of Nasik Trimbak. Although Kamgar Khan stated that Shah Jahan "resolved that he would hasten immediately to the Emperor his father"[2] in order to save him from his abductor, most believe that the prince wanted to gain whatever advantage he could for himself out of the unsettled situation.[3]

Although Shah Jahan had not yet chosen sides, it would eventually become clear to him that his best chances lay in an alliance with Mahabat Khan. The two were not friends—in fact, they had most recently been on either ends of a pursuit that had veered all over India—but Mahabat Khan was now a fugitive and his natural animosity toward the imperial court would be an especially beneficial factor to the exiled prince. Eventually, Shah Jahan would see such an alliance as eminently agreeable to both the failed minister and to himself: Mahabat Khan was an excellent soldier and an experienced courtier who, only because of circumstances, had been unable recently to exhibit the loyal qualities for which he was best known.

On the way north, Shah Jahan found it difficult to get troops together. Both Khan Jahan and Raja Nar Singh Deo made excuses when asked to join the prince and after reaching Ajmer, where Raja Kishan Singh died, Shah Jahan saw that his men had dwindled to only about four or five hundred in number. Because "it was impossible for him to carry out his design of going to the Emperor" with so small an army,[4] Shah Jahan resolved to go to Tatta, where he would "wait patiently for a while"[5] in the hopes of recruiting more troops. But the route was unusually dry and barren and "his journey was attended with great hardship,"[6] and when he reached Tatta in October of 1626, he found that patient waiting was impossible. Under Sharifulmulk, the governor of the district and a devoted supporter of Shahryar's through Nur Jahan, three to four thousand cavalry and ten thousand infantry stopped Shah Jahan's progress at the gate. Though overpowering, Shahryar's forces were afraid to strike and retreated to within the city, thus encouraging some of Shah Jahan's men to attack anyway despite their prince's insistent instructions not to.[7] Many men died in the attack, and although he knew beforehand that it was a futile seige, Shah Jahan was nevertheless "greatly affected by his ill-success."[8]

Spurned at Tatta, Shah Jahan now thought to enlist the aid of his old friend, Shah Abbas of Persia. He wrote several letters to the shah, but none of them received a promising response; the second of the replies, in fact, made quite clear to Shah Jahan that Abbas thought the prince should lay low and submit to his father.[9] With Persia no longer an obvious source of support, then, and still so weak and ill that "he was obliged to travel in a *palki*,"[10] Shah Jahan now turned around and went back through Gujarat to the Deccan.[11] There he was warmly greeted by the son of Malik Ambar, who had taken over the government after his father died. The new ruler "received Khurram with honor and helped him with whatever he required,"[12] and in the time that followed, Shah Jahan was able to strengthen further his alliances with the noble families of the Deccan.[13]

On his way back to the Deccan, Shah Jahan received the news that his older brother Parviz had died. Suffering from intemperance, the family affliction, Parviz had succumbed "after a long illness"[14] on October 28, 1626, at the age of thirty-eight.[15] Jahangir's grief had been "immeasurable," for he loved deeply this [illegible] "was more gentle and obedient than the other sons . . . [and who had] always submissively obeyed the King's commands."[16] Rumors persisted that Shah Jahan had had a hand in his brother's death, that "he [had] caused his second brother, Sultan Parveen, to be poisoned,"[17] but such stories by all accounts were illfounded. Parviz's body was taken back to Agra, where it was eventually entombed in his own garden.[18]

Parviz's death raised new questions about the future of the crown, and Nur Jahan watched as Jahangir grew increasingly "anxious as to who should succeed to the throne after his death."[19] Shah Jahan was heartened by the news of Parviz, however, for it reduced his competition by one and left him with only Shahryar and Dawar Bakhsh, a son of Khusrau nicknamed Bulaqi, with whom to contend.[20]

About this time, as Shah Jahan proceeded toward the Deccan, Mahabat Khan began to make overtures of alliance to him.[21] Mahabat Khan had been forced into hiding by Nur Jahan's seizure of his Bengal treasure outside of Delhi,[22] and, as a result, had taken refuge in the forests of Mewar[23] and had sought asylum, said De Laet, with the Rana of Udaipur.[24] Exceedingly depressed over the death of his protégé Parviz,[25] however, and having been in the Rana's district for a while, Mahabat Khan now sought to reverse the infamy by which "his very name . . . seemed to have ceased to exist."[26]

Furious that Nur Jahan was still harassing his nobles and taking money from them,[27] and knowing that her pursuit of him would not abate quickly, Mahabat Khan came out of hiding and approached Shah Jahan.[28] Sending messengers to the prince "to express his contrition," Mahabat Khan's gamble was successful; the "Prince received his apologies kindly, called him to his presence, and treated him with great favour and kindness."[29] After submitting to Shah Jahan—all "that I have, my treasure and my person, till I die, will be employed in your service"[30]— Mahabat Khan was pardoned and the alliance between the two confirmed.[31] Gifts were exchanged, and both men vowed to work companionably together from this point on to secure Shah Jahan's accession. Said Mundy: Mahabat Khan "never left him [Shah Jahan] till hee brought him to Agra where hee became King by Asaph Ckauns and this mans helpe."[32]

Jahangir and Nur Jahan, meanwhile, had been keeping court in Lahore. Safe for the time from abductors and rebellious children, they had resumed the ordinary trappings of imperial life, receiving gifts from visitors[33] and effecting the usual promotions and demotions necessary to hold the continued interest of the court. Fidai Khan, "who had for a long time been in refuge in the territory of Bharat Singh"[34] after the initial Mahabat Khan abduction, came out of hiding now and made his way to Nur Jahan and Jahangir in Lahore. There he was elevated in rank by the queen and made governor of Bengal.[35] Nur Jahan also ordered at this time "a great gathering" to be held in Shahryar's garden in honor of her son-in-law's appointment as commander of 40,000 *suwar*. There "all the nobles who were present in the palace or the camp made obeisance (Salam) to him, which signified that he was to succeed to the Kingdom"[36]—a gesture that seems, by later events, to have held little legal or moral force.

Jahangir, however, was not doing well. The seasonal heat of Lahore had exacerbated his sickness, and unable to bear the approaching summer, he left with the court for Kashmir in March of 1627. Included in his retinue, besides the queen, were Asaf Khan, Shahryar, and Bulaqi. In Kashmir, however, his declining health got even worse. Each day "his illness increased," and as he "was unable to ride on horseback . . . [he had to be] carried about in a *palki*." "He lost all appetite for food, and rejected opium, which had been his companion for forty years. He took nothing but a few cups of wine of the grape."[37] Suffering from asthma, Jahangir found that the air of "the elevated country," against expectation, was not good for him.

As Jahangir's health got worse and his asthma became progressively debilitating, another member of the imperial retinue got desperately ill. Shahryar, the youngest son and at least in Nur Jahan's view the heir apparent, came down with a kind of leprosy known as Fox's Disease. His hair, whiskers, eyebrows, and eyelashes fell out, leaving him pale and denuded to the end. The doctors were unable to prescribe any medicine that would help, and thus thoroughly shamed, Shahryar decided to return to Lahore where the warmer climate might prove more beneficial.[38] Although it was planned that Shahryar would proceed to Lahore first so that he could make immediate arrangements for his treatment,[39] the whole imperial retinue, including Jahangir, was to leave Kashmir quickly thereafter. Some suggest that Jahangir needed to go back for reasons of his own health,[40] but by now Nur Jahan had become obsessed with the imminent issue of succession. It is quite probable, then, others would argue, that Jahangir had been persuaded to leave not because of his health but because his wife wanted to be near her son-in-law when Jahangir died. Proximity to Shahryar would mean that Nur Jahan could ensure his accession to the throne as soon as the occasion demanded.

On Jahangir's way back to Lahore from Kashmir, a tragic hunting accident occurred. As the emperor's party reached Bairam Kala—the place where "one enters India"[41]—Jahangir decided to hunt. The local people drove the deer up to the area where the emperor was sitting, and Jahangir raised his gun, shot a deer, and watched as the wounded animal scurried off to its females and fell. One of Jahangir's men ran after the stricken deer but lost his balance and fell over the cliff to his death. "The fate of the poor man greatly affected the Emperor. It seemed as though he had thus seen the angel of death. From that time he had no rest or ease, and his state was entirely changed."[42] Although Jahangir must have known, given the desiccated state of his body, that he did not have long to live, the death of a servant for no reason but his own imperial whim struck him as frighteningly ominous. His own death now seemed very close, and for a man who had so feared the morbid throughout his life,[43] the actuality was horrifying. Some preparation for death had already taken place, for earlier in 1620 while in Kashmir, Jahangir experienced difficulty in breathing and mused, "I hope that in the end, please God, it may all go well."[44] Now that it was upon him, however, the terror was great.

As it turned out the waiting was not long, for shortly after the accident, on October 28, 1627, Jahangir died—exactly a year to the day after the death of his second son Parviz.[45] The imperial entourage had just left Rajauri for the next [illegible], Chingaz Hatli near Bhimbar, the day before. On the way, Jahangir had [illegible] a glass of wine but could not swallow it. As the night wore on, he grew worse and early the next morning he died. Nuruddin Jahangir Padshah was fifty-eight and had just completed the twenty-second year of his reign.[46]

Despite his public waverings in favor of the weak Shahryar and, we would like to believe, his private hopes for the better suited Shah Jahan, Jahangir had not officially appointed an heir to his throne. His death, then, set in motion a struggle for succession that lasted over three months and cost the imperial line almost all of its possible legatees. The struggle began in earnest on the day of Jahangir's death when Nur Jahan, still with the imperial party outside of Rajauri, called all the nobles to her side for a conference. According to the anti-Nur Jahan *Padshahnama* of Lahori: "Nur Mahal, who had been the cause of much strife and contention, now clung to the vain idea of retaining the reins of government in her grasp, as she had held them during the reign of the late Emperor."[47] The conference never materialized, however, having been foiled by Asaf Khan, who managed to evade his sister's brief play for power on one pretext or another. Said the *Iqbalnama*, "he made excuses, and did not go."[48] Clear that his sister would make a strong bid to control the succession, Asaf Khan, with the support of all the nobles and after years of secret duplicity, now came out in the open against her. In order to prevent Nur Jahan from putting Shahryar on the throne, Asaf Khan "put the queen under arrest,"[49] confined "her to her tent; and gave strict orders that none should be admitted into her presence."[50] In this way, with Nur Jahan under watchful guard, Asaf Khan could not only check his sister's movements but also lay plans for his own security.

Asaf Khan began by sending the Hindu runner Banarasi from Chingaz Hatli to Shah Jahan "with intelligence of the death of Jahangir."[51] Shah Jahan had by now returned to the Deccan after his unsuccessful campaign to Tatta and was "at a distance of three months' journey from the place where the Emperor Jahangir had died."[52] Because there was no time to write the prince, Asaf Khan sent his own signet ring with Banarasi "as a guarantee" that the news from the north was authentic.[53] Even at that moment, as his father-in-law was making plans for his succession, Shah Jahan was being urged by his supporters in the Deccan "to make a bid for the Empire"[54]—a bid, as history proved, it was unnecessary to make.

Asaf Khan and the *mir bakhshi*, Iradat Khan, then saw that they had to stall for time in the interval before Shah Jahan's arrival. Because it was "well known to politicians that the throne of royalty cannot remain vacant for a moment,"[55] they decided to bring Dawar Bakhsh, son of Khusrau and otherwise known as Bulaqi, "out of confinement" and place him on the throne.[56] The move was never thought to be more than a stratagem, a way of gaining time and of holding off bids by other claimants.[57] But it had the appearance of a real accession and Dawar Bakhsh himself eventually came to believe in the sincerity of his promoters. On October 29, 1627, then, "the *khutba* was read in Dawar Bakhsh's name near Bhimbar."[58]

To onlookers at the time, the outcome of the struggle was still unclear. Van den Broecke, writing in the midst of the succession days, assessed the candidates as frankly as he could and drew conclusions as wavering as the situation they described. Dawar Bakhsh, he said, had been named successor to Jahangir by the emperor himself on his deathbed[59]—a claim repeated by Mundy,[60] Manucci,[61] and at great length by Tavernier, who argued that Jahangir had from the time of the blinding of Khusrau thought Bulaqi should succeed him through the auspices of primogeniture. Although Nur Jahan also had promised, van den Broecke continued, "to follow the King's wishes in the matter" and although Bulaqi was loved "for his father's [Khusrau's] sake," he was young and had very little following of his own.[62] Moreover, Nur Jahan (never a favorite of the Dutchman's) was not to be trusted, and Jahangir, not discovering "even till the end the cunning nature of his wife . . . died like a blind man"[63]; "can it be believed that that vicious woman, who is filled with cunning up to the throat, will be deterred from her purpose on account of a simple word of promise?"[64] Van den Broecke concluded, then, "that there is very little hope or chance for Bulaqi,"[65] given his scanty resources and the active opposition of the lately widowed queen.

Shahryar, he thought at first, had a greater chance of winning the throne. His primary asset, of course, was "his cunning mother-in-law, who has both the Kingdom and the treasure in her power."[66] Enjoying at this time an income of 40,000 *suwar*, Shahryar could also count on the financial resources of Qasim Khan, Nur Jahan's sister's husband, who was governor of Agra. In the imperial treasury there lay most of the estate left by Akbar, whose gold had been little touched. Kept there also was the treasury of Jahangir and of Nur Jahan, the latter described by van den Broecke as "the very great amount of wealth which the Queen has amassed during 15 years, which is more than that left by the King."[67] Moreover, Nur Jahan had recently acquired new followers among the nobles, who were beholden to her for their rank and wealth and who would certainly back the candidacy of Shahryar.[68] For these reasons, then, van den Broecke predicted that Nur Jahan's quest on behalf of her son-in-law "may now be realised."[69]

Van den Broecke's predictions on Shah Jahan's chances were more ambiguous. The third son was now in exile in the Deccan, and although he had many friends, they had been "compelled to leave him in the course of his flight on account of his terrible distress and adversity."[70] Van den Broecke's initial assessment was suitably pessimistic: "how else could one talk about Khurram except as a rebel and a traitor who deserved to die. He was suspect and his fortunes were uncertain."[71] He knew, however, that many were urging Shah Jahan on to the throne and that there were networks of alliances all over the country this prince could activate when appropriate. Although van den Broecke seemed unaware of the effort on Shah Jahan's part being made by Asaf Khan, he was writing in late 1627 from an underlying assumption that Shah Jahan would ultimately accede to the throne. At the end of his account, in fact, he noted that Mahabat Khan and the other nobles "will prepare the way for Khurram"[72]—an admirable prophecy given the current great "confusion in the Empire of Hindustan."[73]

The deciding factor for van den Broecke was the future success or failure of Nur Jahan. The Dutchman's account is unusually eerie in this regard, for not only, in the vacuum following Jahangir's death, was he unable to pick clearly who the successor would be, but he seemed singularly unaware of the doings of Asaf Khan either for Shah Jahan or against Nur Jahan. Ordinarily very detailed and in touch with activities at the imperial court, van den Broecke here, perhaps because bazaar gossip to him was slow, had lost his usual familiarity with the ruling clique. Against hindsight knowledge, then, his worries about Nur Jahan seem odd. Van den Broecke was most concerned that the queen and her family would grab for power and send the empire into chaos. Although they could not "divide the Empire among themselves" without thought for the legitimate rules of sovereignty, they could be, he feared, oblivious to the need for order. "In view of the existing circumstances," he mused, "no improvement can be expected, unless fickle fortune smiled upon Khurram and he became King."[74]

The civil war van den Broecke feared might happen did not materialize, for Nur Jahan was immediately rendered powerless by her imprisonment. After placing Dawar Bakhsh at the head of the government on October 29, Asaf Khan proceeded to fix her isolation by taking the three sons of Shah Jahan out of Nur Jahan's apartments. Dara Shikoh, Shah Shuja, and Aurangzeb, who had been in the care of the empress since Shah Jahan's revolt, were now considered not "safe with Nur Mahal" and were removed from her charge and kept for the moment with Asaf Khan and Iradat Khan. Then, to assuage a hesitant supporter of the great trust the nobles had in him, the three sons were placed under the watchful care of Sadiq Khan.[75]

Formal funeral ceremonies for Jahangir had been performed the day after his death, when the royal retinue had come "down from the mountains to Bhimbar,"[76] which was on the plains. Dawar Bakhsh, apparently, could not have the *khutba* read in his name until after the preceding emperor's reign was officially over, so closing rites needed to be performed immediately. Jahangir's body was then "sent on under escort to Lahore, where it was interred in a garden which Nur Jahan had made."[77] Asaf Khan sent the corpse to Lahore for burial under the supervision of Maqsud Khan and other nobles,[78] with strict instructions that Nur Jahan was to accompany her dead husband at every stage through to the very end. The long royal procession then left Bhimbar for Lahore in two stages. Asaf Khan and Iradat Khan, having "placed Bulaki on horseback, and, with a party of men in whom they had full confidence, . . . commenced their march, taking care to keep one day ahead of Nur Mahal."[79] Nur Jahan, with the body of Jahangir, then followed a day behind as they made their way to his final resting place in Shahdara.

Nur Jahan had not been idle, however. In spite of the fact that Asaf Khan, who "was not at ease in respect of Nur Jahan," had "kept watch over her, and would allow no communication with her,"[80] the queen had managed to send a message to Shahryar in Lahore. Because she had long hoped to raise Shahryar to the throne when Jahangir died and in spite of her promise to her dead husband to support Dawar Bakhsh,[81] Nur Jahan now urged her son-in-law in Lahore to collect soldiers and bring them quickly to her: "She wrote to Na-shudani ["Good-for-Nothing," for example, Shahryar], advising him to collect as many men as he could, and hasten to her."[82] This message from the camp at Bhimbar to Shahryar to mobilize troops was to be her last known political act. Asaf Khan, in his apprehension, had isolated her, and apparently her sister Khadija,[83] so thoroughly that her political and military choices now became very few. Moreover, sentiment against her was running high, and if van den Broecke's malicious vision of her at this time was widespread (as it must have been given his sources among the people), then she would have had trouble commanding any kind of popular support. Nur Jahan, finally, was Jahangir's wife and her need to go quietly with his body in its final public hours carried substantial political and personal weight.

Shahryar, meanwhile, was in Lahore when he heard of the emperor's death. Urged on "by his intriguing wife,"[84] "the poor bald Shahriyar"[85] proclaimed himself emperor there with all the incumbent rights and privileges. In spite of the fact that his erstwhile connections, and the potential revenue they could call up, might have given him a real chance for the throne,[86] Shahryar did not have the character, experience, or stamina for the job. The proclamation, then, almost from the beginning, was a futile act and only a few nobles recognized the accession as genuine. Shahryar, however, was serious. He proceeded to seize "the royal treasure and everything belonging to the State which was in Lahore." In order to guarantee his place as the head of the government and of the troops, he distributed the treasury to would-be supporters, giving "to every one what he asked for."[87] In the course of a week, said the *Iqbalnama*, "he distributed seventy *lacs* of rupees among the old and new nobles, in the hope of securing his position."[88] Mirza Bayasanghar, son of Daniyal, late brother of Jahangir, had fled to Lahore when the emperor died and now joined Shahryar. Taking command of the forces, Bayasanghar brought the troops over the river and stood with Shahryar against the royal claims of others.[89]

Asaf Khan and Dawar Bakhsh had, by now, advanced considerably from Bhimbar. Keeping one day ahead of Nur Jahan's army, they had moved quickly to Lahore and were within three miles from the city when they met Shahryar's forces. The opposing armies gave battle but at "the first attack Shahriyar's mercenaries, unable to face the old and loyal servants of the State, broke, and fled."[90] Shahryar himself had stayed back in Lahore with two or three thousand cavalry "awaiting the course of events." When a Turki slave brought him the news of his troops' defeat, he panicked. "Unable to understand his position and danger," Shahryar turned back and entered the fort, "thus placing his own foot in the trap."[91]

When, on the next day, Asaf Khan's men arrived at the fort, some of Shahryar's followers "had an interview with Asaf Khan, and made terms." One of the *vakil's* men, Azam Khan,[92] had posed as Shahryar's friend and had detained the prince as he waited for news from Bayasanghar at the front. When news of Bayasanghar's defeat outside of Lahore arrived, Shahryar locked himself in the fort,[93] and Azam Khan moved quickly to let in Asaf Khan's men.[94] Searching for Shahryar, Iradat Khan and Abu Talib Shayista Khan found that he had "fled for refuge into the female apartments of the late Emperor." From there, he was brought out and led, in chains, into the presence of Dawar Bakhsh. "After making the regular bows and homage, he was placed in confinement, and two or three days afterward he was blinded."[95]

So ended the brief and blighted reign of Shahryar. With his troops gone and his eyesight compromised, there was no hope for any return to power. If one wonders why Nur Jahan was not able to do more, why she could not mobilize more troops on his behalf or why there was not a greater outpouring of support as her son-in-law proclaimed himself emperor, one need only look at the circumstances of Shahyar's rise. Clearly, events happened so quickly in the end that a large mobilization effort was out of the question. But, whatever his mother-in-law could or couldn't do, Shahryar's defeat was due more to the astuteness and force of his enemies, namely Asaf Khan, and to his own lack of imperial charisma than to the military exigencies of the time. Says Prasad: "If Nur Jahan had been free to act, she might have prolonged the affair, but even she could hardly have succeeded in the end."[96]

Meanwhile, the runner Banarasi, who had left Chingaz Hatli with the signet ring, arrived in Junnair in the north Deccan after twenty days on November 18, 1627. He made his way to the house of Mahabat Khan, "who had just before been received by Shah Jahan." "Mahabat Khan sent word into the private apartments of the Prince, who came out and received from the runner the signet ring of Asaf Khan."[97] The content of Banarasi's message was that Shah Jahan "must leave his place of refuge by whatever method he could devise . . . [and] come to court [in Agra where] he should [be] made king, . . . [as] everything was in readiness."[98] At the news of his father's death, Shah Jahan observed "the proper rites and term of mourning," and abandoning plans to march to Bengal with Mahabat Khan,[99] he proceeded northward by way of Gujarat.

Although the first intelligence from Banarasi could not have carried with it the report of Asaf Khan's victory in Lahore, Shah Jahan did come to know of it along the way, after he had crossed the Narmada, and his "march to the north was like a triumphal procession" with drums "beaten to celebrate the victory."[100] Not all saw Shah Jahan's march northward as reason to cheer, however, for van den Broecke, whose account ends just as the prince had reached the fort at Surat, was consistently unsure just how many districts would fall in with him as he proceeded toward Agra. The Dutchman said with characteristic vagueness, for example, it "is more or less a fact that every one is more or less afraid of him, and no one follows him seriously except Mahabat Khan."[101] Nevertheless, once he had heard the news of Shahryar's defeat, Shah Jahan began to feel and act more and more as if he were the emperor-designate.

What he did next, however, was an unnecessary act of desperation, which changed the rules of all successions to come. Certain now that his benefactor Asaf Khan was ascendant, Shah Jahan sent orders from Gujarat to Asaf Khan to execute Shahryar, Dawar Bakhsh, and two of the sons of Daniyal, Tahmuras and Hoshang.[102] "Shah Jahan sent a *farman* to Yaminu-d daula Asaf Khan, to the effect that it would be well if Dawar Bakhsh the son, and (Shahriyar) the useless brother, of Khusru, and the sons of Prince Daniyal, were all sent out of the world."[103] With this, he was convinced, all possible competition for the throne would be gone.[104]

Matters now moved quickly. On January 19, 1628, as Shah Jahan was still proceeding toward Agra, he was "proclaimed [emperor] at Lahore . . . by general consent." Dawar Bakhsh was thrown into prison and, with the concurrence of all the nobles, Asaf Khan had the *khutba* read in Shah Jahan's name.[105] On

January 21, Asaf Khan received the *farman* ordering the execution of the remaining contenders for the crown. On January 23, he carried it out: "Dawar, his brother Garshasp, Shahriyar, and Tahmuras and Hoshang, sons of the deceased Prince Daniyal, were all put to death."[106] Surprisingly, De Laet suggested that the princes were strangled by the very assassin who was said to have strangled Khusrau in 1621, Raza Bahadur: "In accordance with these instructions [of Shah Jahan] Bahador reached Lahor in eight days by means of the post- horses. Assoffghan handed over to him the princes, whom he cruelly strangled at night, and then buried by the side of the dead king in a garden."[107] It is not clear how true De Laet's account of the strangling of the princes may have been, but with their execution, Shah Jahan's hold on the throne was certain. Saksena suggests, with reason, that the five princes died unnecessarily and that Shah Jahan was assured of a secure throne even without their elimination. Whatever the course of history might have been had they lived, however, Shah Jahan was to see these events repeated when, at the end of his own life, "he had to witness the execution of two of his sons, and the disappearance of a third."[108]

On January 24, 1628, Shah Jahan entered Agra. He had celebrated his thirty-eighth birthday on the way north with Raja Karan and in Ajmer, "according to the practice of his great ancestor, [he had] paid a visit on foot to the tombs of the saints."[109] Now having come "with a powerful army *via* Gujarat and Ajmir, . . . [he] soon arrived in Agra, which was the seat of his and his forefathers' government."[110] On January 23, he camped outside the city in the recently refurbished Nur Manzil gardens[111]—much to the great fury, we imagine, of the former queen who, discovered that his host there was none other than her brother-in-law and former poetry partner, Qasim Khan—and the next day "he entered the city, and was universally recognized as King."[112] After waiting twelve days for an auspicious time fixed by the astrologers, Shah Jahan was crowned emperor on February 4, 1628,[113] and "distributed largesses and rewards among his subjects."[114] Finally, on February 26, the agent of all these events, Asaf Khan, arrived in Agra and was met by his own daughter, the new queen, and by Jahanara, the favorite daughter of Shah Jahan. Asaf Khan was honored with great fanfare, and with these festivities, the official coronation celebrations of Shah Jahan came to an end.

Meanwhile, Jahangir's body was buried in state. A false grave had been constructed initially at Chingaz Sarai near a Mughal mosque, where the emperor's entrails had been interred.[115] But his official resting place was in Lahore, the city that during his reign "had been considered as the capital of the empire."[116] Jahangir had been fond of Lahore, calling it "one of the greatest places in Hindustan"[117] and had often held his court and entertainments there.[118] Finch had reported that Lahore was "one of the greatest cities of the East,"[119] and Monserrate had calculated that it was "second to none, either in Asia or in Europe, with regard to size, population and wealth."[120] Early speculation had been that Jahangir would be buried near Agra in his father Akbar's tomb. Hawkins said, for example, in 1613 "there came into my memory another feast, solemnized at his [Jahangir's] fathers funerall, which is kept at his sepulchre, where likewise himselfe, with all his posterity, meane to be buried."[121] There was also a tradition that he wanted to be buried in his garden at Vernag in Kashmir,[122] his last and perhaps most beautiful obsession. Shah Jahan's desire to have a grand and centrally accessible public monument that would ultimately affirm his own right to rule, however, overrode any other claims, and it was there in Lahore, at Shahdara on the old bank of the Ravi river in the Dilkusha garden, where Jahangir was finally buried. The garden belonged to Jahangir's "lovely and accomplished wife, Nur Jahan," and with his interment inside its bounds he was "thus paying . . . [his wife] the last tribute of affection."[123]

Local tradition says that the design and construction of Jahangir's tomb were in Nur Jahan's hands. A number of later scholars such as Havell,[124] Fergusson,[125] P. Brown,[126] Prasad,[127] Haywood,[128] and Gascoigne[129] follow this tradition, all stating that Nur Jahan spent the early years of her retirement actively overseeing the tomb's construction. Latif, however, following Muhammad Salih's *Shahjahan-nama*, attributes the tomb primarily to Shah Jahan who, three years later in 1631, would be building a contemporaneous monument for his wife Arjumand Banu Begam. The Shujauddins, uncharacteristically, support this view, arguing that because Nur Jahan was in strict confinement by now and had a very limited purse, she could play no major role in the building process. Rather than neglect his father's memory, they argue, Shah Jahan glorified it, for the "mausoleum of Jahangir was constructed as a State building under royal orders."[130] Nur Jahan most certainly watched, but the final decisions of design, layout, and decoration may, in all probability, not have been hers alone to make.

Jahangir's widow had no recourse now but exile. Although De Laet suggested that Nur Jahan actually accompanied her brother Asaf Khan to Agra and personally handed over the royal treasure to Shah Jahan,[131] there is no other contemporary evidence for this. She would certainly have wanted to stay at court as was the normal practice for imperial widows, but her most influential relative, Asaf Khan, had no intention of sharing power with her again, and without a consort or offspring on the throne, any claim she had to authority was minimal. From the meager accounts of Nur Jahan for the period after Jahangir's death, we know that having been made a prisoner by her brother Asaf Khan, she was brought to Lahore under strict guard.[132] Giving up the body of her husband to be buried in state by his son, Nur Jahan retired there on a fixed annual pension from Shah Jahan of two *lakh* rupees,[133] or as Dow notes twenty-five thousand pounds.[134] Ironically, the man she had promoted for so long to such good fortune and then worked almost equally long to defeat now had almost total control over the means of her livelihood.

We know little of Nur Jahan's life in Lahore. All accounts indicated that for the next eighteen years, until her death in 1645, she spent her time in relative seclusion in her own personal house in the city.[135] According to tradition, after Jahangir's death Nur Jahan "never went to parties of amusement of her own accord, but lived in private and in sorrow."[136] The woman who had "obtained such an ascendency over, . . . [Jahangir,] and exercised such absolute control over civil and revenue matters,"[137] was now without any authority at all as "her power [had] ceased with the death of her consort."[138] Being "too proud even to speak of public affairs, . . . she, therefore, gave up her mind to study, retirement, and ease."[139] The Shujauddins have suggested that Nur Jahan, whose daughter Ladli (also now a widow) was living with her, was frustrated by her limited state of affairs but, whatever complaints she may have had about her now severely curtailed powers, she had no alternative but to accept her fate.[140] As Gascoigne notes, Nur Jahan was "too positive a character to quibble when her defeat was plain."[141]

What Nur Jahan did with her time can only be a matter of speculation. Some have suggested that she spent many of her hours in charitable giving. We know that in addition to the two *lakh* rupees granted her by Shah Jahan, Nur Jahan also had money of her own. In the treasury at Agra, for example, Nur Jahan had a "very great amount of wealth . . . amassed during 15 years, which is more than that left by the King."[142] Depending upon how much of this fortune from her reign Shah Jahan allowed her to keep or to use, Nur Jahan would certainly have had some monies with which to spend philanthropically.[143] That she would turn to charity was well within the bounds of her character, for the *Iqbalnama* noted of her time as empress that:

> Whoever threw himself upon her protection was preserved from tyranny and oppression; and if ever she learnt that any orphan girl was destitute and friendless, she would bring about her marriage, and give her a wedding portion. It is probable that during her reign no less than 500 orphan girls were thus married and portioned.[144]

Through giving, then, Nur Jahan may have been able to exercise the patronage she was used to and to maintain a benevolent contact with the people of her erstwhile reign.

It may also be that a widow in Nur Jahan's circumstances would have turned increasingly to religious activities. As is often the case, lay religious in India were frequently women, and often women of means. The early seventeenth century was no exception and we know of many women active in religious work then who supported, with all they had, the traditions of Jainism,[145] Hinduism, and Islam. Nur Jahan was still, we presume, a piously devout Shia, practicing the religion brought by her family when they emigrated from Persia. Although Lahore had originally been Hindu, its recent history had been primarily Muslim. Under the Mughals spacious mosques had been built, minarets had been erected, and Islamic poets and scholars had gathered in numbers, making it a seat of great learning. To what extent Nur Jahan participated in this religious life is not known. She would certainly have carried out the appropriate domestic rites and prayers as befitted a woman of her station, but any odd conversations with religious scholars, any regular commitments to textual study, or any patronage of religious buildings or vocations there are now lost to history.

The "old Queene Noore mohol,"[146] as Mundy so aptly called her in 1632, lived eighteen years as a widow. During that time, she saw her niece Arjumand Banu Begam (Mumtaz Mahal) die in 1631 and most of the Taj Mahal completed as her tomb (1632–48). She lived through the completion of her husband's tomb in 1637 and the death of her brother Asaf Khan, Shah Jahan's chief minister, in

1641. Saksena indicates that Nur Jahan, throughout all this time, remained faithful to the memory of her dead husband,[147] and the Shujauddins suggest that she "was often seen visiting the grave of her beloved husband accompanied by her slave-girls and attendants."[148] No doubt Nur Jahan spent much of her time at Jahangir's tomb, as it was a custom then for a widow to keep physical proximity to her husband's remains as a way of honoring the couple's marriage vows. Of Akbar's widows, for example, Finch said:

> Alongst the way side is a spacious moholl for his fathers women (as is said) to remayne and end their dayes in deploring their deceased lord, each enjoying the lands they before had in the Kings time, . . . so that this should be to them a perpetuall nunnery, never to marry againe.[149]

Nur Jahan would certainly have felt the weight of social custom in her regular visits to Shahdara, but her own feelings as she went there were no doubt of real affection and substantial personal loss.

Against the prevailing tradition of keeping widowed queens at court, Nur Jahan's isolation in Lahore was virtually complete. The Shujauddins note that "Shah Jahan and Asaf Khan came to Lahore many a time during this interval but they did not appear to have met Noor Jahan."[150] The rivalry between brother and sister not only survived Jahangir's death,[151] but so colored Asaf Khan's behavior that to safeguard his current success he could not bring himself to have any further contact with his sister. Moreover, through his court chroniclers, painters, and artisans, Shah Jahan worked hard to sully the memory of his once-powerful stepmother, with the result that almost all of the historical works from his reign were explicitly critical of Nur Jahan and blamed her for much of Shah Jahan's early misfortune.[152] This invidious spirit was so contagious that European writers of the early Shah Jahan years were infected and the opinions of valuable historians like van den Broecke and Pelsaert, for example, became hostile whenever they turned to Nur Jahan. Shah Jahan did not stop with defamation, however, but launched a contemporaneous campaign "to wipe out all memory of her erstwhile sway."[153] As if to erase her presence from history, he withdrew from circulation all coins stamped with her name, contravening current practice of keeping coins issued by predecessors in circulation,[154] and he cleansed his administration however else he could of her ubiquitous hand.

Nur Jahan died in Lahore on December 18, 1645, over halfway through Shah Jahan's reign. There had been rumors current in the country that she had been secretly murdered,[155] but they appear to have been the benign creation of the ever working Indian imagination. Local custom and religious law forbade the murder of a woman in any case, and Lahori's *Padshahnama* gave a clear and explicit notice of her death by natural causes.[156] Her funeral was, says Prasad, "a modest one,"[157] and she was buried in a tomb near Jahangir she had constructed for herself. Her marble sarcophagus was "of most chaste workmanship" and her daughter Ladli Begam lies likewise by her side. Today her restored tomb reflects only a moment of the brilliant flora and geometric design she once preferred.

Appendix I
Selected Members of Jahangir's Family

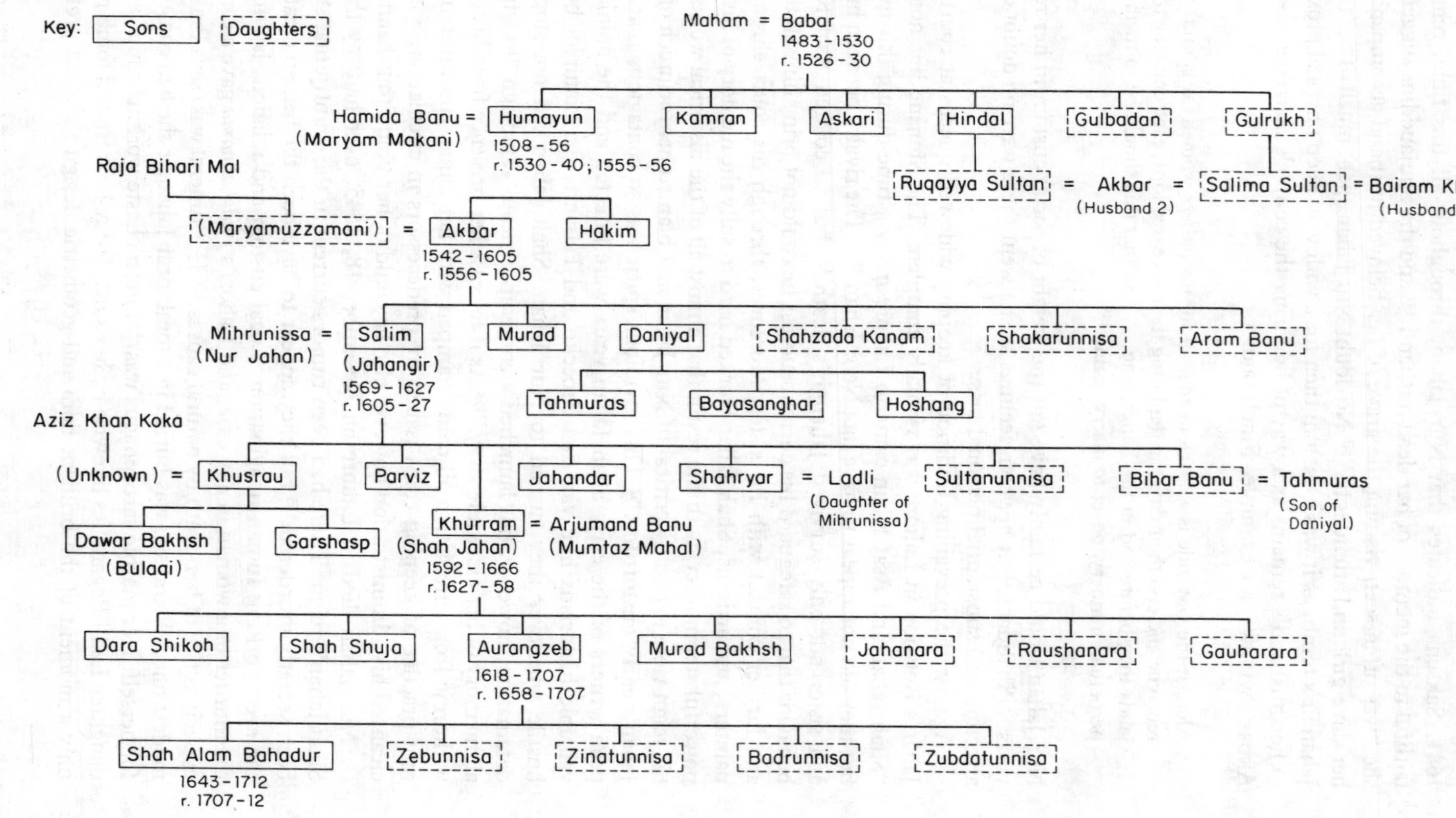

Appendix II
Selected Members of Nur Jahan's Family

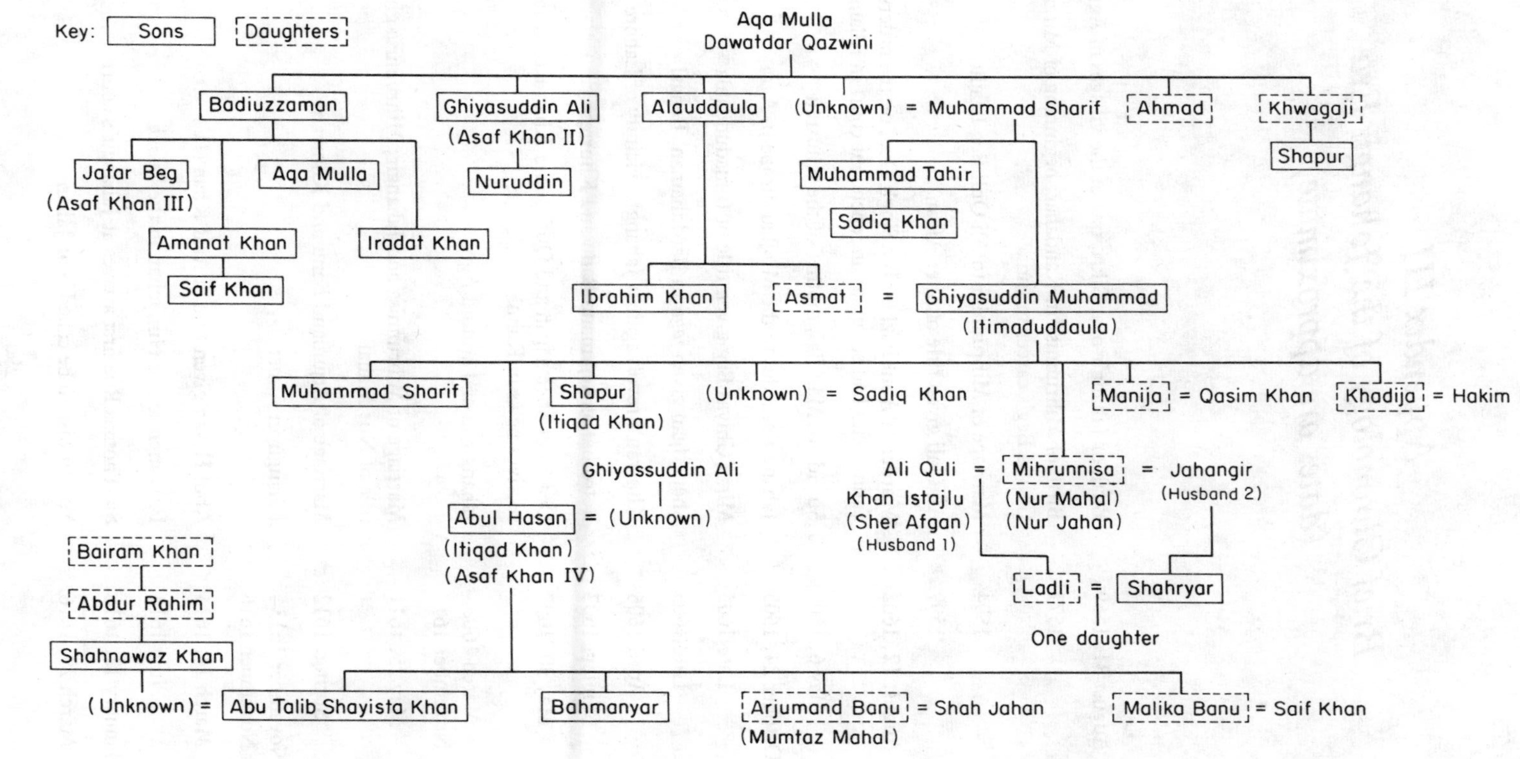

Appendix III
Brief Chronology of the Jahangir Era (dates are approximate)

August 31, 1569	Birth of Jahangir near Sikri, one of the villages of Agra
1577	Birth of Mihrunnisa in Kandahar; beginning of Mirza Ghiyas Beg's career in India
1594	Marriage of Mihrunnisa to Ali Quli Beg Istajlu
1599	Ali Quli given title of Sher Afgan
August 12, 1602	Murder of Abul Fazl by Bir Singh Deo, on the orders of Salim, who had set up an independent court in Allahabad
May 6, 1605	Suicide of Man Bai, mother of the Khusrau
October 24, 1605	Jahangir accedes to the Mughal throne in Agra
Late 1605	Mirza Ghiyas Beg given title of Itimaduddaula
Late 1605	Sher Afgan given *jagir* in Barddhaman, Bengal
April 1606	Khusrau's revolt against Jahangir, vicinity of Lahore
Winter, 1607	Betrothal of Arjumand Banu and Khurram
May 30, 1607	Deaths of Sher Afgan and Qutbuddin Khan Koka; Jahangir receives news in Kabul
March 1608–November 1613	Jahangir in and around Agra
May 25, 1611	Marriage of Mihrunnisa and Jahangir; Mihrunnisa given title of Nur Mahal
Spring, 1612	Marriage of Arjumand Banu and Khurram
November 1613–November 1616	Jahangir in Ajmer
March 24, 1614	Abul Hasan given title of Asaf Khan (IV)
July 1614	First mention of Nur Jahan in the *Tuzuk*
January 12, 1616	Sir Thomas Roe first arrives at Jahangir's court
March 29, 1616	Mihrunnisa to be called Nur Jahan

March–October 1617	Jahangir in Mandu; Khurram given title of Shah Jahan for victories in the Deccan
January–February 1618	Jahangir in Ahmedabad
Early 1620	Beginning of regular trips to Kashmir
April 1621	Marriage of Ladli Begam and Shahryar in Agra
October 10, 1621	Death of Asmat Begam, mother of Nur Jahan
End of Jan. 1622	Death of Itimaduddaula near Kangra
Jan. 29, 1622	Jahangir hears news of Khusrau's death, occurring as early as August 1621
March 29, 1623	Battle between forces of Jahangir and Shah Jahan near Baluchpur
Early summer, 1623	Death of Maryamuzzamani, mother of Jahangir, in Agra
September 4, 1623	Daughter born to Ladli Begam and Shahryar
March 1626	Shah Jahan surrenders to Jahangir
March–September 1626	Rebellion of Mahabat Khan
October 28, 1626	Death of Parviz in Burhanpur
October 28, 1627	Death of Jahangir in Chingaz Ḥatli, near Bhimbar
January 1628	Deaths of Shahryar, Dawar Bakhsh, Garshasp, Tahmuras, and Hoshang
February 4, 1628	Shah Jahan accedes to the Mughal throne in Agra
November 10, 1641	Death of Asaf Khan
December 18, 1645	Death of Nur Jahan in Lahore

Notes

Prologue: Standing in the Legend

1. Ali Sardar Jafri, May 9, 1985, Bombay.
2. Saksena, p. xx.
3. Van den Broecke, p. 97.

Chapter 1. The Immigrant Persians

1. See Blochmann, *Ain-i Akbari* 1.572.

2. See C. Pant, pp. 19ff; Blochmann's note, *Ain-i Akbari* 1.572; *Ikbal-nama-i Jahangiri* E&D 6.403.

3. C. Pant, p. 19.

4. *Ikbal-nama-i Jahangiri* E&D 6.403; C. Pant, pp. 19–22; Blochmann, *Ain-i Akbari* 1.572; Prasad, p. 158; Shujauddins, p. 1.

5. A comet was seen in India in 1577. According to the opinion of Mughal astrologers, "the effects would not be felt in Hindustan, but probably in Khurasan and Irak. Shortly afterward, Shah Ismail, son of Shah Tahmasp Safawi, departed this life, and great troubles arose in Persia" (*Tabakat-i Akbari* E&D 5.407).

6. *Ikbal-nama-i Jahangiri* E&D 6.403; Blochmann, *Ain-i Akbari* 1.572.

7. Manucci 1.171.

8. C. Pant's sources (p. 26) and the *Ikbal-nama-i Jahangiri* (E&D 6.403) noted that Ghiyas Beg and his wife at this time, that is, prior to the birth of Mihrunnisa, had two sons and only *one* daughter. Blochmann (*Ain-i Akbari* 1.576), however, gives a genealogical table for the family in which Mihrunnisa had *two* older sisters, Manija and Khadija. Van den Broecke (p. 93), who was writing around 1627, went on to record that ultimately Nur Jahan had four sisters and two brothers, the latter number reflecting the addition of a younger brother, Itiqad Khan Mirza Shapur, and the execution of an elder one (Muhammad Sharif) in 1607 for his role in the Khusrau rebellion, and the former number the result either of later births to the family after arriving in India or of inflationary reports from the bazaar. C. Pant (p. 55) discusses the careers of three son-in-laws to Ghiyas Beg (excluding those married to Mihrunnisa) indicating that there were at least that many sisters to the future empress: Manija married to Qasim Khan, Khadija married Hakim Beg, and an unknown sister married to Sadiq Khan.

9. *Ikbal-nama-i Jahangiri* E&D 1.403–4; C. Pant, pp. 25–26; Blochmann, *Ain-i Akbari* 1.572. According to Dow's sources (p. 22), the young girl did not receive the name Mihrunnisa until the family reached Lahore.

10. Cf. Manucci 1.159; see also C. Pant, pp. 26–27. Most if not all stories about Mihrunnisa's birth seems to be apocryphal and narrated in such a way by later chroni-

clers so as to reflect, for good or ill, upon Nur Jahan's later career. For an evaluation of this Khafi Khan material, see C. Pant, p. 27n.

11. Dow 3.20–21.

12. Blochmann, *Ain-i Akbari* 1.572; C. Pant, p. 27; Prasad, pp. 159–60. Della Valle (1.53) said Mihrunnisa "was born . . . the Daughter of a Persian, who [was] coming as many do into *India*, to the service of the *Moghol*."

13. *Ikbal-nama-i Jahangiri* E&D 6.404.

14. Terry, p. 65.

15. Pelsaert, p. 1. Finch (in Foster, *Early Travels*, p. 182) noted early in Jahangir's reign that "Agra hath not been in fame above fiftie yeeres, being before Acabars time a village."

16. Monserrate, pp. 35–36.

17. Said Bernier (pp. 284–85):

> For not having been constructed after any settled design, it wants the uniform and wide steets that so eminently distinguish *Dehli* . . . the consequence is that when the court is at *Agra* there is often a strange confusion.

18. Mundy 2.207.

19. Pelsaert, p. 1.

20. Mundy 2.207.

21. Withington in Foster, *Early Travels*, p. 227.

22. *Tuzuk* 1.3.

23. Bernier, p. 284.

24. A. S. Beveridge in Gulbadan, p. 6.

25. A. S. Beveridge in Gulbadan, p. 1.

26. Gascoigne, p. 15.

27. Bernier, p. 3.

28. Monserrate, p. 196.

29. Monserrate, pp. 196–97.

30. Du Jarric, pp. 8–9.

31. For details, see C. Pant, pp. 29–32.

32. C. Pant, pp. 32, 163; Blochmann, *Ain-i Akbari* 1.572. The *mansab* system was a system of rank based on the number of infantry (*zat*) and cavalry (*suwar*) a given noble was assigned. Said Roe (1.110):

> The great men about him are not borne Noble, but Iauourites raised. . . . They are reckoned by Horses; that is to say; Coronels of twelue thousand Horses, which is the greatest . . . so descending to twentie Horses. . . . The King assigneth them so much land as is bound to maintaine so many Horses as a rent, each horse at fiue and twentie pounds sterling by the yeere.

33. Terry, p. 75.

34. C. Pant, pp. 32, 163; see *Tuzuk* 1.45.

35. *Ikbal-nama-i Jahangiri* E&D 6.404.

36. Guerreiro, p. 139. This remark, like those of the *Iqbalnama*, most certainly reflected Ghiyas Beg's later position as projected back onto his place at Akbar's court. Although Guerreiro was reporting information from Benedict Goes collected in 1604, long before Ghiyas Beg's daughter would have made permanent inroads into the Mughal dynasty, the remark could easily have been of the self-inflationary style used by Persians, in this case by a Ghiyas Beg who clearly here had messengerial status.

37. Prasad, p. 160.

38. *Ikbal-nama-i Jahangiri* E&D 6.404.

39. Van den Broecke, preface, p. 1.

40. Brij Narain and Sri Ram Sharma note misguidedly that among "contemporary accounts the Ballad of Pholodi reproduced by Tessitori in his Bardic and Historical Survey of Rajputana (in J.R.A.S.B.) corroborates Palsaert's (sic) account of Jahangir's earlier love for Mehr-un-Nasa" (Van den Broecke, p. 101, n. 83).

41. Van den Broecke, p. 42. Joannes De Laet (p. 181), who based his 1631 account on Pelsaert and van den Broecke, noted that Salim "had been in love with her when she was still a maiden, during the lifetime of his father Achabar."

42. As paraphrased in the Shujauddins, pp. 5–6. Khafi Khan's story came from Muhammad Sadiq Tabrizi, who was in the service of Prince Shuja. Because it dated then from Shah Jahan's reign, the Shujauddins (p. 5n) speculate that it "means that the germs of the romance, as it is described now, had begun to sprout as early as the reign of Shah Jahan, either due to anti-Noor Jahan bias of the age or the extreme attachment between the two led people to speculate in this way."

43. Dow 3.22.

44. From Maulana Muhammad Husain Azad's (d. 1910) *Darbar-i Akbari*, as recorded in the Shujauddins, pp. 8–9. The Shujauddins (pp. 4–18) also record other late histories carrying apocryphal stories of Nur Jahan.

45. Sources that were silent about any acquaintance between Mihrunnisa and Salim prior to their meeting in March of 1611 at the New Year's bazaar and their subsequent marriage in May of that year are many, e.g., *Akbarnama*, *Ain-i Akbari*, *Tuzuk-i Jahangiri*, *Iqbalnama-i Jahangiri*, *Maasir-i Jahangiri*, William Hawkins (in Foster, *Early Travels*), John Jourdain, Thomas Roe, Edward Terry, Francisco Pelsaert, Joannes De Laet, Pietro Della Valle, Peter Mundy, and others. We must be persuaded, then, that all stories depicting any aspect of an earlier romance foiled by Akbar or by other circumstance were apocryphal and have their base not in historical fact but in courtly rumor or bazaar gossip.

46. *Ikbal-nama-i Jahangiri* E&D 6.402. It has been suggested that *safarchi* refers instead to a protocol officer, someone who makes arrangements for travel and social occasions on behalf of the ruler.

47. Abdur Rahim Khankhanan was the son of Bairam Khan, early regent to Akbar, and was at one time a tutor to the prince Salim. *Tuzuk* 1.21. On the Tatta campaign, see van den Broecke, p. 23; De Laet, p. 159.

48. *Tuzuk* 1.113; *Ikbal-nama-i Jahangiri* E&D 6.402, see p. 397; C. Pant, p. 42; Blochmann, *Ain-i Akbari* 1.591.

49. *Tuzuk* 1.113.

50. Van den Broecke, p. 42.

51. As given in the Shujauddins, p. 6. See Blochmann, *Ain-i Akbari* 1.591.

52. Blochmann, *Ain-i Akbari* 1.591–92.

53. Van den Broecke, p. 42.

54. Dow 3.23.

55. Manucci 1.157.

56. Jahangir was called king and there was no mention of an interfering father.

57. See the discussion in C. Pant, pp. 156–57.

58. *Ikbal-nama-i Jahangiri* E&D 6.402. Della Valle (1.53) was also quite clear that Sher Afgan (Ali Quli) had been in the service of Jahangir.

59. Exactly when he received the title is not known. The *Iqbalnama* placed it sometimes before and sometimes after Jahangir's accession to power in 1605 but other sources placed it, as is more likely, before. *Ikbal-nama-i Jahangiri* E&D 6.402, 404; *Tuzuk* 1.113–14; Prasad, p. 161; C. Pant, p. 42; Blochmann, *Ain-i Akbari* 1.592.

60. Jafa, pp. 44–45.

61. Or alternately: "In battle she is a man-smiter and a tiger-slayer." *Tuzuk* 1.375. See Blochmann, *Ain-i Akbari* 1.592.

62. Van den Broecke and De Laet indicated that there may also have been a son who, at the time of Sher Afgan's death, was handed over into the custody of the *amirs* in Agra together with Sher Afgan's brother. No other sources confirm this. Van den Broecke, pp. 39, 41; De Laet, p. 180. The name of the daughter of Mihrunnisa and Ali Quli has been given variously as Mihrunnisa (again), Banu Begam, and Bahu Begam, but following Prasad (pp. 162, 297), we use the name Ladli Begam.

63. Van den Broecke (pp. 41–42) said that the child was five or six when her mother and Jahangir met in 1611, and De Laet (p. 181) that she was six or seven, putting her birth roughly in the year 1605.

64. See Della Valle 1.55.

Chapter 2. Death of Sher Afgan and Marriage to Jahangir

1. See van den Broecke, pp. 24–25. Abul Fazl, Akbar's trusted "head chancellor and former tutor of Shah Murad" had been sent to wean him from drink but was too late. De Laet, pp. 161–62; *Akbar-nama* E&D 6.97; *Tuzuk* 1.34.

2. See van den Broecke, pp. 29–30; De Laet, p. 168; *Takmila-i Akbar-nama* E&D 6.114; *Tuzuk* 1.34–35.

3. Badauni (2.390) noted:

> In this year the Emperor's constitution became a little deranged and he suffered from stomachache and colic, which could by no means be removed. In this conscious state he uttered some words which arose from suspicions of his eldest son, and accused him of giving him poison.

4. Van den Broecke, p. 27; *Akbar-nama* E&D 6.99; Du Jarric, p. 182.

5. De Laet, pp. 164–65; *Akbar-nama* E&D 6.98–99. Later Jahangir would say:

> Short-sighted men in Allahabad had urged me also to rebel against my father. Their words were extremely unacceptable and disapproved by me. I know what sort of endurance a Kingdom would have, the foundations of which were laid on hostility to a father, and was not moved by the evil counsels of such worthless men, but acting according to the dictates of reason and knowledge.

Tuzuk 1.65. Other sources as well would re-envision the Allahabad days as the work of bad advisors. Note this account of Kamgar Khan in the *Ma-asir-i Jahangiri* (E&D 6.442):

> A body of seditious and turbulent people . . . were in the habit of spreading false reports openly and clandestinely against that ornament of the crown the Prince Salim. Sometimes they represented that he had conferred upon his servants the titles of Khan and Sultan, and at other times they said that he had ordered coins to be struck in his name. By such misrepresentations they every day attempted to excite the alarm of the Emperor, who, being endowed with a very enlightened and noble mind, was but little affected by their insinuations. In truth, in the relation of father and son, there were those ties of love and affection between the Emperor and the Prince which existed between Jacob and his son Joseph.

6. See Temple in Mundy 2.229n; Latif, *Agra*, pp. 165–66.

7. For an account of this attempt on Agra, see Hawkins in Foster, *Early Travels*, p. 107.

8. See Beach, *Grand Mogul*, pp. 33–41.

9. The coins, inscriptions, and *farmans* (royal orders) of this period are detailed in Jalaluddin, pp. 121–25. On the *jagir* system, see Bernier, p. 5.

10. Van den Broecke, pp. 28–29; De Laet, pp. 166–67.

11. *Ma-asir-i Jahangiri* E&D 6.442.

12. In his memoirs Jahangir said: "[Abul Fazl's] feelings towards me were not honest, [and] he both publicly and privately spoke against me . . . if he obtained the honour of waiting on him (Akbar) it . . . would preclude me from the favour of union with him (my father)" (*Tuzuk* 1.24–25). Said van den Broecke (p. 29):

> Prince Shah Salim came to know what Abul Fazl had written to the king, and that he was actually on his way. This alarmed him greatly, for he thought "Abul Fazl is my old enemy. If he sees my father, my ruin is certain. I must consider what is to be done about it."

De Laet, p. 167; *Takmila-i Akbar-nama* E&D 6.106–107. See also Latif, *Agra*, p. 262.

13. Van den Broecke, p. 29; De Laet, p. 167; *Takmila-i Akbar-nama* E&D 6.107; Beach, *Imperial Image*, p. 83.

14. *Ma-asir-i Jahangiri* E&D 6.443.

15. Van den Broecke, p. 29; De Laet, p. 167; Latif, *Agra*, p. 262.

16. Rizvi, p. 489; *Tuzuk* 1.13.

17. Van den Broecke, p. 29; see De Laet, pp. 167–68. Said Asad Beg (*Wikaya-i Asad Beg* E&D 6.155), that "day and night he neither shaved, as usual, nor took opium, but spent his time in weeping and lamenting." See *Tuzuk* 1.25; *Ma-asir-i Jahangiri* E&D 6.444.

18. *Takmila-i Akbar-nama* E&D 6.107, 108, 113. Said Du Jarric (p. 183): "[the murder of Abul Fazl] greatly enraged the King, and filled the whole court with consternation."

19. There is no doubt, however, that Jahangir harbored some remorse over the deed particularly with respect to his father. See the discussion in Findly, "Vow of Non-Violence," pp. 248–52. Perhaps as part of this, Jahangir raised Abul Fazl's son, Abdur Rahman, to the rank of 2,000 *zat* and 1,500 *suwar* a year or so after his accession. *Tuzuk* 1.105.

20. *Takmila-i Akbar-nama* E&D 6.108–9. Salima Sultan Begam was the widow of Bairam Khan, regent of the young Akbar, who after her husband's death married Akbar himself. *Tuzuk* 1.232.

21. *Takmila-i Akbar-nama* E&D 6.108–9; van den Broecke, p. 26; Mundy 2.102. It was probably at this time that the black slate throne was inscribed for Jahangir (1603), for this "was two years before the death of his father, Akbar, and he was then only Prince Salim. The throne was therefore, probably made to commemorate the recognition by Akbar of his son's title to the succession" (Havell, *Agra*, p. 56).

22. Du Jarric, p. 188.

23. Prasad, p. 53.

24. *Tuzuk* 1.114. C. Pant, p. 42.

25. Pelsaert, p. 71; Terry, p. 411; Maclagan, p. 68. Said Della Valle (1.55): "[Khusrau] was a Prince of much expectation, well-belov'd, and, as they say, a friend in particular of the Christians."

26. *Tuzuk* 1.55–56. The *Takmila-i Akbar-nama* (E&D 6.112), alternately, said that Khusrau's mother, reportedly an ambitious and difficult woman, took her life in a fit of anger over harem politics. Finch reported (in Foster, *Early Travels*, pp. 178–79) seeing "a sumptuous tombe" for Khusrau's mother "who upon the newes of her sonnes revolt poysoned her selfe." See also Finch in Foster, *Early Travels*, p. 164; Beach, *Grand Mogul*, pp. 33, 93; A. K. Das, *Mughal Painting*, p. 50.

27. Said Hawkins (in Foster, *Early Travels*, pp. 107–8): Salim's "father dispossessed him and proclaimed heire apparant his eldest sonne Cossero, being eldest sonne to Selimsha;" Finch (in Foster, *Early Travels*, p. 159): "Sha Selim, upon some disgust, tooke

armes in his fathers lifetime . . . whereupon Acubar gave the crowne to Sultan Cusseroom his sonne." And Terry (p. 408): "Achabar-Sha . . . resolved to break that ancient custom [of succession by a son]; and . . . protested, that not he [Salim], but his grandchild Sultan Coobsurroo, whom he always kept in his court, should succeed him in that empire."

28. See the excellent discussion in A. Husain, pp. 61–69.

29. Jahangir (*Tuzuk* 1.138) would later call Raja Man Singh "one of the hypocrites and old wolves of this State." See Mundy 2.103.

30. A. Husain, pp. 62–63.

31. Du Jarric, p. 204.

32. Guerreiro, p. 3.

33. Nizami, "Naqshbandi," p. 47. The tradition is that, having extracted a promise from Salim earlier, Shaikh Farid raced to Salim's side as Akbar was dying to congratulate him on his accession in the hopes of beating out the pro-Khusrau forces. On the future Jahangir's relations with the Sufis, see Findly, "Jahangir and the Sufis."

34. Du Jarric, p. 63.

35. Guerreiro, p. 3.

36. A final plot to arrest Salim while he was visiting his father was disclosed prematurely by Ziyaulmulk Qazwini. Another move to rally open support for Khusrau was opposed by the Barha Sayyids, who felt skipping a generation in the succession was a violation of Chaghatai law. *Wikaya-i Asad Beg* E&D 6.169–71; Prasad, pp. 65–67.

37. Van den Broecke, p. 30; De Laet, p. 168; *Takmila-i Akbar-nama* E&D 6.113.

38. Van den Broecke, p. 30; De Laet, p. 168.

39. Van den Broecke, pp. 30–31; see De Laet, p. 169.

40. On the number of days in confinement and on Salim's consumption of opium during that time, see Prasad, p. 63.

41. There was a tradition that even until the very last Salim "was suspected" of trying to poison Akbar, although if true may have been a ruse by supporters of Khusrau. Said Du Jarric (p. 204): "Up to this time [just before Akbar's death in October of 1605], the Prince had not ventured to appear before his father. Some said that this was because his father suspected him of having given him the poison." Said De Laet (p. 170): "The members of the royal household had filled the suspicious mind of the old king with the fear that his son was plotting to kill him, and hence Xa Selim was in future admitted to his father's presence [only when] accompanied by four companions."

Others, however, reported that Akbar did die of poison but by accident and by his own hand. It was the custom, apparently, for the emperor to give secretly poisoned pills to nobles who had displeased him and whom he wanted to eliminate. On one such occasion, having two pills in his hand, Akbar "by a mistake took the poisoned pill himself . . . [and fell] immediately into a mortal flux of blood" and died a few days later (Terry, pp. 408–9; see also Mundy 2.103). Manucci (1.146) elaborated this story by saying that the emperor often honored people by personally presenting betel made from the contents of a box: in the first part the leaves, in the second restorative pills, and in the third poisonous pills.

> It happened one day that the king wished to kill one of the grandees, and took by oversight one of the poisoned pills and ate it, taking it for one of the restoratives, with the object of giving confidence to the other man. After a little time he recognised the mistake he had made; but there was no remedy, and thus, through his own death, was disclosed the way that he had killed others.

Prasad (p. 68n) argues that both stories are questionable: that, in the first case, Salim would have had "little opportunity and little motive" to hasten Akbar's demise, and that, in the second, the intended "grandee" was given variously, and therefore suspiciously, as Raja Man Singh (for attempting "to disturb the line of succession") or Mirza Ghazi of Tatta. The second group of stories, he argues further, were probably invented when the actuality of the first group was perceived as impossible.

42. *Wikaya-i Asad Beg* E&D 6.168–69. Asad Beg calls Khusrau's elephant Chanchal instead of Apurva. See also Mundy 2.102.

43. *Wikaya-i Asad Beg* E&D 6.169.

44. Van den Broecke, p. 32; De Laet, p. 170; *Wikaya-i Asad Beg* E&D 6.171; Du Jarric, p. 205. Mundy (2.103) maintains that Akbar, to the end, wanted Khusrau on the throne.

45. According to Payne (in Du Jarric, p. 278, note 2), the usual date given for Akbar's death, October 17, 1605 (see Prasad, p. 68), is based on the old reckoning in place in Great Britain until 1752. According to the new reckoning, based on the reformed calendar in use in Roman Catholic countries by 1582, the death date was October 27. Akbar was buried in Sikandra, a village three miles northwest of Agra, in a mausoleum begun by him and finished by Jahangir. See, e.g., Terry, pp. 291–92.

46. Jahangir's penchant for political hyperbole was evident from the beginning. His new name, Jahangir, "World Conqueror," and new title, Nuruddin, "Light of the Faith," marked the beginning of an increasingly idealized and, by any account, highly unrealistic vision of his political abilities as a ruler. *Tuzuk* 1.3; van den Broecke, pp. 32–33; De Laet, p. 172; *Wikaya-i Asad Beg* E&D 6.173. *Padshah*, usually "Emperor," signifies "headship of the house of Timur and . . . independent sovereignty" (A. S. Beveridge in Gulbadan, pp. 1–2).

47. *Tuzuk* 1.7ff.; see E&D 6.284–87; *Wakaya-i Asad Beg* E&D 6.173–74; van den Broecke, p. 33; De Laet, p. 172.

48. *Ikbal-nama-i Jahangiri* E&D 6.402; *Tuzuk* 1.22, see also 1.45; c. Pant, pp. 34–35.

49. *Tuzuk* 1.13.

50. *Tuzuk* 1.24.

51. *Tuzuk* 1.24.

52. *Tuzuk* 1.114.

53. Particularly on the part of Afghan discontents. It is no coincidence, then, that Dow opens volume three of his *The History of Hindostan* with a long dissertation on the origins of despotism in India and the particular problems of Bengal. See 3.vii-cliv.

54. C. Pant, p. 42.

55. Blochmann, *Ain-i Akbari* 1.345–46.

56. *Tuzuk* 1.15–16, 75; Blochmann, *Ain-i Akbari* 1.362–63.

57. *Tuzuk* 1.78, see also 1.75, 77. Expressing sentiment common toward elder women in the "family," Jahangir said of his former wet-nurse that he loved Qutbuddin's mother more than his own and that her children were to him like his own brothers. Qutbuddin, in fact, was "the foster brother . . . most fit for fosterage." Qutbuddin's mother died in early 1607, just a short time before the governor himself was assassinated. Whether there were any lasting strains from this that might have agitated him unnaturally during his confrontation with Sher Afgan later, we can only guess. *Tuzuk* 1.84–85.

58. See Prasad, pp. 65–66; *Wikaya-i Asad Beg* E&D 6.169–73; van den Broecke, p. 32; De Laet, p. 171.

59. Guerreiro, p. 4.

60. For a good discussion, see D'Silva, pp. 267–81.

61. *Tuzuk* 1.52; see also van den Broecke, p. 33; De Laet, p. 173.

62. *Tuzuk* 1.52–53. Van den Broecke (p. 36) stated that Khusrau heard "that his father was not well-disposed towards him, and wanted to have him watched. Khusrau

was frightened and resolved to fly and get away from his father." He also stated that Khusrau, on his flight, actually did go to the grave of his grandfather, Akbar, and there offered a prayer. See also De Laet, pp. 173–74; Della Valle 1.55–56.

63. *Tuzuk* 1.62–63. Van den Broecke, pp. 36–37; De Laet, pp. 173–75; Guerreiro, pp. 4–5; Finch in Foster, *Early Travels*, p. 159.

64. Itimaduddaula was shortly recalled from Agra, however, to be at Jahangir's side in the Punjab. *Tuzuk* 1.57; C. Pant, pp. 35–36.

65. *Tuzuk* 1.57ff. Van den Broecke, pp. 36–37; De Laet, pp. 174–75.

66. The Sayyids of Barha were a family, said Jahangir (*Tuzuk* 2.269), belonging to the twelve (*bara*) villages near each other in the region of Muzaffarnagar, north of Delhi. They were known for their great bravery and as being "the averters of calamity," "for there has never been a battle in this region in which they have not been conspicuous, and in which some have not been killed." See Blochmann, *Ain-i Akbari* 1.424–27.

67. Coryat in Foster, *Early Travels*, p. 279.

68. *Tuzuk* 1.52.

69. Payne in Guerreiro, p. 91n.

70. Finch in Foster, *Early Travels*, p. 159.

71. *Tuzuk* 1.53–68. Van den Broecke, p. 38; De Laet, pp. 175–76; Finch in Foster, *Early Travels*, pp. 159–60; Guerreiro, pp. 5–7.

72. *Tuzuk* 1.68–69. See also van den Broecke, p. 39. The *Tabakat-i Akbari* (E&D 5.359) noted an earlier version of this punishment in which prisoners had "cow-hides placed on their necks in a strange fashion."

73. Guerreiro's story (p. 10) behind the freeing of Abdur Rahim was as follows: "In the end, however, he was set free; for a courtier who was desirous of marrying his daughter interceded for him to such good purpose that he obtained his pardon; but for this he had to pay His Majesty something over a hundred thousand crowns." Jahangir may also have noted that Abdur Rahim's association with Khusrau had been last minute and was only because he was too "lethargic and timid" to do otherwise (*Tuzuk* 1.59). In general, it seems, Jahangir was not well-disposed to the Khankhanan and tended at times to "belittle . . . his services" (H. Beveridge in *Tuzuk* 1.88n). However, as the son of Akbar's former regent, Bairam Khan, Abdur Rahim had sentimental sway at court (having been a former tutor of Jahangir himself) and went on after this affair to become known as a significant patron of poetry and the arts.

74. *Tuzuk* 1.69; Mundy 2.104; van den Broecke, pp. 38–39; De Laet, pp. 176–77; Della Valle 1.56; Guerreiro, pp. 8–10; Coryat in Foster, *Early Travels*, p. 279.

75. Jahangir himself did not mention Khusrau's elephant ride down this road. According to Terry (p. 410): "His father immediately after caused to be impaled, or put upon stakes (that most cruel and tormenting death) eight hundred in two several ranks in one day, without the city Lahore, and then carried his son most disgracefully through them, bidding him to behold the men in whom he trusted." See van den Broecke, pp. 38–39; De Laet, pp. 176–77; Della Valle 1.56; *Ikbal-nama-i Jahangiri* E&D 6.401; Coryat in Foster, *Early Travels*, p. 279.

76. Van den Broecke, pp. 38–39. See also Guerreiro, pp. 10–11.

77. Guerreiro, p. 11.

78. *Tuzuk* 1.72–73; Guerreiro, p. 12. Guru Arjun was buried in Lahore.

79. *Tuzuk* 1.69ff; see also 1.324, 325.

80. *Tuzuk* 1.70.

81. *Tuzuk* 1.78.

82. *Tuzuk* 1.114; *Ikbal-nama-i Jahangiri* E&D 6.402.

83. According to the *Iqbalnama* (E&D 6.402): "It was . . . reported that he was

insurbordinate, and disposed to be rebellious," and was in general exhibiting disloyal behavior. The extent of Sher Afgan's involvement in pro-Khusrau activity is unclear, but many secondary sources assume that Jahangir suspected the soldier of complicity in the 1606 revolt as well as of continued seditious activity on his son's behalf. Prasad, p. 161; Shujauddins, p. 22; C. Pant, p. 43. The discussion of rewards bestowed upon Qutbuddin just after the capture of Khusrau certainly implied that Qutbuddin had exhibited anti-Khusrau loyalties, in contrast presumably to Sher Afgan. *Tuzuk* 1.75ff.

84. Note that Jahangir made it very clear, at least in hindsight, that he did not issue orders for Sher Afgan's death.

85. *Tuzuk* 1.114; see also 1.75, 208.

86. *Ikbal-nama-i Jahangiri* E&D 6.402; C. Pant, p. 43. According to the *Iqbalnama* (E&D 6.402), Qutbuddin first summoned Sher Afgan to him but was given "unreasonable excuses" for not coming; then, so concerned was he about the "evil designs" that Sher Afgan may have been harboring, that Qutbuddin finally went to him.

87. *Ikbal-nama-i Jahangiri* E&D 6.402–403. Mutamid Khan called the Kashmiri avenger Pir Khan instead of Amba Khan. Note that Jahangir, unlike Mutamid Khan, called Mihrunnisa's husband Ali Quli, regressing to the time before he had conferred upon him the title of Sher Afgan. *Tuzuk* 1.114.

88. Van den Broecke (p. 39) stated that it was "the brother (sister's son), of Qutb-ud-Din named Shaikh Ghias-ud-Din and the son of Qutb-ud-Din named Kishwar Khan . . . [who] cut to pieces with arrows and their swords the traitor Sher Afghan, and sent his head to the King."

89. *Ikbal-nama-i Jahangiri* E&D 6.403. Sher Afgan was buried in a tomb in Barddhaman, Bengal. See Blochmann, *Ain-i Akbari* 1.592; Wali, pp. 184–86. Contrary to local tradition that he was buried next to Sher Afgan in Barddhaman (H. Beveridge in *Tuzuk* 2.73n), Qutbuddin Khan Koka, as the son of the daughter of Shaikh Salim Chishti, was buried by the tomb of the *shaikh* at Fatehpur Sikri. *Tuzuk* 2.73; Blochmann, *Ain-i Akbari* 1.557.

90. C. Pant, pp. 43–44. While many of these details may be accurate, Haidar Malik's description of his own initial acts of heroism are absent from other sources.

91. Van den Broecke, p. 39.

92. *Tuzuk* 1.115; see also 75, 77, 78, 84–85.

93. *Tuzuk* 1.113, 115.

94. *Tuzuk* 1.115.

95. *Tuzuk* 1.208.

96. *Khulasat ul-tawarikh*, as quoted in Shujauddins, p. 4.

97. Khafi Khan, as recapitulated in Shujauddins, pp. 5–6. See also C. Pant, pp. 44, 156–57.

98. Manucci 1.157.

99. Dow 3.27.

100. Dow 3.23–30.

101. Van den Broecke, p. 42.

102. De Laet, p. 181.

103. Hawkins in Foster, *Early Travels*, pp. 94, 101.

104. E.g., Roe 1.118.

105. E.g., Terry, p. 406.

106. Della Valle 1.53–55.

107. Mundy 2.205–206.

108. See Prasad, pp. 163–68; Shujauddins, pp. 12–16; C. Pant, pp. 44–45, 156–57.

109. See Prasad, pp. 163–68; Shujauddins, pp. 4–6; C. Pant, pp. 44–45, 156–57.

110. *Ikbal-nama-i Jahangiri* E&D 6.404.

111. *Tatimma-i Wakiat-i Jahangiri* E&D 6.398.

112. Khafi Khan as reported by the Shujauddins, pp. 5–6.

113. Mundy 2.205–6.

114. See the *Tarikh-i Kashmir* account in C. Pant, pp. 44–45. Haidar Malik's protection of Mihrunnisa after Sher Afgan's death (see H. Beveridge in *Tuzuk* 2.154n) most certainly afforded him special status with the future empress in years to come. We know for sure that his efforts were central in the planning and execution of many of her gardens and that their friendship may have been in part responsible for her attraction to Kashmir, his native region. If there were any other aspects to their relationship besides the long-term affection and loyalty so understandable given the circumstances, they are now lost to history.

115. Van den Broecke, p. 41; De Laet, p. 180.

116. Prasad (p. 162) wrongly follows the *Maasir-i Jahangiri* and Khafi Khan and states that Mihrunnisa was placed in the care of Salima Sultan Begam. Most other sources state that it was Ruqayya Sultan Begam who was Mihrunnisa's sponsor and protector at court. *Ikbal-nama-i Jahangiri* E&D 6.404; van den Broecke, p. 41; De Laet, p. 180; *Tatimma-i Wakiat-i Jahangiri* E&D 6.398.

117. Oddly, C. Pant (p. 45) says "no motives can be attached for royal orders calling Mehrunnisa to Agra by the Emperor." She goes on to say, however, citing an example from the *Humayunnama*, that after a death like this royal instructions are needed before the family can move.

118. C. Pant, p. 45. Or, one might argue, placing Mihrunnisa in the service of Ruqayya Begam was the only way to secure the court against the mischievous designs of a traitorous woman.

119. Blochmann, *Ain-i Akbari* 1.321, 573; *Tuzuk* 1.48. Could this early association between Mihrunnisa and Khurram under the care of Ruqayya Sultan Begam have laid the foundation for their work together in the junta?

120. Van den Broecke, p. 41; see De Laet, p. 180. Mihrunnisa was about thirty when she first became lady-in-waiting to Ruqayya Begam. There would have been a span of at least a full generation between them and there is every indication that the elder treated the younger much like a daughter.

121. Van den Broeck, p. 39; De Laet, p. 178. Itimaduddaula's greed was perceived to have been one of his few faults. Muhammad Hadi said: "Mirza Ghiyas Beg was so charitably disposed, that no one ever left his door dissatisfied; but in the taking of bribes he certainly was most uncompromising and fearless." *Tatimma-i Wakiat-i Jahangiri* E&D 6.397.

122. The plot was made known to Jahangir by Khurram, who heard about it from his *diwan*, Khwaja Waisi. *Tuzuk* 1.122.

123. *Tuzuk* 1.122. According to van den Broecke's account, the men had planned to attack Jahangir on his way through the Khyber Pass to Kabul, but were unsuccessful, and Jahangir arrived safely. Van den Broecke, p. 39.

124. Van den Broecke, pp. 39–40; De Laet, pp. 178–79. Jahangir himself did not mention this offense of Itimaduddaula's, but there was much that Jahangir did not mention. The emperor did apparently demote the minister: in 1605 (*Tuzuk* 1.22) Jahangir gave him the title of Itimaduddaula and the rank of 1,500, while in 1608 (*Tuzuk* 1.140) he promoted him to the rank of 1,000 *zat* and 250 *suwar*, indicating that in between these years the minister somehow lost rank and had to be upgraded again. By the time of Mihrunnisa's meeting of Jahangir, Itimaduddaula was again at the rank of 1,500 (*Tuzuk* 1.197), suggesting that between 1608 and 1611 he had been promoted again. Van den

Broecke (p. 42), however, did make a great deal of the embezzling charge, suggesting it later as a reason Jahangir's ministers were opposed to the emperor's marriage to Mihrunnisa. He was one of the very few chroniclers, though, to pursue the matter.

125. Van den Broecke, p. 40; De Laet, p. 179. Jahangir mentioned that he ordered capital punishment for the leaders of the plot, but he did not give names, perhaps out of deference to Itimaduddaula. *Tuzuk* 1.123.

126. Said Jahangir (*Tuzuk* 1.122): "Although Khusrau had repeatedly done evil actions and deserved a thousand kinds of punishment, my fatherly affection did not permit me to take his life. . . . I averted my eyes from his faults, and kept him in excessive comfort and ease."

127. See *Tuzuk* 1.122.

128. See Gulbadan, pp. 114, 201.

129. He did preserve, however, the story of a later incident in which someone pretended to be Khusrau and had, as a part of his disguise, placed recognizable scars around his eyes presumably to be from an earlier blinding. *Tuzuk* 1.173–74.

130. See, e.g., H. Beveridge's discussion in *Tuzuk* 1.174n; Foster's discussion of Finch's evidence in Foster, *Early Travels*, p. 160n; and the Shujauddins, p. 31.

131. Payne in Guerreiro, p. xiii. Payne (in Guerreiro, pp. 102n–3n) argues that

> this must be regarded as the most authentic account we possess of the blinding of Prince Khusru; for, though Father Xavier [whose account, in a very abridged form, Guerreiro preserved] may not have been in Jahangir's camp at the time the punishment was inflicted, he must have reached it a few days afterwards, and must have heard a great deal about it. He states in his letter that the juice of the "leiteira" was applied to the victim's eyes. . . . We are also told that after the blinding Khusru was taken about with a bandage over his eyes, from which Xavier inferred that he was not totally bereft of sight.

132. Guerreiro, pp. 47–48.

133. Finch in Foster, *Early Travels*, p. 160; see Mundy 2.103–4.

134. Hawkins in Foster, *Early Travels*, p. 108.

135. Terry, p. 410.

136. Della Valle 1.56.

137. Van den Broecke, pp. 36, 40: "They took leaves called Aech and pressed out their juice. This was rubbed into his eyes as the result of which one eye completely lost the power of vision and the other retained only a little of it."

138. Tavernier, p. 268.

139. *Intikhab-i Jahangir-Shahi* E&D 6.448; see also 6.452.

140. Roe 2.378, 404.

141. *Intikhab-i Jahangir-Shahi* E&D 6.448–49, 452.

142. Prasad, p. 152; Shujauddins, p. 31. See also the discussions by H. Beveridge in *Tuzuk* 1.174n and Foster in *Early Travels*, p. 160n.

143. The story was told as if it were shortly after Mihrunnisa's arrival in Agra but Della Valle, in fact, said simply "after her Husband's death" and, in the abbreviated chronology of his account, this could mean "four years after," that is, in 1611 when she actually met and married Jahangir. Della Valle 1.53.

144. Della Valle 1.53–54. See also Villiers Stuart, p. 128.

145. Van den Broecke, pp. 41–42; De Laet, p. 181.

146. Van den Broecke, p. 42; De Laet, p. 181. These Dutch renditions of the early meetings of Mihrunnisa and Jahangir were the product of many stories conflated together to form a somewhat contradictory narrative with at least two problems. First, both van den Broecke and De Laet suggested that it was during the couple's two encounters at the New

Year's festival (in 1611), a few days apart, that they actually met and first fell in love. But both sources went on to report that the love that arose at this time was actually the revival of an old love from the days of Akbar—neither account, however, ever attempting to explain the inconsistency. Second, both sources stated just earlier that Mihrunnisa was in the charge of Ruqayya Begam and presumably lived in her compound. Why then did Jahangir have to travel to the house of Itimaduddaula to see his love? We know that Ruqayya Begam and Itimaduddaula lived close, if not next, to each other in Agra (see Pelsaert, pp. 2–3), but if secret meetings were actually being arranged, away from Mihrunnisa's place of residence, they certainly would not be held at the home of her father!

147. Roe 1.142.

148. Blochmann, *Ain-i Akbari* 1.192–93, 286.

149. *Tuzuk* 1.48–49.

150. Hawkins in Foster, *Early Travels*, p. 117.

151. Roe (1.143) noted, e.g., in 1616, pictures of "the King of England, the Queene, my lady Elizabeth, the Countesse[s] of Sommersett and Salisbury, and of a Cittizens wife of London; below them another of Sir Thomas Smyth, gouernor of the East India company."

152. Hawkins (in Foster, *Early Travels*, p. 118) noted that Jahangir would not accept the gifts as presents, but insisted on paying "what his praysers valew them to bee worth; which are valewed at halfe the price."

153. E.g., *Tuzuk* 1.49.

154. Roe 1.142–44; Terry, pp. 375–76; Hawkins in Foster, *Early Travels*, pp. 117–19; De Laet, pp. 99–101.

155. Blochmann, *Ain-i Akbari* 1.286–87; Tod 1.274.

156. Hawkins in Foster, *Early Travels*, p. 118.

157. Coryat in Foster, *Early Travels*, p. 278.

158. Coryat in Foster, *Early Travels*, p. 278. Coryat (pp. 278–79) also noted that any item of phallic shape, such as a radish, was in such demand at the festival that it was "cut and jagged for feare of converting the same to same unnaturall abuse."

159. Tod 1.274.

160. See Bernier's (pp. 272–73) description of the Khushruz fairs at Shah Jahan's court.

161. *Tuzuk* 1.192.

162. *Ikbal-nama-i Jahangiri* E&D 6.404–5; *Tatimma-i-Wakiat-i Jahangiri* E&D 6.398; van den Broecke, p. 42; De Laet, p. 181.

163. Shujauddins, p. 132. This description is according to "almost all the chroniclers," but they remain unnamed in the Shujauddins's text. Latif (*Agra*, p. 95) also sees Nur Jahan as "independent . . . handsome . . . a figure tall and graceful."

164. Dow 3.22.

165. Shujauddins, p. 53.

166. Pelsaert, p. 83.

167. Van den Broecke, p. 42; De Laet, pp. 181–82. Both sources describe opposition to the marriage from nobles at court.

168. Terry, p. 285; Pelsaert, pp. 81–84.

169. Terry (p. 406) noted, however, that Jahangir was not as interested in using marriage to solidify political alliances as his father Akbar had been. He said:

> The Mogul, in the choice of his wives and women, . . . was guided more by his eye and fancy, than by any respect . . . to his honour, for he took not the daughters of neighboring princes, but of his own subjects, and there preferred that which he looked upon as beauty, before anything else.

170. Note his 1608 marriage to the granddaughter of Raja Man Singh. *Tuzuk* 1.144; see also 1.138.

171. Dow 3.xxviii–xxix.

172. His promotion to the rank of 1,500 in 1605, which came with his title, had apparently been taken away from him as a result of the events of 1607 and in increments been fully reinstated by March of 1611. *Tuzuk* 1.22, 140, 197.

173. *Tuzuk* 1.197, 199. Van den Broecke (p. 42) gave the figure at 5,000 *suwar*. C. Pant (pp. 162–93) has excellent tabulations for all the promotions in Nur Jahan's family.

174. *Tuzuk* 1.202–3.

175. *Tuzuk* 1.260. Crowe et al. (p. 92) even make the suggestion that Mihrunnisa was married to Jahangir "through the intervention of her brother, Asaf Khan," presumably to reap rewards such as these.

176. *Tuzuk* 1.266.

177. *Tuzuk* 1.319.

178. *Tuzuk* 1.15, 19, 144, 145, 160.

179. A. S. Beveridge in Gulbadan, p. 3.

180. C. Pant, p. 45.

181. M. M. A. Husain, pp. 3, 17; see also Havell, *Agra*, p. 51. See also Tavernier, p. 89; Latif, *Agra*, p. 79.

182. Hawkins in Foster, *Early Travels*, p. 94.

183. In a footnote H. Beveridge notes that the *Iqbalnama* said Jahangir first saw Mihrunnisa on New Year's Day (see E&D 6.404) and that Jahangir himself noted that he married Mihrunnisa on the fourteenth of Khurdad, or the end of May 1611. *Tuzuk* 1.192n.

184. This was actually a small promotion given that Itimaduddaula was already ranked at 1,500. It could have been a betrothal present, the rest to come when the marriage was finalized, or it could have been increased later when Jahangir was certain the marriage would go through, or when he began to realize just what a gem his new wife was.

185. The information on which this argument is based is in H. Beveridge's notes, *Tuzuk* 1.224n–225n. See *Shah Jahan Nama*, pp. 5, 6, 70–71, 74.

186. Della Valle 1.53–54.

187. E.g., *Tuzuk* 1.319; *Ikbal-nama-i Jahangiri* E&D 6.405; Della Valle 1.54–55; Roe 1.118, 156; 2.281, 293; Terry, pp. 406–7; Hawkins in Foster, *Early Travels*, p. 101.

188. *Tuzuk* 1.319; *Ikbal-nama-i Jahangiri* E&D 6.405; van den Broecke, p. 42; De Laet, p. 182.

189. Blochmann, *Ain-i Akbari* 1.170–76.

190. As quoted in Rizvi, p. 388.

191. Rizvi, p. 389.

192. *Tuzuk* 1.3.

193. *Tuzuk* 1.10–11.

194. *Tuzuk* 1.11–12.

195. *Tuzuk* 2.198.

196. *Tuzuk* 1.46–47.

197. *Tuzuk* 2.79.

198. *Tuzuk* 2.75–76, 197.

199. *Tuzuk* 2.192, 220; Mundy 2.78–79.

200. *Tuzuk* 2.197, 199–200.

201. *Tuzuk* 1.141.

Chapter 3. Rise of the Junta (1611–1620)

1. "There is no clique so close and so odious as a family clique—it is nature's own clique" (Prasad, p. 179).

2. Dow 3.34.

3. C. Pant, p. 50; Dow 3.35; A. K. Das, *Mughal Painting*, pp. 110, 111; Shujauddins, p. 27; Gascoigne, p. 136. A good discussion of all the family fortunes can be found in I. Habib, pp. 74–95.

4. Hasan, pp. 324–35.

5. Her book, in fact, is designed to dispel "the commonly prevalent myth . . . that during the reign of Emperor Jahangir the reins of power were wielded wholly and solely by Nur Jahan who exercised this power for the upliftment of her family members" (C. Pant, pp. 5, 50–52). Misra (p. 34) charges, somewhat out of hand, that the existence of a junta "is not fully supported by contemporary or other reliable documents" and that the theory is "based on speculation and not corroborated by facts." Her dismissal of non-Indian documents as "often based on gossips and . . . not very reliable" (p. 35) is overly hasty, as the charge could be made of all the texts and artifacts used for information here. Moreover, her assessment of Nur Jahan (p. 35) is simply not born out by the material: "Whatever influence Nurjahan exercised over Jahangir was of a purely personal nature, based possibly on her emotions and her devotion to him. It will be unfair to attribute purely political ambition to her acts of interference or her active participation in political matters." A similar plea for a nonpolitical, altruistically minded Nur Jahan can be found in Lal (pp. 79–82) and, as follows, in Varadarajan (p. 411): "The descriptions given by Jahangir show that the ascendancy achieved by Nur Jahan over him was based on her submission to him, rather than on the force of her dominant personality. This submission constituted the essence of her feminine magnetism which so allured the Emperor."

6. C. Pant, pp. 29–30.

7. *Ikbal-nama-i Jahangiri* E&D 6.403; C. Pant, pp. 30–32.

8. *Tuzuk* 1.16.

9. *Tuzuk* 1.103.

10. *Tuzuk* 1.58, 74.

11. As narrated in Guerreiro, p. 139. Although we have noted in Chapter 1, note 36, that this remark may be a slight overstatement, there is no doubt that Ghiyas Beg had by this time already made a place for himself.

12. *Ikbal-nama-i Jahangiri* E&D 6.404.

13. *Tuzuk* 1.22.

14. *Tuzuk* 1.140, 197, 199, 200, 217, 218, 260, 280, 320, 351, 384; 2.82. See C. Pant, pp. 52–54, 163–64.

15. *Tuzuk* 1.202, 203.

16. *Tuzuk* 1.217, 260, 281, 317, 381; 2.1, 90, 175, 230, 261. See C. Pant, pp. 54, 167–68.

17. *Tuzuk* 1.218, 283–84, 320; 2.2, 7, 159, 215, 238. C. Pant, pp. 54–55, 166.

18. *Tuzuk* 1.260, 281, 286, 287. See C. Pant, pp. 56, 165, and van den Broecke, p. 51.

19. *Tuzuk* 2.2, 82, 88, 177, 228, 230, 281; Blochmann, *Ain-i Akbari* 1.559–60, 576; C. Pant, pp. 55, 170.

20. *Tuzuk* 2.5. The year was 1618. See also *Tuzuk* 2.88, and C. Pant, p. 55.

21. C. Pant, pp. 55, 173.

22. Based on data collected in I. Habib, pp. 74–95.

23. Van den Broecke, p. 39; De Laet, p. 178.

24. Hawkins in Foster, *Early Travel*, p. 94.

25. Pelsaert (p. 50), e.g., said that

> Jahangir, disregarding his own person and position, has surrendered himself to a crafty wife of humble lineage, as the result either of her arts or of her persuasive tongue. She has taken, and still continues increasingly to take, such advantage of this opportunity, that she has gradually enriched herself with super-abundant treasures, and has secured a more than royal position.

See also Della Valle 2.53; Dow 3.35.

26. Dow 3.184.

27. The best list is in the *Ikbal-nama-i Jahangiri* E&D 6.405, reproduced almost intact in the *Tatimma-i Wakiat-i Jahangiri* E&D 6.398–99.

28. Pelsaert, p. 50; Dow 3.56.

29. Pelsaert, p. 50. And again (p. 56): "It is the practice of the King, or rather of his wife, to give rapid advancement and promotion to any soldier, however low his rank, who has carried out orders with credit, or has displayed courage in the field."

Said Della Valle (1.54): "having also in the court made many alterations by deposing, and displacing almost all the old Captains and Officers, and by advancing to dignities other new ones of her own creatures, and particularly those of her blood and alliance."

Said van den Broecke (p. 93): "[People] with gifts and presents to the Queen easily get themselves transferred from one province to another."

30. The *Ikbal-nama-i Jahangiri* E&D 6.405, of all the sources, showed special interest in Nur Jahan's promotion of other women.

31. *Ikbal-nama-i Jahangiri* E&D 6.405.

32. Of these coins Pelsaert (p. 29) said: "Very little trade, however, is done with these gold coins, seeing that most of them must come from the King's treasures, and further the great men hoard them, and search for them for their *khazana* [treasuries]." Manucci (p. 157), however, said that "in her time these [zodiac coins] were current money." See also Dow 3.53.

33. Pelsaert, p. 4.

34. Letter from John Browne to the East India Company, February 10, 1617, and from James Bickford to Sir Thomas Smythe, March 4, 1617, *East India Company Letters* 5(1617).80, 133.

35. Roe 1.109.

36. Jahangir recorded the mutual exchange of letters and rare gifts between Nur Jahan and the mother of Imam Quli Khan, the ruler of Turan. *Tuzuk* 2.205.

37. Pelsaert, p. 50. For details, see chaps. 9 and 10.

38. Dow 3.53.

39. Prasad, p. 169; *Tuzuk* 1.232, C. Pant, p. 5.

40. Van den Broecke, p. 77.

41. Pelsaert, p. 50.

42. *Tatimma-i Wakiat-i Jahangiri* E&D 6.398.

43. *Tatimma-i Wakiat-i Jahangiri* E&D 6.398; Shujauddins, p. 99.

44. Gulbadan, p. 161. The striking of coins and the reading of the *khutba* seem to have gone hand in hand as new acts of sovereignty (*Tabakat-i Akbari* E&D 5.245, 359), and the fact that Nur Jahan's ascendancy was marked by one of them is remarkable indeed.

45. *Ikbal-nama-i Jahangiri* E&D 6.405.

46. Letter to Sir Thomas Smythe, January 16, 1617, *East India Company Letters* 5(1617).329.

47. Bernier, pp. 5, 275.

48. Manucci 1.157.
49. E&D 6.451–52.
50. Manucci 1.165.
51. Pelsaert, p. 50.
52. Pelsaert, pp. 50–51.
53. *Tuzuk* 1.20.
54. Della Valle 1.55. See also Srivastava, pp. 479–92.
55. Terry, p. 407.
56. *Tuzuk* 1.51–52.
57. Dow 3.61.
58. *Tuzuk* 1.12, 51–52, 54, 122.
59. *Tuzuk* 1.51.
60. *Tuzuk* 1.55.
61. *Tuzuk* 1.54.
62. *Tuzuk* 1.134.
63. *Tuzuk* 1.122, 294, 338.
64. Guerreiro (p. 11) contended that in the wake of the 1606 rebellion, Jahangir "deprived him of his titles and his right to succeed to the throne, transferring these to his second son," or rather, to his third. The Jesuits were quite sympathetic to Khusrau, as he was known to be open to Christianity. Du Jarric, pp. 62–63.
65. Pelsaert, p. 38.
66. Roe 1.90–93. See also 1.192–93.
67. Hawkins in Foster, *Early Travels*, p. 117.
68. *Intikhab-i Jahangir-Shahi* E&D 6.450.
69. Prasad, p. 296.
70. Jahangir (*Tuzuk* 1.306), ironically, given his own drinking habits, urged continued restraint saying, "Thou must observe the path of moderation, for wise men do not consider it right to drink to such an extent as to destroy the understanding."
71. "With much trouble wine was given to him" (*Tuzuk* 1.307). See *Shah Jahan Nama*, pp. 6, 9.
72. Saksena, pp. 18, 27
73. Manrique 2.219–20.
74. E.g., *Tuzuk* 1.288.
75. Saksena, pp. 15–31.
76. *Tuzuk* 1.20; see also 1.322.
77. *Tuzuk* 2.27. Said Roe (1.109): "Prince Sultan Coronne [was] his third sonne by byrth but first in fauour."
78. *Tuzuk* 1.20. At the beginning of the new year, in March of 1619, Jahangir (*Tuzuk* 2.78). called Khurram "my prosperous son . . . who is the star of the forehead of accomplished desires, and the brilliancy of the brow of prosperity."
79. E.g., *Tuzuk* 1.282, 325, 329, 377, 380, 387.
80. *Tuzuk* 1.338, 395.
81. Letter to Sir Thomas Smythe, January 16, 1617, *East India Company Letters* 5(1617).332.
82. *Tuzuk* 1.277.
83. *Tuzuk* 1.277–78. See *Shah Jahan Nama*, p. 6.
84. A. K. Das, *Mughal Painting*, p. 115.
85. 1.388. See also *Shah Jahan Nama*, pp. 5, 6, for alternate calculations.
86. H. Beveridge in *Tuzuk* 1.224n–25n. Saksena (p. 8) gives the date as March 21, 1607.

87. In 1609 Khurram married the daughter of Mirza Muzaffar Husain (*Tuzuk* 1.159), a cousin of his through Jahangir's sister. In the absence of a reasonable explanation given the groom's long-standing betrothal to Arjumand Banu, Saksena (pp. 11–12) speculates that Jahangir had already seen and fallen in love with Mihrunnisa and, in order to press her into marriage with him, was making things difficult for her niece.

88. *Badshah-nama* E&D 7.27; Manucci 1.176; Saksena, p. 310. In spite of his love for Nur Jahan's niece, however, Shah Jahan developed a reputation for being a ladies' man after her death with occasional histories of abuse. See, e.g., Manucci 1.186–90; Dow 3.141, 147.

89. Della Valle 1.56.

90. Della Valle 1.56:

> His Wife on the contrary, who lov'd him as well as he lov'd her, obtain'd to be the person allotted to serve him in the prison, and accordingly went thither, and liv'd with him so long as he was there, never ceasing to persuade him to marry *Nurmahal's* Daughter, that so he might be deliver'd from those troubles; that for her part she was content to live with him as a slave, provided she saw him free and in a good condition; but he could never be prevailed with.

91. Della Valle 1.56. Foster (*Early Travels*, p. 277n) went so far as to claim that Khusrau's scornful rejection of the marriage proposal "cost him his chance of the succession and consequently his life." See also Foster in Roe 2.404n–5n.

92. *Tuzuk* 1.395. See *Shah Jahan Nama*, p. 7.

93. *Tuzuk* 1.397.

94. *Tuzuk* 1.401.

95. Roe 2.329.

96. E.g., *Tuzuk* 1.277, 278; 2.190. Mundy (2.106), however, reported a tradition of their intimacy that apparently lasted into Shah Jahan's reign: "For the king [Jahangir] being incensed against him [Khurram] on some occasions (and as they say, for haveinge too secrett familiaritie with Nooremoholl)." Temple's note here (2.106n) says: "Mundy seems to be confusing Prince Khurram with his father, Jahangir, and is repeating a story current in Finch's time."

97. *Ikbal-nama-i Jahangiri* E&D 6.404. See also Sarkar, pp. 154–64.

98. *Tuzuk* 1.278.

99. *Tuzuk* 2.80.

100. *Tuzuk* 2.222.

101. E.g., *Tuzuk* 1.235, 280.

102. *Tuzuk* 2.2, 120, 153, 286. Said Hawkins (in Foster, *Early Travels*, p. 94): "[He was] a man that in outward shew made much of me and was alwayes willing to pleasure me when I had occasion to use him." Roe (2.453), however, noted that Itimaduddaula was "always indifferent," perhaps because he was less involved in and less sure of the wisdom of opening up trade with the west.

103. *Tuzuk* 1.373.

104. *Tuzuk* 2.194.

105. Guerreiro, p. 139.

106. *Tuzuk* 1.249; 2.201.

107. *Tuzuk* 2.73.

108. *Tuzuk* 2.80.

109. *Tuzuk* 1.281.

110. *Tuzuk* 1.351; Dow 3.53.

111. *Tuzuk* 1.378.

112. *Tuzuk* 1.384.

113. *Tuzuk* 2.26–27, 37.

114. E&D 6.397.

115. Van den Broecke, pp. 39–40.

116. De Laet, pp. 178–79.

117. Dow 3.55.

118. *Tuzuk* 1.202.

119. *Tuzuk* 1.260.

120. *Tuzuk* 2.37.

121. *Tuzuk* 2.81.

122. *Tuzuk* 2.168.

123. Dow 3.172.

124. *Tuzuk* 2.24, 81, 200, 211.

125. Although a letter of February 1618 from Roe to Thomas Kerridge indicated that on at least one occasion Asaf Khan was supported in his deals by the work of his father Itimadduddaula. *English Factories* (1618–21), pp. 4–5.

126. Hawkins in Foster, *Early Travels*, p. 94.

127. See Terry, p. 195.

128. Terry, pp. 395, 406–07. Foster, in fact, calls him "avaricious, crafty, and unscrupulous" (Roe 1.xlv). See also Dow 3.56.

129. Letters from John Browne to the Company, February 10, 1618, and William Biddulph et al., to the Council at Surat, November 23, 1621, *English Factories* (1618–21), pp. 9, 335.

130. Terry, pp. 364–65.

131. This dislike of Nur Jahan was especially prominent during the height of the Khusrau affair. See Roe 2.293–94.

132. For a popular account, see Srivastava, pp. 479–92.

133. Referred to during this period as "the unhappy affair of Khusrau." E.g., *Tuzuk* 1.251.

134. *Tuzuk* 1.261.

135. Coryat in Foster, *Early Travels*, p. 277.

136. *Tuzuk* 1.336. See *Intikhab-i Jahangir-Shahi* E&D 6.452.

137. Roe 2.281.

138. Roe 2.281.

139. Roe 2.282.

140. Roe 2.299.

141. *Tuzuk* 1.336.

142. Roe 2.324; see also 2.379.

143. Roe 2.404.

144. Roe 2.407.

145. *Tuzuk* 2.107.

146. In December of 1616, Roe (2.363) noted: "Ther is now a great whisper at court about a new affinitye of Sultan Corsoronne and Asaph chan, and great hope of his liberty."

147. *Tuzuk* 1.380.

148. Roe 1.267.

149. *Tuzuk* 1.385.

150. It is not clear here from Roe's description whether Asaf Khan or Shah Jahan was the dominant member of their relationship: Asaf Khan was the father of the beloved wife of Shah Jahan, but Shah Jahan was still the prince.

151. Roe 1.118.

152. Roe 2.281.
153. Roe 2.293.
154. Roe 2.281.
155. Roe 2.294, 293.
156. See, for example, Roe's description (2.376–77) of being brought to Jahangir's side to speak intimately in broken Persian.
157. Roe 1.109. Nur Jahan may well have expressed doubts as to whether Roe was a properly accredited ambassador, or whether like his predecessors only an emissary of the merchants.
158. Roe 2.444; 1.111. See also Roe 1.249.
159. Roe 2.363–64.
160. Roe 2.453. Roe went on to imply that whatever relationship he had with Itimaduddaula was because his son Asaf Khan had openly facilitated it.
161. Roe 1.249.
162. Roe 1.262.
163. Best, p. 253.
164. See Hawkins in Foster, *Early Travels*, p. 94.
165. E.g., Roe 2.458. He complained, in fact, in a letter dated January 25, 1616, that "they did expect ten times as much from me as from Mr. Edwards, and spake it openly: that now an ambassador was come, a great man, they should receive proportionable gifts" (*East India Company Letters* 4[1616].13).
166. Roe 2.498. In writing to Kerridge once, Roe (2.290n) urged haste in sending presents for he sensed that he had neglected Nur Jahan that year and "I haue felt [it] heauely."
167. Roe 1.119.
168. Roe 1.169–170.
169. Roe 1.174.
170. Roe 1.174–75, 176. In summing up the gifts given to him by the king a month later, Roe (1.176n) included "hoggs flesh, deare, a theefe and a whore."
171. Roe 2.295.
172. Pelsaert, p. 50.
173. See Foster in Roe 1.xxxvii.

Chapter 4. "The World Conqueror"

1. Terry, p. 386.
2. Roe 1.xlv.
3. Dow 3.xxv–xxvi.
4. A. K. Das, *Mughal Painting*, p. 8.
5. "I made holes in my ears and drew into each a shining pearl" (*Tuzuk* 1.267).
6. *Tuzuk* 1.143.
7. *Tuzuk* 1.5, 116, 119.
8. *Tuzuk* 1.5–6.
9. *Tuzuk* 2.292–93.
10. Many of Jahangir's wine cups have survived. See, e.g., the collection in the Victoria and Albert Museum, London.
11. *Tuzuk* 1.384.
12. A. K. Das, *Mughal Painting*, pp. 10–11.
13. Terry, pp. 400–401.

14. Roe 1.112.

15. In spite of the Jains' perspective as captured in the *Sribhanucandraganicarita* (p. 47):

> Jahangir enjoyed and amused himself as *Indra* does in heaven—sometimes residing in wonderful rest-houses, sometimes on the banks of the Indus, sometimes on pleasure-mounts, sometimes in mansions of variegated colours, sometimes revelling in the exquisite performance of the best female dancers, sometimes listening to the soft music of beautiful damsels, and sometimes attending to dramatic performances.

16. A. K. Das, *Mughal Painting*, p. xxi.

17. Roe 1.120.

18. Terry, p. 373.

19. Hawkins in Foster, *Early Travels*, p. 106.

20. Withington in Foster, *Early Travels*, p. 225.

21. Gascoigne, p. 134.

22. A. K. Das, *Splendour*, p. 1.

23. H. Beveridge in *Tuzuk* 2.vi. Hawkins (ca. 1612) said: "In such sort that what this mans father, called Ecber Padasha, got of the Decans, this king, Selim Sha, beginneth to loose." In Foster, *Early Travels*, pp. 106–7. And Manucci (1.153) began his discussion of Jahangir by saying: "It is a truth tested by experience that sons dissipate what their fathers gained in the sweat of their brow."

24. H. Beveridge in *Tuzuk* 2.vi. Beveridge (*Tuzuk* 2.v) compares Jahangir to the Emperor Claudius, for both were "weak men . . . in their wrong places as rulers . . . [and had] Jahangir been head of a Natural History Museum, . . . [he] would have been [a] better and happier" man.

25. *Tuzuk* 1.1–2; see *Tabakat-i Akbari* E&D 5.332–34; A. K. Das, *Mughal Painting*, p. 3.

26. See Findly, "Visionary Paintings."

27. *Tuzuk* 2.210, 211.

28. E.g., *Tuzuk* 1.168, 435; Roe 2.498.

29. See, e.g., Roe 2.416.

30. There are oblique references, however, to "those who travel round the world" and to various aspects of trade with Europeans, especially the English. *Tuzuk* 1.269, 274–75, 338, 416–17.

31. A. S. Beveridge in Gulbadan, p. 3. See *Tuzuk* 1.191ff where mention of the marriage should appear. He did, however, mention marriages to other wives, e.g., to the daughter of Jagat Singh, eldest son of Raja Man Singh (1608), to the daughter of Ram Chand Bundela (1609), and to the daughter of Kalyan of Jaisalmer (as a prince), as well as the deaths of two of his wives, Jodh Bai, daughter of the Mota, or "Fat," Raja (Udai Singh) (1619), and the Padshah Begam, Saliha Banu Begam (1620) (*Tuzuk* 1.144, 160, 326–27; 2.84, 159), so it is even more significant that his marriage to Nur Jahan went unnoted.

32. *Tuzuk* 1.24–25. Note that he did, however, promote Abul Fazl's son Abdur Rahman to the rank of 2,000 *zat* and 1,500 *suwar* a year or so after his accession. *Tuzuk* 1.105.

33. *Tuzuk*, 1.33–34, 37–45.

34. A. K. Das, *Mughal Painting*, pp. xxi, 5; Gascoigne, p. 131.

35. Roe 1.112, 124, 363, 364.

36. Van den Broecke, p. 91.

37. Gascoigne, p. 131.

38. *Tuzuk* 1.432.

39. Terry, p. 387; Roe 1.215.

40. The eunuch was trampled to death by an elephant (or alternately cut into pieces) before her as she stood in the pit—an event that took place close to the houses of Terry and Roe. Trampling to death by an elephant was a common form of execution at both the Mughal and Rajput courts (Roe 1.123; Hawkins in Foster, *Early Travels*, p. 108) and, of this kind of punishment, Roe (1.108) said, "And some tymes [he] sees with too much delight in blood the execution done by his Eliphants."

41. Terry, p. 388; Hawkins in Foster, *Early Travels*, pp. 109–10.

42. Guerreiro, pp. 34–35.

43. *Tuzuk* 1.254–55; see 2.226.

44. Manucci 1.155.

45. Terry, p. 362.

46. *Tuzuk* 1.365–67.

47. Terry, pp. 362–63.

48. See Findly, "Vow of Non-Violence," pp. 245–56, where there is discussion of Jahangir's strong ambivalence on crimes committed against one's family.

49. Although Shahryar had been born not to a legal wife of Jahangir but to one of his concubines, this would not in and of itself account for the emperor's behavior here. *Tuzuk* 1.20.

50. Hawkins in Foster, *Early Travels*, p. 117. Roe (1.198–99) told another story of Jahangir's baiting of Shahryar: the emperor had wanted one of his nephews who had become a Christian (probably a son of Daniyal's) to lose favor with the people and accordingly asked the boy to strike a lion on the head. When the boy refused, Jahangir asked Shahryar to do it, which he "did so without any harme" (the lion apparently being tame). The emperor then sent his nephew to prison "where hee is neuer like to see day light."

51. *Tuzuk* 1.294. Later he was to discover through an ambassador of Shah Abbas that this eldest son, Safi Mirza, if not executed, "would certainly have attempted the Shah's life. As this intention became manifest from his behavior," his father had had him killed (*Tuzuk* 1.338).

52. *Tuzuk* 1.122; see also 1.111.

53. *Tuzuk* 1.432.

54. Prasad, p. 152.

55. *Tuzuk* 2.28.

56. *Tuzuk* 2.211–12.

57. Terry, pp. 388–89.

58. Gascoigne, p. 135.

59. Note, however, his abrupt and severely retributive treatment of the Portuguese when they captured the *Rahimi*, his mother's trading ship, in 1613. Foster, *Early Travels*, pp. 191–92, 203; *East India Company Letters* 2 (1613–15).213; *East India Company Letters* 3 (1615).4. For a discussion, see Findly, "Maryamuzzamani," pp. 227–38.

60. Hawkins in Foster, *Early Travels*, p. 108.

61. Withington in Foster, *Early Travels*, p. 225.

62. Terry, p. 389.

63. Van den Broecke, p. 91.

64. *Tuzuk* 1.13.

65. See, for example, Moreland, pp. 32–35.

66. *Tuzuk* 1.10.

67. *Tuzuk* 1.7–10.

68. *Tuzuk* 1.7.

69. *Tuzuk* 1.7. H. Beveridge notes that Du Jarric, using missionary reports, implied that the chain was silver and that Jahangir "was following the idea of an old Persian king." Note here Guerreiro's report (p. 13) that Jahangir

> displayed so great a love for justice that, calling to mind what one of the ancient kings of Persia had done, he gave orders that a silver bell with a chain twenty cubits long should be suspended close to his own apartments, so that all who felt that they had grievances and were unable to obtain redress at the hands of the law or the officers of the State, might pull this chain, when the King would immediately come forth and deliver justice verbally.

70. Hawkins in Foster, *Early Travels*, p. 113.

71. A custom apparently taken up by lesser rulers in imitation. *Tuzuk* 1.204–5.

72. Hawkins in Foster, *Early Travels*, p. 115; Terry, pp. 370–71, 383. Tavernier (pp. 260–61), during Shah Jahan's reign, recorded the custom as requiring "these Kings to show themselves in public three times every week, or, at the very least, every fifteen days." According to Hawkins' account, when in Agra Jahangir's first two showings were presumably from the same window and a third (from three until five) with nobles in open audience. According to Terry, however, in the morning Jahangir appeared at a window on the east, at noon on the south, and in the evening on the west. But, continued Terry, "as soon as the sun forsakes the hemisphere, he leaves his people, ushered in and out with drums and wind instruments and the people's acclamations."

73. Coryat in Foster, *Early Travels*, p. 247. Coryat oddly noted that Jahangir's audience here was nobles, although we know from other sources that a main concern were the grievances of the public. See *Tuzuk* 1.10, 266; 2.14.

74. *Tuzuk* 2.13.

75. Roe 1.108.

76. Terry, pp. 353–54.

77. Said Roe (2.314): "[Many people] will not eate till they haue saluted him in the morning, for which Purpose hee Comes at the Sunnes rising to a wyndow open to a great Playne before his house, where Multitudes attend him."

78. *Tuzuk* 1.172.

79. Dow 3.105–7. This particular relative, says Dow, was the son of a man named Ibrahim who at one time had held the *suba* of Bengal. This would have made the father Ibrahim Khan, a brother of Asmat Begam's and an uncle of Nur Jahan's. The boy, then, would have been Nur Jahan's first cousin not her nephew. Dow narrates that just before the boy finally paid for his crime, the driver of the elephant used to execute him "passed over him several times, without giving the elephant the necessary directions," because he was greatly "afraid of the resentment of the Sultana."

80. Manucci 1.169.

81. From Maulana Shibli Numani's *Jahangiri Justice*, translated here courtesy of Syed N. Haq of Cambridge, Massachusetts. The story is also depicted in such modern Indian films as *Pukar* (Minerva Movietone, 1939), staring Naseem Banu as Nur Jahan and Chandra Mohan as Jahangir, and produced and directed by Sohrab Modi.

The *dirham* is a silver coin of varying weight whose usage goes back to the time of Umar. *Ain-i Akbari* 1.36–38.

82. *Tuzuk* 2.211.

83. *Tuzuk* 1.420–21.

84. Roe 2.413–14. Said Roe:

> I had nothing to giue, nor might fitly goe with nothing, nor stay at home without discourtesie; which made mee venture vpon a faire Booke well bound, filleted and

gilt, Mercators last Edition of the Maps of the world, which I presented with an excuse that I had nothing worthy, but to a great King I offered the World, in which he had so great and rich a part.

85. Terry, p. 351; see also Roe 2.416–17. The situation was not as Jahangir imagined internally either for, said Pelsaert (pp. 58–59):

> The whole country is enclosed and broken up by many mountains, and the people who live in, on, or beyond, the mountains know nothing of any King, or of Jahangir, . . . Jahangir, whose name implies that he grasps the whole world, must therefore be regarded as ruling no more than half the dominions which he claims.

86. A. K. Das, *Mughal Painting*, p. xxii; Das, *Splendour*, p. 1.

87. From the *Kevorkian Album*, inscr. to Abul Hasan, ca. 1650, Freer Gallery of Art, Smithsonian Institution, Washington, D.C. (48.28b), based presumably on a prototype by Abul Hasan, ca. 1623.

88. From the *Kevorkian Album*, inscr. to Abul Hasan, early 19th c., Freer Gallery of Art, Smithsonian Institution, Washington, D.C. (48.19); based on a prototype fr. the *Minto Album*, inscr. to Abul Hasan, ca. 1615–20, A. Chester Beatty Library, Dublin (ms. 7, no. 15).

89. From the *Leningrad Album*, inscr. to Abul Hasan, ca. 1618–22, Freer Gallery of Art, Smithsonian Institution, Washington, D.C. (45.9).

90. From the *Leningrad Album*, inscr. to Bichitr, ca. 1615–18, Freer Gallery of Art, Smithsonian Institution, Washington, D.C. (45.15).

91. See Ettinghausen, pp. 98–120.

92. One could argue as well that Nur Jahan and the junta encouraged such paintings and such views in order to further distance Jahangir from real sovereignty, thereby making their own control that much more complete.

93. A. K. Das, *Mughal Painting*, p. 17. P. Brown (*Painting*, pp. 173–74) argues that Jahangir "fully believed in the divinity of kings; and symbolized his semi-sanctified state by means of the nimbus in all portraits of himself." The use of the nimbus in this way, Brown continues, "was entirely Jahangir's."

94. *Tuzuk* 1.141.

95. Terry, pp. 347, 349.

96. See Roe 2.314; Latif, *Lahore*, pp. 120–21.

97. Varadarajan, p. 412.

98. *Tuzuk* 1.410.

99. Manucci 1.160.

100. *Tuzuk* 1.90–91.

101. E.g., *Tuzuk* 1.215–17, 143; 2.88–89. Note the large number of "animal portraits" painted for him by his artists, especially Mansur, and his habit of taking painters with him on hunts, precisely for the purpose of capturing the likeness of whatever creature befell his fancy. See Alvi and Rahman.

102. *Tuzuk* 2.201.

103. *Tuzuk* 1.139–40.

104. *Tuzuk* 2.16–18, 23ff., 39, 42.

105. *Tuzuk* 1.242–43.

106. E.g., *Tuzuk* 1.83, 120, 121, 129, 136, 163, 166–67, 185–88, 204, 255, 264, 268, 286–87, 341, 362–63, 375, 444; 2.40–41, 181–82, 231, 269, 285.

107. *Tuzuk* 2.43–44.

108. *Tuzuk* 2.119–20.

109. *Tuzuk* 1.118–19.

110. *Tuzuk* 2.125.

111. *Tuzuk* 2.20–21.

112. On Jahangir's physical appearance, see Coryat in Foster, *Early Travels*, p. 245; Maclagan, p. 76.

113. See A. S. Beveridge in Gulbadan, p. 29, and Gulbadan, pp. 99, 131, 189.

114. Murad had died at age thirty while in the Deccan, and Daniyal at age thirty-three while in Burhanpur. Daniyal, though a regular abuser of alcohol, died most immediately of drinking wine from a rusty, powdery gun barrel. *Tuzuk* 1.34–35. See also van den Broecke, pp. 24–25, 29–30.

115. A. K. Das, *Mughal Painting*, p. 5.

116. In his own history of his drinking he said fifteen, but according to two other manuscripts and to H. Beveridge's calculations, Jahangir did not begin wine drinking until he was seventeen and a half years old, that is, in his eighteenth year. Says H. Beveridge (*Tuzuk* 1.307n): "It seems to follow that the MSS. are right, and that we should read 18." Jahangir himself stated earlier, in his opening remarks to his memoirs, that he did not begin drinking until he was eighteen. *Tuzuk* 1.8.

117. *Tuzuk* 1.307.

118. *Tuzuk* 1.307–8. *Araq*, though prepared in a variety of ways, was most commonly made with a distillation of unrefined sugar mixed with the bark of the *babul* tree. "This was the most common and cheapest drink of Rajasthan" (Agre, p. 268).

119. *Tuzuk* 1.308.

120. Hakim Humam, brother of Hakim Abul Fath, came in fact at Salim's request, for the young drunkard seemed to be most aware of his deteriorating condition. *Tuzuk* 1.308.

121. See Jahangir's alternate account at the beginning of his reign. *Tuzuk* 1.8.

122. H. Beveridge's note suggests that *filuniya* may be opium (*Tuzuk* 1.308n), but Jahangir himself noted later that eventually, in the place of *filuniya*, he substituted opium. *Tuzuk* 1.310. A traditional term for opium was *afim*, and poppies for the crop were grown in many areas of Rajasthan. Agre, pp. 269–70.

123. The exception was that on Thursday he drank during the day rather than at night, his usual drinking time, because Thursday had been the day of his accession and Thursday night was the eve of the Muslim holy day. We may assume that he also did not drink on Friday when "there should be an omission . . . to return thanks to the True Benefactor" (*Tuzuk* 1.309). Earlier in his memoirs (*Tuzuk* 1.20) he said: "A year before I became King I had determined that I would drink no wine on Friday eve, and I hope at the throne of God that He will keep me firm in this resolve as long as I live."

124. *Tuzuk* 1.310.

125. *Tuzuk* 1.267.

126. *Tuzuk* 2.11–12.

127. *Tuzuk* 2.11–13.

128. *Tuzuk* 2.35.

129. E.g., *Tuzuk* 2.128, 180. In one story early in his memoirs (1607) (*Tuzuk* 1.105–6), he boastfully noted that while drinking kept many of his courtiers from successfully jumping over a stream, he—aged forty and full of wine—was able to make it, although not "with the activity that I had shown . . . when I was 30."

130. E.g., *Tuzuk* 1.226, 266.

131. *Tuzuk* 1.8.

132. *Tuzuk* 2.41.

133. *Tuzuk* 1.8.

134. *Tuzuk* 2.87; see also 1.134–35, 377.

135. *Tuzuk* 2.165.

136. Roe 2.304; Terry, pp. 387–88; see A. K. Das, *Mughal Painting*, p. 6.

137. E.g., *Tuzuk* 1.370.

138. Jahangir's reputation for being a drunkard, for example, was carried abroad by travelers who took with them eyewitness accounts. Note, for example, Thomas Keridge's letter from Agra to Thomas Aldworth in Surat, September 7, 1613: "The king [is] a drunkard so given to vice that the chief captains care not for him, and willingly would never come near him" (*East India Company Letters* 1 (1602–13).281). Said Roe (1.119): "Ther is nothing more welcome here, nor euer saw I man soe enamord of drincke as both the King and Prince [Shah Jahan] are of redd wyne . . . I thinck 4 or 5 handsome cases of that wyne wilbe more welcome than the richest Iewell in Cheapesyde." See also Roe 2.303.

139. *Tuzuk* 1.306. A weighing ceremony like this one is depicted in "Emperor Jahangir Weighs Prince Khurram," attributed to Manohar, ca. 1610–15, British Museum (1948.10–9069). See *Shah Jahan Nama,* pp. 6, 9.

140. *Tuzuk* 1.115; 2.14.

141. Said Jahangir (*Tuzuk* 1.307): "With much trouble wine was given to him."

142. *Tuzuk* 1.20.

143. Terry, p. 387.

144. *Tuzuk* 1.1–2; 2.70.

145. Pelsaert, p. 77.

146. *Tuzuk* 2.6–7. Said Jahangir: "This usage is my own, and has never been practised until now."

147. *Tuzuk* 1.183.

148. *Tuzuk* 2.6. Jahangir was kept back from the trip by knowledge "which had thrown its rays on my mind through Divine inspiration."

149. *Tuzuk* 2.25, 65.

150. *Tuzuk* 2.70–71.

151. *Tuzuk* 2.151–53.

152. *Tuzuk* 2.159–60.

153. Again, a prophecy based on Jahangir's horoscope. *Tuzuk* 2.203.

154. *Tuzuk* 2.235.

155. *Tuzuk* 2.291.

156. *Tuzuk* 2.74.

157. Van den Broecke, p. 56.

158. Pelsaert, p. 3.

159. As noted in C. Pant, pp. 109–11.

160. Terry, p. 406.

161. Van den Broecke, p. 5.

162. Van den Broecke, pp. 91–92.

163. Della Valle 1.53.

164. E.g., H. Beveridge in *Tuzuk* 2.vi; Das, p. 8; Gascoigne, p. 172. See also Dow's rendition (3.35) of his sources: "The charms of the Sultana estranged the mind of Jehangire from all public affairs. Easy in his temper, and naturally voluptuous, the powers of his soul were locked up in a pleasing enthusiasm of love, by the engaging conversation and extraordinary beauty of Noor-Mahil."

165. Shujauddins, p. 29.

166. A. K. Das, *Mughal Painting*, p. 8; see also C. Pant, pp. 109–11.

167. *Tuzuk* 2.53.

168. *Tuzuk* 2.192; see also 2.215.

169. *Tuzuk* 2.222.

170. *Tuzuk* 2.223.
171. *Tuzuk* 2.228. See van den Broecke, p. 53.
172. *Tuzuk* 2.214.
173. *Tuzuk* 1.266.
174. *Tuzuk* 2.213.
175. *Tuzuk* 2.214.
176. Pelsaert, p. 53; van den Broecke, pp. 91–92.
177. Manucci 1.168.
178. Manucci 1.155–56.
179. Manucci 1.157–58.
180. Van den Broecke, p. 92.
181. *Ikbal-nama-i Jahangiri* E&D 6.404, 405; *Sribhanucandraganicarita* 259–68.
182. Jahangir, (*Tuzuk* 1.358) in fact, described this doctrine: "It is a maxim of the Hindus that no good deed can be thoroughly performed by men in the social state without the partnership of . . . a wife, whom they have styled the half of a man."
183. *Tuzuk* 2.45.
184. *Tuzuk* 2.64.
185. *Tuzuk* 1.77–78, 145–46, 148, 154–55, 230, 239, 248; 2.98.
186. *Tuzuk* 1.81, 145.
187. *Tuzuk* 1.76.
188. Terry, p. 389. 189. *Tuzuk* 1.84–85.
190. *Tuzuk* 2.216.
191. Coryat in Foster, *Early Travels*, p. 278.
192. Du Jarric, p. 190.
193. Maclagan, pp. 70, 93.
194. Hawkins in Foster, *Early Travels*, p. 115.
195. Finch in Foster, *Early Travels*, pp. 163, 184.
196. A. K. Das, *Mughal Painting*, p. 232.
197. Oddly enough, the Jesuit fathers believed up to the time of Jahangir's death that the only thing keeping the emperor from converting to Christianity was Nur Jahan's antipathy to the religion. Maclagan, p. 90.
198. *Ikbal-nama-i Jahangiri* E&D 6.405.
199. *Tuzuk* 2.277.
200. *Sribhanucandraganicarita* 269–79.

Chapter 5. Life in the Women's Palaces

1. Said Manucci (2.319): [For] "all Mahomedans are very fond of women, who are their principal relaxation and almost their only pleasure."
2. A. S. Beveridge in Gulbadan, p. 28.
3. Roe 2.458.
4. *Tuzuk* 1.57. See also *Tuzuk* 1.62 where Jahangir quoted Khusrau: "I will give orders to plunder the city for seven days and to make captive the women and children."
5. Dow (3.xix) reports, e.g.:

> When the governor of a province falls under the suspicion of disaffection for his prince, the first step taken against him, is an order issued for sending his women to court. Even one of his wives, and she too not the best beloved, will bind him to his allegiance. His obedience to this mandate is the true test of his designs.

6. Dow 3.xix.

7. This accounts in part for the practice of killing women of the *mahal* whenever they were in danger of being captured by an enemy. See, e.g., *Badshah-nama* E&D 7.49.

8. See the account in the *Tuzuk* (1.366) where Jahangir noted, with contempt, the practice of Nasiruddin: "They say that he had collected 15,000 women in his harem. He had a whole city of them, and had made it up of all castes, kinds, and descriptions—artificers, magistrates, qazis, kotwals, and whatever else is necessary for the administration of a town."

9. Altekar, pp. 166–79.

10. Roe 1.21.

11. Terry, p. 203.

12. Roe 1.32; 2.457.

13. Terry, p. 180.

14. Terry, pp. 283–84.

15. Terry, p. 283.

16. *Tuzuk* 1.351.

17. Dow 3.xix.

18. Misra, pp. 71–75; A. K. Das, *Mughal Painting*, p. 46.

19. *Tuzuk* 1.73.

20. Said Gulbadan (p. 98), Babur "commanded buildings to be put up in Agra on the other side of the river, and a stone palace to be built for himself between the *haram* and the garden." Later she said (p. 103) of Babur, the "emperor gave houses to all the begams."

21. Pelsaert, pp. 2–3; see also Finch in Foster, *Early Travels*, pp. 148–49.

22. Pelsaert, pp. 3–4; see De Laet, pp. 38–39.

23. Pelsaert, p. 4.

24. Pelsaert, p. 64. See also, e.g., Gulbadan, p. 101.

25. Terry, p. 187; Pelsaert, p. 66.

26. Both Terry (pp. 187–88) and Pelsaert (p. 66) described waterworks found in establishments of a great variety of classes.

27. Pelsaert, p. 66; Finch in Foster, *Early Travels*, p. 178. According to Bernier (p. 267):

> They inform me that the seraglio contains beautiful apartments, separated and more or less spacious and splendid according to the rank and income of females. Nearly every chamber has its reservoir of running water at the door, on every side are gardens, delightful alleys, shady retreats, streams, fountains, grottoes, deep excavations that afford shelter from the Sun by day, lofty divans and terraces, on which to sleep coolly at night.

28. Terry, p. 188.

29. Pelsaert, p. 67.

30. Roe 1.145.

31. Pelsaert, p. 64.

32. Finch in Foster, *Early Travels*, pp. 163–64.

33. Terry, p. 283.

34. Finch in Foster, *Early Travels*, p. 163.

35. Finch in Foster, *Early Travels*, p. 164.

36. Finch in Foster, *Early Travels*, p. 164.

37. Finch in Foster, *Early Travels*, p. 163.

38. Hawkins in Foster, *Early Travels*, p. 101.

39. Terry, p. 406.

40. *Tuzuk* 1.366. Manucci (2.308, see also 320), however, noted that Aurangzeb's royal household included "two thousand women of different races."

41. Manucci 2.308.

42. On spies in the harem, see Manucci 2.311–12.

43. A. S. Beveridge in Gulbadan, p. 75; see also Du Jarric, pp. 42–43.

44. Misra, pp. 11–12, 156–57.

45. Maclagan, pp. 72, 74.

46. See Manucci 2.310–11. He said (2.315) that the "kings are very choice about giving names to suit the persons receiving them."

47. *Tuzuk* 1.319. These are the official dates, of course; it seems, however, that the name Nur Mahal was used of her throughout her career especially by European travelers and was perhaps contemporaneous with the name Nur Jahan, which may have been a private title from the very beginning of her time on the throne. The title Nur Mahal also belonged to the first wife of Dara Shikoh, who was much beloved by him and took her life by poison when she saw that her husband would eventually come to his end through the treachery of his brother Aurangzeb. Manucci 1.330–32, 342, 343.

48. Terry, p. 406.

49. Blochmann, *Ain-i Akbari* 1.49n.

50. See *Tuzuk* 1.76.

51. As reported in Misra, p. 59.

52. She was also called Queen Aliya Begam. *Badshah-nama* E&D 7.27.

53. As reported in Misra, p. 60.

54. Manucci 2.311. Khanam, on the other hand, signified that the woman was "of the royal household."

55. E.g., A. S. Beveridge in Gulbadan, p. 62.

56. Lall, p. 32.

57. A. S. Beveridge in Gulbadan, p. 37.

58. Dow 3.xiv.

59. Dow 3.xiv. See Manucci 2.319.

60. Pelsaert, pp. 64–65.

61. Pelsaert, p. 65.

62. Dow 3.xviii.

63. See Blochmann, *Ain-i Akbari* 1.343–47. In spite of Aziz Koka's offenses, Akbar was attached to him his whole life long, for between "me and Aziz is a river of milk which I cannot cross."

64. *Tuzuk* 1.84–85.

65. *Ain-i Akbari* 1.46; see also Manucci 2.308, 312.

66. Manucci 2.309; *Ain-i Akbari* 1.46.

67. Misra, p. 78.

68. Misra, pp. 78, 78n–79n.

69. *Tuzuk* 2.110. Likewise, Muhammad Hadi reported that an old servant named Dila Rani took over from Haji Koka as superintendent of the women servants in the palace about the time of Nur Jahan's second marriage and that without her seal stipends could not be paid. *Tatimma-i Wakiat-i Jahangiri* E&D 6.398. Said Blochmann (*Ain-i Akbari* 1.574): "[Nur Jahan] provided for all her relations; even hur nurse, Da,i Dilaram, enjoyed much influence, and held the post of "Sadr of the Women" (*sadr-i anas*), and when she conferred lands as *suyurghals* the grants were confirmed and sealed by the Sadr of the empire."

70. *Ain-i Akbari* 1.47.

71. Manucci 2.328.

72. *Ain-i Akbari* 1.46–47; Manucci 2.308–9, 326–28.

73. A. S. Beveridge in Gulbadan, p. 40.

74. As reported by Foster in Roe 1.253n.

75. Eunuchs were responsible for preventing all illicit foods, beverages, and drugs from coming into the harem. Manucci 2.328.

76. *Ain-i Akbari* 1.46–47; Manucci 1.288.

77. Manucci 2.328, 309.

78. *Ain-i Akbari* 1.47; Manucci 2.328.

79. Pelsaert said (p. 64) of Jahangir's harem that each wife "has a regular monthly allowance for her *gastos*," *gastos* referring to housekeeping or traveling expenses (p. 64n). See also Manucci 2.308, 310, 319. The highest allowance on record is 10 *lakh* rupees per year given to Arjumand Banu Begam under Shah Jahan. Blochmann, *Ain-i Akbari* 1.574n.

80. *Ain-i Akbari* 1.46.

81. Manucci 2.315–16.

82. *Tuzuk* 1.10.

83. Manucci 2.328.

84. *Tuzuk* 2.192.

85. Pelsaert, p. 64.

86. Lall, p. 32.

87. A. S. Beveridge in Gulbadan, p. 67.

88. Gulbadan, pp. 118–23.

89. See Terry, p. 376.

90. A. S. Beveridge in Gulbadan, p. 10.

91. Gulbadan, pp. 116–17. A. S. Beveridge says (p. 9): "In some cases which are mentioned by Babur, adoptions were made by a childless wife of high degree from a slave or servant, but no such reason seems behind those from Dil-dar."

92. *Tuzuk* 1.75, 130.

93. *Ikbal-nama-i Jahangiri* E&D 6.404.

94. Blochmann, *Ain-i Akbari* 1.321.

95. Saksena, p. 15.

96. *Tuzuk* 2.45. Shah Shuja, apparently, was quite prone to accident and illness (at least if the *Tuzuk* accounts were representative) and had to be followed very closely by attendants and astrologers. *Tuzuk* 1.45, 151–52, 203.

97. See Manucci 2.74–75.

98. Pelsaert, p. 65; Manucci 2.326–28. Their responsibility to the emperor was, said Fitch (in Foster, *Early Travels*, p. 18), to "keepe his women."

99. Terry, p. 284.

100. Manucci 2.72.

101. *Tuzuk* 1.168. Said Jahangir earlier (*Tuzuk* 1.150–51):

> At this time [late 1608] I issued an order that hereafter no one should follow this abominable custom, and that the traffic in young eunuchs should be completely done away with. . . . In a short time this objectionable practice will be completely done away with, and the traffic in eunuchs being forbidden, no one shall venture on this unpleasant and unprofitable proceeding.

102. In both life and death for, as Tavernier (1.91) noted, a eunuch with command over two thousand men guarded the tomb of Arjumand Banu Begam. See also Manucci 1.176.

103. Finch in Foster, *Early Travels*, p. 163.

104. Manucci 2.74, 309, 328; Bernier, p. 374; Monserrate, p. 79.

105. Pelsaert, p. 66; Manucci 2.326–27.

106. Peslaert, p. 65. The good will of the male principal was exceedingly important for the eunuch, and he went out of his way to curry favor with his employer. See Manucci 1.277; 2.31, 50–51, 177.

107. Manucci 1.212.

108. Pelsaert, p. 66.

109. Terry, p. 89.

110. Bernier, p. 131.

111. Roe 1.215.

112. The two stories differ somewhat. Roe (1.215) said that her head and both arms were exposed to the sun and that the eunuch was condemned to the elephants, while Terry (p. 387) said that only her head was above ground and that the eunuch was "cut all into pieces."

113. Dow 3.xix–xx.

114. Said van den Broecke (p. 51), e.g.: "Shaikh Qasim put to death all his mahel or women, so as not to be hampered by them (in his fight) or prevent their falling into the hands of his enemy."

115. Manucci 1.144; 2.175–77; see also Mundy (2.202–3): "[The] Great Mogolls or kings daughters are never suffered to marrie (as I am informed), being an auntient Custom."

116. Bernier, p. 12.

117. *Tuzuk* 1.81. Since Parviz was already a contender for the throne, however, no new threat to Jahangir was posed by this marriage.

118. *Tuzuk* 2.91.

119. Manucci 2.175–77. Aurangzeb was quite open to marriage for princesses, and Bernier (pp. 126–27) preserved a story of a daughter of Dara Shikoh, whom the emperor tried to marry to his third son and intended successor, Sultan Akbar. The princess refused, however, making known the "utmost repugnance to the marriage" and declaring that she would rather "die by her own hand . . . than be united to the son of him who murdered her father."

120. Tavernier 1.313.

121. Blochmann, *Ain-i Akbari* 1.45.

122. Terry, p. 406.

123. Pelsaert, p. 66.

124. Tavernier 1.300.

125. As Tavernier noted (1.313), the custom was that the firstborn (except the son of a slave) succeeded to the throne, so "when the Princesses in the imperial harem become aware that there is one among them with child, they immediately use all conceivable methods to cause a miscarriage." He reported further that when he was in Patna in 1666 Shayista Khan's surgeon told him that Shayista Khan's wife had "in one month . . . caused miscarriages to eight women of his harem, as she would not permit any children but her own to survive." Again, note the reverse in Gulbadan (pp. 112–13), who described a woman recently taken into Humayun's harem who was so desirous of giving him a son that she kept up the fraud of a pregnancy for over eleven months.

126. Terry, p. 387.

127. Terry, p. 405.

128. Said Manucci (2.329): "Thus the women, being shut up with this closeness and

constantly watched, and having neither liberty nor occupation, think of nothing but adorning themselves, and their minds dwell on nothing but malice and lewdness. Confession of this was made to me once by one of these ladies herself."

129. Pelsaert, p. 66.

130. Pelsaert, p. 68.

131. Terry, p. 284. Note the often-illustrated Punjabi folk tale of Sohni and Mahinval, lovers of different castes, who had to meet at night in secret. When brothers of the high-born Sohni discovered her liaison, they substituted an unbaked pot of clay for the baked one she had been using to cross the river, causing her thus to drown.

132. Tavernier 1.300. Manucci (1.210) preserved stories of Jahanara's many lovers, one of whom was her music teacher, "the son of the chief dancer in her employ." He was brought into the harem when he was very young and given the title "Born in the House"—like an adoptive son of the women there. "Under the cover of this title these princesses and many great ladies gratify their desires." Another story in Manucci (1.209) told of a lover of Jahanara who had to jump into a stove when he heard Shah Jahan coming. The emperor, however, "caused it to be lighted, and thus secured his death." An alternate version of this story can be found in Bernier (pp. 12–13) in which the unfortunate lover had no place to hide except "in the capacious cauldron used for the baths." Sensing its new contents Shah Jahan suggested that Jahanara heat water and take a bath and did not himself "retire until they [the eunuchs] gave him to understand that his wretched victim was no more."

133. Bernier, pp. 132–33.

134. Said Manucci (1.212): "[the] wife of Jafar Khan, being mistress of Shahjahan, moves about with the same dignity" as other women of rank in the *mahal*. And again (Manucci 1.186): "[the] chief of these women [whom Shah Jahan had intrigues with], one that he thought a great deal of, was the wife of Jafarcan (Jafar Khan), and from the love he bore her he wished to take her husband's life." In general (Manucci 2.16), Aurangzeb accused his father "of being a corrupter of others' wives."

135. Terry, p. 383.

136. Terry, p. 406.

137. *Sribhanucandraganicarita* 4.221–40; Desai in *Sribhanucandraganicarita* (pp. 52–53): "O Lord! your form is stately enough to make you a king. You have youth hotly in your veins. Your age is meant for the soft pleasure of contact with the body of red-blooded damsels. Why, then, do you waste it upon the desert of severe austerities?"

138. We cannot discount either the possibility that these boys might simply have been court or harem gofers, around to perform the odd task or errand too menial for someone else.

139. Tavernier 1.275. See *Shah Jahan Nama*, pp. 309–10.

140. Tavernier 1.295.

141. Said Mundy (2.203), i.e.: "This Shaw Jehan [Shah Jahan], amonge the rest, hath one named Chiminy Beagum, a verie beautifull Creature by report, with whome (it was openly bruited and talked of in Agra) hee committed incest, being verie familiar with him many tymes in boyes apparrell, in great favour and as great meanes allowed her."

142. Bernier, pp. 11.

143. Manucci 1.208–9.

144. Coryat in Foster *Early Travels*, pp. 278–79.

145. Manucci 2.328.

146. Gascoigne, p. 162.

147. See *Ain-i Akbari* 1.47.

148. Said Manucci (2.328): "What forces the eunuchs to such strict measures is the

continual fear in which they exist that some young man in disguise might enter in female dress."

149. E.g., Manucci 1.192.

150. *Tuzuk* 1.351.

151. *Sribhanucandraganicarita* 4.87–92, and Desai in *Sribhanucandraganicarita*, p. 41.

152. See Misra, pp. 90–91.

153. Manucci 2.328.

154. Purchas, as reported by Foster in Roe 2.500n–501n. Purchas went on to say that the eunuch once put a thinner cloth over Steele's head purposely so that he might actually see the women he passed by, "there being of them some hundreds."

155. *Tuzuk* 2.278–79; H. Beveridge in *Tuzuk* 2.279n.

156. Manucci 1.295.

157. Bernier, pp. 404–5.

158. Manucci 2.319, 351.

159. *Tuzuk* 2.53. Jahangir said: "Nur-Jahan Begam had been ill for some time, and the physicians who had the good fortune to be chosen to attend on her, Musalmans and Hindus, perceived no gain from all the medicines they gave her, and confessed their helplessness in treating her."

160. *Tuzuk* 2.66.

161. Manucci 2.328–29. Said Bernier (p. 267):

> I have sometimes gone into it [the *zanana*] . . . [as] in the case of a great lady so extremely ill that she could not be moved to the outward gate, according to the customs observed upon similar occasions; but a *Kachemire* shawl covered my head, hanging like a large scarf down to my feet, and an eunuch led me by the hand, as if I had been a blind man.

162. Tavernier 1.241.

163. Tavernier 1.242.

164. Tavernier 1.242.

165. Manucci 2.329; see also 2.328, 331.

166. Tavernier 1.279. See Bernier, p. 90.

167. *Tuzuk* 1.110.

168. *Tuzuk* 1.241.

169. *Tuzuk* 1.129, 130, 361, 390.

170. *Tuzuk* 1.131.

171. Roe 1.247.

172. E.g., Roe 2.324.

173. A. S. Beveridge in Gulbadan, pp. 70–71; *Tabakat-i Akbari* E&D 5.457. 465. Manucci (2.69), however, said that "although the princesses and ladies start last, they always arrive the first, having taken some other shorter route. Ordinarily the women start after the baggage and move quickly."

174. See A. S. Beveridge in Gulbadan, p. 20.

175. A. S. Beveridge in Gulbadan, p. 95n.

176. Bernier, p. 361.

177. *Ain-i Akbari* 1.47.

178. "On account of the crowding of camp-followers, and the number of the troops themselves, it would take a soldier days to find his tent" (*Ain-i Akbari* 1.49).

179. *Ain-i Akbari* 1.49–50.

180. See Roe 2.324–26.

181. For another description of the modes of travel, see Misra, pp. 105–8.

182. Said Terry (pp. 143–44): "The men of the inferior sort go all on foot, their

women that cannot so travel ride on little oxen, inured to carry burdens, or on asses, which carry their little children with them; the women like the men astride."

183. Tavernier 1.37–38; Bernier, p. 372.

184. Manucci 1.212.

185. Bernier, p. 372.

186. Bernier (pp. 372–73) gave an excellent and very elaborate description of one of the processions of Raushanara and her many attendants saying of the women's section of the entourage: "There is something very impressive of state and royalty in the march of these sixty or more elephants; in their solemn and, as it were, measured steps; in the splendour of the *Mikdembers*, and the brilliant and innumerable followers in attendance."

187. Manucci 1.212.

188. Bernier, p. 373.

189. Bernier, p. 372. Abul Fazl (*Ain-i Akbari* 1.123–39) spent some time describing this "wonderful animal" (1.123) and, although he did not say how many elephants Akbar had in all his stables, the emperor did keep one hundred and one for his own use (1.137). Tavernier noted that "the Great Mogul keeps 3,000 or 4,000 elephants" with about five hundred reserved for household usage (1.223–24). Roe noted (2.321) of one trip that Jahangir had fifty elephants in use for his women. See also Manucci 2.340.

190. Roe 2.321, 324. Said Terry (p. 405), the *haudas* were "pretty receptacles, surrounded with curtains, which stand up like low and little turrets upon their [the elephants'] backs." See also Manucci 2.66–67, 330–31.

191. *Tuzuk* 2.79.

192. Monserrate, p. 79. See also Bernier, p. 372.

193. Terry, pp. 144–45.

194. Terry, p. 404. Della Valle (1.44) described these as "close Coaches."

195. Roe 2.324; see also Roe 1.118–19.

196. A. S. Beveridge in Gulbadan, p. 45.

197. A. S. Beveridge in Gulbadan, p. 20; Gulbadan, p. 169. Della Valle 1.44.

198. Gulbadan, p. 169.

199. Terry, p. 405.

200. Tavernier 1.117.

201. Roe 2.274.

202. *Tuzuk* 1.401.

203. A. S. Beveridge in Gulbadan, p. 20; Gulbadan, p. 100.

204. *Tuzuk* 2.123.

205. Gascoigne, pp. 160–61.

206. Note the complaint by Bega Begam to Humayun in Gulbadan (p. 130):

> She began a complaint, and said to him: "For several days now you have been paying visits in this garden, and on no one day have you been to our house. Thorns have not been planted in the way to it. We hope you will deign to visit our quarters also, and to have a party and a sociable gathering there, too. How long will you think it right to show all these disfavours to us helpless ones? We too have hearts. Three times you have honoured other places by visits, and you have run day and night into one in amusement and conversation."

207. Shujauddins, p. 97.

208. *Ain-i Akbari* 1.59. See Manucci 2.309–10.

209. Pelsaert, pp. 64–65.

210. As reported in Misra, p. 93.

211. Pelsaert, p. 66. The best of all the foods apparently went into the *mahal*, and

Jahangir told (*Tuzuk* 1.435), e.g., of receiving a present of 1,500 melons and of sending a full 500 into the harem.

212. Pelsaert, p. 67.

213. Pelsaert, pp. 67–68. See Roe (1.241–42) for a description of a meal he had at the house of Mir Jamaluddin Husain.

214. *Ain-i Akbari* 1.59–64.

215. Pelsaert, p. 68.

216. For a full description, see Findly, "Maryamuzzamani," pp. 227–38. See also Misra, pp. 60–64.

217. *Tuzuk* 1.46; Manucci 2.319. See *Shah Jahan Nama*, pp. 447–48.

218. *Tuzuk* 1.146, 239; Manucci 1.206; see Foster, *Early Travels*, p. 101n; Gulbadan, pp. 94–95.

219. *Tuzuk* 1.401.

220. *Tuzuk* 2.80.

221. *Tuzuk* 2.228. The rule of escheat, by which all lands and monies reverted to the ruler upon the death of the noble and were then distributed around as the ruler saw fit, was the norm during Mughal times in spite of the following pronouncement at the beginning of Jahangir's reign (*Tuzuk* 1.8): "In my dominions if anyone, whether unbeliever or Musalman, should die, his property and effects should be left for his heirs, and no one should interfere with them."

222. Pelsaert, p. 4.

223. Said Tavernier (1.310):

> This wife of Jafar Khan is the most magnificent and the most liberal woman in the whole of India, and she alone expends more than all the wives and daughters of the Emperor put together; it is on this account that her family is always in debt, although her husband is practically master of the whole Empire.

224. Khafi Khan as paraphrased in the Shujauddins, p. 133.

225. See *Tuzuk* 1.397.

226. *Tuzuk* 2.237.

227. *Tuzuk* 2.260.

228. See Tavernier 1.301–2.

229. See Misra, pp. 116–18. Note the large ruby Maryam Makani gave to Akbar on the occasion of the birth of Salim (*Tuzuk* 1.409) and the "large store of wealth" she left behind with instructions that it be distributed "amongst her sons and grandsons" (Du Jarric, p. 188).

230. Tavernier 1.240.

231. See Latif (*Lahore*, pp. 131–32) on the mosque of Maryamuzzamani.

232. Pelsaert, p. 5.

233. Manucci 1.212–13.

234. A. S. Beveridge in Gulbadan, pp. 76–77; Manucci 1.209; Misra, pp. 109–10.

235. See Findly, "Maryamuzzamani," pp. 232–34.

236. Pelsaert, p. 4.

237. Manucci 2.350–51.

238. See Misra, p. 61.

239. Gulbadan, pp. 89, 111.

240. Misra, pp. 60–62; see *Tuzuk* 1.46.

241. *Tuzuk* 1.380.

242. *Tuzuk* 2.235–36.

243. He noted, e.g., an especially lavish feast and entertainment held in Nur Jahan's *jagir* of Ramsar. *Tuzuk* 1.342.

244. Pelsaert, p. 66. See *Shah Jahan Nama*, pp. 309–10.

245. Finch in Foster, *Early Travels*, p. 162. The extravagance of Finch's statement is offset by Manucci's observation (2.317, 318) that the princesses changed their clothes at least once a day, if not several times a day, and that the used garments were not worn again but given away to their servants.

246. Pelsaert, p. 64.

247. Della Valle 1.44–45, 46.

248. Terry, p. 204.

249. On clothes, see Ghurye. See Manucci 2.318; Misra, pp. 119–28. On muslin, see Tavernier 1.46–47.

250. Manucci 2.317. "This mirror they use to look at themselves, an act of which they are very fond, at any and every moment." On jewelry, see Manucci 2.316–17.

251. Terry, p. 204. Said Della Valle (I.45):

> Those that have them adorn themselves with many gold-works, and jewels, especially their ears with pendants sufficiently enormous, wearing a circle of Gold or Silver at their ears, the diametre whereof is often times above half a span and 'tis made of a plate two fingers broad, and engraven with sundry works, which is a very disproportionate thing.

And De Laet (p. 81): "Some pierce one of the nostrils in order to be able to wear a gold nose-ring ornamented with gems when they so desire." See also Terry in Foster, *Early Travels*, p. 309.

252. Manucci 2.317.

253. Manucci 2.318.

254. Terry, p. 204.

255. Manucci 2.318.

256. See Altekar, pp. 300–301.

257. See Altekar, pp. 300–301.

258. Manucci 2.316, 318.

259. Said Fitch (in Foster, *Early Travels*, p. 22): "They are marked with a great spot of red in their foreheads and a stroke of red up to the crowne."

260. A. S. Beveridge in Gulbadan, p. 79. See Manucci 2.323.

261. See Misra, p. 89, and on the whole subject, pp. 87–92.

262. *Sribhanucandraganicarita* 4.87–92, and Desai, in *Sribhanucandraganicarita*, p. 41.

263. Copies of this manuscript can be found in the Bombay University Library and at the Deutsche Staatsbibliothek in Berlin.

264. *Ain-i Akbari* 1.309; Misra pp. 88–89.

265. See Misra, p. 91.

266. See A. S. Beveridge in Gulbadan, p. 58.

267. *Ain-i Akbari* 1.166. In later times Aurangzeb would move to ban music and to have all instruments broken if they were heard being played but, as Manucci (2.6) noted, in "spite of this, the nobles did not cease to listen to songs in secret."

268. Gulbadan, p. 95.

269. Gulbadan, p. 178.

270. Finch in Foster, *Early Travels*, p. 183. Said Withington (in Foster, *Early Travels*, pp. 208–9): "At our beeing here, the women of the towne came into our caravan and daunced, everye man givinge them somethinge; and afterwards they asked openly: Whoe wants a bedfellow? Soe shamelesse they were."

271. Manucci 1.211.

272. A. K. Das, *Mughal Painting*, p. 46; Misra, p. 94n.

273. Manucci 2.308, 313–14.

274. Roe 1.119, 171, 254; 2.386; 488, Foster in Roe 2.352n.

275. E.g., Finch in Foster, *Early Travels*, pp. 163–64.

276. She was buried in the building in the Mandakar Garden, which she herself had made. *Tuzuk* 1.232–33.

277. See Chapter 9.

278. Sarkar 1.70; 3.62.

279. See Misra, pp. 110–12.

280. Manucci 1.213.

281. *Tuzuk* 1.106

282. *Tuzuk* 2.64.

283. *Tuzuk* 2.75–76.

284. *Tuzuk* 2.192.

285. *Tuzuk* 2.110–11.

286. Pelsaert, p. 65 and 65n.

287. *Ain-i Akbari* 1.72–78.

288. *Ain-i Akbari* 1.78.

289. *Ain-i Akbari* 1.80–87.

290. A popular fragrance in Akbar's time. *Ain-i Akbari* 1.79, 80. Manucci (2.316) noted that women in the harem were "fond of, scents and flowers, [and that] they disburse a great deal for essences of many kinds, for rosewater, and for scented oils distilled from different flowers."

291. *Tuzuk* 1.270–71; 2.115.

292. Manucci 1.158–59.

293. Manucci (2.4–5), e.g., noted that so "accustomed are the Mahomedans to intoxication that the poor people, who have not enough funds to procure spirits, invented another beverage, called in the language of the country *bang* (*bhang*)." The orthodox Aurangzeb then, he continued, banned the intoxicant when he took office and not "a day passed that on rising in the morning we did not hear the breaking by blows and strokes of the pots and pans in which these beverages are prepared."

294. See Bernier (pp. 39–40) for a description of the effects of opium on Rajput warriors.

295. *Tuzuk* 1.19, 55–56.

296. Pelsaert, p. 65.

297. Manucci 1.211. He also reported on (2.99–100) a wife of Aurangzeb from Georgia who loved drinking so much that the emperor would find her "all in disorder, her hair flying loose and her head full of drink," on (2.139–40) Jahanara's gift of wine to the wives of the *qazi* and other learned men when they visited her, and on (2.328) the unsuccessful attempts of the eunuchs to "search everything with great care to stop the entry of *bhang*, wine, *ophion* (opium), nutmegs (*noix muscades*), or other drugs which could intoxicate" into the harem.

298. Note here Agre, pp. 263–71.

299. A. S. Beveridge in Gulbadan, p. 40. Said Roe (1.106): "His [Jahangir's] weomen watch within, and guard him with manly weapons."

300. Gulbadan, pp. 120–21.

301. Gulbadan, pp. 170, 197.

302. *Tuzuk* 1.348.

303. *Tuzuk* 1.375.

304. See Findly, "Vow of Non-Violence," pp. 245–56.

305. *Tuzuk* 2.104–5.

306. *Tuzuk* 1.363; 402–3; 2.40, 105, 133.
307. *Tuzuk* 2.105.
308. *Muntakhab ul-Lubab* as paraphrased in the Shujauddins, p. 94.
309. Gulbadan, pp. 120–21.
310. See Misra, p. 85.
311. Manucci 2.318.
312. As quoted by Blochmann in *Ain-i Akbari* 1.217.
313. Shujauddins, p. 97.
314. A. S. Beveridge in Gulbadan, p. 75.
315. Note, however, Roe's 1616 comment (2.293) about Khusrau's women in the event that the prince was murdered by the junta: "If hee dye ther will 100 of his kindred burne for him in memorye of the kinges bloudines to his woorthyest sonne."
316. Withington in Foster, *Early Travels*, p. 219.
317. Badauni as quoted by Blochmann in *Ain-i Akbari* 1.215, 216.
318. Hawkins in Foster, *Early Travels*, p. 119.
319. Withington in Foster, *Early Travels*, p. 219.
320. Terry, pp. 303–7.
321. Della Valle 1.83–85.
322. Mundy 2.34–36 (with illustration), 179.
323. Bernier's account (pp. 306–14) included many detailed examples of the *sati* and of his own involvement in several cases:

> But not to tire you with the history of every woman whom I have seen perish on the funeral pile, I shall advert to only two or three of those shocking spectacles at which I have been present; and first I shall give you some details concerning a female to whom I was sent for the purpose of diverting her from persevering in her dreadful intention.

324. Tavernier 1.175.
325. *Tuzuk* 1.150.
326. *Tuzuk* 1.358; see also *Manusmriti* 9.45, 46.
327. *Tuzuk* 2.181.
328. A. S. Beveridge in Gulbadan, pp. 68–69.
329. Or, alternately, as A.K. Das (*Mughal Painting*, p. 000) suggests:

> The picture of Jahangir's celebration of the "holi" festival in the company of Nur Jahan and the members of the *zanana* . . . may depict the celebration of the "feast of Basant-bari" described in the *Tuzuk*. It was the day when a valuable pearl and a ruby lost by Nur Jahan while hunting were found, the news of the defeat of Suraj Mal was received, and the emperor's lunar weighing was held.

330. *Tuzuk* 2.70–71. Although it remains a possibility, there is no clear evidence that the sorceress was trying to get back at the *shaikh* for some reason.
331. *Tuzuk* 2.235.
332. Misra, p. 83.
333. See Pelsaert's (pp. 73–75) description of the Ramadan *id* and of the commemoration of the Ali family. See also Misra, p. 13.
334. Lall, p. 74. 335. *Ain-i Akbari* 3.317–21.
336. A. S. Beveridge in Gulbadan, pp. 76–77. See also Gulbadan, p. 111.
337. *Ikbal-nama-i Jahangiri* E&D 6.405E; see also *Tatimma-i Wakiat-i Jahangiri* E&D 6.399.
338. *Ain-i Akbari* 3.282–84; see also Misra, pp. 109–10.
339. See A. S. Beveridge in Gulbadan, p. 49.
340. Du Jarric, p. 60.

341. A. S. Beveridge in Gulbadan, pp. 69–75; *Tabakat-i Akbari* E&D 5.391.
342. Roe 2.418.
343. Tavernier 1.171.
344. *Tuzuk* 1.110; see also Jahangir's visit to Akbar's tomb, *Tuzuk* 2.101.
345. *Tuzuk* 2.109.
346. See the list of Hindu pilgrimage sites in *Ain-i Akbari* 3.303–7.
347. Pelsaert, p. 72.
348. E.g., *Tuzuk* 1.418.
349. Roe 2.321.
350. As reported in Misra, pp. 32–33. See also Blochmann, *Ain-i Akbari* 1.345, and Gascoigne, p. 165.
351. A. S. Beveridge in Gulbadan, p. 38.
352. Prasad, pp. 50–51. A. S. Beveridge in Gulbadan (p. 76) notes her author's involvement in this affair as well.
353. A. S. Beveridge in Gulbadan, pp. 47–48.
354. *Tuzuk* 2.205.
355. Roe 2.293.
356. Roe 2.299–300.
357. See Misra, pp. 68–71.
358. See Misra, pp. 149–51.
359. *Ikbal-nama-i Jahangiri* E&D 6.405.
360. See Misra, pp. 154, 67, and A. S. Beveridge in Gulbadan, pp. 237–41.
361. Tirmizi, pp. 124–25. See Misra, pp. 155, 67.
362. Tirmizi, pp. 103, 111, 117, 128, 129, 133, 134, 135. See Misra, pp. 152, see also p. 67.
363. See Misra, pp. 153, see also p. 67.
364. Misra, p. 67.
365. *Ikbal-nama-i Jahangiri* E&D 6.405.
366. Finch in Foster, *Early Travels*, p. 166. It was Foster who, in his note (p. 166n), interpreted Finch as saying Anarkali was Daniyal's mother, a story for which there "is no corroboration." Jahangir noted at the beginning of the *Tuzuk* (1.34) that Daniyal "was born to one of the [Akbar's] concubines." 367. Terry, p. 408.
368. Finch in Foster, *Early Travels*, p. 166.
369. Latif, *Lahore*, p. 186. Later tradition said that Anarkali was Akbar's lover not his wife, as Finch would have it, and it may well be that (whether the legend is true or not) a relationship between Salim and one of his "mothers" was simply intolerable for the collective memory of the time. If Finch's version is true, however, it would give a good reason for the vehemence of Akbar's response. Robert Skelton has further suggested that Nadira Begam (also known as Anarkali) supported Salim during his Allahabad revolt and that, perhaps because of this, there were political reasons as well for Akbar's displeasure with her. She may also have been a painter of miniatures.
370. Finch in Foster, *Early Travels*, p. 166.
371. Finch in Foster, *Early Travels*, p. 166.
372. Latif, *Lahore*, pp. 186–87; see Shujauddins, pp. 95–96.
373. The list is based in part on the tabulations of the Shujauddins (pp. 93–98), Prasad (pp. 26–29), and Blochmann in *Ain-i Akbari* 1.323.
374. *Tuzuk* 1.56; *Tabakat-i Akbari* E&D 5.447. See Moreland (pp. 245–46) for a discussion of this dowry. If Man Bai and Raja Man Singh (sister and brother) were, as Jahangir stated (*Tuzuk* 1.15–16), both children of Raja Bhagwan Das and had as their grandfather Raja Bihari Mal, then Man Bai, Jahangir's first wife, was also his first cousin,

for Jahangir was a grandchild of Raja Bihari Mal as well, through his mother Maryamuzzamani, sister of Raja Bhagwan Das.

375. *Tuzuk* 1.15.
376. *Tabakat-i Akbari* E&D 5.456; *Tuzuk* 1.15; *Firishtah* 2.161.
377. *Tuzuk* 1.56.
378. *Tuzuk* 1.15–55.
379. *Tuzuk* 1.55–56.
380. *Tuzuk* 1.56.
381. Finch in Foster, *Early Travels*, p. 178. The whole reference (pp. 178–79) is: "[I saw] a sumptuous tombe for this kings first wife, mother to Sultan Cusseroon and sister to Raja Manisengo, who upon the newes of her sonnes revolt poysoned her selfe."
382. See van den Broecke, p. 54; Pelsaert, p. 71; Mundy 2.100.
383. *Tuzuk* 1.19; see 1.128; Blochmann, *Ain-i Akbari* 1.323.
384. H. Beveridge in *Tuzuk* 2.84n.
385. *Tuzuk* 1.19–20.
386. Shujauddins, p. 95.
387. *Tuzuk* 2.84. See *Shah Jahan Nama*, p. 8.
388. *Tuzuk* 1.18–19; H. Beveridge in *Tuzuk* 1.19n; Haig in Badauni 3.327n; Hawkins in Foster, *Early Travels*, p. 101; Blochmann, *Ain-i Akbari* 1.323, 533n.
389. Shujauddins, pp. 95–96.
390. *Tuzuk* 1.325–26; Blochmann, *Ain-i Akbari* 1.533n.
391. *Tuzuk* 1.326.
392. Blochmann, *Ain-i Akbari* 1.533n; Shujauddins, p. 96.
393. H. Beveridge in *Tuzuk* 2.86n, 159n; Blochmann, *Ain-i Akbari* 1.401, 533n.
394. *Tuzuk* 2.86. Of her brother Jahangir said: "He was not devoid of sluggishness and self-indulgence, and was a young man fond of pleasure. He wished to pass his whole life at ease, and was devoted to Hindu music and did not understand it badly. He was a man void of evil."
395. *Tuzuk* 2.159; H. Beveridge in *Tuzuk* 2.159n. Prasad (p. 169) says the title was given to Nur Jahan in 1613 when Salima Sultan Begam died.
396. H. Beveridge in *Tuzuk* 2.86n.
397. *Tuzuk* 2.160.
398. Hawkins in Foster, *Early Travels*, p. 101.
399. *Tuzuk* 1.19; H. Beveridge in *Tuzuk* 1.19n; Blochmann, *Ain-i Akbari* 1.323.
400. *Tuzuk* 1.19; H. Beveridge in *Tuzuk* 1.19n.
401. On Ali Rai, see *Tuzuk* 2.288; Blochmann, *Ain-i Akbari* 1.323.
402. H. Beveridge in *Tuzuk* 2.288n.
403. Blochmann, *Ain-i Akbari* 1.686. The Chak family were the former rulers of Kashmir.
404. Blochmann, *Ain-i Akbari* 1.686.
405. Blochmann, *Ain-i Akbari* 1.533n.
406. Blochmann, *Ain-i Akbari* 1.533n.
407. Blochmann, *Ain-i Akbari* 1.533n.
408. Blochmann, *Ain-i Akbari* 1.323; *Firishta* 2.160.
409. H. Beveridge suggests that this was Salim's third marriage. Blochmann, *Ain-i Akbari* 1.533n.
410. *Tuzuk* 1.144, 145; Blochmann, *Ain-i Akbari* 1.323. That this marriage was in 1608 supports the argument that Jahangir did not know Nur Jahan in 1607 or earlier, but only met her in 1611. Charismatic as she apparently was, if he had met Nur Jahan in 1607 or before, not only would he have married her immediately but he also would not have married anyone else afterward.

411. *Tuzuk* 1.160; Blochmann, *Ain-i Akbari* 1.533n

412. Said Roe (2.293): "The king giues fayre woordes, protesteth no intent of ill toward the Prince, and promiseth his deliuery and sendes Narmahall to appease these enraged ladyes, but they Curse, threaten, and refuse to see her."

413. See the Shujauddins, pp. 94–95.

414. Della Valle 1.54.

Chapter 6. The English Embassy

1. Moreland, pp. 132–33.

2. Badauni (2.203) as quoted in Blochmann, *Ain-i Akbari* 1.181. See also Mujeeb, pp. 240, 240n, and Simkin, pp. 174–75.

3. See Fitch in Foster, *Early Travels*, p.35.

4. Roe 1.228; see also *Tuzuk* 1.417.

5. Terry, p. 130

6. Roe 2.482; Terry, pp. 117–18.

7. Hawkins in Foster, *Early Travels*, p. 62; Mundy 2.29; *Tuzuk* 1.415–17.

8. Hawkins in Foster, *Early Travels*, p. 63.

9. Roe 1.112; Copland in Best, p. 208.

10. Pelsaert, p. 41.

11. Mundy 2.28n.

12. See Findly, "Maryamuzzamani," pp. 227–38.

13. *English Factories* (1618–21), p. 81; Roe 2.440, 467. See also Simkin, pp. 176–77, 179, 181; Mukerjee, p. 102.

14. Badauni (2.203) as quoted in Blochmann, *Ain-i Akbari* 1.181.

15. Withington in Foster, *Early Travels*, p. 203; see letter of Thomas Aldworthe and William Biddulph to the East India Company, August 19, 1614, *East India Company Letters* 2 (1613–15).96. Note that the names Aldworth/Aldworthe, Keridge/Kerridge, Smith/Smythe, etc., are here spelled as they appear in each text and so will differ.

16. Danvers suggests that the capture of the Queen Mother's ship marked Portuguese "displeasure at the favourable reception accorded to the English," a view accepted on strong circumstantial evidence by most historians. *East India Company Letters* 2 (1613–15).xvii. See Foster in Roe 1.x.

17. Withington in Foster, *Early Travels*, p. 203.

18. Foster, *Early Travels*, pp. 191–92.

19. *East India Company Letters* 2 (1613–15).96. In a letter of September 20, 1614, Thomas Keridge noted "The king here hath caused the Jesuits' churches to be shut up, debarring them from public exercise of their religion and hath taken their allowances from them, yet their goods untouched, the merchants and their goods embargoed, the ports shut up and no passage by sea." *East India Company Letters* 2 (1613–15).107. In a letter of February 25, 1615, Thomas Elkington noted that:

> the Great Mogul had debarred the Portingall from trade in any of his dominions, by reason of a ship they took at the bar's foot of Surrat of very great value pertaining to his subjects, as also had besieged a town possessed by them some twelve leagues to the southward of Surrat called Damon, which siege as yet continueth, though with little hope of prevailing.

East India Company Letters 3 (1615).4.

20. Letter of William Edwards to the East India Company, received December 2, 1615, *East India Company Letters* 2 (1613–15).149.

21. *East India Company Letters* 2 (1613–15).150.

22. Letter of Thomas Mitford to Sir Thomas Smith, Governor, and the Committees of the East India Company, December 26, 1614, *East India Company Letters* 2 (1613–15).236. The articles of the treaty of peace that concluded this war are reproduced in Tirmizi, pp. 97–98.

23. Letter of John Sandcrofte to the East India Company, November 29, 1614, *East India Company Letters* 2 (1613–15).213.

24. *East India Company Letters* 2 (1613–15).229.

25. Foster in *East India Company Letters* 3 (1615).xxxvii–xxxviii.

26. See Maclagan, pp. 79–80.

27. *Tuzuk* 1.274.

28. Roe 2.512.

29. Moreland and Geyl in Pelsaert, p. x.

30. Pelsaert, pp. 21–23.

31. Moreland and Geyl in Pelsaert, p. x; Foster in *English Factories* (1618–1621), p. xxxvi; Danvers in *East India Company Letters* 1 (1602–13).xxii.

32. Moreland and Geyl in Pelsaert, pp. x–xi; Foster in *English Factories* (1618–1621), pp. xxxvi–xxxviii. This trade remained hampered, however, by the imports of the English and Portuguese. See Pelsaert, p. 28; Bernier, pp. 292–93.

33. Despite comments like Roe's (2.490–91), which foreshadow attitudes of the later British Empire: "Pray for vs, that God wilbe Pleased to keepe vs, that among heathens wee may bee as light in darknes."

34. Roe 1.120; see Roe 2.286–87, 467.

35. Foster, *Early Travels*, p. 188.

36. Note William Edwards' comment in a letter of February 26, 1615: "One principal cause of this hopeful entrance [at court] and more than ordinary entertainment hath been a late fight between the Portingalls and our ships" (*East India Company Letters* 3[1615].15).

37. *East India Company Letters* 2 (1613–15).236.

38. Foster in Roe 1.xlv.

39. Danvers in *East India Company Letters* 1 (1602–13).xxii–xxviii; Foster in Best, pp. ix–x.

40. Danvers in *East India Company Letters* 1 (1602–13).xxviii–xxx.

41. Hawkins in Foster, *Early Travels*, p. 81. Some of the other Englishmen who passed through the court at this time also knew one of the locally spoken languages. Thomas Coryat, for example, knew Persian and preserved for us a copy of the speech he gave Jahangir in that language, as well as his translation of it. Coryat in Foster, *Early Travels*, pp. 263–65.

42. Hawkins in Foster, *Early Travels*, p. 83.

43. Hawkins in Foster, *Early Travels*, p. 95.

44. Foster in Best, p. xi.

45. Foster, *Early Travels*, p. 188.

46. Foster, *Early Travels*, p. 188; Foster in Best, pp. xxii–xxxiv; Best, pp. 142–43, 233.

47. Foster in Roe 1.iii. Best had listed earlier (pp. 31–33) the terms he had agreed upon with "the Governor of Amadevar, the Governor of Suratt, and 4 principall merchants," but did not note whether these are the terms agreed to by Jahangir.

48. Best, pp. 34, 114; Roe 1.66; Foster, *Early Travels*, pp. 189–90; letters of Thomas Keridge to Thomas Aldworth, September 7, 1613, and of Ralph Willsonn to the East India Company, September 11, 1613, *East India Company Letters* 1 (1602–13).282–86, 300.

49. M. Brown, p. 28.
50. M. Brown, p. 29.
51. Best, p. 32.
52. *East India Company Letters* 1 (1602–13).307; Foster in *East India Company Letters* 3 (1615).xxxix.
53. Foster in Roe 1.iv.
54. Terry, p. 54.
55. Foster in Roe 1.iv–vi.
56. Foster in Roe 1.vi.
57. Foster in Roe 1.254n–255n.
58. Roe 1.254–56.
59. Roe 2.484.
60. Foster in Roe 1.255n.
61. Roe 1.119.
62. Roe 1.98; Foster in Roe 1.98n.
63. Foster, *Early Travels*, p. 192; Danvers, *East India Company Letters* 2 (1613–15).xix.
64. Roe 1.45.
65. Roe 1.47.
66. Roe 1.45.
67. Roe 1.98.
68. Roe 1.119. Roe, in fact, noted several times that Spain would not send an ambassador to India precisely because of the poor reception he would receive: "The King of Spayne would neuer send any Ambassadour hither, out of greatnes, knoweing they are not receiued with proportionable honour" (2.310); and Jahangir "hath often demanded an Ambassador from Spayne but could neuer obteyne it, for two reasons: first, because they would not giue Presentes vnwoorthy their kinges greatnes; Next, they knew his reception should not answere his qualety" (2.351).
69. Roe 2.351.
70. Roe 1.245.
71. As quoted in Foster in Roe 1.246n.
72. Roe 1.76–77.
73. Foster in Roe 1.xx.
74. Foster in Roe 1.xx–xxi; Roe 1.152–56.
75. Terry, p. 378; see p. 411.
76. Roe 2.547.
77. Letter of Roe to Shah Jahan, May 1, 1616, *East India Company Letters* 4 (1616).101.
78. Foster in Roe 1.xliv.
79. Roe 1.42.
80. Roe 1.61.
81. Roe 1.43–86.
82. Roe 1.90–93.
83. Roe 1.106.
84. Roe 1.109.
85. Roe 1.114–15.
86. Roe 1.118.
87. E.g., Roe 1.142, 145; 2.413, 415.
88. Roe 1.150.
89. Roe 2.392–93.

90. Roe 2.439, 453, 454.

91. Roe 2.451.

92. Roe 2.469.

93. Roe 2.479.

94. Foster in Roe 1.xlii.

95. E.g., Roe 1.111.

96. Moreland in Floris, p. xxv.

97. Roe 1.111.

98. Van den Broecke, pp. 33–35.

99. Hawkins in Foster, *Early Travels*, pp. 99, 101–3, 112.

100. Coryat in Foster, *Early Travels*, p. 246.

101. Roe 1.120.

102. Roe 1.252; see also 2.322.

103. Roe 1.228; Letter of Roe to the East India Company, January 25, 1616, *East India Company Letters* 4 (1616).13.

104. Moreland, pp. 186–89.

105. Pelsaert, p. 77.

106. Roe 2.310.

107. Roe 1.42.

108. Roe 1.xxix, xxxvi.

109. Roe 1.109; see also 1.165.

110. Roe 2.317.

111. Letter of Joseph Salbank to the East India Company, November 1616, *East India Company Letters* 4 (1616).234.

112. Danvers in *East India Company Letters* 3 (1615).xl, and in *East India Company Letters* 4 (1616).xxxi.

113. Roe 2.283.

114. Letter of Roe to East India Company, January 25, 1616, *East India Company Letters* 4 (1616).11.

115. In a September 17, 1619, letter from Surat to William Biddulph in Agra, Thomas Kerridge and Thomas Rastell noted: "Itt is rumorde heare thatt the Prince C[horoo]m is disgraced by his father; which were much to be desired, for so longe as the master is not our favorer, his servantes will little befrind us" (*English Factories* [1618–1621], p. 122).

116. Roe 1.188–89.

117. *English Factories* (1618–1621), p. 38.

118. Hawkins in Foster, *Early Travels*, p. 94.

119. See the letter of Edwards to the East India Company, February 26, 1615, and of Keridge, March 20, 1615, in *East India Company Letters* 3 (1615).14, 63.

120. Foster, *Early Travels*, p. 67.

121. Said Roe (1.138): "The Jesuite had much Poysoned Asaph Chan, in whom was the fault, and I resolued to startle him."

122. Roe 1.171.

123. Roe 1.127, 125.

124. Roe 1.171.

125. Roe (1.202) was fully aware of the difficult position he was in with regard to Asaf Khan. His demands were irremovably in the minister's hands, and to cross Asaf Khan would be to ruin any chance he had of finalizing the agreement. His only course was to remain neutral and not take any sides whatsoever, and to that end had to pledge

diplomatic troth to both Asaf Khan and Shah Jahan. "But," he said, "really I trusted neither."

126. Roe 2.435.

127. Roe 2.452.

128. Foster, *Early Travels*, p. 63.

129. Hawkins in Foster, *Early Travels*, p. 71.

130. Letter of Thomas Mitford to Sir Thomas Smith, Governor, and the East India Company, December 26, 1614, *East India Company Letters* 2 (1613–15).237.

131. See Hawkins in Foster, *Early Travels*, p. 75.

132. Best, pp. 27, 233; letter of Keridge at Agra to Thomas Aldworth and Council at Surat, September 7, 1613, *East India Company Letters* 1 (1602–13).278, 280, 284, 286; of Aldworthe to Keridge, October 22, 1614, *East India Company Letters* 2 (1613–15).138.

133. E.g., Roe 2.457.

134. Letter of Keridge at Agra to Thomas Aldworth and Council at Surat, September 7, 1613, *East India Company Letters* 1 (1602–13).284–85.

135. Letter of Roe to the factors at Surat, October 15, 1616, *East India Company Letters* 4 (1616).204.

136. Terry, p. 112.

137. Terry, p. 112; Floris, p. 115.

138. Terry, p. 112; Pelsaert, p. 7; see Bernier, p. 203, however.

139. Terry, p. 112.

140. Terry, p. 112.

141. Terry, p. 112.

142. Terry, pp. 373–74; see *Tuzuk* 1.314–16.

143. Terry, p. 109. See Roe 1.134; Fitch in Foster, *Early Travels*, p. 47.

144. Pelsaert, pp. 44–45.

145. Pelsaert, p. 45.

146. Pelsaert, p. 46; Blochmann, *Ain-i Akbari* 1.58.

147. Fitch in Foster, *Early Travels*, p. 34.

148. Fitch in Foster, *Early Travels*, p. 46.

149. Fitch in Foster, *Early Travels*, p. 46; letter of Aldworthe and Biddulph to the East India Company, August 19, 1614, *East India Company Letters* 2 (1613–15).100.

150. Pelsaert, p. 35.

151. Moreland and Geyl in Pelsaert, p. xi. See the list of spices and other commodoties (with prices) sold in Patna. Mundy 2.153–56.

152. Letter of Aldworthe and Biddulph to the East India Company, August 19, 1614, *East India Company Letters* 2 (1613–15).99.

153. Terry, p. 109; although see Roe 1.134.

154. Terry, p. 111.

155. Terry, p. 111.

156. Letter of Edwards to Sir Thomas Smith, Governor of the East India Company, December 26, 1614, *East India Company Letters* 2 (1613–15).246.

157. Roe 1.134; see Roe 2.346.

158. Roe 1.134; Terry, p. 111.

159. Pelsaert, p. 9.

160. Floris, pp. 115, 127, 137; Letter of Aldworthe and Biddulph to the East India Company, August 19, 1614, *East India Company Letters* 2 (1613–15).99; Terry, p. 105; Roe 2.345, 478.

161. Pelsaert, p. 13.

162. Pelsaert, pp. 10–11; Terry, pp. 107–8; letter of Francis Fettiplace to the East India Company, September 1 and November 26, 1616, *East India Company Letters* 4 (1616).241.

163. Pelsaert, p. 13.

164. Pelsaert, pp. 10–11.

165. Roe 1.227; Roe 2.273, 283; Roe to the East India Company, January 25, 1616, *East India Company Letters* 4 (1616).18.

166. Roe 2.336–37. The price of indigo is said to have gone down "by reason of the wars between the Portingals and the Moors." Letter of Aldworthe to the East India Company, December 27, 1614, *East India Company Letters* 2 (1613–1615).247.

167. Pelsaert, p. 30.

168. Letter of Richard Cocks to the Governor of the East India Company, November 30, 1613, *East India Company Letters* 1 (1602–13).317.

169. Roe 1.120.

170. Said Terry (p. 105): "Of that [cotton] wool they make divers sorts of callico, which had that name (as I suppose) from Calicute, not far from Goa, where that kind of cloth was first bought by Portuguese." See Best, p. 235.

171. Terry, pp. 108–9. Said Fitch (in Foster, *Early Travels*, p. 34): "They [the Indian ships] bring thither also much cotton yarne red coloured with a root . . . which will never lose his colour; it is very wel solde here, and very much of it commeth yerely to Pegu."

172. Temple in Mundy 2.362.

173. Letter of Roe to the East India Company, December 1, 1616, *East India Company Letters* 4 (1616).250.

174. Terry, p. 111.

175. Terry, p. 110.

176. Pelsaert, p. 8.

177. Moreland, pp. 167, 171–72, 273.

178. Roe 2.480.

179. Foster, *Early Travels*, p. 67n.

180. *Tuzuk* 1.338; Roe 1.66, 67, 112, 118–19; 2.324, 329, 347; Terry, pp. 367–68.

181. Best, p. 244; Terry, p. 368.

182. Best, pp. 235, 245; Terry, p. 368. Ultimately swords and knives did not fare well as presents being of "little estimation" among the Mughals. Roe 2.167, 165. Said Keridge: "Your sword-blades now brought hither are not such as are in request, neither in goodness or fashion. They desire not swords out of want, but because they cannot temper their metal as well as in Christendom" (letter to the East India Company, March 20, 1615, *East India Company Letters* 3 [1615].67).

183. Best, p. 244; Roe 1.93, 119, 159, 169, 172, 208; Terry, p. 188. Said Roe: "I think four or five handsome cases of that wine will be more welcome than the richest jewel in Cheapside" (letter to the East India Company, January 25, 1616, *East India Company Letters* 4 [1616].11).

184. Said Roe (2.498): "The King . . . reguardes no trade but what feedes his vnsatiable appetite after stones." Again: "Fair pearls, ballast rubies and emeralds of extraordinary great sizes surely would vend here to the King in infinite quantities" (letter of Francis Fettiplace to the East India Company, September 1 and November 26, 1616, *East India Company Letters* 4 [1616].243).

185. Roe 1.182; 2.288, 385, 388; Terry, p. 140.

186. Roe 1.147; 2.288, 387; letter of Edwards to the East India Company, received December 2, 1615, *East India Company Letters* 2 (1613–15).152; Bernier, p. 203.

187. Roe 2.288.

188. Foster in Roe 2.352n.

189. Terry, p. 202; Bernier, p. 203. The list of luxury items desired by Muqarrab Khan in 1614 included armor, swords, knives, satins, velvets, broadcloths, pictures (only on cloth, not on wood), leathers, mirrors, cabinets, dogs, and parchments. Compiled by Nicholas Downton, *East India Company Letters* 2 (1613–15).173–74.

190. Roe 1.143.

191. Roe 1.119; see 1.150, 171, 182.

192. Terry, p. 368; letters of Thomas Keridge to the East India Company, March 20, 1615, and Thomas Mitford to the East India Company, March 25, 1615, *East India Company Letters* 3 (1615).67, 88; Pelsaert, p. 26.

193. Roe 2.386–87.

194. Roe 2.478.

195. Terry, pp. 128, 129.

196. Letter of Edwards to Smith, December 26, 1614, *East India Company Letters* 2 (1613–15).246.

197. Letter of Keridge to the East India Company, March 20, 1614, *East India Company Letters* 3 (1615).67.

198. Best, p. 235; Bernier, p. 203.

199. Best, p. 245.

200. Roe 2.418.

201. Roe 1.165.

202. Terry, pp. 397, 161. He said (p. 144): "These coaches are covered for men of quality, with something that is costly; much of our English broad-cloth, that is dyed red, is there bought from us, and employed for that use."

203. Letter of Aldworthe and Biddulph to the East India Company, August 19, 1614, *East India Company Letters* 2 (1613–15).97.

204. Letter of Edwards to the East India Company, December 2, 1615, *East India Company Letters* 2 (1613–15).154.

205. Letter of Keridge to the East India Company, March 20, 1615, *East India Company Letters* 3 (1615).65, 66.

206. Letter of Joseph Salbancke to the East India Company, November 1616, *East India Company Letters* 4 (1616).232.

207. Letters of Aldworthe and Biddulph to the East India Company, August 19, 1614, of Edwards to the East India Company, December 2, 1615, of Keridge to Captain Downton, November 22, 1614, of Aldworthe to the East India Company, December 27, 1614, *East India Company Letters* 2 (1613–15).100, 151, 181, 248; of Thomas Elkington to the East India Company, February 25, 1615, of Keridge to the East India Company, March 20, 1615, *East India Company Letters* 3 (1615).8, 9, 10, 66; of Joseph Salbank to the East India Company, November 1616, of Francis Fettiplace to the East India Company, November 26, 1616, of the factors at Surat to the East India Company, March 10, 1616, of the factors at Surat to Sir Thomas Roe, July 23 and 26, 1616, *East India Company Letters* 4 (1616).232, 243, 296, 324. Among the things Bernier (pp. 203–4) listed as important imports for India from all over Europe, Asia, and Africa were copper, cloves, nutmeg, cinnamon, elephants, broadcloth, horses, fresh and dried fruits of all kinds, seashells, ambergris, ivory, musk, porcelain, and pearls.

208. Terry, pp. 112–13; Foster in Roe 1.164n. Said Bernier (p. 202): "It should not escape notice that gold and silver, after circulating in every other quarter of the globe, come at length to be swallowed up, lost in some measure, in *Hindoustan*."

209. Roe 1.165.

210. Roe 1.165.

211. Fitch in Foster, *Early Travels*, pp. 34–35.

212. Best, p. 158.

213. Floris, p. 145.

214. Fitch in Foster, *Early Travels*, p. 35.

215. Letter of Edwards to the East India Company, December 2, 1615, *East India Company Letters* 2 (1613–15).152.

216. Roe 1.119.

217. *East India Company Letters* 2 (1613–15).108.

218. *East India Company Letters* 3 (1615).68.

219. Roe 2.386.

220. Pelsaert, pp. 7, 19.

221. Letter of John Sandcrofte to the East India Company, November 29, 1614, *East India Company Letters* 2 (1613–15).213.

222. *East India Company Letters* 1 (1602–13).163, 167, 178, 179, 183, 184.

223. Finch in Foster, *Early Travels*, pp. 129–30.

224. *East India Company Letters* 1 (1602–13).188, 187. The rates set down were so that "every ship should be taxed to pay for her freedom," and the *Rahimi* was used as a standard, apparently, because she was so large. Her tax was set at fifteen thousand rials (1.186).

225. Letter of Richard Cocks to the Governor and Committees of the East India Company, November 30, 1613, *East India Company Letters* 1 (1602–13).317; Foster, *Early Travels*, p. 123.

226. See Withington in Foster, *Early Travels*, p. 203.

227. Letter of Thomas Elkington to John Oxwicke and Christopher Farewell, December 16, 1614, *East India Company Letters* 2 (1613–15).229.

228. Pelsaert, pp. 4–5.

229. Roe 2.436–37.

230. Roe 2.444.

231. *East India Company Letters* 5 (1617).80.

232. Roe (2.421) mentioned "the Queen Mothers ship" on October 5, 1617, but since the *Rahimi* was burned in 1614, this is either another one of Maryamuzzamani's ships or one belonging to her daughter-in-law, Roe making a mistake here in ownership. The next day Roe (2.425) referred to a ship, presumably the same one, as "the Queenes ship," and since he always referred to Nur Jahan as "the Queene" (2.281) or "Normahall" and Maryamuzzamani as "the Queene mother" or "the Kings Mother" (2.299, 420), the owner of the vessel in question seems clearly to be the current queen.

233. Note the references of 1617 (*Tuzuk* 1.401) and early 1619 (*Tuzuk* 2.66).

234. *East India Company Letters* 5 (1617).133.

235. *English Factories* (1618–1621), p. 335.

236. Letter of Kerridge, Biddulph, Thomas Rastell, and Giles James at Surat, *English Factories* (1618–1621), p. 81.

237. *English Factories* (1622–1623), p. 204.

238. Hawkins in Foster, *Early Travels*, p. 89.

239. Hawkins in Foster, *Early Travels*, p. 119.

240. Terry, pp. 378–79.

241. Roe 1.115.

242. Roe 1.114.

243. Roe 1.119.

244. Roe 2.498.

245. Roe 1.171.

246. Roe 2.487.

247. *Tuzuk* 1.167, 168, 192, 206–7, 236, 260, 281, 371, 388, 435; *Tuzuk* 2.81, 95, 211.

248. Roe 1.167, 171, 183.

249. Letter of Roe to the factors at Surat, March 10, 1617, *East India Company Letters* 5 (1617).338. Said Keridge earlier: "Those Jesuits do so bewitch the king etc. with daily presents"; and Biddulph: "These lying Jesuits feeding the king daily with presents and strange toys so that what they desire is granted" (letters to Thomas Aldworth, September 7, 1613, and Sir Thomas Smith, October 28, 1613, *East India Company Letters* 1 [1602–13].282, 300).

250. Roe 2.487.

251. Roe 1.121.

252. Roe 2.326.

253. Roe 2.487.

254. Hawkins in Foster, *Early Travels*, p. 94. In a letter of March 20, 1615, to the East India Company, Thomas Keridge noted that "Mr. Edwards presented . . . unto the favoured queen . . . a perfumed bag embroidered, a cabinet with a looking-glass and some other toys" (*East India Company Letters* 3 [1615].64).

255. Roe 1.119.

256. Roe 2.384–86.

257. Roe 2.427.

258. Roe 2.458.

259. Letter of Roe to the East India Company, January 25, 1616, *East India Company Letters* 4 (1616).13.

260. Letter of Roe to the factors at Surat, October 15, 1616, *East India Company Letters* 4 (1616).207.

261. Letter from the factors at Surat to Roe at Ajmer, May 26, 1616, *East India Company Letters* 4 (1616).310.

262. Roe 1.159, 171, 215; Roe 2.391, 393.

263. Roe 1.150, 174–78; Roe 2.305.

264. E.g., Roe 1.170, 172.

265. Roe 2.416.

266. Roe 1.137.

267. Roe 2.284, 416.

268. Roe 2.390.

269. Terry, p. 378; see also Terry p. 41.

270. Roe 2.498.

271. Roe 1.47–50.

272. Roe 1.73–74.

273. Roe 1.56.

274. Roe 2.460.

275. Roe 1.120.

276. Roe 2.310.

277. Della Valle 2.418–19.

278. Letter of Roe to the East India Company, January 25, 1616, *East India Company Letters* 4 (1616).15.

279. Terry, pp. 114–20.

280. Roe 1.93.

281. Roe 1.134.

282. Roe 1.113.

283. Roe 1.114.
284. Roe 1.68.
285. Roe 2.351.
286. Terry, p. 511.
287. See Roe 2.456.
288. E.g., Roe 1.147–48.
289. Roe 1.112.
290. Roe 1.165.
291. Roe 2.310.
292. Letter of Roe to the East India Company, January 25, 1616, *East India Company Letters* 4 (1616).13–14.
293. Letter of Roe to Sir Thomas Smythe, January 16, 1617, *East India Company Letters* 5 (1617).329.
294. M. Brown, p. 60; see also M. Brown, p. 70.
295. Roe 1.167, 171, 183.
296. Roe 1.230, 232; Roe 2.459.
297. Roe 2.325.
298. Roe 2.390–91.
299. See Best, p. 245; Terry, p. 397.
300. Roe 1.136–37.
301. M. Brown, p. 66.
302. Although he did mention the January 1615 battle between English and Portuguese ships (*Tuzuk* 1.274–75), and the English coach (*Tuzuk* 1.338), though this last reference was to Jahangir's copy and not the original.
303. E.g., Roe 2.557–60.
304. M. Brown, p. 96.
305. Roe 2.469.
306. Roe 2.498.
307. Pelsaert, p. 25.

Chapter 7. Breakup of the Junta (1620–1627)

1. Prasad, p. 270.
2. *Tuzuk* 2.65; *Ikbal-nama-i Jahangiri* E&D 6.405–6. See also Commissariat, pp. 139–52.
3. Terry, p. 393.
4. *Ikbal-nama-i Jahangiri* E&D 6.406.
5. Terry, p. 393; *Ikbal-nama-i Jahangiri* E&D 6.407.
6. Terry, pp. 393–94; *Ikbal-nama-i Jahangiri* E&D 6.407.
7. *Ikbal-nama-i Jahangiri* E&D 6.407.
8. Roe 2.436. The English would again make early reference to the rift between emperor and prince as in this passage from a letter from Thomas Kerridge and Thomas Rastell to William Biddulph, written September 17, 1619: "Itt is rumorde heare [in Surat] thatt the Prince C[horoo]m is disgraced by his father; which were much to be desired, for so longe as the master is not our favorer, his servantes will little befrind us."
9. *Tuzuk* 1.19. See also Blochmann, *Ain-i Akbari* 1.323.
10. *Tuzuk* 2.84. See *Shah Jahan Nama*, p. 8.
11. *Tuzuk* 2.84. See also Shujauddins, p. 57.
12. *Tuzuk* 2.176.

13. *Tuzuk* 2.212.

14. *Tuzuk* 2.213. Hakim Sadra, after this terrible breach of professionalism and good manners, had the nerve to ask Jahangir later for leave to go on pilgrimage. Jahangir gave him permission (*Tuzuk* 2.217) "with an open brow."

15. *Tuzuk* 2.213.

16. *Tuzuk* 2.213.

17. *Tuzuk* 2.213–14.

18. E.g., *Tuzuk* 2.217.

19. *Tuzuk* 2.246.

20. His other wives included a descendant of Shah Ismail of Persia (the daughter of Mirza Muzaffar Husain, his cousin) and a granddaughter of Abdur Rahim, the Khan-khanan, by his eldest son Shahnawaz Khan. *Tuzuk* 1.159, 180; Lall, p. 101.

21. Della Valle 1.56–57.

22. Coryat in Foster, *Early Travels*, p. 277. See also Della Valle 1.57.

23. Roe 2.407; see also 2.404, Foster in Roe 2.404n-405n.

24. Prasad, p. 296. See also Amar, pp. 437–55, esp. p. 437.

25. Van den Broecke, p. 84.

26. *Badshah-nama* E&D 7.5.

27. Hawkins in Foster, *Early Travels*, p. 117.

28. *Tuzuk* 2.187–88.

29. *Tuzuk* 2.202–3. See also Pelsaert, p. 34; Della Valle 1.55.

30. Prasad, p. 298.

31. *Tuzuk* 2.216.

32. *Tuzuk* 2.216.

33. *Tuzuk* 2.216.

34. *Tuzuk* 2.222.

35. *Tuzuk* 2.222.

36. Pelsaert, p. 5; van den Broecke, p. 53. On Itimaduddaula's career, see Sarkar, pp. 154–64.

37. *Tuzuk* 1.303.

38. *Tuzuk* 1.336.

39. *Tuzuk* 1.373.

40. C. Pant, p. 59.

41. *Tuzuk* 2.222; *Ikbal-nama-i Jahangiri* E&D 6.404.

42. Said Roe (1.110): "He is euery mans heire when he dyeth, which maketh him rich, and the Countrey so euill builded." Manucci (1.198) stated "that the Mogul kings were the heirs of the men in their service, taking all the wealth left at their death," and Tavernier (p. 15; see p. 44) that "when a great noble dies the Emperor inherits his property, his wife remaining only mistress of her jewels."

43. *Tuzuk* 1.321; *Tuzuk* 2.18, 161. At the beginning of his reign (*Tuzuk* 1.8), he had ruled against the process of escheat even though he seems to have followed it most of the time: "In my dominions if anyone, whether unbeliever or Musalman, should die, his property and effects should be left for his heirs, and no one should interfere with them." Said Hawkins (in Foster, *Early Travels*, pp. 104–5):

> The custome of this Mogoll Emperour is to take possession of his noblemens treasure when they dye, and to bestow on his [their] children what he pleaseth; but commonly he dealeth well with them, possessing them with their fathers land, dividing it amongst them; and unto the eldest sonne he hath a very great respect, who in time receiveth the full title of his father.

See also Pelsaert, pp. 54–55.

44. *Tuzuk* 2.228. See also van den Broecke, p. 53.

45. Said Pelsaert (pp. 54–55):

Immediately on the death of a lord who has enjoyed the King's *jagir*, be he great or small, without any exception—even before the breath is out of his body—the King's officers are ready on the spot, and make an inventory of the entire estate, recording everything down to the value of a single pice, even to the dresses and jewels of the ladies, provided they have not concealed them. The King takes back the whole estate absolutely for himself, except in a case where the deceased has done good service in his lifetime, when the women and children are given enough to live on, but no more.

46. *Tuzuk* 2.228. See also van den Broecke, p. 53. Blochmann (*Ain-i Akbari* 1.575) notes, however, that by the time of his own death in 1641, Asaf Khan had amassed property "said to have been more than double that of his father."

47. According to Roe, Jahangir distrusted Shah Jahan's powers as early as 1617.

48. Van den Broecke, pp. 52–53.

49. Shujauddins, pp. 46–47.

50. Dow 3.60.

51. Dow 3.60. Tavernier (p. 268), perhaps more accurately, reported that Shah Jahan's argument was twofold: the accompaniment of Khusrau would (1) remove a "distressing . . . object" from the emperor, and (2) provide the elder son a "life with greater comfort in the Deccan." Moreover, Jahangir did "not penetrat[e] the designs of Khurram, [and] consented without difficulty."

52. Terry, p. 394. See also Della Valle 1.58.

53. Roe 2.281–83. See Dow 3.53.

54. Della Valle 1.57.

55. Van den Broecke, p. 52.

56. Della Valle 1.57–58. Terry (p. 412) also noted that Shah Jahan promised good care for his brother, for he "told his father that he would have both his eyes upon him, and further so provide, that he should never have cause to fear him any more."

57. *Tuzuk* 2.190, 243; van den Broecke, p. 52.

58. They say: "It was a good game to do away with one claimant to the throne through the other. The end of Khusrau under Khurram's charge was bound to make him unpopular among the admirers of the former" (Shujauddins, p. 58).

59. C. Pant, p. 57n.

60. E.g., Della Valle 1.57; Dow 3.53.

61. Dow 3.61.

62. *Tuzuk* 2.206–8; van den Broecke, pp. 52–53.

63. *Tuzuk* 2.196, 202, 208.

64. Van den Broecke, p. 53.

65. *Tuzuk* 2.201.

66. *Tuzuk* 2.228. See *Shah Jahan Nama*, p. 10.

67. Van den Broecke, p. 54; De Laet, p. 199.

68. Terry, p. 412.

69. Pelsaert, p. 71; van den Broecke (p. 54) has Riza Gholam; De Laet (pp. 198–99) has Reza; and Peter Mundy (2.105) has Raza Bahadur.

70. Van den Broecke, pp. 54, 57; Pelsaert, pp. 70–71; De Laet, pp. 198–99.

71. Della Valle 1.58. Della Valle also offered the story that Shah Jahan himself killed his brother publicly and "with his own hand."

72. Mundy 2.104–5. Again, according to Tavernier (p. 269):

[Shah Jahan] had this poor prince in his power . . . [and] knew how to rid himself of him by the most secret means, and used the most plausible pretexts to conceal his crime from the view of men, not considering that he was unable to conceal it from the eyes of God.

73. Dow 3.62–63.

74. See Khafi Khan as noted in Shujauddins, p. 49.

75. As noted in Shujauddins, p. 49. On the charges of murder, see Srivastava, pp. 479–92.

76. See H. Beveridge "Sultan Khusrau," pp. 599–601.

77. Foster, *English Factories, 1622–1623*, p. xxv.

78. See Coryat in Foster, *Early Travels*, p. 277.

79. Guerreiro in Payne, p. 38.

80. Van den Broecke, p. 54; De Laet, p. 199. Says Dow (3.63): "She ran about distracted, and called down the vengeance of God upon the murderers."

81. Van den Broecke, p. 54.

82. Dow 3.63.

83. Van den Broecke, pp. 54–55.

84. Van den Broecke, p. 54; Pelsaert, p. 71; Finch in Foster, *Early Travels*, pp. 178–79. This is an ironic end to what must have been a sorrow-filled relationship between mother and son: this was the mother who committed suicide by an opium overdose on May 6, 1605, when her son seemed destined to rebel openly against his father.

85. Terry, p. 412. Even though Terry left India with Roe in 1619, he did not present his chronicles to the English king until 1622, having written them "shortly after my return from East-India." This means information about Khusrau's death in 1621 and Shah Jahan's complicity in it could have reached him via secondhand sources, probably late-arriving merchants, after he had returned to England. Terry, p. iv. Moreover, at least once Terry (p. 425) refers to Jahangir as the "late Mogul," indicating that some editing of the text did not take place until after Jahangir's death in 1627. De Laet (p. 199) also said, "the king mourned deeply for the death of his son."

86. *Tuzuk* 2.228. On this see Varadarajan, pp. 403–18, esp. 410.

87. See H. Beveridge's note, *Tuzuk* 2.228n. Pelsaert (p. 71) erroneously stated that the death took place in February of 1621 (see the note of Moreland and Geyl in Pelsaert, p. 71n). The death could have been as early as August 1621, when Shah Jahan heard of Jahangir's declining health and decided to do something to secure his own future. *Tuzuk* 2.212–14. For a full discussion, see Prasad, pp. 308n–311n.

88. De Laet, p. 199; van den Broecke, p. 54.

89. De Laet, p. 199. See *Shah Jahan Nama*, p. 10.

90. Van den Broecke, p. 54; De Laet, p. 199.

91. Della Valle 1.58–59. Della Valle (1.59) was of the opinion that this action indicated there was "some conspiracy of *Asaf Chan*, and *Nurmahal*" with Shah Jahan, beginning with the Khusrau death, and that the King of Persia, who at this moment moved against Kandahar, was also in league with all of them against Jahangir.

92. *Tuzuk* 2.230, 233; van den Broecke, p. 55.

93. *Tuzuk* 2.233. See *Shah Jahan Nama*, p. 10.

94. Van den Broecke, p. 55.

95. Van den Broecke, p. 55.

96. Van den Broecke, p. 55.

97. *Tuzuk* 2.234.

98. Van den Broecke, p. 55.

99. *Tuzuk* 2.234. See the *farman* in Tirmizi (p. 122) urging Shah Jahan on against Shah Abbas.

100. C. Pant, p. 61n.

101. *Tuzuk* 2.234. An account of the beginnings of Shah Jahan's rebellion can also be found in Amar, pp. 437–55.

102. *Tuzuk* 2.234–35.

103. *Tuzuk* 2.235; Dow 3.66. Dholpur contained an old garden belonging to Babur, the Lotus Garden, which was now in the hands of Nur Jahan and therefore much beloved by her. See Moynihan, pp. 103–9.

104. *Tuzuk* 2.236.

105. *Tuzuk* 2.236. For the large properties and extent of powers of Shah Jahan, see van den Broecke, pp. 56–57.

106. *Tuzuk* 2.237, 245. Nur Jahan's pleasure at this appointment was shown in her presentation, immediately thereafter, of two large pearls she bought from a merchant for Rs. 60,000 to her obviously flattered husband. *Tuzuk* 2.237.

107. *Tuzuk* 2.239.

108. *Tuzuk* 2.239.

109. Van den Broecke, p. 56.

110. Van den Broecke, pp. 55–56.

111. *Tuzuk* 2.245; van den Broecke, p. 56; Della Valle 1.47, 59.

112. Van den Broecke, pp. 55–56.

113. Della Valle 1.47. Prasad (p. 327) entertains a third possibility: that Nur Jahan had asked Mahabat Khan to come from Afghanistan to help out in the Kandahar affair and, when he refused because he thought the summons was a ruse by his enemy Asaf Khan to get him into his power, Nur Jahan tried to regain Mahabat Khan's faith by sending her brother away to Agra, presumably on the makeshift errand of retrieving the treasury.

114. *Tuzuk* 2.243.

115. *Tuzuk* 2.246ff. Note an early use of the term for a denuded mountain in *Tuzuk* 1.103.

116. *Tuzuk* 2.246.

117. *Tuzuk* 2.248.

118. Van den Broecke, p. 56; see Della Valle 1.59 and C. Pant, p. 64.

119. *Tuzuk* 2.247.

120. *Tuzuk* 2.247–48.

121. Van den Broecke, p. 57.

122. *Tuzuk* 2.249–50; van den Broecke, pp. 57–58.

123. Van den Broecke, p. 58.

124. *Tuzuk* 2.251.

125. Van den Broecke, p. 58.

126. *Tuzuk* 2.253–54.

127. *Tuzuk* 2.254–55.

128. Van den Broecke, p. 59.

129. *Tuzuk* 2.255–56; Dow 3.68–70.

130. *Tuzuk* 2.256.

131. *Tuzuk* 2.256ff. See C. Pant, p. 65.

132. *Tuzuk* 2.257–60; van den Broecke, p. 65; Dow 3.70. Prasad (p. 333) suggests that Parviz, despite his father's repeated requests to come and help stop his brother's rebellion, had been playing a waiting game—perhaps to avoid taking sides, which was now, obviously, out of the question.

133. *Tuzuk* 2.260–61; Blochmann, *Ain-i Akbari* 1.346.

134. *Tuzuk* 2.261.

135. Prasad, p. 334.

136. See Findly, "Maryamuzzamani," pp. 227–38

137. *Tuzuk* 2.261.

138. *Tuzuk* 2.276. See Blochmann, *Ain-i Akbari* 1.324.

139. *Tuzuk* 2.262; van den Broecke, p. 65.

140. *Tuzuk* 2.271ff. See C. Pant (pp. 66–67) for the various family connections at stake here.

141. *Tuzuk* 2.277.

142. *Tuzuk* 2.277–78.

143. *Tuzuk* 2.278. Shah Jahan was married to the daughter of the eldest son of Abdur Rahim in an alliance that seems to have been primarily political. Prasad (p. 340) suggests that this Khankhanan gambit was only a way of toying with Shah Jahan, that Parviz and Mahabat Khan had no intention of granting any peaceful terms to the prince at all. And van den Broecke (p. 65) suggested that the whole thing was the Khankhanan's idea, "that he might be sent to Purwez as he was certain of being able to arrange peace between the two." For another account of this Khankhanan episode, see Amar, pp. 437–55.

144. *Tuzuk* 2.279. Shah Jahan had imprisoned the Khankhanan because of a secret letter he had written to Mahabat Khan. Blochmann, *Ain-i Akbari* 1.358–59. Van den Broecke (p. 66) characterized the Khankhanan as a traitor in league with Bairam Beg and noted that several of Shah Jahan's aids warned him about the treachery involved in sending the Khankhanan over to Parviz.

145. *Tuzuk* 2.279; Dow 3.72–73.

146. *Tuzuk* 2.281.

147. *Tuzuk* 2.281–82; van den Broecke, p. 67.

148. *Tuzuk* 2.282; see also C. Pant, p. 65.

149. *Tuzuk* 2.289; van den Broecke, p. 67; *Ikbal-nama-i Jahangiri* E&D 6.407–408.

150. *Tuzuk* 2.289–90.

151. *Tuzuk* 2.297–98; van den Broecke, p. 67. See *Ikbal-nama-i Jahangiri* E&D 6.408; Dow 3.73.

152. *Tuzuk* 2.298–99; van den Broecke, p. 67; *Ikbal-nama-i Jahangiri* E&D 6.408; Tavernier, p. 102. See also C. Pant, pp. 68–69.

153. Van den Broecke, p. 67.

154. Van den Broecke, pp. 67–68; *Ikbal-nama-i Jahangiri* E&D 6.408–10; Dow 3.73.

155. Van den Broecke, pp. 68–71; Dow 3.74–77; *Tatimma-i Wakiat-i Jahangiri* E&D 6.393–94; *Ikbal-nama-i Jahangiri* E&D 6.408–11.

156. Prasad, p. 360. See *Ikbal-nama-i Jahangiri* E&D 6.413–18; Dow 3.78.

157. *Tatimma-i Wakiat-i Jahangiri* E&D 6.396.

158. *Tatimma-i Wakiat-i Jahangiri* E&D 6.396E; Dow 3.78–79.

159. *Tatimma-i Wakiat-i Jahangiri* E&D 6.396; *Ikbal-nama-i Jahangiri* E&D 6.419; van den Broecke, pp. 72–73.

160. E.g., van den Broecke, p. 52; Della Valle 1.57.

161. Dow 3.66–67.

162. Van den Broecke, p. 56.

163. Dow 3.66.

164. See Prasad, p. 362.

165. Dow 3.79.

166. Van den Broecke, p. 52; Della Valle 1.57, 59.

167. Van den Broecke, p. 56; Della Valle 1.59.

168. *Tuzuk* 2.282.
169. Della Valle 1.59.
170. C. Pant, p. 7.
171. *Tuzuk* 2.230.
172. *Tuzuk* 2.247.
173. *Tuzuk* 2.250.
174. Van den Broecke, p. 56.
175. Prasad, p. 179.
176. Dow 3.184.

Chapter 8. Nur Jahan and Religious Policy

1. Roe 1.142; *Ain-i Akbari* 1.286–87.
2. *Tuzuk* 1.365.
3. *Tuzuk* 2.72, see 71–73.
4. Guerreiro, p. 49.
5. *Tuzuk* 1.34.
6. *Tuzuk* 1.33; a few pages later (*Tuzuk* 1.37–45), however, Jahangir gave an extended account of his father's character and achievements.
7. Nizami, "Naqshbandi," pp. 46. See the letter written by Sirhindi to Shaikh Farid urging the return to Islamic tradition, as reproduced in Mujeeb, pp. 269–70.
8. Mentioned by Jahangir (*Tuzuk* 1.22) only as follows:

> Whilst I was prince and before my revered father's illness, and during that time, when the ministers (pillars of the State) and the high nobles had become agitated, and each had conceived some idea of gain for himself and wished to become the originator of some act which could only bring ruin on the State.

9. *Tuzuk* 1.13, 20, 30, 53. For an excellent account of Shaikh Farid Bukhari, see Mujeeb, pp. 264–70.
10. *Tuzuk* 1.21.
11. *Tuzuk* 1.21.
12. *Tuzuk* 1.27.
13. *Tuzuk* 1.30–31.
14. H. Beveridge in *Tuzuk* 1.31n; *Tuzuk* 1.71–72. See Friedmann, pp. 79–80; Nizami, "Naqshbandi," pp. 46–50.
15. Du Jarric, p. 204.
16. Guerreiro, p. 3.
17. We know this to be true of at least Mirza Aziz Koka and Khwaja Abdullah.
18. Du Jarric, pp. 62–63.
19. Blochmann in *Ain-i Akbari* 1.343–47.
20. *Tuzuk* 1.59, 68, 69.
21. *Tuzuk* 1.53, 57, 64, 69.
22. Nizami, "Naqshbandi," p. 47; and see Ahmad, "Sirhindi," pp. 259–71. Presumably following Nurul Haqq's *Zubdatut Tawarikh*, Mujeeb's (p. 266) scenario of the accession is as follows: Raja Man Singh and Mirza Aziz Koka had been maneuvering to put Khusrau on the throne while Akbar lay dying. Shaikh Farid, who "did not belong to any party" and who had no particular allegiance to Salim, nevertheless decided to bring about a peaceful accession to the throne and went to Salim's house and congratulated him on becoming emperor. "This bold move decided the course of events" and the other nobles soon fell in line, making it easier for Salim to go to Akbar and receive his final blessings.

Rizvi's excellent discussion of the evidence (pp. 298n–299n), however, argues instead that the Naqshbandis, and especially Sirhindi, were in fact fairly neutral players in Jahangir's succession and that arguments like Nizami's for a strong connection are based on thin material.

23. A. S. Beveridge in Gulbadan, p. 75.

24. *Tuzuk* 1.2; Finch in Foster, *Early Travels*, pp. 148–50, 171; Pelsaert, p. 70; Mundy 2.226, 243–44. See also *Tabakat-i Akbari* E&D 5.328, 371.

25. *Tuzuk* 2.72–73; Finch in Foster, *Early Travels*, p. 150.

26. *Tuzuk* 2.70–71.

27. See A. Husain, pp. 61–69.

28. Blochmann in *Ain-i Akbari* 1.530; A. Husain, p. 62.

29. Blochmann in *Ain-i Akbari* 1.552–53.

30. *Tuzuk* 1.32, 79.

31. *Tuzuk* 1.29; A. Husain, pp. 62, 65.

32. *Tuzuk* 1.31–32.

33. A. Husain, p. 65; Blochmann in *Ain-i Akbari* 1.556ff.

34. *Tuzuk* 1.78.

35. *Tuzuk* 1.75, 77, 78.

36. *Tuzuk* 1.113–15.

37. A. Husain, pp. 63–64.

38. A. K. Das, *Mughal Painting*, p. 14.

39. Sharma, p. 88.

40. Sharma, p. 72.

41. *Tuzuk* 1.205.

42. The list is almost inexhaustible. E.g., *Tuzuk* 1.27, 28, 29, 30–31, 60, 71–72, 135.

43. *Tuzuk* 1.77.

44. *Tuzuk* 2.91–93.

45. *Tuzuk* 1.157, 182.

46. *Tuzuk* 1.45–46.

47. Pelsaert, pp. 74–75.

48. *Tuzuk* 2.94–95. See also A. K. Das' comments on Figure 5-2 (Chapter 5).

49. Such as the refusal to eat fish without scales as practiced by the Shias (*Tuzuk* 1.188) and the use of a "*khichri* of *bajra* (a mixture of split peas and millet boiled together") as a vegetarian alternative to dishes made with animal flesh (*Tuzuk* 1.419).

50. Like the Jami mosque in Mandu in the winters of 1617 and of 1618 (*Tuzuk* 1.365, 424).

51. Like that of Shaikh Nizamuddin Auliya in 1606 (*Tuzuk* 1.58), of Shaikh Ahmad Khattu in the winter of 1618 (*Tuzuk* 1.428–29), and of Shaikh Salim Chishti in the winter of 1619 (*Tuzuk* 2.70–71).

52. Like the tomb of Humayun in 1606 (*Tuzuk* 1.58) and of Akbar in 1608 and in 1619 (*Tuzuk* 1.152; 2.101–2).

53. *Tuzuk* 2.34–35.

54. *Tuzuk* 2.149.

55. *Tuzuk* 2.101–2.

56. *Tuzuk* 1.46, 58, 305–6.

57. *Tuzuk* 2.101–2.

58. *Tuzuk* 1.30–31, 102; *Tuzuk* 2.119.

59. *Tuzuk* 1.102.

60. *Tuzuk* 1.303–4.

61. *Tuzuk* 2.119.

62. *Tuzuk* 2.210.

63. *Tuzuk* 1.1.

64. *Tuzuk* 1.152; Pelsaert (p. 70) mistakenly said, "King Akbar . . . went there [to Muinuddin] from Agra on foot with his wife Miryam Makani." Maryam Makani was Akbar's mother, and we presume that here Pelsaert meant Akbar's wife and Jahangir's mother, Maryamuzzamani.

65. See, e.g., Begg, pp. 82–84.

66. *Tuzuk* 1.168. An aged Khwaja Husain was the subject of one of Jahangir's later allegorical paintings, "Jahangir Preferring a Sufi Shaikh to Kings," ca. 1615–20, inscribed to Bichitr, Freer Gallery of Art (45.15), discussed in Beach, *Grand Mogul*, p. 105.

67. *Tuzuk* 1.189.

68. *Tuzuk* 1.253, 257.

69. *Tuzuk* 1.340.

70. *Tuzuk* 1.249.

71. *Tuzuk* 1.341.

72. *Tuzuk* 1.256. This occasion took place in February (1614), corresponding to Pelsaert's (p. 70) account: "The pilgrimage to his [Muinuddin's] tomb is in February, when immense numbers of people from all quarters gather near Sikandra, beyond Agra, and march thither like an army, accompanied by even greater numbers of mendicants than the devotees, who there take various parties under their standards for protection."

73. Coryat in Foster, *Early Travels*, p. 280.

74. *Tuzuk* 1.28, 264–65, 334–35.

75. *Tuzuk* 1.267.

76. *Tuzuk* 1.267–68.

77. *Tuzuk* 1.297.

78. *Tuzuk* 1.329.

79. *Tuzuk* 1.340–41.

80. *Tuzuk* 1.340.

81. *Tuzuk* 2.109.

82. *Tuzuk* 1.38.

83. Aslam, p. 135.

84. Roe 2.382.

85. Terry, p. 418. And again (p. 253): "because every one there hath liberty to profess his own religion freely, and if he please may argue against theirs, without fear of an inquisition."

86. See A. K. Das, *Mughal Painting*, pp. 12–14. Bernier (p. 176) noted that Shah Jahan, however, was "a more rigid Mahometan than his father" and did not tolerate other religions as his predecessors had done.

87. *Tuzuk* 1.32–33; see again *Tuzuk* 1.361.

88. *Tuzuk* 1.102.

89. *Tuzuk* 1.244–46.

90. *Tuzuk* 1.357–59.

91. *Tuzuk* 1.58.

92. *Tuzuk* 1.245, 268.

93. *Tuzuk* 1.361, 246–47.

94. Bernier, p. 326.

95. *Tuzuk* 1.254.

96. *Tuzuk* 1.32–33.

97. *Tuzuk* 1.254–55.

98. *Tuzuk* 1.255.

99. *Badshah-nama* E&D 7.36.
100. *Tuzuk* 1.32–33, 254.
101. *Tuzuk* 1.355–59.
102. *Tuzuk* 2.49, 52–53.
103. *Tuzuk* 2.104–8.
104. *Tuzuk* 1.356. See also Chaghatai, pp. 119–30.
105. *Tuzuk* 1.355–56.
106. *Tuzuk* 2.52.
107. *Tuzuk* 1.356.
108. *Tuzuk* 2.52.
109. *Tuzuk* 2.105.
110. *Tuzuk* 2.130–31.
111. *Tuzuk* 1.142–358. Note his discussion in early 1617.
112. *Tuzuk* 2.181. The practice did, however, continue and he noted later, without comment, the immolation of two wives and eight concubines "in the fire of fidelity" of Raja Bhao Singh. *Tuzuk* 2.218. Hawkins (in Foster, *Early Travels*, p. 119) gave a moving account of Jahangir's attempts to dissuade some wives from their voluntary deaths in the fires of their husbands.
113. *Tuzuk* 2.35, 218. This he did in spite of the obvious hypocrisy of so many of the holy men, as vividly and contemptuously described by Manucci (2.9–11).
114. *Tuzuk* 2.203–4.
115. *Tuzuk* 2.226–27.
116. *Tuzuk* 2.224–25.
117. Terry, p. 308.
118. Roe 1.123–24.
119. Manucci 1.152, 151.
120. For a more thorough treatment of Jahangir and the Jains, see Findly, "Vow of Non-Violence," pp. 245–56.
121. *Tuzuk* 1.9.
122. Desai in *Sribhanucandraganicarita*, pp. 19–22.
123. *Sribhanucandraganicarita* 4.114–15; Desai in *Sribhanucandraganicarita*, p. 59.
124. Desai in *Sribhanucandraganicarita*, p. 62.
124. Desai in *Sribhanucandraganicarita*, p. 18.
126. This list is a selected and abbreviated version of what appears in Desai in *Sribhanucandraganicarita*, pp. 79–91. See also the account of these Mughal documents in Tirmizi, pp. 82, 83, 99–100.
127. The specified days were the Thursday and Sunday of every week, as so ordered in Jahangir's eleventh regulation of 1605 (*Tuzuk* 1.9), the new moon day in every month, feast days, every new year's day, "in the month of Navroj" (presumably, during the nineteen days of the Nauroz festival under the sign of Aries), and on the day of Jahangir's birthday weighing. "On those days there shall be no killing of animals in (our) protected Kingdom; and no one on that day shall hunt and catch and kill birds and fish and such like" (Desai in *Sribhanucandraganicarita*, p. 84). See also Pelsaert, p. 49.
128. Desai (in *Sribhanucandraganicarita*, p. 86n) notes that Chandu Sanghavai is probably the Samghapati Candrapala of Agra, who consecrated the installation of two images of Sumatinatha, one of them being of the deity Mulanayaka.
129. Roe 1.124.
130. Terry, p. 335.
131. Pelsaert, p. 49.
132. Desai in *Sribhanucandraganicarita*, pp. 62–64.

133. *Sribhanucandraganicarita* 4.168–73.

134. Desai gives these dates because the text refers to the substantial role played in the following incident by Nur Jahan. Since the text calls her Nur Mahal, Desai argues that the incident must have taken place before Jahangir gave her the title Nur Jahan in 1616. Certainly the incident happened after her 1611 marriage to Jahangir and most probably during the immediately succeeding years, but the years after 1616 cannot be excluded for even after receiving the title Nur Jahan, she was called Nur Mahal by Terry (in 1618, e.g., pp. 393, 406) and Roe (in 1617, e.g., 2.377, 384, 386, 404, 407, 427, 436, 437, 458).

135. *Sribhanucandraganicarita* 4.221–334.

136. *Sribhanucandraganicarita* 4.338–46.

137. *Sribhanucandraganicarita* 4.347–58.

138. *Tuzuk* 1.437–38.

139. Desai in *Sribhanucandraganicarita*, p. 18.

140. *Tuzuk* 1.437.

141. *Tuzuk* 1.438.

142. Desai in *Sribhanucandraganicarita*, pp. 18–19.

143. *Tuzuk* 2.35.

144. *Tuzuk* 2.36; 1.24–25. For my full argument on this, see Findly, "Vow of Non-Violence," pp. 245–52. Note that Jahangir would subsequently tie the taking of the vow in his "fiftieth year" to the illness of his beloved grandson, Shah Shuja. The life of the young boy, then, "would become the means of preserving the lives of many animals. . . . By the grace of Allah his illness [then] diminished" (*Tuzuk* 2.45).

145. *Tuzuk* 2.236–37. Note also that it was in 1619 that Jahangir finally gave freedom to Khusrau, again indicating that it was a pivotal year for the resolution of tensions between fathers and sons.

146. Desai in *Sribhanucandraganicarita*, p. 91.

147. Du Jarric, pp. 62ff.

148. Payne in Guerreiro, pp. xvii–xviii.

149. Foster in Roe 2.314n–15n. For a general discussion of the history of the Jesuit missions, see Maclagan, pp. 75–77.

150. Roe 2.314–15.

151. Terry, p. 422.

152. Guerreiro, p. 49.

153. Guerreiro, pp. 49–62.

154. Guerreiro, p. 50.

155. Guerreiro, pp. 51–52, 57.

156. Guerreiro, p. 49.

157. Roe 2.314; Terry, pp. 419–22. Roe's short account of this was made in 1616.

158. Terry, pp. 419–22.

159. Terry, p. 424.

160. E.g., Du Jarric, p. 69.

161. Guerreiro, pp. 24–31.

162. *Tuzuk* 1.27–28.

163. Note that Muqarrab Khan was one of the physicians who bled Jahangir. *Tuzuk* 1.226.

164. E.g., *Tuzuk* 1.144, 153–54, 163, 167, 215, 237, 322, 415.

165. *Tuzuk* 1.172.

166. Maclagan, p. 78. Note, however, the great difficulty he must have had when the Portuguese seized Maryamuzzamani's ship during the "wars" between them and the

Mughals, especially since he had been put in the position of leading a retaliatory attack against the Portuguese at Daman. See Danvers in *East India Company Letters* 2 (1613–15).xviii.

167. *Tuzuk* 1.217, 224, 229, 231, 234, 237, 255, 303, 322, 323, 375, 378.

168. *Tuzuk* 1.275, 295, 297, 331, 332, 334.

169. Maclagan, pp. 72–73. Some traditions said only two nephews (e.g., Roe 2.315; Terry, p. 425, Bernier, p. 287).

170. Finch in Foster, *Early Travels*, pp. 101, 147, 148.

171. *Tuzuk* 1.28, 74–75.

172. Finch in Foster, *Early Travels*, p. 148. According to Roe (2.315):

> And to that end he [Father Francisco Corsi] kept a Schoole some yeares, to which the King sent two Princes, his brothers sonnes; who beeing brought vp in the knowledg of God and his sonne our Blessed Sauiour, were solemly Babtised in the Church of Agra with great Pomp, being Carried first vp and downe all the Citty on Eliphants in triumph; and this by the Kings expresse order, who often would examen them in their progression, and seemed much contented in them.

173. Hawkins in Foster, *Early Travels*, p. 116. See also Roe 1.198; Roe 2.315–16. Maclagan (pp. 72, 74) suggests a second reason for the conversions to Christianity and that was to bring in Portuguese wives for Jahangir.

174. Van den Broecke, p. 74. On the cruel and tortuous lengths Jahangir often went to to convert Christian children to Islam, see Guerreiro (pp. 13–23), where the emperor proved to be not above forced circumcision and the eating of pig flesh to test young boys' faiths. See Maclagan, pp. 73–74.

175. Manucci 1.156. Indeed Bernier (p. 288) preserved a story from the Jesuits that maintained "that . . . on his death-bed he [Jahangir] expressed a wish to die a Christian, and sent for those holy men, but that the message was never delivered."

176. Guerreiro, pp. 49–62.

177. Guerreiro, pp. 63–76; Della Valle 1.98.

178. Finch in Foster, *Early Travels*, pp. 177–78. M. Brown (p. 53) notes that Jahangir's Agra throne was surrounded by paintings of St. John, St. Anthony, and St. Bernardine.

179. Van den Broecke, p. 91.

180. Du Jarric, p. 186.

181. Terry, pp. 384–85; Roe 2.318. For a full discussion of this incident, see Maclagan, pp. 88–89.

182. Terry, pp. 260–61, 389. According to Coryat (in Foster, *Early Travels*, p. 246): "Hee speaketh very reverently of our Savior, calling him in the Indian tongue *Isazaret Eesa* [*Haxarat Isa*], that is The Great Prophet Jesus."

183. Guerreiro, p. 67.

184. Guerreiro, p. 70.

185. Hawkins in Foster, *Early Travels*, pp. 114–15; see Terry, pp. 255–56. On the black throne, see note 299.

186. Terry (p. 426) described Shah Jahan as "no favourer of the Christians" and Roe (2.317) described him as "hater of all Christians."

187. *Tatimma-i Wakiat-i Jahangiri* E&D 6.399.

188. *Ikbal-nama-i Jahangiri* E&D 6.405.

189. Coryat in Foster, *Early Travels*, pp. 262, 280.

190. Foster, *Early Travels*, p. 280n.

191. Coryat in Foster, *Early Travels*, p. 280; see Foster in Roe 2.314n.

192. Desai in *Sribhanucandraganicarita*, p. 41.

193. Although the account is undated, we can probably narrow the period down to about 1611–13, as, first, the text calls the empress Nur Mahal placing the likely parameters of the event at 1611 and 1616, at least according to Desai (in *Sribhanucandraganicarita*, p. 54n), and, second, it took place when the court was in Agra (*Sribhanucandraganicarita* 4.228–36) presumably occurring before Jahangir transferred his court to Ajmer for three years to watch over the campaign in Mewar. Desai concurs (in *Sribhanucandraganicarita*, p. 65) with this period, but can give no more exact estimate than that the discussions occurred after the marriage with Mihrunnisa and before the move to Ajmer.

194. *Sribhanucandraganicarita* 4.221–334. Jahangir had found wives for others, notably William Hawkins, for whom he supplied the daughter of Mubarik Shah, an Armenian Christian, to cook his food. Hawkins in Foster, *Early Travels*, pp. 84–85. Desai in *Sribhanucandraganicarita*, p. 52n.

195. *Sribhanucandraganicarita* 4.259–83.

196. Ahmad, "Sirhindi," p. 259; Mujeeb, p. 243.

197. Nizami, "Naqshbandi," pp. 41–47; Mujeeb, pp. 269–70.

198. Nizami, "Naqshbandi," pp. 46–47; Friedmann, pp. 81–83.

199. E.g., *Tuzuk* 1.13, 20, 21, 27, 30.

200. E.g., *Tuzuk* 1.53, 57, 64, 69.

201. Rizvi, pp. 444–45.

202. Mujeeb, pp. 244, 270; Rizvi, pp. 444–45. Friedmann (p. 79), however, understands Sirhindi's position to be that he did not want to be appointed to the post and was apprehensive that Jahangir might ask him.

203. *Tuzuk* 2.91–93; Ani Rai, formerly Anup Rai, had been given his full title after courageously stepping in to receive a tiger's attack and so preventing serious injury to Jahangir. *Tuzuk* 1.185–88. See Temple in Mundy 2.74n.

204. *Tuzuk* 2.161.

205. *Tuzuk* 2.276.

206. Nizami, "Naqshbandi," p. 49; Friedmann, p. 85.

207. *Tuzuk* 2.91–93.

208. Mujeeb, p. 244; Nizami, "Naqshbandi," pp. 47–48; Ahmad, "Sirhindi," pp. 259–70; Ahmad, *Islamic Culture*, pp. 182–90. Sirhindi's response to Jahangir when questioned about his claim (Sharma, p. 80) had been, first, that when even the lowest of servants came to the emperor, he passed through the stations of all the *amirs* and thus stood closer to the emperor than even the highest of the others and, second, that his own assertion that he had passed beyond the *khalifas* in no way gave him any higher status than before.

209. Nizami, "Naqshbandi," p. 48; Mujeeb, p. 244.

210. Findly, "Jahangir and the Sufis."

211. *Tuzuk* 2.35, 45.

212. *Tuzuk* 2.83.

213. Aslam, pp. 137–39; Sharma, pp. 80–81. Sharma (p. 85) and Aslam (p. 141) argue that the reconciliation that took place a year later between the emperor and the *shaikh* was based, at least in part, upon Jahangir exempting Sirhindi from prostration, in the same way that he had other religious at his court. See, e.g., *Tuzuk* 1.203, 205.

214. Friedmann, pp. 84, 108; Nizami, "Naqshbandi," pp. 48, 49; Aslam, pp. 135–36; Schimmel, p. 367.

215. Friedmann, pp. 51–52.

216. Friedmann, pp. 52–53.

217. *Tuzuk* 1.380–81.

218. In April of 1621, *Tuzuk* 2.187–88, 202–3.

219. In October of 1621 (Asmat Begam) and January 1622 (Itimaduddaula), *Tuzuk* 2.216, 222.

220. Aslam, p. 137.

221. Friedmann, p. 84.

222. A. Husain, pp. 63–64.

223. A. Husain, pp. 63–64. It may be only circumstantial evidence that it was the ranks of Abdur Rahim Khankhanan that Sher Afgan had joined in Multan when he had first entered India from Iran (*Tuzuk* 1.113). Abdur Rahim would later be a court correspondee of Shaikh Sirhindi, whose Naqshbandi *silsila* would rival for influence the Chishti *silsila* of Qutbuddin Khan Koka's family.

224. See Maclagan, p. 90. If anybody actively worked at dissuading Jahangir from Christianity, it may have been Shah Jahan. In 1616, e.g., Roe (2.317) described a discussion on Christian miracles at the court and said of Shah Jahan: "The Prince . . . [was] a most stiff Mahometan and hater of all Christians." Said Terry (p. 426): "The Prince Sultan Caroome . . . was no favourer of the Christians." See Della Valle 1.98.

225. De Castro's letters of July 26, 1627, and August 15, 1627, in *JASB* 23 (Hosten, 1927), pp. 154, 162. See Maclagan, p. 91.

226. See the argument in Aslam, p. 135.

227. A reworking of the argument in Findly, "Religious Resources," p. 144.

228. Guerreiro, pp. 66, 67.

229. Terry, p. 389.

230. Du Jarric, p. 190.

231. Finch in Foster, *Early Travels*, pp. 163, 184; Guerreiro, p. 64.

232. Guerreiro, p. 64.

233. Hawkins in Foster, *Early Travels*, p. 115. Of this black throne Jahangir (*Tuzuk* 1.177) said:

> Daulat Khan, who had been sent to Allahabad to bring the throne of black stone, came on . . . (15 September, 1610), and had an audience and brought the stone safe and sound. In truth it was a wonderful slab, very black and shining. Many say it is a species of touchstone . . . . I ordered stone-cutters to carve suitable couplets on the sides of it. They had attached feet to it of the same kind of stone. I often sat on that throne.

See Havell (*Agra*, p. 56), who notes that by the inscription "ve learn that it was made in 1603 for Jahangir." Either there was more than one black throne, or Jahangir back-dated the inscription, or (as is probable given that it was coming from Allahabad where Jahangir's court was in 1603) the throne arrived fully worked by the stonecutters. Jahangir was in Agra when he recorded the above entry, and the throne now sits on "the terrace in front of the Diwan-i-Khas" of the Agra Fort.

234. Du Jarric, p. 190.

235. Guerreiro, pp. 66–67.

236. Guerreiro, p. 63.

237. Du Jarric, pp. 160–62.

238. Du Jarric, p. 192.

239. Terry, p. 427.

240. Du Jarric, pp. 66–67; A. K. Das, *Mughal Painting*, p. 231.

241. Du Jarric, p. 81.

242. See, for example, "Darbar of Jahangir," from a *Jahangirnama* manuscript attrib-

uted to Manohar, ca. 1620, Museum of Fine Arts, Boston (14.654), discussed in Beach, *Grand Mogul*, Pl.14. Jahangir also placed European paintings of Madonnas in his albums. Note here Finch in Foster, *Early Travels*, pp. 163, 184.

243. Della Valle 1.98.

244. Gulbadan, p. 104.

245. Roe in a letter to Sir Thomas Smythe, January 16, 1617, *East India Company Letters* 5 (1617).328.

246. Van den Broecke, p. 77.

Chapter 9. Arts and Architecture of Nur Jahan

1. See Skelton, p. 15.
2. E.g., Shujauddins, p. 101.
3. Khafi Khan, as quoted by Misra, p. 122.
4. See Pelsaert p. 29.
5. *Tuzuk* 1.10–12.
6. *Tuzuk* 2.198. In 1615, Jahangir noted that the *nurjahani muhr* was equal in value to Rs. 6,400 (*Tuzuk* 1.298) and later that it weighed 500 *tulcha* (*Tuzuk* 1.300).
7. Pelsaert, p. 29. See also *Tatimma-i Wakiat-i Jahangiri* E&D 6.398.
8. Unlike his predecessors, Jahangir "alone . . . dared to put his own portrait on coins intended for circulation. He habitually disregarded the Prophet's prohibition of strong drink, and was not ashamed to show himself on the coinage holding a goblet of wine" (Smith, p. 188). See also R. Vanaja, "Islamac Coinage in India," in Khandalavala and Doshi, p. 75.
9. Shujauddins, p. 100. See also Vanaja in Khandalavala and Doshi, pp. 73, 75.
10. As quoted in the *Ikbal-nama-i Jahangiri* E&D 6.405.
11. *Tuzuk* 2.6–7. See Smith (p. 188), who notes that the "figure of *Virgo* is a Europeanized angel."
12. Many of Nur Jahan's coins survive in today's museums and private collections. See the Shujauddins (p. 100n) for a selected list of references.
13. Pelsaert, p. 29.
14. Manucci (1.157) suggested (1) that zodiacal coins were indeed introduced by Nur Jahan, and (2) that they were present in substantial quantity in the public domain: "They struck coin in her name, which had for symbol the twelve signs of the zodiac, and in her time these were current money." See *Tatimma-i Wakiat-i Jahangiri* E&D 6.398.
16. E.g., *Tuzuk* 1.5, 116, 119.
17. E.g., *Tuzuk* 2.292–93.
18. E.g., Roe 1.137; 2.284, 390, 416.
19. My thanks to Mr. Galib Bachooali of Madras. The knife and companion dagger are published in M. L. Nigam, "The Mughal Jades of India," in Khandalavala and Doshi, pp. 78–79.
20. Fabri, pls. 20–25 and accompanying texts.
21. *Tuzuk* 1.384. See also *Tuzuk* 1.299, 377–78; *Tuzuk* 2.49, 191.
22. *Tuzuk* 1.384.
23. Dar, pp. 38–43, 59–61.
24. See C. Pant, p. 118; Blochmann, *Ain-i Akbari* 1.101, 574, 574n; Lal, p. 76. For some of the women's wear pieces popular in trade at the time, see Pelsaert, p. 19.
25. Note, e.g., Nur Jahan's requests for embroidered articles from Roe: on October 15, 1616, he ordered the "fairest embroidered sweetbag," an "embroidered folding case,"

and an "embroidered pillow" (letter to factors at Surat, *East India Company Letters* 4 [1616].207–8). And note *Tuzuk* 1.342.

26. My thanks to M. C. Joshi of the Archaeological Survey of India, New Delhi.

27. Again, my thanks to M. C. Joshi of the ASI, New Delhi.

28. See Fabri, pl. 21 and accompanying text.

29. E.g., Lal, p. 77.

30. A. K. Das, *Mughal Painting*, pp. 46, 235–36. Das also gives a list of some of the women known to have painted, as well as modern locations of some of their works. One of the signatures found on two of the paintings is that of Nadira Banu, tentatively identified as the legendary Anarkali. The Nadira Banu of these paintings was a colorist, guided in her renderings of European reproductions by the Jesuits resident at the court, and was a student of Aqa Riza's in the Salim studio of ca. 1598–1600. A. K. Das, *Mughal Painting*, pp. 234, 238.

31. Beach, *Grand Mogul*, pp. 24–26.

32. Since Sher Afgan was not a supporter of Salim's independent court in Allahabad, it is more likely that Nur Jahan's training, if any, would have been through artists at Akbar's court.

33. A. K. Das, *Mughal Painting*, p. 83.

34. Leach, in Gray, pp. 143–45.

35. *Tuzuk* 2.37.

36. As quoted by Foster in *Early Travels*, p. 67n; see also p. 65. For a full discussion of the shifts in European influence on Jahangiri painting, see P. Brown, *Painting*, pp. 163–79, and A. K. Das, *Mughal Painting*, pp. 231–39.

37. Best, p. 244.

38. See letters of Aldworthe to Keridge at Agra, October 22, 1614, *East India Company Letters* 2 (1613–15).138; of Edwards to the East India Company, February 26, 1615, of Keridge to the East India Company, March 20, 1615, and of Mitford to the East India Company, March 25, 1615 *East India Company Letters* 3 (1615).15, 63, 85.

39. Letter of Edwards to the East India Company, February 26, 1615, *East India Company Letters* 3 (1615).16, 19.

40. Terry, p. 368.

41. Letter to the East India Company, March 20, 1615, *East India Company Letters* 3 (1615).67–68.

42. Roe 2.386–87.

43. E.g., letter of Mitford to the East India Company, March 25, 1615, *East India Company Letters* 3 (1615).88.

44. *Tuzuk* 2.205.

45. Pal, pp. 44, 60; see A. K. Das, *Mughal Painting*, p. 46.

46. C. Pant (pp. 121–23) has published a selection of his verse.

47. C. Pant, pp. 124–25.

48. C. Pant, pp. 127–29.

49. C. Pant, pp. 131–33. Blochmann, *Ain-i Akbari* 1.559–60. For the many others of Nur Jahan's family who were accomplished composers of verse, see C. Pant, pp. 121–43.

50. The following material is taken from the Shujauddins (pp. 110–12), with the Persian translated by Prof. Wheeler Thackston of Harvard, to whom I am immensely grateful.

51. C. Pant, p. 114.

52. *Tuzuk* 2.24, 73, 80, 81, 100, 200, 211.

53. Shujauddins, p. 101. See also Crowe et al., p. 92.

54. See Misra, pp. 110–11.

55. Pelsaert, p. 50.

56. Pelsaert, pp. 4–5.

57. Pelsaert (p. 56) charged:

> They . . . keep . . . [the buildings] in repair only so long as the owners live and have the means. Once the builder is dead, no one will care for the buildings; the son will neglect his father's work, the mother her son's, brothers and friends will take no care for each other's buildings; . . . if all these buildings and erections were attended to and repaired for a century, the lands of every city, and even village, would be adorned with monuments; but as a matter of fact the roads leading to the cities are strewn with fallen columns of stone.

58. The name of this building is given variously in tradition and literature as Nur Sarai, Nur Mahal Sarai, and Nur Jahan Sarai. Nur Sarai is the term used by Jahangir (*Tuzuk* 2.192): "On the 21st of the same month I took up my quarters at Nur-saray" See also *Tuzuk* 2.220, 249.

59. *Tuzuk* 2.100. See also *Ain-i Akbari* 1.232.

60. Shujauddins, p. 102.

61. *Tuzuk* 2.192.

62. Alexander Cunningham, "Report of A Tour in the Punjab in 1878–79, U.P. XIV." Archaeological Survey of India, as quoted by C. Pant, pp. 197–99. Cunningham notes (p. 197) that large pieces of old brick and a variety of coins have been unearthed there, some of which date to well before Nur Jahan's time. The Shujauddins (p. 102) give the name of the town on the ancient site as Kot Ghalur.

63. Cunningham in C. Pant, p. 197.

64. Cunningham in C. Pant, p. 197. P. Brown's comment (*Architecture*, p. 100) on the Jalandhar *sarai* is as follows: "a small but attractive structure although somewhat of the 'precious' order, as the designer has aimed at a nicety of detail rather than breadth or strength."

65. Taken from Cunningham's translation in C. Pant, p. 199.

66. Cunningham in C. Pant, p. 197.

67. Cunningham (in C. Pant, p. 198) notes that the walls of the exterior court to the emperor's quarters had disappeared by the time he examined the building in 1838.

68. *Tuzuk* 2.192.

69. See *Tuzuk* 2.220–49.

70. Temple in Mundy 2.78n.

71. Mundy 2.78–79.

72. Temple in Mundy 2.78n-79n; see Cunningham, pp. 159–62.

73. P. Brown, *Architecture*, p. 100; Smith, p. 180; Latif, *Agra*, pp. 183, 184; Havell, *Agra*, p. 85, and *Indian Art*, p. 131; Villiers Stuart, p. 52; Shujauddins, pp. 102–4; Peter Andrews, "The Architecture and Gardens of Islamic India," in Gray, p. 112; Gascoigne, p. 159.

74. Shujauddins, p. 101.

75. Pelsaert, p. 5.

76. Crowe et al., pp. 123–24.

77. Crowe et al., p. 124. See also P. Brown, *Architecture*, p. 101.

78. Andrews, in Gray, p. 112.

79. Crowe et al., p. 124.

80. Andrews, in Gray, pp. 112–13.

81. Andrews, in Gray, p. 113.

82. Gascoigne, p. 159.

83. Smith, pp. 174–75.

84. Gascoigne, pp. 159–60.

85. Smith, p. 198. A contemporaneous example can be found in the Gol Mandal in Udaipur, built around 1623 for Shah Jahan.

86. Gascoigne, p. 159.

87. Gascoigne, p. 159.

88. Andrews, in Gray, p. 113.

89. Haig and Burn, p. 553.

90. Andrews, in Gray, pp. 111–12. See also P. Brown, *Architecture*, p. 102.

91. Gascoigne, p. 159.

92. Joshi, pp. 10, 13.

93. Plaster has been lost on the exterior of the tomb, and it is possible that other patterns may have originally been included. Only these three, however, were remaining at the time of my visit in 1988. See also Welch, *Emperor's Album*, p. 21; Villiers Stuart, p. 53.

94. Again, my thanks to M. C. Joshi of the ASI, New Delhi.

95. Andrews, in Gray, p. 112; Havell, *Agra*, p. 89.

96. Andrews, in Gray, p. 109.

97. Joshi, pp. 11–12.

98. Joshi, p. 15.

99. Joshi, pp. 13, 14; Havell, *Agra*, p. 87.

100. Joshi, p. 15.

101. Andrews, in Gray, p. 112; P. Brown (*Architecture*, p. 100) calls them "broad."

102. Andrews, in Gray, p. 113; see *Tuzuk* 1.152, where Jahangir noted having ordered "a large and lofty gateway with minarets of white stone" to be built at his father's tomb.

103. C.f. *Tuzuk* 1.90–91.

104. Haig and Burn, p. 552.

105. Says Smith (p. 180): "[The *pietra dura* work is] equal to or surpassing in splendour the finest work of the kind executed in Shah Jahan's reign."

106. P. Brown, *Architecture*, p. 100.

107. Kak, p. 80; P. Brown, *Architecture*, p. 88.

108. Shujauddins, p. 44; see also Kak, p. 81.

109. Says P. Brown, *Architecture* (p. 100), e.g.: "[Jahangir's] mausoleum . . . was probably constructed after his death under the order of his remarkable consort, Nur Mahall Begum." See Fergusson, p. 304; Havell, *Indian Art*, p. 137; and the discussion in chapter 12.

110. Shujauddins, p. 124.

111. *Badshah-nama* E&D 7.70.

112. Shujauddins, p. 126.

113. Its exact limits, however, cannot now be traced because of the general decline and disrepair of the site. Moynihan, p. 129.

114. Shujauddins, p. 127.

115. Says Villiers Stuart (p. 131): "Its [Jahangir's tomb] model was that of Itimad-ud-Daulah . . . but . . . on an immense scale."

116. "The central platform of the roof seems to have contained a Bara Dari" (Shujauddins, p. 127).

117. Shujauddins, pp. 127, 128, 129; Latif, *Lahore*, p. 109.

118. Shujauddins, p. 127.

119. All taken, says Latif, *Lahore* (p. 110), when Ranjit Singh, "stripped the building of its costly ornamental stones."

120. According to the Shujauddins (p. 127n), the *Ibratnama* of 1854 noted that Nur Jahan's tomb "was not completed."

Chapter 10. In the Gardens of Eternal Spring

1. Villiers Stuart, p. 126; see pp. 42–43.
2. *Tuzuk* 1.106.
3. *Tuzuk* 2.232.
4. *Tuzuk* 2.64.
5. See Findly, "Idea of Kashmir."
6. Bernier, p. 284.
7. *Tuzuk* 2.178.
8. Crowe et al., p. 17.
9. Crowe et al., pp. 19–20.
10. Villiers Stuart, pp. 13–14.
11. Terry in Foster, *Early Travels*, p. 303.
12. Mundy 2.214–15.
13. Mundy 2.215.
14. *Tuzuk* 1.5. On Kashmiri flowers in the borders of miniature paintings, see P. Brown, *Painting*, pp. 139–40.
15. Shujauddins, p. 105.
16. Pelsaert, p. 5.
17. *Tuzuk* 1.3.
18. The identification of the modern Ram Bagh with the site of Babur's first Agra garden is fairly well accepted by modern scholars. See Villiers Stuart, p. 42; Crowe et al., p. 63; Havell, *Agra*, pp. 92–94; Latif, *Agra*, pp. 188, 189.
19. *Tuzuk* 1.4
20. *Tuzuk* 1.5
21. *Tuzuk* 2.95.
22. *Tuzuk* 2.197. The question, then, is whether Nur Jahan acquired the garden before or after her first trip to Kashmir: if before, then a burgeoning love of gardens would have occasioned the trip north; if after, Kashmir would have so aroused her to garden that she began, perhaps, by appropriating the Nur Afshan as her own. Given the ascendance of another garden likely hers as well (the Nur Manzil) *before* the first trip to Kashmir, it is most probable that Nur Jahan had the Nur Afshan in hand prior to trekking north and that she acquired it only after seeing what a beautiful job Khwaja Jahan had done in maintaining it. According to Latif (*Agra*, p. 188), the Ram Bagh was "one of the oldest garden enclosures in Agra in which was the garden palace of Nur Afshan."
23. *Tuzuk* 2.198.
24. *Tuzuk* 2.199–200.
25. *Tuzuk* 2.205–6.
26. Villiers Stuart, p. 5; Crowe et al., p. 63.
27. Crowe et al., pp. 63–66.
28. H. Beveridge in *Tuzuk* 2.76n.
29. *Tuzuk* 1.232, 252.
30. Havell, *Agra*, p. 95; Latif, *Agra*, p. 190. See also Temple in Mundy 2.214n. Mundy himself (2.188, 190) visited the Dahra Bagh, for instance, in June of 1632 on the occasion of Shah Jahan's return to Agra from "warringe against Decan." It is interesting

that the Englishman called it the "Darree ca baag," indicating that the name Nur Manzil had had a short life (as one would expect under the anti-Nur Jahan campaigns of the new emperor).

31. *Tuzuk* 2.75–76, 84.
32. *Tuzuk* 2.98.
33. Pelsaert, p. 5.
34. Mundy 2.214.
35. Mundy 2.78–79.
36. Temple in Mundy 2.79n; see Latif, *Agra*, p. 190.
37. Pelsaert, p. 5. His Charbagh, a generic name, could be any of the Persian-style gardens strung along this far bank, including perhaps the "Char Bagh, or garden palace of Babar, . . . situated to the east of the Kachpura village" (Latif, *Agra*, p. 191).
38. Temple in Mundy 2.214n.
39. Mundy 2.215.
40. Temple in Mundy 2.215n.
41. Mundy 2.83–84.
42. Crowe et al., p. 131.
43. Villiers Stuart, pp. 132–33.
44. *Tuzuk* 1.91–93. See Jahangir's account of Kashmir's land and culture in *Tuzuk* 2.140ff.
45. *Tuzuk* 1.91–93.
46. *Tuzuk* 1.406, 412, 442.
47. Pelsaert, p. 35.
48. *Tuzuk* 1.96.
49. Pelsaert, p. 35.
50. Bernier, p. 350. Bernier (p. 385), in fact, went so far as to attribute the heat of the plains to Kashmir itself:

> This extraordinary heat is occasioned by the high mountains of *Kachemire*; for being to the north of our road, they intercept the cool breezes which would refresh us from that quarter, at the same time that they reflect the scorching sunbeams, and leave the whole country arid and suffocating.

51. *Tuzuk* 2.35.
52. *Tuzuk* 2.134.
53. H. Beveridge (*Tuzuk* 2.164n) suggests that this is the Gurais Valley mentioned in Lawrence, p. 16.
54. *Tuzuk* 2.164.
55. *Tuzuk* 1.92.
56. *Tuzuk* 1.93; 2.177.
57. E.g., *Tuzuk* 2.151.
58. *Tuzuk* 2.134, 178, 238; Bernier, pp. 406–7.
59. E.g., *Tuzuk* 2.163.
60. Pelsaert, p. 35. Jahangir (*Tuzuk* 2.146, 159), however, said that Kashmiri pears were "better than those of Kabul, or Badakhshan," and that the cherry "of Kashmir is not inferior to that of Kabul; it is even better grown."
61. *Tuzuk* 2.144, 145, 146, 159, 161.
62. Pelsaert, p. 34.
63. *Tuzuk* 1.92.
64. Bernier, p. 414.
65. *Tuzuk* 2.174.
66. Pelsaert, pp. 33–34; *Tuzuk* 1.92.

67. E.g., *Tuzuk* 2.144–45; Pelsaert, p. 34.
68. Villiers Stuart, p. 157.
69. Lawrence, pp. 19–21.
70. Pant, p. 117.
71. Villiers Stuart, p. 159.
72. Pant, p. 117.
73. *Tuzuk* 2.150–51.
74. *Tuzuk* 2.162.
75. *Tuzuk* 2.238.
76. *Tuzuk* 2.154.
77. *Tuzuk* 2.151.
78. Bernier, pp. 399–400.
79. Crowe et al., p. 96.
80. Villiers Stuart, pp. 163–66.
81. *Tuzuk* 2.151.
82. Villiers Stuart, p. 191.
83. Crowe et al., pp. 78–80.
84. *Tuzuk* 2.173, 237; Pelsaert, p. 33.
85. Bernier, p. 413.
86. Bernier, p. 413.
87. Villiers Stuart, pp. 191–95.
88. Shujauddins, p. 40.
89. *Tuzuk* 1.94.
90. *Tuzuk* 1.92–93; *Tuzuk* 2.141–42, 173.
91. *Tuzuk* 1.92.
92. Crowe et al., p. 110.
93. Villiers Stuart, pp. 130, 185.
94. *Tuzuk* 1.92; *Tuzuk* 2.142, 173–74.
95. *Tuzuk* 1.92; *Tuzuk* 2.173.
96. Villiers Stuart, pp. 185–86.
97. *Tuzuk* 1.92.
98. *Tuzuk* 2.174.
99. Bernier, p. 414.
100. *Tuzuk* 2.173.
101. *Tuzuk* 2.174.
102. Pelsaert, p. 33.
103. *Tuzuk* 2.174.
104. Two inscriptions at the site date the building of the structures at the spring to 1609 and 1616 (Villiers Stuart, pp. 187–88), and Jahangir remarked that when he saw the garden in 1620 what he had ordered done had been completed (*Tuzuk* 2.173).

Chapter 11. The Rebellion of Mahabat Khan

1. Prasad, p. 385. Mahabat Khan's "sovereignty" over Jahangir's imperial camp lasted from the end of March to the beginning of August 1626, a little over a hundred days. *Ikbal-nama-i Jahangiri* E&D 6.419, 429. See also Dow 3.84, 93.
2. See *Tuzuk* 1.24.
3. Van den Broecke, p. 96.
4. *Tuzuk* 1.24.

5. *Tuzuk* 1.146, 241, 248, 397; *Tuzuk* 2.121, 124–25, 231.
6. *Tuzuk* 1.147, 258, 279; *Tuzuk* 2.85, 160–61, 212.
7. *Intikhab-i Jahangir-Shahi* E&D 6.452.
8. *Tuzuk* 2.251, 246.
9. *Tuzuk* 2.259–60.
10. *Tuzuk* 2.231.
11. Shujauddins, pp. 70–71.
12. Said van den Broecke (p. 96): "[The] King loved him not as a servant, but like a father in times of difficulty, which indeed he had shown himself to be."
13. *Tuzuk* 2.271ff., 288; van den Broecke, pp. 65, 96.
14. Dow's account (3.82), though, does suggest that Mahabat Khan had been "shocked at . . . [Shah Jahan's] reiteration of treachery" against the crown.
15. Prasad, p. 330.
16. Van den Broecke, p. 96.
17. Dow 3.81.
18. Dow 3.83; see also van den Broecke, p. 74.
19. Dow 3.83.
20. E&D 6.451–52.
21. Roe 1.262; see Mundy 2.204.
22. C. Pant, pp. 69–70. Manucci's late account (1.164), written during Shah Jahan's reign and therefore quite sympathetic to Mahabat Khan, suggested that many courtiers were envious of Mahabat Khan's long-standing intimacy with Jahangir and that Asaf Khan and Nur Jahan had for some time toyed with assassination, e.g., "they placed ten thousand armed horsemen on the roads, hoping to get him killed."
23. Van den Broecke, p. 96; see De Laet, p. 222.
24. Van den Broecke, p. 74.
25. De Laet, pp. 222–23, 224.
26. A key player in the whole of this event, Fidai Khan had been an attendant of the emperor's since Jahangir's childhood under the name Sulaiman Beg. He received the title by which was best known in late 1607. *Tuzuk* 1.131.
27. Van den Broecke, p. 75.
28. De Laet, p. 224.
29. Van den Broecke, p. 74.
30. *Ikbal-nama-i Jahangiri* E&D 6.420.
31. Prasad, p. 367. Bits and pieces of an alternate version of the story had Mahabat Khan consent to go to Bengal and receive his recall to the imperial court there (*Ikbal-nama-i Jahangiri* E&D 6.420). Another alternate narrative had Parviz, "acting on bad advice," apparently believing the ill reports about his minister, asking Jahangir himself to recall Mahabat Khan (Van den Broecke, p. 74). Finally, Dow (3.83) suggests that Mahabat Khan was ordered to court, but before he got the orders, he had set out with Parviz to Bengal.
32. Van den Broecke, p. 75.
33. Misra, p. 36. Dow (3.83) argues that Mahabat Khan had kept the elephants he had taken in the battle of Benares, which ordinarily should have reverted to the crown. His son also had presents he had received in resettling the province that had to be returned. C. Pant (p. 70) calls the material in question "the Bengal booty."
34. Van den Broecke, p. 75; see also De Laet, p. 224; Dow 3.84.
35. *Ikbal-nama-i Jahangiri* E&D 6.420; van den Broecke, p. 75; De Laet, p. 225; Dow 3.84. Mutamid Khan called the Rajputs "brave men united in one cause," presumably because they had, in their loyalty, the vindication of their chief solely in mind.

36. *Ikbal-nama-i Jahangiri* E&D 6.420; van den Broecke, p. 75; De Laet, p. 225. Van den Broecke did not have him personally forbidden from the court as Mutamid Khan did, though in the Dutch account Mahabat Khan did not himself go at first. Also, van den Broecke said that Nur Jahan and her brother wrote to the minister when they heard of his approach asking him "why he was coming without the order of the King, and warned him that it might lead to evil consequences."

37. De Laet, p. 225.

38. *Tatimma-i Wakiat-i Jahangiri* E&D 6.396. See Appendix C, "Institutes of Jahangir" in E&D 6.512.

39. *Tatimma-i Wakiat-i Jahangiri* E&D 6.396–97; *Ikbal-nama-i Jahangiri* E&D 6.420.

40. *Ikbal-nama-i Jahangiri* E&D 6.420; Dow 3.85. According to van den Broecke's colorful narrative, as "soon as Mahabat Khan's son-in-law came to the King, every one brought serious charges against him and, instigated by Asaf Khan, the King ordered him to be soundly beaten with shoes." De Laet (pp. 225–26) offered another scenario: "He was paraded through the camp with uncovered head, mounted on an elephant for all to see."

41. *Ikbal-nama-i Jahangiri* E&D 6.420.

42. *Ikbal-nama-i Jahangiri* E&D 6.421. According to De Laet's narrative (p. 226), the first attack was made by Nur Jahan:

> In order to bring about his destruction, they crossed the river with a great army, which is said to have numbered 50,000 horse, at a time when the king was asleep in his tent, and made a violent attack upon the army of Mahobotghan, which only consisted of 5,000 Raspots.

43. *Ikbal-nama-i Jahangiri* E&D 6.421–22.

44. *Ikbal-nama-i Jahangiri* E&D 6.422.

45. *Ikbal-nama-i Jahangiri* E&D 6.422; Dow 3.86–87. Van den Broecke described Jahangir's fear upon being startled by Mahabat Khan as follows: "[Finding] no guards or attendants either to his right or his left, he almost died of fear, which changed his whole being."

46. *Ikbal-nama-i Jahangiri* E&D 6.422–23. See van den Broecke, pp. 76–77; De Laet, p. 226; Dow 3.87–88.

47. Manucci 1.164.

48. *Ikbal-nama-i Jahangiri* E&D 6.423. Says Dow (3.88):

> [The] Sultana, when Mohabet was busy in securing the person of the emperor, made her escape to her brother. He considered, that nothing was done, so long as that haughty woman remained out of his power. He resolved to prosecute his plan, with the same resolute boldness with which it was begun.

49. *Ikbal-nama-i Jahangiri* E&D 6.423.

50. *Ikbal-nama-i Jahangiri* E&D 6.424.

51. *Ikbal-nama-i Jahangiri* E&D 6.424. See Dow 3.89.

52. Manucci 1.164.

53. *Ikbal-nama-i Jahangiri* E&D 6.424. Dow 3.89. Prasad (p. 374) argues that neither Jahangir nor Mahabat Khan wanted battle, Jahangir because he felt the imperial forces were outnumbered by the Rajputs and doomed to lose and Mahabat Khan because a battle would expose the hostile nature of his actions. He had hoped, argues Prasad, to preserve the illusion that Jahangir had come with him willingly, and the battle therefore was not in his best interest. See also the Shujauddins, p. 77.

54. *Ikbal-nama-i Jahangiri* E&D 6.424.

55. *Ikbal-nama-i Jahangiri* E&D 6.425.

56. *Ikbal-nama-i Jahangiri* E&D 6.425.

57. Dow 3.89.

58. *Ikbal-nama-i Jahangiri* E&D 6.425.

59. *Ikbal-nama-i Jahangiri* E&D 6.426.

60. *Ikbal-nama-i Jahangiri* E&D 6.425.

61. Mutamid Khan (*Ikbal-nama-i Jahangiri* E&D 6.426) confessed: "I was paralyzed at this sight, as if a mill-stone had been revolving on the top of my head."

62. *Ikbal-nama-i Jahangiri* E&D 6.426.

63. Dow 3.89.

64. The *Iqbalnama* (E&D 6.425) said that Asaf Khan set out to do battle "determined to pass the river in attendance upon Nur Jahan Begam."

65. *Ikbal-nama-i Jahangiri* E&D 6.426.

66. Van den Broecke, p. 76.

67. Dow 3.89; *Ikbal-nama-i Jahangiri* E&D 6.426.

68. *Ikbal-nama-i Jahangiri* E&D 6.426–27. Dow (3.89) says that it was Nur Jahan's daughter Ladli who received the arrow wound.

69. Dow 3.89–90.

70. *Ikbal-nama-i Jahangiri* E&D 6.427. It is odd that Dow (3.184), in referring probably to this event, should be so critical: "Her passions were indeed too masculine. When we see her acting the part of a soldier, she excites ridicule more than admiration; and we are apt to forget that delicacy, beyond which her sex ceases to please."

71. Van den Brocke, p. 76.

72. *Ikbal-nama-i Jahangiri* E&D 6.427–28; see De Laet, pp. 227, 229–230.

73. Van den Broecke, p. 76.

74. Van den Broecke, pp. 75–77.

75. *Ikbal-nama-i Jahangiri* E&D 6.428; van den Broecke, pp. 76, 77; De Laet, p. 227.

76. *Ikbal-nama-i Jahangiri* E&D 6.427.

77. Van den Broecke, pp. 77. Dow's rendition of the story (3.90–91) says that initially Nur Jahan had been able to escape to Lahore, but after receiving letters from the emperor saying that he was being treated well under Mahabat Khan and urging her for "his peace and safety" to return to camp, she came back and submitted to Mahabat Khan.

78. Van den Broecke, p. 77. According to De Laet (p. 227): "For the Queen Nourziahanbegem, who had hitherto been worshipped like a goddess, was now neglected and deserted by her usual entourage."

79. Dow 3.91.

80. Dow 3.92.

81. Dow 3.92.

82. *Ikbal-nama-i Jahangiri* E&D 6.428.

83. Van den Broecke, p. 77.

84. *Ikbal-nama-i Jahangiri* E&D 6.428.

85. Van den Broecke, p. 77; De Laet, p. 227; see also Mundy 2.204.

86. *Ikbal-nama-i Jahangiri* E&D 6.428.

87. *Ikbal-nama-i Jahangiri* E&D 6.429.

88. Van den Broecke (p. 77) calls her "Mouniza Begum."

89. De Laet, pp. 223, 228.

90. De Laet (p. 228) made an odd remark here—that Manija Begam "easily persuaded him to restore her husband to his governorship" because "she had long had an understanding" with him. No other source suggests such a relationship.

91. Van den Broecke, pp. 77–78; De Laet, p. 228.

92. *Ikbal-nama-i Jahangiri* E&D 6.428–29.

93. Van den Broecke, p. 78.

94. *Ikbal-nama-i Jahangiri* E&D 6.429; van den Broecke, pp. 78–79.

95. *Ikbal-nama-i Jahangiri* E&D 6.429. Dow (pp. 93–94) says that Mahabat Khan decided to leave Kabul for Lahore because of the fight that broke out between his men and the emperor's.

96. *Ikbal-nama-i Jahangiri* E&D 6.429.

97. *Ikbal-nama-i Jahangiri* E&D 6.429.

98. Van den Broecke, p. 79.

99. *Ikbal-nama-i Jahangiri* E&D 6.429; De Laet, p. 229.

100. Van den Broecke, p. 79.

101. Van den Broecke, p. 79; see Dow 3.93–94.

102. *Ikbal-nama-i Jahangiri* E&D 6.429; see Dow 3.92–93.

103. *Ikbal-nama-i Jahangiri* E&D 6.429.

104. *Ikbal-nama-i Jahangiri* E&D 6.429.

105. Jahangir was apparently able to convince Mahabat Khan that he had been a helpless pawn in the hands of his wife and of Asaf Khan.

106. Dow 3.92. Nur Jahan "concealed her schemes so effectually," says Dow (p. 93), "that they escaped the penetrating eyes of Mohabet."

107. Van den Broecke, p. 79.

108. *Ikbal-nama-i Jahangiri* E&D 6.430; De Laet, p. 229.

109. Van den Broecke, p. 79.

110. Mutamid Khan gave the number at 2,000 men. *Ikbal-nama-i Jahangiri* E&D 6.430.

111. Van den Broecke, pp. 79, 80. Van den Broecke (p. 80) also noted that Shahryar played an important role in gathering troops from Lahore for his mother-in-law.

112. *Tatimma-i Wakiat-i Jahangiri* E&D 6.430n; *Ikbal-nama-i Jahangiri* E&D 6.430. Van den Broecke (p. 80), however, portrayed Mahabat Khan not as resigned to his fate, but overconfident about the powers of his army: "Mahat Khan was not at all concerned about it, having the greatest confidence in his Rajputs. He said, 'They are like sheep before me. God willing, I shall destroy and scatter them like sand in the wind.' "

113. *Ikbal-nama-i Jahangiri* E&D 6.430. Dow's account (3.94) of the transfer of power says simply that Mahabat Khan "took a sudden resolution to throw up his power" and negotiated a quiet deal. Nur Jahan's subsequent demand for his death was overruled by her husband, who "commanded her to be silent."

114. Prasad, p. 386; see Dow 3.95.

115. *Ikbal-nama-i Jahangiri* E&D 6.430–31; see van den Broecke, pp. 79–81.

116. *Ikbal-nama-i Jahangiri* E&D 6.431. Van den Broecke (p. 80) reported that Asaf Khan was kept more freely now, as one of his legs was taken out of chains and he was given better food. He also reported (p. 81) that, characteristically, Mahabat Khan throughout the ordeal maintained his staunch loyalty to the emperor and refused to be seen as a traitor.

117. Van den Broecke, p. 81.

118. Van den Broecke, p. 81.

119. *Ikbal-nama-i Jahangiri* E&D 6.431.

120. Van den Broecke, p. 82. De Laet, p. 232.

121. Van den Broecke (p. 82) said that Asaf Khan, ever mindful of his need to appear faithful to the emperor, assured Jahangir that in doing whatever he needed to fulfill the obligation "he would have nothing to do with any one trying to bring about his

[Jahangir's] ruin." We know, however, that Mahabat Khan, along with Asaf Khan, became great favorites at Shah Jahan's court.

122. De Laet, p. 232.

123. De Laet, p. 232.

124. *Ikbal-nama-i Jahangiri* E&D 6.431; van den Broecke, p. 82.

125. Van den Broecke, p. 82.

126. Van den Broecke, pp. 82–83; De Laet, p. 233; see Latif, *Lahore*, p. 39. Blochmann (*Ain-i Akbari* 1.359) notes that Nur Jahan "contributed herself twelve lacs of rupees to the expedition" of the old Khankhanan against Mahabat Khan.

127. Van den Broecke, p. 81.

128. Dow (3.95) says further that "Asiph disapproved of his sister's violence. He knew the merit of Mohabet: he was not forgetful of his kindness to himself, when under his power. He was tired, besides, of the weakness of Jehangire, and of the Sultana's tyranny. He, however, observed a cautious silence."

129. *Ikbal-nama-i Jahangiri* E&D 6.434. Dow (3.95–96) preserves a tradition that believes Mahabat Khan, once in flight, made his way to Asaf Khan, who was at that time on the road between Lahore and Delhi. Mahabat Khan entered Asaf Khan's camp about nine o'clock at night and, finding his way into the inner passages, asked that the *vakil* come see him. Asaf Khan met his former captor and, seeing how miserable he was now and foreseeing what a good ally he would eventually make, was overjoyed to hear the visitor suggest an alliance with Shah Jahan on the grounds of Parviz's weakness and Shah Jahan's excellent skills in the field. Asaf Khan then sent Mahabat Khan off with the promise of a pardon and an army, both "having sworn fidelity to one another."

130. Van den Broecke, p. 96.

131. Van den Broecke, p. 96.

Chapter 12. Death of Jahangir and Retirement to Lahore

1. *Ma-asir-i-Jahangiri* E&D 6.444. Kamgar Khan said that Shah Jahan was "in a very feeble state of health."

2. *Ma-asir-i-Jahangiri* E&D 6.444.

3. Saksena, pp. 53–54; Prasad, p. 391.

4. *Ma-asir-i-Jahangiri* E&D 6.444. The *Iqbalnama* (E&D 6.432) gave the troop number as three or four hundred.

5. *Ma-asir-i-Jahangiri* E&D 6.444.

6. *Ma-asir-i-Jahangiri* E&D 6.444.

7. *Ikbal-nama-i Jahangiri* E&D 6.432–33; *Ma-asir-i-Jahangiri* E&D 6.444–45.

8. *Ma-asir-i-Jahangiri* E&D 6.445.

9. *Ikbal-nama-i Jahangiri* E&D 6.432; Saksena, pp. 54–55. For a history of Shah Jahan's relations with Persia and especially with Shah Abbas, see Saksena, pp. 210ff.

10. *Ikbal-nama-i Jahangiri* E&D 6.433.

11. Kamgar Khan (*Ma-asir-i-Jahangiri* E&D 6.445), obviously partisan, said:

> Just at this time [of the defeat at Tatta] a letter reached him from Nur Jahan informing him that his march had alarmed Mahabat Khan, whose forces had been driven away and dispersed, and that the Prince had better return to the Dakhin, and await a change of fortune. The advice of the Begam seemed good, so the Prince determined to return to the Dakhin by way of Gujarat.

12. Van den Broecke, p. 85.

13. Van den Broecke, p. 88.
14. Van den Broecke, p. 84.
15. *Ikbal-nama-i Jahangiri* E&D 6.432; De Laet, p. 233.
16. Van den Broecke, p. 84.
17. Terry, p. 412. See also Tod 1.294; 2.33. Van den Broecke (p. 84) said that various of Parviz's nobles were arrested for questioning after his death "for it was they who had always given him food and drink."
18. Shujauddins, p. 91.
19. Van den Broecke, p. 84.
20. Saksena, p. 55. Bulaqi was the nickname of Dawar Bakhsh, given to him "from *bulaq*, the ring worn by women in the septum of the nose. A boy is ornamented in this way in order that he may be supposed to be a girl, and thus escape from the effects of the Evil Eye" (Ball in Tavernier, p. 67n).
21. *Ikbal-nama-i Jahangiri* E&D 6.434; van den Broecke, p. 89; De Laet, p. 237.
22. De Laet, p. 236.
23. Saksena, p. 53.
24. De Laet, p. 236; see *Ikbal-nama-i Jahangiri* E&D 6.434 and van den Broecke, p. 88.
25. Van den Broecke, pp. 84–85; De Laet, p. 234.
26. Van den Broecke, p. 85.
27. Van den Broecke, pp. 85–86.
28. Dow (3.94ff), as noted above, suggests that the decision to approach Shah Jahan was not initially Mahabat Khan's but Asaf Khan's, who acted as midwife to the alliance.
29. *Ikbal-nama-i Jahangiri* E&D 6.434.
30. Van den Broecke, p. 89.
31. Dow (3.96) contends that the pardon of Mahabat Khan was from Jahangir and was engineered by Asaf Khan. See *Shah Jahan Nama*, p. 12.
32. Mundy 2.204.
33. Van den Broecke, pp. 86–87.
34. Van den Broecke, p. 85.
35. Van den Broecke, p. 88.
36. Van den Broecke, p. 88.
37. *Ikbal-nama-i Jahangiri* E&D 6.435. See also H. Beveridge in *Tuzuk* 2.vi.
38. *Ikbal-nama-i Jahangiri* E&D 6.435.
39. Saksena, p. 56.
40. De Laet, p. 237; Dow 3.101.
41. *Tuzuk* 2.180.
42. *Ikbal-nama-i Jahangiri* E&D 6.435.
43. Terry, pp. 381–82.
44. *Tuzuk* 2.176.
45. *Ikbal-nama-i Jahangiri* E&D 6.435. See also *Badshah-nama* E&D 7.5; De Laet, p. 237; Manucci 1.172; Prasad, p. 393.
46. *Ikbal-nama-i Jahangiri* E&D 6.435. Dow (3.101), oddly, gives Jahangir's death date as November 9, 1627, and van den Broecke (p. 89) gave Jahangir's age at death as 63.
47. *Badshah-nama* E&D 7.5.
48. *Ikbal-nama-i Jahangiri* E&D 6.436.
49. De Laet, p. 238.
50. Dow 3.108. See *Shah Jahan Nama*, pp. 12, 13.
51. *Ikbal-nama-i Jahangiri* E&D 6.436. See Dow 3.107.

52. *Majalisu-s Salatin* E&D 7.137.
53. *Ikbal-nama-i Jahangiri* E&D 6.436.
54. Van den Broecke, p. 90.
55. *Majalisu-s Salatin* E&D 7.137.
56. *Ikbal-nama-i Jahangiri* E&D 6.436. In this way Asaf Khan and his nobles hoped "to guard against mutinies and disturbances which might otherwise arise" (*Majalisu-s Salatin* E&D 7.137). See also De Laet, p. 238; Manucci 1.172; C. Pant, p. 76; and Saksena, p. 57. Initially, Dawar Bakhsh had been placed "by Nur Mahal's contrivance" under the care of Shahryar, but when Shahryar left for Lahore, he "had been put under the charge of Iradat Khan by Jahangir" (*Badshah-nama* E&D 7.6).
57. *Ikbal-nama-i Jahangiri* E&D 6.436. See *Shah Jahan Nama*, p. 12.
58. *Ikbal-nama-i Jahangiri* E&D 6.436. The *Badshah-nama* (E&D 7.5–6) suggested that Dawar Bakhsh (Bulaqi) was not raised to the throne in Bhimbar but sometime after the journey had recommenced, perhaps even as far in their journey as Lahore.
59. Van den Broecke, p. 89. Dow (3.107) claims, however, that "the will of Jehangire had been opened immediately upon his demise. He had, at the instigation of the Sultana named his fourth son Shariar, as his successor in the throne."
60. On the kingdom Mundy (2.107) said: "Jehangueere [Jahangir] left it to Sultan Bulake [Bulaki] Cozrooes sonne."
61. Manucci 1.169, 172.
62. Van den Broecke, p. 89. Tirmizi (p. 137), however, preserves a *nishan* of Dawar Bakhsh in which he said he came to the throne with the support of Nur Jahan.
63. Van den Broecke, p. 89.
64. Van den Broecke, p. 90.
65. Van den Broecke, p. 90.
66. Van den Broecke, p. 90. See *Shah Jahan Nama*, p. 12.
67. Van den Broecke, p. 90.
68. Van den Broecke, p. 90.
69. Van den Broecke, p. 97.
70. Van den Broecke, p. 90.
71. Van den Broecke, p. 90.
72. Van den Broecke, p. 96.
73. Van den Broecke, p. 97.
74. Van den Broecke, p. 93.
75. *Badshah-nama* E&D 7.5–6; Saksena, pp. 57–58.
76. *Ikbal-nama-i Jahangiri* E&D 6.436.
77. *Ikbal-nama-i Jahangiri* E&D 6.436.
78. Latif, *Lahore*, p. 50. See *Shah Jahan Nama*, p. 13.
79. *Badshah-nama* E&D 7.6.
80. *Ikbal-nama-i Jahangiri* E&D 6.436; see Dow 3.108.
81. Van den Broecke, p. 89.
82. *Badshah-nama* E&D 7.5.
83. C. Pant (p. 77) notes that Nur Jahan "along with her sister was virtually reduced to the position of a state prisoner." Since Manija was probably back in Agra with her husband Qasim Khan (he was to welcome Shah Jahan there upon his arrival), the sister in question here may have been Khadija.
84. *Ikbal-nama-i Jahangiri* E&D 6.436.
85. Gascoigne, p. 179.
86. Van den Broecke, p. 90. Again, note Dow (3.107) who suggests that Shahryar had been named "as his [Jahangir's] successor in the throne" in the late emperor's will.

87. *Ikbal-nama-i Jahangiri* E&D 6.436.

88. *Ikbal-nama-i Jahangiri* E&D 6.436.

89. *Ikbal-nama-i Jahangiri* E&D 6.436. Dow (3.108) claims that Shahryar appointed Bayasanghar commander of his forces because he was "ill of a venereal disorder himself."

90. *Ikbal-nama-i Jahangiri* E&D 6.436–37; see also *Majalisu-s Salatin* E&D 7.137.

91. *Ikbal-nama-i Jahangiri* E&D 6.437.

92. Saksena (p. 58) gives him as Afzal Khan.

93. Saksena, pp. 58–59.

94. *Ikbal-nama-i Jahangiri* E&D 6.437; Dow 3.108.

95. *Ikbal-nama-i Jahangiri* E&D 6.437; Dow 3.108.

96. Prasad, p. 401.

97. *Ikbal-nama-i Jahangiri* E&D 6.437.

98. Manucci 1.174.

99. Prasad, p. 402. In spite of Shah Jahan's inclination toward observing a period of mourning, Saksena (p. 60) notes that his counsellors "advised him to hasten; and the astrologers were asked to choose the auspicious time for the journey to the north."

100. Saksena, p. 61. Part of the *Iqbalnama* account (E&D 6.438) stated that "On reaching the boundaries of the Rana, Shah Jahan was waited upon by Rana Karan at Kokanda, who, as well as his father Rana Amar Singh, had shown great loyalty. He offered his tribute, and received great gifts and honours."

101. Van den Broecke, p. 95.

102. Tahmuras and Hoshang were included, argued Tavernier (2.270–71), because even though they had become Christian and were thus not in the running for the throne, being "kind-hearted," they had warned Bulaqi early on of the duplicitous designs of Asaf Khan. The fate of the third brother and son of Daniyal, who fought to the end with Shahryar, is stated by Maclagan (p. 74) as follows: "After being signally defeated in battle near Lahore, [Bayasanghar] vanished into oblivion."

103. *Ikbal-nama-i Jahangiri* E&D 6.438; Dow 3.109–10.

104. Says Dow (3.111): Shah Jahan, "either by the dager or bowstring, dispatched all the males of the house of Timur; so that he himself and his children only remained of the posterity of Baber, who conquered India."

105. *Ikbal-nama-i Jahangiri* E&D 6.438.

106. *Ikbal-nama-i Jahangiri* E&D 6.438. Manucci (1.175) preserved a version of the story in which Dawar Bakhsh, upon Shah Jahan's accession, was not killed but fled to Persia "where he ended his life in destitution." Tavernier (1.271–72) also preserved this story (but see 1.66–67!), noting that the young emperor Bulaqi took to flight, wandering

> for a long time in India as a sort of *Fakir*. But at length, wearied with that kind of life, he took refuge in Persia, where he was magnificently received by Shah Safavi, who bestowed upon him a pension worthy of a great Prince. He enjoys it still, and I had an opportunity of conversing with him during my travels in Persia, and drank and ate with him.

Ball's note here (in Tavernier 1.272n) offers support to confirm Tavernier's account.

107. De Laet, p. 240; see Mundy 2.105 and Dow 3.110. In Manucci's version (1.175), two of the princes, presumably the two sons of Daniyal in question, were bricked up inside a room and left to die.

108. Saksena, p. 63. As Bernier (p. 199) had noted earlier:

> In *Hindoustan* the right of governing is usually disputed by all the sons of the deceased monarch, each of whom is reduced to the cruel alternative of sacrificing his brothers, that he himself may reign, or of suffering his own life to be forfeited for the security and stability of the dominion of another.

109. *Ikbal-nama-i Jahangiri* E&D 6.438. According to Saksena (p. 62), Shah Jahan visited the tomb of Shaikh Muinuddin Chishti and, in fulfillment of a vow he made at the time of the Mewar campaign, ordered a marble mosque to be built.

110. *Majalisu-s Salatin* E&D 7.137.

111. See *Tuzuk* 2.75–76.

112. *Ikbal-nama-i Jahangiri* E&D 6.438; Prasad, p. 402. C. Pant (p. 79) gives the date of arrival outside Agra as January 28 and Dow (3.110) as January 31. Although C. Pant (p. 79) notes that Shah Jahan had "encamped in the Nur Manzil garden"—confirmed by Dow's (3.110) "in the garden which from its beauty was called the Habitation of Light" (i.e., *nur manzil*)—the *Iqbalnama* (E&D 6.438) said simply "the gardens," and Saksena (p. 63) says "in the Dahara garden," confirming in this last that the Nur Jahani name for the site was indeed short-lived.

113. *Majalisu-s Salatin* E&D 7.137, 141. The *Badshah-nama* (E&D 7.6) gave the date as February 6.

114. *Majalisu-s Salatin* E&D 7.137.

115. Say the Shujauddins (p. 122), by

> the roadside the corpse was given the last wash and was prepared for burial according to the prevalent Muslim rites. At Chingas Serai, close to the Mughal mosque, there is a grave on a platform with a green flag fluttering over it. The common people take it to be Jahangir's grave. It is said that the last bath to the body was given here and the entrails, ripped out to save the corpse from early decomposition were entombed here.

116. Dow 3.178.

117. *Tuzuk* 1.63.

118. Latif, *Lahore*, pp. 44ff.

119. Finch in Foster, *Early Travels*, p. 161.

120. Monserrate, p. 159.

121. Hawkins in Foster, *Early Travels*, p. 120.

122. See, e.g., Villiers Stuart, p. 185; Lawrence, *Kashmir*, p. 194; and Moynihan, p. 128.

123. Latif, *Lahore*, p. 106.

124. Havell, *Indian Art*, p. 137.

125. Fergusson, pp. 304–5.

126. P. Brown, *Architecture*, p. 100.

127. Prasad (p. 399): "Here [in Shahdara in the garden of Nur Jahan] in time the widowed empress erected a magnificent mausoleum at her own expense."

128. In Crowe et al., p. 93.

129. Gascoigne (p. 179): "[Nur Jahan in retirement] occupied herself with building a tomb for her husband at Lahore."

130. Shujauddins, p. 123.

131. De Laet, p. 240.

132. Dow 3.123.

133. *Badshah-nama* E&D 7.70.

134. Dow 3.184.

135. Dow 3.184.

136. As noted by Dowson in *Badshah-nama* E&D 7.70n.

137. *Badshah-nama* E&D 7.69–70.

138. Dow 3.184.

139. Dow 3.184.

140. Misra (p. 40) argues instead, oddly, that after Jahangir's death Nur Jahan chose

voluntarily to retire from political life, thus leading "one to conclude that her interests were [always] confined to Jahangir and Jahangir alone." Had she wanted to, Misra continues, she could have retained power within the inner circles of the imperial palace where her knowledge and expertise would have been especially useful. Instead she freely committed herself to the life of a recluse now that Jahangir, "with whom were bound all her interests," was gone.

141. Gascoigne, p. 179.
142. Van den Broecke, p. 90.
143. That there were some monies kept as hers was suggested by the following remark of Manucci's (1.199): "While Aurangzeb was king, the whole of these treasures, and the treasures of Queen Nurjahan, were expended, owing to the falling off in the revenue." Irvine's note, however, says the "statement is not literally exact, for both Bahadur Shah in 1707 and the Sayyid brothers in 1719 disinterred large hoards within Agra Fort," presumably referring to the treasure of Nur Jahan which may still have been intact then. The implication in both accounts, however, is that although Nur Jahan did have a sizable treasure at the time of Jahangir's death, she was not allowed to use it by Shah Jahan.
144. *Ikbal-nama-i Jahangiri* E&D 6.405.
145. Desai in *Sribhanucandraganicarita*, pp. 45, 49.
146. Mundy 2.78; see also Mundy 2.101.
147. Saksena, p. vi.
148. Shujauddins, p. 124.
149. Finch in Foster, *Early Travels*, p. 186.
150. Shujauddins, p. 125.
151. Saksena, p. 130.
152. Saksena, pp. iv, vii.
153. Prasad, p. 403. See *Shah Jahan Nama*, pp. 333–34.
154. Prasad, p. 403; Shujauddins, p. 99.
155. Prasad, p. 403; Shujauddins, p. 125.
156. *Badshah-nama* E&D 7.69–70.
157. Prasad, p. 403.

Abbreviations and Selected Annotated Bibliography

(References have been left as published, with the exception of the diacriticals. Bibliographic narrative uses standard form.)

Primary Sources

Ain-i Akbari

Blochmann, H., trans. The *Ain-i Akbari by Abul-Fazl Allami*. Vol. 1. 1873. 2d ed., revised by D. C. Phillott. Calcutta: Royal Asiatic Society of Bengal, 1927.

Jarrett, Colonel H. S., trans. *Ain-i Akbari* by *Abul Fazl Allami*. Vols. 2, 3. Calcutta: Asiatic Society of Bengal, 1910, 1894.

The *Ain-i Akbari* is the third volume of Abul Fazl's *Akbarnama*. Volume one covers the history of the Timurid line up through Humayun, volume two is a detailed history of Akbar's reign, and volume three (the *Ain-i Akbari*) is a discussion of information about Akbar's reign arranged thematically.

Baburnama

Beveridge, Annette Susannah, trans. The *Baburnama in English* (*Memoirs of Babur*). Translated from the original Turki text of Zahirud-din Muhammad Babur Padshah Ghazi. 2 vols. London: Luzac, 1922. Reprint. New York: AMS Press, 1971.

Badauni

Lowe, W. H., trans. *Muntakhab-ut-Tawarikh by Abd-ul-Qadir bin Maluk Shah known as al-Badaoni*. Vol. 2. Calcutta: The Asiatic Society of Bengal, 1884. Reprint. Karachi: Karimsons, 1976.

Haig, Sir Wolseley, trans. *Muntakhabu-t-Tawarikh, by Abdu-l-Qadir ibn-i Mulukshah, known as al-Badaoni*. Vol. 3. Calcutta: The Asiatic Society of Bengal, 1925. Reprint. Karachi: Karimsons, 1978.

Written in secret between 1590 and 1596, this account of the Mughals, and especially of Akbar's reign, gives the view of a conservative Muslim.

Bernier

Constable, Archibald, ed. *Travels in the Mogul Empire, A.D. 1656–1668, by Francois Bernier*. London: Oxford University Press, 1891. 2d ed. New Delhi: S. Chand & Co., 1968.
This is a revised edition based upon Irving Brock's translation. Bernier was a celebrated French physician who was in the Mughal empire from 1658 to 1665. Among other things, he traveled with Tavernier to Bengal in 1665 during the latter's sixth and final voyage to the subcontinent.

Best

Foster, Sir William, ed. *The Voyage of Thomas Best to the East Indies (1612–14)*. London: Hakluyt Society, 1934.
Best sailed on the tenth voyage of the East India Company to India. Although his account tells us relatively little of Jahangir's court, it was a successful trip, marked by a victory over the Portuguese and the settlement of a factory at Surat.

De Laet

Hoyland, J. S., trans., and S. N. Banerjee, annot. *The Empire of the Great Mogol, A Translation of De Laet's "Description of India and Fragment of Indian History."* 1928. Reprint. Delhi: Idarah-i Adabiyat-i Delli, 1975.
Joannes De Laet's text is a 1631 Latin translation of materials originally written by Pelsaert and chronicled by van den Broecke, as well as materials from other travelers to India. Although he never went to India, he was a Director of the Dutch East India Company and concerned himself primarily with gathering information about the subcontinent.

Della Valle

Grey, Edward, ed. *The Travels of Pietro Della Valle in India*. 2 vols. London: Hakluyt Society, 1892.
This is from the old English translation of the original Italian done in 1664 by G. Havers. Della Valle was in India from February of 1623 to November of 1624 and left a detailed account of his somewhat limited travels in eight letters published beginning in 1663.

Du Jarric

Payne, C. H., trans. *Akbar and the Jesuits: An Account of the Jesuit Missions to the Court of Akbar by Father Pierre Du Jarric, S.J.* London: George Routledge & Sons, Ltd., 1926.
This translation from the French is of that portion of Du Jarric's *Historie* (completed in 1614) that deals with the reign of Akbar. It is an account of the Jesuit missions to the court of the early Mughal compiled from the letters and reports written by the Portuguese Fathers while on service there, and it provides one of the earliest European accounts of the Mughal empire. Du Jarric himself never went to India, residing much of his life in Bordeaux, and many of his Jesuit

authorities are left unnamed. A major source of information, however, was certainly Father Fernao Guerreiro, S.J.

E&D

Elliot, H. M., and John Dowson, trans. and ed. *The History of India as told by its Own Historians. The Muhammadan Period*. Vols. 5, 6, 7. London: Trübner and Co., 1873, 1875, 1877. Reprint. New York: AMS Press, Inc. 1966.
These volumes include selected translations of historical texts contemporary to the reigns of Akbar, Jahangir, and Shah Jahan.

Tabakat-i Akbari E&D

Vol. 5: *Tabakat-i Akbari* of Nizamu-d din Ahmad, Bakhshi, also known as the the *Tabakat-i Akbar-shahi* and the *Tarikh-i Nizami*. This work is a history of India, unusual because for the first time India alone is the subject and not other Asian countries as well. The author, Nizamuddin Ahmad, was for a long time *bakhshi* for Akbar in Gujarat and was throughout his life a loyal and devoted minister to the emperor.

Akbar-nama E&D

Vol. 6: *Akbar-nama* of Shaikh Abul Fazl. Abul Fazl Allami was the second son of Shaikh Mubarak, the elder being Shaikh Abul Fayz (better known as Fayzi), a popular poet of the time. Abul Fazl was a close companion and learned minister of Akbar's, whose two-volume *Akbarnama*, a historical account of the Mughal dynasty down through Akbar, and *Ain-i Akbari*, a detailed description of Mughal government, are essential sources for Akbar's reign.

Ikbal-nama-i E&D

Ikbal-nama-i Jahangiri of Mutamad Khan. This text is a history of the Mughal dynasty, whose third volume deals with Jahangir. Up until the middle of 1624, this part of the *Iqbalnama* is more or less an abridgment of Jahangir's own memoirs, the last two years of which (1623–24) Mutamid Khan himself transcribed; after the memoirs cease, the *Iqbalnama* continues the chronicle of the reign up to and beyond Jahangir's death in 1627. For these last three years of Jahangir's life, it is one of the best of the Persian sources available.

Intikhab-i Jahangiri-Shahi E&D

Intikhab-i Jahangiri-Shahi, by a contemporary and a companion of Jahangir's, possibly a certain Shaikh Abdu-l Wahab, author of *Akhlak-i Jahangiri*. Many of the narratives herein are firsthand, eyewitness accounts.

Ma-asir-i Jahangiri E&D

Ma-asir-i Jahangiri, of Kamgar Khan. Although the exact name of the text is unclear, Khwaja Kamgar Ghairat Khan intended with this text (completed early in the reign of Shah Jahan) to make up for the incompleteness of Jahangir's own memoirs.

Takmila-i Akbar-hama E&D

Takmila-i Akbar-nama, of Inayatu-lla, or Muhammad Salih. This text is the supplement to the *Akbarnama*, containing an account of the last four years of Akbar's reign after the murder of Abul Fazl.

Tatimma-i Wakiat-i Jahanairi E&D

Tatimma-i Wakiat-i Jahangiri, of Muhammad Hadi. This work is a completion of Jahangir's memoirs covering the years 1624 to 1627; included in it is an account of the rest of Jahagir's life taken in large part from the *Iqbalnama*. That Muhammad Hadi was a writer from the first quarter of the eighteenth century makes this text somewhat less useful than other chronicles.

Wikaya-i Asad Beg E&D

Wikaya-i Asad Beg. Also called *Halat-i Asad Beg*, this text is a personal memoir from the latter part of Akbar's reign and is especially good on the death of Abul Fazl.

Majalisu-s Salatin E&D

Vol. 7: *Majalisu-s Salatin*, of Muhammad Sharif Hanafi. Composed in the early part of Shah Jahan's reign, Hanafi compiled an abridged history of India using long histories of the period.

Badshah-nama E&D

Badshah-nama, of Abdu-l Hamid Lahori. This contemporary history of the first twenty years of the reign of Shah Jahan is intended to be in the style of Abul Fazl.

East India Company Letters

Danvers, Frederic Charles, ed. *Letters Received by the East India Company, From Its Servants in the East, Transcribed from the Original Correspondence Series of the India Office Records*. 5 vols. (1602–13, 1613–15, 1615, 1616, 1617). London: Sampson Low, Marston & Company, 1896, 1897, 1899, 1900, 1901. Reprint. Amsterdam: N. Israel, 1968.

English Factories

Foster, William, ed. *The English Factories in India, 1618–1621; The English Factories in India, 1622–1623. A Calendar of Documents in the India Office, British Museum and Public Record Office*. Oxford: The Clarendon Press, 1906; 1908.

Firishta

Briggs, John, trans. and ed. *History of the Rise of the Mahomedan Power in India Till the Year A.D. 1612, Translated from the Original Persian of Mahomed Kasim Ferishta*. London, 1829. Reprint. Calcutta: R. Cambray and Co., London: K. Paul, Trench, Trubner & Co., Ltd., 1908–110.

Firishta's *Gulshan-i Ibrahimi* was written in the early part of the seventeenth century. He had worked for rulers in Ahmadnagar and Bijapur but had traveled throughout much of the Mughal empire.

Floris

Moreland, W. H., ed., *Peter Floris: His Voyage to the East Indies in the* Globe, *1611–1615, The Contemporary Translation of his Journal*. London: Hakluyt Society, 1934.
Peter Floris was a Dutch merchant who took up the name Floris for use in England, his real name being Pieter Willemsz van Elbing. He was just over thirty when he joined the East India Company in London, and the voyage by the *Globe* was the seventh for the company.

Foster, *Early Travels*

Foster, William, ed. *Early Travels in India, 1583–1619*. Humphrey Milford: Oxford University Press, 1921.
This collection includes personal travel accounts of Ralph Fitch (1583–91), John Mildenhall (1599–1606), William Hawkins (1608–13), William Finch (1608–11), Nicholas Withington (1612–16), Thomas Coryat (1612–17), and Edward Terry (1616–19).

Guerreiro

Payne, C. H., trans. *Jahangir and the Jesuits, With an Account of the Travels of Benedict Goes and the Mission to Pegu, From the Relations of Father Fernao Guerreiro, S.J.* New York: Robert M. McBride & Co., 1930.
The most important material here comes from three letters written by Father Jerome Xavier to the Provincial of Goa, dated September 25, 1606, August 8, 1607, and September 24, 1608.

Gulbadan

Beveridge, Annette S., trans. *The History of Humayun (Humayun-nama), by Gulbadan Begam (Princess Rose-Body)*. 1901. Reprint. Delhi: Idarah-i Adabiyat-i Delli, 1972.
This volume includes the Persian text and English translation, and a long introduction and biographical data on women of the period.

Jourdain

Foster, William, ed. *The Journal of John Jourdain, 1608–1617, Describing his Experiences in Arabia, India, and the Malay Archipelago*. Cambridge: Hakluyt Society, 1905. Reprint. Nendeln/Liechtenstein: Kraus Reprint Limited, 1967.

Keshavadasa

Jahangirjaschandrika. In *Keshav Granthavali*. Edited by V. P. Misra. Vol. 3. Allahabad, 1959.
This Hindi text is a eulogistic tribute to the emperor Jahangir written in April of

1612 in reply to a question posed to Keshavadasa by Irij Khan, son of Abdur Rahim Khankhanan. The question was whether *udyam* ("effort") or *karma* ("fate") was superior and, in answering, the Hindi poet-laureate praised Jahangir's justice and the splendor of his court. The final verdict, predictably, was that both *udyam* and *karma* were equal.

Manrique

Luard, Lt.-Col. C. Eckford with Father H. Hosten, trans. and ed. *Travels of Fray Sebastien Manrique, 1629–1643; a translation of the Itinerario de las missiones orientales*. Oxford: for the Hakluyt Society, 1927.

Manrique was an Augustinian friar who came to the Bengal mission in 1629 and for the next six years remained in Arracan. After a long voyage to the Philippines and China, he traveled through northern India during the years 1640 to 1641 on his way back to Europe. His work *Itenerario* was published in 1649.

Manucci

Irvine, William, trans. *Storia do Mogor, or Mogul India, 1653–1708, by Niccolao Manucci, Venetian*. Vol. 1. London, 1907. Reprint. Calcutta: Editions Indian, 1965.

A native of Venice, Manucci arrived in India in 1656 as a gunner and a "physician." Over time he fought in military units under the Mughals and Hindu chieftains and held various positions of responsibility at the Mughal court until his death in India in 1717. His narrative is florid and rambunctious and appears to depend on local gossip for its many stories.

Manusmriti

Bühler, Georg, trans. *The Laws of Manu*. Oxford: Clarendon Press, 1886. Reprint. New York: Dover Publications, Inc., 1969.

Mehri

Sarapa-i Mehri. This manuscript is available through the Deutsche Staatsbibliothek, Berlin, and University Library, Bombay.

This is a work by a Persian poetess, who was brought up and patronized by Nur Jahan and used Mehri as her pen name.

Monserrate

Hoyland, J. S., trans., and S. N. Banerjee, annot. *The Commentary of Father Monserrate, On his Journey to the Court of Akbar*. Humphrey Milford: Oxford University Press, 1922.

Monserrate, one of the three members on the first Jesuit mission to Akbar, was at the Mughal court from 1580 to 1582. The original Latin text of this manuscript was edited by Father H. Hosten, S.J., and published in the memoirs of the Asiatic Society of Bengal (3:513–704).

Mundy

Temple, Sir Richard Carnac, ed. *The Travels of Peter Mundy, in Europe and Asia, 1608–1667*. Vol. 2, *Travels in Asia, 1628–1634*. London: Hakluyt Society, 1914.
Mundy arrived at Surat in 1628, was appointed to the Agra factory in 1630, and remained in India for eight years. His travels included the surrounds of Agra and Patna, from which he was able to give excellent and very detailed descriptions of local monuments. His historical sections appear to come from "common report," rather than from contemporary Persian chronicles and, therefore, have their own historical value. The text is illustrated with Mundy's own delightful line drawings of things he saw.

Pelsaert

Moreland, W. H., and P. Geyl, trans. *Jahangir's India, The* Remonstrantie *of Francisco Pelsaert*. Cambridge: W. Heffer & Sons Ltd., 1925.
Pelsaert was in Agra from 1620 to 1627. As a senior factor for the Dutch East India Company, he was a subordinate of van den Broecke's. His account was intended as a commercial report, and seems to be a combination of his own firsthand historical and linguistic knowledge and material gleaned from contemporary Persian sources.

Roe

Foster, William, ed. *The Embassy of Sir Thomas Roe to the Court of the Great Mogul, 1615–1619, As Narrated in His Journal and Correspondence*. 2 vols. London: Hakluyt Society, 1899.
Roe was in India as the first official ambassador from England to the Mughal court from August 1615 to February 1619 and with Jahangir's court from January 1616 to August 1618.

Shah Jahan Nama

Begley, W. E., and Z. A. Desai, ed. and comp. *The Shah Jahan Nama of Inayat Khan*. Delhi: Oxford University Press, 1990.
Using A. R. Fuller's almost complete translation (1851) of Inayat Khan's *Shah Jahan Nama* as a basis, Begley and Desai have produced a fully revised edition. Inayat Khan's text is an abridged chronicle of the history of Shah Jahan's reign based on the *Padshahnama*.

Sribhanucandraganicarita

Desai, Mohanlal Dalichand, ed. *Bhanucandra Caritra by His Pupil Gani Siddhicandra Upadhyaya*. Ahmedabad-Calcutta: The Sanchalaka-Singhi Jaina Granthamala, 1941.
This Sanskrit text is both a biography of the great Guru Upadhyaya Bhanucandra Gani and an autobiography of his student Siddhicandra Upadhyaya. Both Jain monks were present at the courts of Akbar and Jahangir and give us eyewitness accounts of intimate events in the inner chambers. Desai's lengthy introduction is an excellent account of the history of the Jains at court under these two emperors.

Taj Mahal

Begley, W. E., and Z. A. Desai, comp. and trans. *Taj Mahal: The Illumined Tomb. An Anthology of Seventeenth-Century Mughal and European Documentary Sources*. Cambridge, Mass. The Aga Khan Program for Islamic Architecture; Seattle and London: The University of Washington Press, 1989.

Tavernier

Ball, V., trans., and William Crooke, ed. *Travels in India by Jean-Baptiste Tavernier, Baron of Aubonne*. Vol. 1. 2d ed. London, Humphrey Milford: Oxford University Press, 1925.

This text was translated from the original French edition of 1676. Tavernier was a jewel merchant who, in all, made six voyages to India to buy and sell precious and semiprecious gemstones. His voyages covered the years 1631–67.

Terry

Terry, Edward. *A Voyage to East-India*. London: J. Wilkie, W. Cater, S. Hayes, E. Easton, 1777.

This text was reprinted from the edition of 1655. The young Edward Terry had just arrived in Surat in September of 1616 when he was called upon by Thomas Roe to be the ambassador's chaplain in the stead of John Hall who had recently died. Terry remained with Roe and accompanied him back to England in 1619. The original version of this account was presented to the throne in 1622; subsequent versions contained updated information from travelers returning from the Mughal empire.

Tod

Tod, Lieut.-Col. James. *Annals and Antiquities of Rajasthan, or, the Central and Western Rajpoot States of India*. 2 vols. Popular edition. London: George Routledge & Sons Ltd.; New York: E. P. Dutton & Co., 1914.

Tod compiled this extensive history of Rajasthan (1782–1835) from his own work in India.

Tuzuk

Rogers, Alexander, trans., and Henry Beveridge, ed. *The Tuzuk-i-Jahangiri, or Memoirs of Jahangir*. 2 vols. 1909–14. 2d ed. Delhi: Munshiram Manoharlal, 1968.

Jahangir wrote the memoir himself during the years 1605 to 1622; the years 1622 to 1624 were transcribed from Jahangir by Mutamid Khan; and for the years 1624 to 1627 there is no contemporary text. An eighteenth century addendum by Muhammad Hadi has been attached to the text, but it is derived primarily from Mutamid Khan's *Iqbalnama*. For lengthy discussions of the Jahangiri text, see E&D 6.276–83 and H. Beveridge, *Tuzuk* 1.v–vii.

Van den Broecke

Narain, Brij, and Sri Ram Sharma, trans. and ed. *A Contemporary Dutch Chronicle of Mughal India* (by Pieter van den Broecke, supposed author). Calcutta: Susil Gupta (India) Ltd., 1957.
Van den Broecke's chronicle seems to be derived primarily from that of Pelsaert, his senior factor in Agra with whom he returned to Holland from India in 1627. Van den Broecke was director of what was officially known as the "Western Quarters" for Holland, that is, north and west India, Persia, and Arabia.

Secondary Sources

Agre

Agre, Jagat Vir Singh. "Use of Intoxicants in Medieval Rajasthan." *Medieval India: A Miscellany*, vol. 1. Centre of Advanced Study, Department of History, Aligarh Muslim University. New York: Asia Publishing House, 1969.

Ahmad, *Islamic Culture*

Ahmad, Aziz. *Studies in Islamic Culture in the Indian Environment*. 1964. New edition. London: Oxford University Press, 1969.

Ahmad, "Sirhindi"

Ahmad, Aziz. "Religious and Political Ideas of Shaikh Ahmad Sirhindi." *Rivista Degli Studi Orientali* 36.3–4 (1961):259–70.

Altekar

Altekar, Anant Sadashiv. *The Position of Women in Hindu Civilization: From Prehistoric Times to the Present Day*. Benaras: Culture Publications House, Benaras Hindu University, 1938. 2d ed. Delhi: Motilal Banarsidass, 1956 (1973 printing).

Alvi and Rahman

Alvi, M. A. and A. Rahman. *Jahangir—The Naturalist*. New Delhi: National Institute of Sciences of India, 1968.

Amar

Amar, V. B. "Shah Jahan's Rebellion and Abdur Rahim Khan Khanan." *Journal of Indian History, Golden Jubilee Volume* (1973):437–55.

Aslam

Aslam, Muhammad. "Jahangir and Hadrat Shaikh Ahmad Sirhindi." *Journal of the Asiatic Society of Pakistan* 10.1 (June 1965):135–47.

Aziz

Aziz, Abdul. "A History of the Reign of Shah Jahan (Based on Original Persian Sources)." *Journal of Indian History* 6.1–3(1927):235–57.

Beach, *Grand Mogul*

Beach, Milo Cleveland. *The Grand Mogul: Imperial Painting in India, 1600–1660*. Williamstown, Mass.: Sterling and Francine Clark Art Institute, 1978.

Beach, *Imperial Image*

Beach, Milo Clevland. *The Imperial Image: Paintings for the Mughal Court*. Washington, D.C.: Freer Gallery of Art, Smithsonian Institution, 1981.

Begg

Begg, Shri W. D. *The Holy Biography of Hazrat Khwaja Muinuddin Chishti of Ajmer*. 1960–61.

H. Beveridge, "Mother of Jahangir"

Beveridge, H. "The Mother of Jahangir" *Journal of the Asiatic Society of Bengal* 56.1(1887):164–67.

H. Beveridge, "Sultan Khusrau"

Beveridge, H. "Sultan Khusrau." *Journal of the Royal Asiatic Society* 39:599–601.

M. Brown

Brown, Michael J. *Itinerant Ambassador: The Life of Sir Thomas Roe*. Lexington: The University Press of Kentucky, 1970.

P. Brown, *Architecture*

Brown, Percy. *Indian Architecture* (*Islamic Period*). Bombay: Taraporevala's Treasure House of Books, 1956. 5th ed. 1968.

P. Brown, *Painting*

Brown, Percy. *Indian Painting Under the Mughals, A.D. 1550 to A.D. 1750*. Oxford: Clarendon Press, 1924. Reprint. New York: Hacker Art Books, Inc., 1975.

Chaghatai

Chaghatai, M. Abdullah. "Emperor Jahangir's Interviews with Gosain Jadrup and His Portraits." *Islamic Culture* 36.2(1962):119–30.

Chopra

Chopra, Pran Nath. *Some Aspects of Society & Culture during the Mughal Age (1526–1707)*. Agra: Shiva Lal Agarwala & Co. (P.) Ltd., n.d.

Commissariat

Commissariat, Prof. M. S. "The Emperor Jahangir's Second Visit to Ahmadabad (April–September, 1618)." *Journal of the Bombay Historical Society* 1(1928): 139–52.

Crowe et al.

Crowe, Sylvia, et al. *The Gardens of Mughul India, A history and a guide*. London: Thames and Hudson, 1972.

Dar

Dar, S. N. *Costumes of India and Pakistan, A Historical and Cultural Study*. Bombay: D. B. Taraporevala Sons & Co. Private Ltd., 1969.

A. K. Das, *Mughal Painting*

Das, Asok Kumar. *Mughal Painting During Jahangir's Time*. Calcutta: The Asiatic Society, 1978.

A. K. Das, *Splendour*

Das, Asok Kumar. *Splendour of Mughal Painting*. Bombay: Vakils, Feffer & Simons Ltd., 1986.

M. Das

Das, Mahamahopadhyaya Kaviraja Shyamal. "The Mother of Jahangir." *Journal of the Asiatic Society of Bengal* 57.1(1888):71–75. Remarks on the above paper by H. Beveridge: 75–77.

Dow

Dow, Alexander. *The History of Hindostan*. Vol. 3, *From the Death of Akbar to the Settlement of the Empire Under Aurunzebe*. London: S. Beckert & P. A. De Hondt, 1770. Reprint. New Delhi: Today & Tomorrow's Printers & Publishers, 1973.
A historical compendium derived from Persian sources contemporary to and later than Jahangir.

D'Silva

D'Silva, John A. "The Rebellion of Prince Khusru according to Jesuit Sources." *Journal of Indian History* 5.2(1926):267–81.

Esposito

Esposito, John L. *Women in Muslim Family Law*. Syracuse: Syracuse University Press, 1982.

Ettinghausen

Ettinghausen, Richard. "The Emperor's Choice." *De Artibus Opuscula* 40. Reprinted in *Essays in Honor of Erwin Panofsky*, edited by Millard Meiss. New York: New York University Press, 1961.

Fabri

Fabri, Charles. *Indian Dress, A Brief History*. New Delhi: Sangam Books, 1977. Originally published as *A History of Indian Dress*. New Delhi: Orient Longman Ltd., 1960.

Fergusson

Fergusson, James. *History of Indian and Eastern Architecture*. Revised and edited by James Burgess and R. Phene Spiers. Vol. 2. 1876. Reprint of 1910 rev. ed. London: John Murray. Delhi: Munshiram Manoharlal, 1967.

Findly, "Idea of Kashmir"

Findly, Ellison Banks. "Nur Jahan and the Idea of Kashmir." In *B. K. Thapar Commemorative Volume*, edited by M. C. Joshi. New Delhi: Archaeological Survey of India, forthcoming.

Findly, "Jahangir and the Sufis"

Findly, Ellison Banks. "Jahangir and the Sufis." In *Discovering Hidden Connections, Norvin J. Hein Commemorative Volume*, edited by John Carman and Robert Lester. forthcoming.

Findly, "Jain Influence"

Findly, Ellison Banks. "Jain Influence on Early Mughal Trade with Europeans." In *Jains in Indian History and Culture*, edited by John E. Cort. Cambridge, Mass.: Harvard University Press, forthcoming.

Findly, "Maryamuzzamani"

Findly, Ellison Banks. "The Capture of Maryam-uz-Zamani's Ship: Mughal Women and European Traders." *Journal of the American Oriental Society* 108.2(1988):227–38.

Findly, "Pleasure"

Findly, Ellison Banks. "The Pleasure of Women: Nur Jahan and Mughal Painting," *Asian Art*, (Winter 1993).

Findly, "Religious Resources"

Findly, Ellison Banks. "Religious Resources for Secular Power: The Case of Nur Jahan." In *Women and Religion* volume, edited by Debra Campbell. *Colby Library Quarterly* 25.3(September 1989):129–48.

Findly, "Visionary Paintings"

Findly, Ellison Banks. "The Visionary Paintings of Jahangir's Later Years," *Proceedings, 33rd International Congress of Asian and North African Studies*, 1992.

Findly, "Vow of Non-Violence"

Findly, Ellison Banks. "Jahangir's Vow of Non-Violence." *Journal of the American Oriental Society* 107.2(1987):245–56.

Fischel

Fischel, W. J. "Jews and Judaism at the Court of the Moghul Emperors in Medieval India." *Islamic Culture* (1951):105–32.

Friedmann

Friedmann, Yohanan. *Shaykh Ahmad Sirhindi, An Outline of His Thought and a Study of His Image in the Eyes of Posterity*. Montreal and London: McGill-Queen's University Press, 1971.

Gascoigne

Gascoigne, Bamber. *The Great Moghuls*. New York: Harper & Row, 1971.

Ghurye

Ghurye, G. S. *Indian Costume*. Bombay: Popular Prakashan, 1951. 2d ed. 1966.

Goswamy and Grewal

Goswamy, B. N. and J. S. Grewal. *The Mughals and The Jogis of Jakhbar, Some Madad-i-Maash and Other Documents*. Simla: Indian Institute of Advanced Study, 1967.

Gray

Gray, Basil, ed. *The Arts of India*. Oxford: Phaidon, 1981.

I. Habib

Habib, Irfan. "The Family of Nur Jahan During Jahangir's Reign." *Medieval India, A Miscellany*, Vol. 1. Centre of Advanced Study, Department of History, Aligarh Muslim University. New York: Asia Publishing House, 1969.

I. Habib, *Atlas*

Habib, Irfan. *An Atlas of the Mughal Empire; Political and Economic Maps with Detailed Notes, Bibliography and Index*. Delhi, New York: Oxford University Press, 1982.

M. Habib

Habib, Mohammed. "Chishti Mystics Records of the Sultanate Period." *Medieval India Quarterly* 1.2(October 1950):1–42.

Haig and Burn

Haig, Lt.-Colonel Sir Wolseley, plan., and Sir Richard Burn, ed. *The Cambridge History of India*. Vol. 4, *The Mughul Period*. Cambridge: The University Press, 1937.

Hambly

Hambly, Gavin. *Cities of Mughul India*. Photographs by Wim Swaan. New York: G.P. Putnam's Sons, 1968.

Hasan

Hasan, Nurul. "The Theory of the Nur Jahan Junta," *Proceedings of the Indian Historical Congress*, Trivandrum Session (1958):324–35.

Havell, *Agra*

Havell, E. B. *A Handbook to Agra and the Taj, Sikandra, Fatehpur-Sikri and the Neighbourhood*. London: Longmans, Green, and Co., 1904.

Havell, *Indian Art*

Havell, E. B. *A Handbook of Indian Art*. 1920. Reprint. London: John Murray, Albemarle Street, W., 1927.

Hodgson

Hodgson, Marshall G. S. *The Venture of Islam*. Vol. 1, *The Classical Age of Islam*. Chicago and London: The University of Chicago Press, 1974.

A. Husain

Husain, Afzal. "The Family of Shaikh Salim Chishti During the Reign of Jahangir." *Medieval India* 2(1972):61–69.

M. M. A. Husain

Husain, Maulvi Muhammad Ashraf. *An Historical Guide to the Agra Fort (Based on Contemporary Records)*. Delhi: The Manager of Publications; Calcutta: Government of India Press, 1945.

Jalaluddin

Jalaluddin. "Sultan Salim (Jahangir) as a Rebel King." *Islamic Culture* 47(1973):121–25.

Joshi

Joshi, M. C. "Bada Batashewala-Mahal: A Study." In *Dr. Moti Chandra, Commemorative Volume*, part 2, edited by Umakant P. Shah and Krishna Deva. *Journal of the Indian Society of Oriental Art* New Series 9(1977–78):10–19.

Kak

Kak, Ram Chandra. *Ancient Monuments of Kashmir*. London: The India Society, 1933. Reprint. New Delhi: Sagar Publications, 1971.

Khandalavala and Doshi

Khandalavala, Karl, guest ed., and Dr. Saryu Doshi, ed. *An Age of Splendour, Islamic Art in India*. Bombay: Marg Publications, 1983.

Krishnamurti

Krishnamurti, R. *Akbar: The Religious Aspect*. Baroda: Maharaja Sayajirao University of Baroda Press, 1961.

Lal

Lal, K. S. *The Mughal Harem*. New Delhi: Aditya Prakashan, 1988.

Lall

Lall, John, text, and D. N. Dube, photographs. *Taj Mahal & the Glory of Mughal Agra*. 1982. Rev. ed. New Delhi: Lustre Press Pvt Ltd., 1985.

Latif, *Agra*

Latif, Syad Muhammad. *Agra: Historical and Descriptive, with an Account of Akbar and his Court and of the Modern City of Agra*. Calcutta: Calcutta Central Press Company, Ltd., 1896.

Latif, *Lahore*

Latif, Syad Muhammad. *Lahore: Its History, Architectural Remains and Antiquities*. Lahore: The "New Imperial Press," 1892.

Lawrence

Lawrence, Walter R. *The Valley of Kashmir*. London: Henry Frowde, Oxford University Press, 1895.

Lowry and Nemazee

Lowry, Glenn D., and Susan Nemazee. *A Jeweler's Eye, Islamic Arts of the Book from the Vever Collection*. Washington, D.C.: Arthur M. Sackler Gallery, Smithsonian Institution, in association with University of Washington Press, Seattle and London, 1988.

Maclagan

Maclagan, Sir Edward. *The Jesuits and the Great Mogul*. London: Burns Oates & Washbourne Ltd., 1932.

Marshall

Marshall, D. N. *Mughals In India: A Bibliographical Survey*. Vol. 1, Manuscripts. Bombay: Asia Publishing House, 1967.

Misra

Misra, Rekha. *Women in Mughal India (1526–1748 A.D.)*. Delhi: Munshiram Manoharlal, 1967.

Moreland

Moreland, W. H. *India at the Death of Akbar, An Economic Study*. Delhi: Atma Ram & Sons, 1962.

Moynihan

Moynihan, Elizabeth B. *Paradise As A Garden In Persia and Mughal India*. New York: George Braziller, 1979.

Mujeeb

Mujeeb, M. *The Indian Muslims*. London: George Allen & Unwin Ltd., 1967.

Mukerjee

Mukerjee, Radhakamal. *The Economic History of India, 1600–1800*. Allahabad: Kitab Mahal, 1967.

Mukherjee

Mukherjee, Ramkrishna. *The Rise and Fall of the East India Company, A Sociological Appraisal*. Berlin: Veb Deutscher Verlag der Wissenschaften, 1958.

Nath

Nath, R. *Agra and Its Monumental Glory*. Bombay: Taraporevala, 1977.

Nizami, "Indo-Muslim Mystics"

Nizami, Khaliq Ahmad. "Early Indo-Muslim Mystics and Their Attitude Towards the State." *Islamic Culture* 22(1948):387–98; 23(1949):13–21, 162–70, 312–21; 24 (1950):60–71.

Nizami, "Naqshbandi"

Nizami, Khaliq Ahmad. "Naqshbandi Influence on Mughal Rulers and Politics." *Islamic Culture* 39(1965):41–53.

Nizami, "Literature"

Nizami, Khaliq Ahmad. "Persian Literature Under Akbar." *Medieval India Quarterly* 3.3, 4(January, April 1958):300–328.

Nizami, "Shattari"

Nizami, Khaliq Ahmad. "The Shattari Saints and Their Attitude Towards the State." *Medieval India Quarterly* 1.2(October 1950):56–70.

Nizami, "Suhrawardi"

Nizami, Khaliq Ahmad. "The Suhrawardi Silsilah and its Influence on Medieval Indian Politics." *Medieval India Quarterly* 3.1–2:109–49.

Pal

Pal, Pratapaditya. *Court Paintings of India, 16th–19th Centuries*. New York: Navin Kumar, 1983.

C. Pant

Pant, Chandra. *Nur Jahan and Her Family*. Allahabad: Dan Dewal Publishing House, 1978.

D. Pant

Pant, D. *The Commercial Policy of the Moguls*. Bombay: D. B. Taraporevala Sons & Co., 1930.

Prasad

Prasad, Beni. *History of Jahangir*. Allahabad: B. N. Mathur at The Indian Press (Pubs.) Private Ltd., 1922. 5th ed. 1962.

Pullapilly

Pullapilly, Cyriac K., and Edwin J. Van Kley, eds. *Asia and the West, Encounters and Exchanges From the Age of Explorations; Essays in Honor of Donald F. Lack*. Notre Dame, Ind.: Cross Cultural Publications, Inc., Cross Roads Books, 1986.

Qaisar

Qaisar, Ahsan Jan. *The Indian Response to European Technology and Culture* (*A.D. 1498–1707*). Delhi: Oxford University Press, 1982.

Rizvi

Rizvi, Saiyid Athar Abbas. *Religious and Intellectual History of the Muslims in Akbar's Reign*, with *special reference to Abul Fazl* (*1556–1605*). New Delhi: Munshiram Manoharlal, 1975.

Roberts

Roberts, Robert. *The Social Laws of the Qoran*. 1925. New edition. London: Curzon Press, Ltd., 1971.

Saksena

Saksena, Banarsi Prasad. *History of Shahjahan of Dihli*. Allahabad: Central Book Depot, n.d.
Ph.D. thesis for the University of London, 1931.

Sarkar

Sarkar, Ashok Kumar. "Itimad-ud-daulah—A Sketch of his Life and Career." *The Quarterly Review of Historical Studies*. 10.3(1970–71):154–64.

Schimmel

Schimmel, Annemarie. *Mystical Dimensions of Islam*. Chapel Hill: The University of North Carolina Press, 1975.

Sharma

Sharma, Sri Ram. *The Religious Policy of the Mughal Emperors*. Humphrey Milford: Oxford University Press, 1940.

Shujauddins

Shujauddin, Mohammad, and Razia Shujauddin. *The Life and Times of Noor Jahan*. Lahore: The Caravan Book House, 1967.

Simkin

Simkin, C. G. F. *The Traditional Trade of Asia*. London: Oxford University Press, 1968.

Skelton

Skelton, Robert, et al. *The Indian Heritage: Court Life and Arts under Mughal Rule*. Catalogue, Victoria & Albert Museum, 21 April–22 August 1982. London: Victoria & Albert, 1982.

Smith

Smith, Vincent A. *A History of Fine Art in India & Ceylon*. 2d ed. Revised by K. de B. Codrington. Oxford: Clarendon Press, 1930.

Srivastava

Srivastava, Brij Bhushan Lal. "The Fate of Khusrau." *Journal of Indian History* 42.2(1964):479–92.

Steingass

Steingass, F. *A Comprehensive Persian-English Dictionary*. 1892. rev. ed. London: Routledge & Kegan Paul (with Iran University Press), 1984.

Thomas

Thomas, Edward. *The Revenue Resources of the Mughal Empire in India*. Delhi: Munshiram Manoharlal, 1967.

Tirmizi

Tirmizi, S. A. I. *Mughal Documents (1526–1627)*. New Delhi: Ramesh Jain Manohar Publications, 1989.

Topsfield

Topsfield, Andrew. *Indian Court Painting*. London: Her Majesty's Stationery Office, 1984.

Varadarajan

Varadarajan, L. "Jahangir the Diarist—An Interpretation based on the 'Tuzuk-i-Jahangiri'." *Journal of Indian History, Golden Jubilee Volume* (1973):403–18.

Villiers Stuart

Villiers Stuart, C. M. *Gardens of the Great Mughals*. London: Adam and Charles Black, 1913.

Wali

Wali, M. Abdul. "Antiquities of Burdwan." *Journal of the Asiatic Society of Bengal* 13(1917):184–86.

Welch, *Emperor's Album*

Welch, Stuart Cary, et al. *The Emperor's Album: Images of Mughal India*. New York: Harry N. Abrams, Inc., for the Metropolitan Museum of Art, 1987.

Welch, *Imperial Mughal Painting*

Welch, Stuart Cary. *Imperial Mughal Painting*. New York: George Braziller, 1978.

Wescoat et al.

Wescoat, James L., Jr., Michael Brand, and Naeem Mir. "Gardens, roads and legendary tunnels: the underground memory of Mughal Lahore." *Journal of Historical Geography* 17.1 (1991):1–17.

Wilber

Wilber, Donald Newton. *Persian Gardens and Garden Pavilions*. 2d ed. Washington, D.C.: Dumbarton Oaks, Trustees for Harvard University, 1979.

Fictional Accounts

Jafa

Jafa, Jyoti. *Nur Jahan: A Novel, A Historical Novel of Mughal India*. Calcutta: A Writers Workshop Publication, 1978.

Moore

Moore, Thomas. *Lalla Rookh: An Oriental Romance*. Illustrations by Edmund Evans. London: Routledge, Warne, & Routledge, Farringdon St., 1860.

Index

Abdul Qasim Namakin, 44
Abdulla Khan, 72, 167, 175
Abdur Rahim, Khankhanan, 14, 21, 25, 26, 49, 168, 173, 177, 179, 180, 186, 267, 273, 294 *n.* 47, 299 *n.* 73, 341 *n.* 20, 345 *n.* 143, *n.* 144, 353 *n.* 223, 365 *n.* 126, 376
Abdur Rahim (Tarbiyat Khan), 125, 330 *n.* 394
Abdur Rahman, 296 *n.* 19, 311 *n.* 32
Abu Talib Shayista Khan, 267, 268, 270–72, 282
Abul Fazl, 20, 24, 28, 30, 65, 114, 120, 185, 189, 198, 205, 207, 295 *n.* 1, 296 *n.* 12, *n.* 17, *n.* 18, *n.* 19, 311 *n.* 32, 373, 374
Abul Hasan, brother of Nur Jahan, 9, 37, 39, 44, 55. *See also* Asaf Khan (IV); Itiqad Khan
Abul Hasan, painter, 73, 224, 314 *n.* 87, *n.* 88, *n.* 89
Achabal, 257–58
Achin, 149
Afghan, 75, 173, 174, 188, 298 *n.* 53
Afghanistan, 181, 344 *n.* 113
Afim, 315 *n.* 122
Africa, 128, 149
Agra, 3, 10, 11, 13, 20, 24–26, 31–34, 36, 38, 41, 45, 63, 80, 90, 94, 105, 111, 114, 121, 125, 130, 131, 133, 134, 139, 141, 144, 145, 151, 153, 162, 165, 171, 172, 174–76, 181, 182, 189, 200, 201, 202, 206, 214–16, 220, 222, 228, 230, 231–37, 240, 241, 244, 245, 248–53, 263, 270, 277, 280, 283–86, 293 *n.* 15, *n.* 17, 295 *n.* 62, *n.* 7, 298 *n.* 45, 299 *n.* 64, 301 *n.* 117, 302 *n.* 143, 303 *n.* 146, 313 *n.* 72, 316 *n.* 138, 318 *n.* 20, 322 *n.* 141, 344 *n.* 113, 348 *n.* 64, *n.* 72, 349 *n.* 128, 351 *n.* 172, *n.* 178, 352 *n.* 193, 353 *n.* 233, 358 *n.* 18, *n.* 22, *n.* 30, 367 *n.* 83, 369 *n.* 112, 377
Agra Fort, 38, 70, 89, 91, 250, 353 *n.* 233, 370 *n.* 143
Ahadi, 95, 261, 269, 271, 272
Ahmad Beg Khan Kabuli, 44, 180
Ahmadnagar, 168, 170, 180, 275, 375
Ahmedabad, 11, 134, 141, 177, 220, 251, 264
Ajmer, 134, 139, 177, 184, 185, 187, 189–91, 193, 203, 204–6, 213, 251, 270, 276, 284, 352 *n.* 193
Akbar, 3, 6, 11
- and Abul Fazl, 20, 28, 295 *n.* 1, 296 *n.* 12, *n.* 17, *n.* 18
- and the arts, 63, 114, 247
- court/camp, 8–10, 12, 64, 106, 107, 222, 293 *n.* 36, 294 *n.* 47, 319 *n.* 63, 323 *n.* 178, 324 *n.* 189, 355 *n.* 32, 371, 372, 373, 374, 376
- death, 16, 19–24, 284, 298 *n.* 45, 346 *n.* 8, *n.* 22
- description, 11–12
- grandson of Babur, 11
- and Guru Arjun, 27
- honor of mother, 85, 94
- involvement in Mihrunnisa's marriage, 13–15, 294 *n.* 41, *n.* 45
- and Itimaduddaula family, 10, 12, 43–45
- in Kashmir, 255
- loves Khurram, 48, 50, 125
- and Nauroz, 35
- relations with Salim/Jahangir, 20–24, 25, 64, 68, 74–75, 78, 85, 122, 184–87, 198–99, 205, 215, 252, 295 *n.* 3, 296 *n.* 21, 296–97 *n.* 27, 297–98 *n.* 41, 346 *n.* 6
- religious tolerance, 23, 117, 118, 129, 184, 185, 189, 191, 195–96, 201, 203, 207–8
- service to, 12, 95, 122, 171
- tomb, 189, 198, 238, 284, 298 *n.* 45, 299 *n.* 62, 347 *n.* 52, 357 *n.* 102
- wealth, 141
- women, 91, 95–97, 100, 108, 109, 111, 114, 121, 123, 124, 177, 226, 244, 245, 287, 296 *n.* 20, 325 *n.* 229, 329 *n.* 366, *n.* 369
- worship of the sun, 40, 74

Akbarnagar, 180
Akbarpur, 196
Aldworthe, Thomas, 130, 134
Ali, 210, 328 *n.* 333
Ali Quli Khan Istajlu. *See also* Sher Afgan
- death, 16
- marriage to Mihrunnisa, 13–18
- posted to Bengal, 15
- receives title Sher Afgan, 16
- Turkish background and service, 14, 15, 16, 18

Ali Rai, 126
Allah, 186, 209, 350 *n.* 144
Allahabad, 19, 20, 21, 25, 124, 171, 172, 180, 185, 198, 205, 207, 224, 295 *n.* 5, 329 *n.* 369, 353 *n.* 233, 355 *n.* 30, *n.* 32

Allahabad Khan, 167
Amar Singh, 50
Amba Khan, 28, 300 *n.* 87
Ambar, 114, 115
Amber, 124, 149
American, 146
Amir, 72, 97, 126, 167, 295 *n.* 62, 352 *n.* 208
Amir ul-umara, 32
Anarkali (Nadira Banu Begam; Sharifunnisa), 123–25, 329 *n.* 366, *n.* 369, 355 *n.* 30
Andha Nag, 254
Anglican, 199
Ani Rai Singh Dalan, 208, 330 *n.* 401, 352 *n.* 203
Animal slaughter, 68, 192, 193, 195–96, 198–99, 205, 349 *n.* 127, 350 *n.* 144
Anne, 141, 153
Apurva, elephant, 24, 298 *n.* 42
Aqa Aqayam, 95, 114
Aqa Mulla, 9, 44
Aqa Riza, 224, 355 *n.* 30
Arabia, 121, 128, 131
Arabian Sea, 128, 129
Arabic, 227
Araq, 77, 315 *n.* 118
Arjumand Banu Begam
  daughter of Abul Hasan/Asaf Khan, 39, 51
  death, 49, 51, 94
  entombed in Taj Mahal, 39, 49, 233, 285, 286, 320 *n.* 102
  and Khurram/Shah Jahan, 39, 51, 164, 320 *n.* 79
  receives title Malika-i Jahan, 94
  receives title Mumtaz Mahal, 39, 94
  at Shah Jahan's accession, 284
Arjun. *See* Guru Arjun
Armenian, 66
Asaf Khan (IV). *See also* Abul Hasan; Itiqad Khan
  appointed to Bengal, 179
  appointed as *vakil,* 182
  buildings, 228
  bypassed in inheritance, 82–83, 110, 167, 342 *n.* 46
  daughter Arjumand Banu Begam, 39, 51, 60, 165, 167, 309 *n.* 150
  death, 240, 242, 286
  at death of mother, 85, 165
  and the English, 60, 137, 139, 142, 143, 152–55, 157, 161, 309 *n.* 125, *n.* 128, 310 *n.* 160, 334 *n.* 121, 334–35 *n.* 125
  given title in 1614, 37, 44, 55
  and Khusrau, 57–58, 164, 168–72, 309 *n.* 146, 343 *n.* 91
  and Mahabat Khan, 263, 264, 266–74, 344 *n.* 113, 361 *n.* 22, 362 *n.* 36, *n.* 40, 363 *n.* 64, 364 *n.* 105, *n.* 116, *n.* 121, 365 *n.* 129
  as member of junta, 37, 48, 55–56, 59–61, 73, 162
  against Nur Jahan, 278–84, 365 *n.* 128, 367 *n.* 56, 368 *n.* 102
  and the Portuguese, 143, 334 *n.* 121
  promoted at time of Nur Jahan's marriage, 37, 43, 304 *n.* 175
  receives *Jahangirnama,* 55, 224
  and Shah Jahan, 37, 49, 55, 165, 167, 175–77, 181, 182, 275, 279–84, 286, 309 *n.* 150, 364–65 *n.* 121, 366 *n.* 28
Ashrama, 207
Asia, 64, 65, 74, 111, 128, 129, 141, 144–47, 284
Asir Fort, 178, 181
Askari, 121, 122
Asmat Begam
  attar of roses, 114–15
  death, 85, 165, 183, 231, 234
  at death of Sher Afgan, 31
  family, 9, 12, 45, 116, 180, 214, 289, 313 *n.* 79
  flees Persia to India, 8, 9, 10
  gives birth to Mihrunnisa, 9, 292 *n.* 8
Ataliq, 177
Attock, 75, 268, 269, 271
Aurangzeb, 35, 50, 96, 99, 100, 102, 104, 114, 171, 181, 254, 256, 281, 319 *n.* 40, *n.* 47, 321 *n.* 119, 322 *n.* 134, 326 *n.* 267, 327 *n.* 293, *n.* 297, 370 *n.* 143
Azam Khan, 282
Aziz Khan, 173
Aziz Khan Koka. *See* Mirza Aziz Khan Koka

Babul, 315 *n.* 118
Babur, 11, 90–91, 97, 111, 114, 187, 244, 248, 318 *n.* 20, 320 *n.* 91, 344 *n.* 103, 358 *n.* 18, 359 *n.* 37, 368 *n.* 104
Bada Batashewala Mahal, 235–38
Badauni, 19, 40, 117
Badla, 222
Badrunnisa Begam, 100
Bagh-i Bahar Ara, 255
Bahadur Shah, 370 *n.* 143
Bahlwan, 166
Bairam Beg, 179, 345 *n.* 144
Bairam Kala, 278
Bairam Khan, 25, 244, 294 *n.* 47, 296 *n.* 20, 299 *n.* 73
Bajwaral, 271
Bakhshi, 24, 261, 373
Balaghat, 181
Baluchpur, 177, 178, 181, 261
Banarasi, 279, 283
Baniya, 93, 141, 144, 195, 196, 198
Bantim, 149
Baoli, 114
Baqir Khan, 177, 264
Baradari, 231, 241, 246, 247, 249, 255, 256, 357 *n.* 116
Baramula, 193
Barddhaman, 17, 24, 27–29, 31, 32, 180, 188, 211, 300 *n.* 89
Baroda, 134
Bayana, 145, 244

Bayasanghar (Don Carlo), 201, 282, 368 *n.* 89, *n.* 102
Bazaar gossip, 13, 30–31, 36, 103, 104, 207, 281, 292 *n.* 8, 294 *n.* 45, 305 *n.* 5, 322 *n.* 141, 376, 377. *See also* Oral traditions
Bega Begam, 324 *n.* 206
Begam, 18, 122, 318 *n.* 20
Benares, 144, 361 *n.* 33
Bengal, 15, 17, 18, 21, 24, 25–27, 29, 30, 38, 39, 44, 98, 111, 146, 151, 173, 180, 182, 188, 211, 264, 273, 277, 283, 298 *n.* 53, 300 *n.* 89, 313 *n.* 79, 361 *n.* 31, *n.* 33, 372, 376
Bengali Mahal, 91
Bernier, Francois, 47, 99, 102, 103, 104–5, 107, 118, 192, 254, 256–59, 372
Best, Thomas, 60, 133–34, 137, 148, 224, 332 *n.* 47, 372
Beveridge, Annette S., 38, 65, 88, 94, 118, 120
Beveridge, Henry, 64, 88, 171, 244, 249, 315 *n.* 116
Bhang, 327 *n.* 293, *n.* 297
Bhanucandra (Guru Upadhyaya), 195–97, 206
Bharat Singh, 277
Bhimbar, 278, 279, 281, 282, 367 *n.* 58
Bhutan, 111, 151
Bibi Akbarabadi, 114
Bibi Fatima, 95
Bible, 225
Bichitr, 314 *n.* 90, 348 *n.* 66
Bickford, James, 153
Biddulph, William, 130
Bigha, 196
Bihar, 173, 180
Bihar Banu Begam, 126
Bihroz, 269
Bijapur, 121, 168, 180, 375
Bika Begam, 114, 244
Bikaner, 126, 197
Bilqis Makani, 94, 125. *See also* Jagat Gosaini
Bindu, 112
Bir Singh Deo, 20, 24
Blinding, 33–34, 302 *n.* 129, *n.* 131, *n.* 137
Borneo, 149
Brahman, 177, 192, 193
Broach, 134
Brown, Michael, 157, 159
Brown, Percy, 238, 285
Browne, John, 152, 153
Bukhara, 173
Bulaqi. *See* Dawar Bakhsh
Bundela, 20, 126, 311 *n.* 31
Burhanpur, 11, 49, 134, 139, 141, 170–72, 179, 180, 181, 188, 196, 201, 263, 270, 315 *n.* 114

Calicut, 146, 336 *n.* 170
Cambay, 71, 129, 133, 134, 139, 196, 201
Canning, Lancelot, 134
Canning, Paul, 134
Cartaz (pass), 128–30, 150–51
Central Asia, 95, 161, 218
Chadar, 92, 247
Chaghatai, 11, 297 *n.* 36
Chahar chanar, 255
Chain of Justice, 70, 74, 313 *n.* 69
Chajja, 231, 233, 237
Chak, 330 *n.* 403
Champa, 66, 67
Chand Bibi, 3
Charbagh, 231, 237, 241, 246, 250–52, 257, 359 *n.* 37
Chardara (Nurpur), 256
Chenab River, 26, 272
China, 149, 376
Chinese porcelain, 52, 145, 235
Chingaz Hatli, 278, 279, 283
Chingaz Sarai, 284, 369 *n.* 115
Chingiz Khan, 11, 26
Chishti, 187–91, 204, 211, 353 *n.* 223. *See also* Shaikh Muinuddin Chishti; Shaikh Salim Chishti
Christ. *See* Jesus Christ
Christian, 23, 64, 66, 68, 85, 86, 94, 137, 142, 186, 191, 200–203, 210, 212, 214–17, 312 *n.* 50, 352 *n.* 194, 368 *n.* 102
Christianity, 5, 86, 117, 199–203, 206, 317 *n.* 197, 351 *n.* 173, *n.* 174, 353 *n.* 224. *See also* Jesus Christ; Madonna
Chuwa, 114
Clothing, 21, 24, 63, 111–12, 149–50, 218, 219, 221–22, 226, 326 *n.* 245, *n.* 249, 354 *n.* 24. *See also* Textiles
Coach, 53, 108, 146, 324 *n.* 194, 337 *n.* 202, 340 *n.* 302
Cocks, Richard, 145
Coins, 40, 43, 46, 148, 219–21, 287, 295 *n.* 5, 306 *n.* 32, *n.* 44, 354 *n.* 6, *n.* 8, *n.* 12, *n.* 14, 356 *n.* 62
  Zodiac, 46, 80, 220, 306 *n.* 32, 316 *n.* 146, 354 *n.* 14
Concubines. *See* Women
Corsi, Father Francisco, 200, 351 *n.* 172
Coryat, Thomas, 57, 70, 85, 103, 141, 164, 184, 189, 205, 206, 332 *n.* 41

Dacca, 180
Dahra Bagh, 125, 249–50, 358 *n.* 30, 369 *n.* 112. *See also* Nur Manzil
Dal Lake, 255–57
Daman, 331 *n.* 19, 350–51 *n.* 166
Dana, 120
Daniyal, 123, 329 *n.* 366
  children of, 94, 97, 100, 126, 201, 202, 269, 272, 282–84, 312 *n.* 50, 351 *n.* 172, 368 *n.* 102, *n.* 107
  death, 19, 23, 75, 315 *n.* 114
Dara Shikoh, 104, 181, 281, 319 *n.* 47, 321 *n.* 119
Darbar, 35, 215
Darogha, 95
Darogha Bagh, 255

Darya Khan, 174
Das, Ashok Kumar, 63, 64, 191, 224
Dastar ul-amal, 68
Dasuha, 271
Daulat Khan, 353 *n.* 233
Dawar Bakhsh (Bulaqi), 177, 269, 275, 277–84, 366 *n.* 20, 367 *n.* 56, *n.* 58, *n.* 60, *n.* 62, 368 *n.* 102, *n.* 106
De Castro, Father Joseph, 200, 212
De Laet, Joannes, 30, 32, 55, 260, 264, 270, 277, 284, 285, 294 *n.* 41, 302 *n.* 146, 372
Decapitation, 20, 26, 28
Deccan, 19, 20, 49, 50, 51, 58, 109, 111, 124, 144, 161, 163, 167–70, 172–75, 179–82, 210, 261, 263, 270, 275–77, 279, 280, 283, 311 *n.* 23, 315 *n.* 114, 342 *n.* 51, 358 *n.* 30, 365 *n.* 11
Delhi, 11, 114, 176, 177, 191, 229, 235, 245, 251, 273, 277, 293 *n.* 17, 299 *n.* 66, 365 *n.* 129
Della Valle, Pietro, 30, 34, 35, 40, 51, 81, 118, 126, 156, 164, 170, 175, 182, 215, 372
Dervishes, 188, 189, 244
Devi, 215, 216
Dholpur, 111, 174–75, 181, 344 *n.* 103
Dila Rani, 319 *n.* 69
Dildar, 97, 320 *n.* 91
Dirham, 71, 313 *n.* 81
Diu, 153
Divali, 120, 192
Diwan, 12, 13, 25, 32, 33, 44, 167, 224, 301 *n.* 122
Diwan-i am, 38, 256
Diwan-i buyutat, 12, 24
Diwan-i khas, 256, 353 *n.* 233
Diwan-i kul, 44, 167
Diyanat Khan, 33, 167
Dow, Alexander, 9, 10, 14–15, 16, 29, 36, 46, 55, 56, 89, 94, 95, 99, 169, 171, 183, 260, 263, 269, 285, 292 *n.* 9, 298 *n.* 53
Downton, Nicholas, 136
Du Jarric, Father Pierre, 12, 23, 85, 186, 214, 215, 313 *n.* 69, 372
Dudami, 222
Durga, 193, 204, 216
Dust Muhammad (Khwaja Jahan), 89, 248, 358 *n.* 22
Dutch, 13, 30, 35, 55, 105, 130, 131, 144, 170, 199, 224, 228, 250, 268, 280, 283, 302 *n.* 146, 375

East India Company (Dutch), 372, 377
East India Company (English), 129, 130, 133, 134, 136, 141, 143, 145, 147–49, 152, 153, 155–57, 159, 160, 224, 303 *n.* 151, 372, 375
Edwards, William, 130, 136, 142, 148, 155, 224, 310 *n.* 165, 339 *n.* 254
Elephants, 24, 28, 31, 41, 50, 51, 55, 63, 67, 71, 75, 78, 104, 107, 108, 110, 116, 126, 148, 169, 219, 253, 264, 265, 267, 273, 298 *n.* 42, 299 *n.* 75, 312 *n.* 40, 313 *n.* 79, 321 *n.* 112, 324 *n.* 186, *n.* 189, *n.* 190, 351 *n.* 172, 361 *n.* 33, 362 *n.* 40
Elizabeth I, Queen of England, 132
Elkington, Thomas, 131
English, 47, 56, 60, 65, 72, 103, 108, 113, 128–60, 164, 179, 199, 215, 224, 225, 250, 251, 263, 311 *n.* 30, 331 *n.* 16, *n.* 30, 332 *n.* 32, *n.* 35, *n.* 36, *n.* 41, 340 *n.* 302, *n.* 8, 377
Escheat, 82–83, 110, 141, 167, 325 *n.* 221, 341 *n.* 42, *n.* 43, 342 *n.* 45
Eunuch, 66, 89, 93, 98–99, 102, 104–7, 267, 271, 312 *n.* 40, 320 *n.* 75, *n.* 98, *n.* 101, *n.* 102, 321 *n.* 106, *n.* 112, 322 *n.* 132, 322–23 *n.* 148, 323 *n.* 154, *n.* 161, 327 *n.* 297
Europe, 35, 85, 93, 105, 111, 113, 128, 144, 146, 160, 199, 214, 225, 284, 376
European, 4, 40, 46, 56, 63, 65, 84, 86, 103, 104, 130, 144–47, 149, 152, 157–59, 170, 196, 206, 224, 311 *n.* 30
European art, 147, 213–16, 218, 224, 251, 351 *n.* 178, 353–54 *n.* 242, 354 *n.* 11, 355 *n.* 30, *n.* 36. *See also* Painting; Pictures
European sources and travelers, 6, 7, 10, 11, 30, 31, 118, 123, 219, 250, 287, 305 *n.* 5, 319 *n.* 47, 343 *n.* 85, 372

Factory system, 129, 133, 134, 137, 142, 143, 152, 159, 179, 372, 377
Falanja, 114
Far East, 93
Farman, 43, 46, 84, 87, 122–23, 133, 137, 152, 159, 195, 196, 197, 199, 221, 264, 270, 283, 284, 295 *n.* 9, 344 *n.* 99
Farsh-i chandani, 222
Farzandi, 56
Fatehpur Sikri, 8, 10, 12, 121, 176, 177, 185, 187, 229, 300 *n.* 89
Fathjang. *See* Ibrahim Khan
Faujdar, 271
Fidai Khan (Sulaiman Beg), 264–66, 268, 277, 361 *n.* 26
Filuniya, 77, 315 *n.* 122
Finch, William, 21, 33, 93, 113, 123, 150, 201, 214, 284, 287, 326 *n.* 245, 329 *n.* 366, *n.* 369
Fiqh, 209
Florence, 231
Floris, Peter, 375
Flowers/fruits, 112, 114–15, 218, 222, 237, 241, 244, 246–49, 251–55, 258, 259, 287, 327 *n.* 290, 358 *n.* 14. *See also* Gardens
Foster, William, 171, 329 *n.* 366
French, 104, 147, 372

Ganga Bai, 123
Ganges River, 180
Gardens, 3, 46, 91, 110, 114, 147, 218, 228, 237, 238, 241, 244–59, 277, 284, 301 *n.* 114, 318 *n.* 20, *n.* 27, 324 *n.* 206, 344 *n.* 103. *See also* Flowers/fruits

Achabal, 257–58
Bagh-i Bahar Ara, 255
Darogha Bagh, 255
Khusrau Bagh, 171
Mandakar, 244, 327 *n.* 276
Moti Bagh, 230, 250–51
Nawal Ganj, 230, 250
Nur Afshan, 41, 248–50, 358 *n.* 18, *n.* 22
Nur Afza, 255–56
Nur Mahal Sarai, 41, 82, 114, 176, 219, 222, 223, 228–30, 246, 356 *n.* 58, *n.* 62, *n.* 64, *n.* 67
Nur Manzil, 41, 114, 249–50, 284, 358 *n.* 22, 369 *n.* 112. *See also* Dahra Bagh
paradise garden, 246, 257
Shahdara, 240–43, 251–52, 281, 285, 369 *n.* 127
Shalamar, Dal Lake, 256–57
tomb of Itimaduddaula, 114, 166, 222, 230–38, 241–43, 251–52, 357 *n.* 115
tomb of Nur Jahan, 18, 114, 239–43, 275, 287, 357 *n.* 119, 358 *n.* 120
Vernag, 252–54, 258–59, 285
Garshasp, 284
Gascoigne, Bamber, 66, 104, 108, 235, 285, 286
Gastos, 320 *n.* 79
Gemstones, 35, 49–50, 51, 53, 56, 66, 106, 107, 110–12, 120, 141, 144, 146–50, 155, 157, 165, 170, 189, 202, 215, 221, 231–33, 235, 269, 310 *n.* 5, 316 *n.* 138, 325 *n.* 229, 326 *n.* 250, *n.* 251, 328 *n.* 329, 336 *n.* 183, *n.* 184, 337 *n.* 207, *n.* 208, 341 *n.* 42, 342 *n.* 45, 344 *n.* 106, 357 *n.* 119
Georgia, 146, 327 *n.* 297
Ghari, 77
Ghazi, 267
Gifts, 60–61, 109–10, 129, 139, 143, 146–49, 152–56, 158, 159, 201, 204, 248, 303 *n.* 152, 306 *n.* 29, *n.* 36, 310 *n.* 165, *n.* 166, *n.* 170, 313–14 *n.* 84, 324–25 *n.* 211, 333 *n.* 68, 336 *n.* 182, *n.* 183, 337 *n.* 189, 339 *n.* 249, *n.* 254, 354 *n.* 25, 368 *n.* 100
Giranbar, elephant, 24
Globe, 375
Goa, 129, 130, 137, 153, 200, 201, 215, 336 *n.* 170, 375
Gobindwal, 27
Goes, Brother Bendict, 44, 293 *n.* 36
Gol Mandal, 357 *n.* 85
Golconda, 168, 179, 180
Gopal Das, 178
Gosain Jadrup, 192–94, 203–4
Govardhan, 42
Guerreiro, Father Fernao, 12, 23, 33, 185, 186, 200, 202, 214, 293 *n.* 36, 373
Gujarat, 44, 50, 77, 91, 128, 131, 133, 134, 141, 143, 168, 173, 175, 177, 179, 195–97, 201, 221, 253, 276, 283, 284, 365 *n.* 11, 373
Gul Afshan, 248
Gulalbar, 106
Gulazar Begam, 91, 121
Gulbadan Begam, 6, 90, 97, 112, 113, 116, 117, 120, 121, 126, 216
Gulf of Cambay, 129
Gulkari, 242
Guru Arjun, 27, 299 *n.* 78
Gwalior Fort, 167, 204, 208

Hafiz, 224
Haidar Malik, 28, 31–32, 255–56, 259, 300 *n.* 90, 301 *n.* 114
Haji Begam, 121
Haji Koka, 319 *n.* 69
Hajipur, 32
Hajj, 120, 121
Hakim Abul Fath, 33, 315 *n.* 120
Hakim Abul Qasim, 162
Hakim Beg (Hakim Khan), 45
Hakim Humam, 315 *n.* 120
Hakim Nuruddin, 167
Hakim Ruhullah, 82, 162
Hakim Rukna, 162
Hakim Sadra, 34, 162, 341 *n.* 14
Hall, John, 137
Hamida Banu Begam, 88, 93, 97, 117, 123, 213. *See also* Maryam Makani
Hammam, 256
Haram, 122
Harem, 6, 24, 32–34, 36, 46, 49, 50, 55, 56, 80, 88, 90, 91, 93–101, 104–10, 112, 113, 116–18, 120, 121, 123, 126–28, 132, 183, 206, 207, 212, 213, 245, 249, 296 *n.* 26, 318 *n.* 8, *n.* 20, *n.* 27, 319 *n.* 42, 320 *n.* 79, 321 *n.* 125, 322 *n.* 132, *n.* 138, 325 *n.* 212, 327 *n.* 290, *n.* 297. *See also Mahal;* Women; *Zanana*
Hari Parbat Fort, 255–56
Hasan, Nurul, 43
Hauda, 107–8, 116, 265, 267, 324 *n.* 190
Hauz, 246–47
Hauz-i jahangiri, 38
Havan, 120
Hawkins, William, 21, 30, 33, 38, 46, 56, 64, 66, 67, 70, 93, 94, 118, 125, 133, 136, 141–43, 154, 155, 164, 165, 201–3, 214, 284, 352 *n.* 194
Hazrat Mian Mir, 109
Hector, 133, 145
Himalayas, 75, 252, 253
Hindal. *See* Mirza Hindal
Hindi, 41, 74, 112
Hindu/Hinduism, 11, 13, 19, 66, 102, 162, 198, 201, 203, 204, 215, 226, 256, 279, 286, 376
arts and crafts, 142, 145, 150, 158, 330 *n.* 394
caste system, 66, 71, 191–93
charity, 120
consort images, 5, 213, 216, 217
doctors, 82, 105, 323 *n.* 159

Hindu/Hinduism (*continued*)
  festivals/rituals, 118, 120, 121, 192, 193, 257, 258, 329 *n.* 346. *See also Sati*
  food, 109
  holy men, esp. Gosain Jadrup, 191–94, 204
  icons/idolatry, 66, 191, 192, 193–95, 219, 225, 229
  intoxicants, 115
  sun worship, 40
  temples, 191–93, 256–58
  theology, 193
  women, 37, 87, 94, 99, 111, 112, 117, 118, 120, 121, 124–26, 177, 213, 216, 217, 219, 225, 245, 317 *n.* 182
Hiran Minar, 238
Holi, 118–20, 192, 328 *n.* 329
Holland, 158
Hoshang (Don Henrico), 201, 272, 283, 284, 368 *n.* 102
Hoshang Shah, 233
Hoshiyar Khan, 271
Hukm, 123
Humayun, 6, 24, 88, 93, 95, 97, 111, 116, 121, 122, 216, 229, 235, 321 *n.* 125, 324 *n.* 206, 347 *n.* 52, 371
Humayunnama, 6, 90, 301 *n.* 117
Huqqa, 115
Husain Beg, 25, 26
Husain Chak, 126
Hyderabad, 221

Ibrahim Husain, 235
Ibrahim Khan (Fathjang), 45, 180, 313 *n.* 79
Ibrahim Lodi Afghan, 11
Id, 47, 188, 226, 328 *n.* 333
Iffat Banu, 126
Imam Quli Khan, 122, 306 *n.* 36
Inayat Khan, 75
Indigo, 129, 131, 145, 146, 149, 151, 336 *n.* 166
Indra, 311 *n.* 15
Intikhab-i Jahangir-Shahi, 34, 47, 263
Iqbalnama, 10, 12, 19, 30, 36, 43, 44, 120, 123, 161, 260, 265, 268, 269, 279, 282, 286, 293 *n.* 36, 294 *n.* 59, 304 *n.* 183, 373, 374. *See also* Mutamid Khan
Iradat Khan, 279, 281, 282, 367 *n.* 56
Iran, 224, 237, 258, 353 *n.* 223
Iraq, 173, 292 *n.* 5
Irij Khan, 376
Isfahan, 8, 121
Ishtadevata, 120
Islam, 11, 23, 37, 86, 99, 110, 115, 129, 186, 188, 196, 201, 204–10, 212–14, 286, 346 *n.* 7, 351 *n.* 174. *See also* Muslim
Islam Khan (Shaikh Alauddin), 32, 187, 204
Italy, 146, 231
Itibar Khan, 176, 177, 182
Itimaduddaula. *See also* Mirza Ghiyas Beg
  allowed among unveiled women, 55, 90, 104, 109, 167
  buildings, 228
  charges of embezzlement against, 32–33, 37, 38, 45, 55, 166, 264, 301 *n.* 121, *n.* 124
  death, 82, 110, 165–67, 183
  during 1606 revolt of Khusrau, 26, 229 *n.* 64
  and the English, 59, 308 *n.* 102, 309 *n.* 125, 310 *n.* 160
  family, 292 *n.* 8
  gives kind favors, 32, 53–55, 167, 244
  grandfather to Arjumand Banu Begam, 39, 289
  honored at Jahangir's accession, 24, 44, 301 *n.* 124, 304 *n.* 172
  as member of junta, 48, 53–55, 57–59, 73, 162, 165, 341 *n.* 36
  and Nur Jahan, 35, 303 *n.* 146
  power of family, 43–45, 49, 51, 101, 289, 304 *n.* 173
  promoted at Mihrunnisa's marriage to Jahangir, 37–39, 44, 301–2 *n.* 124, 304 *n.* 172, *n.* 184
  receives *Jahangirnama*, 55, 224
  receives title, 24, 44, 304 *n.* 172
  receives title Madarulmulk, 53
  son to assassinate Jahangir, 33, 45
  tomb, 114, 166, 222, 230–38, 241–43, 251–52, 357 *n.* 115
Itiqad Khan, 37, 39, 44, 55. *See also* Abul Hasan; Asaf Khan (IV)
Itiqad Khan (Shapur), 44, 292 *n.* 8

Jadrup. *See* Gosain Jadrup
Jadu, 38, 133, 141–44, 155
Jafa, Jyoti, 16
Jafar Beg, Asaf Khan (III), 12, 44
Jafar Khan, 102, 110, 322 *n.* 134, 325 *n.* 223
Jafari, 257
Jagat Gosaini (Jodh Bai), 49, 116–17, 124–26, 162, 311 *n.* 31. *See also* Bilqis Makani
Jagat Singh, 126, 179, 311 *n.* 31
Jagir, 20, 24, 25, 27, 96, 111, 123, 151, 174, 175, 180, 181, 268, 295 *n.* 9, 325 *n.* 243, 342 *n.* 45
Jagjot, elephant, 55
Jaguli, 221
Jahanara (Sahibatuzzamani), 94, 99, 103, 107, 109, 110, 111, 113–15, 123, 284, 322 *n.* 132, 327 *n.* 297
Jahandar, 79
Jahangir. *See also* Salim
  ability to rule, 63–67, 311 *n.* 23, *n.* 24
  and Abul Fazl, 20, 24, 30, 65, 296 *n.* 12, *n.* 19
  accession to throne, 12, 16, 19–24, 25, 40, 44, 68, 69, 86, 98, 182, 199, 205, 209, 294 *n.* 59, 297 *n.* 33, *n.* 36, 346 *n.* 8
  on Ali Quli/Sher Afgan, 14, 16, 24–25, 27–28, 300 *n.* 83, *n.* 84, *n.* 87, 355 *n.* 32
  and the arts, 63–65, 93, 355 *n.* 36
  bestows title Sher Afgan, 16, 294 *n.* 58
  building projects, 93, 114, 356 *n.* 57
  charity, 185, 188–90

and Chishtis, 187–88. *See also* Shaikh Muinuddin Chishti
and Christianity, 199–203, 212, 214, 351 *n.* 174, *n.* 175, *n.* 178, *n.* 182, 353 *n.* 224
coinage, 219–21, 316 *n.* 146, 354 *n.* 6, *n.* 8
cruelty, 62, 66–68, 199, 205, 217, 312 *n.* 40, 351 *n.* 174
death, 13, 18, 45, 251–52, 258–59, 278–79, 283, 287, 366 *n.* 46, 369 *n.* 115, 369–70 *n.* 140, 370 *n.* 143, 373
and deaths of Qutbuddin and Sher Afgan, 27–31
drinking and drug habits, 3, 19, 57, 63, 75–79, 81, 83–84, 115, 119, 162–63, 167, 253, 278, 297 *n.* 40, 307 *n.* 70, 310 *n.* 10, 311 *n.* 15, 315 *n.* 116, *n.* 120, *n.* 122, *n.* 123, *n.* 129, 316 *n.* 138
and the English, 65, 108, 133, 134, 136, 137, 139, 147, 154, 155, 157–59, 310 *n.* 156, 311 *n.* 30, 332 *n.* 41, *n.* 47
handing of power over to Nur Jahan, 46–48
and Hinduism, 118, 119, 142, 191–95, 328 *n.* 329, 375–76
and hunting, 57, 75, 106, 109, 116–17, 155, 221, 245, 278, 314 *n.* 101
and Islam, 188–92
and Itimaduddaula, 51, 53–55, 90, 166
"*Jahangiri itr*," 115
and Jainism, 195–98, 206–7, 322 *n.* 137
and the junta, 56, 59, 61, 65
in Kashmir, 253–59
and Khusrau, 49, 57, 68, 168–72, 186–87, 199, 205, 296–97 *n.* 27, 342 *n.* 51, 343 *n.* 85, *n.* 91, 350 *n.* 145
love of justice, 62, 68–72, 205, 217, 269, 313 *n.* 69, *n.* 71, *n.* 72, *n.* 79, *n.* 81
love of Madonna pictures, 23, 85–86, 147, 212–16, 353–54 *n.* 242
and Mahabat Khan, 20, 176–77, 260–74, 360 *n.* 1, 361 *n.* 12, *n.* 22, *n.* 31, 362 *n.* 40, *n.* 45, *n.* 53, 363 *n.* 77, 364 *n.* 105, *n.* 113, *n.* 121, 366 *n.* 31
memoirs, *Tuzuk-i Jahangiri*, 4, 6, 7, 30, 38, 41, 55, 64, 82, 83, 162, 170, 178, 186, 191, 193, 197, 198, 203, 211, 224, 248–50, 253, 315 *n.* 116, *n.* 123
and mother, 94, 105, 130, 150, 177–78, 191, 216. *See also* Maryamuzzamani
nature of relationship with Nur Jahan, 4, 5, 80–87, 306 *n.* 25, 316 *n.* 164
no children with Nur Jahan, 18, 79, 98
other marriages, 38, 81, 93, 117, 123–26, 303 *n.* 169, 304 *n.* 170, 311 *n.* 31, 329 *n.* 373, 330 *n.* 409, 351 *n.* 173
and Parviz, 276–77
and the Portuguese, 23, 86, 130, 131, 147, 199, 212, 214, 317 *n.* 197
refusal to execute Khusrau, 33, 49, 67, 302 *n.* 126
relationship with Akbar, 25, 64, 68, 74–75, 78, 122, 184–86, 191, 195, 198–99, 205, 209, 215, 252, 255, 295 *n.* 3, 296 *n.* 21, 297–98 *n.* 41, 346 *n.* 6
religious tolerance, 129, 184, 185, 191, 201, 203–5, 348 *n.* 85
response to *sati*, 118, 349 *n.* 112
role of Naqshbandis in accession, 22–24, 186–87, 207–8, 346 *n.* 8, 346–47 *n.* 22
and Shahryar, 49, 66, 68, 164–65, 312 *n.* 49, *n.* 50
and Shaikh Salim Chishti, 119–20
sickness, 38, 83, 162–63, 168, 170, 175, 189, 204, 205, 253–54, 277–78, 343 *n.* 87
and signs and portents, 79–80, 118–20, 316 *n.* 148, *n.* 153
silence on blinding of Khusrau, 34, 65, 67, 205, 302 *n.* 129
silence on marriage to Nur Jahan, 37–40, 65, 311 *n.* 31
and Sirhindi, 188, 203–4, 208–9, 352 *n.* 202, *n.* 208, *n.* 213
and sisters, 97, 122
1611 meeting of Nur Jahan, 3, 35–37, 45, 86, 155, 302 *n.* 143, *n.* 146, 304 *n.* 183, 330 *n.* 410
1607 assassination plot against, 33, 301 *n.* 122, *n.* 123, 302 *n.* 125, *n.* 126
and 1606 rebellion of Khusrau, 25–27, 197, 205, 298–99 *n.* 62, 299 *n.* 73, *n.* 75, 307 *n.* 64
and 1622 rebellion of Shah Jahan, 142, 161, 172–83, 199, 205, 270, 340 *n.* 8, 342 *n.* 47, 343 *n.* 87
and Spain, 333 *n.* 68
stories of early meetings with and love for Mihrunnisa, 13–16, 28–32, 39, 301 *n.* 117, 302 *n.* 146, 308 *n.* 87, 330 *n.* 410
succession fight at his death, 61, 279–84, 367 *n.* 56, *n.* 58, *n.* 59, *n.* 60, *n.* 62, *n.* 83, *n.* 86, 368 *n.* 99, *n.* 102, *n.* 104, *n.* 106, *n.* 107, *n.* 108
sun imagery, 40–41, 71, 74, 185, 313 *n.* 72, *n.* 77
takes name Nuruddin Muhammad Jahangir Padshah Ghazi, 24, 40, 279, 298 *n.* 46, 314 *n.* 85
tomb, 240–43, 251–52, 281, 284–87, 357 *n.* 109, *n.* 115, 369 *n.* 115, *n.* 129
vow of non-violence, 116, 192, 195–96, 198–99, 203–5, 209, 296 *n.* 19, 349 *n.* 127, 350 *n.* 144, *n.* 145
wealth, 108, 141, 150, 280, 342 *n.* 46
and women of harem, 89, 90, 91, 93–96, 100–101, 111–13
Jahangiri, 40
Jahangirnama, 55, 224
Jain, 87, 103, 104, 112, 195–99, 203, 205–7, 209, 286, 349 *n.* 128. *See also* Shvetambara; Siddhicandra
Jaisalmer, 125, 270, 311 *n.* 31
Jalandhar, 41, 114, 222, 223, 228–30, 246, 356 *n.* 64

James I, King of England, 60, 134, 136, 142, 154, 159, 303 *n.* 151
Jami mosque, 185, 347 *n.* 50
Jammu, 257, 258
Japan, 60, 149
Jesuits, 12, 23, 86, 94, 129, 130, 133, 154, 185, 186, 199, 200–202, 212, 214, 224, 307 *n.* 64, 317 *n.* 197, 331 *n.* 19, 334 *n.* 121, 339 *n.* 249, 350 *n.* 149, 351 *n.* 175, 355 *n.* 30, 372–73, 376
Jesus Christ, 23, 85–86, 129, 147, 202, 203, 210, 212, 214–16, 224, 225, 351 *n.* 182. *See also* Christianity; Madonna
Jharoka, 46, 70–71, 74, 80, 313 *n.* 71, *n.* 72
Jhelum River, 258, 260, 264, 265, 267, 272
Jiddah, 150
Jizyat, 196
Jodhpur, 124
Joshi, M. C., 235–38
Jotik Rai, 80, 120, 125
Junnair, 283
Junta, 37, 43–61, 65, 132, 139, 142, 143, 152, 153, 155, 156–57, 158, 161–83, 204, 205, 210–11, 217, 224, 301 *n.* 119, 305 *n.* 1, *n.* 3, *n.* 5, *n.* 11, 314 *n.* 92, 328 *n.* 315
Junta debate, 43–45, 305 *n.* 5
Jusat, 114

Kabul, 12, 13, 26, 27, 33, 108, 114, 115, 125, 126, 244, 254, 260, 261, 264, 265, 270, 271, 301 *n.* 123, 359 *n.* 60, 364 *n.* 95
Kabul River, 106
Kajawa, 108
Kali, 5, 215–17
Kalyan, 67, 311 *n.* 31
Kama, 245
Kamgar Khan, 20, 81, 275, 373
Kandahar, 3, 8, 9, 12, 14, 27, 64, 173–76, 181, 343 *n.* 91, 344 *n.* 113
Kangra, 166, 167
Karamsi, 125
Karan. *See* Raja Karan Singh
Karma, 376
Karnatic, 63
Kashmir, 3, 28, 32, 63, 75, 95, 104–5, 109, 115, 126, 144, 162, 163, 166, 179, 180, 188, 193, 204, 205, 212, 230, 238, 239, 244, 246–49, 251, 252–59, 277, 278, 285, 300 *n.* 87, 301 *n.* 114, 323 *n.* 161, 330 *n.* 403, 358 *n.* 14, *n.* 22, 359 *n.* 44, *n.* 50, *n.* 60
Keridge, Thomas, 144, 148, 149, 153, 225
Khadija, 5, 213–14
Khadija Begam, Nur Jahan's sister, 45, 281, 292 *n.* 8, 367 *n.* 83
Khafi Khan, 9, 10, 13, 15, 29, 31, 110, 116, 219, 221, 293 *n.* 10, 294 *n.* 42, 300 *n.* 97, 301 *n.* 112, *n.* 116
Khalifa, 208, 209, 352 *n.* 208
Khan Jahan, 173
Khan Jahan Lodi, 264, 276
Khanam, 319 *n.* 54
Khandesh, 126, 175
Khankhanan. *See* Abdur Rahim
Khanzada Begam, 122
Khazana, 306 *n.* 32
Khichri, 184, 205, 347 *n.* 49
Khirki, 170
Khizr Khan Hazara, 126
Khurasan, 8, 173, 292 *n.* 5
Khurram. *See also* Shah Jahan
  and Arjumand Banu Begam, 39–40, 49, 51, 94, 308 *n.* 87, *n.* 88
  birth, 125
  under care of Ruqayya Sultan Begam, 32, 97–98, 301 *n.* 119
  description, 49–50
  drinking habit, 79, 307 *n.* 70, *n.* 71, 316 *n.* 141
  and Ladli Begam, 51
  loved by Akbar, 48, 50, 125, 182
  as member of junta, 48, 49–53, 59, 189, 301 *n.* 119
  mother Jagat Gosaini, 49, 125
  receives title Shah Jahan, 51
  third son of Jahangir, 32, 125, 307 *n.* 77, *n.* 78
Khushruz, 36, 303 *n.* 160
Khusrau
  birth, 124
  blessed by Guru Arjun, 27
  blinding, 33–34, 65, 170, 205, 261, 280, 302 *n.* 129, *n.* 131, *n.* 137
  description, 48–49, 296 *n.* 25
  imprisoned, 51, 57, 58, 164, 308 *n.* 90
  and Jahangir, 33, 49
  mother, 21, 115, 124, 171, 296 *n.* 26, 329 *n.* 374, 330 *n.* 381, 343 *n.* 84
  move to replace Salim as heir to Akbar, 16, 19–24, 25, 45, 48, 115, 122, 123, 186–87, 296 *n.* 26, 296–97 *n.* 27, 297 *n.* 33, *n.* 36, *n.* 41, 298 *n.* 44, 346 *n.* 22
  problem for junta, 56–58, 84, 122, 308 *n.* 91, 309 *n.* 131, *n.* 133, *n.* 146
  pro-Christian, 23, 61, 142, 186, 296 *n.* 25, 307 *n.* 64
  rejects Ladli Begam in marriage, 18, 51, 57, 164, 168, 308 *n.* 90, *n.* 91
  relation to Mirza Aziz Koka, 21, 25, 122, 171, 186
  1607 assassination attempt on Jahangir, 33, 34, 44, 45, 57
  1606 rebellion against Jahangir, 25–27, 33, 34, 44, 57, 106, 122, 186–87, 197, 208, 292 *n.* 8, 298–99 *n.* 62, 299 *n.* 72, *n.* 73, *n.* 75, 300 *n.* 83, 307 *n.* 64
  son Dawar Bakhsh, 177, 269, 280, 283
  suspicious death, 57, 58, 124, 163, 168–72, 181–82, 205, 284, 342 *n.* 51, *n.* 56, *n.* 58, *n.* 71, 342–43 *n.* 72, 343 *n.* 75, *n.* 85, *n.* 87
  wife, 51, 57, 122, 164, 171, 308 *n.* 90, 343 *n.* 80

women favorable to him, 33, 49, 122, 328 *n.* 315, 331 *n.* 412
Khutba, 47, 221, 279, 281, 283, 306 *n.* 44
Khwaja, 189
Khwaja Abdullah, 186, 346 *n.* 17
Khwaja Abdus Samad Shirinqalam, 224
Khwaja Abul Hasan, 167, 267, 268, 271
Khwaja Baqi Billah, 208–9
Khwaja Barkhurdar, 264–65
Khwaja Hasan, 125
Khwaja Hashim, 188
Khwaja Husain, 189, 348 *n.* 66
Khwaja Jahan. *See* Dust Muhammad
Khwaja Muinuddin Chishti. *See* Shaikh Muinuddin Chishti
Khwaja Muhammad Sharif, 8, 9, 226
Khwaja Umar Naqshbandi, 264
Khwaja Waisi, 301 *n.* 122
Khwaja Zakariya, 186
Khwaja-i Jahan, 126
Khwajagi Razi, 226
Khyber Pass, 301 *n.* 123
Kinari, 222
Kurimarg, 254

Ladli Begam
buried next to Nur Jahan in Lahore, 18, 241, 287
at court with mother under care of Ruqayya Begam, 32, 34, 87, 295 *n.* 63
married to Prince Shahryar, 18, 49, 163–65, 210
only child of Nur Jahan, 18, 84, 286, 295 *n.* 62, *n.* 63,
own daughter, 178, 267
in rebellion of Mahabat Khan, 267, 363 *n.* 68
rejected by Khusrau in marriage, 18, 57, 164, 168, 308 *n.* 90
Lahore, 11, 13, 14, 15, 18, 22, 25–27, 33, 93, 123–25, 145, 169, 171, 175, 176, 178, 180, 186, 212, 214, 220, 227–29, 238, 239–43, 248, 251–53, 260, 264, 271, 272, 277, 278, 281, 282, 284–87, 292 *n.* 9, 299 *n.* 75, *n.* 78, 363 *n.* 77, 364 *n.* 95, *n.* 111, 365 *n.* 129, 367 *n.* 56, *n.* 59, 368 *n.* 102, 369 *n.* 129
Lakh, 33, 131, 240, 273, 282, 285, 286, 320 *n.* 79, 365 *n.* 126
Lakshmi, 216
Lancaster, James, 132–33
Lar, 255
Latin, 200
Levant, 145
Little Tibet, 126

Maasir-i Jahangiri, 30
Macao, 149
Madho Singh, 124
Madonna (Virgin Mary; Mary), 5, 23, 52, 85–86, 129, 147, 202, 203, 212–16, 224, 225, 353–54 *n.* 242. *See also* Christianity; Jesus Christ
Mahabat Khan (Zamana Beg)
and Asaf Khan, 263, 264, 266–74, 365 *n.* 128, *n.* 129, 366 *n.* 31
during 1606 revolt, 26–27
and the English, 59
honors at Jahangir's accession, 24
against Nur Jahan, 47–48, 260–74, 275, 277, 344 *n.* 113, 362 *n.* 48, 364 *n.* 106, *n.* 113, 365 *n.* 126
and Parviz, 177–82, 261–62, 264, 277, 345 *n.* 143, 361 *n.* 31
rebellion, 45, 260–74, 360 *n.* 1, 361 *n.* 22, *n.* 31, *n.* 33, 362 *n.* 36, *n.* 40, *n.* 42, *n.* 45, *n.* 53, 363 *n.* 77, 364 *n.* 95, *n.* 105, *n.* 112, *n.* 116, 364–65 *n.* 121, 366 *n.* 31
receives title, 24
service to Salim/Jahangir, 20, 73, 176–77, 261
and Shah Jahan, 179, 180, 183, 261–62, 272, 274, 276–77, 280, 345 *n.* 144, 361 *n.* 14, 365 *n.* 129, 366 *n.* 28
urges blinding of Khusrau, 33, 261
Mahal, 90–93, 96–104, 109–13, 115–18, 120, 121, 123, 126, 226, 235, 287, 318 *n.* 7, 321 *n.* 114, 322 *n.* 134, 324–25 *n.* 211. *See also* Harem; Women; *Zanana*
Mahaldar, 95
Maham Begam, 97, 216
Mahinval, 322 *n.* 131
Makhfi, 113, 226
Maktubat, 209–210
Malik Ambar, 73, 168, 170, 180, 270, 276
Malik Masud, 9, 10, 12
Malika Jahan, a wife of Jahangir, 125
Malika-i Jahan. *See* Arjumand Banu Begam
Malwa, 144, 173, 175, 178, 225
Man Bai, 21, 115, 124, 171, 296 *n.* 26, 329 *n.* 374, 330 *n.* 381, 343 *n.* 84
Man Singh, 197–98, 203, 205, 209
Manar, 75
Mandakar, 244, 327 *n.* 276
Mandala, 73
Mandu, 51, 141, 173, 174, 176, 178, 185, 191, 221, 251, 261, 347 *n.* 50
Manija Begam, 45, 226, 270, 292 *n.* 8, 363 *n.* 90, 367 *n.* 83
Manohar, 22, 54, 262, 316 *n.* 139, 353–54 *n.* 242
Manrique, Sebastian, 49, 376
Mansab, 12, 14, 16, 24, 25, 27, 44, 45, 71, 165, 167, 171, 174, 177, 178, 182, 187, 201, 293 *n.* 32
Mansur, 247, 314 *n.* 101
Manucci, Niccolao, 15, 16, 29, 30, 47, 83, 96, 100, 103–5, 110–15, 195, 202, 265, 280, 376
Maqsud Khan, 281
Marathas, 168, 248
Marble, 218, 230–33, 235, 237, 238, 287, 369 *n.* 109
Mary. *See* Madonna

Maryam Makani, 20–21, 24, 85, 93, 94, 114, 122, 123, 213, 244, 325 *n.* 229, 348 *n.* 64. *See also* Hamida Banu Begam
Maryamuzzamani, 85, 94, 96, 105, 108, 111, 122, 123, 126, 130–31, 145, 150–53, 165, 177–78, 189, 213, 216, 244, 312 *n.* 59, 325 *n.* 231, 330 *n.* 374, 331 *n.* 16, 338 *n.* 232, 348 *n.* 64, 350 *n.* 166
Master Steele, 104, 323 *n.* 154
Matab Nuruddin Quli, 172
Mathnawi, 113
Mathura, 216
Mecca, 30, 106, 111, 120, 121, 128, 149, 150, 159, 203
Mehri, 113, 227, 228, 376
Mercator's atlas, 72, 313–14 *n.* 84, 314 *n.* 85
Mewar, 16, 19, 50, 168, 177, 191, 225, 277, 352 *n.* 193, 369 *n.* 109
Middleton, Sir Henry, 133, 143, 150–51
Mihrunnisa. *See also* Nur Jahan
  abandonment narrative, 9–10, 12–13
  beauty, 36–37, 41, 303 *n.* 163
  birth, 9, 292 *n.* 8, 292–93 *n.* 10
  daughter Ladli Begam with Sher Afgan, 18, 32, 34
  family advancement on marriage to Jahangir, 37, 301–2 *n.* 124, 304 *n.* 173, *n.* 184
  first marriage, to Ali Quli/Sher Afgan, 13–18, 21, 28, 39, 188, 256, 300 *n.* 87, 301 *n.* 114
  given title Nur Jahan, 40, 41, 94
  given title Nur Mahal, 40, 41, 45, 94
  lady-in-waiting to Ruqayya Sultan Begam, 3, 31, 32, 34, 36, 50, 97, 301 *n.* 116, *n.* 117, *n.* 118, *n.* 119, *n.* 120, 302 *n.* 143, 303 *n.* 146
  parentage, 8–9, 24
  Persian heritage, 13, 15
  second marriage, to Jahangir, 31, 37–40, 126, 303 *n.* 167, 352 *n.* 193
  1611 meeting of Jahangir, 35–37, 304 *n.* 183
  stories of early contact with Salim/Jahangir, 13–16, 28–32, 34–35, 39, 294 *n.* 40, *n.* 41, *n.* 45, 301 *n.* 117, 302 *n.* 146, 308 *n.* 87, 330 *n.* 410
  widowed, 3, 31, 32, 37, 39
  youth, 10, 13, 14, 293 *n.* 12, *n.* 36
Mina Bazaar, 14, 36, 37, 294 *n.* 45
Mir bakhshi, 20, 24, 279
Mir Husamuddin, 178
Mir Jamaluddin Husain, 325 *n.* 213
Mir Mansur, 266
Miran Shah, 11
Mirza Alauddaula, 9
Mirza Ali Beg, 189
Mirza Aziz Khan Koka, 21, 23–25, 95, 122, 171, 186, 319 *n.* 63, 346 *n.* 17, *n.* 22
Mirza Fathulla, 33
Mirza Ghazi, 298 *n.* 41
Mirza Ghiyas Beg (Mirza Ghiyasuddin Muhammad). *See also* Itimaduddaula
  arrives in India, 10, 12, 293 *n.* 12
  betrothal of Mihrunnisa, 15, 126
  flees Persia, 8, 9
  honored by Jahangir on accession, 24
  poet, 226
  receives title Itimaduddaula, 24
  service to Akbar, 12, 13, 44, 53, 293 *n.* 36, 305 *n.* 11
  son of Khwaja Muhammad Sharif, 8, 9
Mirza Ghiyasuddin Ali, Asaf Khan (II), 12, 33, 44
Mirza Hasan, 25
Mirza Hindal, 32, 97, 121
Mirza Kamran, 26
Mirza Muhammad Hakim, 75, 201
Mirza Muzaffar Husain, 91, 125, 235, 308 *n.* 87, 341 *n.* 20
Mirza Nuruddin, 33, 45
Mirza Rustam, 116
Mirza Sanjar, 126
Mirza Shah Rukh, 25
Mirza Wali, 100
Miyan Shaikh Muhammad Mir, 188
Mocha, 128, 141, 150, 153
Mongols, 11
Monserrate, Father, 10, 108, 284, 376
Moor, 23, 27, 137, 191, 200, 202, 214, 336 *n.* 166
Moscow, 94
Mosque, 23, 47, 141, 185, 188, 238, 239, 248, 254, 284, 286, 347 *n.* 50, 369 *n.* 109, *n.* 115
Mota Raja. *See* Udai Singh
Moti Bagh, 230, 250–51
Moti Mahal, 250–51
Mubarak Chak, 126
Mubarik Shah, 352 *n.* 194
Muhammad, 23, 213, 214
Muhammad Hadi, 43, 374
Muhammad Khan Sharifuddin Ughlu Taklu, 8
Muhammad Sadiq Tabrizi, 294 *n.* 42
Muhammad Salih, 285, 374
Muhammad Sharif, 9, 33, 45, 55, 292 *n.* 8
Muhammad Tahir, 9, 226
Muharram, 120, 188
Muhr, 219, 220, 354 *n.* 6
Mulanayaka, 349 *n.* 128
Mulla, 103, 200, 202
Multan, 14, 173, 353 *n.* 223
Mumtaz Mahal. *See* Arjumand Banu Begam
Mundy, Peter, 30, 31, 53, 103, 118, 171, 230, 247, 250, 251, 277, 280, 286, 308 *n.* 96, 358–59 *n.* 30, 377
Muqarrab Khan (Shaikh Hasan; John), 60, 71, 130, 133, 142, 143, 152, 201, 337 *n.* 189, 350 *n.* 163
Murad, brother of Jahangir, 19, 75, 100, 295 *n.* 1, 315 *n.* 114
Murad, son of Shah Jahan, 181
Muslim, 11, 13, 19, 21, 37, 40, 59, 66, 71, 79, 82, 85, 86, 94, 95, 102, 105, 111, 117,

118, 120, 121, 125, 126, 128, 129, 142, 159, 162, 186, 188, 192, 193, 200, 202, 203, 205, 207, 208, 213, 215, 216, 217, 225, 229, 238, 323 *n.* 159, 325 *n.* 221, 341 *n.* 43, 371. *See also* Islam
Mutamid Khan, 43, 81, 163, 175, 255, 260, 265, 267–69, 300 *n.* 87, 362 *n.* 36, 363 *n.* 61. *See also Iqbalnama*
Muzaffar Khan, 270
Muzaffarnagar, 299 *n.* 66
Mystic Feast, 97, 116

Nadim, 267
Nadiri, 63, 221
Naqarkhana, 107
Naqib Khan, 189
Naqshbandi, 21, 23, 24, 186–87, 207, 208, 264, 347 *n.* 22, 353 *n.* 223. *See also* Shaikh Ahmad Sirhindi
Narmada River, 178, 179, 283
Nasik, 181
Nasik Trimbak, 275
Nasiruddin, 66, 67, 93, 318 *n.* 8
Nauroz
  general, 35–36, 103, 128, 147, 185, 349 *n.* 127
  in 1611, 3, 35, 40, 45, 86, 302–3 *n.* 146
Navaratra, 120
Nawal Ganj, 230, 250
Nayika, 225
Nazir, 96, 98
Nilgau, 189
Nimbus, 41, 52, 74, 119, 314 *n.* 93
Nishan, 123, 195, 196, 367 *n.* 62
Nizami, Khaliq Ahmad, 23, 186
Nizamuddin, 126
Nur, 74
Nur Afshan, 41, 248–50, 358 *n.* 18, *n.* 22
Nur Afza, 255–56
Nur Gaj, elephant, 41
Nur Jahan. *See also* Junta; Mihrunnisa
  and Arjumand Banu Begam, 39
  arts, 218–43, 244–59
  and Asaf Khan. *See* Asaf Khan (IV); Junta
  beauty, 36–37, 41, 79, 84, 269, 316 *n.* 164
  birth, 8, 9
  brothers. *See* Asaf Khan (IV); Itiqad Khan; Muhammad Sharif
  brothers-in-law. *See* Hakim Beg; Qasim Khan Juvaini; Sadiq Khan
  buildings, 46, 82, 87, 91, 96, 114, 218, 222, 228–43, 356 *n.* 57, 357 *n.* 109
  charity, 4, 46, 83, 87, 111, 120, 184, 205–6, 286
  and Christianity, 206, 212, 317 *n.* 197
  coins, 3, 46, 123, 219–21, 306 *n.* 32, *n.* 44, 354 *n.* 6, *n.* 12, *n.* 14, 356 *n.* 62
  daughter Ladli Begam, 3, 18, 35, 57, 79, 81, 84, 86, 87, 98, 164–65, 210, 241, 267, 286, 287, 295 *n.* 62, 363 *n.* 68
  death, 3, 31, 240, 287
  at deaths of parents, 165–67, 183, 210
  domestic trade, 46, 96, 111, 151
  edicts, 122–23
  exile to Lahore, 3, 30–31, 240, 284–87, 369 *n.* 129, 369–70 *n.* 140
  family fortunes on marriage to Jahangir, 37–39, 44–45, 304 *n.* 173, *n.* 175
  and family of Shaikh Salim Chishti, 206, 211
  foreign trade, 3, 111, 113, 151–53
  gardens/flowers, 3, 4, 46, 82, 87, 114, 115, 218, 228, 244–59, 344 *n.* 103, 358 *n.* 22
  granddaughter, 178, 267, 271
  influence on Jahangir, 10, 14, 28–30, 41, 46–48, 57, 58, 62, 71–72, 80–87, 98, 101, 126–27, 163, 183, 184, 211–17, 285–86, 305 *n.* 5, 306 *n.* 25, 313 *n.* 79, 316 *n.* 164
  influence over Shahryar, 18, 49, 165, 168, 172, 174–75, 177, 181–83, 278–83, 344 *n.* 106
  inherits father's holdings, 82–83, 110, 167, 183
  at Jahangir's death, 279–82, 285, 367 *n.* 56, *n.* 83
  and junta, 43–61, 132, 161–83, 205, 305 *n.* 5, 314 *n.* 92
  as Khadija, 5, 213–14
  and Khurram/Shah Jahan, 50–53, 58, 87, 109, 111, 116–17, 162, 167–69, 173–74, 179–83, 211, 252, 284–87, 308 *n.* 96, 365 *n.* 11
  against Khusrau, 51, 57–58, 122, 126, 164, 168–72, 308 *n.* 90, *n.* 91, 309 *n.* 131, 331 *n.* 412, 343 *n.* 91
  landholdings, 96, 111, 123, 151, 174, 181, 325 *n.* 243, 344 *n.* 103
  and legend of Sher Afgan as tiger slayer, 16, 295 *n.* 61
  as the Madonna, 5, 85–86, 213, 216
  against Mahabat Khan, 48, 260–74, 275, 277, 361 *n.* 22, 362 *n.* 36, *n.* 42, *n.* 48, 363 *n.* 64, *n.* 77, *n.* 78, 364 *n.* 105, *n.* 106, *n.* 113, 365 *n.* 126, *n.* 128
  marksmanship, 16, 116–17, 328 *n.* 329
  marriage to Jahangir, 37–40, 44, 62, 86, 126, 220, 352 *n.* 193
  as Nur Mahal, 40, 41, 45, 50, 51, 53, 58, 59, 94, 99, 152, 153, 155, 164, 169, 184, 189, 230, 250, 254, 259, 279, 281, 286, 308 *n.* 96, 316 *n.* 164, 319 *n.* 47, 331 *n.* 412, 338 *n.* 232, 343 *n.* 91, 350 *n.* 134, 352 *n.* 193, 357 *n.* 109, 367 *n.* 56
  and painting, 6, 87, 113, 224–26, 355 *n.* 32
  parents. *See* Asmat Begam; Itimaduddaula
  as Parvati, 5, 217
  personality, 10, 14
  political effectiveness, 7, 46–48, 58–59, 60, 61, 183, 225, 245, 266–69, 306 *n.* 29, *n.* 30, *n.* 36
  prowess in battle, 31, 266–69, 275, 363 *n.* 70
  religious practices, 184, 189, 204–12, 286–87, 328 *n.* 329

Nur Jahan (*continued*)
rivalry with Jagat Gosaini, 116, 125, 126
and Roe, 59–61, 108, 121–22, 129, 131, 132, 139, 149, 152–58, 160, 310 *n.* 157, *n.* 166, 338 *n.* 232, 354 *n.* 25
seal, 43, 46, 123, 224
servants, 66, 68, 99, 152, 155, 312 *n.* 40, 321 *n.* 112
sickness, 105, 323 *n.* 159
and Siddhicandra, 197, 206–7, 350 *n.* 134
and Sirhindi, 206–11
sisters. *See* Khadija Begam; Manija Begam
1611 meeting of Jahangir, 3, 35–37, 45, 86, 155, 302 *n.* 143, *n.* 146, 330 *n.* 410
title given in 1616, 38, 41, 319 *n.* 47, 330 *n.* 395
tomb, 18, 114, 239–43, 275, 287, 357 *n.* 119, 358 *n.* 120, 369 *n.* 127
tomb for father, 114, 222, 230–38, 241–43, 251, 252
wealth, 47, 80, 110, 183, 230, 242, 252, 280, 285, 286, 370 *n.* 143, 356 *n.* 62
writings, 6, 87, 112, 113, 226–28, 355 *n.* 49
youth, 10
Nur Mahal. *See* Mihrunnisa; Nur Jahan
Nur Mahal Sarai, 41, 82, 114, 176, 219, 222, 223, 228–30, 246, 356 *n.* 58, *n.* 62, *n.* 64, *n.* 67
Nur Manzil, 41, 114, 249–50, 284, 358 *n.* 22, 369 *n.* 112. *See also* Dahra Bagh
Nurdaulat, 40
Nur-i Nauroz, elephant, 41
Nurjahani, 40, 220, 354 *n.* 6
Nurkaram, 40
Nurmahal, district, 230
Nurmahali, 219, 222
Nurmihr, 40
Nurpur, 256
Nurshahi, 40
Nursultani, 40
Nuruddin Muhammad Jahangir Padshah Ghazi. *See* Jahangir
Nurunnisa Begam, 125

Oral traditions, 7, 219. *See also* Bazaar gossip
Orissa, 44, 179, 180
Ornament, 218, 219, 229, 232, 235, 237, 238, 242, 249
Oudh, 180

Padshah Begam, 94
title given to Nur Jahan, 125, 330 *n.* 395
title given to Saliha Banu Begam, 80, 125, 311 *n.* 31
Padshahnama, 51, 164, 279, 287
Pahunchi, 116
Paijama, 221
Painting, 20, 63, 75, 102, 104, 113, 117, 148, 222–26, 254, 355 *n.* 36, 358 *n.* 14. *See also* European art; Pictures
allegory, 64–65, 72–74, 147, 225, 314 *n.* 92, *n.* 93, 348 *n.* 66
Paintings. *See* Pictures
Pal, Pratapaditya, 225
Palki, 107, 108, 276, 278
Pampur, 253, 254
Panchtoliya, 222
Pandit, 191, 192
Panipat, 11
Pant, Chandra, 6–7, 43, 47, 169
Parda, 36, 59, 89, 90, 102, 104, 107, 108, 113, 152, 158
Pargana, 58, 111, 174
Parhez Banu, 98
Paris, 107
Parliament, 134, 136, 147, 225
Parricide, 66–68, 312 *n.* 48
Parvati, 5, 216, 217
Parviz, 49, 58, 100, 110, 125, 139, 176–82, 212, 261, 263, 264, 270, 276–78, 321 *n.* 117, 344 *n.* 132, 345 *n.* 143, *n.* 144, 361 *n.* 31, 365 *n.* 129, 366 *n.* 17
Parwana, 123
Pass system. *See Cartaz*
Pathan, 271
Patna, 29, 32, 151, 321 *n.* 125, 335 *n.* 151, 377
Pattar Masjid, 238–39
Pegu, 336 *n.* 171
Pelsaert, Francisco, 13, 37, 46, 48, 61, 79, 80, 83, 92, 94, 99, 101, 109, 111, 114, 115, 121, 144, 145, 151, 159, 196, 220, 228, 230, 248, 250, 253, 254, 287, 294 *n.* 40, 348 *n.* 64, 372, 377
Persia, 3, 8, 9, 12, 14, 34, 105, 115, 131, 146, 158, 162, 165, 173, 218, 235, 254, 270, 276, 286, 292 *n.* 5, 343 *n.* 91, 365 *n.* 9, 368 *n.* 106
Persian, 9, 10, 12, 29, 31, 35, 39, 44, 53, 63, 64, 81, 104, 111, 112, 113, 139, 141, 143, 148, 170, 171, 173, 176, 185, 188, 204, 205, 210, 218, 219, 225, 227, 228, 237, 245, 246, 251, 252, 256, 293 *n.* 12, *n.* 36, 310 *n.* 156, 313 *n.* 69, 332 *n.* 41, 376
Persian sources, 6, 7, 9, 28, 30, 36, 38, 373, 377
Phalor, 229
Pictures, 23, 35, 41, 85, 86, 91, 92–93, 104, 111, 113, 118, 129, 136, 147–48, 155, 159, 185, 200, 214–16, 222–26, 231, 251, 255, 303 *n.* 151, 329 *n.* 396, 337 *n.* 189, 351 *n.* 178, 353–54 *n.* 242, 354 *n.* 8, 355 *n.* 30. *See also* European art; Painting
Pietra dura, 166, 231–33, 235, 242–43, 247, 357 *n.* 105
Pilgrimage, 106, 111, 120–22, 128–30, 132, 150, 159, 187, 188, 189, 206, 245, 252, 329 *n.* 346, 341 *n.* 14, 348 *n.* 72
Pinheiro, Father Emmanuel, 201
Pintado, 146
Pitre de Lan, 105
Polish, 94

Portuguese, 12, 23, 60, 94, 102, 128–33, 137, 139, 142–44, 146, 147, 150–54, 156, 158, 199, 200, 201, 214, 215, 224, 312 *n*. 59, 331 *n*. 16, *n*. 19, 332 *n*. 36, 336 *n*. 166, *n*. 170, 340 *n*. 302, 350–51 *n*. 166, 351 *n*. 173, 372
Prasad, Beni, 34, 47, 164, 177, 283, 285, 287
Pravarsena II, 256
Prophecy, 79–80, 118–20, 125, 197, 205, 209, 220, 278, 316 *n*. 148, *n*. 153, 320 *n*. 96, 328 *n*. 330, 368 *n*. 99
Protestant, 199, 214, 225
Puja, 120
Punjab, 25, 44, 55, 173, 230, 272, 299 *n*. 64, 322 *n*. 131

Qaba, 221
Qaim Khan, 125
Qarisha, 116
Qasim Khan Juvaini (Mir Qasim), 45, 226, 270, 280, 284, 292 *n*. 8, 367 *n*. 83
Qazaq Khan, 8
Qazi, 37, 318 *n*. 8, 327 *n*. 297
Qazi Nasir, 188
Qulanj, 170
Qulij Khan, 186
Qumar Sultan, 32
Quran, 120, 179, 188, 208, 246, 272
Qutbuddin Khan Koka (Khubu)
  appointed to Bengal, 25
  death, killing of Sher Afgan, 27–32, 33, 211, 298 *n*. 57, 300 *n*. 86, *n*. 87, *n*. 89
  death of his mother, 28, 85, 187–88, 211, 213–14, 298 *n*. 57
  grandson of Shaikh Salim Chishti, 20, 187–88, 211, 353 *n*. 223
  loyal service to Salim, 20, 21, 22, 95, 187–88, 300 *n*. 83
Qutbulmulk, 180

Radha, 217
Ragini, 225
Rahimi, 130–32, 145, 150–51, 153, 312 *n*. 59, 331 *n*. 16, *n*. 19, 338 *n*. 224, *n*. 232
Rai Singh, 126, 197
Raja Ali Khan, 126
Raja Bhagwan Das, 124, 329–30 *n*. 374
Raja Bhao Singh, 349 *n*. 112
Raja Bihari Mal, 329–30 *n*. 374
Raja Bikramajit (Sundar), 177
Raja Kalyan, 125
Raja Karan Singh, 50, 73, 284, 368 *n*. 100
Raja Kesu Das, 125
Raja Kishan Singh, 276
Raja Man Singh, 21, 24–27, 124, 126, 180, 297 *n*. 29, 298 *n*. 41, 304 *n*. 170, 311 *n*. 31, 329 *n*. 374, 330 *n*. 381, 346 *n*. 22
Raja Nar Singh Deo, 276
Raja Sarup Singh, 104
Raja Surat Singh, 122, 123
Rajauri, 251, 278
Rajput, 71, 94, 95, 100, 117, 124, 125, 173, 178, 189, 206, 225, 235, 263–69, 271, 312 *n*. 40, 327 *n*. 294, 361 *n*. 35, 362 *n*. 42, *n*. 53, 364 *n*. 112
Ram Bagh. *See* Nur Afshan
Ram Chand Bundela, 126, 311 *n*. 31
Ramadan, 120, 188, 328 *n*. 333
Ramsar, 151, 325 *n*. 243
Rana of Udaipur, 15, 16, 277
Rani Durgavati, 3
Ranjit Singh, 357 *n*. 119
Ranthambhor, 173, 263, 264
Rathor, 126
Raushanara Begam, 102, 107, 114, 324 *n*. 186
Ravi River, 15, 240–41, 251, 285
Rawalpindi, 173
Raza Bahadur, 170, 171, 284, 342 *n*. 69
Raziyya Sultan, 3
Red Sea, 128, 129, 131, 133, 141, 146, 150, 157
Roe, Sir Thomas, 30, 34, 43, 47–50, 53, 56–61, 63–65, 70, 72, 79, 88, 89, 99, 108, 121, 122, 128, 132, 134–37, 139, 140–49, 152–61, 164, 168, 191, 195, 196, 199, 200, 217, 225, 251, 263, 310 *n*. 156, *n*. 157, *n*. 165, *n*. 166, *n*. 170, 332 *n*. 33, 334 *n*. 125, 338 *n*. 232, 350 *n*. 134, 354 *n*. 25, 377
Rohtas, 181, 268, 271, 272
Roman Catholicism, 129, 133, 199, 200, 225, 298 *n*. 45
Ruqayya Sultan Begam, 31, 32, 34, 36, 50, 87, 91, 97, 121, 213, 301 *n*. 116, *n*. 118, *n*. 119, *n*. 120, 302–3 *n*. 146
Russian, 94

Sachaq, 126
Sadhu, 192
Sadiq Khan, 45, 281, 292 *n*. 8
Sadurkhun, 255
Safarchi, 14, 294 *n*. 46
Safavid, 235
Safi Mirza, 312 *n*. 51
Sahib Jamal, 125
Sahibatuzzamani. *See* Jahanara
Said Khan Ghakkar, 126
Saksena, Banarsi Prasad, 7, 284, 287
Salar Jung Museum, 221
Saliha Banu Begam, Padshah, 80, 125, 311 *n*. 31
Salim. *See also* Jahangir
  and Anarkali, 123–24, 329 *n*. 369
  birth, 64, 118–19, 211, 325 *n*. 229
  court in Allahabad, 19–21, 25, 207–8, 295 *n*. 5, 329 *n*. 369, 355 *n*. 30, *n*. 32
  early love for Mihrunnisa, 13–16, 294 *n*. 40, *n*. 41, *n*. 45
  effects of alcohol, 19, 24, 75–78
  final relations with Akbar, 20–24, 25, 122, 346 *n*. 22
  orders murder of Abul Fazl, 20, 195
  rivalled by son Khusrau as heir to Akbar, 19–24, 346–47 *n*. 22

Salim (*continued*)
and Shaikh Salim Chishti, 119–20, 211
and tigress, 16
wet-nurses, 85
work with Ali Quli, 15, 16
Salim Shah, 20
Salima Khanam, 121
Salima Sultan Begam, 20, 47, 85, 112–14, 121, 122, 213, 244, 296 *n.* 20, 301 *n.* 116, 327 *n.* 276, 330 *n.* 395
Samghapati Candrapala, 349 *n.* 128
Samskara, 192
Sanad, 123
Sannyasi, 192, 193, 204
Sanskrit, 40, 112, 113
Sarai, 46, 68, 110, 114, 222, 228–30, 250, 252, 273, 356 *n.* 64
Sarandaz, 37
Sati, 117–18, 193, 328 *n.* 323, 349 *n.* 112
Satyr, 147, 225
Sayyid Abdullah, 20
Sayyid Ahmad, 16
Sayyids, 26, 173, 271, 297 *n.* 36, 299 *n.* 66, 370 *n.* 143
Shab-i Barat, 188
Shah Abbas, 67, 74, 173, 175, 181, 276, 312 *n.* 51, 343 *n.* 91, 344 *n.* 99, 365 *n.* 9
Shah Begam, 47
Shah Burj, 70, 91
Shah Hamadan, 32
Shah Ismail, 14, 270, 292 *n.* 5, 341 *n.* 20
Shah Jahan. *See also* Khurram
anti-Nur Jahan propaganda, 30–31, 47, 116–17, 279, 287, 294 *n.* 42, 359 *n.* 30, 370 *n.* 143
and Arjumand Banu Begam, 94, 164, 320 *n.* 79
and Asaf Khan, 37, 55, 165, 167, 175–77, 181–82, 275, 279–87, 309 *n.* 150, 366 *n.* 28
as Bidaulat, 161, 173, 175, 177–79, 261
death of a daughter, 55
disdain of Hinduism, 192, 256, 348 *n.* 86
enemy of Christians, 142, 203, 215, 348 *n.* 86, 351 *n.* 186, 353 *n.* 224
and English trade, 139, 141–42, 152, 157, 159, 161, 179, 334 *n.* 115, 334–35 *n.* 125
and Khusrau, 168–72, 342 *n.* 51, *n.* 56, *n.* 58, *n.* 71, 342–43 *n.* 72, 343 *n.* 75, *n.* 85, *n.* 91
and Mahabat Khan, 179, 180, 183, 261–62, 272, 274, 276–77, 345 *n.* 143, *n.* 144, 361 *n.* 14, 364–65 *n.* 121, 365 *n.* 129, 366 *n.* 28
as member of junta, 48, 61, 73, 162, 163, 164, 205
and mother, 94, 116–17, 162
and Nur Jahan, 50–53, 87, 109, 111, 161, 164, 173–74, 181–83, 252, 308 *n.* 96
and Parviz, 277
pro-Portuguese, 142–43
receives *Jahangirnama*, 55
receives title, 51
sickness, 105, 365 *n.* 1
1622 rebellion, 3, 80, 106, 111, 161, 169, 172–83, 199, 205, 261–62, 270, 275–76, 334 *n.* 115, 340 *n.* 8, 342 *n.* 47, 343 *n.* 87, 344 *n.* 99, *n.* 101, *n.* 105, 365 *n.* 9, *n.* 11
successor to Jahangir, 32, 48, 61, 252, 275, 279–84, 307 *n.* 64, *n.* 77, *n.* 78, 368 *n.* 99, *n.* 100, *n.* 104, *n.* 106, 369 *n.* 109, *n.* 112
and Taj Mahal, 233, 235, 247
women, 96, 102–5, 110, 308 *n.* 87, *n.* 88, 322 *n.* 132, *n.* 134, *n.* 141, 325 *n.* 223, 341 *n.* 20, 345 *n.* 143
Shah Salim, 20
Shah Shuja, 80, 84, 98, 281, 294 *n.* 42, 320 *n.* 96, 350 *n.* 144
Shah Tahmasp Safawi, 8, 292 *n.* 5
Shahabad, 273
Shahdara, 240–43, 251–52, 281, 285, 369 *n.* 127
Shahi, 47
Shahjahannama, 285
Shahnawaz Khan, 43, 267, 271, 341 *n.* 20
Shahr Banu Begam, 114, 244
Shahryar
birth, 79
death, 18, 283–84
description, 49, 261
and Dholpur, 174, 181
at end of Jahangir's reign, 276–83, 367 *n.* 56, *n.* 59, *n.* 86, 368 *n.* 89, *n.* 102
marriage to Ladli Begam, 18, 163–65, 210, 267
as *Nashudani*, 164, 165, 281
as Nur Jahan's puppet, 18, 165, 168, 172, 174–75, 177, 181–83, 269, 275–83, 344 *n.* 106, 367 *n.* 59
own daughter, 178, 267
in rebellion of Mahabat Khan, 261, 266–69, 364 *n.* 111
religious instruction, 195, 196
youthful encounters with Jahangir, 49, 66, 68, 164–65, 312 *n.* 49, *n.* 50
Shahzada Khanam, 91, 95, 121, 125, 155, 235
Shaikh, 118, 120, 159, 185, 187, 203, 208–11, 300 *n.* 89, 352 *n.* 213
Shaikh Abul Fayz (Fayzi), 373
Shaikh Abul Fazl. *See* Abul Fazl
Shaikh Ahmad, 187
Shaikh Ahmad Khattu, 347 *n.* 51
Shaikh Ahmad Sirhindi. *See also* Naqshbandi
Jahangir moves against, 188, 203, 204, 208–9, 352 *n.* 202, *n.* 208, *n.* 213
letters to courtiers of Akbar, 23, 186, 346 *n.* 7, 346–47 *n.* 22, 353 *n.* 223
and Nur Jahan, 206, 207–11
Shaikh Alauddin. *See* Islam Khan
Shaikh Baha, 201
Shaikh Bayazid Muazzam Khan, 187
Shaikh Farid Bukhari, 346 *n.* 9
conveys news of Abul Fazl's death to Akbar, 20

death, 210
letters from Shaikh Ahmad Sirhindi, 186, 208, 210, 346 *n.* 7
role in 1606 revolt of Khusrau, 26, 187, 208
supporter of Salim at accession, 23, 24, 186, 204, 297 *n.* 33, 346–47 *n.* 22
Shaikh Husain Jami, 186
Shaikh Ibrahim, 187
Shaikh Ibrahim Baba, 188
Shaikh Kabir, 187
Shaikh Mubarak, 373
Shaikh Muinuddin Chishti. *See also* Chishti
founder of Chishti *silsila*, 189
veneration by Akbar, 187, 189, 348 *n.* 64
veneration by Jahangir, 184, 189–91, 203, 204, 213, 348 *n.* 72
veneration by Nur Jahan, 205–6
veneration by Shah Jahan, 369 *n.* 109
Shaikh Nizamuddin Auliya, 191, 204, 347 *n.* 51
Shaikh Pura, 91
Shaikh Salim Chishti. *See also* Chishti
family, 21, 187–88, 204, 211
family of, and Nur Jahan, 204, 206, 211
grandfather of Qutbuddin Khan Koka, 20, 187–88, 211, 300 *n.* 89
and prophecy, 80, 118–20
and Salim/Jahangir, 64, 80, 187, 211
tomb, 185, 187, 233, 347 *n.* 51
Shaikhzada, 173, 271
Shalamar, Dal Lake, 256–57
Shapur. *See* Itiqad Khan
Sharifa, 178
Sharifulmulk, 276
Shayista Khan, 321 *n.* 125
Sher Afgan. *See also* Ali Quli Khan Istajlu
brother Qumar Sultan, 32, 295 *n.* 62
daughter Ladli Begam, 18, 79, 87, 98, 163, 295 *n.* 62
death, killing of Qutbuddin, 18, 27–34, 38, 39, 87, 188, 211, 256, 298 *n.* 57, 300 *n.* 86, *n.* 87, *n.* 88, *n.* 89, 301 *n.* 114
Jahangir's view of, 14, 16, 24–25, 27–28, 300 *n.* 83, *n.* 84, *n.* 87, 355 *n.* 32
marriage to Mihrunnisa, 15
mother, 32
possible son, 295 *n.* 62
posted to Bengal, 18, 24, 25, 29
receives title "Tiger Slayer," 16, 294 *n.* 59
service to Akbar and Jahangir, 15–18, 39, 45, 294 *n.* 58, 353 *n.* 223
sides with Akbar and Khusrau against Salim in Allahabad, 21, 25, 45, 299–300 *n.* 83, 355 *n.* 32
tomb, 17
Turkish background, 3, 15
Shia, 13, 120, 184, 204, 209–12, 286, 347 *n.* 49
Shikasta, 53
Shiraz, 186
Shiva, 217
Shivaratri, 192
Shri, 216
Shujauddin, Mohammad and Razia, 6, 34, 36, 117, 124, 125, 169, 228, 229, 239–42, 285–87, 294 *n.* 44, 303 *n.* 163
Shvetambara, 196–98, 205, 209. *See also* Jain
Siddhicandra (Upadhyaya), 103, 104, 112–13, 196–97, 206–7, 322 *n.* 137
Sikandra, 25, 46, 111, 151, 177, 189, 238, 250, 252, 298 *n.* 45, 348 *n.* 72
Sikhs, 27
Silsila, 21, 186, 187, 189, 207, 208, 353 *n.* 223
Sind, 14, 21
Sind Canal, 255
Sir, 47
Sirhindi. *See* Shaikh Ahmad Sirhindi
Sita, 216
Skelton, Robert, 329 *n.* 369
Smith, Sir Thomas, 148, 153, 303 *n.* 151
Sohni, 322 *n.* 131
Solomon, 70
Sosanwar, 257
South Asia, 148
Spain, 333 *n.* 68
Spanish Armada, 132
Spices, 131, 133, 144, 151, 335 *n.* 151
Sribhanucandraganicarita, 103, 311 *n.* 15, 352 *n.* 193
Srinigar, 145, 238, 255, 257–59
Suba, 25, 177, 188, 201, 272, 313 *n.* 79
Subhan Quli, 67
Sufi, 21, 23, 74, 159, 186, 187, 189, 191, 193, 203, 204, 206, 210, 297 *n.* 33
Sultan Salim Shah, 20
Sultanam, 121
Sultanate, 94, 95
Sultanpur, 229
Sultanunnisa, 124
Sumatinatha, 349 *n.* 128
Sumatra, 149
Sun imagery, 40–41, 71, 80, 185, 313 *n.* 72, *n.* 77
Sundar. *See* Raja Bikramajit
Sunni, 204
Suraj Mal, 328 *n.* 329
Surat, 128–31, 133, 134, 136, 137, 139, 141–43, 150, 152, 153, 156, 158, 159, 283, 316 *n.* 138, 331 *n.* 19, 332 *n.* 47, 372, 377
Surkh, 77
Suwar, 37, 39, 45, 165, 174, 177, 277, 280, 293 *n.* 32, 296 *n.* 19, 301 *n.* 124, 304 *n.* 173, 311 *n.* 32
Suyurghal, 319 *n.* 69
Swally, 129, 131

Tahmuras (Don Philippe), 97, 126, 201, 272, 283, 284, 368 *n.* 102
Tahwildar, 96
Taj Mahal, 39, 49, 230–38, 247, 285, 286
Takhallus, 113
Talib Amli, 227
Tapti River, 129, 133, 179

Tatar Sultan, 8
Tatimma-i Wakiat-i Jahangiri, 55
Tatta, 14, 270, 272, 273, 276, 279, 294 *n.* 47, 298 *n.* 41, 365 *n.* 11
Tavernier, Jean-Baptiste, 34, 100–103, 105, 108, 118, 121, 280, 372
Tehran, 3, 8, 167
Telingana, 180
Terry, Rev. Edward, 8, 21, 30, 33, 37, 62, 64, 67, 70, 72, 74, 79, 81, 85, 89, 93, 94, 98–103, 108, 111, 112, 118, 134, 137, 144, 146–48, 154–57, 168, 170, 171, 191, 195, 196, 199, 200, 214, 215, 225, 244, 247, 350 *n.* 134
Textiles, 129, 131, 133, 145–51, 154, 155, 158, 218, 221–22, 237, 238, 326 *n.* 249, 336 *n.* 170, *n.* 171, 337 *n.* 189, *n.* 202, *n.* 207, 339 *n.* 254, 354–55 *n.* 25. *See also* Clothing
Thailand, 149
Theological debate, 129, 185, 193, 200, 202
Tibet, 144
Timur, 11, 298 *n.* 46, 368 *n.* 104
Timurid, 11, 371
Tirtha, 196
Tiryaq, 124
Toda, 58, 111, 151
Tola, 40, 219, 220, 222
Trade
  centers as sources of information, 31, 162
  with the English, 61, 65, 113, 128–60, 161, 199, 214, 311 *n.* 30, 332 *n.* 32, *n.* 36, *n.* 41, 340 *n.* 302
  with Europeans, 46, 56, 93, 308 *n.* 102, 311 *n.* 30, 332 *n.* 22, *n.* 32
  items of, 144–50, 336 *n.* 182, *n.* 183, 337 *n.* 189, *n.* 202, *n.* 207
  at Mina Bazaar, 36
  with the Portuguese, 23, 128–60, 199, 214, 331 *n.* 16, *n.* 19, 332 *n.* 32, *n.* 36, 336 *n.* 166, 340 *n.* 302, 350–51 *n.* 166
  women and, 3, 36, 96, 110, 111, 113, 132
Transoxiana, 188
Troy, 108
Trully, Robert, 134
Turan, 122, 306 *n.* 36
Turki, 11, 112, 133
Turkish, 11, 95, 120, 141
Tuzuk-i Jahangiri, 6, 7, 30, 33, 38, 39, 88, 114, 159, 161, 162, 170, 173, 186, 191, 193, 197, 198, 203, 211, 219, 220, 221, 244, 248–50, 253, 256, 320 *n.* 96, 346 *n.* 6

Udai Singh (Mota Raja), 124, 162, 311 *n.* 31
Udaipur, 15, 16, 357 *n.* 85
Udyam, 376
Ujjain, 192, 193, 204
Ulama, 208, 209, 239
Umm Kulsum, 121
Umma, 37
Una, 195
Upanayana, 192
Urdubegi, 95
Urs, 205–6
Uttam Chand, 32

Vakil, 96, 182, 229, 264, 272, 282, 365 *n.* 129
Vakil khilat-i khas, 44
Van den Broecke, Pieter, 7, 13, 15, 26, 30, 32–34, 37, 55, 65, 68, 80, 81, 84, 131, 141, 164, 171, 173, 175, 176, 182, 202, 217, 260, 261, 268–70, 273, 275, 279–83, 287, 292 *n.* 8, 302 *n.* 146, 362 *n.* 36, 372, 377
Van Ravesteyn, Pieter Gillesz, 131
Varaha, 192, 193, 204
Vedanta, 193
Venice, 148, 376
Venus, 147, 224, 225
Vernag, 252–54, 258–59, 285
Vijayadeva Suri, 196
Vijayasena Suri, 196
Villiers Stuart, Charlotte, 244, 252, 257
Vina, 113
Virgin Mary. *See* Madonna
Vishnu, 192, 193

Wazir, 8, 39, 44, 155
Wazirulmulk, 26
Withington, Nicholas, 11, 64, 118, 130
Women. *See also* Harem; *Mahal; Sati; Zanana*
  abuse of, 198
  after age thirty, 66, 79, 84–85, 95, 101
  and the arts, 91–92, 111–15, 218–43, 326 *n.* 267, *n.* 270
  bearing arms, 115–17, 327 *n.* 299
  and children, 94, 97, 101, 320 *n.* 91, 321 *n.* 125, 322 *n.* 132
  clothing/jewelry/toilet, 111–12, 114, 116, 149–50, 219, 221–22, 321–22 *n.* 128, 326 *n.* 245, *n.* 250, *n.* 251, 326 *n.* 259, 327 *n.* 290, 354 *n.* 24
  concepts of beauty, 5
  concubines, 34, 49, 79, 93, 94, 97, 100, 164, 312 *n.* 49, 329 *n.* 366, 349 *n.* 112
  diplomacy among, 46, 122
  drug/alcohol use, 115, 327 *n.* 293, *n.* 297, 343 *n.* 84
  and education, 112–13
  emperor's relationship with, 39–40, 94–95, 109, 317 *n.* 4
  female infanticide, 193
  festivals, 36
  food, 109, 221, 324–25 *n.* 211, 325 *n.* 213
  gardens, 244–59, 324 *n.* 206
  gifts, 51, 53
  in government, 48, 121–23, 179, 306 *n.* 30
  guarding of, 94–96, 98, 107, 116, 323 *n.* 161, 327 *n.* 299
  and honor, 89, 99–100, 317 *n.* 5, 318 *n.* 7, 321 *n.* 114
  and illness, 105, 106, 108
  importance of mother, 50, 53, 85–86, 213, 216, 298 *n.* 57

inheritance, 109–10
and leisure, 245–46, 257, 317 *n.* 1
life in apartments, 13, 88–96, 245–46, 319 *n.* 40
literature by, 226
marriage, 5, 37, 46, 51, 100–101, 118, 120, 121, 193, 202, 205, 213, 214, 216, 217, 219, 287, 303 *n.* 169, 311 *n.* 31, 317 *n.* 182, 321 *n.* 115, *n.* 119
models, 5, 6
painters, 224, 329 *n.* 369, 355 *n.* 30
pictures of, 224–26
physical residences, 90–93, 114, 318 *n.* 20, *n.* 27
religious practices, 117–21, 328 *n.* 323, *n.* 329
rivalries, 94–95, 101, 109, 321–22 *n.* 128, 324 *n.* 206
seclusion, 89–90, 104–6, 108, 111, 117, 226, 257, 260. *See Parda*
secret intrigues, 96, 101–2, 322 *n.* 132, *n.* 134, 322–23 *n.* 148
seniority system in harem, 32, 94, 95, 97
sexual life, 99–104, 303 *n.* 158, 322 *n.* 132
titles, 94, 319 *n.* 46, 330 *n.* 395
in trade, 3, 36, 96, 110, 111, 113, 122, 128, 132, 149, 150–53, 178
and travel, 47, 89, 98, 106–8, 245–46, 253, 257, 323 *n.* 173, *n.* 178, *n.* 181, 323–24 *n.* 182, 324 *n.* 186, *n.* 189
unmarried, 5, 100, 121
and wealth, 24, 47, 90, 96, 109–11, 114, 120, 150, 319 *n.* 69, 320 *n.* 79, 325 *n.* 223, *n.* 229

Xavier, Father Jerome, 200, 302 *n.* 131, 375

Yamuna River, 11, 70, 78, 91, 111, 151, 231, 248–51
Yazd, 8
Yogi, 191, 192, 204, 217
Yuga, 207
Yusuf Khan, 28, 31

Zabad, 114
Zahara Bagh. *See* Nur Manzil
Zain Khan Koka, 125
Zakat, 37
Zamana Beg. *See* Mahabat Khan
Zamindar, 197, 269
Zanana, 81, 88–90, 93–100, 102–4, 106, 108–14, 118, 122, 123, 126, 132, 146, 149, 206, 221, 224, 226, 237, 242, 257, 258, 323 *n.* 161, 328 *n.* 329 *See also* Harem; *Mahal;* Women
Zat, 37, 39, 44, 45, 165, 174, 177, 293 *n.* 32, 296 *n.* 19, 301 *n.* 124, 311 *n.* 32
Zebunnisa, 104, 113, 114
Zinatunnisa Begam, 100, 114
Ziyaulmulk Qazwini, 297 *n.* 36